THE ROMAN REMAINS OF NORTHERN AND EASTERN FRANCE

The Roman Remains of Northern and Eastern France provides a thorough area by area companion to the wealth of the region's monuments, excavations and artefacts, from Paris and Boulogne to Lyon and Strasbourg. The author treats over ninety major and lesser sites, providing both a scholarly assessment of the area's extensive visible remains and a practical guide for visitors.

Precise instructions, carefully designed maps and numerous annotated illustrations ensure that readers will be able to find the places and things they wish to see. As well as guiding visitors to great sites like Lyon with its magnificent ruins, superb Roman museums and immense siphon aqueducts, the book encourages the search for hidden temples, brick kilns and Roman roads, often 'lost' in the forest. The book also offers a comprehensive examination of the area's Roman heritage, interpreting the varied surviving remains and exploring the lifestyles and environment of the Gallo-Roman people.

Comprehensively illustrated with photographs, maps and plans, *The Roman Remains of Northern and Eastern France* is therefore a single, unique resource both for academic study and for visitors interested in the region's archaeological and historical background.

James Bromwich was formerly Principal Lecturer at the London Guildhall University and is the author of *The Roman Remains of Southern France: A Guidebook*.

Frontispiece Magnentius, the Gallic usurper emperor 350–53, silver-bronze bust. Photograph: Louis Bonnamour, Musée Denon, Chalon-sur-Saône.

THE ROMAN REMAINS OF NORTHERN AND EASTERN FRANCE

A guidebook

James Bromwich

Routledge
Taylor & Francis Group
LONDON AND NEW YORK

First published 2003
by Routledge
11 New Fetter Lane, London EC4P 4EE

Simultaneously published in the USA and Canada
by Routledge
29 West 35th Street, New York, NY 10001

Routledge is an imprint of the Taylor & Francis Group

Typeset in Garamond by
Florence Production Ltd, Stoodleigh, Devon
Printed and bound in Great Britain by
MPG Books Ltd, Bodmin

British Library Cataloguing in Publication Data
A catalogue record for this book is available from the British Library

Library of Congress Cataloging in Publication Data
A catalog record for this book has been requested

ISBN 0–415–13994–5

CONTENTS

FIGURES

PLATES

ACKNOWLEDGEMENTS

I wish to thank my patient publisher and my editor, Richard Stoneman, the helpful French museum curators and archaeologists – especially Roger Agache – and academic specialists like John Drinkwater. Edward Oliver has transformed many of my plans and maps. Above all my wife, Anne, has given more than anyone; her contribution has been crucial. Any mistakes are mine alone. I hope that this book helps stimulate others to explore the cities, small towns and hidden places of France and experience some of the pleasure that I did in France's Roman heritage.

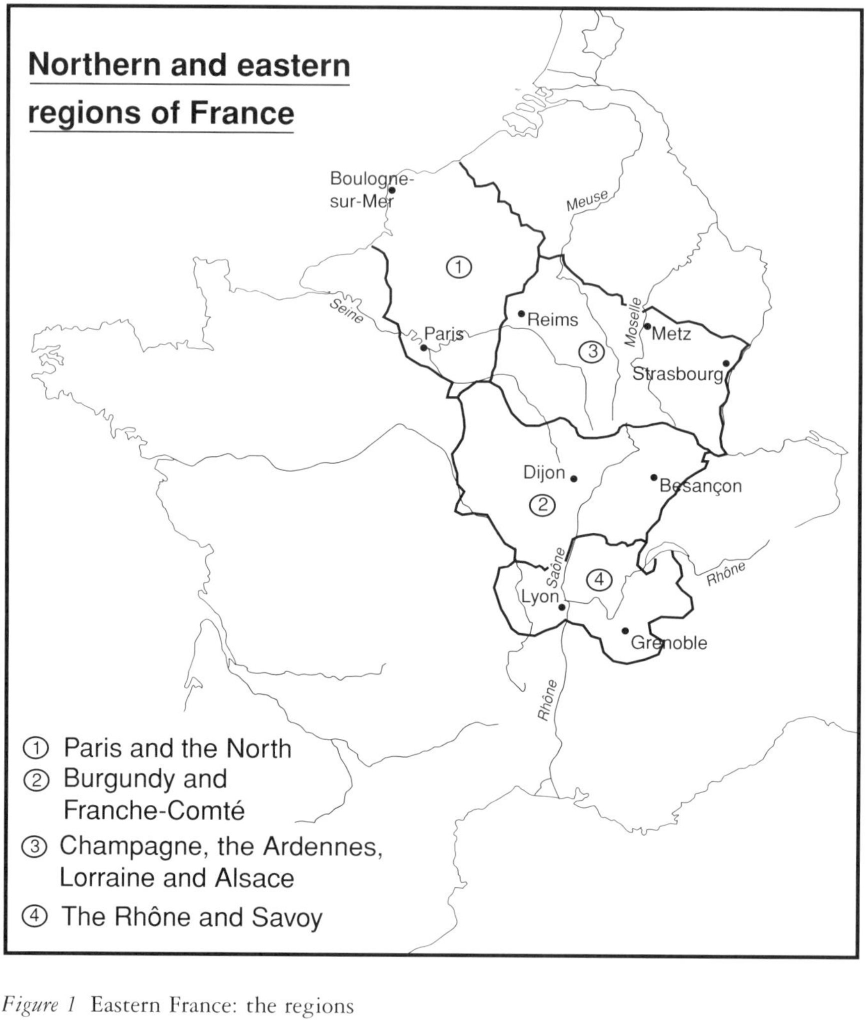

Figure 1 Eastern France: the regions

INTRODUCTION

The Roman archaeology of France

This book is inevitably a limited reflection of archaeology in France. This is not just the natural limitation of a summary approach to the work of hundreds of archaeologists, scientists and scholars who over time have built up the complex picture of the sites covered in this book. It is sure to include descriptions and interpretations that new work will prove to be quite wrong. There are further and unavoidable difficulties. A guidebook's purpose is to identify places where things can be seen, not read about, otherwise why go? But a great deal of Roman France cannot be seen.

Some areas have very few visible remains. This may be due to particular soil types, the wholesale destructive nature of later occupation, or they have simply been poorly researched: Champagne and the Jura have only a thin spread of sites and worthwhile museums (while Burgundy overflows!). A very high proportion of sites are 'rescue' digs. This is really a euphemism; they are actually destroyed: it is only the information derived from the excavation that is rescued. Sometimes, as in all countries, this has entailed the shameful destruction of major remains (as at Bourbonne-les-Bains, page 199). Yet it simply has to be accepted that many painful choices have to be made, that there is a real clash of priorities and that the best result is that skilled archaeologists have drawn as much as possible for posterity from their efforts. There is another type of site that cannot figure in this guide: a great deal may have been revealed but the structural remains are so slight that they are simply covered up again (see Gournay in The ROMANO-CELTIC SANCTUARY, pages 122). Some archaeologists have gone further and have deliberately only carried out partial digs and immediately filled in their excavations (see Ribemont-sur-Ancre, page 121 in the same section); they are trying to balance the demand to extend knowledge now with the certainty that future archaeologists will be able to get more from the material.

The wish to minimize destructive techniques has meant that non-intrusive methods have become more significant. Roger Agache's aerial photographs across the Somme revolutionized our knowledge of the chalk plain villas of

Picardy, not because they led to new excavation (only a handful he found have been dug), but because they made clear the close relationship of villas and road system, enabling new inferences about the market system in Roman Gaul. Other ways of mapping the past, such as field walking and geophysical surveys, are much more widely utilized than even a few years ago. Interesting deductions on land-use and population densities have been possible in the Aisne valley and elsewhere. Many finds are far too degraded ever to be displayed; the enormous expansion of what has been learnt about the environment is often only meaningful as a reflection of change across a number of sites: the antithesis of the site-by-site approach of a guidebook.

Yet this guidebook enables you to interact with the visible structures and many of the artefacts left behind by the Gallo-Roman world. It is written to help you find, observe, consider, analyse and make them part of your life as well. I hope I communicate the excitement that I still feel when I see an aqueduct arch sitting in the landscape: it is the truth in concrete form, raising for me dozens of questions about how and when it was built, why it was done, how it worked, who got the water, and many more. I shall never forget seeing the siphon towers and bridges on the Lyon aqueducts. How did they work? Were they efficient? Why was this technique chosen? I could almost see the water engineers and builders at work. The bronze figure of Epona, side-saddle on her horse, on her shelf in the museum case, may seem a distant and 'dead' goddess for us, but we know about trying to handle the unknown, trying to deal with the unexpected and the need to personalize spiritual feelings.

By seeing the objects and places the Gallo-Romans created we can go some way towards grasping their vision of the world. 'The past is a foreign country. They do things differently there.'[1] Yet it is not an alien environment: you will be seeing the works of fellow human beings and will have the pleasure of exploring how they did things differently. I hope I have provided enough answers in my text and illustrations to help expand your experience and encourage new questions leading you to many other sources.

The region

This book treats more than ninety sites in detail. The problem was where to draw the line. The eastern and south-eastern frontiers of France provide clear markers, even if on occasion I am forced to refer to sites beyond these borders. In the south, the boundary is that of the Midi, covered in my first book. The western limits were more difficult: the mountainous plateaux of the Massif Central forms a western flank in the south, but major geographical features are absent in the north-west. Here, the chosen borders were simply those of the modern French regions: Bourgogne, the Ile de France, Picardie and the Nord/Pas de Calais. How does my region relate to the Roman provincial structure? Not very closely. It clearly excludes nearly all of Narbonensis (see in *The Roman Remains of Southern France*), but does deal with the territory inhabited by the Allobroges tribe, that is much of Savoy, except their capital Vienne, too important to miss out from the earlier guide. The heart of the Three Gauls, the city of Lyon, and the eastern areas of the province of Lugdunensis are included, but western Lugdunensis and Aquitania are excluded. Though much of Belgica is covered, its capital Trier in modern Germany is not; however, most of Germania Superior is taken in. As Europe evolves towards a new identity it may seem more appropriate to write a guidebook that ignores modern boundaries entirely.

Maps and town plans

I hope my maps and plans will help you find the museums and sites described here, but they are best used in conjunction with other sources. Since writing *The Roman Remains of Southern France*, it has become clear that much the easiest, and cheapest, way of finding places is to use a good general map and a detailed map book. Regional maps still have the benefit of lightness and are easy to carry while walking, but road atlases have a very real advantage: at least 9 out of 10 sites are listed in the index. Michelin's standard red maps, the 1/1,000,000 '989' or '916', and its *Road Atlas*, which brings together all the maps produced for the yellow 1/200,000 series, are widely available. The AA *Touring Atlas* uses an even bigger scale, and there are others produced by the Institut Géographique National (IGN), Blay-Foldex, Philips, and Geocenter's *EuroAtlas of France*.

Detailed references. For finding the less obvious **rural sites**, such as sections of aqueducts, temples and rock-cut goddesses hidden in woodland, in addition to my descriptions, maps and plans, there is nothing better than the IGN's large-scale local maps. I refer in the text to the *Série Bleue* or *Top 25*, produced at 1:25,000 (1cm to 250m), four numbers and one or two letters, the E and O standing for Est and Ouest. An orange 1:50,000 *Carte Topographique* would provide more detail, but local *Série Bleue* maps are sold very widely in the localities, while the former are not. Some sites are provided with specific co-ordinates. These use the blue numbers around the map frame; the horizontal (x) number is always followed by the vertical (y) co-ordinator. Note that the *Série Bleue* takes into account the curvature of the earth and the grid formed by these numbers slants to the east.

For **town sites**, Blay-Foldex town plans are comprehensive, usually the clearest, and have street indexes with a simple letter/number grid. Most tourist offices, often found in very small places, will provide free summary plans. Some of the small isolated rural sites can be most easily found by using the marked footpaths (signposted with a mix of crosses, triangles and circles in different colours). The tourist offices can provide details on local walks – and therefore often directions to the archaeological remains – and for more long-distance walks and detailed descriptions of places seen, including archaeological material, consult organizations like the Club Vosgien, based in Strasbourg; its *Guide des Vosges 2, Le Plateau Lorrain et les Vosges du Nord*, is particularly useful for the area around Niederbrunn and Bitche.

Opening times and entry charges

Prices change too often to make them worth inclusion. Times are given, but these cannot be relied upon: I have been to places where the premises were proclaimed open, but were locked up, and others where the hours change annually, but no one seems to know beforehand what the change will be. Tuesday is widely a closing day for state and municipal museums, but where a town has a number of galleries and museums, other days may be used (generally Monday).

Books, journals and the internet

Anthony King's *Roman Gaul and Germany* (1990) remains the best introduction to Roman France, but *Romans, Celts and Germans* (2001) by Maureen Carroll updates material for some of the region. John Drinkwater's *Roman Gaul* (1983) continues to be an excellent description of the political development of Gaul to the 260s, but it does not cover the late empire. Edith Wightman's *Gallia Belgica* (1985) was brilliant and many of her ideas, particularly qualifications made to accepted opinion, have proved to be correct with the advances in archaeology since then. Despite the many biographies and modern historical studies, there is no substitute for reading Julius Caesar's *De bello Gallico*, and I think the best translation with accompanying maps, pictures and background information is that by Anne and Peter Wiseman (*The Battle for Gaul*, 1980).

There are numerous French journals that cover the various regions and localities dealt with in this guide (*Revue du Nord*, *Revue Archéologique de Picardie*, *Revue Archéologique de l'Est*, etc). *Gallia* is the top academic journal for the whole of France. For the general reader who wants to find out about the latest discoveries and see good colour photographs as well, there are now two widely available competing magazines: *Archéologia* and *L'Archéologue.* They are generally written by specialists and, despite their titles, they contain more material on Roman France than on any other period. *Archéologia* has a web-site www.faton.fr where brief summaries of articles can be consulted and journals ordered.

Museum curators and archaeologists are increasingly presenting material on the web. One of the most important websites for researching France is www.bham.ac.uk/ARGE, the Archaeological Resource Guide for Europe produced by Birmingham University. It takes you to Archdata, a French site listing all the major French organizations dealing with Roman archaeology. The website www.portail.culture.fr produced by the French Ministry of

Culture can be used to access both archaeological museums and heritage sites with Roman material. Other useful sites include www.paris.org/musees/ and www.archeologie-aerienne.culture.gouv.fr/. An informal guide to websites targeted on Roman Gaul is www.ukans.edu/history; it reveals that many of the websites are of variable quality.

Note

1 L.P. Hartley, *The Go-Between.*

HISTORICAL DEVELOPMENT

Change and identity

THE PRE-ROMAN INHABITANTS

Since the early twentieth century, western Europe's Iron Age has been divided into two broad cultural groups, the Hallstatt and La Tène, after type sites found in Austria and Switzerland. These terms have continued in use, although broken down both in their development over time and between different regions.

Hallstatt. The site itself shows a long phase of development before the Iron Age, but with Hallstatt C or I the distinctive widely found features emerge: a horse-riding warrior class wielding long swords (iron increasingly replacing bronze), using hill-forts for security, and carrying out inhumation

Table: Broad cultural groups of the Iron Age in western Europe

		Southern Germany	*Central France*	*Peoples and states*
1200/1150 BC	Final Bronze Age	Hallstatt A	Urnfields	**Celtic?**
		Hallstatt B		
800/700 BC	Iron Age I Early	Hallstatt C or **Hallstatt I**		**Celtic?**
625/600 BC		Hallstatt D or Hallstatt II		'Princedoms'
500/475 BC	Iron Age II Middle	**La Tène A**	La Tène I	**Celtic**
*c.*400 BC		La Tène B		Migrations
*c.*250 BC		La Tène C	La Tène II	Gallic tribal states emerging
*c.*120 BC	Iron Age III Late	La Tène D	La Tène III	Roman Transalpine Gaul

Source: Based on Collis (1984) *The European Iron Age.*

burials, at their grandest including four-wheel carts or wagons. At the end of the early Iron Age (Hallstatt D), some small hilltop sites, such as Vix overlooking the upper Seine in Burgundy, embodied features that suggest new extremes of wealth and status, leading to their characterization as 'princely' states. The burials reach a high level of magnificence: large wooden chambers constructed in the ground, the dead laid out on beds, accompanied by a wagon and rich metal goods, weapons and ornaments made of bronze and gold. The chamber was then covered by a large mound. Not only is there trade in products made by skilled local craftsmen, but also evidence of long-distance connections with the Greek world for whom the princedoms acted as intermediaries for the products of the north. These routes collapsed early in the fifth century BC, probably associated in some way with the Etruscans opening new routes to the north cutting out these middlemen and their Greek competitors. In addition, the northern 'periphery' areas that supplied the slaves and metals desired by the Mediterranean traders seem to have experienced destabilizing population growth.

La Tène. What emerged was an even more homogeneous culture, stretching from France to Hungary and, by the end of the Iron Age, through most of the British Isles as well. The decisive identification came with the work of Déchelette (see ROANNE) in 1908, showing common metalwork types ranging from the solid open-ended torc, the most distinctive of necklaces, to the characteristic flowing geometric-based designs, often using foliage or very stylized animal and human forms. It was a dynamic and aggressive society. Starting in the Hunsrück-Eifel area (see BLIESBRUCK), but spreading and flourishing in Champagne, its burial goods demonstrate a new division of wealth. Elite warriors – increasingly cremated rather than interred – were accompanied by weapons and two-wheel chariots, but without mounds; some 250 such burials are known in Champagne alone. Male followers were buried with lances, and others, presumably farmers, were only accompanied by pottery. At the same time migrations took bands of people, called Celts or Gauls by a horrified classical world, to seek their fortunes in the south. The Gallic sack of Rome in 390 BC became fixed in the Roman folk memory.

There followed a period of relative isolation until the second century BC. It was not static. Cremation now became the norm and chariots were first burnt, then disappeared from wealthy burials. Ditch and fence enclosures surrounded farms and distinct sanctuaries were being constructed; settlements with a craft/trade focus emerged. Groups seem to have been coalescing towards tribal structures. Transformed from one contending power to dominance in the Mediterranean, Rome exerted a growing influence. Its wealth and its needs entailed a massive rise in demand, and this, together with its ability to produce a surplus of sought-after wine, helped stimulate further interchange.

In many areas, families and clans drew together into tribes often led by elected kings; some of the larger and richer tribes – such as the Aedui or the Sequani – began to develop states modelled on Roman magistracies. It is clear from Caesar's account of the Gallic wars that political power in all tribes still reflected the social structure of early La Tène: a warrior elite frequently in conflict both between itself and with other tribes, power in each tribe being concentrated in the hands of a few noble families. A mass of dependent farming families and artisans supplied their basic surplus while successful warfare brought new supporters, won slaves and increased wealth. A crucial social cement was the giving of gifts: coinage (gold and silver); craft products (such as the torc, a heavy necklace); beer (the barrel was reputedly a Gallic invention); and imported wine – amphorae in their thousands have been dredged from the Rhône and Saône.

The settlement archaeology of the late La Tène supports this evolving picture. Forests had been extensively cleared, agriculture was well developed and many rich upland soils were being exploited. Population was dense, communications good, farms widespread. Partly as a response to war, when larger concentrations of people possibly offered greater security, and partly because they enabled more social interaction, *oppida* emerge in many of the tribal territories. Research at many sites (see particularly MONT BEUVRAY) has made it abundantly clear that the open-ended Roman term for a settlement, *oppidum*, actually means a town. For Caesar they must have seemed primitive, only using stone in their ramparts and lacking the organized street pattern or distinctive buildings of the Mediterranean city; the enclosure of land for pasture and market gardening must have been confusing. Yet the ramparts were solid enough; there were large numbers of houses – some with distinctive Gallic cellars, linked by roads, even if they were not straight or especially well made. These towns were structured into separate quarters occupied by the houses of craft artisans, farmers and the wealthier. There were both open areas for meetings and religious enclosures, the latter often with a small wooden temple.

Celts, Gauls and Germans

While Hallstatt and La Tène are simply archaeological terms, pointing to how people had similar material styles of life, Celtic, Gallic and German are modern ethnic terms, deriving from past usage but not necessarily carrying the same meaning. From the fifth century BC onwards, Greek writers used 'Celt' to mean people to the north and west of them. Place-names and fragments of script, across central and western Europe, imply a common linguistic heritage as well. Most archaeologists and historians have long agreed that La Tène can be described as the material culture of these Celts; 'Gallus', or Gaul, was simply the Roman name for a Celt.

Yet modern archaeology has revised the traditional picture. There is no significant break from Hallstatt to La Tène, no great movements of people, nor, examining the era where only archaeology can contribute to the debate,

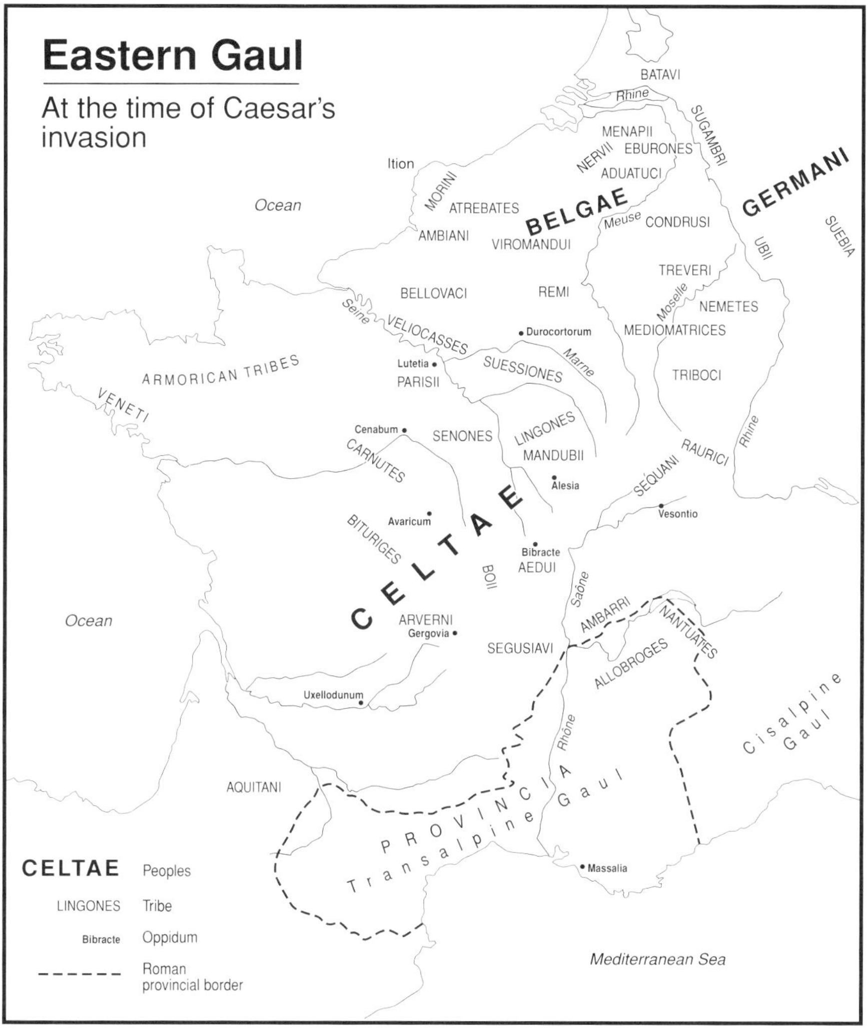

Figure 2 Eastern Gaul at the time of Caesar's invasion

can modern archaeologists see any break from the Bronze Age to Hallstatt. The significance of the absence of any signs of movement in the archaeological record also affects our vision of the extent of the Celtic world. It is clear that neither the British Isles nor Brittany were part of the core Celtic world, only taking on La Tène forms during the later Iron Age. Without evidence of mass migration, the 'Celtic world' is more likely to mean the spread of cultural attributes, both material and social, not the displacement of peoples.

Who then were Caesar's *Belgae* and *Germani*? Caesar was keen to assert that the Rhine was an ethnic division as it provided a clear limit for his conquests and evidence of his entering a new world by crossing it. However, there is no marked break here in La Tène, though there is the archaeological break between southern and northern Germany (La Tène/Jastorf)[1]; to what extent this reflects any meaningful ethnic difference is very difficult to know. Nor is this a sharp break. In northern Gaul stretching up to the Rhine, Caesar used the term 'Belgae' for the more western and settled, and 'German' for the more primitive warlike easterners on both sides of the lower Rhine. It could mean little more, then, than ethnic terminology for what were really contrasts in lifestyle.

Pre-Roman identity

If the terms 'Gaul' and 'German' were simply the crude labels used by Roman imperialists, on a par with 'Red Indian' for native American peoples, then how did these people identify themselves? A critical reading of Greek and Roman writers combined with archaeological research suggests that 'Galli' did have some real meaning: people of similar language(s) together with common cultural and religious beliefs, embodied most concretely in a priesthood of wise holy men, the Druids, recognized and revered throughout the region. For the Germans, it is probable that the term meant no more than the most generalized sense of origin in a particular part of the world; even when they encountered the Roman definition of themselves this failed to create a sharply felt sense of communal identity.

It is possible that people saw themselves as Belgae, but this may have had the same connotations as 'northerner' would have for English or Americans today. Certainly the Romans felt no need to reflect Caesar's pre-Roman tribal affiliations when the provincial boundaries were drawn and redrawn; both Belgica and Germania Superior were to contain German, Belgic and Celtic tribes. The strongest identity was probably the tribe: throughout the wars against (or for) Rome members were prepared to die for it. Even so, Caesar's commentaries are filled with nobles and their followers taking independent lines, and some would suggest that the clan or *pagus* could have been as strong. The Mandubii are seen as a clan or *pagus* who withdrew from one of the larger tribes in the north-west; other tribes, such as the Mediomatrices, are considered to be little more than federations of clans.

THE GALLIC WARS

Increasingly, from the later second century BC, Romans had become familiar figures in Gallic communities. Merchants came to trade and diplomats to make clear Rome's position on tribal disputes and migrations that might

Table: The Gallic wars

		Caesar's Gallic Wars	*Site reference*
60s BC	Allobrogian revolt in Transalpine Gaul crushed German Ariovistus defeats Aedui, allies of Rome		MONT BEUVRAY
59	Caesar made consul and obtains command of Transalpine Gallia (Provincia)		
58	Helvetii migration defeated; Ariovistus defeated	Book I	
57	Remi alliance formed; Caesar launches attack on Belgae; series of victories; north-west tribes concede.	Book II	REIMS BAVAY
56	Rising by north-west tribes and Belgae. Caesar crushes north-west (Venetii, etc.). Aquitani move defeated. Indecisive campaign against Belgae	Book III	
55	German campaign, Rhine crossing. First expedition to Britain Renewed resistance by Belgic coastal tribes	Book IV	
54	Second expedition to Britain. Intimidates Treveri. Winter rising leads to major Belgic revolt. Winters in Gaul to maintain position	Book V	MEAUX
53	Caesar devastates Belgic territories and Treveri. Moves to put down Senones and Carnutes	Book IV	SENS
52	Carnutes slaughter Romans. Vercingetorix of Arveni unites Gauls and has victory at Gergovia. Aedui join revolt, only Remi stay loyal. Alesia campaign and defeat of Vercingetorix and Gallic army	Book VII	ALESIA
51	No major resistance. Bellovaci crushed. Border campaigns in north-east near Rhine. Aquitani submit after defeat at Uxellodunum. Gaul 'at peace'	Book VIII	BEAUVAIS

threaten the stability of the region. Equally, leading figures amongst the Aedui must have gone to Rome as this tribe became Rome's closest 'friends' after 125 BC. Yet when it came, Caesar's invasion was a shattering experience that must have seared a generation.

For more than eight years, Julius Caesar used an army, never less than ten legions, that was two and a half times the size of that used later to conquer Britain, to defeat, ravage, crush and murder its way through Gaul. Brilliant, risk-taking and cool in action, manipulative and totally committed to winning power in Rome and even having the literary skills to produce a masterpiece of war reporting, Caesar, through victory in Gaul, won himself the opportunity to take on Pompey and win absolute power in the Roman empire. For the Gauls, apart, that is, from the Aedui and Remi who were the most consistent of allies, final defeat (51 BC) was followed by a long period of desolation, a time when only the elite who worked for the Romans, often leading cavalry auxiliaries (as they had been forced to do in the Gallic wars), benefited and started to adopt Roman ways. Some historians see this phase as lasting until the middle years of Augustus (20–10s BC), others believe that recovery only came with the favours of Claudius in the middle years of the first century. I would favour the former. Too many places seem to show both investment and growth from the time of Augustus onwards, in both towns and countryside. Despite opportunities, few joined rebellions. A new Gallo-Roman world was emerging.

THE EARLY ROMAN EMPIRE

At first Gallia Comata was simply conquered territory, the Roman empire embodied in two things: Roman troops and the payment of tribute, with little effort made to change it. The road building, initiated by Agrippa in 39 BC, that turned Lugdunum (Lyon) into a virtual capital city, was, in the first instance, undertaken to speed up the movement of Roman armies. A formal **administrative framework** was created under Augustus. First, the three Gauls were established: Lugdunensis, Aquitania and Belgica (see map, Figure 54 p. 253), each province with its own imperial legate or governor;[2] second, tribes were identified as *civitates*, cities with their supporting countryside. Where oppida existed they had to be transformed, or, more commonly, new sites selected to create these *civitas* capitals with as many of the Roman defining elements as possible: made roads on a rectilinear grid, forums, theatres, amphitheatres, baths, temples, grand houses. These urban centres emerged only gradually. Most of Caesar's tribes survived, but changes were made to benefit some and weaken others as clans or *pagi* were transferred from one *civitas* to another (e.g. REIMS). The first census was taken (27 BC) and then repeated to allow more efficient taxation.

The German wars of Augustus, and the periodic campaigns of the first century AD by the Rhine legions, culminated in the formation during the 80s of the two German provinces of Germania Inferior (Lower) and Superior (Upper). Germania Inferior took in the Rhine delta and was governed from Cologne (Köln); Germania Superior took in a far more heterogeneous region. The core was still the old Rhineland with the legionary and Rhine naval base of Mainz as its capital, but it also embraced a large segment of trans-Rhine territory, the Agri Decumates, settled in part by Gallic colonists, and a very large segment of southern Belgica, including north-west Switzerland and not only Alsace but also much of the Lorraine plateau.

First-century events and second-century peace

Politically the German wars of Augustus had a mixed impact on Gaul. Gaul received more attention from the imperial family as the main centre for supplying and backing up the armies; it reinforced Lyon's key role for co-ordinating the military effort and for measures to ensure loyalty such as the foundation of the Condate altar dedicated to proclaiming the greatness of Rome (12 BC). A new priesthood was founded drawn from the leading families of Gaul, who made annual pilgrimages to Lyon to demonstrate their loyalty. While Romanization was hastened, the increase in taxation, and the indebtedness incurred by some of the nobility in their rush to adopt Roman modes of display, also led to some unrest. In AD 21 disaffection was widespread, but a revolt won no significant backing and was easily suppressed (see AUTUN).

The invasion of Britain (AD 43) did not create the same pressures. The military effort was never as great and both the British conquest and the Rhine frontiers were likely to have encouraged the production of surplus food and materials. Gallic *sigillata* pottery[3] replaced Italian; clothing became a major industry (see 'Dress and Appearance'); Gallic wine producers joined those of Italy and Spain. Demand from the army was coupled with that of the growing cities, and industries like quarrying, mining and timber were stimulated. Claudius, perhaps more sensitive to these changes because of his birth in Lyon, took a positive line. In 48, he granted Aeduan nobles the right to undertake careers that would lead to membership of the Senate, and his speech, recorded by Tacitus and on a plaque (see LYON, page 403) shows that he saw this as the beginning of the right of all wealthy Gauls to integration in the Roman aristocracy. While in Spain this led to great senatorial families generating Roman emperors like Trajan or Hadrian, the second century for Gaul was a political blank in which few of its leading men seem to have taken up any kind of career in Rome.

The civil wars that marked the death of Nero may have helped induce this effect though they in no way inhibited overall Romanization. The turmoil of four emperors in two years, ill-disciplined armies, uncertainty if not panic, led to Julius Civilis, a Batavian auxiliary commander, heading a revolt. Although there was some support in the Three Gauls, the main concentration was in the Rhineland and was easily put down. It still shook Roman opinion. For a time a legion was withdrawn from the frontier zone to the interior in Burgundy (see STRASBOURG). After this, Gallic and German troops were not normally kept in the region and their commanders were not locals.

The events of 68–9 did little to stop Gaul's increasing prosperity. Gaul was at peace for the next 120 years. The Flavian period (69–96) saw extensive new building in stone in many cities, a constant feature well into the second century. There was a rural transformation as well. Environmental studies suggest that agriculture suffered badly for a number of years after the Gallic wars, particularly in the north and east of Gaul where land reverted to forest and pasture. It may be that the Gallic wars had an immediate impact on population levels. Excavations have shown that farms everywhere continued to be of an indigenous type (see ARCHEODROME). Recognizable *villas* start to emerge in the Rhône valley before the end of the first century BC, but they were only becoming widespread in eastern Gaul from mid-first century AD. In mountainous regions, like the Vosges, villas were always rare (see SAVERNE).

But the villa farms that by the second century dominated much of the landscape were never simply Roman transplants, even if some had non-Gallic owners. The Somme area in particular has revealed through aerial photography that many were built on or close to their indigenous predecessors and evolved in a distinct way with a central house and its gardens, then a yard with many subsidiary buildings, only some of which were farm buildings – others were smaller homes: they seem to reflect the social structure of the old elite and their dependants. Excavations have traditionally focused on the main living accommodation, revealing the increasingly romanized style of living with stone and painted plaster walls, tiled roofs, mosaic floors and bath systems (see JONVELLE), but at BLIESBRUCK the formal yard has a series of symmetrical houses, presumably the homes of dependent farmers (see also ST ULRICH). Some villa development must have been stimulated by the need to feed the troops on the Rhineland; the Somme villas built close to the main west–east road fall into this category. But by the second century many more villas will have been satisfying the needs of the flowering urban centres.

Another change in the landscape was the emergence of the small town: where inscriptions have survived they usually seem to have achieved the status of *vicus*. Although only meaning a simple type of self-government, this word has generally come to be used for a settlement clearly beyond hamlet size, but without the status of being a city. They range from isolated settlements (COMPIERRE) to major centres. Most of these evolved organically, often with only late attempts to give them any regularity (ALISE-STE-REINE and MALAIN). Occasionally they exceeded the size of provincial cities and had grand temples and theatres attached (MANDEURE).

The importance of *vici* has been underplayed in the past. Too many had been wrongly identified as simply rural sanctuaries. Certainly Arcenant, hidden in woods and obviously poor, was rural (see NUITS-ST-GEORGES). Indeed, even rich sanctuaries like the isolated VILLARDS-D'HERIA or the great complex at GRAND were never towns, but many others, it is now being recognized, formed part of a settlement and, in reality, the sanctuary might not even have been the dominant element. A very few sanctuaries were town substitutes, meeting places for religious and exchange ceremonies recalling the border area temple sites of pre-Roman Gaul (see GENAINVILLE). They are a reminder that the Gallic provinces developed their own distinctive religious practices that accepted Roman and then eastern deities, but clung tenaciously to local Gallic beliefs and developed a distinctive temple design, the *fanum* (see THE ROMANO-CELTIC SANCTUARY).

Population estimates can only be of the broadest kind, based as they are on disputed assumptions about town densities, settlement frequencies, life expectancy data from better-known provinces, generalizations about tax levels, or historical analogy with later societies assumed to be at a similar stage of development. Yet some points are agreed. Most earlier estimates should be revised upwards. The population of Gaul was larger than in the Iron Age (then perhaps 8 million). It is also clear that settlement density in the countryside was much higher than previously assumed, even if town populations might have been smaller – but this tends to be balanced out by the recognition of the size and number of small towns. A recent estimate for the Three Gauls and Germany suggests 1 million or more lived in the small towns, cities and army camps.[4] Ten times more lived in the country: a total of *c.*11–12 million.

Gallo-Roman identity

For the first time, by writing commorative inscriptions, we have explicit statements by Gauls on how they saw themselves. The vast majority are in Latin; a very, very few are in Celtic, but written in Latin or Greek characters. The deceased were presented regularly with their *origo* (stock or origin) as a *civitas*; tribal identity continued to be relevant but it could no longer be fed by semi-permanent war as it had been before conquest. Equally interesting are their personal names. Studies suggest that initially, in the early first century AD, we find two main kinds of inscription: first, the straight Roman names, some with the classic *tria nomina*. These must be the incomers and those keen to demonstrate that they have obtained Roman citizenship: they are concentrated in major urban centres. There are also those families who are gradually adapting, where fathers give sons and daughters Roman rather than Gallic names. But from the mid-second century a new trend emerges, a return to single or double names and a mix of Gallic and Roman names. This is now seen not as a Celtic revival, anti-Roman in spirit, but as a sign that you could indeed carry layered loyalty: you could be Gallic (or German) *and* Roman. It is the same message given by the the distinctive provincial dress: there was no shame in being Gallo-Roman.

The third-century crisis

It is surprising that the Roman empire had not collapsed by the end of the third century: certainly the Gaul that emerged in the fourth century was part of a very different society. There is some debate on how early the problems began. On the German frontiers the 170s saw an upsurge in activity, but the biggest threat faced the Danube provinces, where Marcus Aurelius fought a series of major campaigns to contain the Marcomanni. There is a hint of disorder amongst the Sequani, and Maternus, an army deserter, led a popular bandit movement over a number of years in the 180s. In 193, another year of four emperors, Clodius Albinus as a self-proclaimed Caesar ruled Britain and Gaul with his capital at Lyon, until destroyed in the battle of Lugdunensis by Septimius Severus (197). Lyon never recovered its leading role in Gaul. Yet, under the Severan dynasty (193–235), there is evidence of continued building in many of the cities, and there were no serious incursions across the Rhine.

Few among the generations who lived through the 240s to 270s could have avoided distress of some kind. Civil wars were frequent, usually inspired by army commanders; it was rare for the Rhine garrisons not to be involved. As troops marched across Gaul, looting was common and the frontier was left far less securely guarded. The Alamanni, first mentioned in 213, became frequent marauders from the 230s, and the Franks, first mentioned in 259, made massive and wide-ranging attacks in 259/60 and 275/6. Increased banditry is apparent in the need for *beneficii*, Roman soldiers on detachment as road police. Rewarding troops for their services, whether for being loyal or disloyal, led to the debasement of currency to make the coins go further: it became a period of rampant inflation. Archaeology has provided abundant evidence of the shock and pain: the dramatic rise in coin and treasure hoards after 250; the presence of extensive fire levels – the precise cause does not really matter, when these are so widespread; the pattern of ruined villas whether in Alsace, Picardy or the Rhône valley; the dramatic contraction of towns large and small, some even being totally abandoned (e.g. MALAIN); the decline of many sanctuaries.

Was the distress of the third century more than the interaction of civil war, barbarian invasion and a collapse of the market economy through currency debasement? The plagues that struck widely through the empire, particularly between 165 and 190 and again between 251 and 266, when thousands died every day,[5] would certainly have exacerbated the situation. But were these the products of a deeper malaise present in all pre-industrial economies: the threat of rising population and the inability to do more than push the margins of production? It has been argued that during the second half of the second century the limits had been reached and the surplus could no longer be raised or distributed quickly enough to maintain the standard of living and the needs of government. The numbers of poor would have increased, the poverty of their diet making them increasingly vulnerable to all diseases. So far, the consensus seems to be that plagues were simply an additional stress for people to endure rather than part of a population crisis.[6]

Crisis and identity

The key years were perhaps 260–74. The disorder and constant warfare of the 250s had led to the proclamation of a local military commander, Postumus, as emperor. His successors in Gaul were finally crushed by Aurelian. What was unusual was that the population (or at least its elite) seems to have been prepared to accept what was in practice a regional 'Roman' empire, one that has since been named the Gallic empire. It is the first real sign that being Roman could be separated from rule by Rome. It is equally important in showing that traditional tribal loyalties no longer especially mattered. Perhaps not surprisingly, when the new order of late antiquity emerged, the 'tribe' had become the shrunken city: the old Lutetia becomes Civitas Parisiorum. The multiple problems faced during the crisis were now seen through Gallo-Roman eyes: the interests of both the rich and poor crossed over the old boundaries. For the rich it was the preservation of a Roman lifestyle, for the poor preservation from the depredations of all armies and marauders.

LATE ANTIQUITY IN GAUL

The late Roman empire

That the empire did not disintegrate was the result of the measures taken by two determined and competent men, Diocletian (284–305) and Constantine (306–37). Maybe their least conscious decision concerned Rome itself. Emperors were frequently on the move to deal with the many problems that confronted them. During the fourth century the city stopped being the residence of emperors and therefore a significant political centre, though it remained the cultural and emotional heart. The preservation of Gaul and the German provinces – and with them much of the western half of the empire – focused on Trier (which developed all the features of an imperial capital). In the south, Vienne, and later Arles, provided similar facilities and great warehouses for supplies, linked in turn with the Italian capital at Milan. In our region, Metz maintained a significant role as a junction city.

Diocletian attempted to handle the sheer size of the empire in an era of permanent disarray by formalizing shared responsibilities. His 'tetrarchy' or four-man rule, entailing two full emperors (Augusti) and a supporter for each (Caesars), did not last. It was inherently unstable: strife between the men led back to one-man rule and the desire to perpetuate families led to periodic and usually short-lived child emperors. Usurpers did not disappear. Yet the underlying logic was that the empire was too much for one person; it became the norm for emperors to appoint Caesars as their deputies and an east–west split of responsibilities became common; from 395 it was automatic.

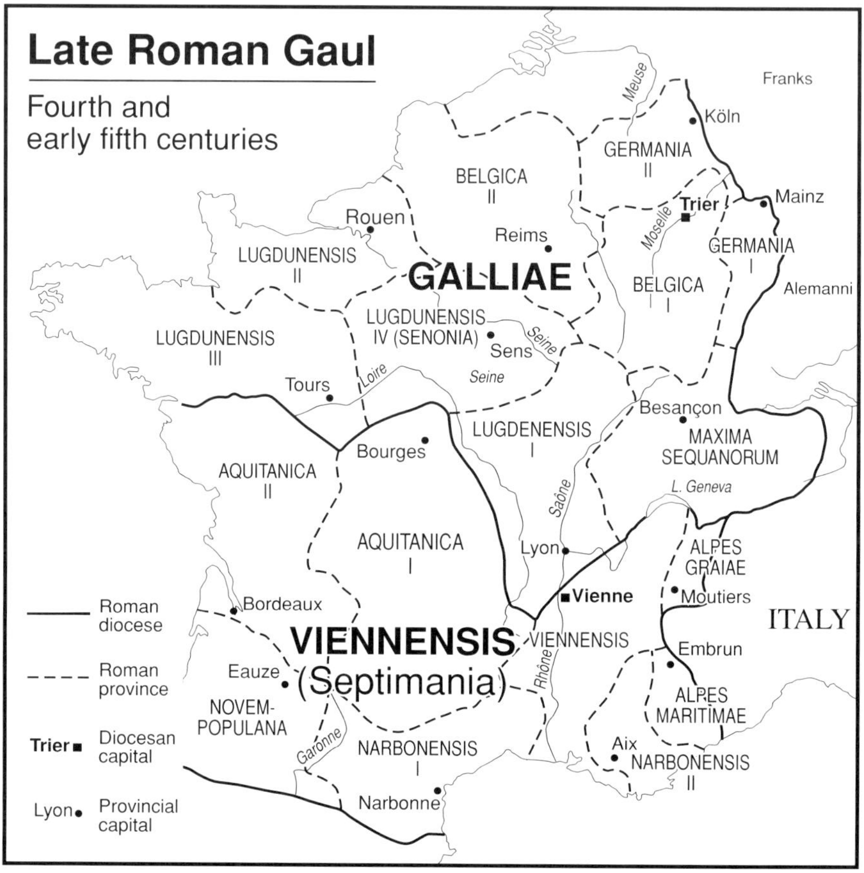

Figure 3 Late Roman eastern Gaul

A major administrative restructuring, aimed at increasing imperial control of the provinces, was undertaken, based on the concept of small provinces organized in large dioceses under 'vicars'. The new provinces were not only much smaller (see Figure 3), but their governors retained control simply of civilian administration, military forces coming under separate commands, led by a *dux* or *comes*.

The army, it is now recognized, was not dramatically changed, but had been evolving and continued to do so into a very different body of men. The need for a mobile force, which Augusti and Caesars could lead to deal with emergencies, had led to the field army or *comitatus*, particularly strong in cavalry. The old legions multiplied in number and frequently became part of the static frontier forces or *limitanei*. These legions were much smaller, *c.*1000+ men instead of the old *c.*5000. It was not perhaps a major change because they had long fought in smaller units or vexillations, but it did reduce the difference between them and auxiliary units. Recruits, too, were different, drawn increasingly from less Romanized sources: Danubians had dominated in the third century; in the fourth Germans, and especially Franks, became the major source for the western armies. There were also more men in the army. The total during the second century is generally thought to have numbered 250–300,000; now there were perhaps as many as 400,000.

Late Roman Gaul, along with the other provinces, had somehow to bear the burden of this much larger army and a much enlarged government administration. It may be that the actual taxes, although more widely collected in kind, particularly to provide the army's *annona* or corn supply, were not raised significantly. However, Diocletian had made tax collection systematic, working out rates for in-kind payments based on a census, and increasingly these were collected through the large landowners as the most convenient method. Inevitably, there was a rise in the numbers of those seeking tax-avoidance, led by the high ranking. Emperors, keen to win loyalty among the elite, responded by increasing the number of senators, who no longer needed to be in Rome, and offering a wide variety of ranks granting tax exemption. Patronage, the norm in the early empire, now became divorced from responsibility. No one wanted the burdens of office – primarily because town councillors, the *decuriones*, had to make up shortfalls in taxes; corruption was rife. While the privileged avoided taxation, the poorest, those now tied to the land, were the prime taxpayers, liable to the harshest punishments for non-payment.

The market economy, even if this had never been an important feature of life for the majority, was severely contracted. The notable trends were to local production, for basic materials like pottery, clothing and daily metalware, and government-controlled production, primarily for the army and bureaucracy. Amiens manufactured shields and swords, Autun armour, others status-defining brooches and belts. The most obvious physical change were the dramatically reduced towns, hidden by their new ramparts, nearly all built upon foundations made from the public buildings and tombstones of the early empire citizens: the break with the past was brutal. Vici that revived were smaller, and where considered strategic, defended (see ANSE). In the countryside, the impact varied. The upland 'native' settlements in the Vosges were abandoned. The valley of the Aisne in northern France saw a decline in settlements – probably a mix of absolute decline in population and a move to larger places for security, both hamlets and larger villas. The Rhône saw a revival in villas. Undoubtedly some of the large landowners prospered. Even in the north-east, villas like those at Bliesbruck and St Ulrich show how a luxurious life on the Roman model could continue for the few.

Christianity only made significant inroads in central and northern Gaul during the fifth century (though martyrs are known in Lyon in the second century and toleration in 313 was quickly followed by active state support).

Few bishops are known and far fewer churches, the earliest notable remains coming at the very end of the fourth and beginning of the fifth centuries (see LYON and GRENOBLE). Pagan sanctuaries may have been less prosperous as a whole, but the economic and political environment is more likely to have been responsible. Destruction levels, such as that at Châteaubleau, have been blamed on Christians and in this case may be true, but barbarian looters, civil strife and accidental fire are likely to have been responsible more generally.

Though Roman Gaul was vulnerable in so many ways, it did surprisingly well at stemming barbarian attack. Perhaps until the 350s it faced lower intensity attacks from barbarians than previously, but when Magnentius, a Gallic usurper (349–52), stimulated a major civil war in the west, which in turn led to an influx of German warrior bands, the new Caesar, Julian, was able to campaign successfully and win a major victory at Strasbourg.[7] Even after Julian died, further German troubles were repressed by Valentinian with campaigns and new forts in Germany in the 360s. As recent work at Vireux-Molhain and at Arras has shown, even in the 380s and 390s both forts and barracks were being occupied by organized troops. Gradually, though, the enormity of the defeat of Valentinian's brother Valens at Adrianople in 378 emerged as the Visigoths ranged at will across the empire. To confront them troops had to be withdrawn widely in the west; this was never adequate to defeat the Visigoths, but it seriously weakened defences. Two major events marked a decisive downturn for Roman Gaul. First, in 406 a mass crossing of the Rhine by Vandals, Alans and Suevi followed by the Alamanni. The Franks remained largely loyal to Rome, though it made little difference as the invaders swept over Gaul and Spain. Second, the Visigoths, now in Italy, turned on Rome itself and sacked the city (410); the magnitude of the shock to the Roman world is reflected in all the literary sources. Whatever was to emerge from these disasters, it could not be Gallo-Roman.

The fifth and sixth centuries

Only briefly, during the 460s and 470s, when the cultured Gallic senator Sidonius Apollinaris produced his invaluable letters, are there dependable local sources for this period. What is certain is that military forces consistently recognizing the authority of Rome were in a minority. The Visigoths in Aquitania were settled as *feoderati*, and so were the Burgundians, who had followed the Vandals across the Rhine and were eventually established in Savoy and the Jura (Sapaudia) in 443. Although their treaty agreements bound them to fight for the empire, this could only be when there was an independent Roman force in Gaul strong enough to persuade them to do so. In the north, occupying Belgica I and a large part of Belgica II, were groups of Franks. In the north-west, Armorica was flooded by refugees fleeing the disorders in Britain. For a time in the 420s and 430s Aëtius, Master of the

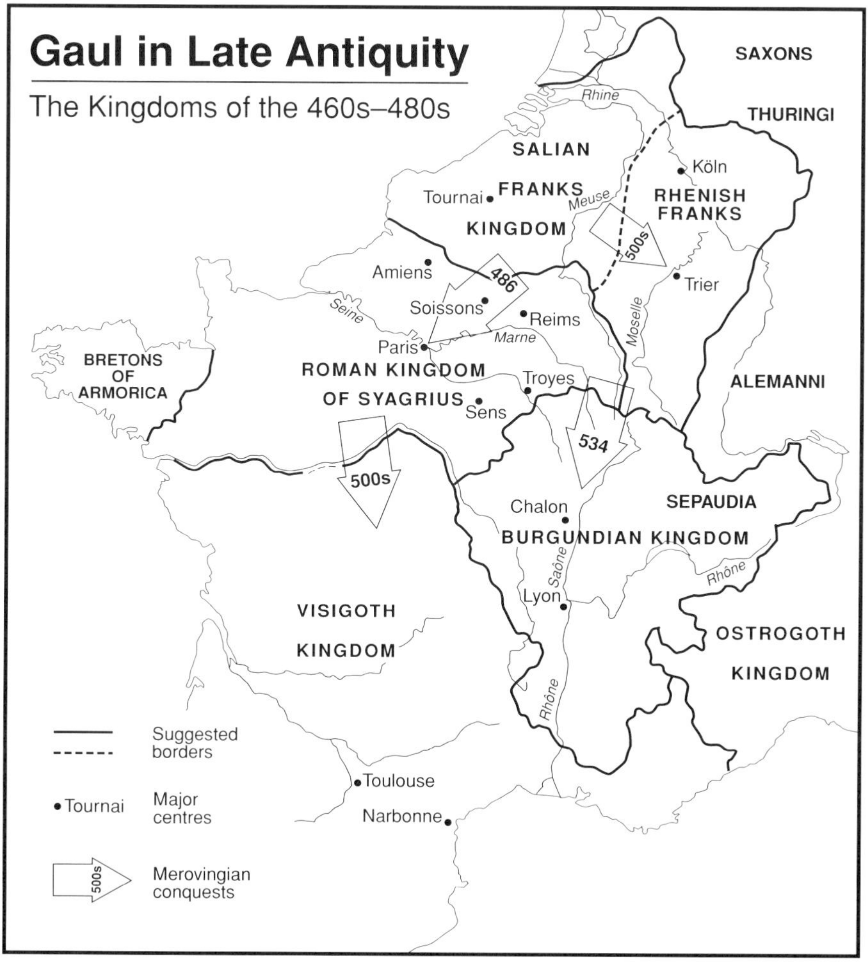

Figure 4 Eastern Gaul in late antiquity

Soldiers, brought up by the Huns and with Hunnish support, was able to assert recognition of the Roman imperial order. When the Huns and their tribal coalition decided to act on their own, crossed Germany and invaded Gaul, Aëtius led the force that defeated them (see TROYES), but his army was almost entirely drawn from the settler tribes of Gaul and his failure to control his friends discredited him for ever.

The last gasps of Roman authority quickly followed. The Visigoths hardened their control of the south-west and the Burgundians moved down into the Saône and Rhône valleys, taking Lyon (469). Further north, Aegidius and then Syagrius, generally considered local warlords rather than servants of the Roman empire, held out briefly against Frankish pressure. Their authority began to crumble when the Merovingian family, led first by Childeric then by Clovis, gave leadership and coherence to the western or Salian Franks; the end came at the battle of Soissons (486). By then the Roman emperors of the west were so insignificant that the child emperor Romulus, 475–6, was retired without replacement – and allowed to live.

The only chance of any meaningful revival of Roman rule in Gaul now depended on the eastern Roman empire; could the west be reconquered? Until the 530s it had too many problems of its own, but Justinian (537–65) made the reconquest of 'remaining countries which the ancient Romans possessed to the limits of both oceans' (Novel 30)[8] a real imperial project. North Africa was regained easily and Italy followed after many years fighting, though soon lost to the Lombards after his death: the only meaningful link with Gaul was an alliance with the Franks to keep them from intervening in Italy. Following the battle of Soissons, Clovis (480–511) had murdered most of his relatives (echoing Roman practice) and turned on his neighbours, defeating fellow Franks to take the northern Rhineland (the Alamanni taking the southern Rhineland), pushed the Visigoths out of most of Aquitania and conquered the territories of the Burgundians. Despite Clovis dividing his state into parts for his sons, through a process of mutual slaughter it was reunited again by 561. The continuous history of France can be traced back to these Frankish founders.

Origins: Frank, Alamanni, Burgundian

'Frank' seems to have been a German term originally meaning 'the fierce', but came to mean 'the free'; it is the most nebulous group of all in the third to fifth centuries. It was first used by the Romans to refer to those Germans living to the north-east of the lower Rhine. Many were recruited to the Roman army to become its foot soldiers and its generals. They were particularly concentrated in north-east Gaul. The Alamanni were simply a federation called 'all peoples' by the Romans, who occupied land south of the Main. The Burgundian tribe may have come originally from Scandinavia via the north German Baltic coast to east of the middle Rhine, but many different tribes were absorbed on the way. Alamanni, Frank and Burgundian were not, then, ethnic identities, but blanket terms. It is not surprising that the Franks with their long experience of defending the empire were the most successful at state building.

The new world

By the mid-sixth century, the old Roman provinces of Gaul were governed by a variety of barbarian kings, some for more than a hundred years. In the south were the Visigoths; in the Jura, Savoy and the Rhône valley the Burgundian kingdom had come and gone; finally, the Regnum Francorum, the kingdom of the Franks, had emerged in the north to take control of much of what would become France, Belgium, the Netherlands and western regions of Germany. The Germanic law codes, such as the later fifth century Burgundian *Liber Constitutionum* and the Frankish *Pactus Legis Salicae* of the early sixth century, have been taken to suggest a sharp divide between a privileged elite of Germans and subject peoples, yet modern research and interpretative framework suggests that the Merovingian world did not have such a simple ethnic divide.

For many Gallo-Romans the world must have seemed to change very little. Warfare was frequent, soldiers and their families settled and civilians relocated to fill depopulated areas (particularly in north-east Gaul): what was new? Governments claimed to rule with the approval of the Roman emperors, yet the difference between Aëtius in the 440s and Clovis, made Consul by Anastasius, must have seemed minimal. The taxes collected were the same as those of the fourth century, the laws that ran were late Roman, modified by royal decree, just as they had been by imperial edict, while petitioning to mollify the oppressiveness of the regime hardly differed. Even if the villas had fallen into ruin and some landowning families were replaced by Germans, the estates had not disappeared; tied labourers and slaves were still present, though they lived much more commonly in small hamlets (see MARLE). The move away from a market economy and low value coins had been continuous since at least the later 200s. Until 576, Frankish gold coins bore the head of the emperor, not the king. Latin was the written language of all educated people and forms of Gallo-Latin were still spoken by the majority; Germanic languages only made progress in the north and east of Gaul.

Identities

How did people perceive themselves in this world? Social class was one deep-seated division between people. The distinction between the *honestiores* – the honourable elite – and *humiliores* – the humble masses – remained. While Roman law was gradually modified in the new states, it did not change the fundamental position of the wealthy, ranking them as *honestiores* who could avoid torture and receive lesser forms of punishment. Given that the power of landlords and military men had not changed (though the holders of that power did), for the mass of 'Roman' inhabitants the strongest identity is likely to have been with family and locality. The study of human remains in rural cemeteries suggests that there may have been little mixing with outsiders. As Christianity spread, so some came to feel the need to assert that side of their identity quicker in the towns than in the country, quicker in the south than the north. Burials without any evidence of Christian belief continue well into the sixth century.

The landowning elite of late Roman Gaul had been gradually adjusting to fit new realities throughout the fourth, fifth and sixth centuries. Of course, numbers were killed, others fled, but to survive as a group and retain as much wealth as possible – primarily their estates – lay in the redefinition of 'Roman'. During the fourth century they lost any realistic stake in military matters; during the fifth century they gradually learnt there was no future in a traditional Roman administrative or political career. The key to the retention of any power now lay in their cultural role. Rhetoric, literature and legal expertise were needed by the barbarian states and families could supply advisers, courtiers and lawyers, just as they once had to governors and emperors. More crucial, because it gave them a status less dependent on the whims and immediate needs of kings, was to adapt their control of communities by becoming bishops in the Christian Church. While the fourth-century bishops are shadowy figures or militants often from a low status background, in the fifth century the great landowners moved in: episcopal sanctity enhanced them as patron brokers between the people and the state. The best known example is Sidonius Apollinaris (432–*c.*480). Drawn from a senatorial family in Lyon, but with extensive estates, he made a career in Rome in the 450s and returned to Gaul as an administrator and then switched to the Church in the 470s. But others such as Germanus (see AUXERRE) had earlier shown the way; in the generation after Sidonius, Remigius (see REIMS) was to baptize Clovis. As the mass conversions of the fifth century were given a parochial structure in the sixth century, so their survival was ensured.

What of the Franks? With the world of Gallic late antiquity we are at the limits of current archaeology and history; identifying this group within the much wider population is especially difficult. Attempts to find them in distinctive clothes, names, language, burial rites, even weaponry, fail because it is clear that none of these can be tied to either a particular place or time. Most have a far wider spread, both chronologically and geographically, than the kingdom founded by Childeric and Clovis in the later fifth century. The Franks must, then, be seen in two ways. Many of the descendants of the German settlers and earlier warriors of the fourth century who had served in the army, *laeti* or *feoderati*, may well have considered themselves Roman by the late fifth and early sixth century when the Regnum Francorum was being established. The fifth-century people who called themselves Salians were a group driven by an ambitious family, the Merovingians, who, as they expanded, developed a new identity for themselves. As we know from contemporary experience, it is not what we wear or consider to be our kinds of goods, not the names we give ourselves and the language we speak, not the religion we follow and not a matter of physical being but ultimately a question of how we are perceived by others and how we perceive ourselves. These Merovingian Franks were the military and political leaders of the state who chose an ethnic label to distinguish themselves from others: they were who they were because they said so, and others accepted this.

Notes

1 In northern Germany and Scandinavia, where forests and a less settled agriculture prevailed, a distinctive middle and late Iron Age culture evolved, characterized by the Jastorf style of ornament.
2 Noting that Savoy was divided between the *civitas* of the Allobroges (part of the province of Narbonne), and the separate, small, Alpine provinces of Alpes Graiae and Poeninae.
3 A mass-produced red ware called Samian in Britain, but known as *sigillata* in continental Europe.
4 Anthony King 1990: 106–8.
5 The first was perhaps an early version of smallpox. The bubonic plague is not firmly identified until the plague of 542–3, but the black rats that carried the fleas with the bacillus are known in France in the second century.
6 The argument that there was a demographic crisis starting before the plagues has been put by Willem Jongman of Groningen University (2001, *Transformation of Economic Life under the Roman Empire*, Conference, Nottingham).
7 See the account of Julian's military career by the last great Roman historian, Ammianus Marcellinus.
8 The 'Novels' were a series of laws. Quoted by Richard Reece 1999: 170.

CHRONOLOGY

Date	*Roman Gaul and the Rhineland*	*Site reference*	*Events elsewhere*	*Central government*
44 BC			Julius Caesar murdered Civil War	Republic
43	Lyon founded	LYON	Octavian wins West	
40	Octavian in Gaul			
39	Agrippa begins road network programme			
31			Octavian wins Actium	
27	Augustus visits Gaul Transalpine Gaul made Narbonensis Province Three Gauls organization begun		Augustus (Octavian)	Principate Augustus 27 BC–AD 14
22	Narbonensis made Senatorial province (no troops)			
16	Augustus in Gaul			
12 BC	Condate Altar founded at Lyon		German wars begin	
AD 9			Destruction of Varus	
14–17			Germanicus revenge campaigns	Tiberius 14–37
21	Rebellion of Florus and Sacrovir put down	AUTUN		
43	Invasion and conquest of Britain			Claudius 41–54
48	Claudian table	LYON		
68	Julius Vindex rebels and proclaims Galba		Civil wars 68–69	Nero's death
69	Julius Civilis and Gallic revolt crushed		Flavian emperors 69–96	Vespasian 69–79
85	Creation of German provinces	LANGRES STRASBOURG		Domitian 81–96
80s	Argentorate (Strasbourg) fortress built of stone 'An age without history'	STRASBOURG		Trajan 97–117 Hadrian 117–38 Antoninus Pius 138–161
160s			Empire-wide plague Marcomanni	Marcus Aurelius
170s			Wars on Danube	161–80

195	Albinus asserts rival claim to empire based on Lyon	LYON		Septimius Severus 193–211
197	Defeat and death of Albinus at battle of Lyon			
213	Caracalla grants citizenship to free in empire			Caracalla 211–17
	Caracalla's German campaign against Alamanni			
233	Alamanni incursions on frontier			
242	Alamanni troubles	STRASBOURG	Withdrawal from Agri Decumates	Short-lived emperors 235–60
254	Alamanni troubles			
259/260	Major incursions of Alamanni and Franks			Gallienus 253–68
260–8	Postumus: Gallic empire			
268–70	Victorinus: Gallic empire			
	Seige and sack of Autun	AUTUN		
273	Tetricus surrenders Gallic empire to Aurelian			Aurelian 270–75
276	Major incursion by Franks			Probus 276–82
280–2	First agreed settlement of Frankish group in empire			
286/7	Carausius, Boulogne fleet commander, sets up independent British empire	BOULOGNE	Diocletian appoints Maximian in West	Diocletian 284–305
296	Constantine Chlorus, Caesar in west, retakes London	ARRAS		
290s	Trier made capital of Galliae provinces	(see map)	Administrative and tax reforms	
	Successes against Alamanni			
310s	Free Franks contained		313 Edict of Milan: Christianity tolerated	Constantine 306–37
	Constantine campaigns in Germany			
349–352	The usurper Magnentius proclaimed at Autun. Wins Gaul and Britain; defeat at battle of Mursa			
355–360	Julian made Caesar and sent to Gaul to repel barbarians (Franks and Alamanni). Victories	STRASBOURG		
360	Julian proclaimed Augustus in Paris	PARIS		Julian 360–63
368	Valentian campaigns in Germany and builds new forts			Valentian (west) 364–75
378			Visigoths triumph at Adrianople	Valens (east) 364–78
392			Law against paganism	Theodosius 379–95

Roman Gaul and the Rhineland		*Site reference*	*Events elsewhere*	*Central government*
395	Trier abandoned as imperial capital. Troops being withdrawn from Gaul and Britain to fight elsewhere	ARRAS	Arles and Milan western capitals	Honorius (west) 395–423
406	Rhine crossing. Invasions by Vandals, Alans, Suevi; Alamanni join them	BIESHEIM CORA	410 Visigoths sack Rome	
	Franks fight in name of Romans	VIRIEUX		
412/419	Visigoths settle in Aquitania and then invade Spain		Vandals leave Spain for Africa in 428	
420s–440s	Roman general Aëtius campaigns in Gaul: Visigoths contained			
	Franks contained	CAMBRAI		
	Burgundians settled in Savoy and Jura			
451	Battle of Catalaunian Fields. Hun invasion defeated by Visigoths and Salian Franks	METZ + PARIS TROYES		
469	Burgundians take Lyon	LYON		
470s	Visigoths take Massif Central			
	Salian Franks established in most of Belgica			
450s–486	Roman warlord territory in north-west: Aegidius and then Syagrius		Last emperor of west	Romulus Augustulus 475–6
486	Clovis destroys Roman warlords	SOISSONS		
496?	Clovis baptized Christian (Catholic not Arian)	REIMS		
	Campaigns against Alamanni			
500	Campaigns against Burgundians			
508	Clovis makes Paris his capital	PARIS		
	Campaigns against Visigoths in Aquitania			
511	Campaigns against Ripuarian Franks (Cologne)			
	Clovis dies and kingdom divided			
530s	534 Merovingians take Burgundy			
	537 Merovingians take Provincia			
530s–560s	Regnum Francorum		Eastern Roman empire reconquers Italy 568 Lombards invade Italy	Justinian 527–65

1

THE SITES OF THE PARIS REGION AND NORTHERN FRANCE

ABBEVILLE, Somme

Museum site.
www.archéologie-aerienne.culture.gouv.fr

Musée Boucher de Perthes

Rue Gontier Patin
80100 Abbeville

Hours:	2 May–30 September	2–6p.m. Closed Tuesday
	1 October–30 April	Wednesday, Friday, Saturday only

This museum is dedicated to two great men. Its name recalls one of the most important founders of prehistory, the Abbeville customs officer, Jacques Boucher de Perthes (1788–1868), who began collecting what we now call Palaeolithic tool axes in the gravel pits of the Somme, and recognized that, as the new geology indicated, objects found in 'antediluvian', that is very old, deposits must be as old themselves. Further, these primitive tools were contemporaneous with his finds of elephant and rhinoceros bones, so man must have been living in a long distant past. It was a shattering combination of logic and evidence. In 1859, he received the recognition he deserved, initially from British scientists who came, saw – and photographed – hand axes in situ and were convinced.

The museum also commemorates the work of Roger Agache. His work as an aerial photographer revolutionized attitudes towards the potential of aerial photography as investigative archaeology. Perhaps his greatest work was demonstrating, at the beginning of the 1970s, that the Somme region had been covered with villas during the Roman period, many of them very large and imposing. He was able to bring out the significance of their discovery through his follow-up mapping, marking both these and their late Iron Age predecessors, pointing to the links between the two eras and the role played by the Roman roads (also revealed in his photographs), giving depth and

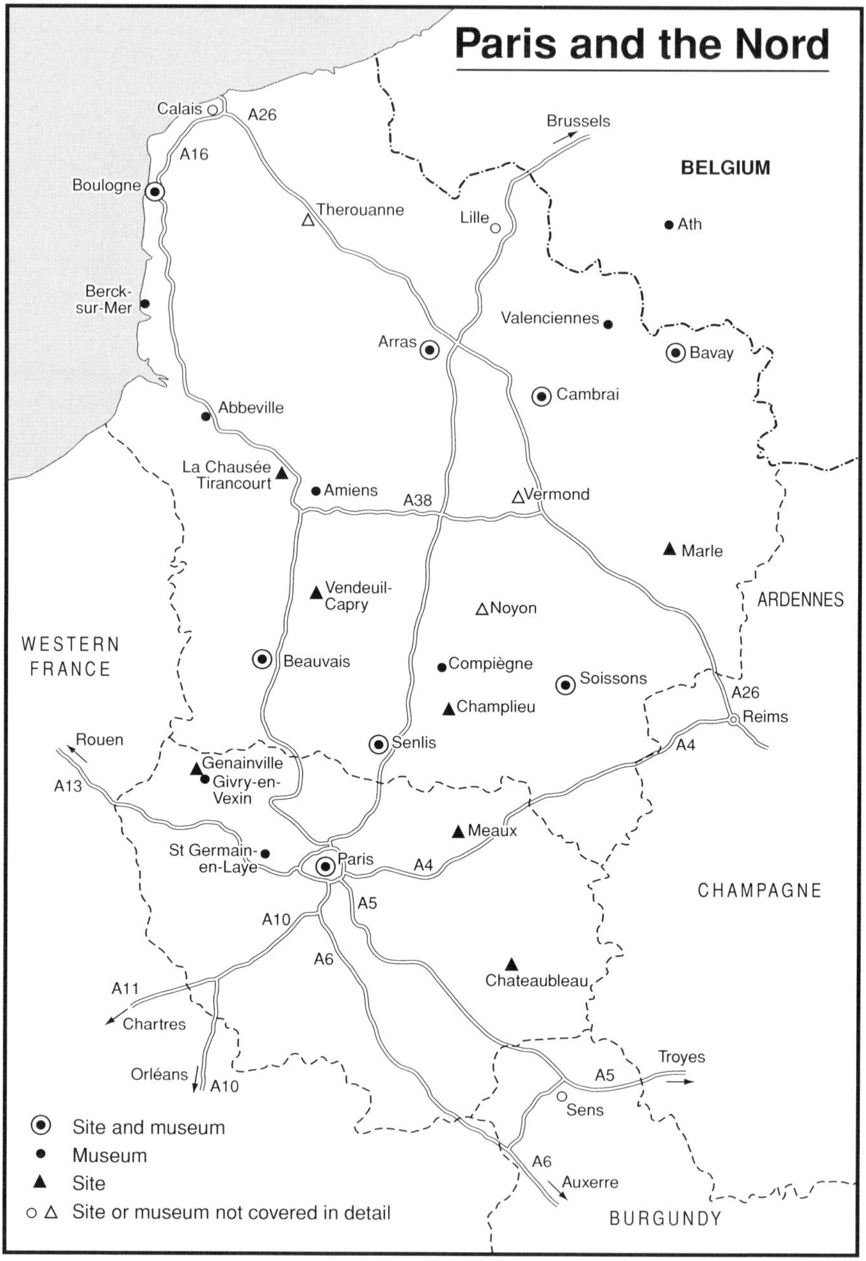

Figure 5 Regional map: Paris and the Nord

raising new questions concerning the relationship between the villas, new cities and long-distance military markets. Equally his work has helped push research in new directions through his photographs of known sites, showing unsuspected ditches and occupation (see LA CHAUSSEE TIRANCOURT). It is not simply that Agache has inspired aerial photographers everywhere, he has also consistently argued that archaeology should communicate, not just with other specialists, but with all people.

The collection

Agache's photographs of the late Iron Age and Gallo-Roman sites are featured in the entrance in a display roundel. Further photographs in the galleries show how his pictures demonstrate not only his superb skill in revealing hidden evidence but also a deep aesthetic sense of the environment.

Displays are periodically rotated between the public galleries and the reserve collection. They include older material such as the miniature flat figures of the late La Tène period suggesting phallic images, a form of male fertility imagery that may suggest Cernunnos, though he is more usually indicated by the addition of stag horns. While there is no evidence that there was any significant settlement at Abbeville during the Gallo-Roman period, isolated finds have been made here, including bronze jugs of high quality, one with a pair of finely wrought hands at the base of the handle. There is also an excellent lamp standard. More recent Gallo-Roman finds from outside Abbeville include an iron grill stand and a wine ladle, the latter found at Béhen, following the site's discovery in one of Agache's aerial surveys. Merovingian burials have provided typical examples of buckles and swords.

AMIENS, Somme

Museum site.

Amiens is frustrating. Well excavated for a number of years, yet there is nothing Gallo-Roman for the visitor to see outside the regional museum. Since the Second World War, local and regional governments have encouraged investigation – though not preservation – and the municipal archaeology service continues the meticulous work started by Vasselle, followed by Massy and Bayard. More has been discovered about the layout and development of the capital of the Ambiani tribe than about most other *civitas* capitals in northern France.

Samarabriva ('Samara crossing') was laid out in a classic grid pattern, on the southern bank of the Samara (Somme) river. No evidence of Gallic settlement has been found, though it is likely that there was a road here, as the gravel terraces would have made the naturally marshy river bed easier to cross. Possibly Julius Caesar identified this as the key point to control the region, but the enigmatic evidence from LA CHAUSSEE TIRANCOURT suggests that military surveillance in the area was done from there, though there are hints of a military presence on the site of Samarabriva from *c.*20 BC, perhaps linked to the construction of the major Lyon–Boulogne road.

In the last years of Augustus' reign city streets were laid out in rectangular blocks, aligned to the slopes of the valley, leaving the road cutting through them at an angle. The new town developed slowly and the grid was changed to squares (385 Roman feet/160m) in the 50s, when it began to grow more rapidly and the *insulae* to fill up. The buildings were still largely wood and cob, but stone foundations were more widely adopted under the Flavians; the forum was finally completed in the 70s/80s, unusually taking up two insulae linking the *macellum*, or commercial market, to the political and business centre in an exceptionally long building. No temple has been identified here or anywhere else in the town.

Evidence of a massive fire towards the end of the first century has been found at many sites in Amiens, but the town was rapidly rebuilt on a grander scale with more stone and better drains. There was a large public baths system with hot and cold swimming pools and an aqueduct to supply it with running water (though only fragments of the latter have been found and its course is unknown). An amphitheatre was constructed, unusually sited at the centre of the town, flush against the forum. Perhaps, as Massy and Bayard suggested, the city council found land deserted and cheap after the fire. Excavating the foundations for the late nineteenth-century Hôtel de Ville revealed the defining oval and foundation walls. Fragments of rich houses that occupied other central insulae have been found decorated with mosaics and wall paintings (none providing very extensive remains) and further building took place, even in the marshy northern areas. Once again major fire struck. Extensive fire levels dated to the 170s were again followed by reconstruction. During the early third century new building still took place but on a smaller scale. By the 240s Samarabriva, like so many other cities in Gaul, was beginning to show signs of contraction. There were renewed fires. Rubbish filled some areas, some insulae reverted to gardens and cemeteries began to encroach on sites previously occupied by the living. The barbarian invasions of the late third century were only the culmination of a declining ability to maintain classical life in Amiens.

Samarabriva was a genuine crossroads site: a major north–south road artery and an important east–west river route. In addition tributary rivers (the Avre and Selle were only the nearest) and roads made Samarabriva a good focal point for the regional economy, which was of course agricultural. Agache's brilliant aerial photography (see ABBEVILLE) revealed the density of villa estates across the Picardy plains. Meat, leather and bones would have helped stimulate local business, but wheat production must have played the key role. The army was a significant market and while much wheat would have gone east to the Rhineland frontier, some will have gone via Samarabriva to the Channel and either along the coast to Germany or more frequently to Britain. Equally, Samarabriva not only consumed the export goods from elsewhere, such as pottery, glass and wine, but must have been responsible for sending at least some of them down the Somme to St Valéry and to Britain; the discovery of both lead and tin ingots suggests that this also was a route for returning imports. There are hints, too, that it was a military transit point where troops perhaps rested when being moved from Britain to the Rhineland and back and that the surges in growth can be linked to the Claudian invasion and its follow-up (AD 43–70), the construction of Hadrian's Wall (120s), and the Severan campaigns in Scotland (early 200s).

It is also probable that what prosperity the late Roman 'city' had in the fourth century was based on the continuing military role of Samarabriva Ambianorum as a continuing link between Britain and the Rhine, as part of the defences against Saxon raiders, and for local control, for example in overseeing barbarians (e.g. Sarmatians) drafted in as settler-soldiers. It must have helped keep the regional villa economy going for a time as well.

Ambiani – as it was increasingly called – had an irregular rampart enclosing about 20ha. This was made with the usual hard-headed disdain for the buildings and funeral monuments of the earlier city. As at BAVAY, the forum walls were used to provide a basic structure and the amphitheatre became the core buttress. One part of the forum became a metal workshop, perhaps the shield and sword *fabrica Ambiensis* referred to in the *Notitia Dignitatum*. Written sources also suggest a Christian presence: an oratory dedicated to St Martin (*c.* 316–397) by one of the gates is mentioned by Gregory of Tours and the story of his conscientious objection here may well be true – he could have been part of the local garrison. However, no archaeological evidence has been found of any churches. During the fifth century, it is impossible to say at what point Ambiani was permanently lost to the empire – the 450s? the 460s? – not simply because the written sources do not tell us, but because whether it was ruled by a local Roman warlord or a Frankish king must have been almost irrelevant to the peasants who worked the land and who no longer had any use for the city.

Musée de Picardie

48 rue de la République
80000 Amiens
Hours: 10a.m.–12.30p.m., 2–6p.m. Closed Monday

Renovation has transformed the basement of this grandiose Victorian building into a modern, tasteful display area. Following collections of ancient Egyptian and Greek – especially Corinthian – material, there are three galleries devoted to the Gallo-Roman period. Here is the visible evidence not only of Samarabriva and Ambiani, but also of other sites in Picardy, most important perhaps being Ribemont-sur-Ancre (see THE ROMANO-CELTIC SANCTUARY).

The most striking portrayal of Ribemont is the re-created ***headless burial***, with the original skeletal remains, bent swords and other weapons. A case shows the wide range of Gallic weaponry found surrounding the sanctuary. The high quality of the decorative stone sculpture on the later Roman temple is hinted at by the expressiveness of the faces.

The earliest material from Amiens is suggestive of a military presence. Arretine ware, *sigillata* from Arezzo in Italy, could indicate army use, and a ***dagger scabbard***, found in the same deposit, has been identified as typical of an Augustan auxiliary. Attractive British enamelled fibulae confirm the cross-Channel connection. There were also travellers and tourists. Someone came to Samarabriva with his or her souvenir **cup commemorating Hadrian's Wall**. It has a list of names enamelled round its rim: they record a number of western forts from MIAE (Bowness) to BANNA (Birdoswald). Perhaps a soldier in transit from the Wall to the German frontier was quartered here? Perhaps a retired man chose to settle in Samarabriva? The elegant carved **bone officer statuette**, which may have been a soldier's offering, was found at the fanum on the Somme *oppidum* of L'Etoile.

The Amiens area has no good clay and little local production. The creamy ***terracotta moulded statuettes***, produced in central France, are mostly simple and cheap representations of fertility and plenty, either classical Venuses or Gallic seated mother figures in their basket chairs, but Amiens has some splendid zoomorphic designs, especially a seated stag. **Glass** was imported as well, some as expensive tableware, some for perfumes and medicines and some as appropriate goods to accompany a person's burial. The collection, largely from the cemeteries, is a fine one, the best being the **chalice from the Rhineland**, with its blue-and-white snake décor.

There are only hints at the appearance of Samarabriva, for example the beautifully decorated column drums with hares, birds and figures surrounded by foliage, but the evidence found so far suggests that the larger houses were unimpressive. Dull geometric **mosaics** are representative of the small number found. Finds of **painted plaster** decorated with candelabra and griffins, discovered in the rue de Jacobins domus excavation, are better than many, but pale beside the sophistication of the section of wall-painting brought back from the Boscoreale villa (Italy). The broken **oscillum**, a marble plaque hung in a house or on a garden tree, is of high quality and shows Pan playing his pipes before a rural altar; it must have been imported. The **small bronzes** are also interesting. There is a strange cross-legged god whose right ear is that of an animal (see also BESANCON). Is the ear a stag's, in which case it might be a personification of Cernunnos, or is it a bull's, identified possibly with Jupiter, symbolizing virility? Another strange statuette is dedicated to the worship of Jupiter–Sabazius. It is a hand, fingers spread in benediction with heads of a bird, frog, tortoise and ram perched on the tips. Sexual prowess is a strong element: tiny chains attach three phalluses to the hand. The snake round the wrist is the most widely found attribute of this secretive eastern religion, originally from eastern Turkey, but brought to Rome and spread, like Mithraism, largely by soldiers. There are unlikely to have been many adherents in Amiens. A cruder form of phallic worship is the **cloaked Priapus** figure.

The more mundane life of the city is hinted at by the heavy grinding stone, a bronze lamp in the shape of two feet, the **50 Roman pounds weight** in the shape of a solid-looking Bacchus, the rare marked **ruler** that must have been used by a local craftsman and the exceptional **bronze disc** with the imperial provinces listed round the edge, used to get a rough estimate of the time in different latitudes. Death too was part of daily life. The most persuasive of the few tombstones on display is the sensitively depicted mother consoling her son next to his father. The end of Ambiani is best represented perhaps by the battered memorial to Valerius, the Thracian cavalryman who died here, and the Frankish trapezoidal coffin with skeleton and grave goods.

A temporary exhibition area is used to show the results of recent excavations.

ARRAS, Pas-de-Calais

Museum and site.

The Roman city of Nemetacum owed its origins to the camp established here by Caesar in the last phase of the Gallic wars. In part to control the local Atrebates, it also served as a base to cover the nearby coastal tribes and the German groups to the north and east. It became a tribal capital, but very little is known about its evolution. It is estimated that it grew to about 35ha during the early empire, and fragments of rampart suggest that about a third of this was enclosed in the late Roman period. In the fourth century, like Amiens and Soissons, it was the headquarters of a *praefectus laetorum*, an official responsible for new settlers, generally German barbarians, given land in return for agreeing to fight for Rome. The *Notitia Dignitatum*, listing late Roman military commands, mentions a troop of Batavian *laeti*. No bishops are known: it seems to have been a military outpost in what a contemporary Christian considered 'a (spiritual) wasteland'. The decision of the court to leave Trier and the withdrawal of troops from Britain were decisive; despite being recovered from the Alamanni after their shattering move across the Rhine in the winter of 406, Arras virtually drops out of history, only emerging again at the end of the century as simply one place in Belgica Secunda ruled by the Merovingian Frankish dynasty.

Though our ignorance of Nemetacum in the first and second centuries largely continues, the town archaeological service has made revealing discoveries about circumstances in what was the fringe of the Roman empire in the fourth century.

Rue Baudimont site

77 Rue Baudimont
The excavation area lies immediately behind the buildings fronting the street.
Hours: Open daily in summer months

The remains exposed here lay by the northern late Roman rampart. When built, this enclosed a sanctuary devoted to the eastern cult of Cybele and Attis. In the 370s this was pulled down and a new sanctuary built, dedicated to a Germanic fertility god. The final phase came in the 390s, only about fifteen years after the German sanctuary had been built, when it was covered by two barrack buildings.

Musée des Beaux-Arts d'Arras

Abbaye St-Vaast
22 rue Paul-Doumer
62000 Arras

Hours:	1 April–15 October	Monday–Saturday 10a.m.–noon, 2–6p.m.
		Sunday 10a.m.–noon, 3–6p.m.
	15 October–31 March	Monday–Friday 10a.m.–noon, 2–5p.m.
		Saturday 10a.m.–noon, 2–6p.m.
		Sunday 10a.m.–noon, 3–6p.m.

Roman Arras is presented in two small rooms. This is a well-lit and revealing display, helped considerably by the use of models. English-speaking visitors are well catered for, with both a guidebook in English and free sheets describing each of the exhibits.

Room 1. The least interesting. The **Duisans sanctuary** was found 7km north-west from Arras. It had at least two *fana*, dating to the beginning of the Roman period. The grave goods were found in early empire cremations at the **Baralle necropolis**, 3km along the Arras–Cambrai road.

Room 2. The **Beaurains treasure** of coins, silverware and jewellery was discovered in 1922 just outside Arras at a time when the state had doubtful title. Property owners and claimants sought to profit as quickly as possible: much disappeared into private collections in the USA and Europe, but a good selection of jewellery – and the only piece of silver to go to a public collection – ended up in the British Museum (London), some fine coins and medallions are in the Cabinet des Médailles (Paris) and others in Brussels. Arras managed to buy some silver *denarii* and three superb *aurea*. These gold medallions – weighing more than the normal coins – were minted at the end of the third century in Trier. Their contemporary value made them each worth the yearly subsistence of a poor family. The finest is that of Constantine Chlorus, the reverse showing the Caesar receiving Londinium's submission after crushing the British independent empire in 295/6. The ship recalls both the domination of the Channel that permitted the landing and the fleet soldiers who crushed the rebels' Frankish mercenaries. The Latin inscription proclaims him as 'Restorer of the Eternal Light [of Rome]'. It is thought they belonged to a senior army officer and were hastily hidden not long after 315, the date of the last coin. No major war is known then: perhaps the treasure had been stolen.

The large central chamber of the **Cybele and Attis sanctuary** is represented by the restored fresco (possibly portraying the Cybele herself) and fragments of marble facing stones. Rooms to the north may have formed a sacristy for keeping sacred goods, such as the flat vine-like candlestick. Some imply the religious syncretism of the third-century Roman world. Once distinct eastern faiths appear together: a perfume jar decorated with Bacchus was found with a porphyry statue of Attis but in Persian dress – and with a penis – which suggests identification with Mithras, reinforced by the double-handled jar or *cantharus* associated with Mithraic ritual. Food preparation equipment (e.g. a pestle and mortar) together with pits have suggested that to the south of the chamber was a *taurobolium* area where the ritual sacrifice of bulls took place.

The **German sanctuary** was the most dramatic discovery. A model recreates the sacred area with its central walled-in trench and four-posted thatch roof. The three skulls, two of children, graphically indicate that worship here could have involved human sacrifice of some kind, and further pits in the area had both human and animal bones. The iron shackles reinforce the impression, while other finds shown here, such as the scythes, hoes, forks and bill-hooks, bring an agricultural aspect to the sanctuary. A carefully folded dismantled sheath serves to emphasize that this sanctuary is highly reminiscent of Gallic practices 400 years before (see THE ROMANO-CELTIC SANCTUARY). The sacrifices were clearly being made to the earth god(s) of fecundity, as the Celts had done, but the discovery of a **stone statue**, totally unlike any known Gallic or Roman portrayal and so far unknown elsewhere in the whole of Roman France, makes the site unequivocally German. This alien bulbous figure clasping his penis depicts Freyr, the leading fertility God of northern Europe. The nearest analogies with this site have been found in the forests of Thuringia. Presumably this was the cult centre of recently settled East German *laeti* in the 'wastelands' around Arras.

The **barracks** are the most surprising find in Arras. Literary sources suggest that Valentinian (365–75) was the last significant restorer of the Gallic/Rhineland frontier region, while under Theodosius (379–95) the western empire is associated with the increasing recruitment of warriors rather than creating trained soldiers. The German sanctuary seems to embody that trend, yet in the 390s two standard-pattern barrack blocks are built, implying that the men here were a coherent force under the command of a qualified officer. Is this the Batavian *laeti* of the *Notitia*, men drawn from the Romanized region of the northern Rhine? Spurs suggest a cavalry troop. Yet it *is* a late empire frontier force: within a couple of years the buildings seem to have been divided into small rooms and, as the finds show, the men lived with their families. Military buckles mix with earrings and spindle whorls. Early in the fifth century the barracks were abandoned and the land deserted – perhaps as the Alamanni swept through.

BAVAY, Nord

Town remains and museum.

25km east of Valenciennes by the N49, Bavay is less than 10km from the Belgian border.

It is now little more than a village, but Bavay has never forgotten that it was a Roman city, Bagacum. The two hectares of the forum, crumbled and then overgrown, were covered by medieval rubbish pits, then a Renaissance foundation and its gardens. Unofficial digs have been a part of Bavay's history for hundreds of years. Typically, in 1818 a weaver dug up a fine bronze statue of Hercules which he then sold to a gentleman collector, an Englishman living in Valenciennes, who, on his death in 1834, bequeathed it to the newly founded British Museum in London. Valenciennes, Douai, Lille and many Belgium museums as well as the BM, have had their collections enlarged by watchful locals for often pitifully small reward. The pillaging only began to end in the twentieth century. A local museum was created in 1906, followed by small-scale excavations between 1910 and 1913, but it was the Second World War that stimulated real progress. The bombardment of 1940 smashed the centre of Bavay, but revealed that there was still extensive Roman building here, and Vichy legislation provided new legal powers of protection. Canon Biévelet then poured his life into exploring the site.

From 1942 to 1966 he excavated continuously to expose one of the largest and best-preserved Roman forums in northern Gaul. Various archaeologists have worked here since, but the most innovative idea came from the director of the museum, J.-C. Carmelez. In the 1970s and 1980s he put excavation and museum tasks into the curriculum of the local lycée. His inspiration transformed the whole spectrum of the school curriculum, covering everything from classics to mathematics. Under his supervision the children learnt how to dig with sensitivity, to observe with precision and to record accurately. The painstaking listing of the museum's large collection and its appropriate labelling is a result of his and their commitment.

During the 1980s the authorities decided it was necessary to adopt a professional approach to some key archaeological questions – such as Bavay's chronology – and also to introduce a comprehensive preservation policy for the site. Departmental and university teams moved in to carry out major excavations from 1988 onwards. Their activities have revised interpretations, but perhaps rather less than at first expected.

Evolution of the town

Bavay was the *civitas* capital of the Nervii. There is as yet no evidence of any meaningful settlement on the site before the Roman conquest and the inhabitants seem to have been among the less urbanized of Belgic peoples. Their territory was spread out on the rich agricultural land on the northern fringes of the Ardennes forest, much of it now in Belgium. Caesar portrays them as fierce warriors, who had rejected that symbol of Roman material civilization, trade in wine, so popular among other Gallic peoples. He claimed to have wiped out their fighting men in 57 BC, yet had to put down a rising in 54. Even after a scorched-earth policy, they sent 5,000 men to help Vercingetorix in 53. It is not surprising that they were recruited as auxiliaries and used in the Augustan German campaigns.

Bavay itself is a prime example of a centre developing as the result of strategic needs. Strabo indicates how Agrippa had mapped out the two main roads north from Lyon, one via Reims to Boulogne, the other via Metz to Köln and the northern Rhine frontier. Bavay lies at the centre of the base of the triangle so formed – the road that linked Boulogne and Köln and allowed the rapid movement of troops between the channel port and the Rhine (see Figure 54, page 254). It was to become a major staging post with the conquest of Britain and the transfer of troops between Rome's two northern frontiers a commonplace. The construction of a road linking Bavay with Reims gave the Roman military an alternative route to the northern Rhineland. An inscription found in Bavay in 1718 records how Tiberius was here in AD 11, when he was leading the forces to avenge the loss of Varus and his legions in the German disaster (AD 9). Bavay became the nodal point for a series of roads leading into the low countries.

Trade and commerce inevitably followed the construction of the roads and the exploitation of the river network (Bavay is not far from the Escaut). It certainly became a major market centre for pottery and workshops have been found in the city itself, dating from the beginning of the first century. Products associated with Roman Bavay include distinctive face pots, a local fine ware copied from *sigillata* called Gallo-Belgic, and coarse wares, including *mortaria*, the characteristic Roman mixing bowl; lamp moulds have been found as well. Bavay was also a centre for the distribution of woollen products. More surprising has been the discovery of large numbers of bronze fittings, suggesting that this could have been a furniture-making centre as well. Some bronze could even have been manufactured locally.

Sadly, excavation has so far given very little picture of what the town was like before the end of the first century. Scraps of early building and roads have been found, and an aqueduct has been traced 20km and dated to about AD 100. Piped water was introduced and public fountains built in the streets. Evidence of some large houses and twenty or so mosaics have been found. Current estimates suggest the town ultimately covered about 40ha and could have had a population of 15,000, maybe three times as many as today.

The orientation of the houses suggested to Biévelet that a town grid was first laid out around the forum in the west of the modern town and then in the second century, with new prosperity, it was decided to extend the town eastwards but with a new orientation for a fresh grid. A review by Patrick Thollard (1994) of the evidence for the two grids suggested an alternative view: the second grid was in fact the first one. 'Grid A' was simply a modification made by the constructors to accommodate the awkward slope of the hill on which this enormous forum was built. Recent excavation suggests that the road alignments to the north and east confirm this. Thollard's revisionism suggests that the forum, as a late first-century structure, could have been built on the edge of the settlement rather than on a site left empty for many years.

The forum site

Excavations and museum
Rue de Gommeries
59570 Bavay

Hours:	July–August	9a.m.–noon, 2–6p.m. Closed Tuesday
	May, June, September	closing at 5p.m.
	October–April	open 2–5p.m.

Thollard's reasoning has been stimulated in part by the new forum excavations. While signs of early occupation have been found in sondages, nothing has turned up to prove Biévelet or Carmelez wrong in their assertion that the forum was first built in the later first century AD. No convincing evidence has appeared of an earlier timber-frame structure.

By the time this forum was built there was a clear notion of the elements that went to make up this symbol of Roman rule: (1) a large **open paved area**, a meeting point of the people as part of the empire – often imperial statues were placed in this area, though none survived here; (2) a **basilica**, the building in which justice was dispensed and a place for merchants and others to meet when the weather was bad; (3) a **religious zone** at the other end, normally consisting of one or more temples enclosed on three sides by a **portico**. Here there appears to have been one temple but even the foundation podium is difficult to make out. Some forums, such as this one, had the portico supported by a basement or a ***cryptoporticus***, whose main use

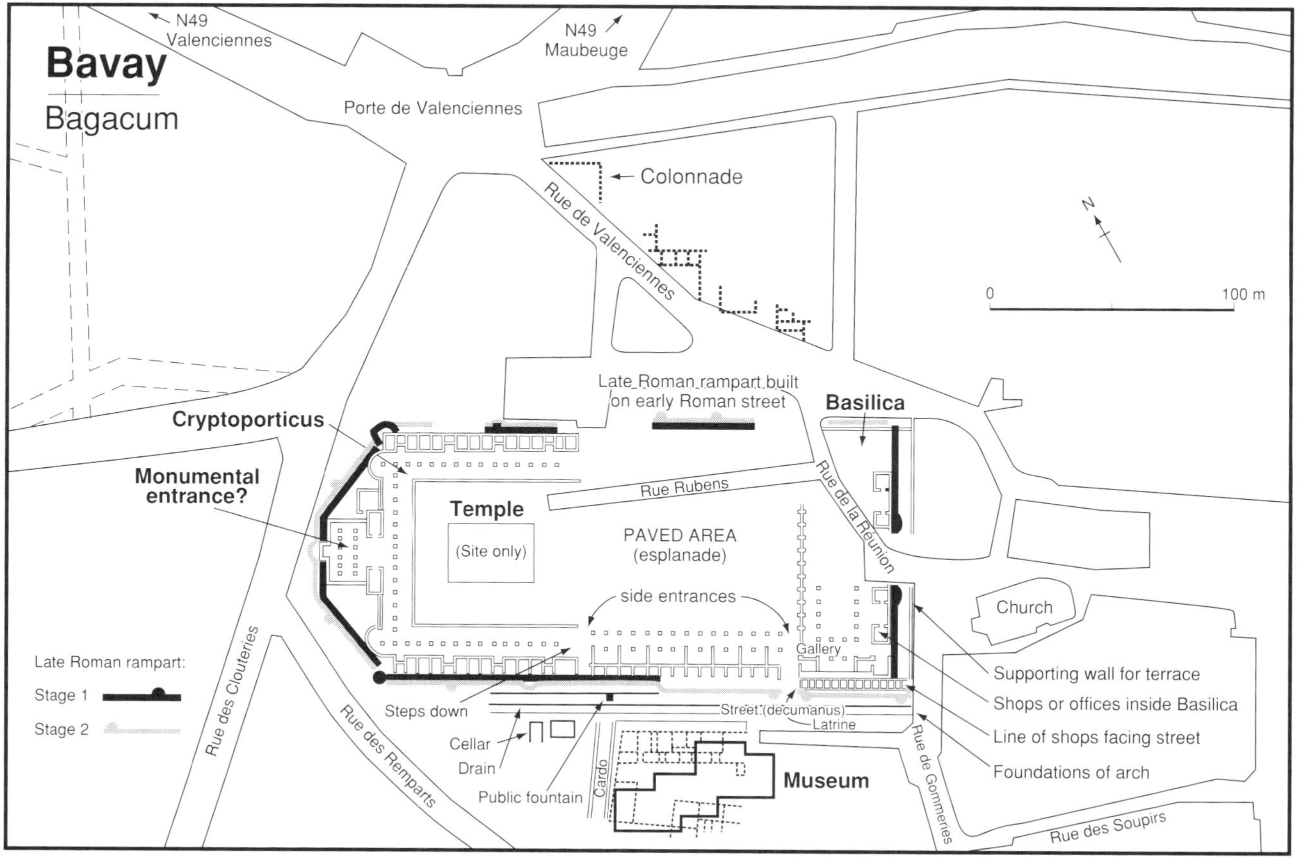

Figure 6 Bavay: site plan

may have been a structural one, providing strong foundations for the portico, but it must also have had other uses: perhaps for communal storage or as a semi-underground walking area. This is well preserved to the upper vaulting. Beyond the western end of the forum extends a triple aisled building; if it had been at the other end, by the basilica, it would have been taken to be a curia for town council meetings. A possible explanation is that this was really a monumental entrance or ***propylaeum***; unfortunately, so much has been excavated away that it seems unlikely anyone will be able to find the answer. Nevertheless, Bavay's forum must have been one of the most impressive in northern Europe.

The forum was first built using a green sandstone fixed with a yellow mortar; it had an enormous basilica. At the end of the second century Severan rebuilding took place. Carmelez, following Biévelet, believed that the forum was burnt down in the 190s and linked it with the rebellion of Clodius Albinus – though of course fires were a constant hazard in ancient cities. The new excavators, at first very dubious, also found a consistent fire level and have come round to this as a major possibility. The new forum, while using the same space, saw a major redesign of the basilica, making it slightly smaller but providing new steps from the forum square, a range of rooms at either end and refitting the eastern rooms (shops?) on the edge of the terrace, so that they now faced inwards, not out to the road, thus creating a gallery round the basilica. The *cryptoporticus* was almost totally rebuilt with the currently fashionable brick and stone courses, plaster-painted walls and vaulting. The stone used was a grey limestone with a pink mortar. At first the new excavators asserted there was a third rebuilding, associated with multi-coloured mortars and new *grand appareil* pillars and pilasters; Carmelez had seen patching and minor modifications. By the mid-1990s they were simply asserting there had been major modifications that were never finished.

Late Roman Bavay and its fortifications

During the later third century and through the fourth century Bavay stood on a vital military highway needing to be secured by a number of fortified points commanded by the Dux Belgicae Secundae. This appears to have been seen as 'bandit country' and bases were needed for the local road police and defence forces, including a legion of Nervii, as well as secure points for the storage of the *annona*, the taxation in kind. The old tribal *civitas* was cut in half and Bavay, like towns elsewhere, was ruthlessly transformed. The forum made an ideal *castrum*: it provided a site raised on a terrace with some ready-made walls, around which could be made a rampart and turrets; as a forum it also represented the essence of Rome and as such the embodiment of Roman rule. The rampart was built in three stages and only received its towers in the second and third phases. No precise dates are available. As usual large stonework from earlier tombs and buildings, even a weights and measures inscription that may have stood in the forum, were used to make the foundations. The *cryptoporticus* continued in use for a time, but by 360 it was filled in, possibly to allow the erection of an internal earth ramp behind the wall. Some of the rooms in the eastern end were occupied and one had a hypocaust installed. Another was used to bury a hoard of fine bronzes. In 1990 Frankish pottery was found, a sign either of the last Roman Germanic troops based at Bavay or of its absorption in the emerging Frankish state.

Museum

The museum is a product of 1970s modern and is rather colourless. Yet it really does enhance the experience of the site. The large model of the town makes clear just how dramatic a change there was in the reality of urban living between the second and fourth centuries, and wall maps give some sense of Bavay's strategic position. The pottery collection is impressive. Sigillata from all the major production centres has been found here (though little is of particularly high quality) in addition to the early Gallo-Belgic tableware, modelled on the mass-produced shiny red product. In the late Roman period Bavay imported a large amount of the roller-stamped geometric patterned **Argonne ware**, attractive with its simple bowl designs and orange finish. There are examples of the earlier second-century black slipped ware, **Metallic Eastern or 'Rhenish' ware**, mainly from the Trier region. The best are the beakers with white barbotine decoration representing scrolls or grapes (some have a motto encouraging drinking); there is a folk art feel to them but they are moulded and were exported much further than just Bavay. The most interesting are the first- and second-century **face pots**. These large jars have been found in cemeteries and the faces are generally seen as divinities; their wild, rich curls and sharply outlined eyes would seem to support this. Some have triple faces; one has seven. It may be that they were seen as protecting the human ashes contained inside. Multiplication of god figures, particularly heads, is a Celtic religious feature. Yet this local product has no history before the arrival of the Romans and they seem to be found most widely in eastern Belgica, the least Celtic and most German part of the region.

The other striking feature in the museum is the **bronze work**. Before 1969 all the best work had ended up in other museum collections, but with the discovery of a bag full of more than 300 bronzes – some with traces of canvas – Bavay had material of which it could be proud. It was presumably a hoard that might have been for melting down, as a number of pieces were small broken elements, others were imported statuettes and fine, locally produced furniture fittings. The purest classical figures include the ***lar familiaris***, a household god, crowned and holding a large cornucopia and patera, and given life by the short, full, almost overflowing tunic. Another more schematic version shows the high quality of this first-century product, which may have come from Italy. A fine **Mercury**, dressed only in his hat, rests on a rock where his emblems, a purse and a tortoise, lie; he once held his *caduceus* (a wand) in the right hand. Other fine statuettes are an imposing Jupiter who has lost both sceptre and seat; a richly bearded **Neptune or Jupiter**, finely balanced, with shining silver eyes; a delicate Cupid; and a rather fey-looking **Minerva**.

Among the **furniture fittings** the best are the **decorative handles**. One uses as a centrepiece the bust of the goddess Cybele set between her two protective lions. The outstretched arms become inverted cornucopias with busts of Attis, her treacherous young lover, at each end emerging from the top of a pine. Other handles are based on Silenus. Further fittings include roundels such as the Ocean mask and decorative bands.

Elsewhere in the museum are the more common bronzes, such as weights and balances, glassware, lamps and keys, iron chains and hipposandals, and white terracotta moulded figurines. They are the normal artefacts that a Roman city such as Bavay consumed and then lost among its rubbish.

BEAUVAIS, Oise

Town site.

On the A16 and N1, 60km south of Amiens and 75km north from Paris.

Caesaromagus, the half-Latin, half-Gallic name for Beauvais, was the capital of the Bellovaci people during the Roman period. Caesar describes them as the strongest of the Belgic tribes, able to mobilize 100,000 fighting men famous for their valour. One suspects Caesar was exaggerating. In 57 BC they surrendered without fighting; in 52 they agreed to send 10,000 troops to help Vercingetorix at Alesia, but in the end only sent 2,000. Certainly they fought in 51, were defeated during Caesar's winter campaign and rose again in 46, to be crushed by the governor Decimus Brutus. It is a mixed record and Caesaromagus, like today's Beauvais, was never more than one of the moderate-sized towns to the north of the Seine.

There seems to be virtually no evidence of pre-Roman settlement on the site and the Bellovaci's leading *oppidum* has been identified with either Mont César 13km to the south-east or Chamont hill at VENDEUIL-CAPLY, without a conclusive case being made for either. Caesaromagus was probably established when the Lyon to Boulogne road was developed by Agrippa for Augustus. The town was set at the point where the river Thérain became navigable down to the Oise and the Paris basin. It served too as a junction for roads from Augustomagus (Senlis), Augusta Suessionum (Soissons) and Bagacum (Bavay). It does not appear to have been enough to have stimulated rapid or long-lasting growth. Though the north–south route, marked by the Rue Gambetta, has been defined as the Cardo Maximus, there is no

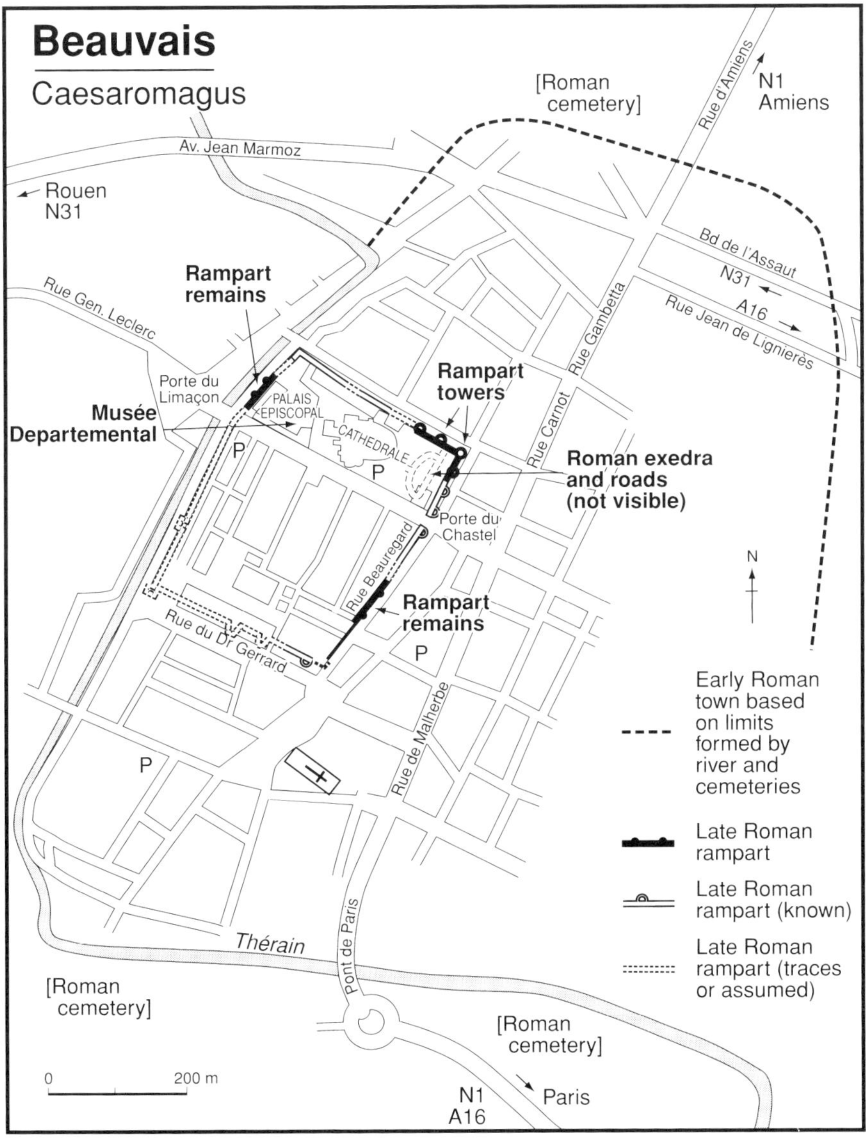

Figure 7 Beauvais: town plan

firm evidence that the town was laid out on a grid pattern. The destruction of the city centre when the fire services were withdrawn at the time of a major bombing raid in 1940 and the failure to use the post-war opportunity to make a coherent archaeological record before rebuilding took place have certainly contributed to the patchiness of the record. However, since 1969 there has been an energetic municipal archaeological service. The thinness of literary references, the lack of inscriptions (none referring to town government), the poverty of sculptural remains and of mosaics, the modern rejection of any serious claim for an amphitheatre here and the failure to discover a forum, still support an interpretation of limited growth.

The case for claiming Caesaromagus as a genuine city is best based on one ancient and two recent excavations. The **'Bacchus temple'** was found in the late seventeenth century. Contemporaries described a massive complex with a unique apsed cella decorated with vine and ivy paintings. Nothing at all has survived. In 1966–9, a curved double wall or ***exedra*** was discovered behind the apse of the cathedral. It has been seen as part of a public square or even a library. In the 1980s, work at the Hôtel de Dieu hospital led to the discovery of the unidentified remains of a **Flavian monumental building** lying on top of earlier first-century housing. Nothing is visible at these sites. The same is true of other major excavations. These include the baths found in the St Etienne precinct – now considered to be too small to be public, though of course they still imply an important private house; a 'round temple' under the war memorial gardens and the evidence of first/second-century housing clustered in the streets round the Place Clemenceau. However, recent excavations have reinforced the view that the centre of the early imperial town lay to the north of the late Roman fortified area, where concentrations of housing have been found and street drains were installed at the end of the first century; their water supply came predominantly from wells. Much of the town appears to have been burnt in the mid-third century. Of late Roman developments little is known apart from the ramparts. No doubt Christianity arrived, but Saint Lucien, a supposed martyr here in the third century, is generally thought to have been a ninth-century invention. His abbey church stands on the remains of a *fanum* temple. The first known bishop was in 632.

The late Roman walls

The only significant remains are these quite impressive walls. They enclosed less than 11ha, about typical for the fortress centres of Belgica Secunda. The foundations include large blocks and stone from the exedra, the baths and cemetery memorials. The walls themselves are 2.5m thick, using *petit appareil* facings with a thick rubble core and, every twelve courses, a double-tile level. The wall was defended by massive towers some 10m high, U-shaped except at the corners. The finest are the Tour St-Hilaire and the north-east corner tower. A second line of walls in front of these has been claimed, but nothing is visible. They were possibly built under Probus (276–82), though the care in construction might suggest a later, less threatening time. Put-holes used to hold the timber scaffolding are visible at various points (e.g. in the rectangular rear section of the U-shaped tower at the corner of Avenue Foch). The northern section is best preserved because it formed the precinct of the cathedral and episcopal palace.

Museum

Musée Départemental de l'Oise
Ancien Palais Episcopal
Rue St-Pierre
60006 Beauvais
Hours: 10a.m.–noon, 2–6p.m. Closed Tuesday

The museum was renovated in the 1970s and re-opened in 1982. The archaeological galleries are still based on excavations made largely outside Beauvais, but exhibits will be altered to reflect new contributions by the archaeological service.

There are two main displays of Iron Age material. There is a reconstruction of three burials cut in chalk with typical metal goods and food offerings from the **Tartigny necropolis** (about 6km north-east of Vendeuil-Caply). From a ditch at **Aulnes du Canada**, a site by the Thérain on the edge of Beauvais, come metalwork, local ceramics and fragments of imported Roman amphorae mixed with frequent pig remains: perhaps it was a sanctuary boundary.

The most interesting Gallo-Roman period sculpture is represented by new and old finds. In 1985, at **St Maur** 25km north-west of Beauvais an unusually large *fanum* temple was found orientated precisely within the ditches of a Gallic sanctuary. The site has been interpreted as a sacred border marker of the Bellovaci tribal lands. In it was found a stiff metallic **warrior** figure. He is made of sheets of brass, hammered into shape and then soldered together, with inlaid silver eyes. He carries a hexagonal shield and wears a kilt with a wide sword belt, a breastplate and a torc round his neck. Dated to the beginning of the first century AD, it has been variously described as a rich gift (an ex-voto), the statue of a Bellovaci god or so un-Gallic that it might be a German import! The **Mercury relief** was found in 1695 on Mont Capron. Not especially well carved, it does show how the Roman Mercury was adopted in Gaul as an equivalent of local multi-functional gods. He wears the Roman cloak and shows his classic attributes – the winged hat, the herald's staff or caduceus and a purse. For Romans his herald role not only included conducting the dead to Hades, but also inspiring trade. This in turn helped lead him to be seen as the embodiment of wealth, inventiveness and general well-being. Here he is given a beard – a common feature on Gallic male gods – and the additional symbols of snakes with ram's horns (on the sides of the statue). These additions both have sexual imagery and turn well-being and prosperity into regeneration. The dedication was probably added shortly after its discovery.

Plate 1 Beauvais. The Gallic warrior from St Maur. © Beauvais, Musée Départemental de l'Oise. Photograph Piero Baguzzi.

The **wall paintings** from the vicus site at St-Martin-Longueau, 50km south-east of Beauvais on the Senlis road, have been placed on the walls of the main Gallo-Roman room. Delicate scenes were painted between and above the panels. One shows victories and a Mars above a pediment, another foliage and birds on top of a hunting scene. The stone sarcophagi are unimpressive but there are some simply decorated lead coffins (second/third century). Found inside a coffin, the excellent **ivory Bacchic scene** with cupids on each side of the child Bacchus, harvesting the vine, is probably the remains of a small casket. It should not be missed.

The Merovingian room assembles material from the enormous cemetery at Bulles, used between the fifth and eighth centuries. It has helped give Beauvais a fine collection of **Frankish weaponry**, including an early long sword, a short single-edged sword or scramasax, a javelin or ango based on the Roman pilum and a throwing axe, the francisca, the most characteristic Frankish weapon until the 600s. Equally impressive are other forms of metal-work, including jewellery and the extensive collection of buckles, some very large, and other belt fittings. The technical progress is apparent: the mastery of manufacturing iron, the use of inlay and the development of damascening, an advanced form of hardening and patterning iron. Equally apparent, though, is how, in contrast to the Gallo-Roman era, power is expressed through personal, not public display.

BERCK-SUR-MER, Pas-de-Calais

Museum.

One of the benefits of new motorways has been the support given to rescue archaeology in the path of construction (or destruction?). Building the A16 in the area between Montreuil and Berck led to the discovery of a number of new sites, the most important of which was at la Calotterie, 4km west of Montreuil, where a large sixth- and seventh-century Merovingian cemetery was discovered, containing some magnificent metalwork. This has been well displayed in the small municipal museum.

Musée Municipal

Rue de l'Impératrice,
62600 Berck-sur-Mer

Downstairs, probably most interesting are the photographs and reconstruction drawings of **Gallic and Roman salt works**, the former found at Sorrus and the latter, slightly different, found at Conchil-le-Temple. The acid soil has helped preserve the large wooden shovels used in the making of salt bricks, many of which were probably exported to other regions.

The Merovingian material is upstairs. No settlement has been found at la Calotterie, but the burials indicate large numbers of well-armed men and richly dressed women, suggesting that this may have been the burial place for a socially privileged warrior elite. Just as the past surrounds us today, so it did then: they probably chose this place as a cemetery because then there were the mounds of Bronze Age burials, built more than 1,000 years before their time.

Though soil acidity has largely destroyed the skeletons of the more than six hundred burials, the metalwork, wood, leather and even fragments of textile and fur have been preserved. The most striking material is not the various Frankish weapons, but the superb **gold and garnet cloisonné work** covering pins, bird-patterned (aviform) brooches and sword sheath decoration. Equally impressive are the very large, silver-inlayed (damascened) iron belt buckles and fittings. While the sophistication and technical virtuosity of this ornamentation links it with the late Roman world, the crudely cut amber and brightly coloured glass bead necklaces seem to derive much more from the lands beyond.

BOULOGNE-SUR-MER, Pas-de-Calais

Classis Britannica fortress and museum

For those prepared to struggle up the hill, the most striking things at Boulogne are the massive medieval walls of the Haute Ville. That the old town covered Roman remains had long been known, but it is only since 1967 that modern excavations, inspired by Claude Seillier, have revealed that the thirteenth-century walls were actually hiding two sets of earlier Roman stone defences. Bringing together the professional work of the municipal archaeological service, the much sketchier earlier archaeological evidence and the literary record, Boulogne emerges as the major Roman naval base for the whole north of the empire.

Although Boulogne's visible Roman remains are slight, its historical significance justifies detailed examination. It was the embarkation point for both Caligula's projected (AD 40) and Claudius' actual invasion (43); it no doubt seemed the obvious choice. Yet plenty of evidence suggests that traditionally the main trade routes between Britain and the continent went via the Somme and Seine to the south and the Rhine to the north. Indeed, the Liane river offered little as a navigable waterway, but its mouth provided a fine harbour on one of the shortest routes to Britain: excellent reasons for a naval base. The Roman road system, designed initially to serve military needs, concentrates on Boulogne as the key Channel port.

Archaeological evidence dates from the Augustan period when the harbour might have been developed as a coastal base for the German campaigns of Drusus and Tiberius. Traditionally, Julius Caesar has been credited with its founding, calling his embarkation port 'Itius', yet throughout the early imperial period it is known as Gesoriacum – a name derived from 'Chersiacus', the local *pagus* or district. There are other sites with perhaps better claims as Caesar's departure point in 54 BC. Gallic settlements have been found at Wimereux, Sangatte and Wissant. The last has the advantage of being much nearer Ptolemy's 'Ition', convincingly identified as Cap Gris Nez.

Tour d'Ordre site

Rue Tour d'Ordre, below allotments and modern lighthouse

Nothing remains of the great lighthouse that stood on the northern cliffs of Boulogne but the site is still worth visiting. Looking down over the port

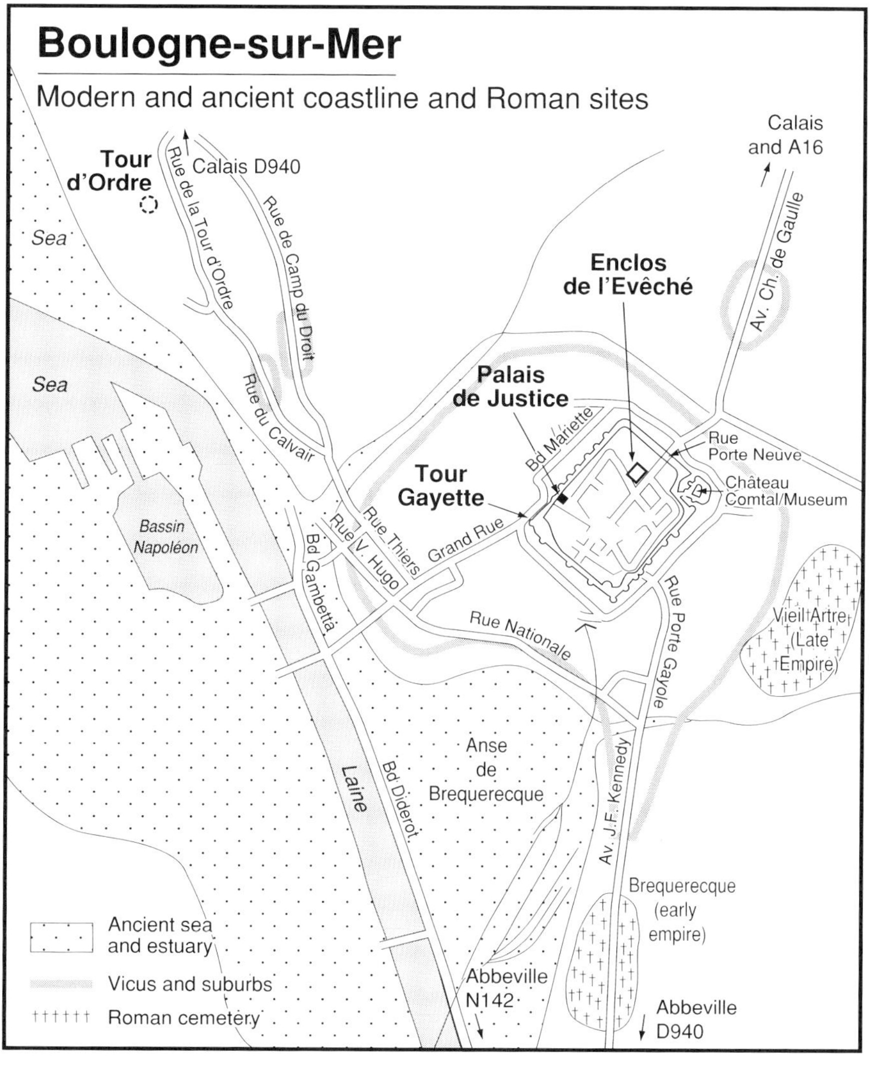

Figure 8 Boulogne-sur-Mer: town plan

area the surface pattern has been transformed by silting and more obviously by the creation of the modern dock area. The *anse* or bay of Brequerecque, now covered by railway sidings, is the best candidate for the Roman fleet harbour with its concentration of military artefacts, especially tiles stamped CL.BR for 'Classis Britannica' – the British fleet. The underlying shape of the place is apparent: a river coming from the south providing, with the

Portel peninsula opposite, a well-protected estuary and harbour. On a fine day it is possible to look out over the Straits and be astonished at the clarity with which the cliffs of Dover sit on the horizon. This perhaps is what Caligula saw when he ordered the construction of the lighthouse after his aborted invasion. Erosion, quarrying and pilfering destroyed it and it is best seen in the seventeenth-century engravings kept (though rarely displayed) in Boulogne's Château Comtal museum. It appears as a stepped octagon some 55–60m high, a design similar to the luckier Roman lighthouse at Dover. The bonding tiles, implying rebuilding in the second century or later, are clearly visible.

Traditional local names suggest interesting British connections. 'Le Vieil Homme' is thought to be a translation of the English 'Old Man' – itself a corruption of the Celtic 'Alt Maen' or High Stone. It was also known as the Pharos St Patrice, in this case recalling a legend that the lighthouse guard was Saint Patrick's father.

The installations of the Classis Britannica

Boulogne was the base of the Roman northern waters fleet from at least the beginning of the second century. Inscriptions record the existence of the prefect or commander and various captains, navigators and seamen. The construction of the Stanegate defences in Britain and the fortified line or *limes* in Germany marked the decision of Domitian and then Trajan to harden the frontiers in the north-west. The fleet, which had operated extensively in British and North Sea waters providing essential support for campaigning troops, was now provided with a permanent headquarters at Boulogne and much smaller subsidiary bases for squadrons along the south coast of Britain (such as Dover, Richborough and Lympne).

Until recently virtually nothing was known about the Roman harbour. However, in the early 1990s excavations by the Rue de l'Ancien Rivage (currently a car park) revealed the first evidence confirming the *anse* of Brequerecque as the likely dock area. Evidence of a finely built second-century warehouse and a rampart was excavated. They may have been part of the vicus or civilian town, but are more likely to have belonged to the fleet. There is no doubt about the buildings in the upper town: Claude Seillier's work confirmed that at the beginning of the second century a great stone fort was built on the hill, covering around 12.5ha, about twelve times the size of the base in Dover.

Palais de Justice site

Rue St Jean

The walls are in fact largely hidden just inside the perimeter of, and below, the medieval Haute Ville defences. Happily, when the Palais de Justice site was extended Seillier and his co-archaeologists managed to persuade the authorities to preserve a stretch of fort wall and a tower; these can be seen by asking the concierge for access.

The wall is about 1.8m thick, constructed on a slightly wider rubble foundation. An outer facing of ashlar blocks covers a concrete mortar and rubble interior. In places the wall rises to 3m. The internal tower is of a typical rectangular shape, originally using small ashlar, but subsequently modified with large, finely cut blocks. The inside of the tower shows remains of a staircase and possibly a well. The external ditch and inner road running beside the rampart are no longer visible.

Enclos de l'Evêché site

Cathédrale Parking

The 1980 excavation of the Notre Dame cathedral precinct revealed the distinctive walling of Roman military barracks – now covered by a car park: panel display only. The men's blocks were smaller than those in Dover, but had the more usual officers' quarters typically offset at the end, perhaps a sign that these barracks were more permanent homes. Here, ship captains, fleet officers called trierarchs, must have once enjoyed the comfort of their underfloor heating and painted plastered rooms. Many such officers were Greek, like the trierarch Tiberius Claudius Seleucus, an ex-slave, whilst local coastal tribes like the Menapii also supplied seamen; perhaps the trierarch Quintus Arrenius Verecundus, with his Celtic-sounding *cognomen*, was one of these (see Château Comtal museum below, page 56).

Porte de Calais

Rue Porte Neuve

Outside, a jumble of large blocks was left here in 1895 when the gate area was cleared for access. The grip holes used by Roman cranes are clearly visible; the blocks must have once belonged to early empire public buildings, subsequently used in the late Roman ramparts. Inside the gate, next to the Notre Dame cathedral, are some enigmatic fort remains. A large rectangular basin, buttressed on the sides, does not seem to be part of a bath system and the excavators suggest it could have been a fishpond or had an industrial use.

Notre Dame crypt

Cathédrale

A Roman temple is claimed to have stood here; the evidence was found in the early nineteenth century. Remains of column, capital and architrave are kept in the crypt.

The late Roman town

During the fourth century, Gesoriacum became Bononia, which before was probably just the name of the fort. It has traditionally been assumed that this symbolized the abandonment of the vulnerable lower town for the security of a refortified *castrum* or strong-point on the hilltop. Certainly there is evidence of abandoned suburbs, and even on the slopes of the hill itself, but the recent discovery of a section of late Roman rampart in the harbour area with evidence of occupation until the beginning of the fifth century suggests that it was a new *civitas* capital in more than just name. Theodosian coins imply that troops still occupied the *castrum* into the early fifth century and Constantine III used the port in 407. After this, only squatters' fires and occasional burials hint at continued occupation.

The late Roman ramparts

The new *castrum* ramparts marked a considerable increase in defensive strength. The most interesting aspect is not the new walls themselves – there are much better examples at BEAUVAIS and SENLIS – it is the context in which they were built which remains unresolved.

The third century was a period of violent disruption in the western empire, for Gaul especially. Boulogne was vulnerable to all the usual problems (see HISTORICAL DEVELOPMENT) and to seaborne attack by Frankish and Saxon raiders. The strategic value of Boulogne remained vital for coordinating any combined coastal defences and for maintaining links with Britain. Yet the last known prefect of the fleet died in the 240s and the barracks were levelled apparently in the mid-third century. Coin finds show that the castrum was built after the time of Tetricus, who ruled the Gallic empire in the early 270s, but no evidence as yet shows how long after.

The traditional interpretation suggests it resulted from the order by Probus that Gallic towns be walled after the German invasions of 275/6. This has been connected with the abandonment of the fleet forts in Britain and the construction of new forts in the later third century, perhaps marking a new defensive strategy in the north with small independent squadrons permanently based at the harbours close by these forts. Boulogne then became a central element in the 'Saxon shore' strategy of funnelling raiders down the channel into the straits where perhaps the Dover–Boulogne lighthouses could help signal combined action. The joint nature of the northern defences is symbolized in the fourth century by the creation of a Count of the Saxon Shore, a term that originally applied to both English and French channel coasts.

An alternative to this has been to argue that Carausius, a usurper who controlled parts of northern Gaul and Britain from 286/7 to 293, refortified the site. After his murder, his successor Allectus was crushed by Constantius Chlorus in 296. The crucial event in this victory was the capture of Boulogne.

The panegyric to Constantius describes how he invested rather than stormed the place because of the strength of the walls. A fourth-century date has also been proposed. Supporters of this point to the care with which the walls were built: they do not suggest a rushed response, the use of tombstones being simply the normal ruthless and pragmatic late Roman response.

Tour Gayette site

A section of the *castrum* wall can be seen at the foot of the medieval Haute Ville walls in the north-west corner. It is a complex jumble of material – simply Roman rubble interior built into the medieval structure.

Château site

Currently the best-preserved part of the late Roman rampart has been revealed under the château, providing the external foundations for the medieval cellar vaulting. A ditch filled with uncut stones and pottery rubble formed a base for 2–3 courses of large block masonry, including architectural pieces and tombstones, which in turn supported a medieval wall twice the width. The facing stones, hiding the mortar and rubble core, are less evenly cut than usual, but otherwise the rampart is typical of the period; as yet no precise dating evidence has been found. A section in the museum basement should now be exposed.

Château Comtal museum

Rue de Bernet
62200 Boulogne-sur-Mer
Hours: Weekdays 10–12.30p.m., 2–5p.m. Closed Tuesday
Sunday 10–12.30p.m., 2.30–5.30p.m.

Boulogne's municipal museum is a disappointment: a town that owes its existence to the Romans has managed to dump a limited and drearily presented collection of Roman material in the oppressive cellars of the castle; it makes a strange contrast with the money spent on presenting a nineteenth-century antiquarian's collection of Alaskan masks.

The Roman rooms still contain unlabelled material including an accomplished bearded head and material brought from elsewhere, such as the fine head of Galba (emperor AD 68–9, after the death of Nero), a bust of Faustina, the wife of Antoninus Pius, and a young Commodus, the vicious late second-century emperor; note also the lamp with a Jewish candelabrum from Carthage, put with the local collection. Most of these derive from the pre-Second World War municipal collection, famous for its glassware sadly destroyed in the bombardment of the city; they are only loosely held together by a 'gods and death' theme, devoid of any imaginative illustration to give context. There are neither artefacts from nor descriptions of the post-1960s excavations.

Most interesting are the tombstones recording seamen in the Classis Britannica. These include a trierarch commemorating the death of his daughter, a poignant three years, one month and sixteen days; another remembering his wife (both were ex-slaves); and a Thracian sailor, from what is today European Turkey, who died at 65 after thirty-five years service in the fleet. What looks like a third- or fourth-century inscription records the dedication to Sol Invictus by the crew of the trireme warship *Radius*, shortened to 'Rad'; perhaps they were giving thanks after a victory over Saxon raiders. Note also the recently recognized statues of the twins Castor and Pollux, sons of Jupiter (when he took on the form of a swan) and the nymph Leda, as well as the early Christian lamp showing Abraham sacrificing his son.

CAMBRAI, Nord

Museum and site.
www.villedecambrai.com/musée

Roman Cambrai was a small junction town on the Boulogne to Bavay road and the river Escaut (Scheldt), providing an alternative method for reaching the North Sea. It achieved minor prominence as a supply base when in the late Roman period it became the capital of a pagus that had previously belonged to the Viromandui or the Nervii, as Civitas Camaracensium. From the later third century the area to the north was increasingly insecure. Cambrai, though, apparently had a bishop in the fourth century, one of the most northerly known. It fell to the Franks during the first half of the fifth century, as they gradually took over Belgica Secunda, but was recovered by Aëtius, to be finally absorbed by the Merovingian kingdom. Gregory of Tours refers to it as part of the inheritance of Clovis in the 480s. There are no visible Gallo-Roman remains in the town.

Museum

15 Rue de l'Epée,
59400 Cambrai
Hours: 10a.m.–noon, 2–6p.m. Closed Monday and Tuesday

Despite the renovation of the museum, which re-opened as recently as 1994, the Gallo-Roman rooms are very thin and no effort is made to portray the background to the period. Best of the exhibits is a fine, large, square, firmly made glass jar used as a cinerary urn. Nevertheless, there is important material displayed here in the collection of skeletons from the Rues des

Vignes site. These have been subjected to very careful osteopathic analysis; sample skeletons indicate a variety of ways in which people suffered in the fifth, sixth and seventh centuries, such as arthritis, rheumatism, leprosy and wounds. Some of the things that caused the last are displayed in another case – spears, throwing axes and the single-bladed scramasaxes.

Rues des Vignes

Archéo-site
62 rue Haute
Hours: March to mid-November 2–6p.m. Closed Monday

12km due south by the N44, turning left (east) to Crèvecoeur by the D15, and then south by the D103. In the Rues des Vignes, the Archéo-site is signposted and slopes down to the river looking east. It is an attractive setting of grass and orchard trees, with clucking chickens in the garden next door.

The site was discovered in 1975 and excavated into the early 1980s, when it was decided to develop it as a reconstruction centre. The earliest finds were Gallo-Roman. These included a number of post holes, brick rooms, a hypocaust, painted plaster, cellars, a pottery, a low firing brick oven and evidence of chalk quarrying. Pottery finds suggest that the village was active in the second and third centuries. It is likely that it was part of 'Viniciacus' as this was the subsequent Frankish name for the local estate, later corrupted to 'Vinchy' when a Merovingian royal house was built nearby. This area of the Gallo-Roman settlement became a sixth- to seventh-century Merovingian cemetery; over 300 burials were excavated. A few bodies had stone coffins, some had goods with them, but little to indicate that these people were Christian or non-Christian. The foundations of a long stone structure were found; this seems to have simply fallen into ruin and no indicators survived to denote its purpose, though its shape and the use of stone rather than wood strongly suggest a small church. During the Carolingian period the area was reoccupied, only to revert to agricultural use in the later Middle Ages when it was terraced for vine cultivation – hence the name of the village.

Gallo-Roman material. One of the nine cellars is preserved. Steps go down into a rectangular chamber with alcoves on each of the other sides. The arches are made of delicate brickwork. The cellars may have been for simple agricultural storage or even religious worship, as there is some evidence that the cellars of villas were used for worshipping local or family gods. Given the settlement's semi-industrial character, it seems most likely that craftsmen used them. The pottery has been reconstructed and the wheel, oven and drying shed are used for demonstrations.

Merovingian material. Ten stone graves made in rough-cut blocks are exposed on the slope. The walling of the 'church' is predominantly poorly cut medium-sized stonework, but the occasional *petit appareil* suggests robbing out of earlier Gallo-Roman structures. There is a bronze 'workshop' and a reconstructed 'tavern' based on a structure and finds excavated in Luxembourg.

Carolingian material. The final group of buildings includes a farm, outbuildings, such as a barn, a smithy, and, the most interesting, a cloth worker's house.

CHAMPLIEU, Oise

IGN 2511 OT
637.7/2479.2

Sanctuary site.

Champlieu lies 16km south of Compiègne on the southern edge of the forest on a narrow country road north of the D123, equidistant from Orrouy and Béthisy-St-Martin (2.5km).

The road actually crosses the site; the temple is to the north, the theatre and baths to the south. It is possible to picnic peacefully either here or on the timber benches in a corner of the forest 200m away. Despite work in both the 1960s and the 1970s, Champlieu has an abandoned feel. The remains have been exposed for many years, but the collapsed fencing, the old wooden hut for a guard no longer present and the small number of visitors all enhance this effect.

The first excavations by the local landowner in 1850 stimulated the active interest of Napoleon III, who had turned the old palace at Compiègne into the centre for his court during the hunting season. Imperial patronage was expressed both in personal visits by Napoleon and in support for further excavations by Albert de Roucy and Viollet-le-Duc. The latter, famous more for his love of the Gothic, reflected in his restoration of nearby Château de Pierrefonds, wrote the first study of the site (1860), in which he presented his vision of the temple and theatre. Modern work by Georges Woimant (1977–81) suggests that, as was his way, Viollet-le-Duc reconstructed what he wanted to see rather than what the evidence warranted.

Champlieu lay beside the Senlis–Soissons road on the Suessiones border with the Silvanectes *civitas*. Environmental evidence hints at a woodland setting. Gallic coin finds and evidence of an insubstantial wooden building on the temple site suggest that there was a pre-Roman religious sanctuary; remains of butchering found under the baths together with early occupation levels under the theatre are certainly first century BC. De Roucy's excavation found evidence of Gallo-Roman settlement to the north of the temple and subsequent aerial photography and small-scale fieldwork has shown the existence of other parts of the settlement spreading over 40ha, including a necropolis to the south-east. It looks as though the whole site was deserted in the fourth century.

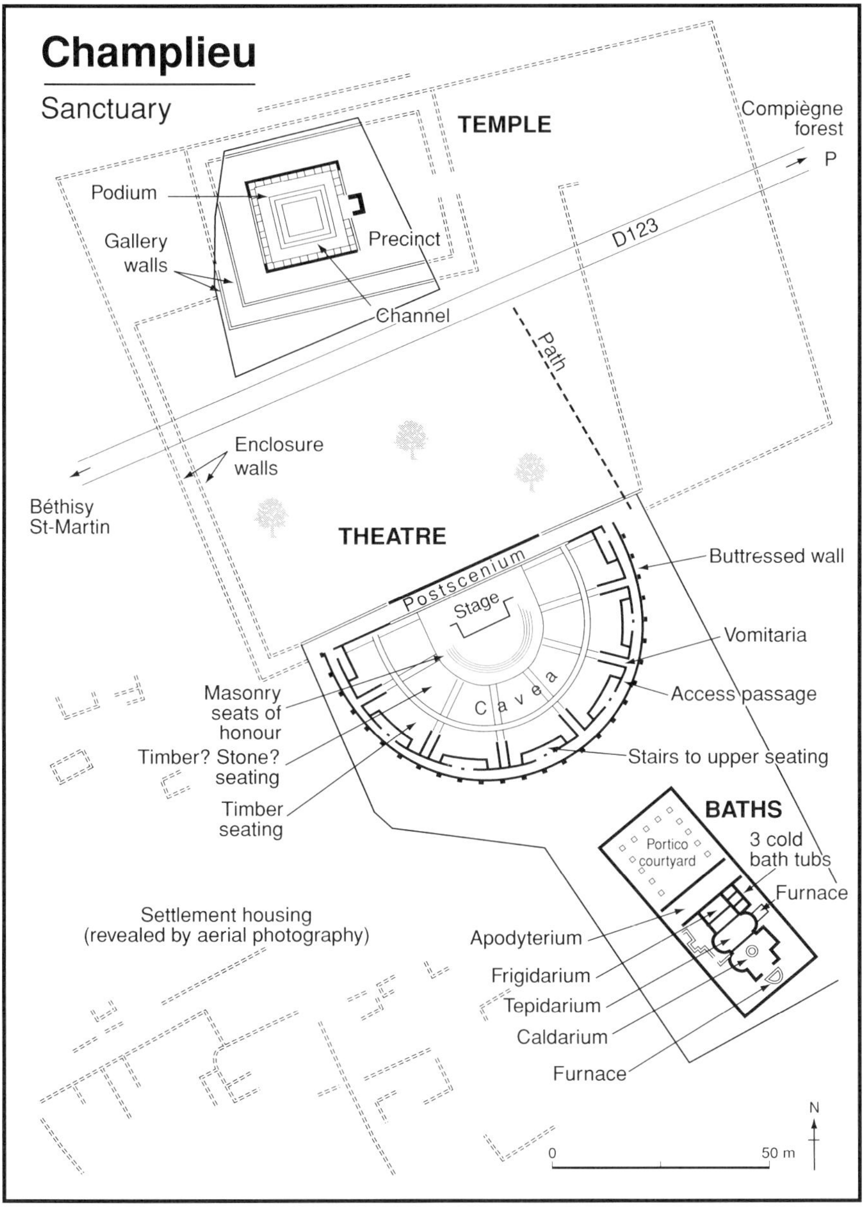

Figure 9 Champlieu: site plan

The temple

The early excavators found a large irregular external enclosure (100 × 130m) and an inner precinct or *temenos*, its double walls perhaps providing a portico for worshippers and a place for their offerings. Neither is exposed.

The visitor sees the remains of the podium and *cella* of the second stone temple on the site, dated to the second century, probably Hadrianic. Cadoux and Woimant in 1977 identified an earlier and simpler *fanum* approached by some steps from the eastern side. They found remains of a mosaic floor and wall painting (see COMPIEGNE) and tentatively dated them to the Claudian period. A channel about a quarter metre wide surrounded the new temple; it is particularly well preserved on the southern side. Only a grass mound recalls the temple walls, yet whether it was reconstructed with an ambulatory around a decorated *cella*, or as a *cella* consisting of walls surmounted by half-columns, the striking aspect is the quality of the decorated stonework scattered around the site.

The confident, pure and delicate classicism of the relief work is rare. The best figurative pieces were removed in the nineteenth century to the Château de Mothe and significant amounts of the best remaining masonry have been stolen, yet the beautiful legs of a nereid (sea nymph) resting on a fish, the confident acanthus and bayleaf pilaster patterns, and the Greek key pattern and firm zigzag decorations show how impressive the temple must once have been.

The theatre

To the south, backing onto the temple enclosure, is the theatre. Meagre dating evidence also suggests the second century. The ***cavea*** is typical of rural theatres. Basically it is a theatre 'exaggerata': a mound to carry the seating held in place by a surrounding wall of masonry. Champlieu theatre has some interesting individual features. Securing the wall are thirty buttresses, suggesting that the builders lacked confidence in the structure. Access is unusual as well. A narrow passage runs round the top of the outermost part of the curving retaining wall, from which spectators could go to any one of the six entrances to the interior tiers of seats. There are also stairs that once provided the way to a gallery constructed of timber scaffolding and seating. At the foot of the *cavea* are the surviving remains of stone seats – probably the seats of honour. Although it is restored, and therefore possibly giving a deceptive contrast with the rest of the *cavea*, the absence of stone elsewhere does support the view that the majority of the mound was covered with wooden seating. Estimates suggest a capacity of 3,000–4,000.

The **performing area** has a large orchestra, half-filled by a protruding stage in front of the long proscenium. The *frons scaenae* is virtually non-existent; instead there is a wall replacing the traditional 'actors' house'. There is no evidence for the standard three doors (only one in the centre) or entries at either end to turn it into a symbolic street. It is extremely unlikely that Roman plays were ever performed here; what religious ceremonies, civic meetings or entertainments took place remain unknown.

The baths

Below the theatre, on the gentle slope down into the Automne valley, is a bath complex, surrounded by a thick wall (53 × 23m). It was probably the last of the public buildings to be erected in the second century. Fortunately the baths have been consolidated after the most recent excavations.

A small, three-sided covered portico provided access and perhaps doubled as a *palaestra* or exercise courtyard. It is only partially excavated but the pillar bases can clearly be seen among the soil and weeds that cover most of it. Next to it is the undressing room or *apodyterium* (originally identified as a swimming pool), and beyond that is the first of the bath rooms proper, a *frigidarium*. On the left, eastern side, of the room is a stone bench with two rectangular and one semi-circular plunge baths; pipes indicate that running water was supplied. The remains of the room to the right of the *frigidarium*, and that beside the main *caldarium* are probably later additions. Both were heated with hypocausts.

The two main hot baths come next: the *tepidarium*, then the *caldarium*, heated by one furnace situated to the south-east of the complex. The hot air passed to the *tepidarium* through seven openings formed by massive stone blocks. Both rooms have tubs, the *caldarium* an additional alcove used as a *sudatorium* (sweating room) and a fine circular stone fountain with the remains of its lead piping in the floor.

CHATEAUBLEAU, Seine-et-Marne

Sanctuary remains.

The small village of Châteaubleau is 15km west of Provins by the N19 and D209.

In the 1960s, after clearing masonry from around La Tannerie spring disclosed a Gallo-Roman enclosure, Châteaubleau seemed to have been just one of many small rural sanctuaries. During the 1970s, another archaeological team dug away a mound, once thought to be the motte of a castle, to find the southern half of a Roman theatre. This was followed by the discovery of a second and larger sanctuary: a triple wall enclosed an enormous rectangular area, with its own spring and no less than four *fana* in a line. Finally, in the 1990s, M.F. Parthuisot exposed numerous houses along two roads, incidentally revealing that the modern village main street of Rue Prosper Desplats was aligned with them and no doubt the modern village buildings cover Gallo-Roman structures. Recent finds have included inscribed tiles using a local patois of Latin and Gallic, one of eleven lines seemingly dealing with a marriage.

This then is a small town or *vicus* in rich agricultural land on the main Sens–Meaux Roman road, though the discovery of La Tène material at La Tannerie shows that this spring at least was known before the Roman conquest. The larger sanctuary was built in the second century and presumably brought a major part of the town's prosperity. Both were used well into the fourth century, but appear to have been deliberately destroyed at the time of Valentinian II (375–92) and the town, too, seems to have died not long after. There is no occupation at all between the fifth and eighth centuries, but, interestingly, the village church, which can be traced back to the Carolingian period, was built within the old sanctuary, perhaps part of a Christianizing act repeated later when two of the *fana* sites were reused by the Hospitaller order, owners of the land in the medieval period. Only remains at La Tannerie and the theatre site are being left exposed.

La Tannerie spring sanctuary

Despite the heavy undergrowth, the reeds, mud and water of the current spring outlets help reveal the rectangular enclosing wall (once part of a plastered portico) and a couple of the semi-circular apses. Three short walls frame what must have been a place for devotions. A pool outside the enclosure, thought to be for pilgrims to wash themselves, and the evidence of the once carefully designed drainage pipes to control the spring's flow, are no longer visible.

The theatre

The southernmost *vomitorium* is quite clear, with four sets of stairs leading up to the single *cavea* platform. The stage wall is also possible to distinguish in the undergrowth. It is touching that a fragment of a player's flute was found in the orchestra area, no doubt thrown away before the theatre went out of use in the third century, though it was reoccupied by artisans for a time during the fourth century.

COMPIEGNE, Oise

Town museum.

80km north-east of Paris, Compiègne is best known for its forest and palace, but it has an interesting municipal museum. Compiègne itself has no Roman remains, nor, it seems, did the forest exist during the Roman period. Environmental evidence points to open wood and farmland, the forest being a product of the collapse of the Gallo-Roman social structure, and, later, deliberate preservation for royal hunting. Archaeological research in the area was stimulated by Napoleon III's fascination with the past and his love of house parties at Compiègne, and led to his appointing Albert de Roucy to carry out a series of excavations in the area during the 1860s. The most important Gallo-Roman finds were made at CHAMPLIEU and at **'La Ville des Gaules'** outside Pierrefonds, approaching Mont Berny, where a large *vicus* was found. Now covered by forest, only odd sections of walling are visible among the tree-roots (IGN 2511 OT, 647.4/2484.9).

Musée Vivinel

2 Rue d'Austerlitz
60200 Compiègne

Hours:	March–October	9a.m.–noon, 2–6p.m.
	November–February	9a.m.–noon, 2–5p.m.
		Closed Mondays and Sunday mornings

The museum is the result of Antoine Vivinel's success as a Parisian entrepreneur. Born in Compiègne, he made a considerable fortune as a property developer under the July Monarchy. The 1848 revolution brought gradual ruin: he died bankrupt and friendless in 1862. However, in the early 1840s he was at the height of his wealth and invested a large proportion of it in fine art, particularly from antiquity. He then pressed his home town to establish a museum with his collection of Egyptian, Greek, Etruscan and Roman pieces as the heart of the display – as indeed they still are.

In the confusion that followed the fall of Napoleon III (1870), some material from the imperial excavations in the Forêt de Compiègne ended up at the Musée Vivinel and further additions (particularly Merovingian) were made from often very disorganized excavations in the late nineteenth century. While Vivinel's original collection still embodies a fine-art approach, recently the collection and its display has begun to be re-examined, properly sorted and displayed on more up-to-date principles. Crucial in this process has been the acquisition of new material, especially late Iron Age and Merovingian.

Pre-Roman rooms

The **Gournay-sur-Aronde** room is the most important. A large low-lying *oppidum* site 15km west of Compiègne on the edge of Bellovaci territory came to prominence following meticulous excavation of its Gallic temple by J.P. Brunaux and his colleagues in the 1970s–1980s. This was a key site in demonstrating the origins of the ROMANO-CELTIC SANCTUARY. It began in the third century BC as a ritual enclosure defined by a ditch and gradually developed new features. A model of the sanctuary on the eve of the Gallic wars, *c.*60 BC, makes clear the general characteristics. By this time, the ditch had been lined with timber and filled with bones. A fence hid the site from casual view and an external ditch emphasized the enclosure's special status. Inside, religious ceremonies were carried out; and from the third century BC sacrifice had played a key role. Various pits had been used for killing and exposure, a large oval one apparently changing function to become temple-like, represented here by the rectangular wood-and-thatch structure.

Cases display various finds. When the ditch was excavated it became clear that the filling was not haphazard. Different animals were laid in alternate sections of the ditch; careful examination of the bones themselves also showed revealing differences in their treatment. The largest group is the bovines. They seem to have been sacrificed using an axe and then, judging from microscopic examination of bone surfaces, some of the body at least was allowed to rot before the bones were placed in the ditch. Two skulls seem to have been set by the entrance, perhaps symbolizing their central role at the site. Sheep and pig bones are rare, but showing signs of butchering, these animals were probably eaten. Horses were buried whole and in isolation – perhaps reflecting their value in contemporary society and so the scale of the sacrifice. There was also a significant number of human bones. Were these human sacrifices? Druids were believed to carry out human sacrifice and finds elsewhere could certainly support this, but the excavators, due to the lack of clear evidence of killing, lean towards burial. Another case is dedicated to metalwork. An amazing 2,000 iron weapons and tools were found on the site. These show clear signs of dedication. Whole weapon kits of sword, scabbard and shield, represented by the central boss, are twisted, bent, bashed or dismantled. The wealth embodied here, and the sacrifice made by those giving, is a reminder that the gold treasures of medieval cathedrals had their deeply felt predecessors.

Gallo-Roman rooms

Non-local exhibits include a fine bronze lamp from southern Italy and some second/third-century glass goblets with snake decoration, probably from the Rhineland. One of the best objets d'art Vivinel bought and gave to the museum was the **young man's torso** found at St Rémy-de-Provence in the early treasure digs of Glanum. It is a fine Roman copy of a Greek original. Interestingly, a capital from CHAMPLIEU temple also recalls Glanum: a head peers between the acanthus leaves, mixing Gallic figures with classical architectural design. There are fragments, too, of the wall painting that decorated the temple *cella* with a simple floral-frame design. Pictures present the reconstruction of the temple by a mid nineteenth-century artist.

Merovingian room

Eventually there will be new displays of the recent finds, hopefully set in a meaningful context. The metalwork exhibited is not the finest Merovingian, but brings together a number of the major early types: francisca axes, scramasaxes and silver-damascened iron belt buckles.

GENAINVILLE, Val d'Oise

IGN 2213 E

Sanctuary site.

About 3km south-west of Magny-en-Vexin. Follow the N183 towards Mantes-la-Jolie and 1.1km after Charmont take the minor turning westwards for 700m to the valley of Vaux de la Celle; 60m short of the fenced site, there is parking space by a large cave used for storage.

The extensive and impressive Gallo-Roman remains are hidden in a lush, narrow valley cut in the soft limestone of the Vexin Français, once part of the Veliocasses Gallic tribal territory. It is possible that Genainville was Petromantalum, a stop identified in the Peutinger Itinerary, as the Lutetia/Paris–Rotomagus/Rouen road (reincarnated in the N14) is close by. However, it is more certain that it received a sudden and short-lived prominence because of heavy investment in an imposing sanctuary.

The rain that helps give the valley its rich green covering also helped hide the site with 2–3m of thick topsoil washed down from the hillsides. The

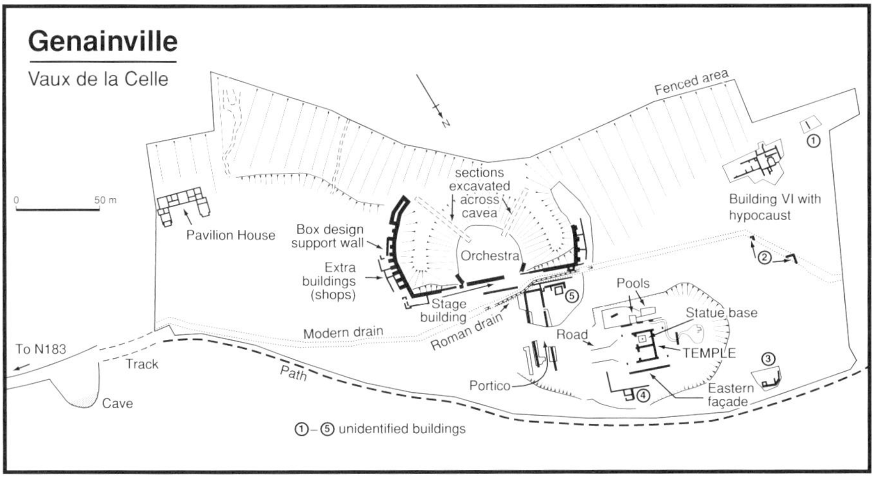

Figure 10 Genainville: site plan

valley's epithet 'de la Celle' hinted at its Roman antiquity, and in 1935 the temple, the theatre and a large Roman house were identified in the first excavations. The potential of the site was so great that 5ha of the valley were bought by the state (1941) and from 1960 it has been continuously excavated by the Centre de Recherches Archéologiques du Vexin Français, for much of that time led by P.H. Mitard. Although the overall outline of its development is clear, and striking finds have been made, more than its name remains obscure.

No evidence has yet been discovered of regular settlement before the construction of a small Augustan temple located beside a spring, which a hydrogeological survey suggests may have been hot, a strong reason for encouraging sacred building here. Yet little is known before the construction of a unique double *cella* temple, a theatre and a complex system of pools around the spring. Most other structures on the site are known only in fragmentary form. Many questions are still unanswered. Where are the public baths that would seem likely at a site like this? Was there a forum? Should it be seen as a *conciliabulum*, the term invented to describe a site with public buildings and few habitations and so aimed to provide Roman public forms for a population that was irredeemably rural? Is it really a small town settlement with widely spread occupation awaiting discovery? Currently, the most likely interpretation is that it was a water sanctuary site like GRAND or Les Fontaines-Salées (VEZELAY). It had a short-lived flowering, beginning either in the mid-second century AD, according to the older archaeological dating, or, by 1990s archaeometric methods, at the start of the third century, then suffered partial destruction in the later third century, to be abandoned in the fourth and turned into a quarry in the fifth and sixth centuries. Under the Merovingians a cemetery was established here.

The temple area

The walls of the **double *cellae*** still rise up to a dramatic 5m, built of *petit appareil* with brick dividing courses; the scaffolding holes are still clearly visible. Internally the walls were decorated with niches and pillars, plastered and painted to suggest marble (see the northern *cella* for surviving plaster). Above the niches were openings for light. The foundations of a statue base are preserved in the southern *cella*.

A corridor with grandiose front and rear façades encircled the *cellae*. Though tumbled down, enough of the eastern façade survived to reconstruct its appearance with vaulted bays over the corridors, and, along the front, divided by pillars and niches for statues, with an entablature, central pediment and side pediments over the corridors. The remains are preserved in GUIRY museum.

Following the discovery of a bronze statuette of Mercury in the northern *cella*, the temple's twin form has been assumed to embody dedications to Mercury and his consort Rosmerta. Burnt remains in the surrounding precinct were seen by Mitard as the result of offerings made to the gods. Also within the precinct is a well-preserved **road** of 35m that led to the centre of the façade from the **portico** that formed the western boundary of the precinct – did it also face a forum?

The pools

Three pools have been identified. They are still waterlogged and excavation has been difficult. The smallest was filled with dumped sculpture from the façade and a votive statue. The largest pool had steps, suggesting immersion by devotees. The second largest appears to have been decorated with an Apollo and at least one nymph, leading to its identification as a *nymphaeum*. This may be so, but there is much more to be found out about this aspect of the site, such as the ancient spring outlet itself. Only one **Roman drain** has been found.

The theatre

About 115m in diameter, like a number of other small-town theatres, it was built into the hillside to ease construction; sadly much of it was wrecked in late antiquity. The best-preserved section is the **eastern side** where *grand appareil* was used to build the rectangular box design that provided strong support for the seating without using excessive amounts of material. An additional row was added, probably shops; later these, and some inner chambers, became makeshift houses. Though little survives of the ***cavea***, it had two tiers of seats, nine of which were found with inscriptions. Traces of three walls at the top of the *cavea* suggest that there was a precinct from which five *vomitoria* gave access to a corridor running round the middle of the *cavea*.

The **orchestra** extends beyond the classic Roman semi-circle, leaving a small stage building and no apparent stage. It led Mitard to call it a theatre-amphitheatre. In 1991 new excavation demonstrated that the long-removed podium wall had left impressions round the orchestra, indicating that it rose to 2.5/3m high: it *could* have been used for dangerous spectacles. However, we really know nothing about what was done here.

Other buildings

The 'Pavilion' was imaginatively named in 1935. There is no evidence to support the implication that it was a sanctuary lodge. The only identified rooms are in the east wing, where two painted plaster rooms had hypocausts, probably part of the house's private baths. It appears to have been occupied in the later second and earlier third century AD. Of the others, only building VI has produced more than fragments: a hypocaust room was found here too, together with a terrace through which a well was later dug.

GUIRY-EN-VEXIN, Val d'Oise

Museum.

Using the N14 Rouen–Paris road, 7km east of Magny-en-Vexin turn south on the D159 to Guiry (1.5 km) and Arthies.

When the Val d'Oise department decided to build a departmental museum, visitors were lucky that they chose this beautiful limestone village. The museum itself is modern but unobtrusive, being partially below ground, and brings together a collection overwhelmingly Gallo-Roman from two sites, Epiais-Rhus and nearby GENAINVILLE: the material from the latter is outstanding.

Musée Archéologique Départemental du Val d'Oise

Place du Château
95450 Guiry-en-Vexin

Hours:	15 March–14 October	9a.m.–noon, 1.30–5.30p.m. Closed Tuesday
	Sat/Sun/holidays	10a.m.–noon, 2–7p.m.
	15 October–14 March	1.30–6.30p.m.

Rooms 1–3 cover local geology and prehistory (mainly Neolithic). Room 4 uses evidence from the two major Gallo-Roman sites to portray Gallic life from Middle La Tène to the arrival of the Romans. While from Genainville come early cemetery goods, the material from Epiais-Rhus gives some idea of life in the context of a Gallic village, gradually extending its links with the outside world and raising its modest level of prosperity. There are broken tools, suggesting a blacksmith's collection for melting down and recasting, locally produced kitchen pottery, a few imported swords and bracelets, and simple personal ornaments. Perhaps most impressive is the **tribal coinage**. A first-century BC gold Veliocasses stater, modelled on the Greek coin, is laid to show its reverse. This depicts a horse and chariot. The design derives from Philip II of Macedon's (fourth-century BC) model, but very distantly! The original horse has become a swirl of dislocated Celtic curves. A chariot wheel takes on the symbolism of the sun, reflecting the head of Apollo on the obverse side. Of course such coins were not used in the market-place but as gifts, whether from leaders to followers or as offerings to the gods.

Room 5 takes developments into the Roman period, again drawing on material from both sites. The focus is still daily life, but now represented by a much wider selection of artefacts including kitchen and table ware, slave manacles, locks and keys, agricultural tools, building materials and a wall painting from Genainville. In the mezzanine room (6) is displayed the magnificent **Mureaux bronzework hoard** bought by the museum in 1985.

Found by the Seine, it hints at the important role played by rivers in the distribution network. The quality of the bronze pieces, all associated with wine drinking, is as high as any found in France; they were made at the end of the second century and could be Italian work. There are four wine buckets or *situlae*, one beautifully decorated with a Silenus figure at the base of the handle; two jugs or *oenochoai* with an Eros-based decor for pouring wine; and deep bowls and matching sieves decorated with palmettes on the handles and incised floral decor around the sieve holes. When the wine was decanted it was necessary to strain off the aromatic herbs – added as preservatives and for taste – as well as the plaster seal fragments from the top of the amphorae.

The main finds from Genainville are in the lower rooms. A model of the temple gives an impression of its possible structure, but no sense of life or colour. Examples of interior plaster, with their streaky faux marble effects, and the paint traces found on the exterior statuary, indicate the much cruder impact the real temple must have had.

The statue group recovered from one of the temple pools dominates the display. The pieces were apparently deliberately placed there, carefully buried under clay, perhaps suggesting a superstitious respect for pagan sanctity in the uncertain Frankish world. A seated goddess holds a *patera* at her knee and once held, it is thought, a cornucopia in her other hand; a child stretches a hand towards the dish. Behind them stands a semi-naked figure, Venus-like with a cloth draped round her thighs, holding an urn from which she pours water. Another nymph lies resting on her elbow on a cloth perhaps draped over a rock. Sadly headless, her shoulders show traces of ringlets. A child stands in the background. The group embodies a very classical vision of life-giving fertility in its fullest sense. Its strongly Hellenistic form, popular in the second century, makes a clear statement of sharing in the heritage of the Graeco-Roman Mediterranean world. Current dating puts its construction under the Severans (193–235), when imperial initiative lay behind many new buildings; craftsmen must have come here from a major centre.

There are no firm indicators concerning the god(s) to whom the temple was dedicated. The statuary implies a figure like Apollo to accompany the seated goddess, yet the best evidence for a male god is a small statue of Mercury (very Celtic), and the charming child holding a tortoise, a fragment that once filled another pediment on the façade. The tortoise is taken to be a reference to the myth that mercury made the first lyre using a tortoise shell. Uncertainty is only increased by the unidentified and battered heads from some fifty other figures found from the temple's decoration. However, even damaged, the architectural fragments, particularly the imaginary marine creatures give a sense of the temple's original splendour.

An unusual **sheet-metal statue head** could have once decorated the interior of the temple or have been left as a votive offering. The face might even be a poor portrait of Hadrian, though this seems unlikely. The head was secured to a wooden core by soldering, then re-secured with nails (perhaps it broke); the most compelling features are the large eyes made of bone and glass paste that give this strange object its Celtic feel. There are other more conventional stone votive offerings ranging from the realistic headless man cradling a bird in his arm to the very Gallic cross-legged figure holding an animal to his chest.

The main exhibits end with finds from Epiais-Rhus. During the Roman period the settlement grew to be a small town of some 20ha, with temples, baths and houses equipped with hypocausts. In the general display the most impressive pieces are **fine glass chalices**. These were made as high-quality goods and used for wine drinking and as grave goods. Trails of coloured glass have been skilfully added to the pale green body in snake designs; in the fourth century these were made in the Rhineland, particularly Köln. In the sunken patio garden are displayed Merovingian coffins found at Genainville.

LA CHAUSSEE-TIRANCOURT, Somme

Oppidum and reconstruction centre.
www.samara.fr

In the Somme valley, 13km west of Amiens by the D191. Well signposted for Samara Park and La Chaussée-Tirancourt.

The *oppidum*

On the north-east side of the road. Access either from the road or via Samara Park.

For Roger Agache, La Chaussée-Tirancourt was 'le plus parfait' promontory fort. Using a spur on the northern bank of the Somme, it demonstrates how a late Iron Age strongpoint could most effectively take advantage of the natural geography of the area. The southern side of the spur runs parallel with the river, the bank rising steeply from the road with the marshland and flood plain beyond. To the north and west, the *oppidum* is protected by a deep valley, formed by the tiny river Acon. But to the east the site had to be artificially defended; a massive flat ditch was dug with a high internal mound (the Fossé Sarrazin). The *oppidum* covers about 35ha.

Identifying its function and purpose once seemed simple. Louis d'Allonville argued in 1782 that, like the other hill fortifications along the Somme, such as nearby Liercourt-Hérondelle and L'Etoile, it was a Roman military camp. The identification stuck: a *camp de César* apparently confirmed by surface finds of Roman coins. Yet as prehistoric works became better understood, opinion switched entirely round. In 1939 Mortimer Wheeler recognized it as one of his Iron Age 'Fécamp' hill-forts. Modern interpretations based on Agache's

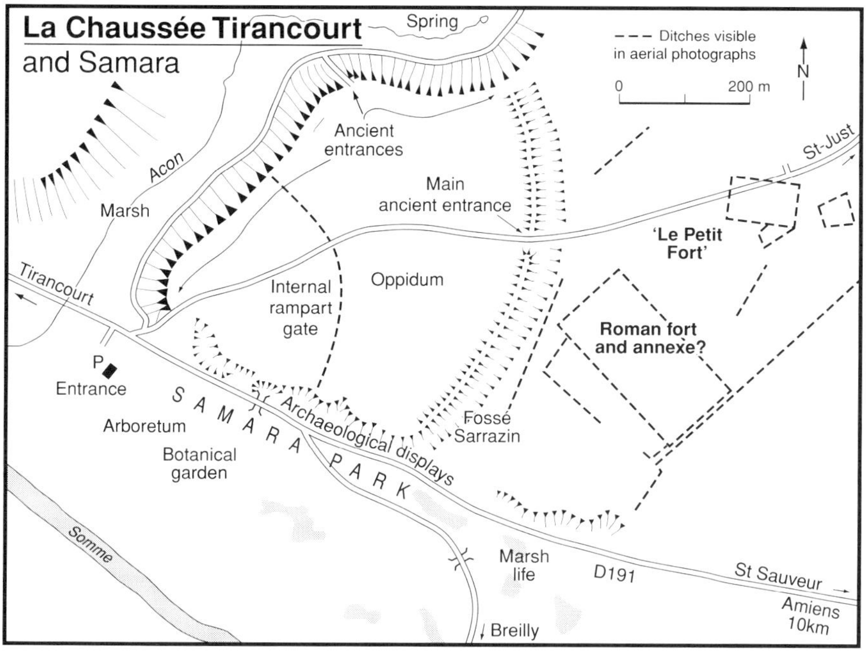

Figure 11 La Chaussée Tirancourt and Samara: local plan

photographs and recent excavations have been forced to reconcile Roman and Gallic in unexpected ways.

The Fossé Sarrazin undoubtedly shows Celtic techniques in its construction and late Gallic pottery has been found in the structure. But the main gate, excavated by Brunaux and Duval in the later 1980s, made clear that this was not built to resist the Romans; they convincingly dated it to an occupation of *c.*50–10 BC, and a subsequent dig on the gate through the second smaller ditch and mound, revealed by an Agache photograph, showed that this, too, was constructed at that time. It therefore seemed possible that this was a post-conquest Gallic town like Villeneuve-St-Germain (Soissons), perhaps a predecessor of Amiens. Yet the excavators rejected this possibility.

The finds made in the 1980s and early 1990s showed that 75 per cent of the coins found are not Belgic, being either Roman or from Marseille; much of the pottery is of a type frequently found at Roman military camps; there are metal fragments of a *gladius* (Roman short sword), a trenching tool and boot nails (Roman military but not legionary). There is also a fair amount of Gallic material, but taken with the lack of any housing within the Fossé Sarrazin, the compromise interpretation is that this was a fort constructed and occupied by Gallic auxiliary forces during the troubled period after the

Plate 2 La Chaussée-Tirancourt. An aerial view of the hill-fort. Photograph: Roger Agache, Ministère de la Culture.

conquest when the neighbouring Bellovaci tribe rebelled in 46 BC and the Morini in 29.

Agache's photographs have also shown important enclosures outside the Fossé, unfortunately not clear at ground level. Some are ancient field boundaries, but soundings made at the 'Petit Fort' site suggest that this could have been a Roman camp and annexe with typical 80cm shallow ditches and even a spiked-stake hole (see ARCHEODROME). Pottery finds suggest occupation connected with either the AD 43 Claudian invasion preparations or the AD 69 Civilis rebellion. Large numbers of late Roman coins indicate that, as elsewhere, previously fortified places were reoccupied during the more dangerous third and fourth centuries.

In addition to the main entrance others have been identified in the north and the west. The steep slope below the northern gate implies that it gave access only to a spring. The western entrance appears to have been large and complex, but medieval quarrying for construction work on Amiens cathedral (evidence of which can be seen all along the south-western side) has severely disturbed the original structure.

Samara (park)

On the south-west side of the D191.

Hours:	summer	10a.m.–7.30p.m.
	winter	9.30a.m.–2.30p.m.

Guided visits available in English at 2p.m.

This regional development project is tastefully and intelligently planned. The archaeological re-creations both inside and outside the slightly bizarre but effective multi-domed central display building are stimulating. It is easy to spend many hours here and, with a free guidebook (various languages), this fully justifies the relatively high entrance price.

Passing through the **arboretum**, the visitor comes first to the **botanical garden**, set in a boxed maze. The plant labels are particularly helpful, giving first known historical uses, e.g. as medicines or dyes. It is possible then to follow the **nature trail**, which takes you through an area of this part of the Somme – the Roman 'Samara' – where something of the traditional marshland has been preserved.

The real pleasure of the re-creations in the display building is that you can walk through them (Palaeolithic to Gallo-Roman), touching and even picking up plates or carvings, real skins or cloth. A Roman shoemaker's counter is re-created with partially cut leather, a wooden sole and a finished hob-nailed sandal, which the visitor can closely examine and consider. A kitchen illustrates the agricultural produce of the Gallo-Roman villa economy of the second century AD: real poultry hangs from the wall, bowls of fruit and cereals lie on the counter, and all the display is based on the analysis of food remains found in Amiens excavations. A Gallo-Roman house interior uses the wall-plaster painting designs and concrete flooring found in Amiens, done with a worn look that is unusual in re-creations. There is an area for special exhibitions which, at the time of writing, displayed a magnificent collection of Roger Agache's aerial photographs, breathtaking in their mix of archaeological revelation and artistic sensibility (see ABBEVILLE).

Outside, the full-scale reconstructions include a **Gallic house** and associated buildings of about 50 BC, based on the excavations at Villeneuve-St-Germain; in addition to the surprisingly large rectangular house, there is a hay loft with a storage pit or cellar, all surrounded by a fence. Yet perhaps the best feature of the outside area is that at set times in the day (these are displayed at the entrance), **craft workers** demonstrate and talk to visitors about the ancient techniques. They cover weaving with various upright loom types; pottery manufacture from four different furnaces; and relief and sculpture work based on original Gallic and Gallo-Roman designs, some available for sale at the park shop. Children can mix and construct cob walling or even, by arrangement, learn how to cast lead Celtic wheel ornaments. The park embodies communication, not commercialization.

MARLE, Aisne

Museum and reconstruction site.

Marle is 20km north-east of Laon by the N2 to Vervins. Taking the road into the centre of Marle to the junction with the D946, follow the (small) sign pointing down the Rue Lehault, which quickly becomes the Rue de la Moulin.

Musée des Temps Barbares

Moulin de Marle
02250 Marle
Hours: 15 April–15 October 2–7p.m. Closed Tuesday

The new museum and archaeology park opposite provide a vivid picture of life in the Frankish period and are based on the work done at the Merovingian site of Goudelancourt-les-Pierrepont, where two cemeteries and a settlement were excavated in the 1980s and early 1990s.

The museum

A renovated watermill houses fresh and imaginative displays, focusing on the cemetery finds. The 458 chalk-cut graves, covering a period from *c.*530 to 690, have revealed most about how long individuals in this small community were likely to live, how they chose to dress and what they valued. A typical burial with skeleton and grave goods is re-created, giving an idea of what the archaeologists found. Disease, particularly the plague, was the major killer among 18–30-year-olds, not violent death (study of the skeletons put life expectancy at 35). The spears, throwing axes and swords certainly give a sense of contemporary insecurity, but equally they indicate how weapons had once again become part of normal masculine attire. The damascened belt buckles, multicoloured beaded necklaces and brooches further emphasize the importance of personal display. Perhaps most interesting is the **ornamented bag**, only its hammered metal and inlaid elements, especially the two beak-like pieces, surviving. Full-size figures help in visualizing the lost belts and dresses, but need to be replaced with less anachronistic shop-window dummies.

Parc Archéologique

The original living site seems to have been a large farming unit with a big house surrounded by huts used in a variety of ways. All were built of timber, though the large house had a hard stone floor. The hamlet was occupied from the first half of the sixth century until the early seventh century; its relationship with the Gallo-Roman settlement at Beauvois, only 1km away, is not known.

The structures are recognized to be possibilities only. However, the archaeologist, CNRS architect and local carpenter/builder all believe that they have put up the simplest and most logical solutions suggested by the post-hole and occupation evidence. They admit that they used many more nails than the few they found on site, but believe this is not significant. Their experiments have contributed to a major debate on the use of small huts in the Frankish period: were they lived in or used purely for a variety of semi- or non-domestic tasks? Only one hut gave a clear hint of usage – bread-making, and their experiments have shown that an oven can work perfectly well inside a hut. The other huts could have housed iron-working, shelter for animals, storage and perhaps textile working, but they could also have been lived in, and one is restored as such. The claim is made that these sunken floor huts are quite amenable to domestic use because this feature actually provides protection from the wind in winter and makes them cool in the summer.

MEAUX, Seine-et-Marne

Late Roman rampart and sanctuary.

43km due east of Paris, Meaux is in the heart of the Ile-de-France basin. Today it is the centre of Brie production; in the Roman period it was Iatinum, the *civitas* capital of the Meldi tribe. The town had grown at a crossing point

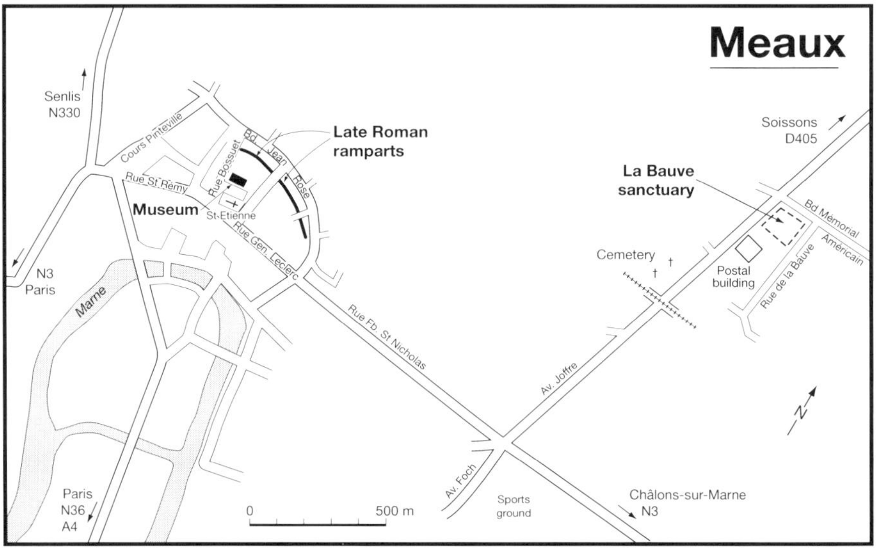

Figure 12 Meaux: town plan

in a loop of the river Marne which the third-century Peutinger Itinerary, or road book, indicates was another route north from Sens, an alternative to either of the major routes via Paris or Reims. The Marne was an important navigable tributary of the Seine, as Caesar implied when he described the Meldi supplying him with sixty ships with which to invade Britain (unfortunately blown off course once they reached the Channel). The Meldi exploited forests to the south of the river and agricultural land to the north, as well as Meaux's position as a staging point on the river. Gallo-Roman traces suggest a town covering approximately 60ha. There is evidence for a grid, but no known forum. The written record suggests a theatre; a fragmentary elliptical wall may have been part of an amphitheatre; an aqueduct and public baths have been claimed. During the late empire Iatinum was renamed after the Meldi tribe; the name subsequently evolved to its contemporary form. The only physical remains are the *castrum* ramparts enclosing around 8ha. A large and well-preserved sanctuary has been found at La Bauve, just outside the town. It is still being researched, but the visible remains are already impressive. The town came under Frankish control during the last quarter of the fifth century.

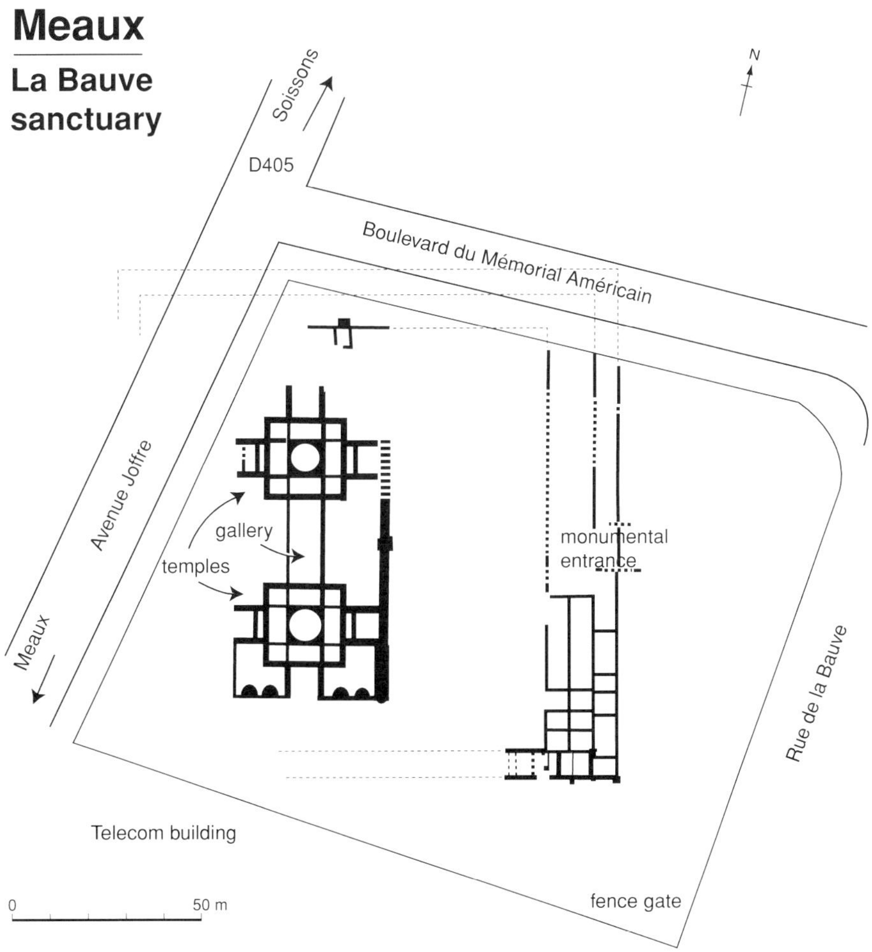

Figure 13 Meaux: sanctuary site plan

Late Roman ramparts

Boulevard Jean-Rose, by the main tourist car park

A major stretch of rampart, *c.*250m of the total 1km, survives to a considerable height; most has been markedly altered over time. The section near the Rue Bossuet has been restored to show its late Roman appearance: facing blocks of *petit appareil* for ten courses followed by three courses of brick. A cellar in Rue Bossuet revealed a stretch of 8m, about 3m thick, with the usual massive foundation blocks, including reused stones, but sitting on its own 2m thick foundation of rough-cut stone courses, set in the sandy bedrock.

La Bauve sanctuary

Corner of Avenue Joffre and Boulevard du Mémorial Américain. Entrance on Rue de la Bauve. 2km from Meaux centre by the D405, Soissons road, next to the Telecom building. At the time of writing, access was restricted to special days only. Much of the walling is over 2m high and can be seen through the wire fencing.

A square double wall encloses nearly 2ha. Excavations since the mid-1980s have revealed a monumental entrance leading into what was probably an open area, though this is not yet fully explored, and separated by a very solid wall from what must be twin but rather enigmatic temples, linked together by a gallery. Twin temples are known (see GENAINVILLE), but, though square, these are far from conventional *fana*. The internal shape of each is unusual, forming a circular structure, the thick walls implying towers. Nor is each surrounded by the normal lightly built gallery: the strong foundation walls suggest something much more substantial. Cornices, marble facings and fragments of sculpture in the debris from its final ruin around 390 suggest richly decorated buildings. A silver Apollo head with gold inlay could represent one god worshipped here. This massive sanctuary certainly existed from the beginning of the second century and went through numerous phases, though how it evolved to the final (third-century?) version is not yet clear. Finds from the fourth/third century BC onwards, including swords, bent scabbards, lance points, coins and animal bones from under both the monumental gateway and the twin temples, strongly suggest a pre-Roman sanctuary.

Musée Bossuet

Palais Episcopal
5 Place Charles de Gaulle
77100 Meaux
Hours: 10a.m.–noon, 2–6p.m. Closed Tuesday

At the time of writing, the entire archaeological collection was in storage.

If exhibited to the public in the future, surely this must include material from La Bauve sanctuary and a selection from the old collection. There is a battered Jupiter column group, in which the shield, portrayed as a wheel, stresses this Jupiter's Celtic imagery symbolizing the power of the sun, turning time and controlling life, while the monster below Jupiter symbolizes the darker forces of the earth. A small altar portrays a child-like Mars and a niche with figures suggests the *lares* or household gods. Among the finds from the Meaux cemeteries are stone coffins, wider at one end than the other, typically Merovingian, yet they have been dated to the fourth century, as have necklaces, fibulae and swords found here: perhaps German/Frankish allies given local land, or perhaps Gallo-Romans fashionably adopting German styles?

PARIS

Museums and sites.

Lutetia was never a major Roman city. At its maximum extent it covered about 60ha, with a population of perhaps only 5,000–8,000. Despite being less than half the size of Samarabriva (Amiens), and succeeded by a capital city that has ruthlessly swept aside the past, more has survived than might be expected. Paris has one of the best preserved Roman buildings in northern France – the magnificent Cluny baths – and, of course, the national collections, including the obvious (e.g. the Louvre) and the rarely visited (e.g. the Cabinet des Médailles).

The outstanding figure in the archaeology of Paris is undoubtedly Théodore Vacquer (1824–99). As the new, very young municipal inspector of historic buildings, he made his name in the 1840s, especially with the 1847 excavation of the Notre Dame square or *parvis*, identifying the remains revealed as Roman. When the medieval and early modern buildings were torn down amid an unprecedented speculative property boom, often the work of Haussmann, Napoleon III's Paris prefect, Vacquer went from site to site. Excavating where possible, rescuing what finds he could and, above all, distinguishing and recording, he was the first person to bring to light the topography of Lutetia. He was made town inspector of archaeological excavations (1860–73) and, finally, *conservateur* of the Musée Carnavalet. Just before his death, the Commission du Vieux Paris was created (1894), a body of the great and good to advise the mayor, protect the Parisian heritage and supervise archaeological work in the city; since then some 1,250 excavations have taken place. The Commission's initial willingness to allow the destruction of a major section of aqueduct in the mid-1990s shows how public belief in the value of the past continues to be just as important in challenging the pressure from developers.

Strabo explained that 'the Parisii live round about the Sequana river, having an island in the river and a city called Lucotocia' (IV, 3, 5). Their power must have been based on control of the Seine highway and its important tributaries the Oise, Aisne and Marne, all of which met in the Paris basin. The Ile de la Cité had been created by the Seine cutting new channels around a mound of silt and bedrock, leaving an old looping meander as a still marshy zone in the Gallic and Roman period, below the heights of Montmartre. Though no one doubts that this island was the one meant by Strabo (and Caesar before him), archaeological evidence to support it has been slim. A modern excavation in the Rue de Lutèce did, however, reveal round huts under far thicker later deposits, suggesting that the Gallic levels are much deeper than previously suspected.

A rough gauge of the Parisii's status in Gaul is provided by their response to Caesar's wars of conquest. They only resisted in the final phase, sending 8,000 troops, a middling number, to help Vercingetorix at Alesia (Caesar,

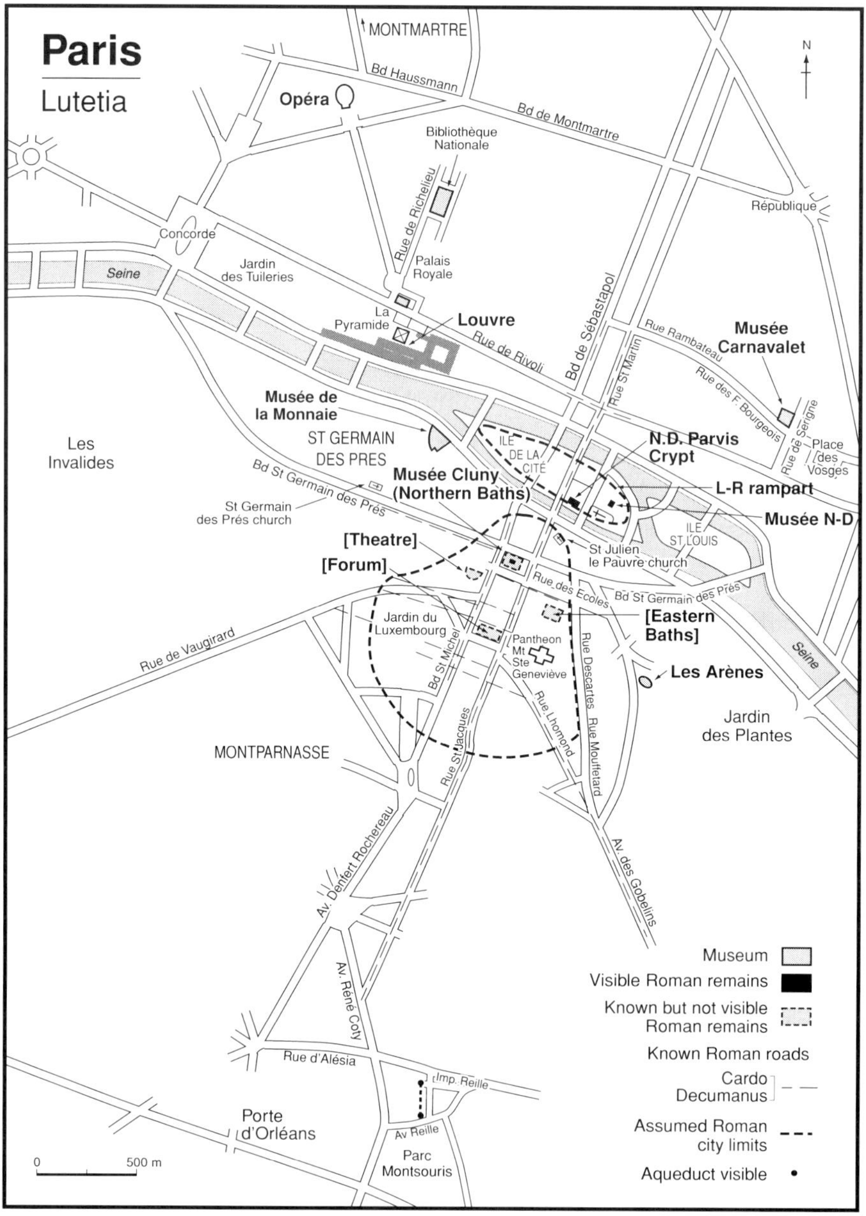

Figure 14 Paris: town plan

Gallic Wars, VII, 75); Labienus, one of Caesar's generals, took Lutetia in battle. This was not a tribe like the Remi or Aedui, key groups who were important in the years of conquest and for many years after prospered under Roman rule. However, it had two strengths. First, Lutetia lay at a good river crossing on one route to the centres that secured the north of Gaul: Rouen, Amiens, Bavay and Boulogne. Second and maybe more importantly, the tribe must have had a significant number of boats and rivermen available to be developed into the inland merchant fleet proclaimed on the Tiberian (AD 14–37) Nautae inscription.

The main road or *cardo* has been found below the modern Rue d'Arcole, bisecting the island; wooden bridges linked each end to the north and south banks. Traces revealed under the Rue St Martin show that to the north the *cardo* was constructed through the damp wood and marshland, sparsely occupied throughout the Roman period. The left bank was different: beyond the marsh thickets of the riverside, Mont Ste-Geneviève provided secure ground and good limestone for building. The main *cardo* has been found under the Rue St Jacques going up and over the hill. The Roman town here dates from the 30s BC. The 1990s excavations at the Collège de France confirmed that large ditches, perhaps quarrying for sand and gravel used for the formal grid roads, destroyed the earliest insubstantial dwellings. Typical Augustan timber and cob buildings followed.

The first stone public buildings appeared in the later first century. The Collège site revealed a large timber building (of unknown function), to be replaced under Trajan by what are known as the eastern baths; these may be slightly later than the northern or Cluny baths, which recent work suggests are Flavian. This in turn must mean that the aqueduct, bringing fresh water from springs at Wissous 20km to the south, is likely to be first century, rather than mid-second century as previously thought. It will also have supplied yet more baths, the 'southern', close by the forum, first identified by Vacquer when the Rue Soufflot was widened. His description of the forum was complemented by 1970–71 excavations preceding final destruction for an underground car park. It was a typical late first-century north of the Alps forum (see FEURS): a long esplanade, 118 × 43m, surrounded by a colonnaded portico with a basilica and classical temple on a podium facing each other across an open square.

Paris had both a small theatre, *c.*72m diameter, of which traces still exist under the Lycée St Louis in the Boulevard St Michel, and an amphitheatre by Rue Monge on the eastern edge of town, both again first recognized by Vacquer. During the twentieth century more trouble was taken to distinguish both homes and industrial premises. Fine houses with wall paintings existed to the south of the forum and most of what is the Luxembourg gardens down to Odéon was inhabited during the early empire. On the right bank there was a large clay quarry, but little habitation before Montmartre hill. Gallo-Roman walling survived here into the sixteenth century; Vacquer, when only 20 years old, revealed here the foundations of what could have been a temple dedicated to Mercury, following the discovery of statuary nearby.

Nineteenth-century excavations showed that the Ile de la Cité, but not the Ile St Louis, was inhabited during both the early and late empire periods. A large structure at the western end was called a 'palace'; a building by the Rue de la Cité considered a 'basilica' and a temple presumed to exist under Notre Dame cathedral. However, firm evidence through a modern stratigraphic dig on the Notre Dame *parvis* (1965–84, M. Fleury) demonstrated that there was a stone quay and housing, subsequently replaced by a late Roman rampart.

Paris in the late third century, like almost all other northern Gallic towns, experienced serious contraction. There is evidence of fires and destruction, but equally deliberate dismantling. The eastern baths were taken down carefully and it is thought other buildings were as well. The cemeteries were scoured and tombstones removed. The stone was used to raise the ground level of the Ile de la Cité and to provide it with firm foundations for a rampart enclosing about 10ha. As the *parvis* excavation showed, within the walls was not just a strongpoint, there were densely packed houses. Nor was the left bank town abandoned. Not only did the forum become a blockhouse with gates filled in with new walling, but houses continued to be occupied, though over a more limited area.

In the fourth century Lutetia became known as Civitas Parisiorum. Famously, Julian described the town as 'my beloved Paris'. He came in 358, again in 359/60, and was proclaimed emperor here. In his letter he noted how it was secure, safe from flooding, had good drinking water (was the aqueduct still in commission?) and that the country around grew vines and figs, suggesting a better climate than today. Ammianus makes clear that it had a military camping ground and that it was a supply base. Other sources show that at the end of the fourth century it was the headquarters of the prefect of a Sarmatian cavalry troop and a (river) fleet prefect. The defence of the north gave Paris a strategic importance without being so close to the action that it suffered constant depredations: its vitality raised its relative importance over many other northern towns.

Paradoxically, firm Christian history of Paris can be dated from 360, during the months spent here by the newly proclaimed emperor Julian, soon to be asserting pagan beliefs and rights. A bishops' council met here and condemned some aspects of Arianism. No bishops of Paris can be firmly assigned before 360, though the martyrdom of Saint-Denis on the hill of Montmartre in the 250s is accepted. His head was taken to the *vicus* of Catulliacus, later to be renamed St Denis. No doubt Christianization was as slow here as elsewhere. The decisive breakthrough undoubtedly came with Sainte Geneviève. Born *c.*422 with a traditional Gallo-Roman aristocratic background, she played the role generally assigned to bishops: proselytizing, working miracles and, when Paris was threatened, securing the city from destruction. Her prayer may have diverted Attila, but it was her drive and leadership that persuaded ships' captains to seek corn when starvation threatened in the 470s and it was her political awareness that led her to cultivate the friendship of Childeric, king of the Franks. By the end of the fifth century Paris was part of the Frankish kingdom and Sainte Geneviève would have known Clovis before she died (500), though Paris was not to become capital of the Merovingian kingdom until 508.

Archaeological remains of palaeo-Christian buildings associated with this shadowy period are rare. A fourth-century church on the site of Notre Dame is likely, but as uncertain as the earlier temple. A church in the cemetery where Sainte Geneviève was buried is certain; it once stood on the top of the hill named after her, but no remains have survived. Firm evidence only comes in the sixth century, the best known being St Etienne, found in the Notre Dame *parvis* excavations; St-Pierre de Montmartre; and St-Germain-des-Prés, used by the Merovingians for royal burial until the later seventh century. At St-Denis, recent excavations have shown that Frankish nobility were buried there for many years before it became the new royal cemetery site.

Cluny (northern) baths and Musée National du Moyen Age

6 place Paul Painlevé (Rue du Sommerard)
5th Arrondissement
Hours: 9.15a.m–5.45p.m. Closed Tuesday

Approaching the baths, you can hardly believe what you are seeing: rising 8–10m high, Roman walling of rectangular stone courses separated by multi-course bricks; its genuineness confirmed by the patching and repairs made over nearly 2,000 years. Still surviving and rising above the rest is the roof of the chamber used as a *frigidarium*. Locked into the baths and merging into the background is the fifteenth-century mansion built as the Paris residence of the abbots of Cluny. The baths are the largest surviving in northern France.

Fortunately, after they went out of use in the fourth century following a great fire, plundering for stones was relatively insignificant and by medieval times it was simply an imposing neglected ruin. The baths were soon enclosed by buildings on all sides and, with land to the east, were bought in 1330 by Cluny monastery. Even when a fine abbot's mansion was built in the 1490s, some bath chambers were integrated within the structure, while plants grew in decorative fashion over others. Eventually rooms were let out for storage. By the late eighteenth century the vaulted chamber was being let to a cooper to store barrels.

It was during the Revolution that the real value of the site was first recognized. The abbot lost his mansion and this eventually came into the hands of Alexandre du Sommerard, an antiquities collector who used the old building for his *cabinet de curiosités*. Abbé Grégoire, who voted for both the dispossession of the clergy and the execution of the king, but believed

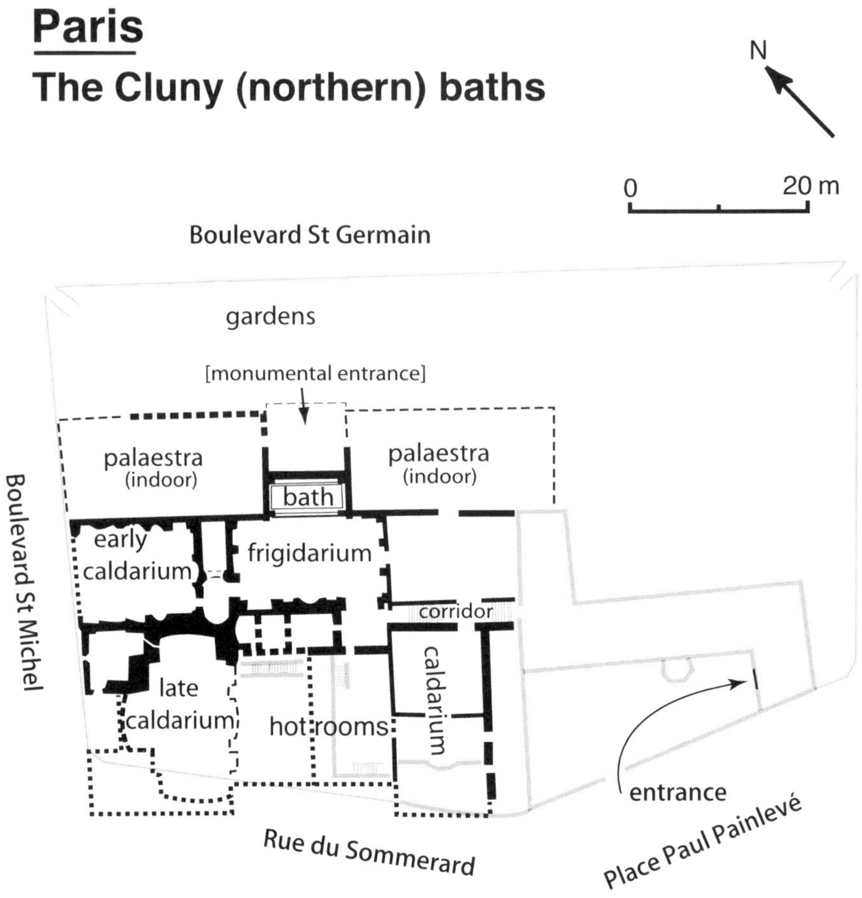

Figure 15 Paris: Cluny (northern) baths: site plan

strongly in the value of the people's heritage, recognized the significance of the Cluny baths when he pointed to 'this unique monument, the only one that Paris has preserved'. Its importance was not forgotten. In the 1830s the architect Moreau excavated here and the first proposals were made for a museum; the logic was to combine the cabinet and the baths. At last, in 1843, Edmond du Sommerard, the collector's son, was named *conservateur*. The museum was to be for both the Roman and medieval heritage. However, by the 1880s the situation had changed. The focus of the collection, particularly after the acquisition of the wonderful Lady and the Unicorn tapestries, was clearly medieval; at the same time Vacquer's work had helped lead to the creation of the Musée Carnavalet with himself as assistant curator; this was where future Roman finds would go.

Inevitably it was Vacquer who carried out the excavations when the surrounding buildings were cleared to make way for the boulevards in the 1850s. He revealed the covered *palaestrae*; he found a monumental entrance, porticos and shops now covered by the Rue du Sommerard and the building south to the Rue d'Ecoles; he cleared the western sections of the baths and he recorded features that were destroyed. What he did not provide was a clear description of the various elements of the baths and how they might have functioned. Following fresh painstaking excavations in 1945–56, this was done by P.-M. Duval. Only in the 1980s–90s has new work revised some of Duval's conclusions, most importantly perhaps expanding the chronology. Where Duval saw one virtually unaltered structure used for a hundred years (150–250), current opinion sees the baths in use from the Flavians to the earlier fourth century (250+years) and experiencing modifications and rebuilding over that time.

The baths

The builders had to contend with the slope of the hill. This was done by creating a basement of **service rooms**. Bathhouse workers – the stokers, cleaners, attendants, masseurs, entertainers – could move freely here. Above this were all the main bathing and exercise rooms, articulated around the great ***frigidarium***. This has a vaulted roof rising 13.5m supported by four unusual capitals made in the shape of ship prows. Sadly the interior skin of this room, along with the others, is missing: the alcoves and pilasters have no more than preparatory plaster layers and one tiny fragment of painted stucco. There was a large pool on the north side for cold dips.

Corbels in some rooms suggest second floors; these were probably for administration and for leaving clothes. To the south was an open palaestra for exercising when the weather was good, and a monumental entrance. To the north there was a second grand entrance, though this was closed off in one of the refittings; this left the large symmetrical rooms still in use, possibly as **indoor palaestrae** or gymnasia. In the first phase, the **main hot room** was on the west (open to the Boulevard St Michel); as there was no access then from the *frigidarium*, there was perhaps a *tepidarium* to the south. However, in the final phase modifications the arrangements were transformed, the *caldarium*'s furnaces were filled in (under the road) and it became another large cold pool. Roman road flagstones were dumped here in 1842. The southern rooms were then converted into a series of hot rooms, the **south-east *caldarium*** being particularly grand with great exedras on three sides. The **central corridor**, by which visitors passed from the medieval mansion into the bath area, was probably the main way in for bathers, who could go on into the northern cold complex or south into the various warm, hot, wet and dry rooms. The **corridor *caldarium*** has traces of Roman windows on its walls.

Plate 3 Paris. The Cluny baths. The *frigidarium* and the indoor palaestra from the garden. Photograph: James Bromwich.

Gallo-Roman and related exhibits

Frigidarium. The **Pillar of the *Nautae***. The blocks were found in 1711 and are believed to have formed a pillar raised on the quayside of the Ile de la Cité. There is the normal mix of Roman and indigenous gods; unusually they are named. The liveliest are the Gallic Cernunnos (see REIMS) and Esus attacking a willow tree. The latter has been linked to Tarvos Trigaranos, a bull, shown here with egrets. The symbolism would then be death and rebirth, Esus cutting down the tree of life but renewed by the fertility of the bull, the two connected by the birds who nest in willows and eat ticks off the backs of cattle. The pillar is inscribed (translated): 'In the reign of Tiberius Caesar Augustus the shippers of the Parisii raised this monument to the very great and very good Jupiter at their own expense.' Around this block are armed figures, carrying Gallic shields; one holds what looks like an arched boat frame. Are these boatmen working for the tribe's shippers (*nautae*) at the time of Tiberius, perhaps demonstrating their contribution to the Roman regime when Florus and Sacrovir had led Gallic revolts in AD 21? The highly unusual *frigidarium* prow capitals might mean that the baths were actually funded by the Parisian nautae, showing their continued importance.

The statue of Julian is a fine life-size fourth-century marble bought in Italy in 1787. He is depicted as the pagan emperor: bearded like a philosopher and wearing a priest's crown and cloak. It was probably made for a pagan senator in Rome after Julian's death, like the very similar example in the Louvre. The sarcophagus relief of lamenting women was also brought from Italy. The **Pillar of St Landry**, reused in the late Roman rampart, is a large block decorated with four reliefs, perhaps from a crossroads. The young woman, usually described as Vesta, has the delicate features and slim curving body more appropriate to Venus; the breastplated young man must be Mars. The **hunting scene**, found at the same time (1829) is a lively relief of dogs and men with nets. The bird roundel mosaic was acquired from Tunisia, but the **cupid on a dolphin mosaic** hints at the decorative splendour of these baths. An inscription from Néris-les-Bains is one of the very rare ones in Gallic, not Latin. Though partially deciphered as a dedication made by Bratronos, a cavalryman, it is now totally unreadable.

Corridor *caldarium*. The **ivory diptychs**. The most important is half of a commemorative pair dedicated to a pagan marriage alliance between the Nicomachi family, shown here, and the Symmachi (in London at the Victoria and Albert Museum). This is a splendid example of late Roman (*c.*400) luxury art; the ivory of the consul Areobindus opening a games (506) is almost as good. The soft form of Ariadne graces decorative ivory made in Constantinople for a chair or bed.

Museum rooms. In a room largely filled with early medieval material, note the first-century BC **torcs**, bracelets and rings from Soucy (Aisne); the Gallo-Roman sea-horse and enamelled dog fibulae; the unsophisticated but impressive **Visigoth votive crowns**; the **crystal lions' heads**, thought to have been made to decorate a late Roman throne, possibly from Trier; and various examples of **Frankish art**, such as the aviform and asymmetrical fibulae, earrings and the superb sword and scabbard. In another room are Egyptian **Coptic textiles**, the earliest of which range from the fourth to sixth centuries; enjoyable are the fragments with a hare and plump ducks.

Archaeological crypt of Notre Dame

Parvis Notre Dame
4th Arrondissement
Hours: 10a.m.–6p.m. Closed Monday

On the Notre Dame square by the Rue de la Cité, with a reproduction of the *Nautae* inscription over the entrance. What began as a rescue dig in 1965 when an underground car park was proposed became a permanently preserved site due to the interest generated by Michel Fleury and his team.

A walkway takes the visitor round **observation points** each equipped with information panels in French and English and light buttons that separate the Gallo-Roman from medieval and later. There are dioramas of the river basin, the late Roman city and the medieval capital. Every effort has therefore been made to clarify these typically complex urban remains.

Gallo-Roman features from walkway observation points

Points 1 and 2. The **late Roman rampart** foundations consist entirely of reused *grand appareil*, architectural decor and tombstones; no walling itself survives. Elements of the gate that opened onto the Roman Petit Pont bridge were found, but are to the west of the public section of the crypt. The **early Roman quay** where the river boats of the nautae tied up are visible as a small section of well-cut blocks at the foot of the dig furthest from point 2. ***Points 4 and 10.*** There is also walling from both early and late Roman public buildings. ***Points 8 and 9.*** Battered evidence of late Roman housing is present as a paved room and a **small bath system with two hypocaust rooms** and associated furnaces. Small finds are presented in wall cases while panels are used to present material on the latest work of the Commission du Vieux Paris. In 2001 this covered the aqueduct.

Nearby are three other places that (just) justify a visit. The **Musée Notre Dame** in Rue du Cloître Notre Dame has a tiny collection of material from the 1847 excavation and a 1711 illustration of the Nautae reliefs. In the **Rue de la Colombe** coloured cobbles mark where the late Roman rampart crossed the street and a plaque records its discovery. Over the Petit Pont bridge, down Rue Gallande (second turning east from the bridge) is the **church of**

St Julien le Pauvre. Inside the courtyard lying flat, and on the right outside standing upright, are two massive pavings from the Roman *cardo* found under the Rue St Jacques.

The amphitheatre (Les Arènes)

Rue Monge/rue des Arènes

Today 'Les Arènes' presents the picture of a sculptured recreation park. Young footballers and older *boule* players happily share the arena while those seeking a quiet break lounge on the reconstructed *cavea* seating; it's attractive, but does not give a strong sense of a building with a past. It is not surprising. When the Rue Monge was being built in 1869, Vacquer was on hand to recognize a Roman amphitheatre; however, a bus company had bought much of the land for a depot and, despite protests, it went ahead. The remaining badly damaged parts of the building were saved in 1883 – Victor Hugo leading the saviours. Excavations were ended by the 1914–18 war and the remains thoroughly consolidated.

This is an amphitheatre-theatre, a summary way of saying that a section of the *cavea* was replaced by a stage building to allow other kinds of performance or ceremonial. Its dimensions are among the biggest in Gaul; it is estimated it could have held 18,000 people in two tiers: clearly many more than the urban population. Of the stage building only the foundations of nine niches survive; fragments, most lost, show that this had a decorative *frons scaenae*, while tile finds imply it was protected by a projecting roof. There was no evidence of *parascaenia* or wings. Presumably dancers and acrobats – or were they priests? – did not need changing rooms. The large arena (52 × 46m) was better served. The podium was pierced to give access to various recesses. In front of the stage and opposite, they were probably chapels for animal fighters or gladiators. By the main entrances were further recesses, these with door-sills, implying they were lockable cages for animals – or people. The largest section of original stonework is the southern main entrance; the alcoves helped resist hillside pressures.

The aqueduct

Regular bulk supplies of water were an essential prerequisite for public baths. The springs tapped for Lutetia were at Wissous (by Orly airport) 20km to the south; this source allowed the aqueduct builders to use the valley of the river Bièvre. The route was well known by 1914. Most of the aqueduct was buried in the usual cut-and-cover method, *c.*50cm to a metre below ground level, using pavings for cover, rather than the more common vaulting. To reach the distribution tank, which must have been near the forum at the top of Mont Ste-Geneviève, the Bièvre valley was bridged and it ran again on arcades for the last stretch beside the road south from Orleans. The redating of the baths implies a construction date at the end of the first century. Fragments are visible at two places.

Rue d'Alesia/Avenue Reille. In 1996 a 300m section was exposed when derelict land by the railway north of the Parc Montsouris was cleared for redevelopment. The Ministry of Culture allowed for the preservation of 2m. Despite the protests of the Commission du Vieux Paris, pressure groups and archaeologists, most of it was destroyed, though a short section will be preserved in a children's playground at the northern end. A one metre (!) long section was 'opened' in 1999 in a glass case on Avenue Reille.

Arcueil-Cachan. From the RER station, *c.*250m. North along Rue Dr Gosselin, turn right into Rue du Chemin de Fer, down the hill parallel with the Belgrand aqueduct (1860s) sitting on top of the Medici aqueduct (1620s), and cross Rue Provigny. The best view is from the Ecole Nationale de Musique's courtyard; go under the Belgrand aqueduct, down Rue Besson and back under the aqueduct; the Ecole is on the right. The surviving Roman pillar is built into the back of the mansion; buttresses support it. Rising to the arch spring (the last arch disappeared in the 1880s), with the channel, it would have been *c.*14m high. The bridge once stretched 330m.

Musée Carnavalet

23 Rue de Sévigné
3rd Arrondissement
Hours: 10a.m.–5.40p.m. Closed Monday

The Prehistoric and Gallo-Roman collections are presented in the newly restored Orangerie (2000). The splendid Neolithic dugouts recently found at Bercy not surprisingly take up a lot of space, while the finds from Lutetia seem few and rather cramped. The graphics of the labelling is modern but small, some of it at a height best suited to 5-year-olds. Equally frustrating are the minimal efforts to give context. Why is a large model reconstruction of Lutetia not related to other exhibits? Why are there so few panels for illustration or explanation? Yet the material is interesting.

Pilaster and architrave blocks, hinting at a portico, imply the splendour of the forum. Thousands of pieces of crumbled **painted stucco** have been brilliantly put together to create an impression of two walls from one of the larger houses; sadly they are relatively simple pilaster and floral compositions, the finest plaster being the miniature idealized **male head**. There is a striking **relief of a blacksmith** – or Vulcan – in his long apron and holding a pair of tongs, but well-made tombstones are scarce and almost devoid of inscriptions. Among the best statuary is the Severan **unfinished head of a leading citizen**.

A pair of hobnailed shoes is shown in context, still lying on the owner's bones. Among the small pieces there are some superb **Parisii gold coins**; the little collection of material devoted to children, including the touching death mask of a baby; and the bronze lion's skin hanging over a hook, as if nonchalantly thrown there when Hercules relaxed from his tasks. Beside fine bone carved handles is the outstanding exhibit: the **surgeon's kit**, found in 1880. This contains knives, tweezers, scalpels, probes, spoons, a mixing palette for medicines, and the remains of a box for carrying them; they are as finely made as any until modern times. Discovered in a sarcophagus, along with coins dating to no later than the 270s, these valuable instruments suggest that they belonged to a proud and highly honoured doctor.

Cabinet des Médailles et Antiques (Bibliothèque Nationale)

58 rue de Richelieu
2nd Arrondissement

Hours:	weekdays	10a.m.–5p.m.
	Sunday	noon–6p.m.

Very few provincial collections in France are able to evoke the immense gulf that separated the elite of the great senatorial families, and above all the imperial rulers, from everyone else. The size of some villas, or the vastness of a mosaic, gives a glimpse; some of the great hoards of silver plate hint at the value of their possessions. Missing are the luxury objects that formed a major store of wealth. The Cabinet has these treasures, displayed according to who collected them (largely dispossessed royalty). It is awkward for anyone interested in examining material specific to a period, but it shows how the property of the privileged few passed from one culture into another.

The **cameo** is a type of worked gem. Rather than intaglio, where a scene is engraved, a cameo is cut to create a relief. The Romans particularly liked to contrast backgrounds and foregrounds by choosing gems layered with different colours. Among the most favoured was sardonyx, a semi-translucent quartz of creamy white and yellow to orange; sometimes three rather than two layers were used. The taste came from the Hellenistic world and the finest craftsmen were Greek; subject matter was the glorification of family and myth – or a combination of both. The earliest are first-century BC, such as Troilus and Polyxena, the children of King Priam of Troy, and the superb woman riding a bull with cupids and dolphins alongside, here seen as **Amphitrite**, wife of Poseidon, rather than Europa. Artistically, the peak for cameos was the Augustan and early Julio-Claudian period: there are figures of Augustus; a young prince, possibly Gaius; and, most astounding of all, the **Grande Camée de France**, the largest cameo known. It depicts a seated Tiberius, surrounded by many figures. The most important is his nephew, the general Germanicus, who has at his feet a small boy, the future Caligula; the divine Augustus presides above and captives crouch below: the dynasty is thus

Plate 4 Paris. Bibliothèque Nationale. Grand Camée de France: Tiberius with his earthly and divine family. Photograph: Bibliothèque Nationale de France.

glorified. From the 40s come the portrayal of Claudius being crowned and the even better cameo of his wife **Messallina** and their two children, Britannicus and Octavia. Lacklustre cameos of Trajan and Hadrian indicate the decline in inspiration, but the **Severan imperial family** attests a short-lived revival.

In the late Roman period **ivory diptychs** continued the concept of family exaltation using the most costly materials and the finest artists. The Cabinet has excellent examples, like that of the Rome consul of 428, Flavius Felix, or the two Constantinople senators **Probus** and **Magnus**, consuls in 517 and 518. By the 520s Christian imagery had become the norm, but the **Dionysiac scene** from Alexandria shows a late flowering of pagan subject matter.

The Cabinet also has two collections with more direct Gallo-Roman links. A nineteenth-century curator bought the treasure of Berthouville from a Normandy farmer. Twenty-five kilogrammes of silver plate was deliberately buried in a chamber under large stones during the third century, not far from a *fanum*; inscriptions on some pieces show that it had been donated to Mercury. It is a rare vision of the kind of offerings made by Gallic nobility, in contrast to the wood, stone and pottery gifts of poorer pilgrims. There is a splendid *oenochoe* with **scenes of Achilles** in his chariot dragging Hector's body around the walls of Troy, and an almost equally good **centaurs cup**. They are both first-century Italian work, but more than half of the material comes from the late second/early third centuries and is Gallo-Roman. The **bowls depicting Mercury** have tell-tale evidence in his un-classical proportions and the use of Gallic attributes, like his purse.

Finally there are the remnants of **Childeric's tomb treasure**. This was one of the earliest-ever archaeological finds properly published. The treasure was found in Tournai by a deaf-mute in 1653, and a book devoted to it was produced by 1655. Its subsequent history after reaching the Cabinet as a gift to Louis XIV is less fortunate. Stolen in 1830, most of the gold was melted down, though a few objects were recovered by divers after being dumped in the Seine. Identified by Childeric's name on a gold signet ring, this was the very rich burial (481) of the founder of the Merovingian state. Missing are the ring itself, massive gold crossbow fibulae, arm-rings, belt decorations and other pieces. All that survives are one gold buckle, golden bee ornaments (once part of horse trappings) and the gold and garnet decorations from his sword and scabbard (for a much more complete example of this type of great man's sword see the Pouan treasure, TROYES).

Musée des Antiquités Nationales

Château, Place Charles-de-Gaulle
78103 St Germain-en-Laye
Yvelines
Hours: 9a.m.–5.15p.m. Closed Tuesday

Frequent RER line A trains from central Paris. Journey *c.*25 minutes.

The museum was founded in 1862 by Napoleon III and is still imbued with the spirit of the time. Sadly, his passion to communicate the excitement he felt at the exploration of Alesia and Gergovia has not remained the dominant force. Instead, it is the nineteenth-century concern with classification and typologies. The museum is helpful in clarifying trends in the development of fibulae or for seeing how Gallo-Roman gods can be recognized through their attributes; it is not the one to visit for any broad vision on how people lived in the past. Napoleon III's models of an onegar and ballista are displayed as no more than curios, but why is there virtually nothing to stimulate the imagination? The collection has many fine objects from all over France and the galleries are easy to visit (there are not many people). If you are lucky enough to find a temporary exhibition, the frustration is moderated; there have been thrilling presentations on relevant topics (sigillata production and early Frankish culture). When will the transformation of the permanent collection take place?

Iron Age section

The material here is almost entirely derived from burial sites and little reference is made to settlements or sanctuaries. However, there are some impressive finds. From the earliest **Hallstatt** phase in France, five **cuirasses** from Marmesse, front and back plates made of beaten incised bronze, are unique military/art pieces of the ninth/eighth centuries. The sixth-century late Hallstatt princedoms are represented by their **four-wheel chariot burials**, particularly the Burgundian Apremont and Sainte Colombe examples; the latter have exceptional gold jewellery.

Early La Tène (*c.*475–275 BC) evolved in Champagne and the Moselle. While finds from the former are extensively displayed here, the more easternly area is not (see BLIESBRUCK). The rich finery and arms of the men and their two-wheeled chariots found at Chassemy, La Bouvandeau and Le Gorge-Meillet, a rare untouched chalk-cut tomb, go towards explaining why a key role has been seen for a warrior class in this culture. Equally significant is the distinctive artistic spirit; this becomes more obvious in **middle La Tène** (*c.*275–140 BC). In part stimulated by Celtic population movements and subsequent mercenary activity, classical realism is encountered, but takes on a swirling disintegrating 'vegetal' appearance. The Amfreville **crown-like helmet** uses a base cap of bronze similar to those made by the Etruscans, but covered by an open iron network with coral and enamel decor and a gold leaf band, incised with almost unrecognizable palmettes. Other more conventional **helmets** with top buttons and neck brims stress the shared development with Italian styles.

Final La Tène (140–25 BC) embodies dynamic growth and change, but again the exhibits give no more than an opaque impression. The **human figure sword grips** hint at the talismanic role of dead bodies and heads revealed in sanctuaries and other representations; barely any effort is made to enliven the nails, hooks, fibulae and pottery, brought here following the nineteenth-century excavations at Mont Beuvray; there is nothing on the current work on the site, the most costly in France. The **Alesia siege** display cries out for drama and explanation. The finds largely derive from the ditches constructed by the Romans leading to the final defeat of the Gauls: they represent the deaths of many people. The **weapons** laid out here are mainly Gallic; Roman equipment could be reused, except for bent or broken *pila* and lost lead slingshots. The **'Alesia type' helmet** shows how the simple oval shape with a rear lip has been modified with the addition of cheek-guards and a double ridge to give more protection from the downward slash. Note the old model of the Caesarian defences; there is a full-scale reconstruction at BEAUNE.

Gallo-Roman rooms

Probably the best section deals with Gallic gods during the Roman period: by bringing together so many examples of individual gods, their characteristic features are brought out clearly. The sixteen bronzes of **Sucellus** demonstrate that his image was one of the least variable. Roman in his Jupiter-like mature face and abundant hair and beard, yet his long-handled hammer is without analogy in the classical world (though its striking quality has been compared to Jupiter's thunderbolt). He wears a short Gallic tunic and cloak or *sagum* and carries a small pot or *olla*. He is generally thought to be a peasant's god, whose hammer brings a spring reawakening and therefore helps fecundity; he is sometimes portrayed with a consort Nantosuetta, reinforcing the protective/re-creating aspects, so important for those tied to the land. The bull seems to have performed a similar function, among the Remi especially: a largely benevolent force, admired for its virility. Although not a specific god, the animal embodied the divine, another un-Roman feature. Note the **triple-horn bulls** – the magic of three and the multiplying quality also widely embodied in the **triple mother-goddesses**.

It is a characteristic of **Cernunnos** that he is always shown cross-legged (see the Nautae pillar in the Cluny Museum (above) for the earliest named example); no other gods are depicted like this – though in contrast to the Romans, Gauls traditionally sat in their houses in this way. His appearance varies more. Normally he wears a torc and is shown with antlers. On one small bronze from **Etang-sur-Arroux** he carries his torc, his antlers are removable and, most unusually, he is three-headed; yet more triplism. The **Bouray bronze** Cernunnos has no horns but is shown with hooves. His lack of classical proportion, bulbous eyes and stylized locks are very Gallic. The most 'primitive' and alien representation in the whole collection is the **Euffigneix god**. A large pillar-like head, perhaps from a wooden model, tops an almost square body; around the thick neck is a massive torc and a wild boar is carved below; decorative eyes perhaps warned off enemy spirits. It may have been a woodland god, but this is a very long way from the Mediterranean world's Silvanus.

Epona is much more reassuring, sitting side-saddle on her horse. She was the only Gallic god to be adopted widely in the Roman world, even having a festival in Rome. Lucius, when transformed into an ass (in the *Metamorphoses*, the late second-century novel by Apuleius), mentions a shrine to Epona in his stable. She was the protector of horses and therefore needed by grooms, breeders and riders. The collection also includes many of the Roman pantheon, but is rather thin on imported eastern gods such as Mithras.

Ways of commemorating the dead express both variety and repetition. The Gallic diversity is represented by the highly Romanized marble **herm** of the *flamen* (priest) Publius brought from Provence, the Vosges house tomb (see SAVERNE) and the chariot burial from Haute Vienne, recalling both the early Iron Age and analogies with contemporary second-century Pannonia. **Apinosus Iclius' relief** from ENTRAINS shows a prosperous, wide-chested man wearing tunic, cloak and fringed scarf: unexceptional, but the essence of numerous memorials to provincial Gallo-Roman men.

Although the army is not well represented here, the **Chassenard burial** (AD 37–41) produced a fine **parade helmet face**, which would have been worn for ceremonial displays. Under this were found the owner's coat of mail, hooks for attaching padding, belt decor and a torc awarded for military service. An early third-century Guisborough-type **cavalry helmet** with cheekpieces missing was found in the river Saône at Chalon in the 1860s. It is finely decorated and looks like a parade helmet, but the bronze is thicker than usual and it could be for battle.

The last part of the museum is filled with cases showing daily life. Almost the only attempt to give human context is 'La Table' with that French curator's delight: oyster shells. Silver and bronze ware, common ware and sigillata, metal fittings and bone all have their individual cases. The three cases used for glassware at least suggest change over time, though eight columns of small writing fail to make it easy to follow. Elsewhere there are individual items of interest. From the world of the countryside, the dramatic bronze of a boar together with the boar-hunting spears. From the prosperous home, a **folding chair**; the metal decoration from a lounge bed; and, among the lamps and candle-holders, a hanging **lantern**; note also the simple and rare earthenware portrayal of a couple sleeping in bed. From the multitude of fibulae and pins, the lively lion brooch and the shoe pins are charming. The displays to illustrate craftwork add little; the mysteries of dodecahedrons and the Egyptian zodiac board from Grand (see EPINAL) are not explored.

The last room contains house decoration, including the only wall painting featuring one of the seasons, an attractive female personification of Summer in a green dress; but it is dominated by the great **mosaic from St Romain-en-Gal**, a suburb of Vienne in the Rhône valley south of Lyon. It illustrated the agricultural year of the Mediterranean world in 40 scenes, 27 of which survive. Showing how close the world of the Roman 'city' was to the rural environment, above all it demonstrates that great householders were landowners; it was their income from the produce of the land that made them rich and respectable and therefore 'honest men'.

Merovingian section

While providing a good collection of weapons and personal ornament (the number of fibulae is almost overpowering); a **stool**, of exactly the same design as a Gallo-Roman example but with the addition of damascening, is exceptional. Since the 1950s excavations at St-Denis have revealed that this was a major centre of wealthy Frankish burials from the fifth century onwards, well before it became the royal cemetery; some of the gold and inlay work is exceptional.

The Louvre: Department of Antiquities

www.louvre.fr/louvrea.htm
Cour Napoléon
1st Arrondissement

Hours:	9a.m.–6.00p.m.	Closed Tuesday
	6.p.m.–9.45p.m.	Monday (evening tours)
		Wednesday (independent visits)

The Louvre is the epitome of Art and Civilization. This museum has not been created to portray ordinary life, religion, social relations, political change or economic activity – though inevitably these are all touched on. The fundamental premise is that this collection, the finest obtainable, has been brought together to proclaim artistic achievement. It is a high-minded and valid purpose, but it sets a book like this a problem. The Louvre does not have a room dedicated to Roman France (unlike the British Museum's 'Roman Britain'); Gallo-Roman objects and Roman finds in France are on display, but they are relatively scarce, scattered around the rooms and periodically moved. Therefore the primary value for the visitor interested in the impact of Rome on Gaul is a comparison, or reminder, of what was being produced elsewhere in the Roman world and, more specifically, a series of portraits of the emperors who ruled Gaul for 500 years.

The ground floor

Salle 30, the ***Mosaic Gallery***. This also has wall paintings and other material, subject to reorganization. The most striking **mosaics** contrast the styles of North Africa and the eastern Mediterranean, both showing an imagination, exuberance and skill rarely touched by finds in Gaul (perhaps in the south, most particularly at Vienne). A sense of the vitality of the busy grand house is apparent in the ***Banquet Preparations*** mosaic from Carthage, particularly the one complete figure of a young man jauntily striding forward, balancing a tray with four round loaves (AD 180–90). The ***Triumph of Neptune and Amphitrite*** was found at Constantine in Algeria. This panel was surrounded by thirty-six medallions covering nearly 60sq m and filled a villa's reception room. The teeming sea, the children fishing, the startled horses, the proud Neptune tenderly held by his wife, fill every space, a colourful if naive fourth-century vision. From the Atrium villa in Antioch comes the ***Judgement of Paris*** mosaic. This is a sophisticated Hellenistic product: illusionist tricks to give depth, highlighting metals and skin, cascading drapery, and a coherent landscape, so unlike the North African products. It formed one of five panels in a 'T' around which diners would have reclined on their couches (*c.* AD 115). The **wall paintings** equally demonstrate a Hellenistic environment in the pre-eruption Pompeian region: especially good is a ***winged male genius*** in the Pompeian second style from a villa in the small town of Boscoreale.

Currently, the centre of the room brings together a disparate group of objects set on three podiums illustrating death, children and the games. This display is being modified; perhaps the recently acquired first/second-century AD **sundial** will be shown here. It is of the rare skyphos type: a large jar with a hole at the top, through which the sun shines moving across a series of lines through the day. It also shows the times of the winter and summer solstices.

Salle 31, the ***Cour du Sphinx***, contains the great fourth-century **Antioch mosaic**, a trapezoidal panel of exotic wild animal hunts, and the massive **Tiber personification**.

Salles 22–27, ***Roman portrait sculpture***. This superb collection enables you to follow both developments in style and the characterization of the Roman imperial family.

The republican patrician elite may have been prepared to have themselves portrayed in all the human variety we still see around us, lumpy, even misshapen, and certainly marked by age (e.g. Aulus Postumus); Augustus was not. His portrait is always compact, smooth-skinned, youthful in an ageless way, noble, with short, groomed hair, combed into carefully posed tufts; the proportions are classic, he is a man above the ordinary. Yet the contrast can be overdrawn. Despite their realism, most Roman portraits had always attempted to embody what the commissioners wished for: expressions of power, dignity and sobriety. While a tradition of death masks gave an exaggerated and harsh truthfulness to some sculpture, the attractions of Hellenistic idealization and the gentler painted portraits of Egypt had increasingly inspired the use of Greek artists in the workshops, and already begun a trend to a more idealized realism (see Agrippa's portrait). A new element was the divine. No portrait of Julius Caesar was contemporary, even the earliest known dates to the empire when his divine status could not be ignored. With Augustus divinity became part of the imperial vision. Of course the many copies that were made around the empire will have been done with varying assurance, which may have undermined the image, but not in the direction of a more accurate depiction of the person. Yet the wish to differentiate emperors and lineages was a perceived need for most of the Roman era, though its intensity inevitably varied; it is only in the fourth century that imperial statue portraiture became totally devoid of individual personality. As the fashion in portraiture of the imperial family changed, so it did for everyone else, moderated only by differing provincial traditions.

First century. The image created by Augustus dominates his family and successors, the Julio-Claudians. They wished to be seen like him and only subtle differences occur. The Flavians revived a more realistic approach; indeed there was no mileage in claiming to be like Nero or Caligula. This feature was maintained by Trajan, but note how, with his double chin, fat jowls, and low forehead, he has his hair represented in the Augustan way. Women fared poorly. Hairstyles certainly varied, but their faces expressed little: Julia is impassive, others, like Agrippina the Elder, are depicted as young goddesses.

Second century. Hadrian is the first bearded emperor, a fashion taken up enthusiastically by artists, to give a richer, hairier look and, when using fine marble, can be contrasted with smooth skin; it is an image that recalls the standard philosopher statues of the ancient world: not inappropriate for Marcus Aurelius at least. Individuality is still apparent when comparing Hadrian, Verus, Commodus or Severus. The women fare worse again, though Faustina the Younger, the wife of Marcus Aurelius, perhaps hints at her matronly status, having produced twelve children.

Third century. There were still significant differences in portraits. Caracalla is shown as a powerful man without delicacy, thick-necked, with furrowed brow; a vision not far from his very real brutality. Gordian III is rather weak-looking, striving for a short-haired, clean-shaven, classical appearance, while Galienus takes a backward look to Verus or Marcus Aurelius combined with a thicker version of an Augustan hairstyle. Finally Constantine Chlorus stands for all those crew-cut military men who featured in the period. The contrasts in artistic presentation reflect the instability of the time. Women feature less, but in Julia Mammea there is a real beauty (as well as a hairstyle) which may, or may not, be at variance with her supposed avarice.

Fourth century. Constantine gives himself Augustan hair, but otherwise is little more than a cuboid god-like face staring forwards, almost devoid of human emotion or intellect – and therefore individual personality. Only Julian stands out against this trend with his backward-looking philosopher-ruler pose. As the head of Theodosius II (408–50) shows, the last elements of genuine individuality have disappeared: the symbols of power are enough – the diadem is turning into the medieval crown.

The first floor

Salles 32–34, Roman silverware, bronze and glass. Room 33 is dominated by the silver. The mask-like faces found at Alençon and the massive shell dish from Graincourt are probably Gallo-Roman temple treasure, but the 109 silver pieces found during the 1890s in the villa at **Boscoreale**, overwhelmed in the Vesuvius eruption of AD 79, are the ultimate in sophisticated household possessions. Baron Rothschild bought almost the entire collection (ninety-four pieces) and gave them to the Louvre. One is a **cup with a**

central female bust, perhaps Cleopatra or an allegorical figure of Egypt; another, a **goblet depicting Augustus**, has a delegation of barbarian chiefs pleading for their children. Many show a skill, exuberance, vitality (and even morbidity with the skeletons' goblets) that would fit a top producer in Greek-influenced southern Italy or imperial workshops and given away at ceremonial celebrations. Alongside are grandiose **bronze lamps**, made only for the very wealthiest, far removed from the usual simple terracotta types, and examples of fine furniture, particularly the **silver-coated iron stool**. The same desire for conspicuous wealth is seen in the very large **cameos**: scenes portray the triumph of Bacchus, Ariadne and Bacchus, and Augustus.

Room 32 focuses on bronzes (half the room containing Greek work). There are inscriptions from Narbonne and Sens; enigmatic hollow **dodecahedrons**; and **military diplomas**. These are the most complete expression of the difference between a warrior force and a regular army embodying a binding feature of any complex society: bureaucracy. Artistically, the most striking for me is undoubtedly the **Eros and Psyche**. Far larger than most bronzes, the pair are portrayed as children and without wings. Psyche is especially good: delicate and tender. Gladiatorial combat is illustrated by the **greave of a murmillo**, who fought with a sword, and the shoulder guard or **galerus of a retiarius**, who wielded a net and trident. Another case contains a fine statuette of a **wrestler** from Autun, balanced beautifully in a kick-boxing pose, his hair in the standard bob to prevent it being grabbed.

Room 34 is devoted to glass, though this is likely to be reorganized. The glassware comes predominantly from the Near East and Italy. There are richly coloured bowls, especially aquamarine and dark green; late vessels decorated with blobs or the extraordinarily skilful cage-cups – a surface blank cut away to create delicate rings barely secured to the main body; mould-made goblets; and wonderful, **delicately shaped birds**, once used to contain cosmetics.

Musée de la Monnaie

11 Quai de Conti
6th Arrondissement
Hours: 1–6p.m. (Wednesday to 9p.m.). Closed Monday

The museum is disappointing, partly due to the smallness of the collection, partly to poor presentation. In the entrance foyer two small cases display Gallic gold and silver coins. There is just space to illustrate the techniques of manufacturing these coins by hand, but nothing on the function of coins in the tribal societies of pre-Roman Gaul. Here too is a mould of a tombstone from METZ; the relief illustrates an imperial treasury (*fiscus*) official

Plate 5 Paris. The bronze wrestler from Autun. Photograph: Musée du Louvre.

taking in a bag of cash to be weighed and checked for forgery – or is he just collecting rent?

The main hall has coins displayed in holes cut through curved plastic transparent screens. Superficially, it looks dramatic and innovative, with coins suspended in the air. In reality, the light glints on them and it is difficult to see the reverses through the thick perspex material. There is only one Roman screen, and though the emperors are well represented, little attempt is made to make sense of the series, either in types or numbers issued, production technology, distribution – or even what to look for on the coins. Equally disappointing is the number of copies included with the originals.

SENLIS, Oise

IGN 2412 OT

Town and rural sanctuary.

45km north-east of Paris, by either the A1 or the N17, and 30km south-west of Compiègne (D932) is the very attractive old town of Senlis, the centre of which is still defined by the best-preserved late Roman ramparts in northern France.

For all its real antiquity, the early history of Senlis is challenging. Augustomagus was the capital of the Silvanectes tribe, but they do not appear in Caesar's account of the Gallic wars. Their territory covered no more than 20 × 25km, the smallest in northern Gaul. The site seems to have been virtu-

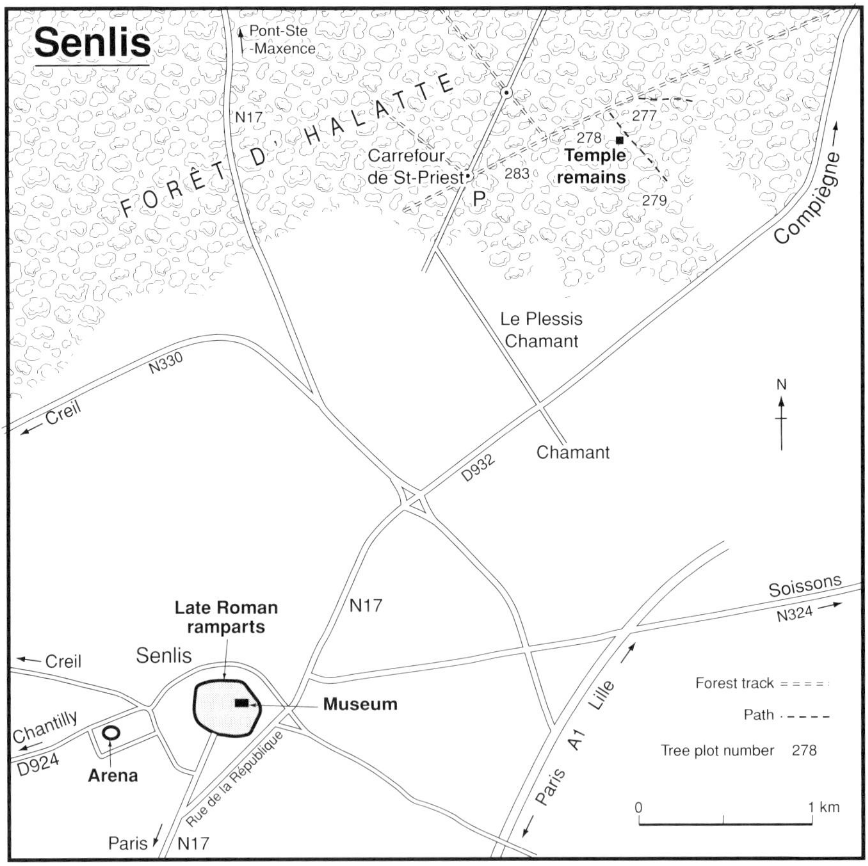

Figure 16 Senlis: local area and L'Halatte temple

ally unoccupied prior to the creation of the Roman city, nor was there a significant *oppidum* nearby, yet it boasted an amphitheatre, capable of holding an audience of 10,000, that could have been built at the beginning of the first century. The sudden appearance of the Silvanectes is best explained as a *pagus* or people being made independent from their previous tribal body. All the surrounding tribes have been credited with that role, but perhaps the Suessiones as the most powerful, and traditional enemies of the Remi (the Romans' closest allies in the north), were most ripe for this treatment. A strategic concern for Roman policymakers immediately after the conquest would be the control of the major south–north routes: the Remi controlled the eastern route, the early western road went via Autun and Meaux through Senlis to Amiens and an independent, enriched, Silvanectes would provide an island of local support. Rapid early development would have been enhanced, too, when Claudius invested in new roads and collected supplies for the conquest of Britain in the 40s; perhaps the bronze statue put up here commemorated an actual visit by Claudius.

The medieval town developed within and around the late Roman walls and not surprisingly, where so many old buildings have survived intact, very little is known about the early Roman city. Because it lay well outside the core of the town, in the 1860s Félix Vernois was able to dig and prove his theory that a local name hid the memory of an amphitheatre. Georges Matherat before and after the Second World War resumed work there and also excavated where he could in the old town; he filled in the rest with his imagination. His forum, temples and markets are no longer accepted as his evidence was so slight. Recent excavations have been confined to occasional cellars, allowing a picture of local inhabitants and their environment to emerge. Rubbish tipped into disused wells indicates countryside not of forest, but of pasture and cereal crops, and a strong preference for eating pork. As well as domestic animal remains, the presence of the black rat was confirmed, long before its supposed arrival with the Crusades. Perhaps the epidemics of the late Roman and Merovingian period really were the plague and not other diseases.

The 6.5ha oval enclosed by the late Roman walls was a *castrum* or stronghold for administrators, food storage and both permanent and mobile troops, with very little room for ordinary city dwellers. Though occupation may have continued in what were now suburbs, no firm evidence has been found and cemeteries seem to have been small, suggesting few inhabitants. Nor were there many in the surrounding countryside. A *praefectus laetorum* was based here: his job was to supply part-time soldiers from ex-prisoners (*laeti*) settled in the area. As these settlers were increasingly drawn from Germanic backgrounds so the seeds were sown for the emergence of the Frankish state.

The amphitheatre

Consult Senlis tourist office, as the amphitheatre has often been closed to visitors.

The track down into the hollow where the amphitheatre is hidden naturally takes the visitor into the eastern passage (once vaulted), where there were holding cells or *carceres*. After the opening parade the passage gates were shut and hapless people or animals were released into the arena. On the north and south sides are traces of chambers or *sacella* where performers dedicated themselves to the gods. Niches survive where statues once stood; a head of Venus and a torso of Hercules were found in the southern *sacellum*. Above were enclosed seating areas for the privileged; in the south sat the president of the games, in the north wealthy Silvanectes. The northern loggia was widened to make a paved area 11.5m × 5.5m, either simply to accommodate larger parties, or, as most writers have argued, a conversion to a stage, so creating a dual-purpose building (see PARIS).

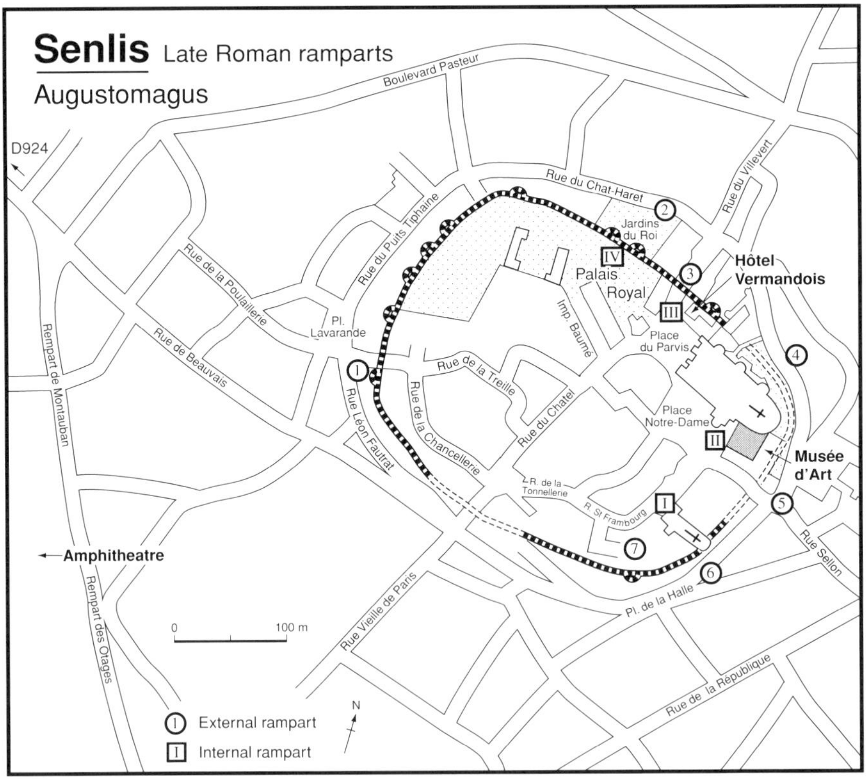

Figure 17 Senlis: town plan (ramparts)

The slopes minimized the need for extensive building to make the three-tier seating. A podium wall with a projecting cornice, 2.5–3m high, protected the front rows; holes found in the top imply that railings gave additional security. The only surviving seats are in the south-east corner. Individual seat size and total amphitheatre size (*c.*90 × 83m) suggest some 10,000 could attend performances; these probably took place on market days when country dwellers were most likely to visit the city.

Augustan coins in the base levels point to foundation in the early first century AD. Out of use by the fourth century, the entrances were walled up to create a 'fortress', maybe for dispossessed town inhabitants. This was finally abandoned in the early Middle Ages to become a rubbish dump, which grew so high that it was suitable for a gun battery in the sixteenth century!

The late Roman rampart

Parking in the Place Notre Dame or Place de la Halle.

The general dimensions of the ramparts, the size and shape of the towers, the construction methods used, including the size of the stonework and use of tile courses here and at Beauvais, Soissons and Amiens, point to common builders (or common instructions) for Belgica Secunda cities. The case is strong for a direct imperial initiative using military architects, perhaps inspired by Probus (276–82) after the major barbarian incursions of the 260s and 270s.

The surviving sections of rampart and towers give an outstanding impression of late Roman fortifications. Originally 840m long, the walls were 3.3m thick and more than 7m high. The foundations used large rectangular blocks or reused stone from earlier public buildings. The wall itself was faced with *petit appareil* both externally and internally, with a massive rubble concrete core, stabilized by tile courses. The rampart was once topped by crenellation to make the walkway a fighting platform. In front, the ground was landscaped to form a slope (*glacis*) down to a wide ditch, found during the excavation of Rue St Hilaire. Sixteen of the estimated 28 towers have been identified, one every 30m, enabling easy covering fire along the rampart. They were U-shaped and had solid cores up to walkway level, making them very difficult to breach, even with sophisticated siege weapons. From their arched windows large crossbows could fire great distances – or down on men struggling in the ditch. Only two gateways are known, both destroyed.

The external face of the ramparts

Rue de la Chancellerie. (1) Retained in the medieval Hôtel de la Chancellerie; despite the glass in the windows and other signs of restoration, the U-shaped tower is unmistakable.

Jardins du Roi. (2) Here the rampart was integrated in the twelfth-century royal palace, ensuring its preservation. Despite some robbing out of facing stones the walls still reach walkway level. Facing the wall, the **tower on the left** has survived best, reaching a full 14m, lacking only a tile roof. The semi-circular windows, four above and three below, are filled in, but their outline is clear. Their alternating tile/stone surrounds may be ninth century (Carolingians liked this kind of patterning as well). The tile courses are clear, but there are only putlog holes above the top course. The **tower on the right** shows the most modification with a fourteenth-century oratory added. The filled-in Roman windows are still recognizable.

Rue de Villevert. (3) The road cuts through the rampart, which is visible in section.

Rue aux Flageards. (4) From the Jardin de l'Evêché, look back towards the Hôtel de Vermandois. The heavily restored tower rises above the surrounding low buildings. Next to the last chapel and joined to the Palais Episcopal is another heavily adapted but clearly Roman tower. The slate roof is not original.

Rue du Chancelier-Guérin. (5) A plaque records how the Roman gateway towers were pulled down in 1805.

Rue St-Hilaire. (6) At the foot of St Flambourg church in the yards on each side are short sections of walling.

Impasse St-Nicolas. (7) The rear of a short section of rampart can be seen from a tiny public garden.

The internal face of the ramparts

St Flambourg. (I) The 1970s excavated base of a tower and part of the *glacis* are preserved in the crypt.

Palais Episcopal. (II) See Museum.

Hôtel de Vermandois. (III) A section of the curtain wall survives in the Grand Salle.

Palais Royal. (IV) The internal faces of two towers and a long stretch of curtain wall are visible from the Jardins du Roi. Note how medieval middle-sized stone was used, particularly at corners, to preserve the towers.

Museum d'Art

Ancien Palais Episcopal
2 Place Notre Dame
60300 Senlis
Hours: Thursday–Monday 10a.m.–6p.m. Closed Tuesday
Wednesday 2–6p.m.
1 November–1 February closes at 5p.m.

Ground floor. **The Claudius statue base and fragments.** Found during the 1950s in the Palais Royal excavations. Serious corrosion problems have required two major conservation treatments. The statue itself was smashed up and burnt at the end of the first century – for reasons unknown. The dedication, beautifully inscribed on the base and perhaps prepared in Lyon, is the only inscription known giving the name of the 'Silbanectes' (the Gallic 'b' being replaced later by the Latin 'v'). Claudius' titles indicate a date of AD 48. The superb craftsmanship of the statue itself is hinted at by the delicate arm remains and most of all by the water god believed to have decorated the centre of the breastplate that Claudius would have been wearing.

Among the small finds, note the two tiny bronze crayfish, hinting at one of the delicacies available in the local rivers.

Basement. **The late Roman rampart.** This was revealed by 1980s restoration work. The variety of reused stonework is obvious in the lower courses, especially the bas-reliefs. It also shows how the rampart cut across some late second- and early third-century houses that stood beside a beaten earth road. On the north, a house with a paved courtyard; to the south, the cellars of houses (see BLIESBRUCK or ALISE-STE-REINE).

Forêt d'Halatte finds. Over two hundred stone figures give a vivid sense of the healing sanctuary, accentuated by an excellent audiovisual display – worth seeing for the use of light to highlight figures, even if you do not understand the French commentary. Visitors to the temple would have bought the figures as offerings to the sanctuary god (unknown to us). Many are simply heads; some have stubby lumps hinting at bodies. A few might portray the god; most will be pilgrims. Several statues specifically draw attention to illness, which the devotee hoped the god would heal. A knee is pointed to, swollen genitals exposed. An open mouth hints at trouble in breathing, wrapped babies at the diseases of childhood. Sometimes the sickness is reduced to the troubled part of the body alone: feet or single and double breasts (feeding difficulties?). Some embody Gallo-Roman provincial realism, but others reduce the features to a very schematic simplicity, which might represent the more fluid approach to religion in Gaul: while Roman traditions focused so clearly on human representation, all that seems to have been needed in the Celtic world were a few key pointers, the god could recognize the rest.

Forêt d'Halatte temple

620.5/2470.7

The site evokes a deep sense of the past because of its romantic setting – whether this was woodland in the Roman period or not. A 2.5km drive and 900m walk. Boots would help as it becomes muddy in poor weather.

From Senlis, take the D932 road for Compiègne, 2km to Chamant. Turn left and drive to the T-junction. Turn right by the pony club to enter the forest. Park at the St Priest crossroads. Take the Chemin Royal (signposted). The forest is divided into plantations, each numbered on trees: 283 is on the right followed by 278. After about 850m the track gently begins to rise; take the path on the right by a tree recording the end of plantation 278; some 50m on the right are the remains.

The site is almost hidden by trees and bushes. Moss- and leaf-covered walls, at most 60cm high, outline the temple, a rectangle about 8.5 × 7m, and part of the surrounding enclosure, at least 40m long. Further walling suggests another building, maybe the temple guardian's house, but only modern excavation might confirm this. It seems to have been in use from the first to the late fourth century. There may once have been a spring, long since dried up.

SOISSONS, Aisne

Town site and museum.

Soissons is about 100km north-east of Paris, and almost equidistant between Senlis (59km) and Reims (57km).

Soissons has a particular claim to fame in the history of Roman Gaul – and France. In 486, ten years after the death of the last western Roman emperor, a Gallo-Roman aristocrat, Syagrius, who governed Soissons and an unspecified region around it, was killed here in battle with Clovis, king of the Franks: it was the last whimper of the empire in Gaul. Though there continued to be people who called themselves 'Romans', all future claimants to be the true successors of the Roman state were barbarian kings, the most important of whom were the Merovingian Franks.

The territory of the Gallic Suessiones straddled the navigable Aisne river with rich agricultural lowlands to the east and extensive forests to the west. The Suessiones had been rated highly among the Belgae and, even though they gave Caesar little serious trouble, the Romans took a firm line in the post-conquest period. In the west, the Silvanectes, previously a sub-tribe of the Suessiones, were grateful to the Romans for their independence; in the east, the Suessiones seem to have lost land to the Remi. Noviodunum, the oppidum surrendered to Caesar in 57 BC, identified with Pommiers hill (5km to the west of modern Soissons), was abandoned and a new centre established at Villeneuve-St-Germain. At this time a Roman garrison probably occupied the nearby Soissons site itself. After thirty years the site became free and a grid was laid out for the new Roman city of Augusta Suessionum. The Roman military presence was to return, probably after the AD 21 disturbances, with the construction of a large fort (4.9ha) at Arlaines, only 11km to the west of the new civitas capital: it was to remain there until the Flavian period.

The excavation of Roman Soissons got off to a brilliant start when, in

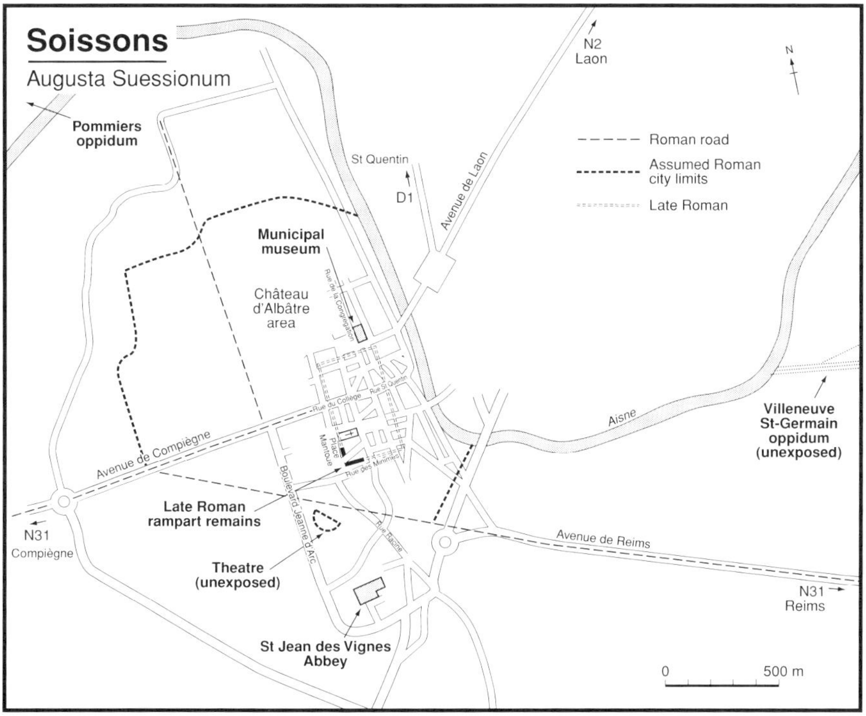

Figure 18 Soissons: town plan

1551, rows of columns, rich mosaics, marble and alabaster remains were found: the area was immediately named the 'Château d'Albâtre'. It could be nothing less than a governor's palace or maybe King Clovis's residence. Unfortunately this interpretation dominated thought into the twentieth century. Growing doubts and modern controlled excavations have clarified the picture. Early Roman Augusta is recognized as a large 120ha settlement, though probably not densely occupied, and, like many others in the north, included agricultural activity. The 'palace' area is now acknowledged to be *insulae*, divided by streets and covered pavements, first- to third-century houses, some wealthy – and maybe richly fitted baths. The only definite public building detected has been a very large theatre, poorly excavated in the mid-nineteenth century; the forum remains unknown and no temple, arena or aqueduct has been found; nor has a circus, mentioned by Gregory of Tours, been identified.

Contraction in the late Roman period was dramatic, a rampart enclosing a mere 13ha. Overlooking the Aisne, the settlement could still control this vital east–west economic link, particularly to the rich fourth-century villas. So far, there seem to have been few areas outside the rampart that remained occupied. The local aristocracy may have survived, but their homes and wealth were surely outside the confined city. During the fifth century the real power may already have been in the hands of the Franks, Syagrius being no more than a shadowy administrator. Certainly their rich burials fill the region and represent the new non-urban society more concretely than the last 'Roman' ruler. However, firm archaeological evidence of Merovingian occupation in Soissons only appears in the seventh century.

Late Roman walls

The walls run in an uneven rectangle some 420 × 260m on a slight eminence parallel to the Aisne. Many of the design features are found in other Belgica Secunda cities (see SENLIS). The odd coin finds support construction by Probus (276–82). Architectural and relief material from cemeteries and public buildings found in the rampart are kept in the museum annexe.

Place Mantoue. In the south-east corner of the square by the chapel next to the Rue de l'Evêché are 19m of rampart and part of a corner tower. The massive rampart foundation blocks stand out clearly; above them the facing stones of *petit appareil* have survived only intermittently along with traces of triple tile rows. The square corner tower survives only as a projecting lower wall (see BEAUVAIS for more complete examples of this type).

Rue des Minimes. At the back of the courtyard of no. 10, there is a considerably modified section of walling rising to the rampart walk height of *c.*7m. It was integrated into an external wall of the long gone bishop's palace.

Musée Municipal de Soissons

Ancien Abbaye de St Léger
2 Rue de la Congrégation
02200 Soissons
Hours: 10a.m.–noon, 2–5p.m. Closed Tuesday

The archaeological section is almost entirely derived from modern excavations.

The **Villeneuve-St-Germain** model, map and finds illustrate the riverside settlement excavated during the 1970s and 1980s. It shows Gallic new town planning without any sign of Roman preconceptions. It has distinct districts and roads, bisected by four fenced and thatched-over drainage ditches forming a cross. Artisans' workshops are concentrated by the ditches. Bronze specialists produced decorative pieces and coins; ironsmiths, tools and wheels; yet others worked in leather. Farm buildings clustered by the rampart that cut off the bottom of the meander. Roman imports occurred as well: oil lamps, amphorae and writing equipment. Wine had always been popular, but the desire to communicate in writing is more surprising: did a Roman tradesman settle here?

The restored **wall paintings** are the result of painstaking work. Found in Rue Paul Deviolaine, at the heart of the Château d'Albâtre area, they have been archaeologically dated to the Flavian period. Above a black dado base is the central zone divided into panels by candelabra, elaborately decorated with tendrils and animals, and, on top, coloured bands. The main panel contains a delicate figure floating on a plain background. The design, reacting against architectural perspectives, is similar to Pompeian Third Style and not too dated (it was popular twenty years earlier in Rome). More Gallo-Roman interiors are reconstructed in the balcony display.

Most interesting of the other Gallo-Roman material are the **bronze furniture fittings**. These once decorated a wooden chair or couch; the swans' necks were a particularly popular Roman furnishing ornament; table legs at Pompeii have been found of very similar design. The rose-coloured pottery from Argonne (in the upper reaches of the Aisne) shows that fine tableware was still in demand during the fifth century. The owner was probably Christian, as it had the Chi-Rho monogram.

Merovingian material: the most important has come not from Soissons itself but from Juvincourt-et-Damary, now under the A26 motorway, on the eastern border of the department. The model of the village shows the reconstruction of large houses and sunken huts, which the excavators consider to have been workshops, storage huts, pigsties, etc., but not dwellings. Those archaeologists who consider many of the huts could be houses they see as 'miserabilists' (see MARLE for contrasting views).

Museum annexe. This is dominated by the large marble statue of *The Teacher and One of Niobe's Sons*. Found in 1831 in the Château d'Albâtre area, the group was considered so fine that for many years it was held in the Louvre. Tastes have changed. It portrays a popular Roman and Greek theme: human power is inadequate before the gods. Niobe, of noble birth and the wife of a king, had foolishly boasted that she had produced six boys and six girls, whereas Leto, of ignoble birth, had only produced two, even if they were gods. Leto then demanded that her children wreak vengeance on the silly boastful woman. Here, a teacher hopelessly tries to fend off Apollo, or his sister Artemis, from killing one of the boys. The skilful but formulaic poses would have made it suitable for the foyer of the public baths or an aristocrat's town house.

Abbaye de St-Jean des Vignes

Hours: 10a.m.–noon, 2–6p.m.

The Soissons archaeological service has reconstructed a full-scale version here of one large house and a hut found at Juvincourt-et-Damary. Although getting a little battered now (built in 1986 to commemorate Clovis' victory 1500 years before), they still give quite a vivid idea of fifth- and sixth-century

Frankish living quarters – and therefore the sort of buildings that local 'Romans' were inhabiting as stone quarrying and masonry disappeared. The house reconstruction is considered 'une ébauche' or 'rough cut': it is now thought that the posts could have supported a higher frame, which in turn might have meant a more sophisticated interior, perhaps including an upper storey.

VALENCIENNES, Nord

Museum.
www.ville-valenciennes.fr

Valenciennes lies on the river Escaut and therefore was part of the navigable route up to the mouth of the Scheldt. There was a bridge carrying the road from BAVAY to Tournai, but the only significant Roman settlement was at Famars. However, the quality of the Gallo-Roman exhibits in the museum is exceptional.

Musée des Beaux Arts de Valenciennes

Boulevard Watteau
59300 Valenciennes
Hours: 10a.m.–6p.m. Closed Tuesday

The museum was renovated in the early 1980s and a small display is full of pleasures.

The pure Gallic material consists of **miniature bronze masks**. They were probably offerings prepared for pilgrims to a sanctuary, enhanced by their stark, impassive look. The large empty oval eyes, the long straight noses and the gently emphasized cheekbones, together with the simplified portrayal of straight hair, give them the particular Celtic look, far from Roman realism.

During the nineteenth century numerous freelance digs at Bavay led to the dispersal of much material, some of which surfaces here. Two typical bronzes enable the visitor to contrast workshop skills. The Eros figure has an extended torso and arms that are too short; the **rearing horse**, however, is superb: the artist has caught the momentary stillness perfectly. In 1877 the Saulzoir oval **silver dish** was found near the Bavay–Cambrai road. During the troubles of the later Roman period it was cut up, along with other pieces of silver, buried in a jar, then covered with paving stones, whether by the owner or by a thief will never be known. As much as possible was restored, though it was incomplete. The craftsmanship is superb. A central thin-necked vase divides a symmetrical design, each of the features of which is associated with Dionysus: on one side, there is a crouching panther and the face of a maenad (one of the female followers of the god); on the other, there is an antelope below the profile of a satyr; a goatskin bottle for his wine rests on some rocks. The handle rim is finished with swans' heads and dolphins swallowing fish. The few pieces of stone sculpture are also of high quality. Nothing is known about the male portrait head, but the fashion for short beards, drilled eyes and hair suggest that it had been created for a second-century funerary monument. The young women are technically less sophisticated, but gentle and attractive.

Six kilometres south of Valenciennes, *Famars*, or Fanum Martis, was a small town of *c.*40–45ha, at its most active in the second century AD. The temple that gave the town its name has not been found, but in the nineteenth century a large baths complex was excavated and it was probably near this. It also seems to have had a major pottery workshop manufacturing first grey, then yellow kitchenware. Economic decline followed in the third century and by the end, Famars was converted into a *castellum* guarding the Bavay–Cambrai road (IGN 2606 E *visible remains*: traces of the late Roman rampart and tower on the southern slope of the hill on which the parish church stands).

Most of the pottery and other evidence of daily life displayed derives from work carried out in the early 1980s. The exceptional though fragmentary **Famars paintings** come from a corridor house decorated in the late second century. The architectural fragment embodies a porch in perspective: on the right, a pilaster and entablature with an outstretched river god; on the left, a bust within a shield. It would have been painted near the top of the wall to be viewed from below. The nymph and the lyre-player once decorated the middle section of the wall, perhaps in some mythical scene around a sacred spring. The ceiling might have been painted in haste: note the poor perspective of the temple roof.

VENDEUIL-CAPLY, Oise

IGN 2310 O
597.5/2512.3

Theatre site.

On the N1 Amiens–Beauvais road at Caply, about 2km south of Breteuil, there is a brown and white sign indicating the Gallo-Roman site. Take the minor road east from here for around 0.5km, following further signs.

This was identified as a ancient site as far back as the sixteenth century, but the decision to excavate Vendeuil-Caply was only taken after Roger Agache's aerial photographs in the 1950s and 1960s revealed evidence of extensive occupation covering at least a square kilometre. Clearly, it was a vigorous small town in the early imperial period and while the initial stimulus might have come from the presence of the army, it also had a sanctuary that attracted

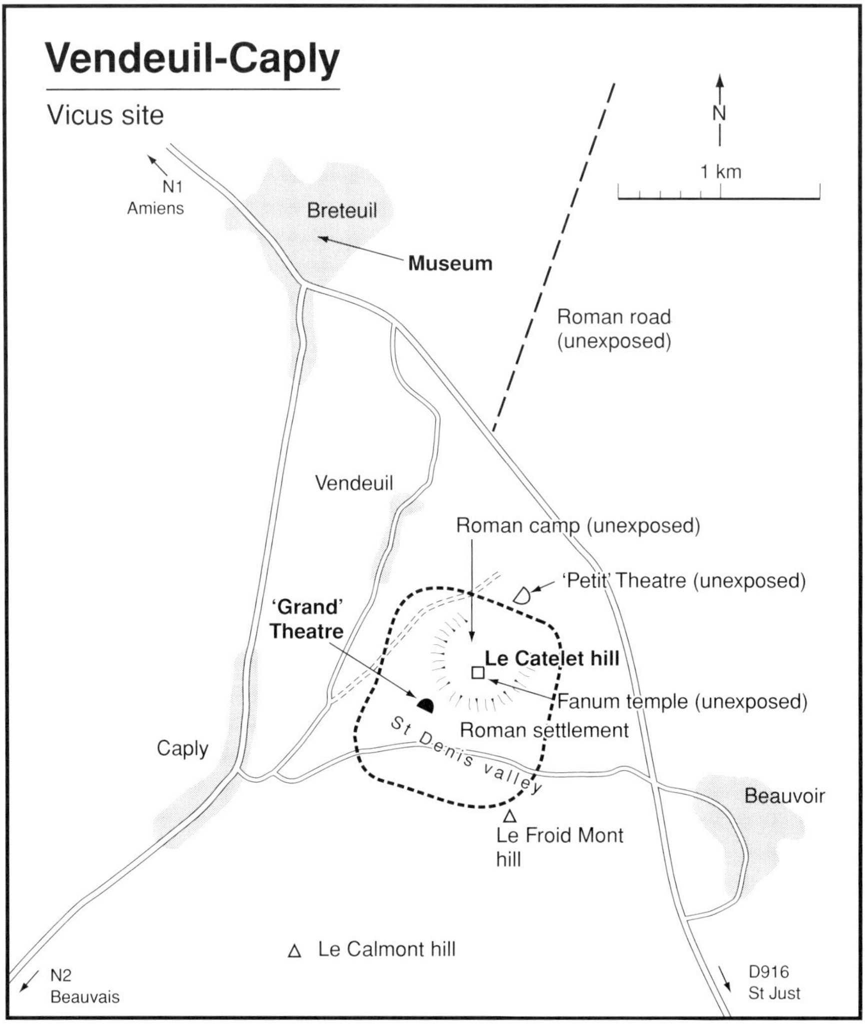

Figure 19 Vendeuil-Caply: local area

enough people to justify two theatres. However, despite the work of teams led by Gérard Dufour and Daniel Piton in the 1970s and 1980s, there are still many questions unanswered.

The earliest occupation they explored is on Le Catelet hill. A Gallic ritual site of the first century BC has been identified under a fanum of *c.* AD 65–70. Also on the hill is evidence of a large Roman camp. However, it has not been possible to decide whether this was built during the conquest campaigns in the 50s BC or later under Augustus. This perhaps supports the identification of Le Calmont hill as Bratuspantium, the *oppidum* where the army of the Bellovaci surrendered to Caesar in the 57 BC campaign, but up to the present this has not been supported archaeologically.

The *vicus* itself was concentrated in the valley of St Denis and on the Catelet slopes. The photographs revealed a mass of streets but no pre-planned grid site. Sadly, fieldwork has not turned the disconnected roads of the photographs into a street plan. Neither the 'baths' identified in a field walk in the 1930s nor the 'forum' suggested by the photographs have been confirmed. **Houses**, though, have been excavated at various points. Augustan wood and cob gave way to stone after a major fire in the Claudian period. These had the cellars so typical of northern and eastern France (see BLIESBRUCK and ALISE-STE-REINE). Destroyed again by fire in the 170s, they were rebuilt. Their subsequent history is obscure. Like many other small towns, it would have suffered in the third century, but unfortunately modern farming has severely disturbed the upper levels. The impression is that the roads were still being used, but that by the fourth century the place was very run down.

The sanctuary has not been sharply defined either. The *fanum* excavation provided little later stratigraphy. Third-century coins and fourth-century pottery suggest some presence, but not of what kind. A small theatre has been excavated as well. Built just after the *fanum* (*c.* AD 75), it was a simple structure hollowed out of the chalk and presumably covered with wooden seating, as it could not have supported stone. Dating evidence was again minimal. It may have been disused as early as the later second century.

The large theatre

This appears as a typical medium-sized, moderately well-preserved Roman theatre. However, the Dufour and Piton teams have revealed a surprisingly complex development in four phases.

(1) A **'ritual enclosure'**. Two *petit appareil* walls, 62.5m apart, were joined at the base by a ditch, while a wall or ditch is assumed to have closed the northern end. Finds under the walls suggest a date in the mid-first century AD. It is assumed to have had a use as part of the sanctuary.

(2) **Theatre I**. The enclosure was converted into a theatre some thirty years later under Domitian or early in Trajan's reign. It was strengthened with new walls added onto the old, so supporting an upper area of rubble cleared by cutting the lower tiers of seats directly into the chalk bedrock. The first theatre had therefore an unconventional rectangular oblong frame with stone seats placed on the bedrock chalk in the lower half and wooden tiers on the loose rubble above.

The **stage** and backstage area are not those of a classical Roman theatre. Performers used a small wooden projecting apron stage, not a platform running the whole width of the orchestra. There was no building – *scaena*

Vendeuil-Caply

Theatre

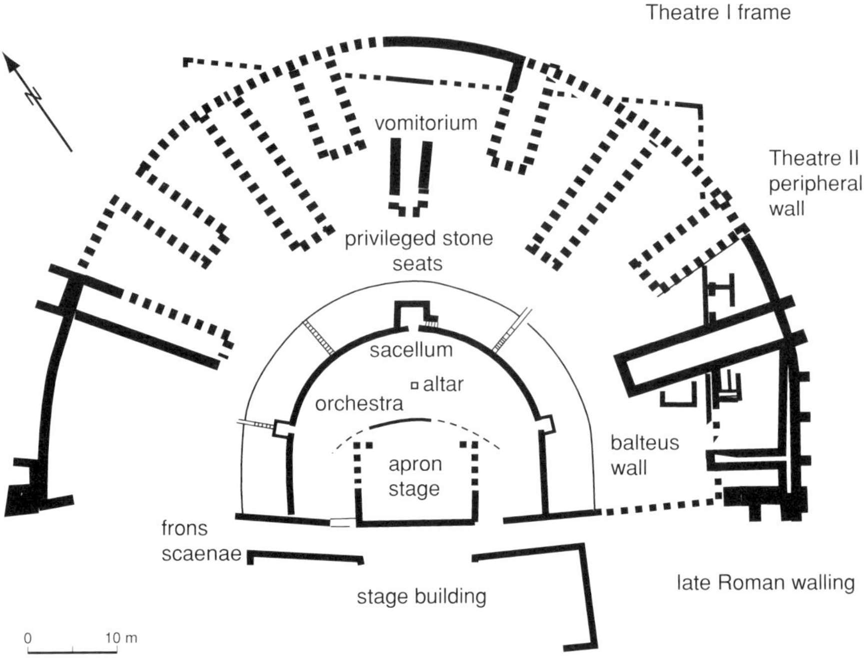

Figure 20 Vendeuil-Caply: theatre

– behind them with windows for scenic effects or to house changing-rooms, instead simply a wall, though with decorative bas-reliefs and architectural features. Fragments showed traces of red, white, blue and yellow paint. A single limestone block marks this *frons scaenae*, while traces of walling filled out with a line of bushes identify the apron stage. Walling parallel with the southern *cavea* (visible on the eastern side), could be that of an independent building where performers might have prepared themselves.

The **orchestra** area was entered by two doors on each side of the stage, represented by the flagstones. Probably performers reached the stage through a central door at platform height but they could have shared these doors with theatre-goers heading for their privileged seats in the orchestra itself or in the lower *cavea*. The floor of the orchestra slopes up gently to the semi-circular wall or *balteus*, so helping drainage to a large pit filled with rubble under the stage, a possible collecting point. The orchestra was covered with paving, almost all of which has been stripped out. The **altar** has been reconstructed from fragments. It is decorated with typical cult images of an offering plate (*patera*) and a libation jar (*oenochoe*), and placed on a paving, perhaps ignored by scavengers because it was disfigured by locating pinholes.

Behind the altar is a miniature temple or ***sacellum*** at the centre of the *balteus* wall. There are examples at Vienne and in Rome of *sacella*, but they are at the top and rear of the *cavea*. Amphitheatres commonly had them (see SENLIS), but the decision to build a *sacellum* in this position in a theatre is rare and has been interpreted as reflecting continuity with the rites of the earlier enclosure. It is built of limestone blocks and would have been painted. The angled lines of the top stones suggest a pedimented roof and broken column remains found in and around the temple have been reconstructed as two supports standing by the steps down from the orchestra. A niche in the back no doubt held an image of the unknown divinity.

(3) **Theatre II**. In the late second century the theatre was significantly modified, perhaps following the fires of the 170s – maybe the wooden tiers were burnt. The orchestra and stage were left unchanged but constructing a new, and 'classical', semi-circular *cavea* enlarged the theatre with stone seating in the upper sections as well. Radiating ditches were dug into the rubble and **twin walls** constructed to provide the stable base needed for stone seats. On the eastern side a pair are visible. Only the central pair, now hidden, seemed to form an access tunnel or *vomitorium*, from the back.

The enclosing **peripheral wall** is impressive. Much has survived and is exposed on the east and north. It is of standard Gallo-Roman construction: rubble concrete core between *petit appareil* facings, the exterior rather better finished. A new late second-century feature is decorative brick on the outside. The wall is not truly curved, but built in short straight sections between pilasters. At the corners, a few *grand appareil* foundation stones survive but most have been removed.

(4) **Late Roman occupation**. The eastern corner of the theatre shows how it lost its identity probably during the late third century. New large-scale walling here has been interpreted as strengthening to make the theatre into a defensive site (this is not unlikely when the conversion of the amphitheatre at AMIENS is taken into account). The impression of general run-down recalls other sites in Vendeuil-Caply. Signs of domestic occupation were found in the orchestra and burnt stones show fires were lit in the *sacellum*. Coins suggest that this continued into the early fifth century, but when Frankish settlement began in the area, it was not here but at the new site of Vendeuil itself.

Le Catelet hill

Although there is little to see on the hill – both the little theatre and the *fanum* were covered again – on a summer's day it is worth taking a few minutes to savour the view across the gentle hills, the cabbage whites fluttering around the meadows and the birds rustling in the copse below the hilltop. Among the trees to the east of the track, you can find traces of the pre-Roman ditches.

Musée de Breteuil

5 Rue de l'Eglise
Hours: 10a.m.–noon, 2–6p.m. Closed Tuesday

Guided tours of site and museum can be provided on application at the museum.

The modern church at the corner of the main street, rather than the tiny street sign, helps in finding the museum in Breteuil. The collection is kept in a single second-floor room, approached by external stairs via the courtyard of what looks like a small converted factory. The prominent words on the front of the building are 'Centre Marcel Dessault'.

The main finds are all from Vendeuil-Caply. From the theatre there are fragments of wall painting and decorative features from the *frons scaenae*, and a stone seat with the name 'Letulus' carved on it – presumably his permanent reservation, or was it ancient graffiti? There is a delicate creamy white terracotta statuette of a soldier with cross-straps over his chest. His head hints at Gallic features: bulbous eyes and schematic locks. There is the usual detritus of daily life, coarse and fine pottery (mainly broken), tiles, nails, pipe work, dice and, most interesting, an **oculist's kit** for treating eyes.

OTHER SITES

Little is known about Gallo-Roman **Laon** (Aisne), but there is a regional museum and a superb mosaic in the Maison des Associations. On the Seine at **Melun** (Seine-et-Marne), the museum displays an interesting collection from the Roman town. At **Noyon** (Oise) poorly made late Roman rampart survives and there is a good local museum. Slight traces of Roman occupation at **Thérouanne** (Pas-de-Calais) are visible and the finds displayed at St Omer. **Vermond** (Aisne) has the remains of an *oppidum* occupied in the Iron Age and Roman period and a small local museum.

THE ROMANO-CELTIC SANCTUARY

Five hundred years ago, Renaissance writers identified a tower standing outside Autun as a 'Temple of Janus', based on the misinterpretation of a local place name. Nevertheless their instincts were right, it was a Roman temple. Though a typical Roman stone structure, its tall square shape was markedly unclassical. By the twentieth century many more had been recognized and to distinguish them from conventional temples, this type became known as a *fanum* (a general Latin word for a shrine): here was the physical expression of the religious synthesis produced by the Roman conquest of Gaul.

The *fanum* temple

The classical temple is a long rectangular building standing on a podium entered through a row of columns leading into a chamber or *cella*, decorated on the sides and rear with pilasters or columns. The Romano-Celtic *fanum* has a tall *cella*, normally square or a squat rectangle (though a few are polygonal or round), surrounded by a gallery. As the exceptionally large 'Temple of Janus' shows, the holes that held the gallery timbers and roofing are set low on the tower: the gallery was therefore a simple one-storey structure, though whether the outer wall was solid (with windows) or a portico set on a low wall is not known. Indeed, the absence of this gallery structure is general, but the gallery wall foundations indicate that they were almost always less substantial than the tower and therefore a low gallery was the norm.

More than 650 *fana* are known, spread through France, Roman Germany and Britain, four hundred of them revealed since 1960. Nearly a third of those found are concentrated in the regions covered by this book. Aerial photography has been decisive and in France Roger Agache led the way with his magisterial survey of the Somme. Before 1960 eight sites were known in Picardy, by 1993, 52 had been found; many still remain unexcavated. Burgundy has been another area with a high concentration of aerial finds; they encouraged the regional archaeologists to ensure that Beaune ARCHEODROME has a full-scale reconstruction of a typical small

Plate 6 Autun. The Romano-Celtic sanctuary. The temple of Janus, a *fanum* temple *cella*. Photograph: James Bromwich.

fanum temple. Other Burgundian sites, such as NUITS-ST-GEORGES (Les Bolards), have been shown to have been much grander sanctuaries with a cluster of buildings around them. There has been considerable debate over the years on the role of sanctuaries. Did they stimulate additional settlement, or were such sanctuaries the normal way of expressing religious belief in smaller Gallo-Roman towns?

Many sanctuaries are closely associated with springs, like SOURCES DE LA SEINE or VILLARDS D'HERIA, hidden away in a mountain valley in the Jura. One has even been discovered on a mountain-top: LE DONON sanctuary looked out from 1,000m (3,300ft) across the expanse of the Vosges. Others, like that in the Forêt de Halatte (see SENLIS) or MOUZON (Le Flavier), were constructed in rural isolation, sometimes using slight hill slopes perhaps to increase their impressiveness. Fewer have been found in cities and even the Temple of Janus was part of a sanctuary complex outside the Aeduan *civitas* capital at AUTUN.

Origins

During the nineteenth and even in the twentieth century, many excavators simply looked for the *fanum* and virtually ignored the rest of the sanctuary that, it has become increasingly clear, holds considerable interest. Like classical temples, the *fanum* stood in a sacred area defined by an enclosing wall or *peribolus*. It was within this area that people interacted with their god(s) and it has become clear that careful excavation could lead to a far greater awareness of how this took place. At the same time, recognition grew that sanctuaries evolved over time. The most dramatic advances demonstrating the evolution from Celtic to Romano-Celtic sanctuary have been made in Picardy. *Ribemont-sur-Ancre* and *Gournay-sur-Aronde*, excavated in the 1970s and 1980s, have excited special interest (neither has exposed remains). Although La Tène material had been observed at Gallo-Roman sites, most opinion still saw Gallic sanctuaries as the Roman poet Lucan described them, 'sacred groves', no more than clearings in forests; the built sanctuary and the *fanum* were seen as purely post-conquest products. Equally, the practices he abhorred, involving piles of offerings in front of crude wooden images combined with human sacrifices, were seen as exaggerations calculated to arouse bitter Roman delight in Gallic barbarian behaviour.

Ribemont was originally identified in one of Agache's photographs as part of a villa, but it was soon recognized by excavation to be a very early, large *fanum* within a much grander complex. J.L. Cadoux, who excavated here for twenty years in the 1970s and 1980s, made full use of aerial photographs to identify where to dig, then trenched in small sections, leaving four-fifths of the surface untouched and filling in after each season. He found that the site covered some 50ha, with a series of courtyards cascading down the hill from the temple near the top; there was a bath complex, a theatre and a number of other large stone structures, including one with a hypocaust. The most dramatic discovery came in 1982 when an 'ossuary' was discovered in the courtyard immediately in front of the temple. Human limbs from over 250 people had been carefully stacked at right angles with horse bones, forming a rectangle around a pit at the centre. No skulls were found. Mixed in with them were spear-heads and shield bosses. As important as this was, the discovery of a ditch and mound, also of La Tène II date, enclosing this court and the site of the later *fanum*, was equally significant as it showed the deliberate creation of a sacred area. Subsequent work in the 1990s has revealed that the trench was later filled with a palisade and a timber lining; beside the ditch were headless human bodies.

At **Gournay**, J.L. Brunaux's meticulous contemporary excavations revealed a series of modifications made to a sacred area within an *oppidum*, defined by an enclosure from the fourth century BC through to the first century AD. He was able to show how the initially open ditch had subsequently been palisaded and then another ditch dug on the inside to be lined with planks. The interior ditch was packed with bones laid out in deliberate zones of horse, cattle, sheep, pigs and human remains. The space inside also evolved. During the third century BC, a large oval pit was dug at the centre of the site and nearby nine smaller circular pits. In addition five post-holes were found, one at the centre and four at the cardinal points. The posts were interpreted as sites for sacrifice, the oval pit for rotting bodies before transfer to the enclosure ditch and the small pits for burying weapons (over 2,000 swords and other weapons were found at Gournay, many deliberately bent). By the beginning of the second century BC small post-holes suggest that the central pit was provided with a roof and, a hundred years later, this was replaced by a square structure, perhaps with a surrounding gallery (the traces are not certain). The final stages came after the Roman conquest. Around 30 BC a square timber *cella* was built open on one side and with a gallery round the other three. Then in the early first century AD the ditches were filled in. The temple was finally abandoned in the 60s when the *oppidum* was deserted.

These two sites clearly demonstrate that the built sanctuary precedes conquest and that it was evolving to the Gallo-Roman form. The central point of the sanctuary had refocused from offering pits to a building embodying a religious presence. Gournay in particular suggests that this is linked in some way with the social changes associated with the emergence of both tribal states and urban living. Roman influence from the south helped to promote these changes and stimulated cultural mutation towards a more concrete expression of faith. The design was already there; the adoption of stone building is simply part of the overall Romanization of Gaul.

The excavation of these and other such sites has made it necessary to treat Lucan's comments on the practice of Gallic religion with rather more respect. The discovery of so many wooden figures at the sanctuary of Sources de la Seine and the 'Jupiter columns' (see METZ, REIMS, CUSSY-LA-COLONNE) make the interpretation of the post-holes of Gournay as decorated pillars inherently more likely. The offering of animal sacrifice was normal in the Roman world, not so the exposure and dislocation of bodies at temples, and in particular not human sacrifice. Brunaux has argued that the human remains found at Ribemont and Gournay might be no more than elaborate burials, the cuts on the bones dismemberment, not wounds. Yet his alternative for the Ribemont pile of bones, given its particular mix, of humans, horses and weaponry, is that it is a battle monument. This seems more convincing to me. La Turbie, a monument near Nice, records a Roman version of a victory pile, different in style but embodying a similar concept. It could be the Ribemont bones were those of dead enemies killed in battle; equally possible, prisoners sacrificed afterwards. Nor is it inherently unlikely that headless bodies found by or in the ditches were human sacrifice: convincing evidence for it has been found in late Iron Age contexts outside France. Greek writers like Diodorus Siculus (*Library of History*, 5, 31, 2–5) identified human sacrifice as a Gallic practice, and the Romans accused the Celtic priesthood specifically of organizing human sacrifice.

'It is impossible to calculate how much is owed to the Romans for suppressing these atrocities, according to which the most religious rite was to kill a man, and the healthiest practice was to devour him' (Pliny the Elder, *Natural History*, XXX, 4). The disgust of civilized people, like the great and open-minded elder Pliny (AD 23–79), gave moral justification for proscribing the **druids**.[1] Though their precise role in sanctuary ceremonial is not known, the top rank of the priestly class, mentioned by many classical writers, and described most fully by Caesar (*Gallic Wars*, VI, 13–14, 16, 18), had been the guiding force of Gallic religious belief. As Caesar explained, druids were deeply respected, not just because they were largely drawn from the nobility, but for a variety of reasons. To become a druid entailed a long education – twenty years was the norm; their teachings on the soul suggest a sophistication that had made earlier writers consider them as Gaul's philosophers; they performed the role of judges; they had the power to decide who could attend sacrifices; and, above all perhaps, they had an organization that crossed tribal borders, drawing from all the tribes of Gaul, meeting annually, electing a national druidic leader and undertaking inter-tribal arbitration. In too many ways they were a potential threat to the new Roman order.

Romanization after the conquest

A series of legislative measures began with Augustus forbidding Roman citizens from becoming druids, forcing Gallic nobles to choose how they saw their personal future, and culminating in the outright banning by Claudius, the same emperor who offered the Gallic elite the opportunity to become senators (Suetonius, *Lives*, V, 25, 5). However, equally important must have been the impact of Gallic defeat. The psychological transformation this produced should not be underestimated: the tribal nobility adopted Roman ways with growing enthusiasm. Uncontrolled fighting was unacceptable within the empire and, as the nobility either entered the Roman army or adopted Roman notions of the good life, gory sanctuaries of the free Gallic era became irrelevant.

Those who found the accelerated change to their culture too much were marginalized. As the aristocracy continued to dominate Gallic society but deserted the traditional priestly order, so the latter became identified with outsiders, the prophetic seers longing for the downfall of the empire. Tacitus (*Histories*, IV, 54), may be simply playing on Roman fears of the Gallic peril, based on the sack of Rome in 390 BC, but it is just as likely that there were druid seers interpreting the Capitol hill fire (AD 69) as a divine sign that Rome's domination of the world was coming to an end, and encouraging rebellion. That these druids were no longer a highly respected elite is shown by the almost total lack of support from Gaul's ruling classes.

How then could an aristocratic family express their commitment to the new order and to the importance of the gods in their lives? The Romans provided an immediate answer: a massive altar at Condate in Lugdunum, established in 12 BC, where delegates from all the Gallic tribes could come and celebrate with a great festival the spirit of Rome and its emperors (see LYON). To be a *sacerdos* (priest) of this altar became the pinnacle of many careers. Its meetings, held in a specially built amphitheatre, were a Roman-inspired substitute for the old druidic gatherings. An intellectual could turn to the new schools, such as that in Autun, and absorb Graeco-Roman philosophy, even share in the delights of debating the merits of Stoicism or Epicureanism (see AUTUN). Nor would there have been anything to prevent those attracted by more time-honoured mystic complexities, such as the astronomical calculations necessary to prepare sanctuary calendars (see LYON and VILLARDS D'HERIA). The Roman empire's pagan tolerance of a multiplicity of gods and practice (as long as they presented no political challenge) made Gauls aware of many more exotic cults as well. An open religious mind could be tempted by Dionysus from Greece, Cybele from Anatolia, Mithras from Persia, Serapis from Egypt, or even the esoteric interpretation of Egyptian astrological tables (see EPINAL).

The Romano-Celtic sanctuary with its characteristic *fanum* could continue to evolve, distinctive, yes, but sanitized. Many must have evolved on the same sites as their Gallic predecessors. While the number firmly identified doing this is still only in the thirties, the real number must have been much greater. Until recently, archaeologists specializing in the Roman period possessed neither the interest nor the technique to interpret La Tène material. In addition, many Romano-Celtic sanctuaries are still unexcavated. Of those that have been dated, it is estimated that more than half had been built by the middle of the first century AD. Ribemont shows one way in which this form of regional Romanization could evolve, with its baths, theatre and other large-scale buildings – features that had not existed before the conquest. Theatre design is not conventional, but like the temple, adapted to local needs and distinctive religious rituals (see MANDEURE). However, even the smallest temples tend to show the evidence of increasing Romanization: good-quality stone construction, painted plaster walls, tile roofs and classical ornamentation. The statuettes took on an increasingly realistic appearance and on the few inscriptions found the gods, once described with Gallic names, have adopted a Latin form of name. By the end of the second century, beliefs may still have been local, but the expression had become Roman.

Gods, priests and people at Gallo-Roman sanctuaries

Surprisingly few of the sanctuaries can be identified with any specific god. Although the portrayal of gods in concrete form, in stone, metal or wood, was prevalent, distinctive identifiable cult statues found in situ have been rare, inscriptions even more so. The most widely found named Roman god in the region is Mercury, frequently portrayed in a Gallic way, only described as 'Mercury' because of attributes such as his hat, wand or tortoise. Apollo and Mars also occur, but were often given another name as well. The problem of identifying the gods of these sanctuaries is made worse by so many finds being un-named crudely made figures, which could be depictions of the gods or simply gifts of worshippers. Many sanctuaries must have been associated with place or peoples and therefore they were more likely to be multi-functional rather than specialized in the Roman way. It has been argued that there was a hierarchy of sanctuaries from local to *pagus* to tribal and beyond, especially perhaps healing centres.

Did ceremony and ritual vary for each god and at each sanctuary or was practice, like the structure, broadly similar? Sadly, no contemporary wrote describing even one ceremony at a Romano-Celtic sanctuary and we are unlikely ever to have more than occasional glimpses. Even the role of the *fanum* gallery is still disputed. At one time it was argued that it provided cover for a ritual involving people circling round the *cella*, but it seems more likely that this is where some at least of the offerings were placed. Yet few have been precisely located here. Were ceremonies mainly carried out in the open, as seems likely? Though stone altars dedicated by visitors have been found, few were discovered where they would be expected, associated with the sacred area around the temple where sacrifices were normally held elsewhere in the empire. The detailed operation of a Romano-Celtic sanctuary will never be really understood, but there is real hope that the kind of care shown at both Ribemont and Gournay to explore and analyse pre-Roman practices could be applied to the finds and the inter-relationship between finds and find spots at the large number of unexplored known sites. It is going to be the secondary buildings of the sanctuaries and the open spaces between structures that reveal the most in future excavations.

Was there a resident priesthood at the sites? A hint at the daily life of a sanctuary is provided by the fragmentary bronze calendars from Coligny (See LYON) and VILLARDS D'HERIA listing regular series of festivals at the sanctuaries. It suggests not only the need for a sophisticated understanding of the lunar month and its reconciliation with the solar year, but also the need for advisers and interpreters at the sanctuaries. When should a sacrifice be made? What kind of animal? Would the visitor want the entrails examined to divine the god's views? Who would carry out the sacrifice? Who were the most appropriate musicians? What hymns should accompany the event? Certainly people would have been needed – and they would probably be local priests – to arrange for the leading figures of the *civitas*, in their capacity as *sacerdotes*, to appear at the festivals, some of which would be major events lasting for many days. At healing sanctuaries, of which there were so many, priests would have acted as medical and spiritual advisers, interpreting illnesses and the role played by the gods in their cure. At great sites, rich visiting pilgrims would have been advised on the interpretation of dreams; with water roaring in the maze of hidden underground aqueducts, GRAND must have provoked the most unsettled sleep. It is likely that they were responsible for guarding temple treasures – and even for hiding the rare survivals (for temple silver plate see PARIS, Cabinet des Médailles). The bronze goddess Sequana on her boat, the spirit of the river worshipped at the Sources of the Seine sanctuary, may have been carried by a priest in procession during festivals (see DIJON).

Sanctuaries would have played a major part in the lives of ordinary people. People met together at festivals, demonstrating support for both their gods and their rulers (who funded them), to witness sacrifices, enjoy the occasion and eat the free meat. Most of all though, sanctuaries allowed people through their personal offerings to seek help in their daily need to survive and, if possible, prosper. Sanctuaries rapidly lost their warrior aspect. Both the bones of animals slaughtered *en masse* and the burial of weapons disappear: they were the symbols of and incitement to tribal war and neither needed nor tolerated. Even useless miniature weapons disappeared from sanctuary offerings (see MOUZON). Instead their offerings increasingly took on the familiar, empire-wide, Roman appearance. The shattered plates, bowls and cups, that would once have carried food to be shared in on-site feasts with the gods, become ubiquitous. Coin finds could be the direct gifts of supplicants or payment for suitable offerings from the sanctuary traders. Offerings ranged from small wheels (associated with sun-gods) to animals, human figures, and limbs – frequent finds at healing sanctuaries where they must have identified the problem part of the body the god was to help. They were made in all kinds of material: stone statues are generally the most Gallic, simplified and crude, often focused on the eyes; wooden objects are inevitably the rarest; bronzes are usually the most Roman; and creamy terracotta

Euffigneix man–boar

A Gallic god

(see PARIS: St Germain-en-Laye)

Epona

A Gallo-Roman goddess

(see BEAUNE)

Freyr

A German fertility god

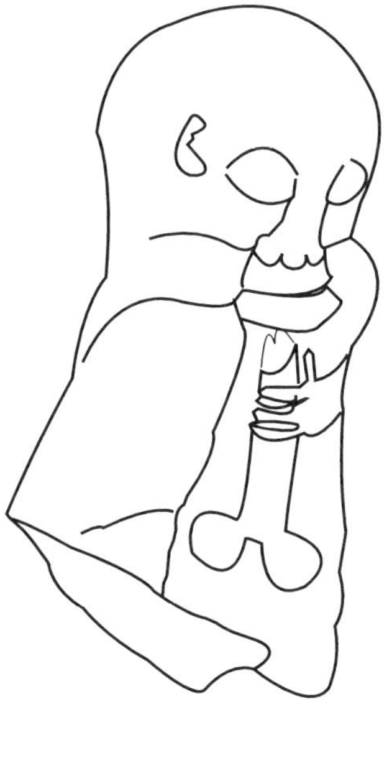

Figure 21 Euffigneix: man–boar god (*top left*)
Figure 22 Epona: Gallo-Roman goddess (*top right*)
Figure 23 Freyr: German fertility god (*bottom*)

figurines, frequently Venus or mother-goddess types, the most widely found, representing that most fundamental of all hopes, procreation.

The Romano-Celtic temple disappeared for ever in the fifth century. The twin assault of Germanic pagans with different beliefs (see ARRAS) and the commitment of the Roman state and then the successor states to Christianity were too much. Along with most aspects of Gallo-Roman life, the momentum for constructing or modernizing Romano-Celtic temples ended in the early third century (only eight new temples are dated to the 200s). In the fourth century, there is some evidence for revival. At Gournay, a new *fanum* was placed on top of the abandoned first-century structure, while elsewhere many saw continued use. Perhaps it was Gallic regionalism rejecting imperial Christianity, perhaps the tenacity of Gallic beliefs. It may be that the pagan gods, Epona, Cernunnos and Mercury, whom the Christians of the fifth and sixth centuries campaigned so hard against, lived on in the minds of the rural poor even when their sanctuaries were in ruin and deserted, worshipped as the Roman poet Lucan had depicted them in the glades and clearings of forests, until they became no more than the superstitions of the countryside.

Note

1 We may doubt whether Roman society as a whole was quite so horrified by its own atrocities: human sacrifice in Rome had only been banned in 97 BC and the public murder of criminals in the amphitheatre was widely appreciated throughout the empire.

2

THE SITES OF BURGUNDY AND THE FRANCHE-COMTE

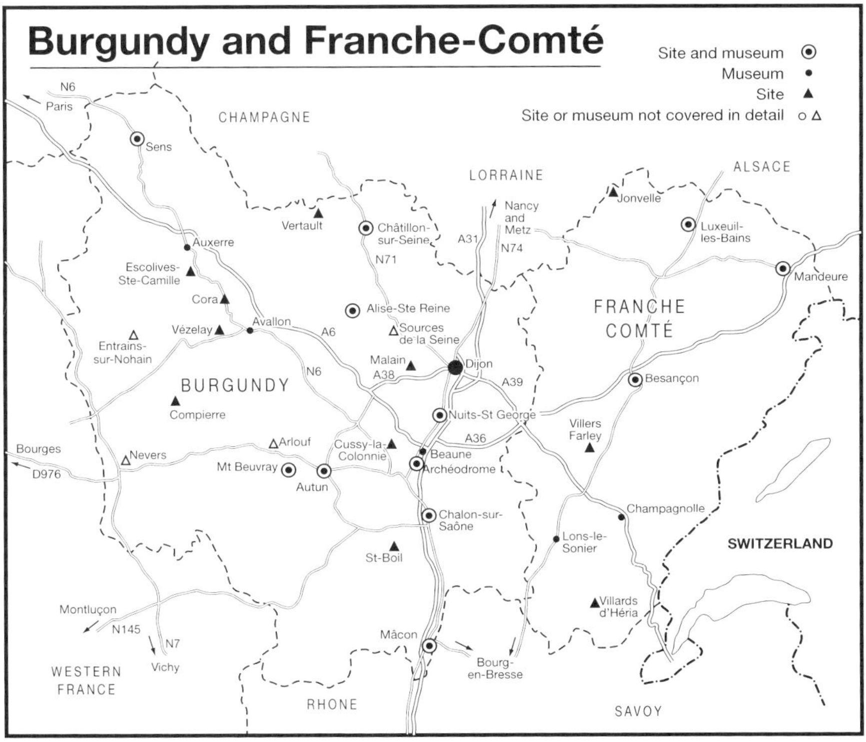

Figure 24 Regional map: Burgundy and Franche-Comté

ALISE-STE-REINE, Côte d'Or

IGN 2921 E/3021 O

Site and museum of Alesia.

3km east of Venarey-les-Laumes, which is 60km north-north-west of Dijon via the A38/D905 and 14km south-east of Montbard.

Alesia has a meaning for the French almost on a par with Hastings for the English. Vercingetorix and Julius Caesar fill the roles of Harold and William the Conqueror, though perhaps the date of 52 BC might not have quite the resonance of 1066. For the French, too, the fact that this was a heroic defeat does not matter too much; just as the 'Normans' have become an absorbed part of being English, so the Gallo-Roman civilization that resulted from Roman victory can be seen as a significant contribution to modern French identity. Yet what we seek from history changes and until the Revolution of 1789 France was perceived largely in terms of its Frankish heritage: king Clovis as the founder of France. During the 1790s, revolutionaries turned to an alternative, untainted Gallic origin. Louis Napoleon (1808–73), Napoleon's nephew and a romantic self-proclaimed man of destiny, facing the royalist backlash of the period 1815–48, saw himself as the inheritor of both the revolutionary and the imperial traditions; he was fascinated by the great struggle between Vercingetorix and Caesar. It is not therefore surprising that, as Napoleon III, in 1861 he initiated the first major national archaeological excavations in France here at Alesia.

Book VII of Caesar's *Gallic Wars* deals with the decisive campaigns of 52 BC, when the Gauls were inspired by the Arverni noble Vercingetorix to unite and wage war together. Caesar had managed to concentrate his troops and those of his chief lieutenant Labienus near Sens, but the scale of the threat posed by the Gauls made his only option withdrawal southwards. The fact that Vercingetorix chose to intercept the Roman army gave Caesar the opportunity to force a decisive confrontation much more on his own terms. The armies first faced each other in a major cavalry engagement, probably in the Armonçon valley north-west of Athie, with both commanders holding back their main forces. It ended with the Gallic horse fleeing from Caesar's Germans. Vercingetorix now decided it was best to withdraw to a strongpoint and rally his troops. From there he might harry the Romans if they continued their retreat or, if Caesar chose to attack, the experience at Gergovia had been that Caesar had suffered severely when trying to take a defended hill-fort against an able defender. Alesia, a particularly strong *oppidum*, was only a single day's march away.

Caesar describes in twenty-eight brilliant paragraphs (Gallic Wars, VII, 63–90) how he pursued Vercingetorix and his army and, recognizing the impossibility of taking Alesia, decided to invest it. How he first built camps to secure his legions; then, after digging a wide ditch joining the rivers on each

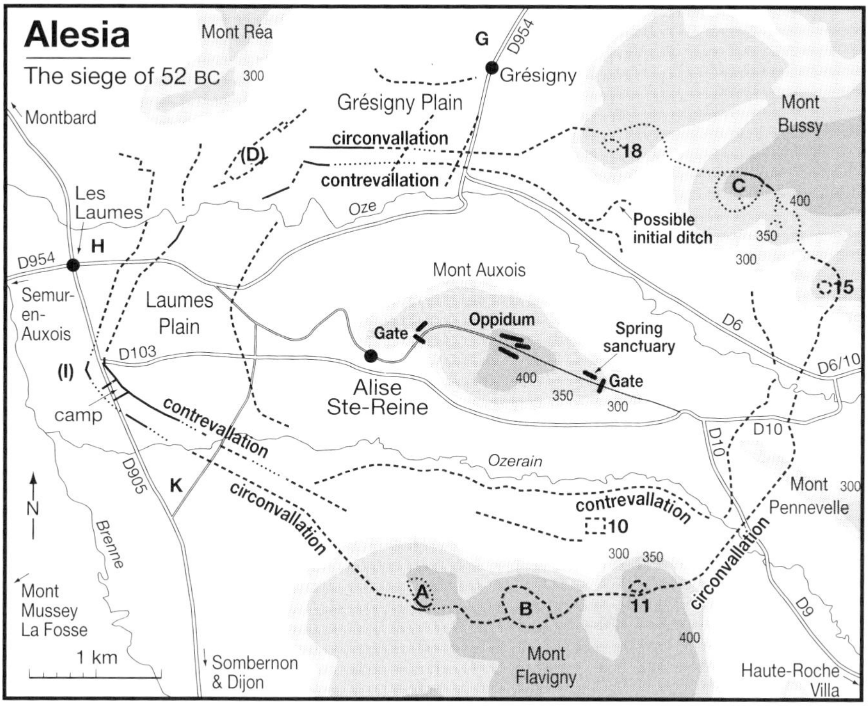

Caesar's ramparts:
—— 1990s excavations
------ Napoleon III's excavations
·········· seen in aerial photographs

The Roman camps:
A, B, C; 10–18
G, H and **K** suspect
(I) and **(D)** no longer accepted

Figure 25 Alesia: the siege of 52 BC

side of the *oppidum*, enclosing fortifications were begun, forcing Vercingetorix to send his cavalry away as they would soon be useless. After these containing defences were built, an external defence line clearly became necessary: a relieving army must come. The fortifications were effective enough to enable Caesar to take on approximately 248,000 men in the relieving force and the 80,000 besieged; Caesar had 40,000–50,000 legionaries plus auxiliaries. The Gallic figures could of course be exaggerated by Caesar, but most scholars do not think the relative numbers inherently unlikely and Caesar led an army familiar with both mass conflict and siege warfare, with many soldiers used to years of battle: professionals versus amateurs. The Gauls tried three times to break the lines. The scale of the effort on the last occasion was so great and its defeat so decisive, that on the following day Vercingetorix came to Caesar to surrender (he then spent six years as a prisoner in Rome before being executed); his soldiers became booty for Caesar's army. They would be sold as slaves, except for 20,000 lucky Aedui and Arverni prisoners, handed back to the tribes to encourage acceptance of Roman domination.

Napoleon III's decision to investigate Mont Auxois and the surrounding area arose from an article published in 1855 arguing that Alaise, a small town in the Jura, was the real Alesia. This challenged the belief going back to the Middle Ages that Mont Auxois was the site. This popular tradition had even been enhanced by the discovery on the hilltop in 1839 of an inscription specifically naming the place 'Alisiia'. To settle the matter,[1] Colonel Stoffel, a top artillery commander, was put in charge; this is not surprising as French army officers were all familiar with Caesar's wars and strategy and were fascinated with identifying where the events occurred. Victor Pernet was made local director of excavations and should be remembered for first noting the significance of crop markings. Within five years it became clear that Mont Auxois was indeed surrounded by an inner fortification 17km long and an outer fortification of 23km, the *contrevallation* and the *circonvallation*. They also identified the ditch linking the rivers and a series of large and small forts on the surrounding heights and plains. Napoleon was able to write his *Histoire de Jules César* (1866) using the work of his team and illustrated with plans based on their discoveries.

Caesar's fortifications

In the 1960s Roger Goguey took a series of aerial photographs of the *oppidum* and its surroundings; they confirmed much of Stoffel and Pernet's identifications, but also raised doubts about camp locations and the precise paths of the defence lines: clearly there had been some confusion of medieval and later ditches with Roman work. In the 1980s, Joël Le Gall, the leading expert on Alesia in the post-war period, re-examined the original records kept by the 1860s excavators. They showed that Napoleon III had misinterpreted the evidence when it did not fit Caesar's descriptions and gaps in knowledge had been ignored. Clearly the time had come for fresh excavations.

A new programme of excavations, begun in the early 1990s, has not yet been completed. However, a number of features have been clarified. There are no doubts about the *c.*6m (20 Roman feet) wide water-filled ditch, but it seems clear that the inner and outer defence lines were never completed, while a number of ditches were significantly shallower than normal military work – evidence of haste. The most important reassessment has involved the camps. Of the twelve identified in the 1860s, only six have so far been confirmed: 18, C and 15 on Mont Bussy and A, B and 11 on Mont Flavigny. Camp 10 may well be genuine; D and I were actually medieval. The others, G, H and K, are considered doubtful as they are all outside the *circonvallation* and would have been vulnerable to attack: it is likely that other camps will be identified inside the corridor created by the inner and outer defence lines. The new excavations at *camps A, B and C* were also individually revealing. Camps C and B were integrated in the *circonvallation*, but still had gates on their outer sides, allowing sallies. Features previously unnoticed were identified: *tituli*, short defensive walls placed in front of the gates to slow any Gallic rush, and a *clavicula*, a curved wall behind a gate, provided further protection if the doors were breached by the Gauls.

Outside camp C lead sling balls, inscribed T.LABI, strongly suggest that this was the camp of Labienus and give support to the traditional identification of camp A as the 'Camp de César'. Finds outside camp B include *tribuli*, four-pointed metal spikes sprinkled on the ground to wound a charging enemy, unmentioned by Caesar. In *Gallic Wars*, VII, 73 and 74, he describes a series of traps to injure and slow down the Gauls. Nowhere is there a complete set in the order he described! German archaeologists have been working in the *Laumes Plain*. They have demonstrated that the *contrevallation* and the *circonvallation* defences were not standardized but varied the mix of formidable barriers. The repertoire included turf ramparts with wooden towers; ditches, some water-filled; *glacis* or slopes with *stimuli*, buried wooden planks with embedded spikes; and open areas with *lilia*, wood spikes set in circular holes. They also found the first definite *castellum* or fortlet formed by two ramparts across the corridor with sally ports at each corner. Hopefully, more of these *castella* will be found and the real camp D identified under Mont Réa, where it is widely believed the final battle took place.

The *oppidum*

The Gallic defences of Alesia are still poorly known. The hill forms a plateau about 2km long surrounded by a ridge, making assault extremely difficult. Erosion had created some gullies and evidence of walling here has been taken to mean the rest was left without a rampart but this is not certain. The eastern end had the shallowest slope and a gateway built using the *murus gallicus* technique was constructed here; traces of a similar gate at the south-east end have also been found linking the natural route along the *oppidum* crest. No trace has been found of the additional defences, probably on the south-west hillside, built to protect Vercingetorix's overflow of troops.

Excavation has revealed only a modest Gallic settlement here. Of the 97ha available on the plateau 1.5–2ha was occupied, apart from a spring sanctuary near the eastern gate, dedicated later to Apollo Moritasgus. Even more surprising perhaps is that the *oppidum* seems to have been founded only a decade before the Gallic wars (70–60 BC). This has been interpreted as being the result of a migration from the north-west by the Mandubii tribe (whose pottery has northern characteristics) to carve out a small territory on the borders of the Aedui, Sequani and Lingones. Like Bibracte (Mont Beuvray), the settlement seems to have been stratified: a public centre by a sanctuary dedicated to the spirit of the tribe or town; a residential area (to the north), and a manufacturing district (to the south, specializing in metalwork). Many of the timber and thatch houses had cellars.

Gallo-Roman Alesia

The archaeological evidence strongly suggests continuity. Caesar (*Gallic Wars*, VII, 78) describes how he refused to let non-combatant Mandubii be sent out from Alesia and that they starved between the lines. They are likely to have been the people who fled into the *oppidum* with their cattle at the start of the siege, not the townspeople. The well-excavated artisans' district shows that in the years immediately after conquest workshops expanded. The pace of change was slower here than at the Aeduan capital of Bibracte: it was a small community and the Mandubii had been made a dependent *pagus* of the Lingones. Yet by the time of Tiberius (AD 14–37), the settlement had grown, houses had developed timber walling, tracks became roads, and the bronze-workers began producing for the market. It seems likely that the metalworkers continued as dependants of the local nobility, not unlike the freedmen clients of the Roman aristocracy. Another more concrete sign of continuity is the main sanctuary. Rebuilt with masonry foundations and a wooden colonnade, in the early post-conquest days it appears to have supported reliefs of severed heads.

From the mid-first century AD, Alesia moved steadily towards a more Romanized form. A regularized road network began to emerge as the town expanded in all directions. Roman stone-building techniques were being adopted, particularly for the cellars. The **bronze workshops** suggest dynamic development. One new block was constructed with a portico facing street 2; inside they were producing bronze for the Rhine army. The Elder Pliny, who had served as an officer in Germany, wrote how in Alesia they plated bronze with silver, 'particularly ornaments for horses and pack animals and yokes of oxen'. Workshops, no doubt run by master craftsmen, show a division of labour between furnace work, moulding, finishing and storage, also apparent at Bibracte (see MONT BEUVRAY museum). Nearby, blacksmiths were making hammers and chisels for them. Before the end of the first century the sanctuary was enclosed by a gallery and decorated with reliefs linking it to Jupiter. To the west was a theatre and, to the south of the open area, a large building interpreted as a *macellum* or meat market.

During the second and third centuries Alesia took on the appearance of a typical Gallo-Roman town. Aerial photographs reveal a site covering *c.*70ha, indicating there were still parts where stock grazed and market gardening went on. At its core, a forum was created, not by wholesale reconstruction, but by adding on a basilica and curia beside the sanctuary and creating a portico around the old open area. There was a monumental entrance on the south side, but elsewhere the porticos were, as at MALAIN, mainly erected by the different property owners to their own design. This 'square' had an equestrian statue and dedications to the emperor. The bronze-workers' corporation or guild built a complex dedicated to Ucuetis. Workshops continued to proliferate, their products now having a regional distribution. Merchants seem to have been concentrated in *insulae* D and E; one ran a multi-goods bazaar selling ceramics, oil, and metals (the 'House of Silenus'). The spring sanctuary by the old east gate became a grand healing centre with a hexagonal *fanum*, pool and baths. Large structures nearby have been interpreted as hostels for pilgrims. This sanctuary zone is not exposed, nor are the *fana* discovered at the western end of the town.

Destruction levels of the later third century are found widely in the town. Districts were abandoned, many cellars filled in and metal production stopped. Recovery of a sort occurred with the occasional hypocaust and a new temple to Cybele, but by the fifth century most of the site was abandoned. What settlement there was clustered around a Christian church (Ste Reine). But movement was away from the hilltop. At the rear of the town cemetery, 200m down the road from the main site of Alesia, are the excavations of a later Merovingian church and small monastery; their distinctive trapezoidal coffins revealing where the faithful were buried inside and outside the buildings. Further down on the south-west slopes, a new village, Alise-Ste-Reine, was to emerge in the early Middle Ages.

The site

Caesar's fortifications. The biggest disappointment is that virtually nothing has been done to help visitors identify the camps, fortlets or lines. Napoleon III had signposts raised where roads crossed the *circonvallation* and *contrevallation*, a few survive; a new broken shield memorial commemorates the battle at the beginning of the D103 by the roundabout on the D905; and that is all. On Mont Auxois there is an orientation table for identifying the surrounding hills – and Napoleon III's giant statue to Vercingetorix.

It is ironic that the decision to undertake the later 1990s excavations was finally provoked when a plan to reconstruct a section of rampart was stopped because the archaeologists did not wish simply to repeat the ARCHEODROME's dramatic full-scale re-creation (see Plate 7, page 142). The problem of course comes down to money and responsibility. Excavations have been carried out on site under the auspices of the Société des Sciences de Semur who maintain both the visitor facilities at Alesia itself and the museum in Alise-Ste-Reine; they do the best they can with very limited resources. The state is not investing in creating the footpaths, reconstructions, panels and new museum essential to bring alive the siege and siege works. Plans have been made for viewing platforms, markers on the hill-top camps, reconstructions in the Laumes Plain, and a renovated museum, but nothing has yet happened (2001). A further irony is that a footpath linking Bibracte with Alesia has been opened. The contrasts are remarkable. Alesia has far more extensive visible remains, an old museum crammed with material and a potential for reconstruction as great, if not greater than Bibracte. Even money to replace the odd tacky cardboard model seems to be absent. Oh to see here a museum a quarter the size of Bibracte's and just some of its re-creations!

The Roman town

Hours:	3 July–3 September	9a.m.–7p.m.
	4 September–1 November, 25 March–2 July	10a.m.–6p.m.

The exposed area open to the public presents one of the largest excavated sites north of Lyon. The Société des Sciences de Semur also provides (free) an excellent pamphlet to guide you round the carefully cordoned area, clearly numbered and interestingly written, and available in English.

The **observation platform** provides an excellent preliminary view.

Roads. The main street (street 1) passes through the town south of the theatre. To the west beyond the excavated area, it eventually curved southwards, near the Vercingetorix statue, and descended the hill. To the east it follows the crest of the hill to the eastern gate. Alesia never achieved a formal quadrangular grid (see streets 2 and 3). The main north–south roads lie to the east, as revealed in aerial photographs of the widest section of the plateau. Sections of road that have survived well show guttering either at the sides or running down the middle.

The **town sanctuary**, like others in Gaul, was not exclusive. Some idea of what gods were worshipped here has been deduced from the sculptural remains: the main temple was associated with Jupiter, but probably derived

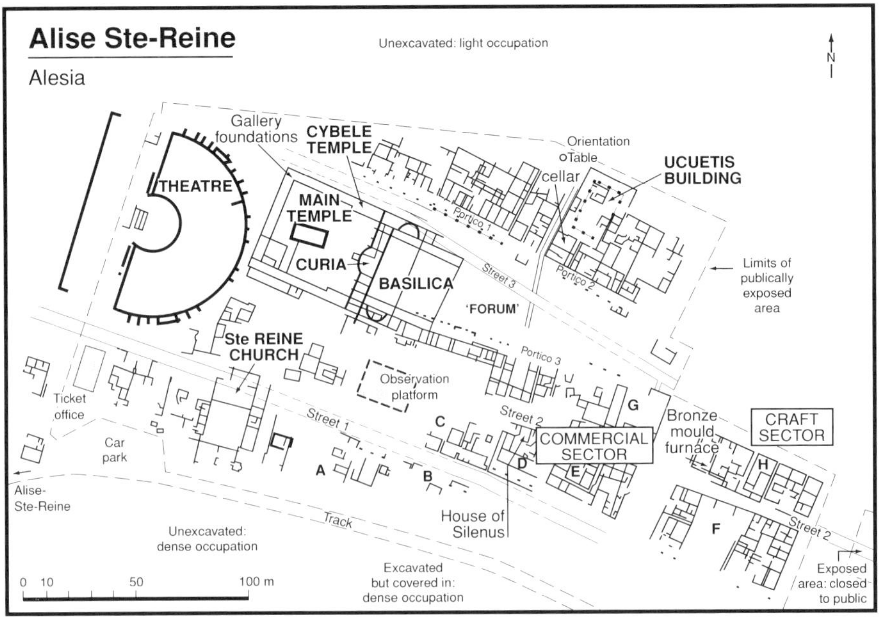

Figure 26 Alise Ste-Reine: the Gallo-Roman town site

from a Gallic sky god. A relief of the Capitoline Triad as a whole (Jupiter with Juno and Minerva) suggests that it might have been extended to include them as well. Other reliefs suggest the sanctuary was also the home of the town's spirit, a goddess of plenty, in one case wearing a crown and a torc. A small temple, little more than a framed altar, could have been her's (its pediment with two cupids is rebuilt in the museum). A temple to Cybele simply provided a home for another powerful mother-goddess, this time from Anatolia.

The **basilica and curia** formed the civil centre of the town. Magistrates (*duumviri*) dispensed justice from the alcoves in the distinctive oblong basilica. The town councillors, the decurions, met in the apsed curia. There were no finds to help indicate the function of any other rooms.

The '**forum**' is now simply a grassed-over trapezoidal area formed by the line of porticoed shops and houses along the south and north sides. Street 3 stopped being a thoroughfare during the second century, simply forming a north-west entrance and blocked off by buildings on the east, beyond which it resumed its path.

The **theatre**. The traces of stage building have been covered in and lie outside the fence. The stage itself was very small and the circle of the orchestra, if extended further, would have almost embraced it. The lack of any stone seating in the *cavea* implies a simple wooden structure. Most performances must have been closely associated with sanctuary and town ceremony rather than any traditional Roman or Greek plays and perhaps included some popular entertainments: animal, even gladiatorial, fights or pantomime stories.

The **Ucuetis building** is the best-preserved structure in Alesia. Stairs (wooden) led down from the forum sidewalk entrance into a two-storied portico of squared stone pillars once covered by a timbered ceiling around a courtyard. A further flight of stairs led down into a cellar, partly cut into rock, in which were found a collection of metalworking tools and a vase inscribed to the divine couple Ucuetis and Bergusia, only known at Alesia. The almost domestic design of the building and the tool finds suggest a guildhall, where many of the town's craftsmen might have come to meet and relax.

The **craft sector**. There were metalworkers in other districts, but the largest concentration was here in *insulae* H and G, and in the partly exposed area closed to the public. The best-preserved remains of workshop houses are in H. Each probably only had enough room for the owner-worker to live, other members of the team coming in from elsewhere to work. Finely finished **cellars** are ubiquitous, serving for storage and for family gods; altars and statuettes have been frequent finds (see similar at BLIESBRUCK).

The **commercial sector** has been identified from two buildings. The cellar in *insula* E with rings and niches designed for amphorae hint at more than personal use, and the variety of goods found in the courtyard house of *insula*

D, named Silenus after the statuette found in its cellar, could easily be that of a prosperous merchant.

Ste Reine church remains were being re-examined at the time of writing. Its position impinging on the town's main street indicates that there was no meaningful traffic left here in the fifth and sixth centuries. This church was abandoned in the early Middle Ages and the saint's relics removed to the monastery by the cemetery, finally ending up in 866 at Flavigny abbey. Medieval Alise-Ste-Reine managed to regain some status for Mont Auxois by linking the saint with a spring in the village, making it a great centre of pilgrimage.

Musée Alésia

Rue de l'Hôpital
21150 Alise-Ste-Reine

Hours:	3 July–3 September	9a.m.–7p.m.
	4 September–1 November, 25 March–2 July	10a.m.–6p.m.

The museum is a shock: like the village it is threadbare in appearance. The adjacent building is available for desperately needed additional space; in 2001 there was no money. Hopefully, you may have the pleasure of seeing a revitalized display.

The entrance room. This contains various reliefs from the sanctuary area, a mixing of Celtic, Graeco-Roman and eastern deities. The most important here is the **Alesia inscription**. Written in Gallic using Latin script, it records that 'Martial, son of Dannotalos, dedicated to Ucuetis this tower [structure] and also with the metalworkers who fashion Ucuetis [the god's name is used here to stand for the bronzemakers' metal] in Alesia.' Imprecisely located in 1839, it is considered to have been built into the walls of the Ucuetis building.

The rear room. The reconstructed **cupids pediment** and the miniaturized votive pots come from the sanctuary and deserve a better context. Past attempts at giving a visual impression of the siege need removing, but Napoleon III's cabinets are charming and though the fine silver cup is a copy, along with the weapons (see PARIS), there is the excellent **appliqué Silenus**. The Christian presence in Alesia is represented by the fourth-century fish-decorated lead plate.

The landing and upstairs rooms. The single most appropriate image for Alesia is the tiny bronze of **the dying Gaul** – surely here is the destruction of independent Gaul embodied by a craftsman living at the site where it took place? Research suggests otherwise. Found in the forum area, it is believed to be a chariot fitting, actually of a well-known Hellenistic type recording the death of a Galatian Gaul of the third century BC. The pottery section contains examples of **grey-black tableware**, using a chemical slip to give a metal-like sheen; the barbotine decoration, using trails of clay like icing, is here used to produce outstanding scenes including Dionysus and Silenus. There are three cases of bronze metalwork and more of iron. Among the bronze fibulae and *phalerae* (horse fittings) note the **vase inscribed to Ucuetis and Bergusia**. Worked bone demonstrates the importance of this material in the life of a small Gallo-Roman town.

Hauteroche Villa

20km east of Alise-Ste-Reine by the D10, down the Oze valley south to Gissey-sur-Flavigny, turn right (south-west) up to the plateau ridge separating the Oze valley from the Ozerain towards Hauteroche and the D9.

By the road at the top of the ridge before descending to Hauteroche, a battered plaque identifies the exposed traces of a few rooms of a medium-sized second-century villa.

ARCHEODROME, Côte d'Or

Re-creation museum site.
www.archeodrome-bourgogne.com
Beaune-Tailly service area, Autoroute du Soleil (A6)
21190 Merceuil

Hours:	July–August	10a.m.–7p.m.
	spring and autumn	10a.m.–6p.m.
	October–March	10a.m.–5p.m. Closed Monday and Tuesday

Motorway parking areas are notorious for their alienation from anything remotely connected with pleasure, but you should not miss one of the most enterprising efforts to communicate archaeological discovery in France.

This 'museum' was the imaginative collaboration of the motorway company and the Burgundy Regional Department of Historical and Prehistoric Antiquities. A winding route (you can listen to a taped description, available in English) takes you through re-creation displays, models, panoramas and panels, all prepared with scholarly precision in a cunningly designed single-storey building. Large windows are deliberately used to look out onto the exterior re-creations of ancient structures, linked to the internal exhibits. Revisions regularly take place, but Iron Age and Gallo-Roman displays still predominate. Roman pottery-making, iron-smelting and casting, barrel-making, lance-throwing and archery competitions have all figured in summer weekend events, but there is little theme park excess even with the tedious, superficial chronoscope and the couple of rather depressing animal enclosures.

Inside the museum building

Prehistoric section. The **Palaeolithic** section has been remodelled to take the visitor (very quickly) through African origins to a number of French sites. The models help identify key changes over time: advanced hunting is implied by driven horses plunging off the Solutré Rock to be butchered at the base, though the panel points out that this is only one possible interpretation of the material. The **Neolithic** simulation of a cooking assemblage and the Ouroux-sur-Saône settlement rather pale before the window view out over the reconstructed Neolithic longhouse. The **Bronze Age** figures only in a rather nondescript metal workshop.

Iron Age Gaul. A recent construction has been the stone passage into a tumulus barrow, modelled on one excavated at Lantilly; a bronze cauldron and a cloaked wax figure animate the early Iron Age eighth-century burial. This naturally leads to the Vix display. A copy of the massive crater peeps from a covering of earth, recalling its discovery in the collapsed mortuary chamber in a tumulus outside the Mont Lassois *oppidum*. It is impressive, but the awesome size and the artistic skill are only obvious in the original (see CHATILLON-SUR-SEINE). Recent work at Mont Beuvray is used to illustrate the emergence of Celtic Gaul with the re-creation of house foundations and a model of the rampart being built using the timber frame, or *murus gallicus*, technique. The main display, though, has refocused away from the Gallic house and farm tools – see now the Gallic farm outside – to transport. There is a full-scale two-wheeled chariot used by the warrior elite, and a *raeda* or four-wheeled cart; note the axle-mounted shock absorbers. A half-size canoe is used to show exploitation of the river network. The violent transformation to the Roman era is portrayed with accurately dressed full-sized figures of two Roman and Gallic soldiers fighting, placed in front of a window looking out on Caesar's siege wall.

The Gallo-Roman period. The transport theme is continued using copies of the LANGRES cart relief and the famous Roman relief from the Calvet Museum, Avignon, illustrating a barge filled with Gallic barrels – naturally a re-created barrel sits behind it. The integration of inside and outside is continued, too, with an evocative re-creation of a typical spring sanctuary surrounded by wooden and stone votive offerings (see DIJON). The many small towns that are a feature of Roman Burgundy are hinted at by the model of a commercial street, based on the excavations at MALAIN; and a whole museum corner is constructed as the wing of a courtyard villa; it is a pity that the farm tools and superb colour aerial photographs of Burgundian sites have been removed; even the small Roman garden needs reviving.

The open-air section

The Neolithic house and shelter. The reconstructions are based on an excavation at Charmoy (Yonne) in 1967 where post-holes of three longhouses and a number of smaller buildings were distinguished, all dated *c.*4000 BC. The shelter has been reconstructed as a barn. This assumes a particular interpretation of longhouse use: as the home of an extended family. An alternative could be a nuclear family sharing with their beasts whilst dependants lived in the small building. Charmoy did not provide conclusive evidence.

The promontory fort and tumulus. Neither the tumulus – a mound of stones – nor the short section of wall and stone huts extend significantly one's appreciation of the later prehistoric period. Only a sense of completion justifies the tumulus, after the earlier and much more exciting visit 'inside', and perhaps it is a help to see just how tiny houses were in the last millennium BC, stressing how much life must have been lived outside, however harsh the weather.

The Gallic farm. This is an attempt to re-create a typical late Iron Age farmstead, consisting of a dwelling, barn and raised granary, based on excavations in the Aisne. All were built scrupulously using Iron Age tool types and techniques, but the buildings are not strictly contemporary, the 'barn' being earlier than the more developed big house and was actually seen as living accommodation by its excavators. Various animals are associated with the farm – and moved into this enclosure in the summer months – including geese, goats and sheep, all traditional breeds selected on the basis of their closeness to the types found in antiquity (see also BLIESBRUCK where a similar re-creation farm focuses on crops).

The Alesia siege works. Despite having stood more than a dozen years (and Caesar's were for the campaign only!), I still find this reconstruction of the Roman siege works brutally dramatic: here you can see why Vercingetorix failed to break out. The ramparts and forward defences re-created here are based on Caesar's own description in the *Gallic Wars*, VII, 63–90. The 1990s excavations showed that nowhere so far examined had all the forward elements he described in one place, though this made them hardly less formidable as the ditches could be wider, also water-filled, and there might be wider zones of outworks.

Ramparts. The bank stands twelve Roman feet (about 3.5m) high, surmounted by a palisade forming a breastwork giving protection to Roman spear throwers, archers, and slingers firing lead shot nicknamed 'glandes' (acorns) by the soldiers. The towers provided even higher platforms; here would be mounted the *scorpiones*, large bolt-firing catapults. *Ditches.* Each is 15 Roman feet (about 4.5m) wide and deep; they would both have slowed any assault on the wall and provided a ready killing area. Generally Roman defensive structures relied on nothing more, as military thinking was consistently offensive. At Alesia, Caesar added further outworks, comparable to barbed wire and mines.

The 'cippi'. The name was a macabre soldiers' pun: 'cippi' means both boundary and tombstones. In front of the ditches are five rows of trenches 5RF deep, dug and filled with sharpened branches that are deliberately entangled with each other.

Plate 7 Caesar's fortifications at Alesia, reconstructed at the Archéodrome. Photograph: James Bromwich.

The 'lilia'. Fire-hardened stakes are secured in the centre of round holes; viewed from above they look like lilies on a pond, but they are set to wound savagely anyone trying to run through them. Note the deliberate offsetting of the eight rows.

The 'stimuli'. Metal spikes are secured in buried wooden blocks. They poke menacingly above ground to slow any attacker at the point where he enters the firing range of the rampart defenders. The name again played on meanings; it was both a name for cattle or slave goads and a sexual term: gruesome, derisive army humour.

Caesar explains how these outer lines were particularly valuable at night, giving time for extra troops to be rushed to the most threatened places. Nor were these additions passive in the strategic sense: they strengthened the line so effectively that even when Vercingetorix made the most persistent efforts to break out, and his men could see the relieving forces fighting beyond the outward-facing ramparts, according to Caesar, they were unable to break through at any point. This failure made the threat of starvation so real that surrender became inevitable.

The *fanum*. A small, square Romano-Celtic temple of a type found widely, not only in Burgundy, but also in the rest of eastern Gaul. It shows the typical square *cella* and surrounding ambulatory. Despite the *cella* being painted with simple fresco work, the reconstruction sadly lacks ambience. Perhaps it is justified by our genuine lack of knowledge of how such temples were actually used.

The cemetery and road. The most surprising and moving experience at the Archéodrome is the final part where you walk along a Roman road by a series of tombstones, recalling the necropolis that lay outside all Gallo-Roman towns. Strangely, the fact that both road and tombs are reproductions seems to matter little – perhaps because these stones are in a recognizable burial context where the grass and trees help evoke a deeper response to the stones' embodiment of people past than they can in a museum where the eye responds much more to the artistic or historical content of gravestones. The originals can be seen at NUITS-ST-GEORGES.

AUTUN, Saône et Loire

Sites and museum.

Augustodunum was a major Roman city, and, excluding Lyon, has more visible Roman remains than anywhere else covered in this book; it also has a small museum packed with interesting material. Some distance from today's French north–south routes, Autun has never recovered its early eminence. In the Middle Ages, the acquisition of the supposed bones of Lazarus brought pilgrims and the superb new Romanesque cathedral of St-Lazare, but did

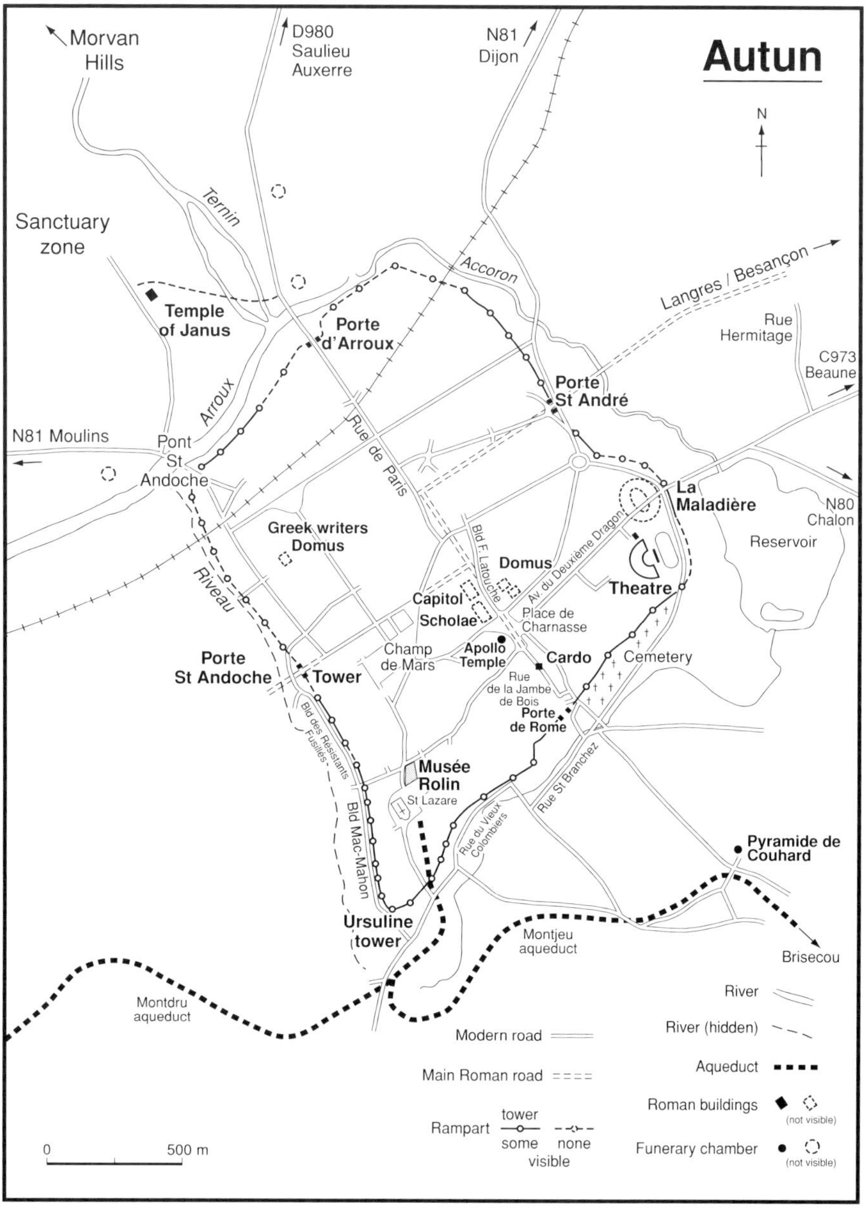

Figure 27 Autun: town plan

little for long-term expansion. Even industrialization has made a marginal impact: locally mined schist, the material for a short-lived oil industry, is almost attractively recalled by the overgrown slag heaps, like inflated prehistoric burial mounds. Autun retains the atmosphere of a provincial town, fortunately now recovering a sense of pride in its oldest heritage.

Prior to the nineteenth century, interest might be expressed, drawings made and finds collected (the majority never to be seen again), but the concept of preservation and a sense of Roman material being part of a living community was absent. Yet while an entire amphitheatre could disappear, gates that might have obstructed the progress of more dynamic cities survived. Here as elsewhere, the Revolution and the encouragement that this gave to new thinking stimulated local societies, dedicated to investigating and understanding the environment. In the 1820s the theatre was explored for the first time, and in 1830 the discovery of the Bellerophon mosaic led to the creation of what became the Musée Rolin to house it. The architectural surveyor, J. Roidot-Deléage, produced a series of fine studies and plans of Roman remains (1872); the archaeologist Harold de Fontenay worked with the historian Anatole de Charmesse to produce the first comprehensive study of Autun (1889). There was a marked decline in interest, except at the theatre site, reaching a nadir during the 1960s–1970s (see also LYON) when modernization justified historical barbarism and extensive Roman finds were not even photographed. The first sign that this could be resisted came when, in 1965, the Musée Rolin managed to save the newly found Anacreon mosaic. In 1984 the municipality finally created an archaeological service led by Alain Rebourg, who established a vibrant, professional and dedicated approach, working closely with the museum. It was a strong foundation for his successors.

Autun sits on a promontory of the Autonois hills, looking out over the plain separating the Morvan hills from the Côte d'Or escarpment. The form was strongly influenced by the river Arroux and two short tributaries: the Accoron, which curled down from the south and flowed into the Arroux to the east of Autun, and the Riveau, on the western side, now hidden underground. Water-meadows still track the Arroux, and on the plain flooding and waterlogged ground must have been common problems in the past.

This 199ha site was chosen by the Romans to be the new capital for the Aedui tribe in about 15 BC, replacing their *oppidum*, Bibracte (see MONT BEUVRAY). Why this site was chosen is still debated. The scale of the sanctuaries to the north beyond the water-meadows could mean that this had been the major religious meeting place of the Aedui and therefore, if a city was to be built at a more convenient site than Bibracte, then close by was a plausible choice. Equally, it has been argued that when Agrippa ordered the main road north from Lyon to be built it naturally came as near as convenient to Mont Beuvray, but the plain was the obvious route for a road from Chalon-sur-Saône to Auxerre and on to Sens, Beauvais and Boulogne. Autun was at the junction with the Langres/Besançon road to Bibracte and subsequently a branching point for roads that followed the Arroux valley or crossed the Loire further north. Some have even argued that the site itself is typical of many military sites; that there must have been a base here in the years after Caesar's victory to support/oversee Rome's chief Gallic ally. No archaeological evidence for a fort has yet been found.

Whatever the reason(s) for this particular site, the political argument for making a major investment in Romanization must have been strong, because it is clear that in the early years this was extensive and must have involved Italian experts. The site was formally laid out with regular blocks alongside the two main roads dividing the city at right angles. The north–south *cardo* took the 'Agrippa' road through the conurbation; however, the slope of the hill prevented an easy east–west *decumanus*, which instead takes a dog-leg through the town. The *insulae*, too, were of uneven sizes to fit the varying widths of the hillside terracing.

The four major roads out of town were given imposing gates, similar in design to those found at the colonies of Nîmes, Narbonne and Augst. The northern Porte d'Arroux and the eastern Porte St André have survived; style strongly suggests that these are Augustan and date from the town's foundation. Almost 6km of rampart was also constructed, together with fifty-four circular turrets and massive semi-circular bastions defending the gates. Although it is difficult to date, it is likely to have been early first century if not part of the foundation programme, but most striking is its very existence: no other *civitas* capital had anything like this. Only colonies normally were given such obvious assertions of Rome's power; even at Lyon, a colony and provincial capital, no firm evidence has been found for an early empire rampart.

Undoubtedly forum, temples, public baths, theatre, the essence of Roman city life everywhere, were also established early in the first century. By AD 21, there seems to have been both a gladiators' training school, and therefore probably an amphitheatre, and more striking still, a 'university', the Maeniana Scholae. Tacitus (*Annals*, III, 43–5) describes how the rebel Aeduan Sacrovir seized young noblemen from all over Gaul being educated here. He goes on to show (*Annals*, XI, 25) that, despite this fresh sign that at least some of the Aedui were not reconciled to Roman rule, twenty-seven years later the Roman Senate was prepared to approve rich Aedui – and only from this tribe – joining them as senators when Claudius pointed out how Romanized the Gauls had become. Pomponius Mela (*De situ orbis*, III, 2), a geographer writing in the 40s, portrays Augustodunum as one of the most opulent cities in Gaul. Implicit in this view is a concept of culture as well. For Romans, to be cultured meant to know Greece: inscriptions were written in Greek here, Greek academics worked here and Autun's nobility were aware of Greek philosophy.

The internal structure of the city and its evolution are still imprecisely known. The exact site of the forum is unknown, but it is now believed to be located under the Centre Hospitalier, west of the Boulevard F. Latouche.

Of Autun's many temples, whether dedicated to Roman or local gods (such as the sanctuary of the obscure Anvallus, recorded only here, but in both Latin and Gallic inscriptions), none has been certainly identified. The sites of three large bath systems are known; none is visible. Fine *domus* have been excavated – in all cases partially – suggesting that in the Flavian period Augustan residences were being replaced with grander buildings, spacious, with integrated gardens, formal peristyles and reception rooms, all finely decorated, characterized by the use of stucco and carved schist. A group of houses to the east of Boulevard F. Latouche, excavated in the 1970s, included the house of Balbius Iassus (after a simple inscription found here), the house of Etui d'Or – the 'gold box' – and the house where the Bellerophon mosaic was found. In the north-west of the town, Rebourg's 1980s excavations in the Rue de la Grille revealed two further fine *domus*, the house of Enseigne (the Sign) and the house of Anacreon or the Greek Writers, after the mosaic found in an enormous reception room. Such houses, modified periodically, peaked in the late second century, as suggested by the mosaics installed then, and remained in use into the later third century at least. Wells have been found widely, but two aqueducts were built, the Montjeu (6.2km), then the Montdru (3.8km). They are undated, but a 'best guess' suggests the first is Flavian. The courses were accurately traced in the nineteenth century, but both are hidden from view. It would be exciting to be able to see the twenty-four underground cascades constructed under Brisecou wood.

Missing is much information on the poorer housing in the city, but it is clear that this was not simply a 'consumer town'. Good evidence of work-shop quarters has been found in both the north-west and south-east of the town and by the Porte St-Andoche, smells, smoke and fire risk putting them on the edge of the town. As well as bone and leather craftsmen, bronze and iron working were clearly important and there is evidence for the manufacture of white earthenware statuettes, made near Porte d'Arroux. The products of the surrounding countryside, including timber and farm produce, in addition to the mining and working of schist, were no doubt controlled from the city.

Barbarian attacks reached Augustodunum from the mid-third century, but it was the creation of the Gallic empire that hurt the city most. The Aedui had supported Postumus (260–68), but at his death they declared for Claudius II. Victorinus (268–70) spent seven months of his short reign besieging the city and taking it, releasing his troops to wreak havoc. An uncertain period followed until Constantius Chlorus appointed his secretary to take charge of the Scholae (*c.*297). Eumenius was a native of Autun whose parents had come from Athens. He invested his own money in reviving the town, was able to persuade Constantine I to visit Autun in 311, and then used his oratory to win the removal of tax arrears and a reduction in taxes to come. The restoration of some of the *domus* and the choice of Augustodunum as a centre for manufacturing armour, mentioned on both a fourth-century inscription and in the *Notitia Dignitatum*, indicates there was some revival at least. Despite finds showing that occupation continued at various sites in the city, it is unlikely that there was a significant population; the ramparts that had been effective for so long in 268 cannot have remained easily defensible. In the cellars and foundations of buildings in a line across the high southern tip of the city have been found architectural blocks and tombstones of early Roman buildings enclosing 10ha. Nothing firmly dates this *castrum* and it could have been erected as an anti-Viking measure in the ninth century, but the most likely context must remain the fourth century when so many other towns and cities were being fortified; surely the site of the bishop's church, baptistery and palace was also the last strongpoint for the Roman state.

The church in Augustodunum showed an early vitality, though there are few remains. Saint Symphorian may be a genuine third-century martyr (he attacked the worship of Cybele in the city) and undoubtedly Reticius, the city's first bishop, participated in councils at both Rome and Arles (313 and 314). But paganism clearly remained significant in the region. Saint Martin came in the 380s and organized the destruction of a pagan sanctuary. Fifth- and sixth-century churches are attested, not firmly identified; the early cathedral could be represented by a crypt, but the only excavated (1976–86) early church is that of St-Pierre l'Estrier. This appears to have been an old villa building next to the late Roman necropolis by the road east to Langres. Made into a church in the fourth century, it went through numerous alterations in the early middle ages. It was here that a poetic Greek-speaking Christian, Pectorios, left his inscribed reflections on the afterlife. Little is known about late Roman Autun's transition into an early medieval town.

The theatre

Avenue du Deuxième Dragon

Using the natural slope has helped preserve the basic form, but quarrying over the centuries prior to 1820, when the municipality bought this 'pasture', has destroyed all of the upper tier and much of the middle, as well as the stage building. Yet the theatre is used in the summer months, and in the winter still makes a good vantage point for spectators watching Autun's football matches on the field beyond. The major excavations by P. Wuilleumier in 1932–38 and the sondages by A. Rebourg in 1984–5 have shown this to be the largest Roman theatre in Gaul. The *cavea* had a diameter wider than any other – 148m – and when complete, its three tiers could have held an estimated 12,000 people. It is recognized as first century, probably Flavian, but even the 1984–5 excavations were unable to come up with a satisfying stratigraphy; it could be a modified earlier building.

In the rear *cavea* are traces of foundations on which stood a two-storey, arcaded structure. The first storey formed a peripheral passage accessible from outside, giving onto the *vomitoria* up and down; the second storey was a

Plate 8 Autun. The largest Roman theatre in Gaul. Photograph: James Bromwich.

Autun

The theatre

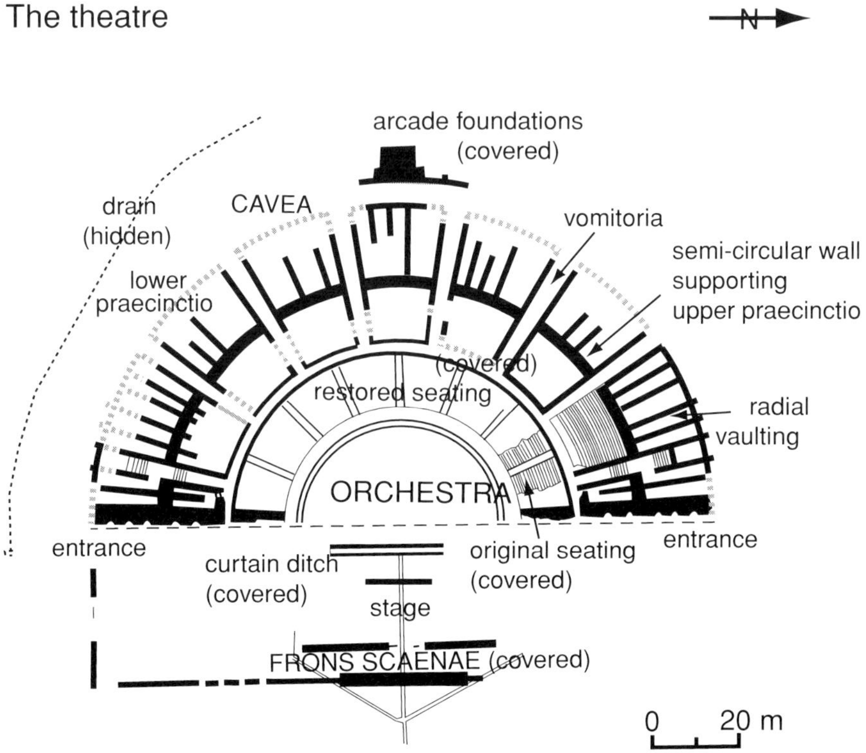

Figure 28 Autun: theatre

classic *porticus*. Remains of the radial walls still retain traces of the vaulting that supported the middle (sixteen rows) and upper tier (twelve rows). Some of the best stonework of *petit appareil* is to be seen in the *vomitoria*. A very thick semi-circular dividing wall not only held the radial walls in place but also carried a *praecinctio* passage. Another *praecinctio* allowed spectators to enter the *lower tier* seating, built on a cement covering over bedrock. These twelve rows are of course reconstructed, largely in the 1930s, but modified in the 1980s for accuracy; the seating originally used sandstone paving. Each wing of the *cavea* was held in place by massive walls. The niches that once may have held statues also functioned as a form of buttressing. The *orchestra* is now grass covered and the *stage building* simply a mound over the foundations.

Decorated house: 'La Maison des Caves Joyaux'

This was constructed in 1845 to house the theatre's caretaker. Built using 'spare' Gallo-Roman stonework, the upper section plaster was covered with ancient and medieval sculpture; most of the reliefs are tombstone figures.

Gates and ramparts

The 6km rampart was about 11m high excluding the crenallation that protected the walkway. It was 2.5m thick with a chalk mortar rubble core and had fine sandstone facing stones – *petit appareil*. The more thinly walled circular towers sat across the rampart 50–100m apart. The rampart was repaired and rebuilt in many places over the following centuries and has been restored in recent years, but parts of Roman construction are still visible. This description starts below the theatre and follows the visible remains north to go round the town.

La Maladière. Some of the distinctive Roman rampart facing stone runs along beside the private La Maladière road, itself below the Rue du Cimetière looking out over the animal park. A semi-circular arch marks a Roman drain exit at the foot of the rampart; it is currently occupied by a pig.

Porte St-André. Built with limestone blocks (*grand appareil*), the eastern gate has two central entrances for carts and two projecting pedestrian passages.

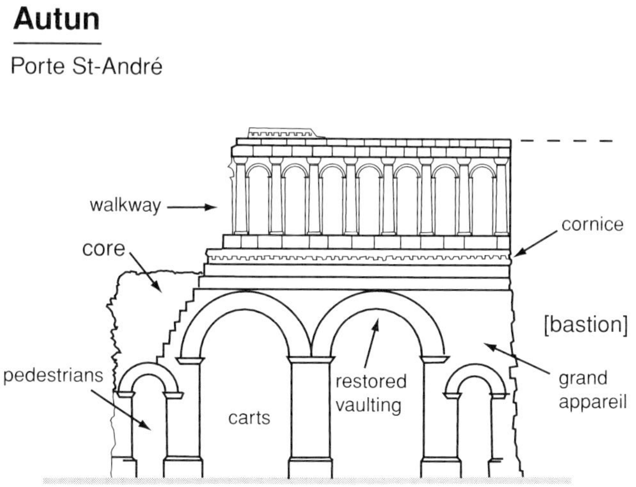

Figure 29 Autun: St-André gate

Above, on top of a cornice, is an arcaded gallery made of sandstone blocks with openings separated by pilasters. A walkway inside suggests the original height of the rampart. On the north, one heavily restored semi-circular bastion owes its survival to becoming first the St-André chapel and subsequently a Protestant church. It is a typical early empire gateway, decorative and, like others, would have had a courtyard on the inner side. The section of rampart visible from the route d'Arnay is largely medieval rebuilding.

Porte d'Arroux. Neither of the north gate's bastions has survived. Although the overall design is obviously similar to that of St-André there are differences: presumably a different team of builders. The dimensions vary slightly, for example, the gateway is deeper and the cart gates are wider. The pedestrian passages do not project and Corinthian, not Doric, capitals top the gallery pilasters. Curiously, both its main gates had a portcullis, as the gateway side grooves show; the St-André gates do not have these and must have had wooden doors. The rampart to the north-east of the gate can be viewed from the footpath by the river, looking back over the market gardens. Along the foot there are a number of small but recognizable sections of Roman facing.

Porte St-Andoche. The western gateway was destroyed in 1584, but excavations in 1850 revealed that its plan was similar to the others. In the Boulevard des Résistants Fusillés, almost opposite the Rue du 19 Mars 1962, the square tower visible above the modern rampart supporting the Institut du St-Sacrement was part of the **southern bastion tower**. There is a mix of original and later *petit appareil* and four-arched windows. Projecting cornerstones hint at the semi-circular frontage that the tower should have had.

South-west rampart and tower remains. Going uphill along the Boulevard des Résistants Fusillés, the first tower after the Rue du 19 Mars 1962 has visible Gallo-Roman foundations, and pieces of Roman walling have been preserved in the following 250m, but most is medieval or modern. More sections on both towers and rampart are visible in Boulevard MacMahon. The best are at the top of the hill, where one tower has at least 2m of *petit appareil*. The Roman circular tower on which the octagonal Ursuline tower was built also has the distinctive stonework.

South-east rampart and tower remains. In the Rue du Vieux Colombier looking up over the gardens, external half-circles of the Roman towers can be seen integrated in the backs of the houses. Scattered Roman stonework is visible in the rampart from the Rue St-Branchez, but the modern bastion by Rue G. Joliet destroyed the Porte de Rome.

Eastern rampart and tower remains. The town-side wall of the cemetery is a continuation of the rampart. The northern half, particularly behind the military burials, has some well-preserved stonework and at the last tower there is solid rubble core and foundations.

Plate 9 Autun. The Porte St-André, a classic early imperial Roman gateway. Photograph: James Bromwich.

Road surface

8 Rue de la Jambe de Bois

By the entrance to the smart residences opposite the Gendarmerie is a 30m section of the *cardo maximus,* the main north–south road that once led down from the Porte de Rome and on to the Arroux gate. The street was 16m wide with gutters and pavements, but exposed here is the 8m-wide road itself. It was made with sandstone foundations of uprights in a herringbone pattern, covered with pebbles and sand and then given the massive red granite surface pavings exposed here. This final version of the road is early fourth-century reconstruction work.

'Temple of Apollo'

Place Charmasse

Hidden behind the houses and only visible down the passages from either the Rue de l'Arquebuse or Rue des Marbres is a 13m-tall piece of Roman masonry made of sandstone *petit appareil* with brick courses. It is slightly curved and is therefore taken to be part of a very large circular structure with a diameter *c.*55m; holes in the masonry seem to be for timber supports implying an external gallery. Undeniably an important public building, it is one of three found alongside the *cardo maximus*, next to a large porticoed structure and then some further heavy foundation. Unfortunately nothing has turned up to confirm the attractive Fontenay/Charmasse (1889) reading of the Eumaneus Panegyric (*PL*, IX, 9, 4), identifying these remains as the temple of Apollo, next to the Scholae and by the Capitol.

Pyramide de Couhard

Chemin de la Cascade

This massive lump, still 10m high and originally far higher, once shone with its white limestone facing (see the parish church of Couhard for its reuse). This was a funeral monument that must have dominated the hillside Roman cemetery overlooking the Agrippa road south to Chalon. It is solid and without a burial chamber – the large hole is a seventeenth-century attempt to find one. A second-century lead tablet was found by the pyramid in the 1970s. It was covered with curses in both Latin and Greek. Was this a memorial to a wealthy but secretly hated professor at the university? The view from here over Autun and the distant Morvan hills is attractive.

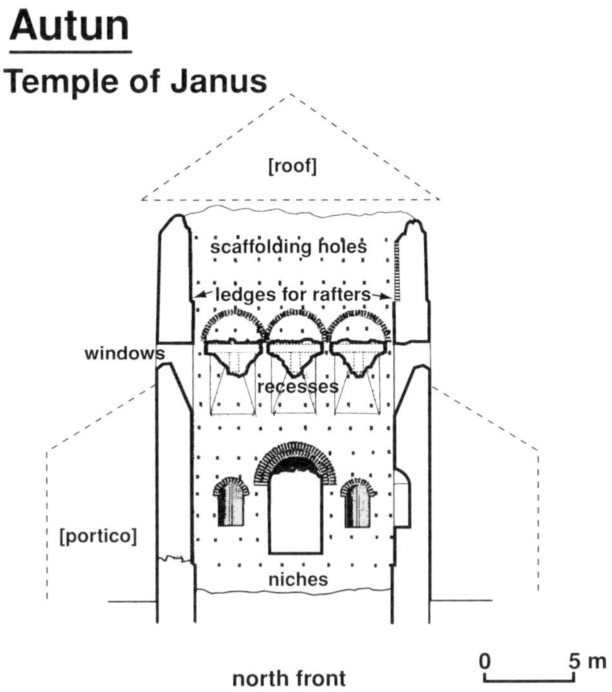

Figure 30 Autun: temple of Janus

'Temple of Janus'

Rue du Pont-St-Andoche

This is the best-known of all *fana*, though the origins for the name 'Janus', the earliest reference coming from the sixteenth century, are obscure and no one has managed a convincing explanation. The flat site, the absence of surrounding buildings and its surviving height (*c.*24m) immediately strike the visitor: this was a massive building, part of a sanctuary area covering many hectares that included other temples and associated buildings together with a large theatre. In the Roman era many pilgrims must have come here and it had perhaps a special significance for the Aedui.

Outside. Though damaged, enough has survived to reconstruct the whole in your mind. The extraordinary scale of the south and west walls makes it easy to see the almost perfect square (16.35 × 16.8m). Certainly we need to reconstruct a roof – pyramid or gable, probably tiled. We also need to remove the large lower 'windows' on both walls: these are really holes dug through after the temple went out of use. The lower external faces, each had four brick-arched niches. Above them are two sets of square holes outlined with brick: twelve lower (and smaller) and six upper holes. These would have held the sloping rafters that supported the roof covering the portico or gallery around the *cella*; traces of the base have been found. Near the top, below the blind arches again defined by bricks, are three triangular openings, once narrow upright rectangular openings covered with a wooden lintel. The evenly spread and much smaller holes were for the constructors' scaffolding.

Inside. The west wall had two large niches, now 'windows', and a smaller curved niche in between, suitable for the statue of the god(s): its central position is taken to imply that the entrance to the *cella* was on the opposite eastern side. On the north wall, the single central niche is still apparent, despite the gouged-out hole, because it has the same double brick arch as the two on the west; it is flanked by two smaller niches. Above, on both walls, the narrow windows, despite the deep recesses below them, must have produced a dim half-light. At a line just above their blind arches, both walls have a narrow shelf that could have supported the vaulting for a ceiling or the rafters for a flat inside roof.

The god(s) worshipped here, the date of construction, and its later abandonment, are all unknown: perhaps when more of the surrounding sanctuary buildings have been excavated some estimates might be made.

Musée Rolin

5 Rue des Bancs
71400 Autun

Hours:	16 April–30 September	9.30a.m.–noon, 2–6p.m; closed Tuesday
	1 October–15 April	10a.m.–noon, 2–4p.m. closed Tuesday
		2.30–5p.m. Sunday all year

The lack of space in the museum has meant that the curators have had to be very selective both in presenting interesting objects and yet giving some sense of the range of finds from a major Roman site. It also means that both the **Reserve Collection** (general) and the **Annexe in St Nicholas** (monumental stonework) have fine material; they like some warning, but both are open to visitors via the desk at the Musée Rolin. Hopefully in the near future, a larger, purpose-built, modern display will help give a better idea of Augustodunum.

The entrance room is an exhibition space as well as an opportunity to buy from the excellent range of postcards. The **sarcophagus** was not found at Autun, but bought by a nineteenth-century bishop and is typical of fine late Roman Arelate marble. Fragments from the second/third century mosaic of Neptune and the decorative decor that surrounded the Bellerophon emblem mosaic are enough to make you aware of the quality of *domus* reception room floors. More striking is the **Greek writers' mosaic**. In 1965 a rushed rescue effort was made to save what was clearly an important panel depicting the sixth-century BC Greek poet **Anacreon** with his lyre; around him are words from two of his poems. In 1990, a more measured excavation by Rebourg revealed another part of the mosaic, this time showing **Metrodorus**, the most famous follower of Epicurus, also with lines from his writing which start 'we are born once only, to be born again is impossible . . .', previously attributed to Epicurus himself; their true author is now known. This mosaic was laid for the admiration of dining guests and not only confirms the quality of mosaic making, but also embodies the city's culture.

Further examples of the decoration of a wealthy *domus* house are the fine marble sculpture, for example the male torso and the head of Venus, and pieces of local **black schist**. This was used to enrich marble flooring and wall facings. It could be cut in architectural patterns or used as an alternative material for suspended rectangular or circular reliefs (*oscilla*); it was even used to make a household shrine (*lararium*). Oysters laid out on a plate in the pottery display may have been for wealthy palates. Autun is a long way from the sea and these are largely unopened; perhaps they were inedible, from a leaking barrel of salt water? Displayed here is a splendid helmet with feather-like decoration. It has been identified as a '**parade helmet**', but it is unlike any other, having a face on the top instead of the normal embossed face visor, and an equally unusual fan neck guard: a commander's review helmet, as one specialist suggested, or is it really from a statue of the warrior goddess Minerva?

The 'daily life' room is packed with interesting articles such as the bronze furniture fitting in the form of an African **acrobat** and the stocky, unromantic bronze **gladiators**. There are white, baked clay figurines, the type mass-produced in Allier, but these were made at a workshop in Autun. Animals, birds, Venus figures, mother-goddesses and chariot racers served the markets for *lararia*, children's toys and sanctuaries in and outside the city. There is not much glass, but two pieces are excellent, a rich **blue carafe** and a **green fish vase**, the applied trails giving the impression of scales and markings. It is to be hoped that the inscribed bobbin weights are on display, which seem more like finds from the local tavern. Two samples: AVE VALE/ BELLA TU – 'Hello, goodbye, you're beautiful' or AVE DOMINA/SITIIO – 'Hello mistress, I'm thirsty'.

The last rooms deal with the gods and human memorials, though the **ducks mosaic** adds a lighter touch. All the elements of the Gallo-Roman religious environment were present in Augustodunum. Celtic traditions continued strongly with the side-saddled goddess Epona well represented; Sucellus the mature hammer god; the triple goddesses with their cornucopia, so typical of the Aedui and Langones; a triple-horned bull; Mercuries, some with his Gallic partner Rosmerta; and local gods, little more than names. There are orthodox Roman gods, such as Jupiter and Diana, but the most striking exhibit here is a rare bronze statuette portraying **Mercury** carrying the busts of a whole pantheon of Graeco-Roman gods on his arms and shoulders: it epitomizes how Roman forms could embody Gallic concepts of multiplication and talismanic reinforcement. The eastern exotic is embodied by the **figurines of Osiris, Isis and Ouchebti** (the servants of the dead); it is easy to forget that during the Roman period ancient Egyptian religious beliefs were still a strong live tradition in the eastern Mediterranean; perhaps the statuettes belonged to households among Autun's Greek inhabitants. Christianity was equally an exotic import at first and the mystical language of **the inscription of Pectoris** could mean an early date – some even suggest the second century – for this Greek adherent. Last, I tend to like **tombstones** that portray the lives of ordinary people; the two that struck me are the simple relief of Sabinianus the shoemaker, hammer-in-hand, his pinking-iron below, and the rare illustration of a woman pouring wine into a tall goblet.

AUXERRE, Yonne

Museum.

Auxerre retained an antiquarian tradition in its approach to archaeology longer than most places; indeed the first serious modern excavation in Auxerre only occurred at the beginning of the 1990s. Until the Vaulabelle parking site dig (1990–92), directed by Annie Bolle, the claim that there had been an important late La Tène occupation on the hill slopes was based on chance finds and first principles: the site looks as though it should have an *oppidum*. Her work showed that at least there were first-century BC houses on this site and therefore a Gallic 'town' was possible, if not proven. The site was certainly attractive for Roman development: a major Roman north–south highway; east–west routes to places such as Entrains and Alesia and an easy crossing over a navigable river (though if there was a bridge it had disappeared by the fifth century).

Gallo-Roman finds had been made in the lower part of the modern town around the Vallan stream since the eighteenth century. However, the Vaulabelle excavation demonstrated that Autessiodurum's development took place in line with that at other urban sites, passing from thatched, timber and clay structures on stone foundations in the Augustan period, to well-built stone houses later, culminating in the luxury dwellings of the second century with cellars and hypocausts. A hint of a public building was found (well-laid *grand appareil*) and an interesting commercial building, interpreted as a covered stockyard. A well, filled with figurines and miniaturized pottery, may have been part of a small sanctuary. Finally, the excavation confirmed that low-lying Auxerre was abandoned in the third century and occupation was then confined, or transferred, to the higher ground, enclosed in a rampart just over 1km long.

Though the rampart was recorded in general outline on ancient maps, between 1830 and 1850 alone eleven towers disappeared. No gates are known and no visible remains have survived. But if the archaeology of late Roman Auxerre is almost non-existent, there is some history, even if based in part on later saints' lives.

Germanus is a classic late Gallo-Roman landowner turned bishop. He was born in the second half of the fourth century of the 'most splendid' family – i.e. owning vast estates in the region – and was clearly intelligent, studying law in Rome to become an advocate in the court of a prefect. He then moved on to a political/military role back in Gaul, maybe as governor of his home region, Lugdunensis IV or, as one source maintained, *ducatus* in charge of all northern Gaul, however shadowy that might have been in reality. In 418 he became bishop of Auxerre. He was considered a powerhouse in the assertion of Christianity in the region and founded a monastery here, but his perspective remained international. He visited Britain twice to combat heresy and even commanded a Romano-British army to victory over barbarian invaders (there were no longer any Roman troops stationed in Britain in 429), returning to Gaul with relics of Saint Alban, the first British saint. He spent his final years in Italy at the imperial court in Ravenna. When he died in 448, his body was brought back for burial at an oratory built outside the ramparts.

Despite antiquarian claims, archaeological evidence for his cathedral, monastery and oratory along with any other fourth-, fifth- or sixth-century churches has not (yet) been found. Attention has focused on **the St-Germain basilica crypt**. It has been claimed that this was the crypt belonging to a new monastic church on the site of his oratory, ordered by Chlotild, the wife of Clovis. However, the claim is based on the suggestion that the core part of the crypt is late fifth/early sixth century: it may have been, but if so, it was entirely replaced by Carolingian masonry. Even a more certainly fifth-century monogrammed paving-stone cannot be directly linked with the crypt, let alone with Saint Germanus: it is first recorded in 1120 and stood under the church altar until 1630! See the cross, and the ninth- and tenth-century wall paintings: they are important, but the crypt does not provide convincing evidence of the palaeo-Christian period.

Archaeological Museum

Abbaye St-Germain
2 Place St-Germain
89000 Auxerre

Hours:	1 June–31 October	10a.m.–6.30p.m.
	1 November–31 December	10a.m.–noon, 2–5.30p.m.
	1 January–31 May	9a.m.–noon, 2–6p.m.

The Iron Age collection draws on finds made in the region. There is a beautiful La Tène **horse from Guerchy**, elongated rather like those found on coins. The most interesting Gallo-Roman material is among the sculpture. There is a delicately carved **classical Mercury** and another much simpler Mercury peering out from the acanthus leaves of a Corinthian capital; tombstones range from the simplistic to the affecting **memorial to Cocilius**, carrying his pet dog. From his neck hangs a *bulla*, an amulet particularly associated with childhood. The first-century **cavalryman** was found in 1789 and given to the museum by Napoleon's valet. Despite the loss of head and legs, it is valuable not simply for the well-balanced swirl of the tunic and decorated horsecloth, but for clearly defining the harness system of straps and phalera, the decorative rings joining the straps, and for suggesting the horns, in front and behind the rider, that held him tightly in his saddle, allowing him to charge into battle rather than trot (as was once thought because of the lack of stirrups).

AVALLON, Yonne

Museum.

Avallon is on the main route linking Autun and Sens and is mentioned as Abello in the third-century Peutinger Table or itinerary for Roman travellers. The spur projecting out by the Cousin river allows it to dominate the area and it is considered to have been a pre-Roman *oppidum*. It would certainly have been an appropriate site for at least late Roman development, and it flourished in the Middle Ages, yet evidence for Gallo-Roman occupation is minimal: there are no visible remains in Avallon. However, the town should be visited, not only because it is attractive today, but also because the museum contains some important Roman sculpture.

Musée de l'Avallonais

Place de la Collégiale
89200 Avallon
Hours: 10a.m.–noon, 2–6p.m. Closed Tuesday

The **Montmarte sculpture** comes from the gallery of a *fanum* at Vault-de-Lugny, 7km north of Avallon, perched on a steep hillside supported by deliberate terracing. The first pieces were discovered in 1822, more were recovered in 1907 and again in 1980–82, when the last attempt was made to research the sanctuary; unfortunately too much had washed down the hill to add any significant details.

The statues here are considered to be products of the same Greek workshop that made the baths façade and Orestes reliefs at SENS (sadly, not so well displayed). Remains of at least a dozen life-size figures were found. The style is pure Graeco-Roman; the material used marble or fine limestone. The three most complete figures are placed in cheaply made alcoves, which disguise rather than enhance their quality. One is a young man, naked bar a strap over one shoulder. He is probably Apollo, though it is now thought that he held a sword in his left hand rather than the more usual bow. Another wears the draped clothes of a priest; he could be the guardian spirit of the sanctuary. The third, on a slightly smaller scale than the others and less certainly restored, should be a young Mars. Other good pieces include a luxuriant, tousle-haired man, rather sombre-faced, set in the 'Alexander' pose, twisted sideways looking up to the heavens. They would all look at home near Pergamon in Asia Minor.

More familiar material in the museum includes a battered Epona on her horse and a fine, richly coloured, late second-century **panelled mosaic** from a local villa, the central panel decorated with a shell, sea creatures, vases and a collared dove, still to be seen around Avallon.

BEAUNE, Côte d'Or

Museums.

Finds from the Bronze Age onwards suggest that there was a pre-Roman settlement taking advantage of a position at an outlet from the valleys of Burgundy onto the Saône plain. When husbanded, it became possible to replace the natural marshland with good agriculture and, of course, vineyards. Certainly an early Roman small town developed here and there is even evidence of Roman land division. The name Beaune derives from the Merovingian 'Beleno Cas', that is the '*castrum* of Belanus', one of the Gallic gods associated with Apollo.

Convincing evidence for a late Roman *castrum* of about 2ha has been found at various places but little is known about it, the last significant section having been destroyed before the end of the nineteenth century. Unmentioned in any ancient sources, it seems to have been an unskilled construction with no more than a 'late Roman' date. As usual, a number of earlier tombstones were used for its foundations and are now in the Museum.

Musée des Beaux Arts

Hôtel de Ville
21200 Beaune
Hours: summer and autumn 2–6p.m.
closed 1 November–31 March

Much of the statuary is battered, but there is a good **Epona**. Her munificence is stressed here, not just by the cornucopia, but also by the foal curled up below her horse. The **'Hermes' relief** is in a poor state, but interesting. Here the central figure of three has three faces, so multiplying his power. On one side an emaciated god offers food to a dog at his feet, on the other is the horned god

Cernunnos, sometimes identified with Mercury/Hermes. Note the rare Gallic inscription from Auxey, a dedication to the goddess Brigindona.

A fine tombstone from Bouilland shows a man holding a purse and goblet wearing a long thick coat for his journey: a typical figure in the region. A well-cut **cornice block** could have decorated a temple; rabbits peep from the foliage – perhaps the team from SENS came down here. A maenad, one of Bacchus' dancing followers, is also likely to come from a temple. Among the small finds, an earthenware **child in swaddling clothes**, found at Les Bolards sanctuary, is the most interesting and important; the child was perhaps sick. There is a good, large, seventh-century Merovingian buckle.

Musée du Vin

Rue d'Enfer
21200 Beaune

Hours:	summer/autumn	9.30a.m.–6p.m.
	1 December–31 March	as above but closed Tuesday

The museum naturally contains references to Roman wine production, but does not provide a coherent picture. A panel records a Constantinian panegyric extolling the delights of the Côtes de Beaune wine, part of a plea to help revive the region after the third-century disasters. A lonely barrel indicates this major Gallic contribution to storing and transporting wine but sadly there is little on Roman wine-making techniques, while wine drinking in the ancient world is limited to presenting Syrian glass cups and a carafe from Brumath (Alsace). An opportunity lost.

BESANCON, Doubs

Remains and museum.
www.besançon.com

The Sequani occupied a swath of territory in the Jura to the west of Geneva. Just how powerful they were in pre-Roman Gaul is not clear: they had defeated the Aedui in 66 BC, but with the help of Germans. However, there are no doubts about Besançon, their key strongpoint. Caesar wrote (*Gallic Wars*, I, 38): 'the river Doubs, winding round in a near perfect circle, surrounds almost the entire *oppidum*, and the gap left by the river, no more than 1,600 feet wide, is closed by a high hill in such a way that on each side the lower slopes come right down to the river bank. A wall encloses this hill, making it into a citadel and linking it with the *oppidum*.' Yet Caesar apparently entered without difficulty, perhaps by the suspected bridge, upstream from Pont Battant. Scattered late Iron Age finds have been made on the eastern side of the site; the western side was damp and marshy, and even during the Gallo-Roman period never fully occupied.

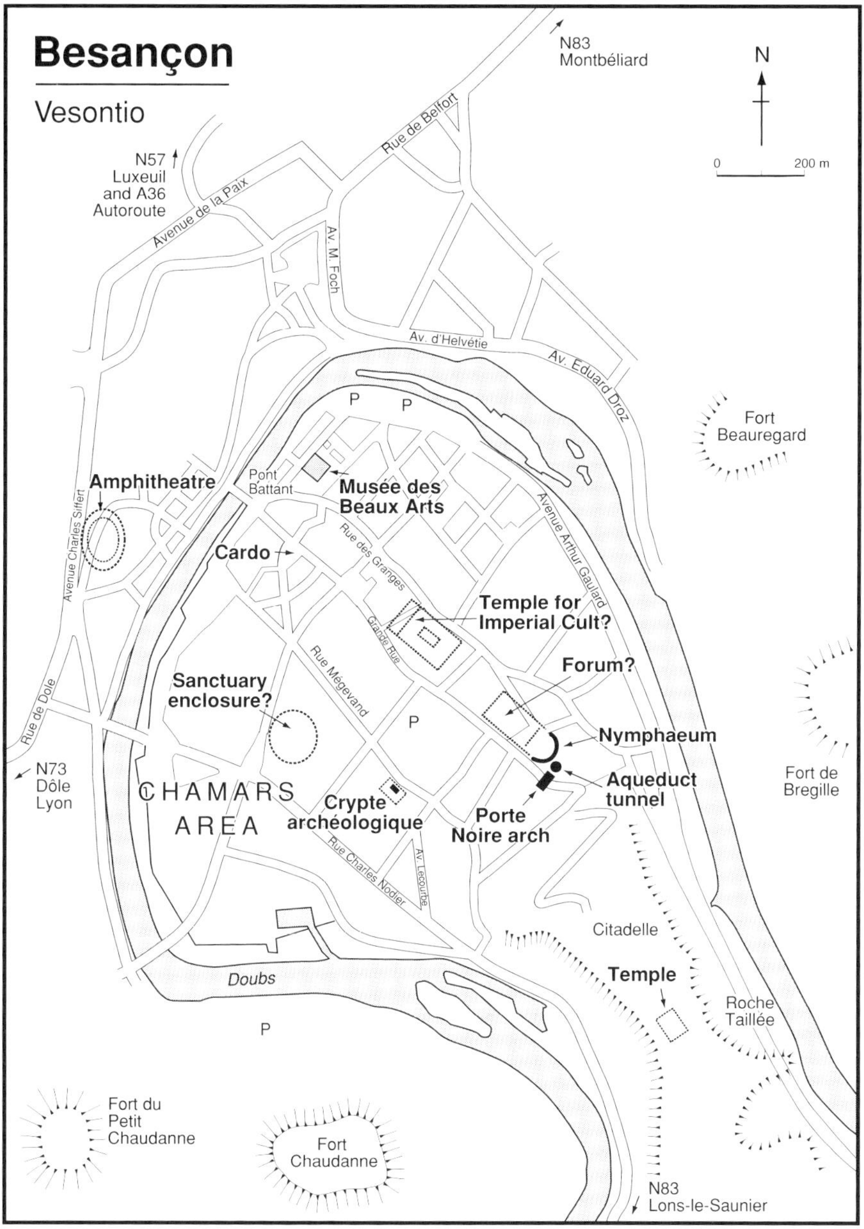

Figure 31 Besançon: town plan

'Vesontio' is most likely to have been named after the tribal God, who was to become the Gallo-Roman Mars Vesontio. Under Augustus the settlement emerged as capital of the Sequani *civitas*. Emperor Domitian (81–96) transferred the *civitas* from Belgica when the new province of Germania Superior was created. Disorders among the Sequani (*SHA*, XXII, 10) led to Marcus Aurelius intervening to settle them, but nothing more is known. Under the late empire, Vesontio became capital of a new, enlarged Maxima Sequanorum that included the territory of the Swiss Raura and Helvetii, but, as Julian described in 360 (*Letters*, 8, To Maximus), though Vesontio's fine buildings still stood, they were outside a shrunken city, little more than the citadel hill. The direct impact of the invasions in both the third and fifth centuries is obscure, but included Alamanni depredations and Burgundian occupation. The beginnings of Christianity here are poorly known, but the first independently attested bishop was Pancharius in 346 and there is little Christian archaeological material, either Roman or early Merovingian.

Though recent work suggests Julio-Claudian growth has been underestimated, most writers have considered the city's greatest prosperity was AD 70–170. It clearly boasted major public buildings, most of which were poorly identified in the nineteenth century from foundations revealed in building work. Two monumental rectangular buildings have been separately identified as the forum and a semi-circular arcade as a nymphaeum. A great circular double wall, built when the city expanded west into the Chamars area, is most likely to have been an exceptionally grand sanctuary enclosure, possibly housing a temple dedicated to Mars Vesontio. There are two suspected theatres on the citadel hillside and an amphitheatre was built in the suburban zone to the west of the Roman bridge. Large public baths, together with public fountains, were supplied by an aqueduct. No doubt many luxury houses also received running water, but the number of wells discovered suggests most inhabitants did not. Probably the last and most permanent of Vesontio's monuments was its triumphal arch.

Porte Noire arch

Grand Rue

Coming up the steep rise that marks the top section of the Grand Rue, once the main Roman *cardo*, the origin for the arch's name becomes obvious: the polluting grime gives it a black veneer only missing where the surface has crumbled away. Seeing large coaches constantly passing through is depressing.

The arch has lost its top section – the attic, the base is buried, and a building partially encloses the eastern pier. The western pier was in such bad shape that in 1825 it had to be restored (rather well, as there was no attempt to re-create Roman reliefs). Nonetheless, Hélène Walter's study, utilizing nineteenth-century moulds made before the effects of pollution became quite so awful, has helped explain much of this not so conventional arch.

Besançon

Porte Noire: north front

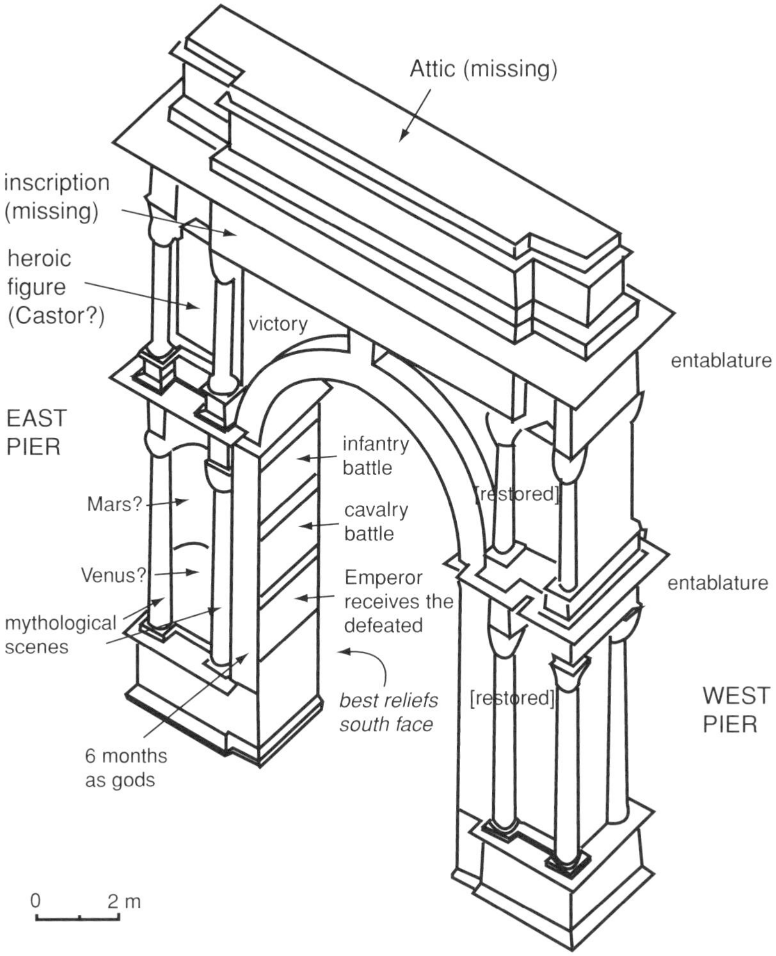

Figure 32 Besançon: Porte Noire arch

The florid, 'baroque' style is later second century, though the desire to cover every possible section of the arch with decorative relief is less usual. So is the split into two tiers with an entablature in the middle and the use of classical myth and hero in so many scenes, apparently eclectic in choice, but perhaps to show the power of gods and heroes (and emperors). Though the overall impact of the arch is clearest on the **north front**, by far the best surviving reliefs are on the **south front**. Here on the eastern pier, the original

Plate 10 Besançon. The Porte Noire, a triumphal arch on the road to the sanctuary. Photograph: James Bromwich.

quality of the relief is most apparent on the **between-column panels** and especially the **outer column**.

No inscription has survived but the **passage decoration** hints at a context. Both sides illustrate military campaigns. On the east, little can be made out. On the west, the reliefs have survived better, particularly the captives, but it is the 'eastern' look of the middle panel, city wall and figure armed with 'Parthian' weapons – bow and arrow – that has led to the proposal that this records the eastern wars of Verus (161–69), while the panels opposite portray the northern campaigns of his 'brother' emperor Marcus Aurelius (161–80). This would then make sense of the two figures on the front face as the Dioscuri: Castor and Pollux, the twin sons of Zeus, semi-divines like 'twin' emperors. The arch would have been constructed in the early 170s to commemorate Marcus Aurelius' role in overcoming the Sequani problem, and his commitment to his recently dead fellow emperor.

A further unconventional touch has been suggested as well. The arch could have marked the beginning of a sacred way up to a temple on top of the citadel hill. A dedication to Mars Vesontio was found there and temple remains survived into the later Middle Ages.

Semi-circular arcade

Square Castan

The park is the creation of Auguste Castan, who excavated here in the 1870s. During the 1860s there had been considerable controversy over exactly what Gallo-Roman buildings stood here. Castan's work gave more precision to the fragments but did not resolve the matter. Finally ruled out were an amphitheatre, a pool for re-creating sea battles and, though he did not admit it, a theatre. He exposed the wide, curving podium with base and top moulding, a large number of pillar drums and capitals, and remains of an entablature. Castan believed an arcade stood on the podium, but could only re-erect it at the side of the new garden; he piled up the remaining fragments in a cross-shaped monument. Interpretation today is divided between a simple decorative exedra and a nymphaeum, where water played in an architectural extravagance. Not enough survives to settle the matter.

He also found evidence of the foundations of another monumental building lower down the hill: a temple? Current thinking suggests that this was the rear of the forum and that what had been considered the forum, the more central Rue Moncey site, is more likely to be an imperial cult site. The difficulty of new excavations – not least the destruction of valuable buildings – prevents sure conclusions.

The aqueduct distribution point (*access via underground passage – but kept locked*). Water from the Acier springs was carried in a 10.26km channel cut into the Doubs valley hillside to a tunnel through the citadel rock (Roche

Taillée, widened and reused in later centuries as a citadel road). Castan explored the final few metres including the *castrum divisiorum*. This was 5m in diameter and had four (lead) pipe exits to carry water to different parts of Vesontio.

Crypte Archéologique

Faculté des Lettres, Institut d'Archéologie building
Rue Mégevand

Ask at Faculty entrance; access during university term. In the 1920s a local bank manager carried out excavations in a park belonging to the bank (subsequently taken over by the university). He dug six rooms of what was clearly a fine *domus*. Later excavation revealed further rooms and a stratigraphy. Rooms 8–9 are Flavian and rooms 1–7 Antonine. Rooms 1–4 were linked together and had mosaic floors; room 5 was empty, whilst room 6 was heated with a hypocaust; room 7 had the finest mosaic but only one corner survives, the rest being sacrificed to the institute of chemistry. The corner of room 8 includes wall painting and a fireplace; room 9 has an excellent black-and-white mosaic and, underneath, the evidence of an earlier first-century building. A small museum exhibits the finds and contrasts the fresco styles of the two periods.

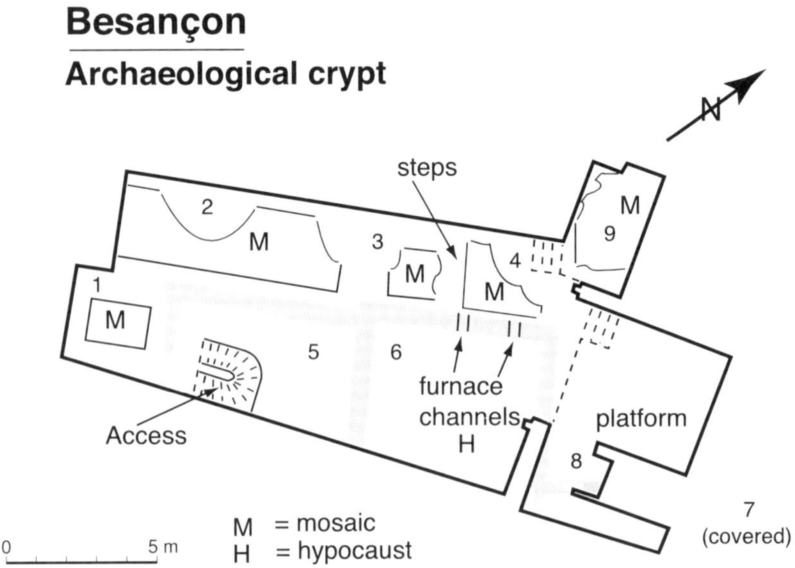

Figure 33 Besançon: archaeological crypt

Pont Battant

The old bridge was replaced in 1953 to allow more traffic; now the need to minimize access means few vehicles use it: too late! All that survives is the foundation of the nearest pier to the old town, now preserved on the embankment. The massive stones, still held by iron clamps secured in place by lead solder, are Roman.

The amphitheatre

(1) Lycée d'Enseignement Professionnel courtyard, Rue Marulaz
(2) Square d'Arènes, Avenue Charles Siffert

Castan first excavated here in the 1880s and Lucien Lerat carried out a 'rescue' dig in 1940, after German soldiers began clearing original walling. He returned again in 1947. This is not an amphitheatre like those at Nîmes or Arles, though it may once have been. With similar dimensions and assuming it had a second floor, it might also have had a first-century date; today, two sections barely hint at its past.

Lycée courtyard. Between buildings, surrounded by a metal fence, a small section of the eastern foundations survives showing the typical cellular structure of the stonework that supported the *cavea* with external pilaster bases and the foot of staircases.

View from the square. From here, look down on the western side where the builders used the Charmont hillside to support the ground floor structure. The 12m-high walling once supported the *cavea* built on the stone cells below. Steps go down the front beside what seems to have been a passage into the arena.

Musée des Beaux Arts et d'Archéologie

1 Place de la Révolution
25000 Besançon
Hours: 9.30a.m.–6p.m. Closed Tuesday

The Iron Age section is drawn from the region and indicates that the Sequani had links beyond Gaul long before the Romans arrived. There are Etruscan bronzes, Campanian pottery and even coins from Emporium (Spain) and Carthage (Africa). The Roman conquest is symbolized dramatically by the wonderful inlaid silver **helmet** – actually the Weisenhau type only came into use during the first century AD. Found in the circular sanctuary, it was probably a pilgrim's gift to Mars-Vesontio.

The richer houses of Vesontio are represented by fragmentary wall paintings, one with an exquisite **white on black wading bird** is the best, and a **bronze faucet** in the shape of a wolf's head, used for tapping into the running water supply. Finds that represent the inhabitants themselves range from a good collection of **fibulae** to bone pins and combs. The large number of loom weights represent both home and workshop activity. The dominance of Lezoux among the sigillata supports the vision of Vesontio at its most vital in the second century. Note the popular lions eating people in the amphitheatre decoration. But the most striking find representing luxury is the very rare first-century **cameo glass jug** depicting a Dionysiac scene at a rural sanctuary, including satyrs, bacchantes, and a Medusa's head.

The most popular small religious **bronzes**, some of which would have been held in sanctuaries, others in the home, are the ubiquitous Mercuries. However, the best bronzes embody an unusually high level of sensitive classical realism, yet with Gallic features. These include a magnificent large **bull** sprouting the magic three horns; an outstandingly detailed **Sucellus**; a seated **youth with an enlarged animal ear**; and the rarely found god of sleep, **Somnus**, wearing a Gallic torc round his neck. The mosaics fit uneasily in another section dedicated to the post-Roman period. The **Neptune mosaic**, found in a 1971 excavation, is large and has an exceptional variety of colour with lively though repetitive horses pulling the god's chariot. Neptune is unsophisticated, clumsy and ill proportioned. There is a varied regional Merovingian collection and a superb **ivory diptych** of the (Byzantine) consul Areobindus opening a session of amphitheatre games in 502. This is from a private collection and was not found in Besançon.

Musée Lapidaire

L'Ancienne Eglise de l'Abbaye St Paul
Place l'Abbaye St Paul
Closed (2000) due to the dilapidated state of the building; it may be re-opened. Enquire at Musée des Beaux Arts et d'Archéologie.

This contains various original architectural fragments from the amphitheatre and the Rue Moncey imperial cult site, and the nineteenth-century moulds of the Porte Noire.

CHALON-SUR-SAONE, Saône et Loire

Museum and ramparts.

The museum breathes traditional display and lacks imagination; the ramparts bear no comparison with those of ANSE, only 100km to the south; yet, this is a place of major interest. Chalon-sur-Saône can claim to be the most important centre for river archaeology in France and it has an outstanding Gallo-Roman collection, significant in a number of ways.

The neighbourhood was occupied since at least the Bronze Age and Strabo (IV, 3, 2) describes the Aeduan settlement of Cabillonum/Chalon as their

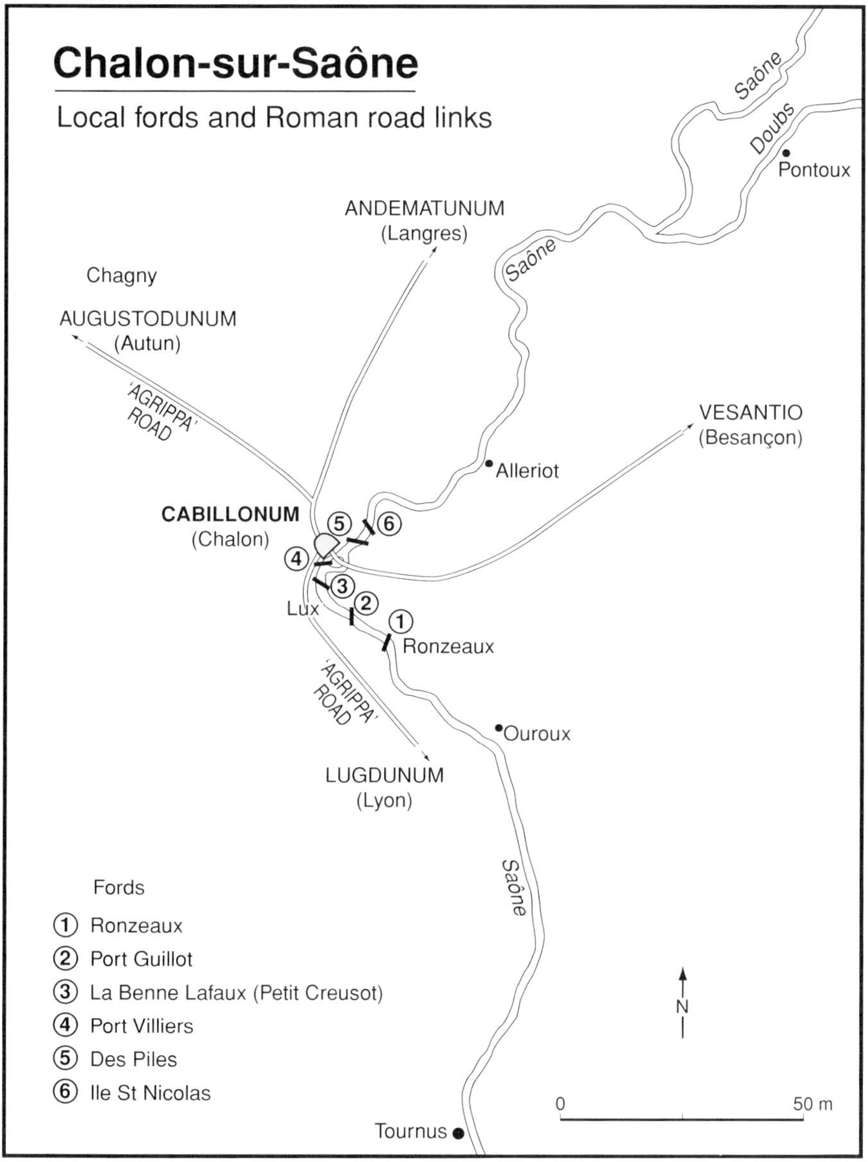

Figure 34 Chalon-sur-Saône: the Saône river and its fords

main city – Bibracte was their political capital and strongpoint. Caesar (*Gallic Wars*, VII, 42 and 90) mentions how there were Roman merchants active at Cabillonum and explains how he based troops here to protect his grain convoys. The discovery of three tombstones recording soldiers in an auxiliary cavalry regiment (*ala*) led to the suggestion that this might imply the continued military occupation of the site through the first century AD, perhaps based on the Ile St Laurent or at Lux.

Roman concern is not surprising: while the Rhône–Saône valley opened up the whole of Gaul to the Mediterranean world (see TRADE AND COMMUNICATIONS), Chalon-sur-Saône was the junction at which many routes from the north coalesced. In addition it was an interchange point for transfer between the river transport of the safe, slow-moving Saône and the road system. Crossing the river was easy too. A high concentration of fords are known: one from Port Villiers across to the Isle St Laurent (and then a short ford across the eastern branch of the river), a further two within 2km upstream, and downstream three fords in less than 5km. Finds show that during the Iron Age the three southern fords were used far more than the others and that these operated as landing stages as well. The Romans continued to use them in this way and Petit Creusot became a major port; two large buildings, interpreted as granaries (*horrea*), were destroyed here when the modern port workings were constructed in 1970.

It seems likely, though excavation has not proved this yet, that the Aeduan settlement was by the southern fords. The Roman *oppidum* – its status is unknown until it became a *civitas* capital in the late empire – developed in the basin on the west bank opposite the Ile St Laurent. From the beginning, its main road or *cardo* was the modern 'Grand Rue'. This suggests that a bridge was planned immediately, although the Villiers ford was strengthened with a ramp to support traffic crossing. In the 1950s two wooden timber piles, strengthened with iron tips, were dredged from the river. In the 1990s a sub-aqua excavation revealed that the old bridge, destroyed in 1944, had indeed been built on Roman stone foundations. Many more oak timbers were found. They protected a 9.3m-long stone pier of which four courses still existed, with iron metal clamps, set in lead, still in place. The scale of first-century AD small finds and the burial grounds on the roads out of the town, especially the large Citadelle cemetery on the Autun road, suggest an active centre, but little precise is known. Cornices and statuary found in the late Roman ramparts suggest public buildings: none is known. The reputation for metalworking in the area and the extensive finds in the Saône suggest many workshops: again, none is known.

The written sources imply the importance of Chalon in the late Roman period. An anonymous panegyric (*PL*, VI, 18, 3) describes Constantine embarking troops here; Ammianus Marcellinus (*History*, XIV, 10, 3 and XV, 11, 11) considered it one of the finest towns in the province of Lugdunensis Prima; the *Notitia Dignitatum* identifies it as the headquarters of the commander of the Saône fleet. The archaeology shows a fortified *civitas* of *c.* 11ha. Typical of the province, the eighteen towers are copied from Autun, around 7m diameter, but with a massive 3.5m-thick rampart. The stretch along the riverside had two projecting sections of rampart each with a tower; it seems plausible that this was where the late Roman river fleet has its quay.

Plate 11 Underwater archaeology in the murky Saône. Photograph: Louis Bonnamour.

The defences failed to stop the Burgundians in the late fifth century and they provided no greater security when the Franks took Chalon in 534. Two things suggest that the town retained its significance during the sixth century. First, it became a bishopric and St-Vincent is believed to have been the episcopal church from the start. Second, when the Merovingian kingdom was divided for a second time, King Guntrum (561–92) with a power base in Orléans chose to build his palace at Chalon, maintaining late Roman administrative forms in his new kingdom of Burgundy.

While the Saône had been heavily used by Roman traffic and its refreshing floods had made it attractive for human settlement and exploitation, its fords, shallows and unpredictability made it less so in the nineteenth century. Iron ships and steam navigation needed a deep and controlled river. Dredging has continued in the twentieth century and the river now runs at least 2.5m higher than it did in the 1840s.

Thanks to Jules Chevrier, the director of the art school and museum, it immediately became clear that the Saône was an archaeological treasure trove. He provided the original core of the Musée Denon's bronze collection by pursuing the dredgers in 1842–4. Further major additions were made following the 1869–70 operations and, off and on, these continued in the twentieth century, with the curators of Chalon's museum, led first by L. Armand Cailliat, then by Louis Bonnamour, ensuring that they obtained the bulk of the finds. In the early 1980s, Bonnamour decided to take the initiative: he organized the first French sub-aqua group dedicated to scientific underwater river research. This has focused on developing appropriate technology for work in the murkiest conditions – for example, sediment penetrators for identifying and recording old river beds – and carrying out planned underwater excavations. The group's work has even been able to throw more light on a key question: why was there so much metalwork in the middle Saône?

There is no single answer. Some artefacts must have been washed in during flooding, when tombs or houses near the river crumbled and their artefacts were carried away by the current; others were lost in harbours when boats sank or packages fell overboard – a number of the finds at the Creusot or Guillot port sites must fit into this category; but it is also clear that a large number of discoveries can be linked to fords. Accidents must have led to the loss of men, horses and wagons, but archaeologists have always been aware that there might be less mundane explanations, especially in Gaul. Were fords where water gods had to be propitiated with gifts? The presence of weapons, especially swords, has traditionally been seen to reflect religious belief from at least the Bronze Age. Significant pre-Roman examples have been found associated with fords, but was this equally so in the Gallo-Roman period? Bonnamour and others are prepared to accept that it was. Roman weaponry was valuable and every effort would have been made to recover it, yet it is still found, supplemented by large amounts of costly bronze tableware. The Gué (ford) de Ouroux excavation revealed in the 1990s that under and between the pavings, placed here during the Gallo-Roman period to make the ford easier, were sealed a bronze casserole, a sword and lance-heads; this could only be deliberate. It is to be hoped that eventually Chalon will create a display that truly celebrates this extended archaeological relationship between the town and its river.

The late Roman ramparts

Rue Edgar Quinet. Two towers and a 30m section of rampart were excavated and cleaned up in the early 1990s. Much of the stonework is medium-sized medieval; even so, the more northerly tower shows two typical Gallo-Roman tile courses and *petit appareil* facing, and along the rampart it rises as high as 5–6m. A further section purely of rough core material lies behind the apse of the cathedral.

Tour de Marcilly. About 20m of robbed-out rampart and tower with some lower *petit appareil* are clearly visible in a yard on the western side of the Passage Marcilly where it meets the Rue l'Ancien Collège.

Tour de Sandon. A heavily restored tower is preserved in the courtyard area between what was 14 Rue du Général Leclerc and the Rue de l'Oratoire. Perhaps there are some original *grand appareil* foundations and *petit appareil* facings here, but not much.

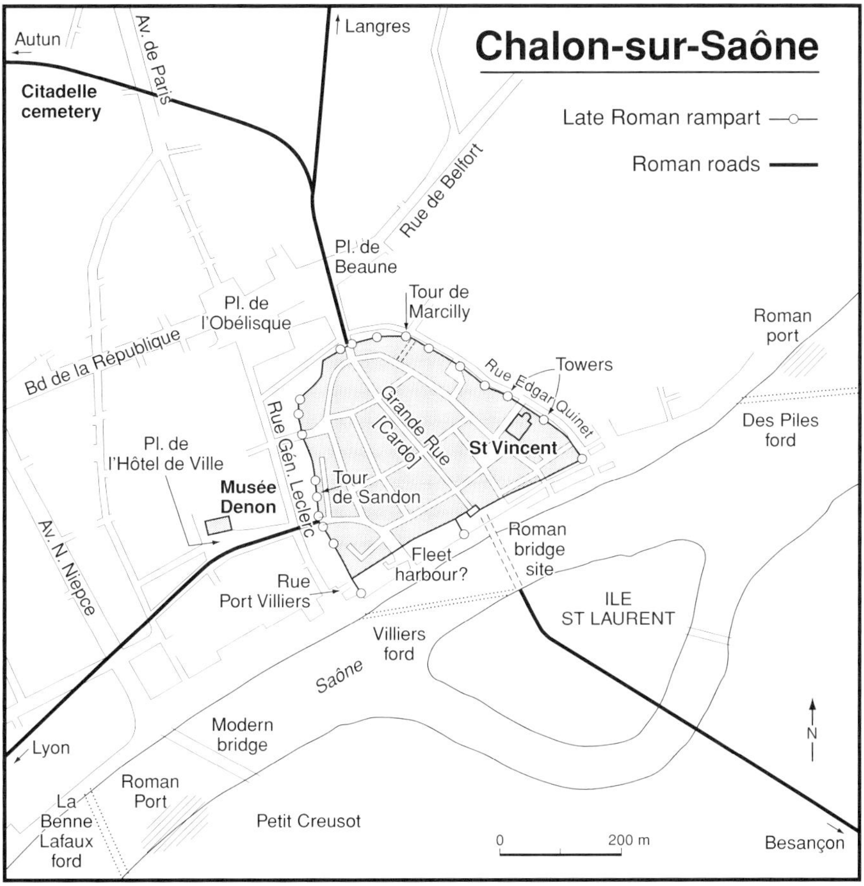

Figure 35 Chalon-sur-Saône: town plan

Port Villiers. In the courtyard behind 4 Rue du Port Villiers, there is a very **small section of rampart** with *grand appareil* foundations *c.*4m long by *c.*4m high.

Musée Denon

Place de l'Hôtel de Ville
71100 Chalon-sur-Saône
Hours: 9.30a.m.–noon, 2–5.30p.m. Closed Tuesday

The fundamentals of good curatorship are here; most things are labelled and the visitor can even see the reserve collection through glass doors. Yet little inspiration has been brought to what is a splendid collection. The stonework is simply lined up and rectangular glass cases filled up with smaller artefacts. Some effort is being made at renewal and the prehistoric and Merovingian rooms were closed at the time of my last visit. It is to be hoped that the Gallo-Roman displays will also be renewed, though the number and importance of new finds from the river Saône makes the case for a new, specialist museum very strong.

Smaller room. This is dominated by the massive statue of a **lion triumphant over a gladiator**. Found in what was later recognized as a cemetery, it probably symbolized the transience of life and stood on a tomb. The gladiator is a 'Thracian': he wears greaves, a skirted, thick leather belt and a feathered helmet; he clutches his short scimitar and kneels on his round shield. There is a small display of the SAINT BOIL **quarry finds**. It is one of the very few exhibits to try to give context, with a large photograph and descriptive panel of the 1970s excavations. There are examples of relief work and cutting tools used, as well as the coin and gold ring hoards found here.

The **cases of weapons** are the most important. Roman **javelins**, the *pila*, have characteristic pyramidal points and long metal shafts, similar to those used by the Roman troops fighting at Alesia. There are a number of Roman **swords**, including the rare long *gladius* found at Boyer in 1993; its importance is in showing the evolution of the Roman sword from the longer general-purpose Republican swords to the short stabbing sword characteristic of the legionary soldier in the first two centuries. Variants of these include 'Mainz' and 'Pompeii' types, the first with a long taper (the waisted look may be deliberate or due to sharpening), the second parallel-edged and with a triangular point. The revival of longer swords in the third and fourth centuries, with examples found at Pontoux and Damerey, is seen as marking the appearance of German recruits in the army and their slashing technique. The first-century AD Alleriot **dagger** is one of the best examples known, a costly addition to a soldier's personal equipment and the kind proud veterans would have chosen to appear on their tombstones; its iron handle is encrusted with silver and the fine iron and wood scabbard inlaid with brass. Last, the **helmets**. The 'Mannheim/Coolus' round-top type seems to me to be strikingly similar to American Second World War examples, except that the lip, rather than being a front peak, is a curl to protect the neck. It is thought the Romans copied the Gauls when they introduced this type during the first century BC. A more specialised piece of equipment is **the *beneficiarius'* lance**. The *beneficiarii* were non-commissioned legionary staff officers and the lance was carried as an insignia of rank rather than as a weapon; the man who owned this one could have been working in a general's or even a governor's office or he could have been on detachment, perhaps as a customs officer. The **stamped tiles** are a reminder that the Eighth Legion was based at Mirabeau (north-west of Dijon) in the 70s and could have had an outpost here when there was concern for Gallic reliability following the Civilis revolt.

Main room. The sculpture and tombstones are not exceptional. An Epona accompanied by a foal, a Mercury as a child, and an army officer on horseback are perhaps the best preserved. Chalon and other local sites have produced mosaic scraps, the usual mix of kitchen and table pottery, white earthenware statuettes and lamps, as well as iron tools and bronze keys. Two cemetery finds are reminders that life could be very short in the Roman period: a beautiful glass bowl accompanied a stillborn baby and a tiny mummified hand still clasps a coin to pay the ferryman for the journey across the Styx.

The people who lived and worked on and by the Saône are recalled by the Severan **lead ingots**, probably lost by rivermen from a holed or overturned boat; the **timber and iron piles** used by Chalon's Roman bridge-builders to provide underwater protection for the buttresses; rarely preserved **eel-pots** used by the river's fishermen. In the port area of Petit Creusot by the Benne Lafaux ford, divers have found **wooden spools**, one with string soaked in resin, **pads of cloth**, also soaked in resin used in caulking, and a spike for working rope. These would be part of the equipment used by shipyard workers for building and repairing boats; perhaps they also once wore the various **leather shoe soles**, including one for a very wide shoe without hobnails – a fashion statement, or did the wearer suffer from a swollen foot caused by gout (often due to preparing syrups in lead containers to flavour wine)?

The reaches of the Saône in the Chalon area have alone produced ninety **bronze vessels** of the Roman era. Those displayed here give a comprehensive picture of the variety of vessels made in this material. It is also possible to see how cooking and eating evolved in the period, with the gradual disappearance of La Tène-style large storage jars (*situlae*) and big cauldrons, used to cook over a fire and linked to a more communal style of life, and their replacement by the jugs and jars, casseroles and sieves, pots and bowls, ladles and spoons more appropriate to a kitchen stove and a villa table. The change in taste and living style of course began before the conquest, as Etruscan, Greek and Italic imports show.

Many of the Gallo-Roman jugs adopted classically based decoration, such as the **jug decorated with Perseus fighting Medusa on the handle base**, while other much simpler jugs have the provincial extended foot handle design. Less usual is the ornate late second-century flat-bottomed **globular pot with a hinged lid** and an arching handle attached to Bacchic faces; a simpler version in iron was found in the same Port Guillot waters. A fine circular **padlock** with chain attached, found in the Doubs at Pontoux, is a reminder that owning expensive metalware demanded security as well. In the final analysis, it was only the power of the emperors and their armies that could provide protection; the damaged **silvered-bronze head of Magnentius** (frontispiece), 350–53, a Gallic usurper with a British mother, symbolizes perhaps their ultimate failure, as it too was found dumped in the river.

Plate 12 Chalon-sur-Saône. Bronze flagon, handle base decoration of Perseus fighting Medusa. Photograph: Louis Bonnamour.

CHAMPAGNOLE, Jura

Museum.

The Combe d'Ain is dominated by **Mont Rivel** (805m). Modern Champagnole is established in the valley to the south-west, but Roman settlement was concentrated on the mountain plateau itself and 3km to the north-east at **St-Germain-en-Montagne**. François Leng undertook modern excavations and sondages at both sites throughout the 1980s and early 1990s. On Mont Rivel a large octagonal, as well as a more common rectangular, *fanum* formed the heart of a 4ha sanctuary with Gallic origins, while at St-Germain there was a small town. Both were at their most vital during the first and second centuries, then abandoned (see also VILLARDS D'HERIA). Small-scale reoccupation occurred in the later third but petered out in the fourth century. They are not simply seen as sites experiencing the same contemporary events, but living a symbiotic existence: St-Germain providing crucial agricultural resources and a commercial road centre for the sanctuary – it may even have been a winter residence for sanctuary workers. A similar relationship is suspected at MONTBRISON (Loire). There are no visible remains.

Late antiquity in the area is represented by the usual cemetery excavations. The two most important are associated with Claude Mercier's founding work at **Monnet-la-ville** and **Crotenay** in the 1960s. The sites perhaps reflect an evolution from a mixed Gallo-Roman/Burgundian environment to a Burgundian-inflected Merovingian world, following the creation of the Burgundian state in the 430s and the acquisition by the Franks at the beginning of the sixth century.

Musée Archéologique

26 Rue Baronne Delort
39300 Champagnole
Hours: July and August only. 2–6p.m. Closed Tuesday

The rooms contain finds from the Gallo-Roman sites and Merovingian graves. There is also a badly damaged medallion mosaic from Tourmont villa, sadly not the magnificent mosaic found in the eighteenth century which made it the most renowned villa in the Jura; despite new excavations in the 1970s, this appears to have been lost for ever.

Apart from evidence of Gallo-Roman daily life, such as wooden platform shoes, it is the barbarian material that is most striking. There is an exceptional collection of **decorative metal**, with which both Burgundian men and women embellished their clothes (usually linen and occasionally embroidered silk). The cemeteries of Monnet-la-ville (fifth and sixth centuries) and Crotenay (sixth and seventh centuries) have provided material ranging through belt buckles and ornamentation, purse clips, pin clips, bracelets and rings, embodying a wide spectrum of metal craft skills, including engraving, punching, gilding and silver damascene work.

CHATILLON-SUR-SEINE, Côte d'Or

IGN 2920 E

Museum and sites.

Musée du Châtillonnais

Maison Philandrier
7 Rue de Bourg
21400 Châtillon-sur-Seine

Hours:	16 June–15 September	9a.m.–noon, 1.30–6p.m.
	16 September–15 November	9a.m.–noon, 2–6p.m. Closed Tuesday
	16 November–31 March	10a.m.–noon, 2–5p.m. Closed Tuesday
	1 April–15 June	9a.m.–noon, 2–6p.m. Closed Tuesday

Châtillon is best known for the magnificent Vix treasure, but this museum has excellent Gallo-Roman exhibits as well, enhanced by its Renaissance building and its modern display techniques: careful placing of material, subtle use of lighting to evoke contexts, aerial photographs and clear, illustrated wall panels and labels. It is one of the best examples of how curators can communicate a belief in their collections.

The Vix treasure

During the Hallstatt Iron Age hill-top settlements together with chariot burials have for some time been seen to show the emergence of small aristocratic states, based of course on the ownership of land, but also on the exploitation of ancient trade routes controlling the distribution of precious commodities beyond the limited areas of production. Mont Lassois overlooks a major route via the Seine valley, between the tin of Cornwall and the Mediterranean world. It was probably control of this trade that enabled their rulers to attract the gifts with which they buried their dead and began the process of familiarization with classical culture before the arrival of the Romans.

At the foot of Mont Lassois by the village of Vix, two large tumuli covering chariot burials were explored in the nineteenth century. A fine **Etruscan tripod and cauldron**, decorated with screeching griffins, were found along with other artefacts displayed here. Fortunately, a smaller tumulus was ignored until 1953 when René Joffroy excavated an untouched mortuary chamber. A glass case with a few wooden slats, sombrely lit, re-creates the actual tomb. The figure of a woman, about 30 years old when she died, lies in the carriage of the dismantled chariot; its four wheels line one side of the tomb. The funereal atmosphere is accentuated by her white dress, but on looking closely we can see how she was covered with jewels: on her dress, seven fibulae; on her arms, two bracelets each; and on her legs, anklets. She wears two necklaces, one amber and hardstones, the other a great **torc of gold**. The torc became a major type of Celtic jewellery, but this is Scythian made on the steppes of Russia, though probably re-exported from the Mediterranean. Delicate winged lions cling to filigree work behind hooves that mark the join with the bulbous ends, themselves decorated with fine chasing. The originals are displayed in wall cases around the room, enabling you to examine them closely.

Dominating everything in the tomb is the biggest **bronze Greek crater** ever found, 1.64m high, decorated with sinister gorgons on the handles and an appliqué frieze of chariots around the neck. It has a perforated lid with a fine statuette at its centre. Joffroy favoured a Greek city in southern Italy while others consider Corinth a more likely source. Further Greek material included a silver bowl and Attic black-figure drinking cups. Perhaps this astounding drinking package, fit for a ruling princess to distribute wine to

Plate 13 Châtillon-sur-Seine. The Vix crater, the largest known Greek bronze (1.64m high). Photograph: Musée du Châtillonnais, Châtillon-sur-Seine.

her followers, was put together in Marseille, the major Greek city in southern France.

The Gallo-Roman collection

The **Nod-sur-Seine mausoleum** remains indicate just how far Romanization had gone among the Gallic elite by the mid-second century AD. Three levelled mausolea were found, decorated with sculptures of the dead in an architectural façade. They stood by an estate perimeter wall overlooking a Roman road: here a family proclaimed its power – just as families did in Rome. Around the mausolea were broken plates and cups with food remains, surely the Roman practice of feasting at the tombs of the dead. Also according to Roman custom, burnt offerings were found inside one mausoleum. Three family heads survive; note especially the beautiful **young woman** with her fashionable hairstyle of coiled plaits.

The material from **Tremblois** presents the typical range of stone offerings found at a healing sanctuary; wooden effigies were available as well, but few were preserved (see DIJON for splendid examples). Small figures, stylized heads and limbs, particularly hands, are clustered together, which achieves a sense of religious devotion, though the sanctuary god is not known. The centrepiece is a statue of a **child carrying a dog**. He wears a knee-length tunic, under a slightly shorter cloak or second tunic. Over his shoulders he is wearing a Gallic hooded cape (*cucullus*), V-necked and seamed down the front with pointed ends. What illness did he suffer, or was it the dog? **Essarois** was another healing sanctuary, with two temples. Apollo Vindonnus is named on inscriptions bringing together the Mediterranean healer and the local god. Another inscribed stone in the shape of a knee was found complete with its classic vow of thanks: V S L M (Votum Solvit Libens Merito or 'in happy and proper fulfilment of my vow'): his prayers had been rewarded, he could walk again. A final and more profane image attracts attention, the sinuous **'Venus' figure** draped against a pillar; it once decorated a nearby villa.

The top floor shows finds from the large *vicus* of Vertillum 23km west-north-west of Châtillon (see VERTAULT). This display presents the twin problems of antiquated excavations and dated presentation. Like a number of small towns, Vertillum seems to have been a significant production centre. Pottery ovens, bone shavings, ingots and iron slag identified some workshops; and tools found suggest that wood, leather and cloth making were equally important. The numerous iron farming tools show the town's blacksmiths must have supplied the region and the number of bone handles suggests a knifemaker at work. There are interesting medical instruments and oculists' ointment stamps. The repellent bronze Bacchus child is of high-quality workmanship while the stone **Matronae** are a classic example of Gallo-Roman triple mother goddesses. The first holds a baby in swaddling clothes, the second has a blanket on her knee open like a scroll and the last carries a bowl and sponge.

Les Sources de Douix

Rue de la Douix

A spring bursts out of the cliffside and fills a pool below the municipal camping site. Underwater exploration in 1993 was followed in 1996 by easier archaeological excavation, when a rockfall blocked the spring. This revealed the earliest known Gallic spring sanctuary with fibulae and votive offerings

Plate 14 Châtillon-sur-Seine. Triple mother goddesses of plenty found at Vertault. Photograph: Musée du Châtillonnais, Châtillon-sur-Seine.

dating from the sixth century. The niche above the pool once held a mother-goddess, not a virgin and child; hairpins were still being thrown in the pool in the eighteenth century.

Mont Lassois

IGN 2920 E

Vix

Seven kilometres north from Châtillon by the N71, then the D118 into the village of Vix. Signposted to Mont Lassois. A parking place at the top, near the Romanesque church of St Marcel, provides an excellent view south, picnic tables and recent orientation panels covering environment and archaeology.

The hill projects out from a line of weathered scarp beside the very young river Seine. Excavation on the hilltop began in 1889, but it was Joffroy's post-war work that revealed the development of the site began in the Neolithic with a major occupation during the Hallstatt and early La Tène periods (*c.*800–450 BC). Small-scale Gallo-Roman occupation followed, which gave way to a large Merovingian cemetery on its slopes. The famous mound tombs lay on the plain below. Aerial photography, geophysical survey and new tomb excavations were carried out in the 1990s.

COMPIERRE, Nièvre

IGN 2623 E
686.9/2247.1

Small town remains.

44km north-east of Nevers by the D977bis to Corbigny, between the villages of St Révérien and Champallement. The site is signposted from St Révérien taking the D140 northwards 2km. A short track from the car park leads to the 'forum' area. There are site panels.

Set in dense woodland, Compierre seems a mysterious and hidden place. This is deceptive: Compierre and its buried treasure have been known for many years. Numerous digs have taken place, remains ruined for ever, finds filling private collections, occasionally still known and kept together, often dispersed and lost for good. French law until 1940 gave no protection to archaeological material. Only in the 1970s did J.B. Devanges bring a professional approach to the site. Yet the forest does give a sense of experiencing the past that few city sites manage.

Compierre was a small Roman town that straggled down the Entrains to Autun road between the Morvan's hilly forests and the plain, ensuring an agricultural mix. Water was available some 3–4m below the sandstone that served as building material. Devanges put together a stratigraphy in the 1970s showing occupation from the first to the fourth centuries. Houses set on low terraces separated by passages lined the main road, which divided into two at the town's centre. Here was a temple in a galleried court, called by the excavators a 'forum'. Typically for a small town, various workshops have been recognized, including a pottery (*c.*150–190), iron and bronze smiths, a boneworker's and a butcher. There was a modest rural theatre, marginally larger than that at ARLEUF.

Temple

The octagonal exterior is rare, though the internal circular shape of the *cella* is found more often. It stands a metre above the surrounding court and though the stairs have gone, the entrance is still clear. When M. Melines excavated here in 1841, he found an altar at the centre, marble facing stones and painted plaster with a vine decor: all gone.

Forum

This irregular area could be the precinct of a temple rather than a market place, but in the north-east corner a building hints at a basilica with its projecting semi-circular wall (though another two semi-circles are enigmatic). Scraps of paving that covered the courtyard are visible. On the lower eastern side were workshops and probably shops at a second-floor level with access from the forum. The discovery in the 1970s excavations of a number of bone handles, pins and ornaments led to the identification of the boneworker's premises. Fragmentary steps indicate a way down from the forum to the lower level where there was a well.

Butcher's house

Devanges's main work was this scrupulous excavation revealing thousands of bones, 80 per cent cattle, the rest sheep, pig and the odd rabbit, piled up in a yard at the back. The butcher probably worked under a portico on the eastern side of his house; a culvert would have allowed the waste to drain away. Inside the house was a meat-smoking oven; the pavings outside the front are worn down: Devanges suggested the butcher had lots of customers. One would have been the boneworker at the forum, another the leather-worker next door. A wooden sandal that must have had leather straps was found in the well between their premises. Beyond his backyard, the concentration of bronze fragments implies that he also had a neighbouring bronze-smith.

Theatre

A poorly marked walk (*c.*600m) leads to little more than a depression on a slope, with fencing preventing access (though the shape can be seen through the wire and trees).

Musée Municipal de Clamecy

Avenue de la République
58500 Clamecy
Hours: 10a.m.–noon; 2–6p.m. Closed Tuesday

30km north. Material found at Compierre since the beginning of the 1970s is normally displayed here, although at the time of writing the archaeological collection was not open to the public.

CORA, Yonne

IGN 2721 E

Late Roman fortifications.

17km north-west of Avallon by the N6, crossing the river to St Moré.

Ammianus (XVI, 2) describes how in 356 his hero Julian was pursuing the Alamanni after they had withdrawn northwards from a raid on Autun. Though Julian chose another and more challenging way north, the obvious route would have been up the 'Agrippa' road to Saulieu and via Cora to Auxerre, as some of his advisers suggested. Like the modern N6, after Avallon the 'Agrippa' used the valley of the Cure. However, at St Moré it avoided the difficult riverside cliff on the east bank by using a ford to cross and then climb north-west over the plateau to join the Yonne valley. In 1897 a 'villa' was found beside the ford, though it is more likely that yards and bath system were part of an official stop for horse changes and accommodation. But the fourth century saw deep barbarian incursions, like the one tackled by Julian, and at some time it was decided to create a strongpoint here. The nearby Villacerre hill was chosen.

Salle d'Exposition

1 Rue de Pont
89270 St Moré

The local society, the Association Cora, has a small display related to the camp, the Roman road and the nearby Merovingian coffin quarry.

Camp de Cora

By Rue de Crot *c.*1km over a level crossing, take the GR13 turning left for Camp de Cora; parking in the Bois de Vosbille. Fifteen minutes signposted walk. On-site panels.

Villacerre is a flat, almost rectilinear promontory site, joined by a narrow isthmus to the main plateau. It was here that Bronze Age occupants first dug a ditch that late Roman troops widened, built up with a ramp on the interior side, and then topped with a rampart. Now 190m long, the rampart survives to over 3m in places. Recent falls show that visitors are not treating it well and when first described in the 1880s it was said to be 270m long. Solid semi-circular towers project out from the 2.7m-wide walls. The stones are roughly cut limestone, but decorated by a horizontal line of stones set in herringbone pattern; it was once whitewashed as well.

Very little is known of the history. Coin finds date from late third to late fourth centuries, while the *Notitia Dignitatum* implies that an irregular troop of Sarmathians may have been based here to protect the approaches to either

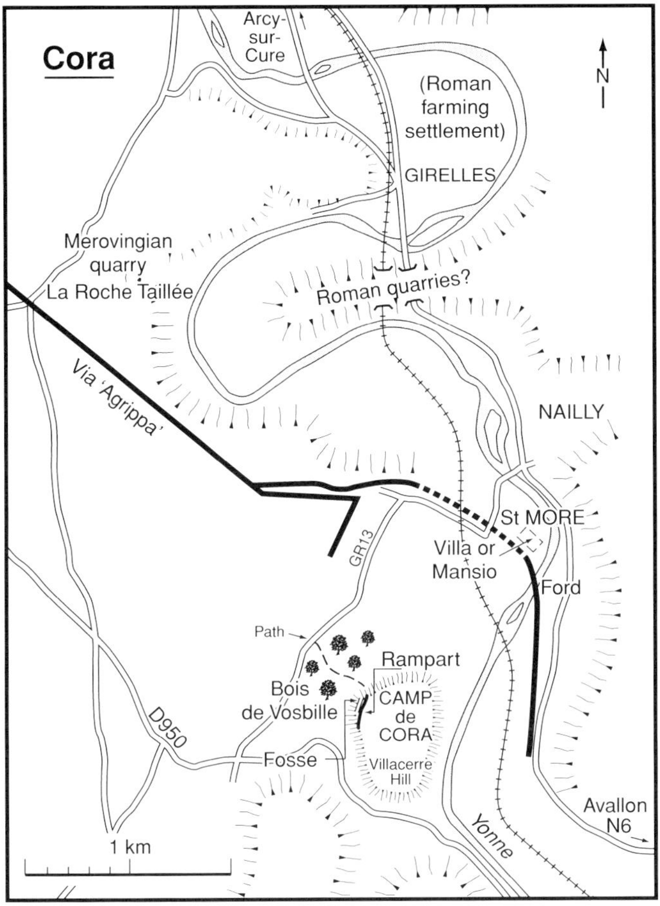

Figure 36 Cora: area map

Paris or Autun. Arrowheads found between the rampart stonework were once interpreted as a Vandal attack in 406 . . .

CUSSY-LA-COLONNE, Saône-et-Loire

IGN 3025 OT
775.1/2230.0

Standing Jupiter Column.

South-east of Arnay-le-Duc 17km by the N6, then the D17 north-east to Cussy-la-Colonne (1km). Passing through the village, at the first junction, left turn for *c.*350m; at the second, right fork for 400m; both are signposted. The elegant grey column then dramatically emerges in the meadows.

Coming upon such an exquisite structure from the past, isolated in the countryside, evokes deep feelings. However much the exploitation of the environment may have changed, grass, trees, cows and birds have not; in that sense the world is the same as it was in the Roman period and we immediately respond to this. Here is the only 'Jupiter' column that has survived standing in its original position (some estimates suggest as many as 150 once stood in eastern Gaul and Roman Germany).

Naturally the column has not stood here unknown and untouched. In 1716, an unsuccessful attempt was made to search for a tomb below; some large cut stones were found and some skeletons scattered around in the area. In 1825 the column was repaired and a capital added, increasing the height from 8.25 to 11.6m; it was then secured by obtrusive metal work and an oval enclosure with a dedication to Charles X.

A four-sided base supports an octagonal pedestal. Each alcove in the octagon has a very weathered figure of a god; they are not easy to identify. Juno is the clearest: she holds a sceptre in her left hand, is veiled and has a peacock at her feet. Following the rest round to your right, next to Juno is Jupiter, sceptre in his right hand. The third is unrecognizable, even as a male or female; perhaps it is Apollo, with an altar on his left that might have supported a lyre. The fourth is equally puzzling: Venus? A nymph? The fifth, a semi-nude figure, may be Diana. The sixth has been interpreted as either Hercules, in which case he carries a club in his right hand, or Mercury, in which case it is a purse (as a god of travellers and merchants looking after their money). On the seventh a beard has been seen on the figure's face; he could be Saturn or Vulcan. Finally a helmeted god, perhaps Mars, but the pose and dress seem feminine; Minerva would be more likely.

The lower part of the column itself is decorated with an attractive diamond pattern filled with foliage and above this overlapping scallop shapes that can be seen as leaves. Sadly, the crowning point of the column is absent: on the basis of many other examples removed to museums, it would have been a triumphant rider crushing an arched-back giant with serpent-like legs. He is widely seen as Jupiter. (The finest examples in France can be seen in METZ and at EPINAL.)

Nothing similar is known in the Mediterranean world. Jupiter as a sky god riding a horse is a Celtic image. So is the holy tree – and the column with its decor certainly recalls that in stone form. Yet the forms are not Celtic: the gods depicted are Roman; the single standing column is found widely in Italy; the Jupiter figure follows a standard Roman image of the triumphant cavalryman; even the agonized broken-backed giant looks back to Hellenistic forms – particularly the gods crushing giants on the Pergamon frieze. The discovery of Antonine coins under the monument and the general

Plate 15 Cussy-la-Colonne. The column, once crowned with Jupiter triumphing over a giant, is still striking in its solitary rural splendour. Photograph: James Bromwich.

dating of other examples suggests these pillars were being put up in the late second and third centuries. They perhaps show how, at this date, Celtic ideas were being clothed more and more in Roman imagery.

Nor would it have stood alone in the countryside. Most are considered to have been erected in sanctuaries and surely it was the same at Cussy. The existence of a local villa might suggest that an important landowner paid for the column and a complex around it – the remains of which were touched on by the eighteenth-century diggers – so demonstrating his Gallo-Roman pride, status and power. As Jupiter was the ruler of the gods, it could be also taken as his expression of loyalty to the emperor. However, recent aerial photographs show that the villa was part of a wider settlement and therefore this could as easily represent a wider expression of faith.

DIJON, Côte d'Or

Museum site.

Gregory of Tours visited Castrum Divionense in the sixth century and was very impressed by its fine rampart and the rich surrounding land. Old inhabitants told him that the walls were ordered by Aurelian (270–5). Archaeology has confirmed that a typical late Roman circuit existed here enclosing 11ha with 1,200m of walling, numerous towers and four gates. The early Roman settlement has proved more elusive. For a time it was even argued that populations, along with suitable stone blocks to build the rampart, were transferred here from the *vici* at Malain and Beaune. The modern excavation of a large cemetery filled with first- and second-century cremations rules this out. Further finds hint at a small core of concentrated settlement to the east of the Place de la Libération, surrounded by a suburban community of workshops, farms and vineyards. In addition, the nearby highway from Chalon to Langres and the navigable river Ouche provided opportunities for distribution and services for travellers, factors that would also explain the decision to fortify the site. Subsequently, the growth of the town was helped by the decision of the bishop of Langres to make Dijon his residence.

Musée Archéologique

5 Rue du Docteur-Maret
21033 Dijon

Hours:	1 June–31 September	10a.m.–8p.m. Closed Tuesday
	1 October–31 May	9a.m.–noon, 2–6p.m.

The abbey of St Bénigne recalls Benignus, a supposed local martyr under Aurelian. A sixth-century bishop constructed a tomb and church dedicated to the saint. The museum is housed on three floors of the eleventh- and thirteenth-century abbey buildings: they are beautiful. The Gallo-Roman collection is excellent. Yet I hesitate: to my eyes modernization has weakened rather than improved the display.

The cellar (Level 0)

The exceptional finds in the museum are the **300 wooden votive offerings** excavated in 1963–7 at SOURCES DE LA SEINE. Abandoned in the late Roman period, the spring washed alluvium down the slopes, sealing and preserving them. They range from thin, tall figures (often 80cm high) to torsos with hearts, lungs, intestines revealed diagrammatically; also included are arms, legs and feet, few of which are more than minimally carved; horses and cattle (it is unclear whether for healing or for sacrifice); heads, largely schematic in shape, with angular surfaces and globular or slash eyes; even a baby in swaddling clothes. The large number of heads illustrates the Gallic concept that they embody the person; the small number of multi-heads may point towards some special ritual, but equally possibly, craftsmen mass-produced heads that were never separated. They are generally crudely made from local oak, clearly for customers more interested in indicating their problems to the healing god Sequana than in reproducing Roman concepts of realism.

Also found at the site were a number of wooden plaques, once painted and probably written on, and the more widely found stone statuettes. Bronze votive sheets are cut to indicate eyes while some offerings focus on genitals, but the stress seems to have been towards general healing rather than eye treatment or fertility problems. The figures with strange discs secured to their chests, and one carrying a ball or fruit in his hand, hint perhaps at the rituals of the site. A **bronze statuette of Sequana**, the river spirit herself, has also survived. Much more classical in style, she stands rigidly on the deck of her duck-prowed boat. She needs, indeed the whole display needs, some sense of context: the mystical and sacred aspects of a healing goddess and her sanctuary are missing and neither the lighting nor the open racks for the wooden offerings provide anything but a dry and formal setting (see SENLIS for how it can be done).

The **Mavilly pillar** came to Dijon via Mavilly parish church (where it was used as a font), and the château park at Savigny-lès-Beaune, where it stood from 1768 to 1975, accounting for its worn state. All four faces are decorated with gods, some Roman, like Neptune, holding a dolphin, or Jupiter, sceptre in hand and eagle at his feet. However, there are strong Gallic elements, especially in a lower-face figure of a mailed warrior holding a shield, a woman resting her hand on his shoulder. This cannot simply be the classical Mars and Venus as his shield is clearly of the late Iron Age type while beside him there is a snake with a ram's head. Despite his warlike appearance, is he really the Gallic therapeutic Mars, fighting here against illness while his consort symbolizes caring? For some this relief is the key that Mavilly was once a healing sanctuary. Another curious seated figure has a bird (often associated with healing) on his left shoulder, with a child covering his eyes – could it indicate a sanctuary specializing in eye treatments?

Dijon's rampart foundations, the cemeteries and other Côte d'Or sites have provided the museum with an excellent collection of tombstone reliefs. Some are barely more than home-made memorials, scratched outlines or simple circle heads on square bodies, but many are craftsman-made. Here are the more prosperous farmers and traders of the Aedui, in their heavy tunics and cloaks, the men in particular looking well fed and reassuringly familiar; they would not look out of place as medieval merchants a thousand years later. One beautifully cut relief shows a stocky man, in hooded cloak, identified as **'a horse dealer'**, behind two young horses led by a man with a whip. Another shows **butchers at work**, a great carcass hanging between two young men with skinning blades in their hands. They wear short Gallic coats secured with waistbands.

The magnificent relief, **'the wine merchant's shop'**, comes from Til-Châtel, 25km north-east of Dijon, a way station on the Chalon–Langres Roman road, probably Peutinger's Tilena. This was only 3.5km from Lux, the transfer port for goods travelling to and from the Saône. It must have been a busy place for travellers and tradespeople. Although only two blocks have survived, they give a vivid picture of roadside shops. The full-scale reproduction of the scene seems unnecessary excess and adds very little to what can be got from a careful look at the relief itself. On the left, a customer holds a jar under a high counter; the shopkeeper holds two jugs, pouring one down a funnel, apparently built into the counter; a bowl catches spillages on the floor. Behind him hang his set of graded jugs and on the right of the counter is possibly a rack of tasting glasses. Next to the wine merchant is a butcher's: pigs' heads and sausages hang from the ceiling and a child works at a table behind a barrel. Beyond are hanging sacks; a grain store? The relief must record the proud owner's income-producing properties.

The upper floor (Level 2)

Prehistoric. The major finds include the Bronze Age **Blanot gold** jewellery treasure (tastelessly displayed) and material from the late Bronze Age and Hallstatt hillfort site at Etaules.

Gallo-Roman. The general display includes household equipment, agricultural tools, cart fittings, hipposandals and pottery from various major and minor sites in the Côte d'Or. Other acquisitions continue the religious theme of the basement exhibits. An Epona, more classical than usual, stretches out languidly along her horse and there is the Moux **god with birds**, moustached and wearing Gallic breeches, with two massive ravens sitting on his shoulders, holding a billhook and fruit in his cloak: he is taken to be a god

Plate 16 Dijon. Funeral relief illustrating a wine merchant's shop. Photograph: Musée Archéologique.

of plenty. Another image stressing munificence is an archetypal **three mother-goddesses** from Alesia, traces of red paint show that they were once brightly painted; from Sainte-Sabine come models of children in swaddling clothes (see also BEAUNE), suggesting there was a sanctuary here specializing in cures for children.

The Mithraic temple material from **Les Bolards** (see NUITS-ST-GEORGES) is given a small dark corner of its own. A private collection from long ago supplied the fine torchbearer, lion and the small column decorated with oak leaves and acorns. Another display focuses on finds from the town of **Mediolanum**, 22km west of Dijon. This was a major urban site in the Ouche valley but abandoned in the third century and superseded by Dijon in late antiquity (see MALAIN). Among the general material the **stone table foot**, decorated with unrealistic adolescent girls wearing only necklaces and arm bracelets, is quite unlike the classical forms found in Italy. It contrasts well with the modest but more classical **Spring goddess** holding her bowl.

In the 1980s both the residence and farm buildings of the well-preserved **Selongey villa** were excavated. Exhibits, arranged around a model of the excavations, include remains of a fragmentary **ivory casket**, inlay and cameo gems and a silvered bronze plate. Unexpected was the corroded military equipment; in addition, there was horse harnessing found in one of the bath's rooms. The equipment cannot be precisely dated. Did a veteran from the Rhineland come to Selongey in the second century as an estate manager? Did a cavalry unit use Selongey in the third century before it was destroyed in a big fire?

Merovingian. Regional cemetery excavations have produced some fine aviform, cruciform and animal fibulae as well as Burgundian and Frankish belt buckles and weapons. The sarcophagi by the museum entrance are largely seventh century.

Musée François Rude

8 Rue Vaillant
21000 Dijon

Hours:	1 June–31 October	10a.m.–noon, 2–5.45p.m. Closed Tuesday
	1 October–31 May	ask at Musée des Beaux Arts

The cellar area of this deconsecrated church, used to display samples of Rude's *Arc de triomphe* dramatics, contains the only visible remains of Dijon's late Roman rampart. Its foundations show the widespread use of re-employed architectural and cemetery stone blocks.

L'Hôtel de Vesvrottes

26 Rue du Palais

Behind the Place de la Révolution, this rich burgher's house presents a façade that initially seems typical of the Renaissance, until you look carefully and see that the decoration is in fact reused Gallo-Roman tombstone material found by the owner. Note the fine shell alcoves, figures dressed in togas and the Roman she-wolf that once decorated the tombs of great Aeduan landowning families.

ESCOLIVES-STE-CAMILLE, Yonne

Excavations.
Signposted west off the N6, 10km south of Auxerre. About 300m along the road, entry by a watermill.

Hours:	1 April–30 September	9a.m.–noon, 2–6p.m.
	1 October–31 March	10a.m.–noon, 2–4p.m, Closed Monday and Tuesday

In 1955 the fortuitous find of a Merovingian burial ground stimulated Raymond Kapps to explore further, leading him to begin a life's work excavating the extensive Gallo-Roman baths, courtyard and the multiple rooms around it. From 1983 the Prosts took over, and, most recently, P. Laurent had been working here – until the funding ran out in the mid-1990s. The results have been impressive, but with many questions unresolved.

The position is a typical one for a settlement, set at the spring line where the Yonne plain reaches the sharp slope up to the limestone plateau. The powerful Creusot spring provided water for the baths and later drove the water

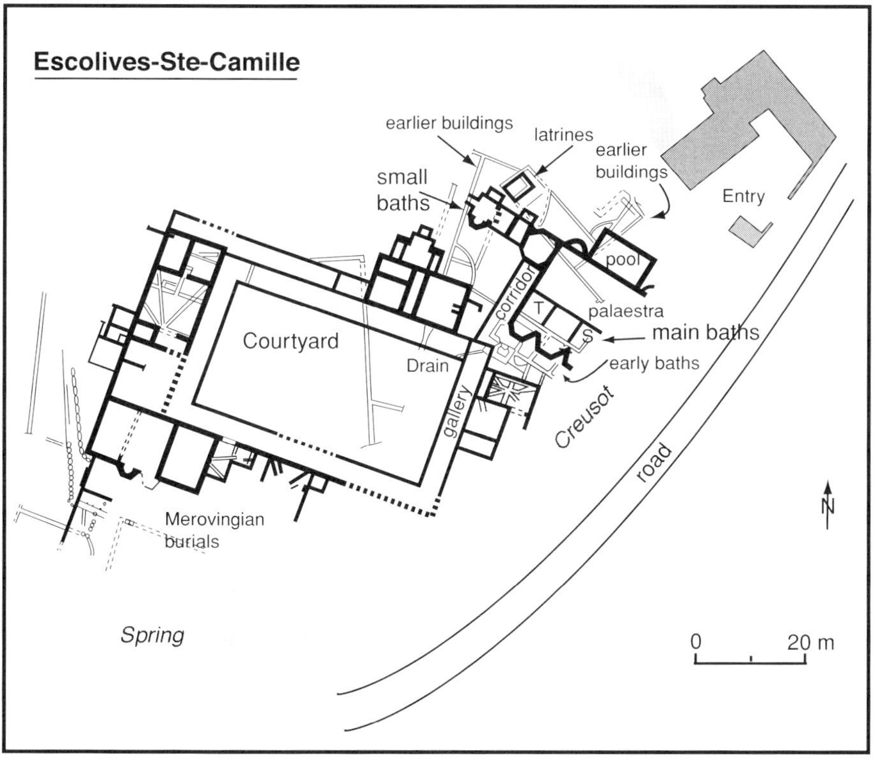

Figure 37 Escolives-Ste-Camille: site plan

mill. Kapps distinguished three major phases of building on different alignments: an early farm or 'villa rustica', a much grander building around a courtyard, and a major modification involving a double bath system linked to the courtyard by a corridor; more recent stratigraphic work suggests that the sequence, at least in the baths area, went through at least eight remodellings. The courtyard was built before the end of the first century and the final most extensive bath system is fourth century. Evidence of fire on the western side of the site suggests that it was abandoned at the end of the fourth century.

But what has been found? A luxurious villa appropriate for a great landowner? The numerous rooms, some large and heated, overlooking the courtyard could have been for dining or reception, and seem strongly to support this interpretation. However, the short distance from the 'Agrippa' road – and its heavy use between the major cities of Sens and Autun – could make this a particularly sumptuous staging post. Or was this really a sanctuary? Is the courtyard a precinct and the bath system for pilgrims? A statuette dedicated to Rosmerta has been found and two four-sided pillar bases decorated with gods, one of which may have been part of a Jupiter column. The magnificent reliefs on display in the depot, found reused in the fourth-century baths, could be interpreted as part of previous baths (see SENS) or appropriate for a religious building. Do the remains revealed so far form part of a much larger settlement? Surface finds and sondages suggest that occupation covered at least 8ha. Or maybe, in part at least, the wrong question is being posed here. This is a site inhabited over four centuries, very incompletely excavated, with many of the rooms found imprecisely identified. Could it have evolved and changed its function over time? Perhaps the more considered reflections of full-scale publication and renewed excavation will provide a clearer picture.

The exposed remains

Tin roofing protects the walls, which are currently being consolidated. A central track takes the visitor along the path of the original corridor joining the baths to the courtyard. The **latrines** lack only the seats that would have rested on the missing upper walls. A stand for the users' cleaning brushes (no paper then) still survives on one side. The **small baths system** was probably reserved for women: pins and jewellery were found here and not in the other bathrooms. To the east is the **large baths system**. Here there is a cold plunge pool and a swimming pool on one side of an open paved area: this could have been a *palaestra* where people could exercise. On the other side of the *palaestra* were a line of hot rooms: the first was possibly a *tepidarium* with a plunge bath, the second a *caldarium* – hot wet heat; and the last, half washed away by the Creusot, was probably a *sudatorium* or hot dry heat room. Beyond lie a series of **earlier and smaller bathing rooms**, themselves repaired and reshaped as well as partially built over by the fourth-century system. All have drains not simply to carry away water from the baths but also to control the constant problem of water seepage from the spring.

The **courtyard** was probably surrounded by a portico or gallery sitting on the parallel walls, sections of which are exposed; note the semi-circular arch that covered a drain under the court. On the **east side**, two large rooms, the first with a corridor-type hypocaust (fourth century) and the second (earlier) with a depleted brick pillar hypocaust floor: reception rooms, but for a villa, pilgrims' and/or travellers' rest? Smaller rooms could have been used for sleeping. On the **west side**, another complex of rooms, split by a narrow corridor, includes two more large rooms, one heated, and a number of smaller chambers.

The unexposed remains

The rest of the court is clearly defined by grey gravel; where the rooms beyond have been excavated, there are coverings. More than twenty rooms had painted plaster walls and seventeen had evidence of marble facings; mosaic tesserae suggest that floors were also of a high quality. The sheer size of the building is impressive.

The depot museum

Lots of keys (possessions of the wealthy? overnight security? sanctuary treasures?), a couple of pavings marked for playing Roman draughts, pottery, pins and jewellery fill simple cases. The seventh-century Merovingian coffins and the associated grave goods are in another corner. But most important are the **architectural pieces** found concentrated in the men's bath area and round about. Enough blocks have been found to give an idea of the kind of wall in which they originally stood. A. Olivier's reconstruction envisages arcades topped by a frieze and cornice. This had grilled windows and was to be viewed from both sides. As yet, no one is prepared to commit him- or herself on its role, but what is quite clear is that this is very high-quality masonry, drawing mainly on Graeco-Roman traditions like SENS and AVALLON. The grapes dangle, foliage swirls and creatures are hidden away: sphinxes, griffins, marine monsters figure, as does Apollo, though here, but not at the other sites, so does Cernunnos.

JONVELLE, Haute-Saône

IGN 3319 O

Villa site.

Jonvelle is beside the D417 Chaumont to Luxeuil-les-Bains road. Signposted, the villa is 2.8km through the village, taking the minor turning for Jussey. The site is sheltered by large green metal sheds.

The excavation here was an inspired local effort, carried out in 1968 by the Abbé, Emile Descourvières, and is essentially simply a bath complex – but a very impressive one. There is a scatter of much rougher walling around the baths and the finer walling of the baths clearly goes further, demonstrating that there was a larger mansion as well. Nothing more of this was revealed in the 1991–2 digs as they focused on the villa's manufacturing work when pottery and tile kilns were explored on the flatter land below. The villa is classically located on the lower slope of a hill, forested higher up, near a spring, overlooking a river, so providing mixed agriculture, fishing, hunting and wood to heat the baths. The major Roman road linking Mandeure, Luxeuil and Langres was half a dozen kilometres away and a landing stage is suspected on the river. Little is known of the villa's history. Coins show first- to fifth-century occupation; the baths are believed to be mid-second century.

The baths

This is a basic system of three 'wet' rooms: hot, warm and cold, but an investment only the very wealthy could afford. Not only did its construction involve plumbers, hypocaust technicians, mosaicists and plasterer/painters, but also workers to maintain it: eight hours alone were needed to stoke and heat the system to a usable temperature.

The ***caldarium*** is exceptional, with a complete hypocaust and pink cement floor on top. On one side are curved-base bathtubs with walls/seats? separating them from the rest of the hot room. A hard residue formed by condensation over the paintwork at the top of the baths indicates the intense heat in the room. Note the wall where clay tubes once carried the heat up to roof level. Damage to the semi-circular area suggests that it was later modified for another bathtub.

The ***tepidarium*** was heated by hot air from the same furnace, but lying further away, at a lower temperature. Here a thin layer of water would cover the floor, no doubt bringing out the colour and quality of the mosaic; this radiated a sense of comfortable pleasure. The inner circle, or plate, portrays familiar Saône fish, the red speckled trout and grey-blue white chub; the rosettes and petals, the wine mixing craters and the dolphins were well-known symbols of the good life; and in a unique touch for Gaul a pair of sandals: here, you can forget the outside world where you wear shoes!

The ***frigidarium*** has steps/seats at both ends forming a cold pool with simple black-and-white tesserae marking out a rectangle at the bottom. The entrance to the baths was presumably from the passage.

The 'museum'

This has a mass of tiles, those with a variety of footprints in the case, others stacked-up below; the nails that held them in place; and the usual fibulae

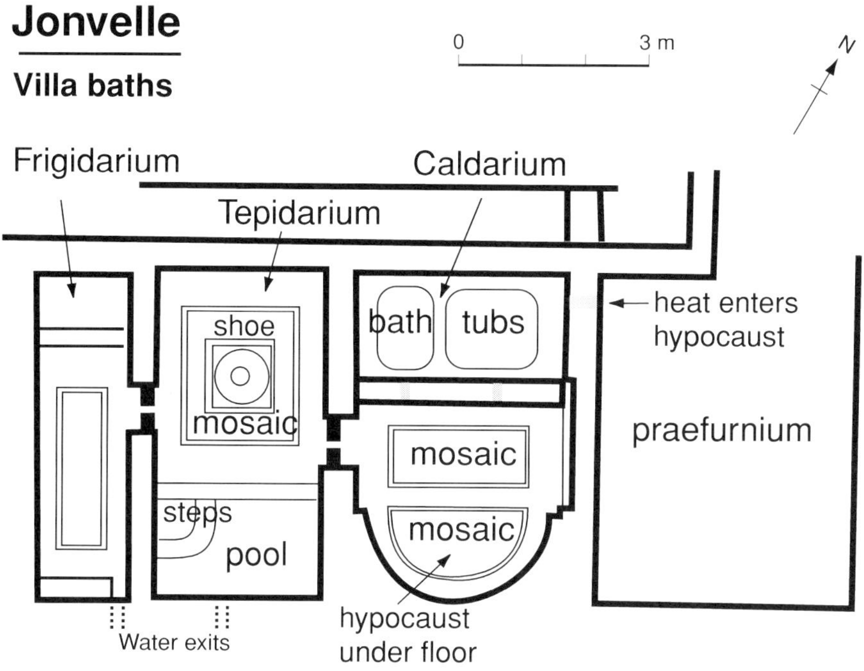

Figure 38 Jonvelle: baths

and pins, inevitably lost in baths. There are plans of the tilery and the two pottery kilns (for exposed examples in the region, see VILLERS-FARLAY and LUXEUIL-LES-BAINS).

Bourbonne-les-Bains

Nineteen kilometres west of Jonvelle on the D417.

The erection of a mix of broken pillars and architectural fragments as a garden feature by the modern *thermes* says it all. Yet this was the site of a genuinely magnificent sanctuary, with pools, porticoes and temples covering 4ha on its own, apart from the community around it. The ruins were once extensive; each renovation since the eighteenth century has destroyed more: understandable in the 1700s, regrettable in the 1880s, but surely just pure philistinism in the 1970s. One French archaeologist has called the wholesale destruction in 1977 a 'massacre'. The **museum** contains two Gallic wooden votive heads rescued in that year, the marble inscription identifying Borvo/Apollo as the chief god worshipped here, and a few other fragmentary finds, tastefully presented, but with absolutely no sense of what once stood here, let alone 'antique thermalisme'.

LONS-LE-SAUNIER, Jura

Museum and site.

During the Roman period, Lons-le-Saunier was a small town of *c.*25ha, on the Rhône–Rhine route via the Saône/Seille port of Châteaurenaud on to Besançon. There had been Neolithic and Gallic occupation, exploiting the Montmorot salt springs, continued in the Gallo-Roman period as traces of large buildings and finds of sculpture and 'CLARIANUS' named tiles brought from the Rhône valley confirm. Excavations in the late 1980s on the Comédie site revealed the Gallo-Roman town had a grid, while evidence of a hypocaust, drains and aqueduct pointed to public baths as well. Suburban villa development was linked to intensive agricultural exploitation.

Musée d'Archéologie

25 Rue Richebourg
39000 Lons-le-Saunier
Hours: 10a.m.–noon, 2–6p.m. Closed Tuesday

Currently the permanent collection is displayed in partial temporary thematic exhibitions, which may, or may not, include the Gallo-Roman material. From 2003 a new larger museum will open.

Among the recent finds from the town itself are 69 **gems** found in the Comédie excavations, rare in such a small area and only rivalled in northern Europe by finds such as those at Caerleon. Once in jewellery settings, particularly rings, then sadly lost, presumably when visiting the baths, the varied gems were incised with figures. They are thought to have had a mainly 'protective' role, though a few may have been seals. The subject matter suggests the first and second centuries: it includes eagles, Eros figures, chariots and a moon and stars.

A major feature will be a room focusing on the Jura's most important site, VILLARDS D'HERIA. Outstanding will be the bronze **Gorgon's head** with silver inlay eyes, the centrepiece of a breastplate that must have decorated a large statue at the temple. This could have portrayed Bellona, a Roman warrior goddess and consort of Mars, mentioned on inscriptions fround at the site. It was found wedged in a crevice under the 'bridge' at Villards d'Héria. There are plans to make an impressive show of the appearance of the temple, especially the **frescoes** restored from thousands of fragments. From Vicourt villa (Pont de Poitte) will be displayed the broken, but very fine and rare, second-century **stucco decoration**. These delicate faces with large almond Gallic eyes, little figures, and varied floral mouldings were found only in the baths and dining area where guests could see them.

LUXEUIL-LES-BAINS, Haute Saône

Museum and site.

Luxovium lay in poor agricultural land but at the crossroads of two major roads: from Langres on to Mandeure and the road from Besançon north to Trier. This gave some potential for development, but the existence of both hot and cold springs was crucial. Their use was undoubtedly pre-Roman; firm evidence for a curative role came with the discovery of wooden votive offerings at one of the springs, dated to the Augustan period. By the mid-first century a large bath complex had been built around the main spring outlets; the attractive eighteenth-century bath buildings cover the Roman remains, but are thought to reflect the original U-shape. The sanctuary, dedicated to Lussoius/Apollo and his consort Bricta, stimulated artisan activity: there is evidence of significant pottery works, including the manufacture of *sigillata*. There were also local specialist mason/sculptors – an inscription of thanks, for those who survived; for those not cured, there were tombstones.

A modern excavation at Haut Borrey has provided a typical chronology for this small but apparently thriving town; contraction in the third century was not as harsh here as elsewhere in Franche-Comté. By tracing the find spots of eighty-eight stelae, it has been possible to work out that a *castrum* rampart was constructed in the centre (late Roman, undated). The discovery of both fifth- and sixth-century material suggests that the town had some kind of continued existence, reinforced by the arrival of the Irish Saint Columbanus (*c.*543–615). The baths still impressed Merovingian writers.

Musée Tour des Echevins

Rue Victor Genoux
70300 Luxeuil-les-Bains
Hours: 10.30a.m.–noon; 3–6p.m. Closed Tuesday and Sunday morning

This attractive fifteenth-century town house has been used as a museum since 1674; it is haphazard, but has charm.

A few of the **funeral stelae** are on display. The best are perhaps the married couple and an elegant lady. Their tombstones have rare dancing bacchantes on each side, expressing the joy of the funeral banquet in memory of the deceased. Others are professional: a woodworker carries a plane, a shoemaker his polisher. Also displayed are the **wooden votive offerings**; some wear hooded capes while one, with hair brushed forward, supports an early first-century date (see DIJON for the finest collection). Upstairs, a small case has finds associated with the baths; note the fine **bronze tap**. Among the nineteenth-century pictures are panels, a model, and finds from the Chatigny pottery workshop, including its *sigillata*, goblets and common ware.

Four des Potiers Chatigny

Rue Sainte-Anne

The site has a large glass structure protecting it (locked). You can visit inside with a guide provided by the very helpful Tourist Office (1 Avenue des Thermes, 03 84 40 06 41).

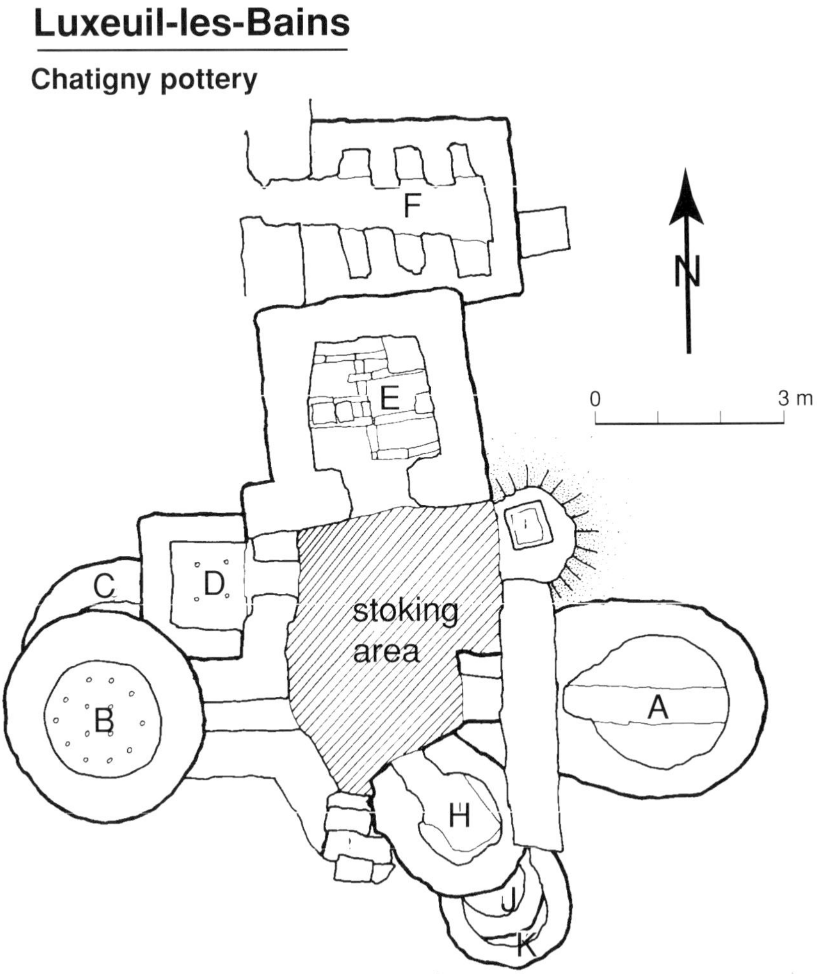

Figure 39 Luxeuil-les-Bains: pottery site

On view are nine of the ten kilns excavated in the 1980s. The A–K identifications are original: 'I' was not used and 'G' lay outside the immediate area. The earliest of the kilns were C and K, beginning at the end of the first century. These were superseded by A and J to be followed by B, D and E. The last phase, some 30–40 years after they began here, is represented by kilns F and H. Clearly the site was convenient; no doubt there was nearby timber – as there still is today – suitable clay and a sandstone bedrock that provided not only building stone, but also a firm base for the hearths. The potters therefore retained the same stoking area where they could stack wood and feed the hearths, simply building new furnaces round it.

The square kiln D is believed to have been used to make the fine goblets; the other small furnaces are more likely to have been used to bake common ware. Kiln B has survived best, is the most sophisticated and was used to make *sigillata*. Here a high indirect heat was required, and therefore the heat entered the chamber through the holes but rose in pipes to the vaulted roof (destroyed); there were additional pipes all round the chamber as well. The workshop where the potter applied his moulds has not been excavated; did he come from central Gaul, or was he a local buying moulds? A stamp with 'REGINUS' is known, though the mould design of 'Luxeuil I' is similar to

Plate 17 Luxeuil-les-Bains. Kiln B at the Chatigny pottery works, exposing the heat-ventilated chamber floor and the piping which carried heat into the (destroyed) chamber roof. Photograph: James Bromwich.

Libertus of Lezoux. Even taking into account the four additional furnaces found in what is now part of the cemetery, *sigillata* was never very important, comprising only 20 per cent of the find material, and had a purely regional distribution. Perhaps it was not good/cheap enough for anything but the local pilgrim market.

MACON, Saône-et-Loire

Museum and early church remains.

The wide alluvial terrace by a ford across the Saône attracted La Tène III settlement and Caesar placed troops at this *oppidum* to secure his supply lines from Provence and Italy after the defeat of Vercingetorix (*Gallic Wars*, VII, 90). Matisco is confirmed by the Antonine Itinerary as a Gallo-Roman settlement in the early Roman empire – the 'Agrippa' road lay just to the west – and by the *Notitia Dignitatum* for the late Roman period, where it was identified as a production centre for arrows. Yet Matisco remains nebulous and archaeologically little is known. No public buildings have been identified, nor is there much sense of whether this was a widely spread minor *vicus* or something larger. Its first known bishop was a Frank in the sixth century. The richest finds made in Mâcon were the wonderful silver statuettes found in a late third-century hoard when the hospital was constructed in 1764: most found their way to the British Museum.

Musée des Ursulines

Allée de Matisco
71000 Mâcon
Hours: 10a.m.–noon, 2–6p.m. Closed Monday and Sunday morning

The seventeenth-century convent has been well renovated. Temporary exhibitions periodically cover the latest work of archaeologists in the region, so filling out the limited local collection. This includes a mosaic of a *murmillo* gladiator, practising his sword work at a post; it lacks fine detail. There is an enigmatic relief of what appears to be a swaying dancer. A small La Tène pottery furnace has been set in a sandy context to give some sense of environment; finds from the Cordier necropolis west of the town are laid out to show various types of ash containers. Among the usual globular glassware, used for finer burials of this kind, is one with a less common pinched-ribbed decoration. A Merovingian stone coffin contains the skeleton with brooches and clasps; a case displays early and late Frankish weaponry, including hand and throwing axes, long-pointed and leaf-type lances.

St Clément church

Place St Clément
Hours: June–September only 10a.m.–noon, 2–6p.m. Closed Tuesday
Sunday 2–6p.m.

At the junction of the Rue de Lyon and the Route de Bioux near the railway station to the south of the centre. The early Christian burial ground along the 'Agrippa' road south of Matisco led to the construction of a cemetery church. St Clément was rebuilt a number of times, then closed in the 1970s. Excavation in the 1980s revealed the sixth-century short-naved, apsed structure, with an annexe on each side. This had been filled and surrounded with some thirty early Christian stone coffins, one decorated with crosses.

MALAIN, Côte d'Or

IGN 3023 O
787.0/2261.0

Site and museum.

24km west of Dijon. Leave the A38 at Pont de Pany, taking the D33 north for Mâlain. At cemetery 500m below Mâlain, turn right on D104c for Ancey. 500m on right, signposted Fouilles (tiny); track up gradient to site entrance.

Currently, the excavation at La Boussière looks as though it has been forgotten. Grass and weeds are protecting the partially excavated lower buildings on the site, the hut near the entrance is dilapidated, and only some of the room/house numbers survive; but a vast hanger covers the main section and has helped preserve the largely 1980s work in remarkably good shape.

Louis Roussel exposed an interesting mix of commercial and residential occupation. In addition, aerial photography, and other small-scale excavations, revealed that Mediolanum extended much further and, as a 100ha town, similar in size to Alesia, was one of the largest in the region. Though its overall layout is not clear, it had a theatre, at least one aqueduct and two independent sanctuaries, one of which had a *fanum* linked to a spring. Its situation at the foot of the north–south Auxois valleys across the Burgundy watershed between the Seine and Saône basins placed it on a major road coming south from Troyes and Châtillon, through Mediolanum and on to Beaune and Chalon. Equally the Roman Langres–Autun road would have passed here to the Roman settlement at Sombernon. The eroded limestone plateau provided varied and rich agriculture and had local iron ore and granite available. Mâlain has produced fifteen inscriptions; they show it formed part of the Lingones *civitas* and that possibly the landowner who left one of the longest testamentary inscriptions known, preserved but then sadly lost in Langres many years ago, actually owned land around Mediolanum: his domain

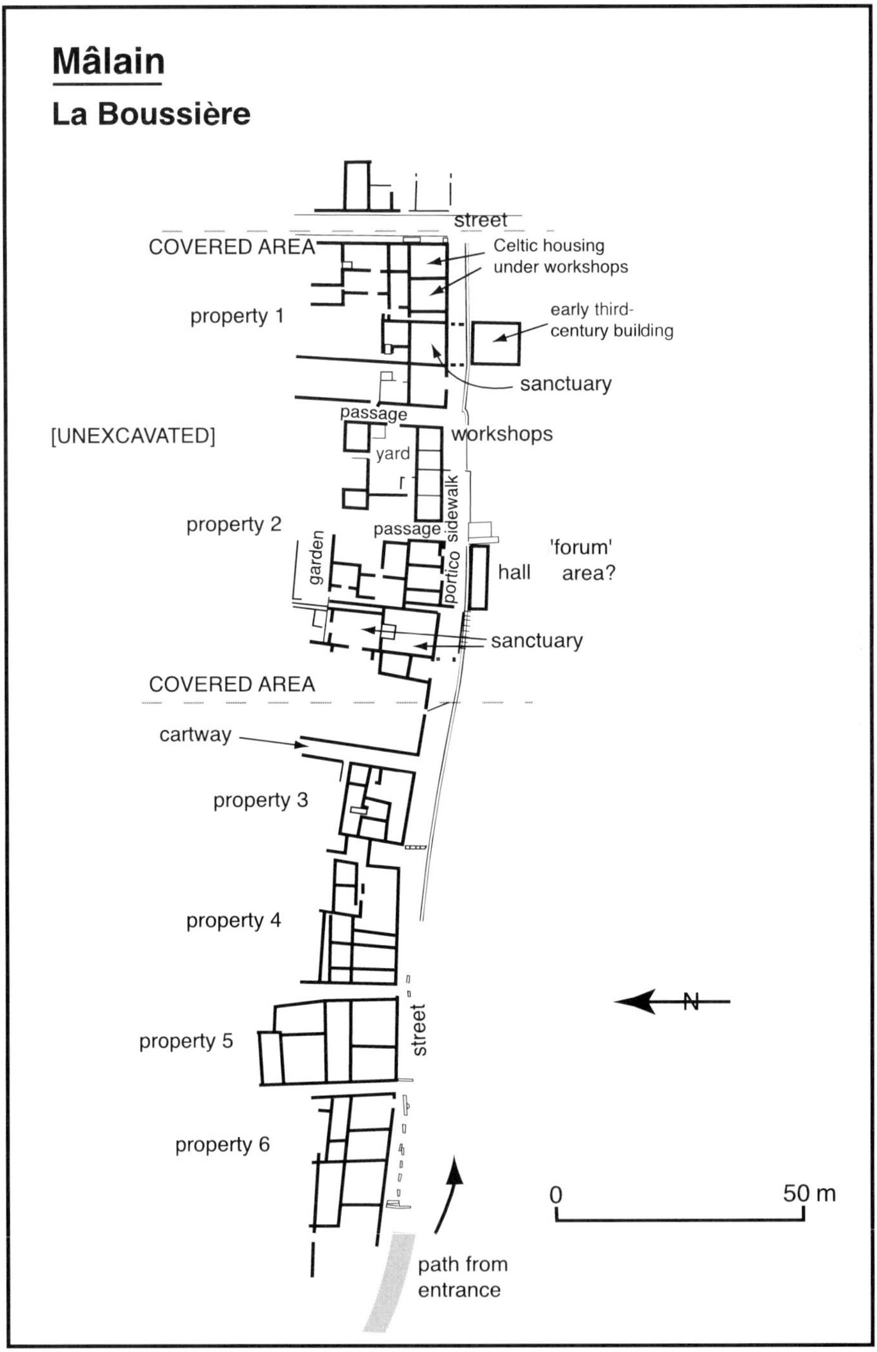

Figure 40 Mâlain: site plan

was named Litavicrari; a sanctuary inscription found here mentions Mars Cicolius and his consort Latavis: the similarity is suggestive.

In the pre-Roman period, the steep hill at Mesmont, 6km east, was the major defended site, but La Boussière was certainly occupied during the first century BC, as a number of rectangular timber and earth houses, storage pits and ovens have been found. Mesmont was abandoned, while Mediolanum prospered. Stone foundations were being used as early as Augustus and there was continuous development until the later second century, when there are signs of withdrawal from the south of the site. The later third century saw dramatic decline, in part linked to fire, but there is also evidence of systematic removal of useful objects: the move back to securer high places had begun. In the early medieval period, Mesmont was once again the main settlement in the area.

La Boussière excavations

The visitor walks up the gentle slope along an east–west road laid out in the first century AD. On the northern side a series of buildings is fronted by a covered sidewalk or portico; to the south excavation showed very few constructions.

The most interesting feature of the site is what has been deduced from the remains and their relationship with the portico. As excavation progressed it became clear that portico construction varied along the sidewalk: a wall and pillars section would lead on to a section of simple wooden pillars to another of finer columns; at one time, a building had even encroached over the entire sidewalk. This encouraged careful examination of the occupation on both sides of the road. What emerged was that to the south, new, possibly public, buildings were constructed: the 'hall' could have been a basilica and part of a more formal market area modelled on the forum of a city.

The north was much more complicated: over 250 years of development had meant considerable changes in house and room use, but what emerged was that unlike BLIESBRUCK, with its strip workshop houses and ownership likely to be concentrated in the hands of one great estate owner whose villa dominates the *vicus*, here we have shops and workshops along the front and, behind, **major residences** with inner courtyards, gardens and running water: here it seems was where the owners of the blocks lived. The model is Pompeii and Herculaneum, where the houses of the rich had rooms and sections rented out to workers: rich and poor lived together in close proximity. The balance between the power of private and public ownership is weighted more heavily to the former in a small town. The portico is not to create a grand vista, but to enable people to move, with minimum impact on landowners. This portico is envisaged as covered with a floor above and split by passageways back into the houses behind; its appearance would have been like many small medieval towns in France, Italy or Germany.

Figure 41 Malain: reconstructed street. Drawing by A. Olivier, CNRS

Property 2 appears to have been much bigger than 1, stretching between the gated passage and the minor road. Modifications of the eastern end may well have transferred ownership here to property 1, as later courtyard use might best be explained as the back yard of the two bronze workers' shops. An interesting feature of both properties is that they have **sanctuaries** integrated into their frontages (identified both by cult statue finds and by their more monumental features). Do they relate to the workers' interests, like the Ucuetis sanctuary at ALESIA, or to the interests of the block owner, or to the community as a whole?

An excellent model of the portico and buildings covered by properties 1 and 2, based on Albéric Olivier's drawing, is on display at the ARCHEODROME. Some finds are displayed in DIJON.

Museum

Rue Gaudot

This depot collection contains small finds, a few architectural pieces and a model of the *fanum*. Metalwork finds, particularly associated with bronze-making, include cinders, slag, moulds, rings, fibulae, keys, statuettes, furniture appliqués and farm tools. The worked stone suggests this was an important craft at Mediolanum: it includes local sculpted limestone and granite millstones.

MANDEURE/MONTBELIARD, Doubs

IGN 3522 E
935.5/2281.6

Theatre and museum.

Epomanduodurum, today the twin towns of Mandeure and Mathay, was one of the largest 'small towns' in the whole of Gaul, covering at its second-century peak an estimated 180ha. For traffic coming up-river, by the Rhône–Saône–Doubs route to Germany, this was the transit point where goods had to be unloaded and taken by road through the Belfort gap to the Upper Rhine. It was also a bridge crossing for the main road from Lyon to Augst and Strasbourg (of key strategic value to the military), mentioned as a stop on both the Antonine and Peutinger itineraries. The commercial potential of the site was considerable and customs stamps found here indicate state exploitation as well.

There had been an Iron Age settlement and sanctuary here, but under the Romans this Sequani border town rapidly developed on both sides of the Doubs. Wharfs must have lined the banks below the bridge. The centre, laid out on a regular grid, lay east of the river in a sweeping bend, the main road from Besançon crossing the bridge and running south of the town. To the south-west was the sanctuary, possibly dedicated to the tribal god and identified with Mars (see BESANÇON), enhanced by a new, immense

Roman-style temple and theatre. To the south-east in Courcelles, rescue excavations revealed large public baths. They may have been part of a second sanctuary; the number of oculists' sets found led to the suggestion that they could have specialized in eye treatments. Alternatively, they may have been part of a travellers' stop; Epomanduodurum must have had a number of *mansio*s.

West of the river there was another group of *insulae* in the Faubourg du Pont, with both housing and artisans' shops; beyond, in the Essarté district of Mathay, lay a major concentration of workshops. Many Gallo-Roman crafts are represented: stonemasons, mosaicists, iron and bronze working, potteries, glassblowing, boneworking and clothmaking. Small-scale smoke-houses found here must have been for local and passing trade, but the region was known in the empire for its smoked meat and the town may have acted as a distributor for surrounding meat producers, particularly to the frontier garrisons.

As elsewhere in Franche-Comté, evidence of trouble grows in the late second century, made worse in the third and fourth centuries by warring Roman factions and invaders. The theatre went out of use and stonework was transferred to build a *castellum* between the town centre and the bridge. Finds from Legio VI Prima Martia suggest a detachment was based here. Excavations to trace the rampart in detail began in 2001. Mandura seems to have survived as a bridgehead site during the Merovingian period, before being replaced by the medieval stronghold of Montbéliard. The pity is that there is so little for the visitor to see. However, the theatre is still impressive and Montbéliard has an excellent museum.

The theatre

From central Montbéliard follow the D34 south through Arbouans to join the N437 at Audincourt. Then via Beaulieu, Courcelles and Mandeure, through town to the sign on the left for the theatre. Free access.

With a diameter of 142m and four levels of seating, the theatre is exceeded in size only by AUTUN. The first digs by antiquarians in the 1820s sadly also made clear that this was an excellent source of cut stone for locals. Eventually this stopped when new excavations took place after the Second World War and staircases and much of the *petit appareil* work were restored.

Using the hillside saved on the human and financial cost of building a free-standing structure, but it also accounts for some of the theatre's peculiarities. The incomplete cellular walling meant the projecting sides of the building had to be strengthened: the cells were therefore filled with earth to act as buttresses to resist the push from the hillside. Blind arcades were added to the side passages, not for decoration, but to help prevent splits caused by hill slippage. Another apparently odd feature is that, despite the

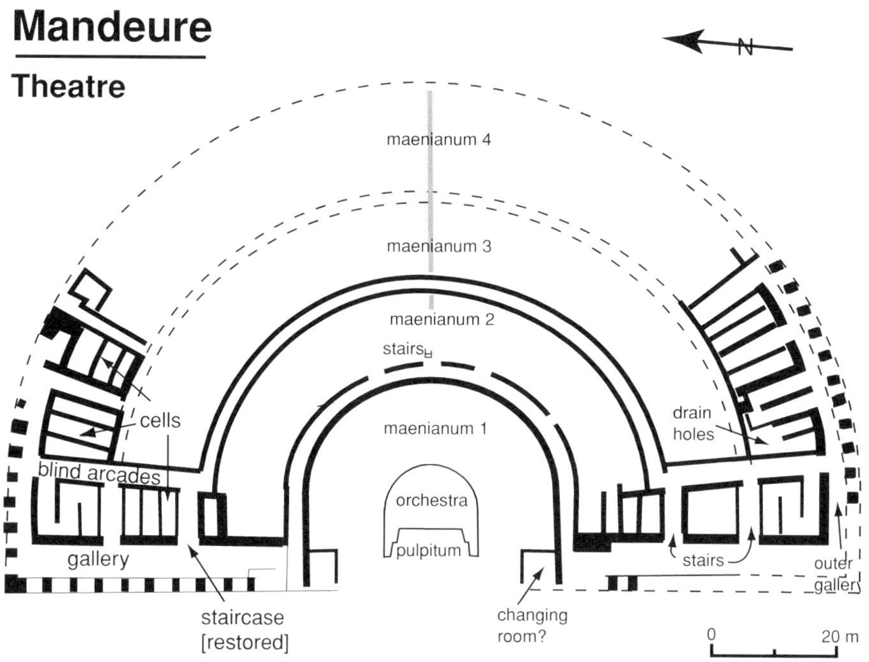

Figure 42 Mandeure: theatre

size of the *cavea*, the orchestra and stage are tiny; nor have excavators found any evidence of a stage building: no stone backcloth for performances, no actors' changing rooms. This can best be explained by reference to the temple, represented by the clump of trees about 300m in front of the theatre. This was not a place for theatrical performance but for religious ritual and ceremony. The audience had an unobstructed view of processions coming from the precinct gates to the theatre, where the elite gathered in the first tier could welcome the priesthood, the rest in the tiers above being reminded of their dependent positions.

Depot/museum. Open during July and August daily except Tuesday. Guided tour available. In addition to architectural fragments, there are small finds including hippo-sandals, Legio VI Prima Martia-stamped bricks and a lead customs' stamp.

Musée de Montbéliard

Château des Ducs de Wurtemberg
25200 Montbéliard
Hours: 10a.m.–noon; 2–6p.m. Closed Tuesday

Plate 18 Mandeure/Montbéliard. The *lares* bronze from a wealthy family's devotional hearth. Photograph: © Musées de Montbéliard.

The Gallo-Roman galleries were reopened in 1997 after an attractive and intelligent remodelling. Most of the material on display comes from Epomanduodurum.

The first room brings together evidence of La Tène occupation, mainly from the temple site: coins, tiny votive bells, fragments of a gilded grill and parts of the Gallic trumpet, the ***carnix***. The Courcelles baths show there was indeed a rich elite with an interest in Epomanduodurum: an inscription, dedicated by a Flavius Catullus, records his gift of 75,000 *denarii* for facing the walls with marble. Finds here included an Etruscan mirror showing two men at ease conversing in what could be a baths and numerous oculists' seals for stamping their preparations, the earliest found here in 1606 by Count Frederick of Württemberg's doctor.

Among the small bronzes the most impressive represent Roman, rather than Gallic, versions of gods, though there is a triple-horned bull with a torc in his nose. The number of Mars finds is perhaps suggestive, though there are more of Mercury, but the finest piece is the **Lares group**: mounted on a plinth, a young man dances, tunic flying, carrying a *patera* and a *rhyton*, at his feet a bearded snake, a double-tailed cockerel and a pig resting against a rural sanctuary; surely the possession of a person of wealth and Roman taste? A well-made priest of Serapis and a crude Mithras head may show the eastern interests of passing travellers.

That catch-all section, 'daily life', has one of the better presentations of *sigillata*, making clear the three major Gallic centres, including examples of the nearby LUXEUIL producers. The lighting section is also good, including a rare **lantern** side, complemented by a picture of a complete example in the British Museum. Mandeure's military associations still need more research, but a legionary's elaborate **personal knife sheath** shows his relative wealth. Most interesting for me is the 'economic' section: the metal-workers' products, including horse fittings – so necessary at this transit station; rare **customs collectors' seals**; a model of a butcher's shop with its smoker, together with the butcher's tools including his paring-knife; and evidence of clothmaking (see DRESS AND APPEARANCE).

The Merovingian room is based on the standard burial finds, nearly all from the Blussangeaux cemetery, excavated in the 1950s and early 1960s. They are carefully divided to show individual burials and some characteristic features of sixth- and seventh-century appearance, weapons and buckles. The most striking thing is the contrast between the restrained Gallo-Roman jewellery displayed in the museum and these brightly coloured stone necklaces and glistening gold brooches.

MONT BEUVRAY, Saône-et-Loire

IGN 2825 OT

Site and museum.
www.bibracte.tm.fr/

30km west of Autun by the N81, then the D61 for St Léger.
Free access. Guided tours available in English; 3p.m. start from the museum (1½ hours).

Napoleon III's fascination with the Gallic wars was decisive in the identification of both Alesia and Bibracte and his subsequent funding vital in stimulating surveys and digs; however, local societies were crucial in continuing excavations through the rest of the nineteenth and into the twentieth century. Today the position is very different. At Mont Auxois (see ALISE-STE-REINE) there has been regular but small-scale excavation carried out over many years and a museum filled with interesting material, but it desperately needs serious money to provide modern facilities; at Mont Beuvray there has been the largest injection of state finance for archaeology in recent times. A costly, architect-designed museum has been built, numerous expert teams brought in, an international centre for research set up.

Once again, personal intervention by the head of state has been crucial: in the early 1980s President François Mitterrand declared Mont Beuvray to be a *Grand Chantier*. The Morvan, a region of winding valleys, hills and mountains, extensive forest cover, a few small lakes, a lot of rain in the winter and a sparse population, has been poor and isolated for many years. It was, though, the political base of Mitterrand. Creating a new cultural-scientific research centre and revitalizing Mont Beuvray as a tourist attraction was a form of regional aid, repaying his supporters and creating a permanent memorial.

The nineteenth-century work on Mont Beuvray was largely the achievement of Jacques Gabriel Bulliot. Napoleon III was persuaded that he was the right man and deserved funding. Bulliot moved to live on the mountain and devoted the rest of his life to its excavation (1867–95). His technique was very crude and devoid of any stratigraphic understanding, but he identified all the major sites being re-worked today and he kept good records. His nephew Joseph Déchelette, one of France's great founding archaeologists (see ROANNE), worked at Mont Beuvray in 1897–1901 and 1907: the site was a cornerstone for his writings on the late Iron Age. When he was killed in the first weeks of war in 1914, Mont Beuvray lost a potential champion. By the 1970s commercial pines covered the hill, their roots were destroying unexcavated remains and they made access extremely difficult.

The first modern team began work in 1984. Since then many different teams (more than twenty-seven!) have worked on the site, some for a short time, some for years; they have come from universities and institutes all over France and Europe (e.g. Budapest, Lausanne, Zaragoza, Sheffield), co-ordinated by an international council, including Christian Goudineau. Whether the investment has been worth while is still difficult to say: a key aim has been to sort out the chronology, and though the archaeologists are some way to doing this, it has proved far more difficult than expected. Bulliot really did destroy the stratigraphic evidence; fresh sites in the *oppidum* are needed and exploration has only just begun. New discoveries have been made, a second rampart, a necropolis (fortuitous: they were laying out the museum car park), a sacred pool and the Roman foundations of a spring sanctuary. Certainly interesting, but enough? An impossible question to answer, but when I think of the obvious poverty at Alesia I have doubts. Perhaps the key benefit has been the sharing of international understanding, a much more difficult result to measure.

The environment

Because the Morvan is part of the plateau separating the rivers Loire, Saône and Seine, Mont Beuvray seems no more than a hill, yet it rises to 821m (2,668ft). In the winter it rains heavily, it is cold, fog is common and snow is not unusual. It is isolated from the major transit routes. Little more than chance finds suggest any occupation between the Neolithic and Middle Iron Age. The decision to make this an *oppidum*, a capital 'city', can only have been a deliberate choice made by the Aedui in the mid-second century BC.

Clearly its height and isolation made it an imposing redoubt; the two ramparts would have been visible miles away. If the climate was gentler then, and there is evidence that this was so, then 'the largest and richest *oppidum* of the Aedui' (Caesar, *Gallic Wars*, I, 23) would make more sense; equally it had a fairly central place in their territory that stretched from Sancerre in the north-west to at least Mâçon in the south-east. It also dominates the immediate area looking south towards the Arroux, west to the Loire, and, via the upper Arroux basin, was within easy reach of routes both north and east. The environment was much more varied then: forest of open oak and beech provided timber; there was good granite and minerals; there was pasture and, on the slopes, limited agriculture was possible for cereals and vegetables; wild fruits were widespread. The hill itself formed a large relatively flat platform with three peaks, and well watered by springs. It has been suggested that an enigmatic rectangular space, 'La Terrasse', may have had sacred significance that could have drawn the tribe to choose this hill.

The Aedui

The transformation of the Aedui tribe into a leading state in Gallia Comata may be linked to the growing influence of the Romans, culminating in the conquest of Provence in the 120s. The Aedui were declared 'allies' and 'brothers' of the Roman people, possibly in recognition of the support given by them against common enemies like the Arverni and Allobroges who threatened the security of Provincia. It was an alliance that lasted, because as Roman traders followed those of Massilia up the Rhône and Saône, so Aeduan strength could protect them; the support of the Roman state would ensure the traders paid their river taxes – at Chalon, their main commercial centre – and at the same time help the Aedui in their struggles with other tribes. Their pivotal position in the centre of Gaul ensured that the relationship continued.

It is clear from Caesar's account that, like other Gallic tribes, they were evolving into a state similar to early Republican Rome with an elected annual magistrate, a 'Virgobret', and like Rome it had a collection of unruly aristocrats, able to call upon numerous clients, who sought status through personal displays of power. They were the dominant partners in links often loosely cemented by marriage with other states around them, like the Boii and Ambarri, and they jostled for position with the Arverni and Sequani. However, in the 60s their position was undermined. A German adventurer, Ariovistus, moved across the Rhine and defeated Gallic forces, including Aeduan, and took territory from the Sequani; at the same time Roman power was enhanced by the crushing of a large-scale revolt by the Allobroges. The decision by the Helvetii to migrate from the Jura to western Gaul provided the excuse for the new Roman proconsul, Julius Caesar, determined to achieve military success, to intervene. Old struggles between nobles for dominance took on a new colouring: pro-Romans like Diviciacus appealed to Rome for help and during the Gallic wars was to become one of Caesar's most trusted allies; his brother Dumnorix, an anti-Roman, was ultimately killed on Caesar's orders, crying out that 'he was a free man and the citizen of a free state' (Caesar, *Gallic Wars*, V, 7).

The leadership of the Aedui remained pro-Roman until Vercingetorix brought the Gauls together and the Aedui had to choose their identity (though once they had, they were annoyed that they were not made leaders of the revolt). Their equal top contribution of troops to the relieving force, 35,000, was three times the size of the next largest, indicating their importance as a state. Though the Aedui must have feared the consequences, Caesar rapidly forgave them, even handing back 20,000 prisoners rather than making them slaves for his troops: the Aedui were to be restored as the linch-pin at the centre of Gaul. Caesar chose Bibracte as his winter quarters and wrote his dispatches here, perhaps in the swirling fog of a Morvan winter. The Aeduan aristocracy, and maybe the people, adapted quickly. Grandiose Roman mansions were built and Roman habits adopted. Under Augustus these *foedorati* were again rewarded; when their new city was laid out at Autun it covered an area as big as the enclosure of Bibracte's outer rampart (200ha), and was surrounded with new Roman-style walls and towers to proclaim their higher status among the tribes that had once been free.

The development of Bibracte

This *oppidum* was a deliberate act of creation. The effort involved in constructing the ramparts alone is impressive: the outer was 7km long and the inner over 5km. Massive tree felling would have been necessary to clear the interior space and to provide the thousands of trunks for constructing the walls and houses. While the external ditches provided the earth fill for the ramparts, facing stone was dug from local quarries. Artisans must have moved in straight away and set to manufacturing the thousands of nails needed; an estimated 25–30,000 tonnes of iron was mined in the neighbourhood. Bulliot identified the main entrance in the north and the *grand voie* that followed the crest of the plateau along which there were various subsidiary roads. Despite the limitations, such as the restricted extent of excavated areas (with the plantation cover it will always be difficult to extend investigation) and the very real difficulties in sorting out the stratigraphy at many places, preliminary conclusions are possible. It is already clear some parts were never occupied and a number of districts were occupied continuously. The first houses were built in the 120s BC and the last houses abandoned in the 20s AD.

The earliest structures are timber-post buildings. Numbers of houses are associated with cellars where goods were stored and perhaps they had a household ritual role as well; in some cases they were very large and, over time, acquired internal timber facings and were divided into sections. From the mid-first century BC there was an influx of new building techniques: constructors using sand and dry stone foundations and clay-daubed walls with a plaster covering; thatch was being replaced in some places by Roman-style tiles and floors were made firmer with beaten earth or amphora fragments, while rooms were heated with clay hearths. During the last quarter of the first century BC masonry became common with stone-built cellars, house walls and flooring. Roads were firmly laid and minor roads set at right angles. Most striking of all is the appearance of grand houses: the nobility were clearly having themselves housed in *domus* on a par with those in Lyon.

Was this a real 'pre-industrial city'? The answer seems to be yes. It had a large population with distinct districts: workshops by the gate(s?); a public zone where the road widens on the Pâture du Couvent; the homes of the elite either near this public district or on the nearby Parc aux Chevaux; sacred sites spread around the south. It is likely there was a commercial area, probably also in the Pâture du Couvent, but shops have not been identified. This is perhaps because of the inherent difficulties when remains above ground are scarce and amphorae in a cellar are open to differing interpretations – personal consumption, or for sale? Coinage has been found quite widely, especially potin, the simple low-value money suggesting a market economy. The lack of Roman coins is surprising; perhaps the 'taxes' collected at Chalon were largely in kind – wine, pottery, bronzes. Most of the pottery was locally produced and must have been made in the Morvan as it is not found in the

Saône valley, but imports including amphorae show a swing from Campania to Etruria and finally include imports from Spain, suggesting the elite were eating olives and *garum* (fish sauce) as well as drinking large quantities of wine. The traditional influence of Massilia is apparent too, not simply in the presence of its obol coins, but in that Greek letters were used for a local Gallic script, indicating some literacy. The archaeological evidence indicates growing Roman influence before the conquest in 52 BC and that following this there was a very rapid adoption of the physical attributes of Roman life – brought to an end at Bibracte by the decision to found an entirely Roman city on a new site. This transformation is not surprising, given the proximity of Roman Provincia and the alliance, but who taught the Aedui to build in the new way? Garrison troops? Craftsmen hired by the elite? Free entrepreneurs? These are questions that hopefully might be reflected upon by the next generation of researchers at Bibracte.

The site

New material is constantly exposed. The visitor will have the pleasure of finding more to look at, and, if you come in the summer, perhaps be able to discuss current thinking with excavators. Sheets displayed at the digs summarize discoveries and objectives. At many points there are tables with information in French, English and German. Just as the *oppidum*'s *grande voie* once did, the D274 follows the crest, but it is best to use the museum car park. (A stiff walk of 500m to the Porte du Rebout.)

1 **Outer rampart**. Identified by the German expert F. Schubert in 1987.

Cut into at points by the inner rampart, it is clearly earlier, but by how much? Nail finds suggest that it had a timber frame construction, but over the whole length and from the beginning? Excavations since 1999 should help on these points. It is possible to walk round, but difficult to follow, as both mound and ditch are barely visible.

2 **Inner rampart and Porte du Rebout**. The mound and exterior ditch are clearly visible here. The rampart was traced by Bulliot.

The gateway. It is a typical late La Tène design, each side of the rampart turned inwards to form a corridor; the gate itself was at the inner end. There is no evidence for a walkway over the gate and some writers suggest that this absence, together with its exceptional width of 19m, would have made it difficult to defend. Modern work has shown it went through five building phases, in which the rampart walling was enlarged before a final phase when much of the gateway appears to have been filled in, along with the ditch. As building now took place outside the gate, its monumental status must have come to an end. By the ditch a **cellar** marked a house next to an **artisan's workshop**, first used for iron then bronze making; the workshop model in the museum is an interpretation of this site.

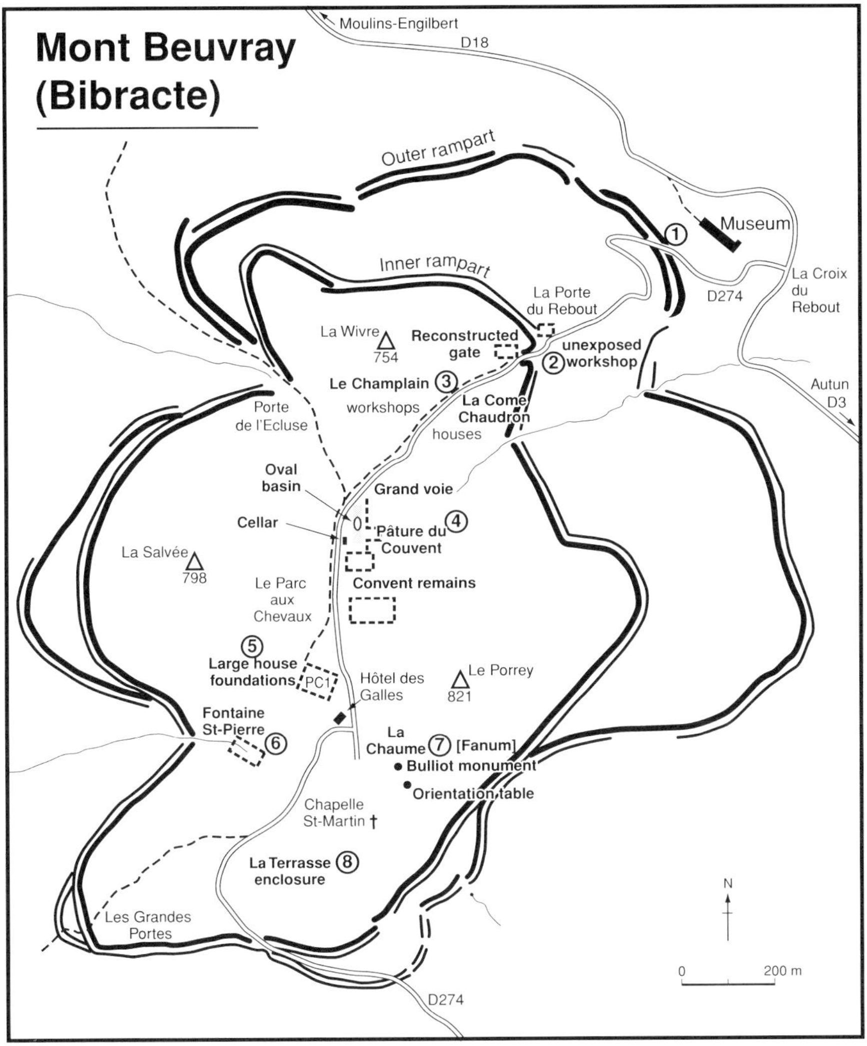

Figure 43 Mont Beuvray: site plan

The reconstruction. Excavations at a number of points along the rampart show that it was entirely built using this wooden box-frame or *murus gallicus* technique. Massive nails secured the timbers; stone blocks covered the exterior face, but left exposed the timber ends; the frame was filled with earth and rubble. Some versions had an internal facing, but here there was a continuous ramp. Caesar described this kind of rampart in his account of the siege of Bourges, explaining that it made an effective defence against battering rams (*Gallic Wars*, VII, 23).

Rampart paths. Despite the modern forest cover, the ditch and the embankment formed from the washed-down earth and stone are still quite prominent and there are paths for each. Though the inner rampart disappears at some gullies and gates it is easy to pick it up again. It takes *c.*1½ hours to walk the 5.2km.

3 **La Come Chaudron**. Filled in and now covered by forest, the slopes on each side of the *grande voie* (a few metres to the north of the modern road) were extensively excavated by Bulliot. It was a densely populated district of houses and workshops. One has recently been re-excavated for reappraisal. As at the gate workshop, these too seem to have followed a two-phase development in usage: in the first half of the first century BC largely working iron and after 50 BC concentrating on bronze products. Is this a response to changing economic circumstance, linked to the *oppidum*'s early and later needs, or is it a product of the social structure where demand was defined by the power of patrons?

4 **La Pâture du Couvent**. This pasture is named after the fourteenth-century Franciscan monastic outpost, burnt down and abandoned in 1650. Though there is nothing to indicate any continuity between the medieval fair held here and the Gallic settlement, the size of the open area makes it likely that this was Bibracte's commercial and political/symbolic centre. The sites in the pasture, including the monastic buildings, were the main focus of attention in the 1990s.

The road and oval basin. The *grand voie* is re-created here. Laid in the later first century BC, this was a well-crafted road with beds of broken amphora pieces and stones set in clay and surfaced with sand and gravel; at 19m, markedly wider than normal. The surprise discovery of the modern excavations was an oval basin, beautifully made of pink granite, set in the middle of the road. Traces of an over-arching superstructure were found and the drain, but not the water supply system. No comparable basin has been found at any other Celtic *oppidum*. It appears to have been aligned with the solstice, implying a sacred meaning. Its central position and a severed head, found nearby in one of the spoil heaps, could signify it was associated with a foundation ceremony.

Houses. The earliest houses can be dated to the 120s. Together with the side roads, these became more carefully aligned in blocks at the same time as stone building was being adopted when Bibracte took on a more Roman appearance. A **cellar reconstruction** in situ here is the work of an Italian team. Carbonized in a fire in the last years BC, it has been possible to restore all the timber frame lining. Other cellars have preserved their stone sill steps. Some houses, which only had the odd room excavated by Bulliot, have now been more completely dug and show that in the final phase these were developing as large Roman town houses.

5 Le Parc aux Chevaux. First excavated in the 1870s. Bulliot soon realized that this was a major district of grand *domus* houses. The modern excavators have been trying to trace their evolution and the point at which they took on their final form. It now seems that they started as isolated houses set in enclosures and culminated in mansions on a par with those in the great cities of Provence.

House PC1 shows this best and the remains are being consolidated. The first two phases were as a timber-post building with cellar, which was then modified by the addition of a wood facing, typical of the second quarter of the first century BC. Between 50 and 25 BC it was rebuilt using basic Roman techniques, insulating foundations, plastered timber and clay walling, tiled roofs and better flooring, including the exposed *opus spicatum*, a herringbone brick design. In the final Augustan phase the stone-built house had its own water supply piped from a spring, a vestibule, an atrium, peristyle, gardens, a bath system, hypocaust rooms and fine floors. It was four times the size of a typical Pompeian house!

Hôtel des Galles. The ruins of J.-G. Bulliot's house, where he lived and entertained his many guests during the summer season, have been restored.

6 St Pierre spring. Numerous springs on Mont Beuvray satisfied basic needs; small finds here could be votive offerings and St Pierre a sacred spring. Archaeological investigation in the 1980s showed that two sets of rectangular **masonry pools** were built, the earlier in the first century BC and the later during the first century AD, which continued in use until the third century. A small wooden frame was discovered around the spring itself. The modern forest helps ensure the site retains a mystical feel that, hopefully, will not be broken by the restoration work.

7 La Chaume. Today this zone is marked by a memorial to Bulliot, the observation table and St Martin's chapel. In the nineteenth century, a rectangular *fanum* with a gallery and enclosure was dug (now covered in), unfortunately destroying all stratigraphic evidence. When the sanctuary was built and whether there was an earlier Gallic temple must wait until scientific techniques are available to see under the chapel.

8 La Terrasse. **A banked enclosure**, almost square (110 × 92m) was created on this promontory and can still be made out. Nothing has yet been found in it, though the timber used in the banking has been dated to the third century BC, apparently much earlier than the Bibracte settlement. Similar *Viereckschanzen* have been found in German *oppida* and they are interpreted as meeting places. Vercingetorix won over the support of the Gallic general council at Mont Beuvray (Caesar, *Gallic Wars*, VII, 63); perhaps it was here.

Musée de la Civilisation Celtique

71990 St Léger-sous-Beuvray

Hours:	July–August	10a.m.–7p.m.
	mid-June/30 June, 1 September/mid-November	10a.m.–6p.m.
	mid-March/mid-June, mid-September/mid-November	10a.m.–6p.m. Closed Tuesday

Audio kits are supplied as part of the entrance fee and cover the permanent displays on the two floors, broadly divided between an overview of the Celtic world and Bibracte itself. Considerable investment has gone into presentation using high-quality materials, precise models and video displays (not always functioning). The presentation is certainly tasteful but, for me at least, clinical and bland, the excitement of discovery missing.

Temporary exhibitions every year cover major themes beyond Bibracte itself. Recent examples have included 'The Druids' and 'The Gauls in Provence'. From 2001, there have been additional smaller exhibitions covering specific protohistoric sites.

Ground floor: Bibracte. As yet the finds have not been exceptional. Of course plenty of pottery has been found widely in living sites and the cemetery, now covered by the car park; 90 per cent was locally made, though no kilns have been found inside the *oppidum*. The fine ware is attractive: some with a lustrous **dark finish** and some with painted spots. A few pieces have Greek-Gallic inscriptions; curiously only feminine endings are found on vessels used for liquids. Imported wares include creamy Campanian and amphorae, Dressel 1, 1B and finally Dressel 20 from Baetica (Spain) providing both dating evidence and support for developing tastes. Equally spread through the exhibits is metalwork produced in Bibracte's many workshops. The small **Rebout workshop model** suggests the way in which its interior was divided for production and storage. Full-scale re-creations include the interior of the Gallic **cellar chambers** from La Pâture du Couvent, suggesting they were used as living accommodation; a section of the rampart shows building technique – adding little to the site reconstruction; and part of PC1 house.

First floor: the Celtic millennium 900 BC–AD 100 throughout Europe.[2] Loan material is drawn from many sites covering both the Hallstatt and La Tène phases. Themes cover general culture: a comparison of *oppida*, such as Manching (Bavaria) and Mont Vully (Fribourg, Switzerland); the typology of gate design using ranks of stylized model gates; various examples of religious sites and burial practices, including a worn stone head found in 1994 at Bibracte; full-scale figures in Gallic checked dress; and a fine model of a Gallic farm, set so high children will not be able to see it! Craft products are used to stress the Celtic economic and technological achievement. A silver coin, stamped with the name Dumnorix, provides one of those rare overlaps with written history and is a poignant reminder of the reality of Caesar's violent presence in Gaul.

NUITS-ST-GEORGES, Côte d'Or

IGN 3024 O

Site and museum.

Nuits-St-Georges lies on the gentle slopes of the eastern edge of the Aeduan heartland in the Morvan hills and the Auxois. The Meuzin river provided a navigable link to the Saône and it was close to prehistoric routes linking the Rhône basin and the Eiffel/Saar regions, as well as an east–west route between Mont Beuvray and Besançon. While near major communications, it was not actually on them. Since the discovery of pre-Roman ditches and Gallic pottery under the Roman 'grand temple' – the name given by the excavator – at **Les Bolards**, 2.5km outside the centre of modern Nuits-St-Georges, development seems more likely to have been based on a Celtic healing sanctuary associated with the Courtavaux warm spring. Peace and the Roman road system gave it the potential to become a moderately successful small town.

There were widespread chance finds in the nineteenth century, sporadic excavations between 1918 and 1948 and regular full-scale work in the Les Bolards area in 1961–89, led by Doctor Planson, a local paediatrician; a necropolis was found when the A31 motorway was built (1973–4), and further evidence was revealed by aerial photography. The settlement – estimated at 25ha – seems to have had a formal layout, but new alignments were adopted over its 500-year history.

The earliest Gallo-Roman *fanum* was surrounded by a few stone structures and some timber and earth houses, given more shape by the first regular streets in the Augustan period. In the mid-first century, the grand temple was built and a new street pattern adopted as the surrounding town expanded. During the second century the town reached its maximum extent, stone building became common, the roads were well made with solid foundations and gutters, and public buildings created including baths, a 'forum', a 'basilica' and, next to the grand temple, a Mithraeum. However, this thriving picture was already threatened by a vulnerability to flooding: numbers of cellars seem to have been deliberately filled in. From the struggle between Severus and Albinus (193–7) onwards, political and economic troubles increased: in the third century the *vicus* was showing serious signs of decline. Its position in the lowlands must have made it a natural target for invaders and by the fifth century the town was in ruins, though coin finds suggest occupation continued until the 450s. Absorbed by the Burgundian kingdom in the late fifth century, it became part of the Frankish realm in 534; the neighbourhood has produced Merovingian cemetery material but no identified settlements.

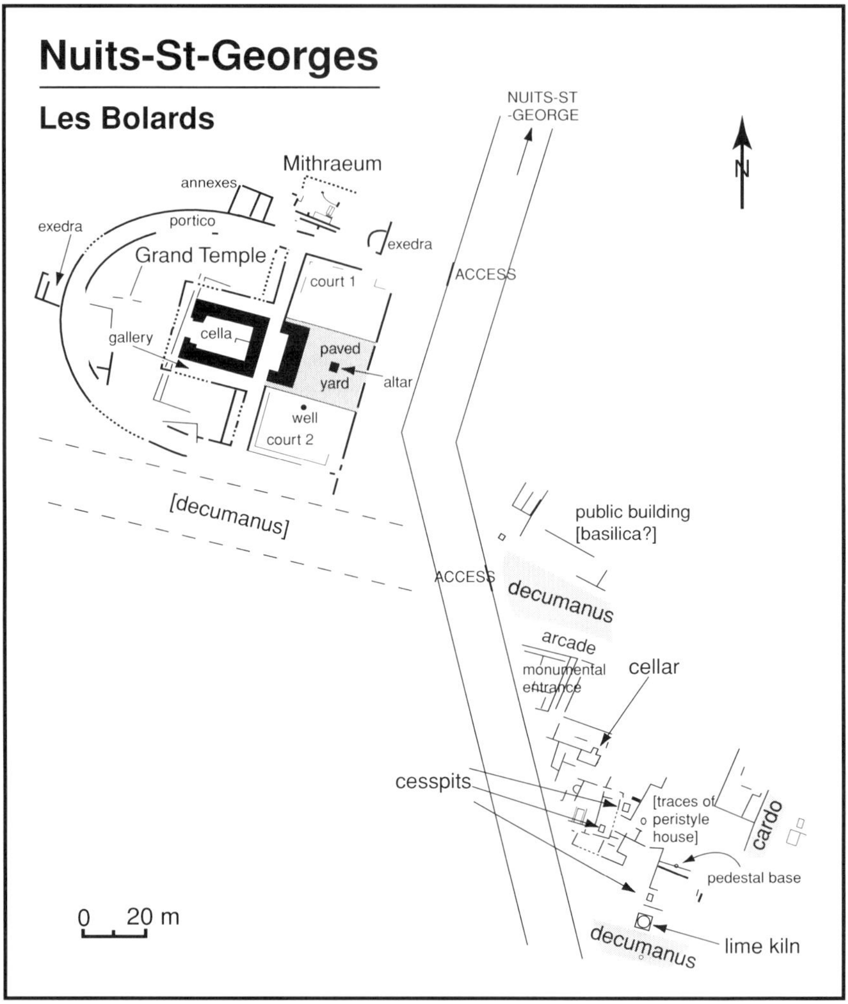

Figure 44 Nuits-St-Georges: Les Bolards

Les Bolards

From the centre of Nuits-St-Georges by Avenue Pasteur, signposted to the A31 motorway, 1.5km to roundabout. Turn right, signposted Seurre and Gerland; 0.75km to minor road on right, signposted Fouilles les Bolards; follow *c.*300m. The road cuts across the excavated area dividing the 'grand temple' from the settlement.

Hours: 2 May–31 Ocober 10a.m.–noon, 2–6p.m. Closed Tuesday

The grand temple

The massive second-century sanctuary walls support a central *cella* and staircase, preceded by a courtyard, enclosed by a semi-circular portico that also provided approaches to the *cella*; but note the narrow walling on a different alignment behind the *cella* that enclosed the earlier *fanum* as well as a scatter of other buildings pulled down for the new sanctuary.

Two features of the **Mithraeum** revealed here seem interesting: first, its size – it is tiny. The exclusive nature of its adherents becomes obvious. Second, its proximity to a much larger sanctuary stresses how this mystery religion, unlike Christianity, in no way challenged other pagan worship, indeed if the grand temple was used to worship a Gallic version of Apollo, then his link with the sun could easily be associated with Mithraic beliefs (see METZ).

The settlement

The fragmentary walls at the northern end of this area are thought to belong to a public building, its length suggesting a **basilica** standing at the end of an open space that in a city would be called a 'forum'; no doubt small towns like this had a market square where people met to discuss business and chat.

Plate 19 Nuits-St-Georges. Cellar with niches, Les Bolards. Photograph: James Bromwich.

On the southern side of the road are traces of a rich **house** that had mosaics and painted plaster walls. The **cellar**, like those at Alesia, could have been used for storage or to hold house divinities in the niches (a Sucellus statuette was found by the entrance). The first-century **sacellum** was identified on the basis of numerous bones mixed with religious material including part of a sacrificial knife. The **basement** has been interpreted as part of a tanner's workshop; post-holes in its floor are seen as representing a scaffold for drying skins, so explaining the nearby pit filled with cattle bones.

Museum

12 Rue Camille Rodier
21700 Nuits-St-Georges
Hours: 2 May–31 October 10a.m.–noon, 2–6p.m. Closed Tuesday

This is an attractive small museum, which uses panels with aerial photographs, models and provides a summary guide in English. There are two rooms; the layout in the larger Gallo-Roman room is broadly thematic. Material that interested me included the following.

The **knife handle** distinctively carved as a crouching monkey wearing a Gallic cape; the numerous **miniaturized offerings** including bells and mirrors, the many white *terre cuite* animals, and the half-metal eye, reflect the desire of the believer seeking the help of the sanctuary to combat hardship, particularly disease. The **triple gods** relief of a three-faced antlered Cernunnos, a hermaphrodite and a conventional mother-goddess with a horn of plenty, sadly rather battered, all encourage fertility and prosperity, reinforced by the animals below feeding at the tree of life. The **Severinus tombstone** shows a thickly built man, wearing a woollen tunic and holding a goblet; many other tombstones follow the same full-face format, some quite competent, some at the 'popular' end, all giving the same impression of small-scale business success; though this simple single-figure relief is typical in the Côte d'Or area, the look is found on many tombstones in eastern Gaul.

The material in the Merovingian room comes from three cemeteries: Arcenant, 9km west of Nuits, Argilly, 9km south-east and Primeaux-Quincey, 3.5km south. From the last comes the earliest material and the only cemetery weapons, including a relatively rare sixth-century Frankish ***angon*** or barbed javelin, based on the Roman *pilum*. Also sixth-century – from Antilly – is an interesting **belt buckle**, decorated with a griffin-headed horse drinking from a cup. The Primeaux cemetery had the most child burials and produced the poorest goods, though one woman was buried here wearing a fine damascened buckle.

Arcenant

788.1/2240.3

Rural sanctuary site.

8km west of Nuits-St-Georges by the D25. The site is situated on the slopes of L'Ecartelot in thick woodland. It can be approached from Arcenant by a number of walks of 2–4km, all attractive and well signposted in the village to the 'ancien site de L'Ecartelot' or, 'Site Gallo-Romain'. The remains are not marked on IGN map.

There are two stone and brick buildings: a **temple** with a small *cella* within a range of rooms and a **house** slightly higher up the hill. Occupation covered the later first to the third century, when fire destroyed them, associated by the local excavators with the invasion of Alamanni and Franks in 259. This was even then hidden by woods and very much a poor persons' place of pilgrimage: there were no votive offerings of the normal kind, instead natural objects like quartz or crystal rocks, fossils, even prehistoric stone tools. Finds in the house suggest that the guardian – perhaps priest as well – lived here, farming a small clearing and exploiting the resources of the forest. A **pool** that collected water running off the hill slope seems to have been for domestic use. Traces of other buildings were found nearby and mark a short-lived return to the site in the later third century.

ST BOIL, Saône-et-Loire

IGN 3025 O

Roman quarry.

On the D981 Chagny to Cluny road, 25km south-west of Chalon-sur-Saône. The quarry is 800m south of the village, on the left-hand side of a track rising a couple of hundred metres to the west of the main road. Though it is surrounded by a wire fence, access is not difficult.

The quarry was recognized as Gallo-Roman in 1971. Backfill and rubble cleared, exploration and painstaking observation followed, led by Gérard Monthel. Ancient quarries give us a rare view of working activity, rather than our having to deduce what was involved from the products of those efforts; certainly the lack of other visitors, its relatively small size (0.5ha), and perhaps its hidden and now partially overgrown nature, make this quarry particularly attractive for such thoughts.

The quarry was one of a number along the slope forming the western edge of the Saône's alluvial plain. Further north at Buxy, Guiry and Fontaines, this white limestone (it fades to a grey or gold patina) was also exploited in the Roman period, but subsequent quarrying has destroyed the Gallo-Roman workings. St Boil limestone was hard and more distant from centres of

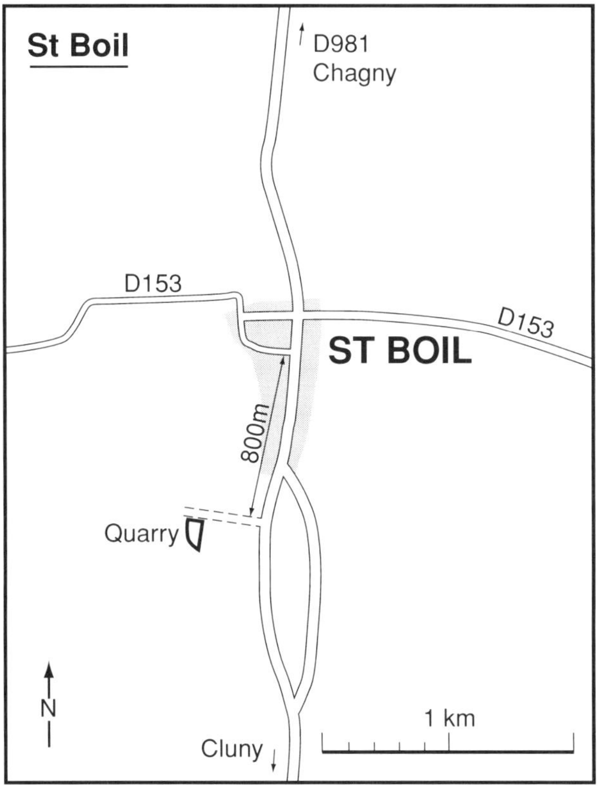

Figure 45 St Boil: area map

demand; exploitation probably began during the first century AD, but quarrying here ended as the second century's dynamic phase of building petered out early in the third century, when towns contracted and disorder grew. Two hoards found here, one of 500 coins, the other of jewellery, suggest that even in the late third century it was rarely visited.

Discarded blocks and columns can still be seen here; possibly they had faults or the orders fell through. The quarry faces show how the quarrymen worked: using simple pickaxes to cut grooves forming the blocks, then partially undercutting the stone; the task was completed by using dampened wooden wedges to split the stone out. The quarry floor was covered with small sandstones used to sharpen their picks after the backbreaking effort. Craftsmen then used hammers, chisels and saws, with sand for grinding and polishing, to complete the orders they received. A forge was an essential element here and two ovens were found where the blacksmith worked at making and repairing tools.

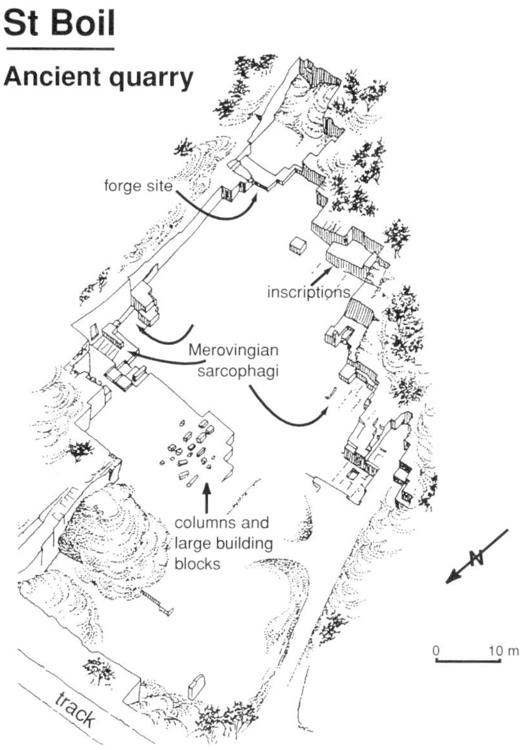

Figure 46 St Boil: the quarry. Drawing by G. Monthel.

An ancient quarry was not just a place for rough-cuts. Skilled craftsmen worked here; if a mistake was made, or a crack appeared, then replacement stone was readily available. A detailed outline of a column – a draughtsman's plan – was drawn on one of the rock faces. The column would have been moved on rollers to the work place. Other drawings and inscriptions were found, some lettering for copying including the 'DM' found on so many tombstones (the abbreviation of *dis manibus*, 'To the spirits of the dead'), some doodles, even some accounts, all done using an oil shale pencil (one was found) made from schist quarried outside Autun. A sculptor worked here as well: unfinished triple mother-goddesses and a broken tombstone suggest his staple work was reliefs.

During the seventh century the quarry was briefly reopened to make coffins. Using the same tools as the workers five centuries before, the new workers cut out the trapezoidal shape fashionable at the time. One lies broken here. But the hardness of the stone must have put them off: local Merovingian burials use sandstone – tombs were no longer a focus for sculptured display.

SENS, Yonne

Sites and museum.

Though not a stronghold of the Senones tribe – it was low-lying and there was marshland on the right bank – Agedincum was already a significant junction for pre-Roman communications. The Yonne provided a major corridor linking the Parisii of the Seine basin and the Aedui of Burgundy, while there were eastern routes into the important territories of the Suessiones and the Remi and to the west, beyond the hills controlled by the Senones themselves, lay the tribes of the Loire basin.

For Caesar, it was obvious that as a pivotal point between his Aedui and Remi allies, he had to secure the Senones' acquiescence. In the early stages of the wars, he was able to use a collaborator, but Cavarinus proved incompetent and in 53 BC an anti-Roman group took over. Caesar rapidly sent in four legions and they capitulated. In the winter months of 53/52 BC, he quartered six legions at Agedincum – more than anywhere else in Gaul. The widespread rising stimulated by Vercingetorix inspired the Senones as well. Caesar showed how important he felt this area to be by crushing the Senones before turning elsewhere; even then, he left Labienus with four legions to intimidate the Senones and Parisii, while Agedincum itself was used to rally two legions of newly drafted men. Only the fall of Alesia brought the Senones finally to recognize Roman control.

Naturally when Agrippa laid out the main strategic roads from Lyon to Boulogne the main road from the south went via Agedincum, yet the Roman city developed slowly. First, to take advantage of the right bank meant a serious programme of drainage: grit, earth and timber to achieve this has been found in many of the deepest occupation levels. Second, as with many places in northern Gaul, recovery from the wars was slow. By the mid-first century AD, though the city had a grid and housing was beginning to fill the blocks, it was sporadic and often poorly built. The second century saw a far greater prosperity, marked by rich houses and major public buildings; more unusually, this continued well into the third century. Recently, D. Perrugot has found strong evidence for a forum in a large block between the modern Grand Rue and the Quai Jean Moulin with a basilica, temple and porticoed shops. A large amphitheatre (160 × 110m), constructed outside the ancient city, was discovered in the 1840s and, searching for springs to satisfy Parisian thirsts in the 1870s, a nineteenth-century engineer traced the path of an aqueduct from St Philibert 16km away. This must have fed the public baths found in the south-west of the town. A theatre is suspected near the forum and the large collection of architectural sculpture suggests that there were other important public buildings, particularly temples. In the suburbs to the south was the large, enigmatic structure called La Motte du Ciar.

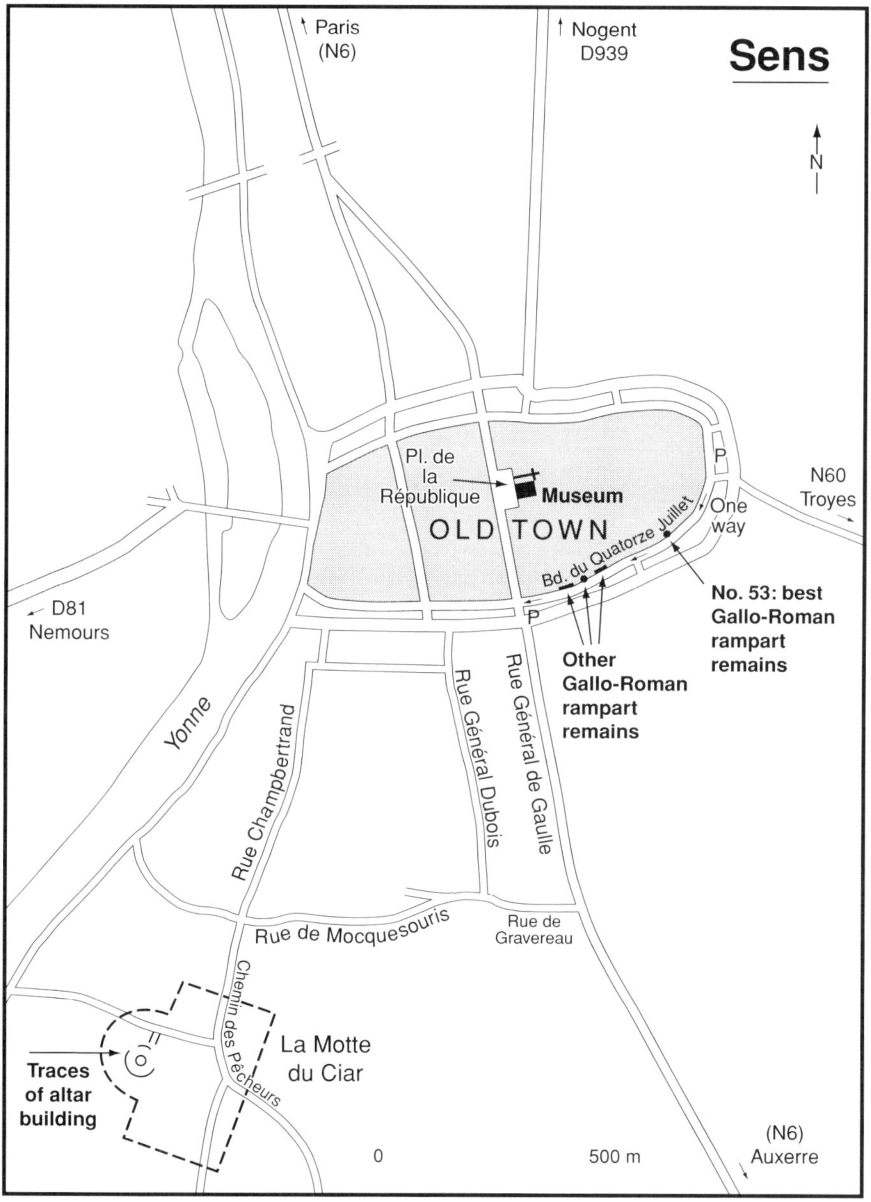

Figure 47 Sens: town plan

The shock of the barbarian invasions was as great here as anywhere. The evidence of the late Roman rampart is that it ignored the earlier street grid, entailed the abandonment and flattening of buildings beyond it, and, to provide stone for the foundations, saw the dismantling of some of the finest buildings in Sens (the south-west baths were severed in half), but enclosed a larger area (34ha) than most towns in Gaul. Its late development perhaps made for more to hang on to and led, when the Gallic administration was reorganised, to the renamed town of 'Senones' becoming the regional capital of Lugdunensis IV, subsequently known as the Christian metropolitan area of Senonia (*c.* 375). Senones frequently figures as an important stopping place for emperors, Caesars and troops in the writings of Ammianus. By the end of the fifth century it was absorbed into the Frankish kingdom.

The late Roman rampart

Boulevard Quatorze Juillet

Nearly 3km of rampart enclosed what became the medieval town of Sens, still clearly defined by a double boulevard. Ramparts are archaeologically identified in many places, but here there are good surviving elements, including part of one semi-circular tower. The extensive reuse of large blocks, *petit appareil* and triple tile courses is apparent. Stephen Johnson has suggested that the technique is very similar to that found at Senlis and Beauvais and therefore implying that the same (army?) team erected this wall. If it was built at the end of the third or early fourth century it seems that it was not finished: Ammianus describes a desperate defence in the 350s because of incomplete walling.

La Motte du Ciar

Chemin des Pêcheurs

In an area abandoned to rubbish and bonfires, all that remains now is a hollow with traces of walling on one side and battered stonework at the centre. The outline was known in the nineteenth century: a large rectangle (nearly 400 × 200m) and an altar-like structure at the centre of a vast apse. An aerial photograph revealed buildings inside the area and two seasons of excavation took place in the 1960s. These remain unpublished. While the excavator saw it as a sanctuary associated with water, D. Parrugot has revived the idea that this was an enormous bath complex. The evidence is the cruciform altar, which is similar to one in the Caracalla baths, and the use of special waterproof cement here. New excavations before the site is finally ruined might provide the answer.

Plate 20 Sens. Late Roman rampart and bastion, Boulevard Quatorze Juillet. Photograph: James Bromwich.

Museum

Ancien Palais d'Archevêché
Place de la Cathédrale
89100 Sens

Hours:	1 June–30 September	10a.m.–noon, 2–6p.m.
	1 October–31 May	Wednesday, Saturday, Sunday, 10a.m.–noon, 2–6p.m. Monday, Thursday, Friday, 2–6p.m.

The museum was renovated in the late 1980s and is an exciting experience. The relief and decorative stonework, both from early Roman public buildings and funeral monuments, are among the best in Gaul.

The baths façade. The basement rooms are entered by a balcony facing the reconstruction of what was probably an external wall belonging to a very magnificent bath system. As various sections of the rampart were pulled down during the nineteenth century, the town museum received a steady flow of carved masonry. In 1891, the curator M. Julliot realized that a number had to have come from the same building, presented drawings of a possible reconstruction and proposed that they came from a baths. The two alternatives to a bath building are basilicas, which did not have rich decoration, and temples, which did not have windows. The revised version presented today follows the 1980s reconstruction of J.P. Adam, the CNRS architect. The blocks form a series of engaged columns, separating large windows. Panel reliefs covered the areas above the windows and there is a frieze running along the foot of the wall. Everywhere there seems to have been a rich decor mixing patterns of twisting foliage and hidden animals.

As the blocks do not come from their original site it is difficult to date. A large, well-cut inscription (in the basement) might be connected: it mentions a portico and ambulatory and is either Trajanic or Hadrianic; however, it is not specific and opinion is split on style: early second to early third centuries. The blocks were all found in the south-west of the wall and the most likely source would be the public baths found in this area, but the Motte site lies not too far beyond. What seems certain is that the work draws on Greek and Roman traditions, without reference to any obvious Gallic influence. This has led to the proposal that they could have been made in a Hellenistic workshop run by a person(s) who came from the eastern part of the empire, settled in Sens. This would account, too, for the number of other architectural pieces reflecting Mediterranean myth rather than Celtic, as well as the equally exuberant material found further down the Yonne at ESCOLIVES and Montmarte temple (see AVALLON).

Probably the finest works of this (possible) Greek workshop are the **Orestes myth reliefs**. Orestes was searching for the altar of Artemis and had come to the land of the Tauri – the Crimea. The inhabitants took all strangers and, after being prepared by a priestess, sacrificed them at the altar. The delicately worked figures show Orestes being brought forward by a bearded guard before the priestess whom Orestes is soon to realize is his sister, Iphigenia. The two were then to escape, carrying away the altar to Attica in Greece. Another block from the same building shows the intelligent bearded Odysseus seeking an explanation from Calchas, the seer who had originally proposed the killing of Iphigenia (by King Agamemnon, her father), from which she had escaped with the help of Artemis. Less impressively worked blocks – perhaps done later by local followers in the workshop – show other figures from Greek myth, such as Ganymede.

The Hellenistic theme is continued in the **mosaic of Phaeton**, sadly missing its central figure, but still impressive with the high quality of the modelling, composition and colour – note the subtle blues and greens. Phaeton was the son of Helios the sun god. He got his unhappy father's permission to drive the sun chariot across the sky only to lose control of the horses. An angry Zeus dispatched a thunderbolt and Phaeton crashed to the earth. We can see the tumble of chariot and horses. The sun imagery is reinforced by the seasons in the corners. It is possible, too, that there was an imperial message as, in the third century, emperors were associated with the sun: not to be tangled with. The **geometric mosaic** is pleasant, less competent and much later, fifth or sixth century, showing the preference for less dense colouring and complex design. It is likely to have decorated a Christian building of some kind.

Two slanting corridors of cellars are filled with **funeral memorials**, distantly evoking a catacomb. One is a veteran of the 22nd Legion. Many involve couples, some full-size, and two figures appear with swords, interpreted to signify that they were landowners. There is a room devoted to craft workers and traders, based on tomb reliefs including wine and textiles, with splendid illustrations of fulling and cropping the cloth, iron working and **a bird seller**. The last stands by a tree with cages on its branches and a large bird (an owl?) standing on a pole: they may have been for sacrifice. The finest portrayal – that Greek workshop again? – is of the **blacksmith Bellicus** holding a hammer, other tools around him and his dog at his feet. His hair is short but a lock is left long; it suggests that he was from Germany where this was fashionable.

The last part of the Gallo-Roman collection is in the two basement rooms. One contains another fifth-/sixth-century **mosaic**. Despite the two deer, suggesting that this might have been laid near or in a baptistery (they were one of the early symbols of Christian faith), this is a rather lifeless work. A case on writing has a diptych, two panels of fifth-century ivory showing complex pagan scenes, demonstrating how traditional culture still survived among the very wealthy. The other room preserves the excavation *in situ* of a first-century hypocaust room and furnace (a nice touch are the steps to climb onto the remains); in a side case numerous fourth-century bone combs.

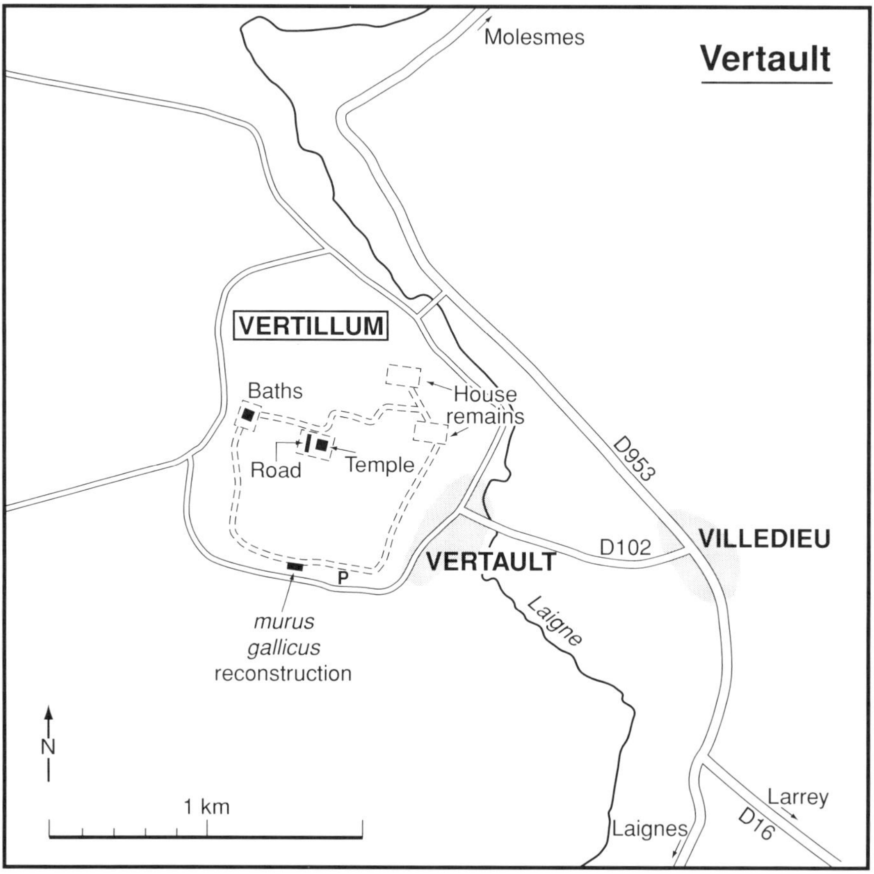

Figure 48 Vertault: area map

VERTAULT, Côte d'Or

Site.

23km north-west of Châtillon-sur-Seine by the D965 and D16 to Villedieu. Following the D102[1] to Vertault, left at the T-junction signposted for 'Vertillum', *c.*250m up the side of the hill to the site parking area.

Panels under a wooden shelter introduce Vertillum; clear signposts indicate the paths round the site; further panels describe the main features. Nothing is outstanding, yet in the rural peace, especially during the spring and summer when the woodland and meadows are blooming, bathed in sunlight, and the butterflies, birds, grasshoppers and dragonflies dart about, then the sense of time and past inhabitants comes most alive.

Vertillum covered most of the plateau, overlooking the tiny Laigne river, which appears to have been navigable as quays and building have been identified to the north-east of the site. A rampart enclosed about 25ha – a decent-sized small town. It was first explored in 1846 and irregular excavations continued until 1939, by which time more than 10ha had been uncovered. Since then, nature has largely taken over; modern archaeologists have focused simply on clarification or exploration below the plateau. René Joffroy excavated the ramparts in 1954 and 1981. The Mangin team in the 1980s began to set out a stratigraphy and was responsible for the 'temple' consolidation. They also undertook a small-scale excavation at a Gallic sanctuary revealed by aerial photography to the south of the town.

Digging in the ruins of the baths in the 1840s, Lucien Coutant found the inscription (taken to Dijon) that indicated both the name and status of Vertillum: a *vicus* in Lingones territory. Its decurions would have been drawn from the estate owners around Vertillum; more than fifty Gallo-Roman villas and farms are known in the area. Like many other small towns this was an active production centre (see CHATILLON). Iron smelting and tool manufacturing, together with bone working, clustered in the north of the town, while shops crowded by and to the south of a large open area (*c.*2ha), loosely called a 'forum', that could also have held district markets – predecessors of the great medieval Champagne fairs.

The nineteenth-century excavators barely recognized stratigraphy and their mapping seems to have been equally poor: new occupation zones found through aerial photographs cannot be added on to the old excavations because they do not 'fit'. Vertillum's pre-Roman history is particularly obscure. Modern sondages and a careful reading of the old reports suggests that the earliest houses were first century BC, but it is not clear if these were before or after the conquest. Even the Gallic rampart could be Augustan. Signs of Romanization are evidence from the early first century AD, with straight roads that formed a loose grid by the time of the Flavians, and the construction of water channels associated with a large number of cisterns. The town probably reached its maximum prosperity under the Antonines. It was badly hit in the third century, but the reconstruction of the baths suggests that in the fourth century there was a revival before widespread burning. Vertillum was abandoned in the fifth century, never to be reoccupied.

The Gallic rampart

Car park site.

The reconstruction was erected in the 1980s, based on Joffroy's exploration of the *murus gallicus* he identified following the edge of the plateau. This formed the face of an 18m-wide mound, 3m high, fronted by a wide, shallow, sloping ditch cut into the flaky bedrock stone. A framework of timber held together with iron pegs was given a smooth surface with well-cut limestone blocks hiding the fill. The ditch seems to have been deliberately filled in by the mid-first century AD.

Excavation hut

On the path following the eastern hill slope.

In the late nineteenth and early twentieth century the hut was used for storing tools and finds. The Société d'Archéologie et d'Histoire du Châtillonnais, the archaeologist in charge, Henri Lorimy, and the diggers come to life in the contemporary photographs and illustrations of the excavations. The overgrown trenches and walls of the old excavations can be glimpsed in the shadows of the bushes and trees around the hut.

Underground rooms

On the path following the eastern hill slope.

Half a dozen or so cellars were cleared again in the 1980s and are now only partially overgrown. The number of houses with cellars is only exceeded by Alesia (see also MONT BEUVRAY). They are known to have Gallic origins, but were still being used during the second century AD. Some are very well built with neatly cut stones, inset niches and stone staircases; the floors were lined and the walls plastered. It is a matter of debate as to why they went to this trouble: were they simply for storage? Or dry, warm places to live and work during the winter? Or were they domestic chapels? Or multi-functional?

The 'temple'

On the south of an open meadow in the centre of the plateau.

The outline of the eastern end of an oblong building with internal apses has been consolidated in concrete. It is orientated east–west, but, as the modern sondages have shown, it went through a series of alterations having started out with a north–south plan supported by pillars down the centre. The failure to distinguish this stratigraphy, identifying the pillars of the early building as a portico for the later one, together with the discovery of an altar in one of the apses, led excavators to identify it as a temple in 1884. It is now thought that it may have been a public building by the 'forum', perhaps a basilica, maybe a market hall or *macellum* (see ALESIA).

The baths

In a depression on the western slope of the plateau, partially protected by metal roofing.

Vertault

Baths

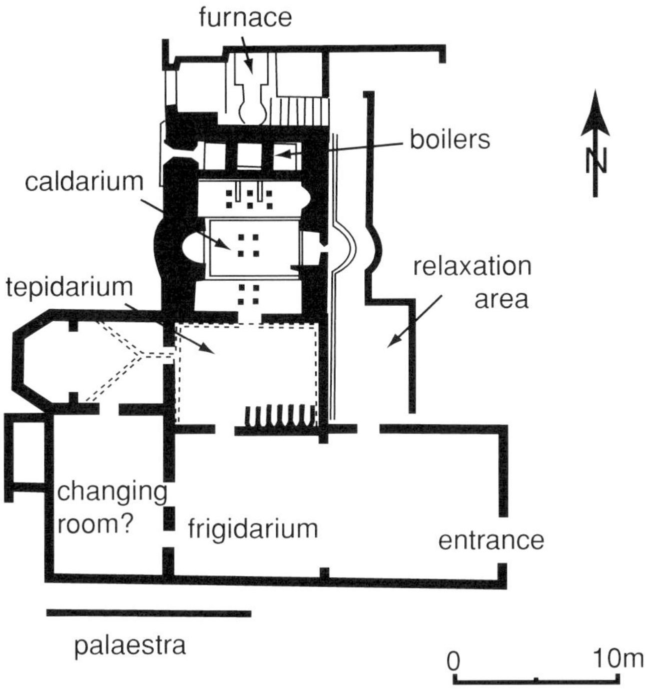

Figure 49 Vertault: baths

The baths were cleared very rapidly in the earlier 1840s, excavated intermittently up to the 1860s and then briefly re-examined in the 1980s. They, too, had gone through various alterations over time, the surviving features being largely those of the third-century reconstruction, perhaps a gift by two leading Lingones citizens whose inscription was found in the *tepidarium*. Sadly, the walls that once stood to 3–4m high have crumbled and inevitably the appearance on an unprotected site is unkempt, but it is still possible to make out the main sections of the baths, though their identification is not totally convincing.

The paths from the temple and from the car park focus naturally on the southern end of the baths. Two parallel walls hint at a portico for a **palaestra** or exercise yard. The **main entrance** appears to have been from the east; fragments of painted plaster, statues and a red marble table suggest that this was impressive. The next room was the ***frigidarium*** in which stood a cold water basin. But the large room beyond has been identified as an ***apolydarium*** or dressing room, though this seems strange coming *after* the *frigidarium*. Two other rooms would have climaxed a baths visit: the heated room (a Y-shaped channel system), possibly an ***unctorium*** used for massage and perfumes. The other was a room and corridor running behind the main baths area, which, because of the luxurious decor of plaster and marble plaques and the glass window alcove to keep out the cold, was identified as a 'conversation' area.

The floor of the ***tepidarium*** was covered with a mosaic and heated in its limited fashion by an under-floor channel running round the room; the walls had clay *tubili* to provide further heat and carry away the gases. Of the sculpture found here, the inscription and the three goddesses (see CHATILLON) are unlikely to have stood here originally, though fragments of decorated frieze suggest some magnificence. The ***caldarium*** was the heart of the whole and must have been impressive. A door from the *tepidarium* led into an entrance area beside a shallow heated pool flanked by semi-circular and rectangular apses with hot plunge basins. On the opposite side of the pool was a semi-dry heated area, where bathers could sit on two benches next to the wall separating them from the three boilers that once stood in a row, heated by a furnace, approached from the outside by steps down into a small yard. In the lower apse a drain, pink cement, and traces of plaster survive clinging to the rough-cut stone, while in the rectangular basin, traces of waterproof concrete flooring and heating *tubuli* can also be seen.

VEZELAY, Yonne

IGN 2722 O

Sites and museum.

Ensure that you visit the breathtaking Romanesque church in Vézelay itself, then visit the nearby Gallo-Roman sites associated with a sulphur water spring and the exploitation of local iron.

St Père-sous-Vézelay

Les Fontaines-Salées sanctuary and baths (708.5/2273.1). St Père is below Vézelay. The site, 1.5km by the D958, is signposted by the river Cure.
Hours: 31 March–1 November 10a.m.–12.30p.m., 1.30–6.30p.m.

Rich salted mineral water – radioactive chlorinated soda with intermittent gas emissions – filled the springs here. Local exploitation to make salt infringed the royal monopoly and Louis XIV ordered the area to be covered over. In 1934, René Louis, a medievalist, decided to look here for a legendary battle mentioned in a twelfth-century poem and instead discovered

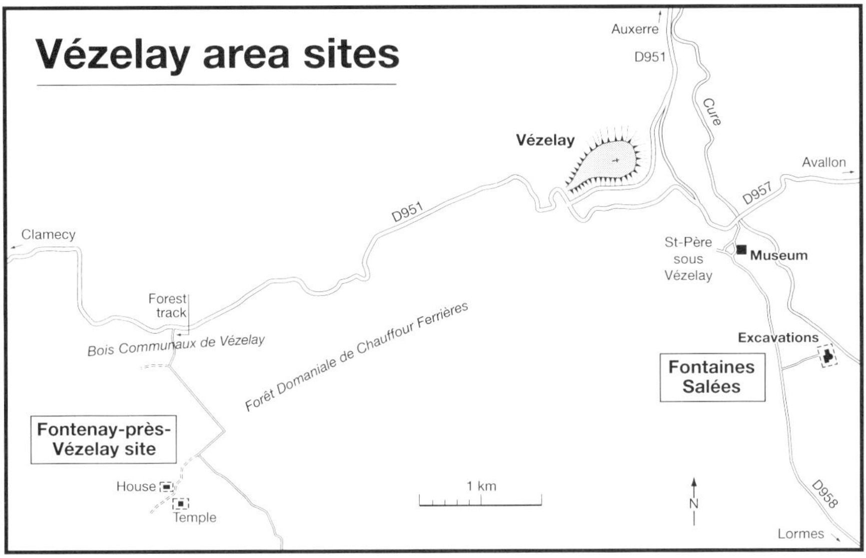

Figure 50 Vézelay: area map

continuous use from the Neolithic to Roman: it became a new life's interest and he led excavations before, during, and after the Second World War. The last major work was carried out by his protégé Abbé Lecroix in the 1960s. It is clear the site could do with more precise dating and the identification of some rooms is questionable.

Oak frames have been found at various points on the site, sunk to channel the spring outlets, and were most recently confirmed as late Neolithic (*c.*2500 BC). The spring's gaseous effects and strange taste must already have given the site a mysterious and religious aura, maybe even attributed healing properties (it is associated with help for rheumatism and skin disorders) – and provided salt. During the Iron Age a **Celtic sanctuary** was constructed. A square stone paved basin known to be first century BC covered an earlier wooden structure. This was encircled by a double ring enclosure, the inner marked by a wall, strongly suggesting a circular *fanum*. The basin was used for offerings into the fourth century AD (500 found).

First-century AD Gallo-Roman building left the Celtic structure untouched. A large rectangular enclosure with a square apse filled with a pool, drawing water from a nearby spring, presumably formed a major new religious focus. A simple bath complex was built for visiting worshippers. During the second century the sanctuary was expanded: an entrance house was built by the road and a second bath system was added to the first, enabling men and women to prepare themselves separately and providing

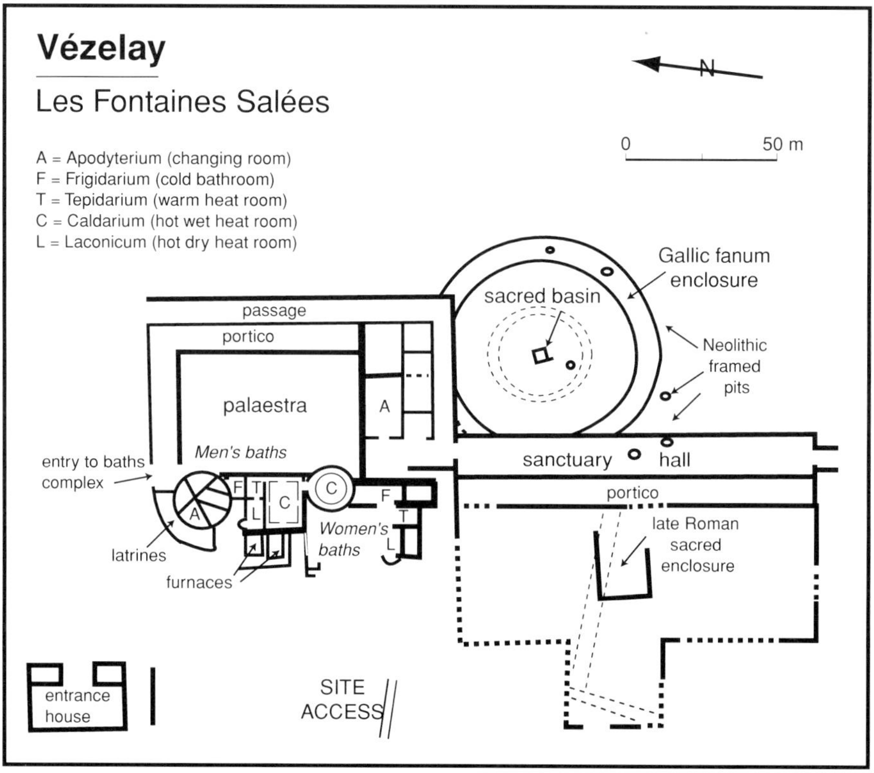

Figure 51 Vézelay: Les Fontaines Salées

both with extra rooms and a *palaestra*. This cut into the circular Celtic structure as did the new 'entrance hall' and portico added to the pool enclosure: clearly the pre-Roman sanctuary was out of use – apart from the basin. The whole sanctuary was destroyed in the later third century. A hut was put up within the enclosure and may represent some form of continuity but was abandoned by the 320s. A farmer occupied rooms around the *palaestra* in the mid-fourth century and a butcher later occupied the entrance house; one room became a smoke-house for curing his meat.

St Père Musée Archéologique

By the church.
Hours: 31 March–1 November 10a.m.–12.30p.m, 1.30–6.30p.m.

From Fontaines Salées come examples of the Neolithic oak pipes that once framed spring outlets, and votive offerings from the Celtic basin. Small Gallo-Roman finds include some typical animal fibulae and there is a collection of

Plate 21 Vézelay. Les Fontaines Salées sanctuary looking across the baths. Photograph: James Bromwich.

late Roman farm tools. Remains of a wooden sluice, a poker, *tuyères*, slag and metal fragments have been brought here from the Fontenay forest excavations.

Fontenay-près-Vézelay

710.9/2272.6

The house and *fanum* are *not* at the village with this name (see IGN Série Bleue 2722 O Vézelay). Take the D951 west from Vézelay to Clamecy. At the 5km stone and signpost *Les Ferrières Centre Sidérurgique*, take a minor road into the Bois Communaux de Vézelay and Forêt Domaniale de Chauffour Ferrières. Pass the picnic site, 400m, then another *c.* 1,200m where the road makes a right-angle turn to the left, you carry straight on, taking the forest track; parking area beyond no entry sign. Walk *c.* 150m to **villa site** on right under metal roofing; *c.* 100m further on left sign to **temple site** *c.* 50m, under metal roofing. Open access all year.

In 1929, local iron companies discovered that the region to the west of Vézelay, now heavily forested, was covered with ancient slag that was so filled with iron it could be economically reworked: many thousand of tons were re-smelted.

Names such as 'Forêt de Chauffour Ferrières' are relics of both Gallo-Roman ironworking and the re-smelting of ancient slag carried out in the 1930s and post-war period. In the 1960s, as this came to an end, not only was a wooden Roman ore washing sluice found and numerous pits where the Roman miners and smelters worked, but also remains of a house and tiny *fanum*. The villa's position strongly suggests that this was an administrator's house; even stucco moulding and wall painting were found. The *fanum* was identified on the basis of a relief suggesting a man beside a god, probably Mercury, and a weathered bronze Mercury: he was identified with commercial prosperity.

VILLARDS D'HERIA, Jura

IGN 3327 OT

Sanctuary site.

About 40km south-south-east of Lons-le-Saunier to the east of Lac de Vouglans (Ain), taking the N78, D52 and the D470 for Moirans. It is also about 38km north from Nantua, by the N84, D984/D436 and D27.

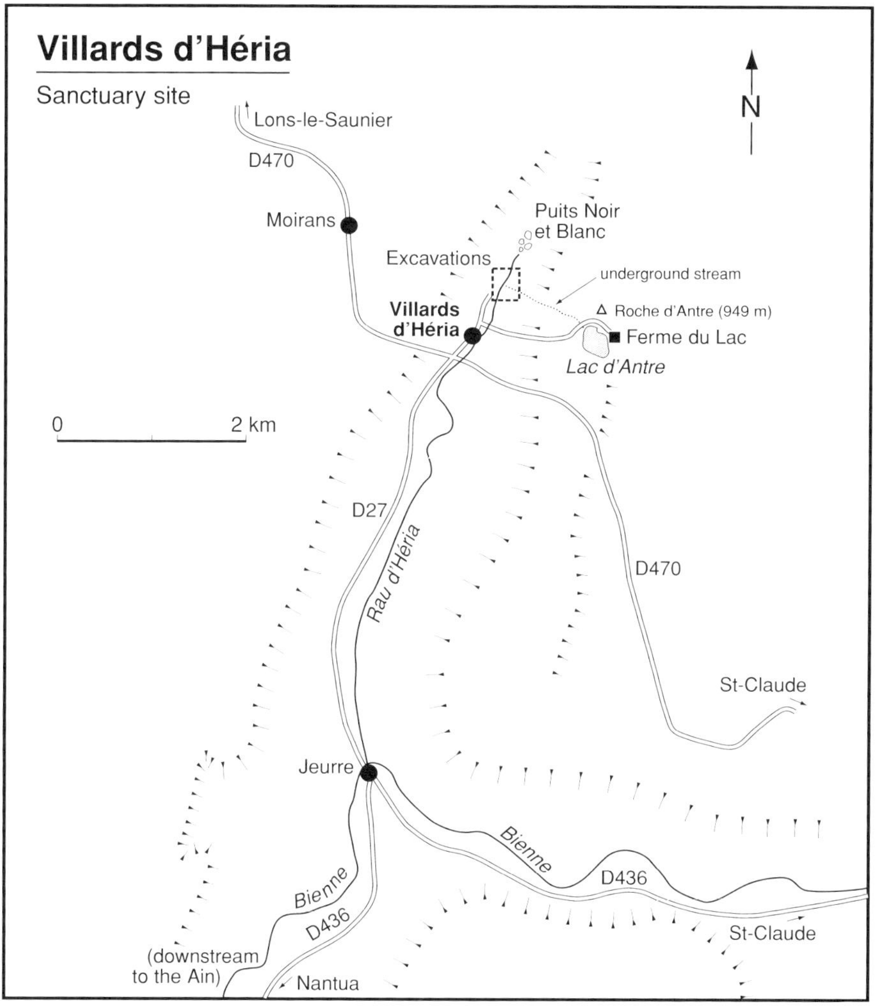

Figure 52 Villards d'Héria: area map

Lac d'Antre

862.5/2162.5

In the heart of the Jura massif is a small, silent mountain lake surrounded by steep tree-covered hills; a towering rock bluff dominates the western side, and at the northern end there is a small meadow clearing with an old, shuttered farmhouse. In 1698, an antiquarian priest, Pierre-Joseph Dunod, described how there was a mysterious but magnificent Gallo-Roman 'city' here. He cited two temples, now largely covered by the farmhouse, and these have been confirmed by modern survey (though no serious excavation has been possible/undertaken), as well as a long wall, interpreted as the sanctuary enclosure. On top of the rock, he also claimed a temple; no traces have survived, but it is considered possible that a small temple or altar stood here. The lake sites are now seen as elements in an upper sanctuary, perhaps earlier than the Val d'Héria temple complex, so explaining the absence of any pre-Roman material at the lower site.

The Val d'Héria sanctuary. Dunod described the remains that survived in his time, and, even allowing for exaggeration, it is clear that much more was then standing than today: one sad effect of his efforts was to attract pillagers. Though Louis XIV issued orders against looting, it was probably the heavy woods and steep slopes that allowed the site's survival, in its modern excavated state, as a charming and atmospheric place.

A badly preserved inscription found by the lake has been read as a dedication by 'the *vicus*'. That this was indeed a community of more than an isolated sanctuary seems likely. In addition to the temple and baths excavated by Lucien Lerat in 1961–82, J.-L. Odouze in the 1970s explored a section of what is likely to have been a pilgrims' hostel 100m to the north and west of the temple, now covered again by forest. Dunod claimed there was an amphitheatre; modern observers have identified a site for a theatre. Slag and bronze fragments, caught in the fissures of the stream, suggest a nearby metal workshop. Surface finds and fragmentary stonework indicate that habitations spread out over an estimated 12ha, where those who worked in the sanctuary lived at least in summer time: winter snow must have helped isolate the place and, with few pilgrims coming then, may have led many to move down the valley. It is likely that most pilgrims approached Villards via the Bienne valley; indeed the river is believed to have been navigable to Jeurre. All the recent finds are kept at LONS-LE-SAUNIER.

'Pont des Arches'/temple excavations

862.1/2163.8

Hours: 10a.m.–noon, 2–6p.m. with guided tours

The massive blocks of the Pont des Arches, through which the Héria crashes in winter and dribbles in the summer, have always been visible, but the installation of modern water piping in 1959–60 led to Lerat's twenty years' excavations here. He revealed exceptionally well-preserved bathing pool remains and an even more unusual temple complex. The key is the water. The 'bridge' marks the junction of the stream and an underground spring, which takes twelve hours to trickle down from the lake. It is this congruence that perhaps gave the site its mystical significance, stimulating the imaginative construction of a unique temple over running water. Dedications, both here and at the upper sanctuary, to Mars and Bellona, his Roman

Villards d'Héria

Sanctuary

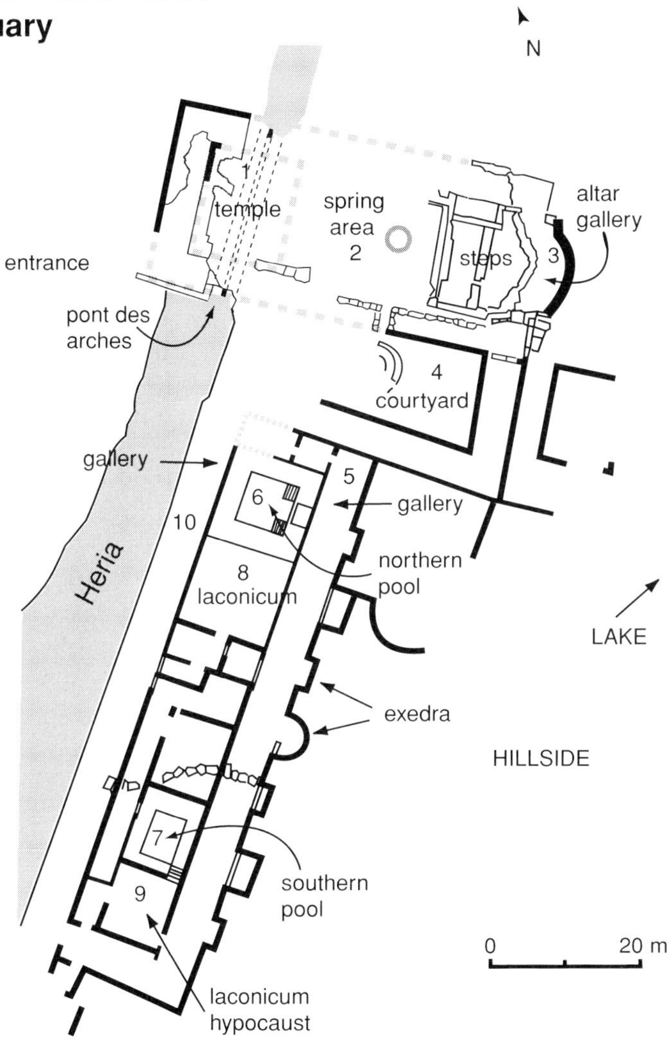

Figure 53 Villards d'Héria: site plan

warrior consort, have been taken to hint that this was an official sanctuary of the Sequani *civitas*.

Though there was a first-century AD building, the temple complex remains that we see today were built in the early second with some later modifications. It was abandoned early in the third century, presumably due to economic and political dislocation, exacerbated in the fourth century by the arrival of Christianity and a long cold phase that led to widespread withdrawal from the upper Jura in the early Middle Ages.

The temple zone. There are three distinct sections. (1) The **temple foundations** are formed by the imposing 23m-long channels constructed with 3m-long blocks of the local limestone, raising the floor 4.2m above the southern exit of the stream. No cement was used, the weight of the floor (and the temple above) holding it in place. Only traces of the *fanum* temple base survive; large broken column fragments suggest that there was a gallery around three sides. The front faced east and had steps down to (2) an **open paved area** with, at its centre, a circular opening where the spring bubbled. This is now capped by a modern stone and metal structure. Flush with the hillside was (3) a **gallery** with a wide stone apse for altars, approached from the central paved area by a monumental staircase. The temple zone was linked to the baths by (4) a **trapezoidal courtyard**, possibly a garden with a circular pool in the middle, surrounded by frescoed galleries. The statue base of an Aeduan priest of the Three Gauls (see LYON) found here is now re-erected in the bath section. Perhaps it was a special thanks by the Sequani for a favour given at the annual council meeting.

The bath area. This 70m-long building with galleries on each side had two separate bath systems. (5) The **hillside gallery** had *exedrae*, each decorated with frescoes of vegetation filled with birds and animals. Food finds, game counters and graffiti suggest the pilgrims rested here before or after their plunge in the holy waters. The central *exedra* had surviving tiles secured to the wall providing extra protection from the damp (snow must have piled up on the outside walls in winter). Light came through glass windows. Most dramatic are the superbly preserved pools, their steps leading down 1.5m. (6) By the **northern pool** is the offering box where the pilgrims could drop coins. The water filled the pools from basins, the one in the north still having its lead lining. (7) The **southern pool** reveals the exit hole. There were **dry heat rooms** (8) and (9) where the pilgrims could warm up after the no doubt very cold dip. The southern hot room still has battered hypocaust piles and a stoke room. These are not true bath systems on the public model; there are no lukewarm or hot damp rooms, but limited versions designed only to enhance the religious experience.

The Héria. The **western gallery** (10) ran along beside the stream and had an open portico for pilgrims to look out over the water. The large blocks running beside the portico may have formed **a quay**, perhaps paralleled by one originally on the other side and a small dam below to create a large pool. There is no conclusive evidence for this, but upstream the rock has been cut to direct the flow through the channels under the temple and there was walling to control **the springs** – *puits noir et blanc* – where the stream began (an easy ten-minute walk by the forestry road).

Plate 22 Villards d'Héria. Northern pool of the mountain valley sanctuary. Photograph: James Bromwich.

VILLERS-FARLAY, Jura

IGN 3224 O

Tile-making kiln.

Villers-Farlay is 45km south-west of Besançon by the N83 and D472. The site is *c.*2.8km south of the village, taking the turning by the post office and the right-hand track at the pond; it rapidly becomes a bumpy forestry road. There is then a 150m walk along a path through the dense serried ranks of young trees. The kiln is on the right under a shelter. Multi-lingual panels describe the site.

Fears of clandestine digging and the destruction threatened by the plantation led to 1990s excavation and excellent protective covering. The kiln, itself built of tiles, is very well preserved. A large square chamber, 4 × 4.2m, it could hold an impressive 10–20,000 tiles at a time. A stack of *imbrices* tiles still stands on one side of the chamber. The heat rose through eighty-eight holes in the chamber floor. Under the floor, it flowed through a central passage and along lateral branches created by tile walls. A vaulted corridor covered the furnace, but the vaults collapsed and are now outlined in timber. A worker standing in the pit at the end of the corridor would have stoked the fire.

The readily available clay makes clear why this site was chosen, but the zones where the workers cut the clay out, cleaned it, moulded the shapes and dried them are not exposed. The workshop manufactured the two standard roof tile types, *tegula* and *imbrex*, and perhaps bricks and tubes. It formed part of a small settlement (*c.*4ha) by the main Roman road from Lyon to Besançon. No doubt this artery provided the workshop with access to its main markets, though these are likely to have been relatively local (Besançon?); sadly the workers did not name their tiles, as at the CLARIANUS works in the Rhône valley. Yet the design conforms to a model found throughout the Roman world, and in their everyday way show Romanization at its most pervasive: something that was not there before the Romans conquered Gaul, nor in the years after.

OTHER SITES

Arlouf (Nièvre), in the hamlet of Bardiaux, has the exposed remains of a rural theatre and a nearby building. **Entrains-sur-Nohain** (Nièvre) had a major sanctuary, but the extensive excavations have been filled in; it has fine, changing summer exhibitions. Little survives of Gallo-Roman **Nevers** (Nièvre), but new excavations are revealing more; it has a small municipal museum and runs special exhibitions. Close to St Germain, the **Sources-de-la-Seine** (Côte d'Or) has nothing visible of the many excavations, but the site is resonant of its healing sanctuary past.

Notes

1 At the time it simply stimulated political enemies to encourage local antiquaries to promote alternatives. By the end of the 1860s, seven other sites were being touted and others have been promoted since. The evidence for Mont Auxois produced then and in recent work seems overwhelming and no serious historian or archaeologist has challenged it.

2 Surprisingly, the large wall-map does not show what they consider to be the Celtic world, though the exhibits focus entirely on continental Europe. This may not be surprising to archaeologists involved in the debate over artefacts, cultures and peoples, but undoubtedly many Irish, Welsh, Scots and even a few Cornish will find it disturbing that they play no part in this vision.

TRAVEL AND COMMUNICATIONS IN ROMAN GAUL

For Strabo, the great geographer (*c.*64–29 BC), the striking feature of Gaul was its excellent communications. He described it as an isthmus between two seas: the 'interior' or Mediterranean Sea and the vast 'exterior' Ocean, which could be reached by sailing past Spain and through the gates of Gibraltar, *or* by crossing Gaul. As he explained,

> The riverbeds are by nature so well situated with reference to one another that there is transportation from either sea into the other; for the cargoes are transported only a short distance by land, with an easy transit through the plains, but most of the way they are carried on rivers – on some into the interior, on the others to the sea.
>
> (Strabo, IV, 1, 2)

One route, long exploited by the Romans as a trade link for British products, went via the Aude and Garonne. However, the key role was now played by the Rhône:

> In the first place, the voyage which the Rhodanus affords inland is a considerable one, even for vessels of great burden, and reaches numerous parts of the country, on account of the fact that the rivers which fall into it are navigable, and in their turn receive most of the traffic. Secondly, the Rhodanus is succeeded by the Arar [Saône], and by the Dubis [Doubs] which empties into the Arar [Saône]; then the traffic goes by land as far as the Sequana [Seine] river; and thence it begins its voyage down to the ocean.
>
> (Strabo, IV, 1, 14)

At the heart of the watershed lay Aeduan territory, criss-crossed with porterages to the Yonne, Armançon and Seine. In the north the watershed between the eastern-draining Maas and Scheldt and the western-draining Oise, Aisne and Marne lay across the plains dominated by the Remi tribe. During the Gallic wars, Caesar always saw the Aedui and Remi as crucial

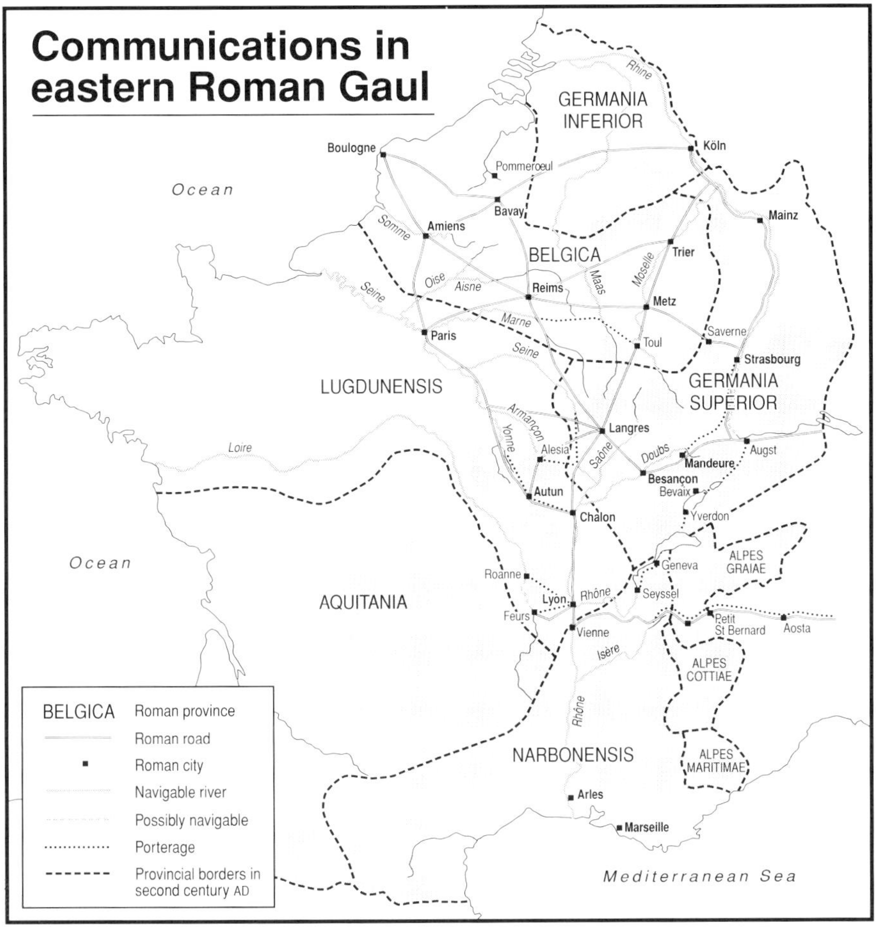

Figure 54 Communications in Gaul: map

Roman allies, so it is not surprising that their capitals Autun and Reims became two of the largest cities in Gaul.

In the following centuries, the rivers linking Gaul and Germany were at times even more important, either via the Doubs and the Belfort gap onto the Alsace plain or via the Saône and the Moselle, joining the Rhine between the major fortresses of Mainz and Köln. Besançon, Mandeure and Strasbourg, Metz and Trier emerged as major inland ports on the Doubs–Alsace and the Saône–Moselle routes. This did not change a feature already obvious to Strabo (IV, 6, 11): 'Lugdunum is in the centre of the country – an acropolis, as it were, not only because the rivers meet here, but also because it is near all parts of the country.' As well as being the linchpin of all movement to and from the north and south, it was the junction for upper Rhône traffic down from the Alps and transport west to the Loire valley and northern Aquitania. Strabo goes on to write: 'And it was on this account, also, that Agrippa began at Lugdunum when he cut his roads.'

Traditionally, Gallic roads have been underestimated by archaeologists, but aerial photography is revealing a network of roads linking major *oppida* and providing communications with farmsteads. The mention of bridges by Caesar implies that many of these roads were more than simple tracks, a view strengthened by the use of Gallic names for a range of two-wheel and four-wheel carts and the Gauls' contemporary reputation for skilful wheel making. What Agrippa and his successors brought was a long tradition in carefully surveyed, direct and well-engineered roads along which traffic could move faster and more reliably than ever before.

The main roads initially focused on the strategic needs of the army. Most followed river valleys, but sometimes more direct routes might be taken, such as the Lyon–Trier highway which shortly after the port of Chalon climbed up onto the Langres plateau, joining the Moselle valley at Toul. Langres itself became a crossroads for an east–west route linking both Mandeure and Besançon with central France. Further north, another road crossed the Moselle highway at Metz, coming from Strasbourg in the east via the Saverne gap, and going to Reims in the west, where branches led to Paris, Amiens or Boulogne. Further north still, another military highway enabled the transfer of troops between the British and Rhine frontiers by joining Boulogne naval base to Bavay and Köln.

Together with other state-owned *viae publicae,* these provided a network for the towns and many *vici*. In addition there were the *viae vicinales*, built and maintained by the *pagi* and therefore often built according to the needs of the local aristocracy. These were generally narrower, though many were still expected to be able to take wheeled traffic. Finally there were paths, used by people and pack-animals particularly in porterage areas and mountainous regions.

As Marcus Varro (116–27 BC) wrote at the beginning of the Gallo-Roman era, 'the transport of produce makes the farm all the more profitable if there are good wagon-roads or navigable rivers nearby' (*On Farming*, I, 16, 6). Heavy loads, ranging from farm produce, such as cereals, fruit and vegetables, to amphorae and barrels of wine, beer, oil and fish sauce; timber and stone; bales of textiles; the stacks of pottery or tiles; or the products of the metal workshops, all could be carried more cheaply and securely by river. But, as Varro hints by putting wagons first, and as recent studies suggest, the cost differences were not so great as to discourage extensive trade by road, though the organization of water-based commercial corporations and the lack of any memorials commemorating road-based transport suppliers implies the profits of water transport were higher. As its magnificent collection of epitaphs

Lyon

The inscription of Sabinianus the river trader

A rich shipper shows his pride and wealth by leaving 3 denarii to all his fellow boatmen, many of whom must must have been significantly poorer, to ensure his importance was recognized by a memorial.

The Latin expanded

Locus datus decreto nautarum rhodanicorum	Caius Julius Sabinianus nauta rhodanicus in honorem nautarum rhodanicorum dat	dedicatione doni hvivs omnibus navigantibus denarios tres dedit

Translated

The site was given by decree of the Rhône shippers	Caius Julius Sabinianus, Rhône shipper, gives (this) in honour of the Rhône shippers	for the dedication of this gift (site) he has given 3 denarii to each of the boatmen shippers

Figure 55 Sabinianus, a Lyon shipper

shows, LYON (Lugdunum) provides a revealing picture of Roman commerce at work.

Sea transport offered the greatest opportunity for profit: a few well-chosen loads could be the making of a businessman (a *negotiator*), as Petronius has Trimalchio boast in the *Satyricon* (76). There were offices of shippers, the *navicularii*, in Lugdunum. **Quintus Capitonius Probatus** (*CIL*, XIII, 1942), from Rome, is commemorated on a tombstone put up by his Greek freedmen. He ran a business linking Lugdunum with Puteoli, one of Rome's two ports; as an Augustan *sevir* in both centres, he must have been a leading figure in each city. Perhaps his ships came up the Rhône to Lugdunum (the pontoon bridge at Arles would have allowed this), or maybe the goods he imported and exported were transferred to specialist river craft, owned by *nautae* (boatmen) like **Caius Julius Sabinianus** (*CIL*, XIII, 2002). They would have been dragged upstream by *heliciarii*, the hauliers or 'human tractors'. It is not simply that men were cheap, they are also more adaptable than animals, particularly as haulage paths seem to have been rare. Even in the fourteenth century, hundreds could be employed to pull one boat; they averaged 5km a day for the 270km journey.

The upper Rhône was rock filled, fast and dangerous. Though light boats could work as far as Seyssel, for cargoes travelling downstream rafts were common. *Ratiarii* brought down stone from the mountain quarries and then sold the raft timbers for building or firewood, returning upstream by road. Lyon also had *Utricularii*, who derived their name from hides. Some writers see them as specialist rafters, using air-filled animal skins; others consider that the name is merely a memory, that they were the lightermen who unloaded goods from larger ships, as their corporation name is usually associated with a town, not a river.

These rivermen, like other traders, had corporations or *collegia*. They were associations whose declared aims were to perform rituals for the gods, collect money for appropriate burials and hold feasts at the cemeteries or in their *scholae*/meeting houses. Undoubtedly they also formed pressure groups: all tried to get patrons who might win them favours. On another epitaph in Lyon (*CIL*, XIII, 1911), the Saône *nautae* and the wine merchants commemorate a patron from Trier, **Caius Apronius Raptor**, no doubt furthering their joint interests on the Moselle.

Considerable river traffic left Lugdunum by the Saône, and its river shippers must have been among the most important. Epitaphs suggest at least three corporations of *nautae* and independants. One *collegium* represented those who operated on the Loire as well, while others combined work on the Rhône and Saône. Some *nautae* inevitably ran businesses that brought together different trades. **Marcus Primius Secundianus** (*CIL*, XIII, 1966) of Lugdunum belonged to both the boat-owners' and the woodworkers' corporations, perhaps as a carrier and boatbuilder. **Toutius Incitatus** (*CIL*, XIII, 1972) was not only a Saône boatman, but also a sackcloth maker and wheat dealer. In the late empire, inscriptions disappear and it is likely that the corporations were absorbed into state-controlled bodies, whose prime concern was the collection and distribution of the army's corn supply, the *annona*.

Beyond Lugdunum, few inscriptions have survived recording corporations of *nautae*. An exception is Paris. Under Tiberius, AD 14–37, a pillar dedicated to Jupiter was erected by the Parisii boatmen (see PARIS). Interestingly, this was a tribal corporation, hinting at two things: first, that their organization dated back to before the conquest when a tribal structure might have been a more natural choice than a purely commercial body; second, that they did not see themselves as confined to the Seine, but operated along the Oise, Aisne and Marne as well. The boatmen of the Moselle are recalled in a different way. Ausonius, the fourth-century poet, highlighted the work of rowers and hauliers: 'For thee two modes of voyaging are appointed: this when boats move down thy stream with current favouring and their oars thrash the churned waters at full speed; that when along the banks, with tow-rope never slackening, the boatmen strain on their shoulders hawsers bound to the masts' (*The Moselle*, 39–42).

Unfortunately, most written sources, when they mention river boats, are as imprecise as Ausonius. Many names are given, but the meaning is vague: context suggests that even *ratis*, the word for raft, can just mean a small boat, though *linter* is used more widely in this general way; *navis*, or ship, is even broader, but could also include river vessels. Models have survived (see AUTUN and DIJON) and suggest the presence of decks and the use of paddles, but they reflect ideal forms suitable for carrying gods. The Althiburus mosaic in Tunisia depicts a range of labelled boats and ships, but precisely how they break down into vessels used at sea, in the harbour and on rivers is not clear; and these may be north African types and might not be applicable in Gaul. The best source has to be archaeological, yet finds are extraordinarily rare. It may be that river boats are naturally scarce: when they sank or were abandoned, they were likely to cause obstructions and sooner or later had to be cleared, equally they could be reused as building timber or firewood, or they might simply rot away.

A Roman boat found at Abbeville in 1808 was found too early for anyone to care; two second-century rafts found at Strasbourg in 1938 were not

Plate 23 Dug-out canoe, late antiquity, Parc de la Tête d'Or, Lyon. Photograph: James Bromwich.

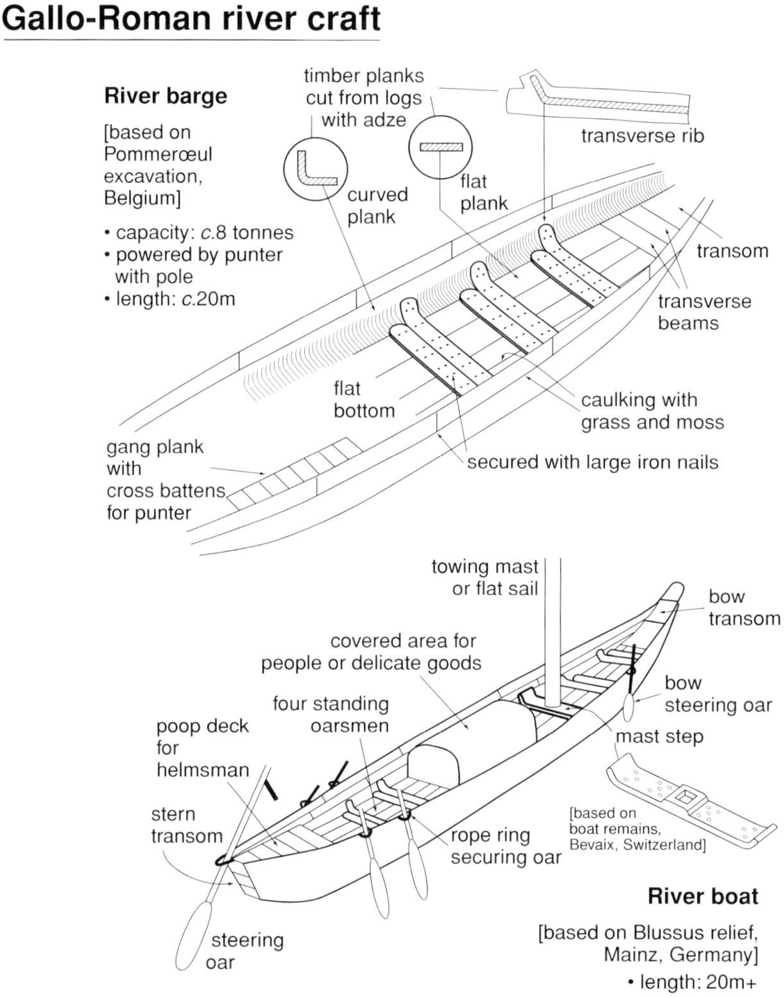

Figure 56 Gallo-Roman river craft

preserved. It may be that many nineteenth-century dug-out *canoe* finds, labelled as prehistoric, are in fact Roman. An excellent example of this widely used craft was found in the Rhône near Aoste. It has an early Middle Ages date and is preserved at LYON. The length of canoes such as this enabled them to carry commercial loads and operate in even very small rivers, needing only the most makeshift landing places. At Pommerœul in Belgium, two second-century Roman canoes of this type were found, both 11.5–12m long. One has been preserved and is displayed in **Ath** museum,[1] along with an even more striking flat-bottomed *barge*, a type that must have been found widely on Gaul's waterways. This was made by cutting canoes in half, then placing planks between secured with cross timbers and washboards added on each side. It was 18–20m long. This had additional planking on one side to allow a puntsman to stand and power the boat along with his pole. Variants of this type of Roman boat have been found in Switzerland at **Yverdon**[2] and Bevaix; in 1990, a section of one of these craft was found on the Rhône riverside in Lyon. The Blussus tombstone from **Mainz** illustrates another and larger version, steered by a long rear oar on a poop deck. It was powered by four oarsmen or by 'human tractors' pulling ropes attached to its thick towing mast, though a simple sail may have been used as well. The Pommerœul barge could carry up to 10 tonnes, a capacity equivalent to thirty carts or 300 mules.

Timber from Gaul was believed to be of particularly high quality and Gallic woodworking skills were admired throughout the ancient world. The sinews of trade were reliable boats and carts and the main liquid carrier of northern Europe, the barrel, was considered to be a Gallic invention. A wide variety of tools was employed, many examples of which have survived. Though the adze was crucial in shaping large pieces of timber, specialist equipment included saws, chisels, gouges, drills and planes. The general availability of iron in the Roman world provided workers with toughened hammers and led Gallic shipbuilders to substitute nails for the wooden tenons used so extensively in Mediterranean boatbuilding. These ranged from the massive foot-long nails to secure main timbers, to tiny nails tacking willow batons along the caulking. Though no doubt specialist commercial shipyards existed in places like Paris and Lyon, and a naval yard was discovered at Mainz,[3] much shipbuilding must have been undertaken locally on timber slipways by landing stages like that found at Pommerœul. Equally there must have been many villa- or *vicus*-based craftsmen capable of making a variety of carts, as well as the sophisticated commercial cart makers in major communications centres.

A cart could average about 2mph pulled by oxen and 4mph pulled by mules. As a relief in Strasbourg shows (see page 332), army transport used mules. They were the strongest traction animals, could work a longer day, were cheaper to feed and lived longer than horses; the Strasbourg legion would expect to have *c.*1,000. Taking into account the needs of the auxiliary troops, the various service providers at an army camp and the wastage rate, mule breeding for the Rhineland frontier must have been big business. Mules were also widely used by administrators and commercial operators. A good muleteer was prized as much as a good cook or doctor. The **Metz relief** shows a manœuvrable two-wheel cart carrying a barrel and pulled by a collared mule held between shafts. The Strasbourg harnessing system seems to have had a much higher collar, more like a yoke (probably using a pole between the animals) and would have pulled on the mule's strong neck rather than shoulder, a system that ruled out potentially faster horses because it constricted their throats: the solid collar that solved this problem was a

Plate 24 Relief of a light cart and mule carrying upright barrel, Metz. © Metz, Musées de la Cour d'Or. Photograph: Jean Munin, all rights reserved.

medieval innovation. Another weakness was the inadequate braking method, using a hook or wheel shoe to slow a vehicle going downhill (see Figure 57). To try to prevent wheels or hooves skating over smooth paving or when roads were cut into bedrock, ruts were deliberately cut (see PETIT ST BERNARD; SAVERNE). Another claimed inadequacy is the lack of turn on front wheels. Certainly reliefs show the wheels above wagon frames, implying rigid axles: a reason for long straight roads? Certainly four-wheelers were kept small (less than 2m long) and 20 per cent play on wide-set front

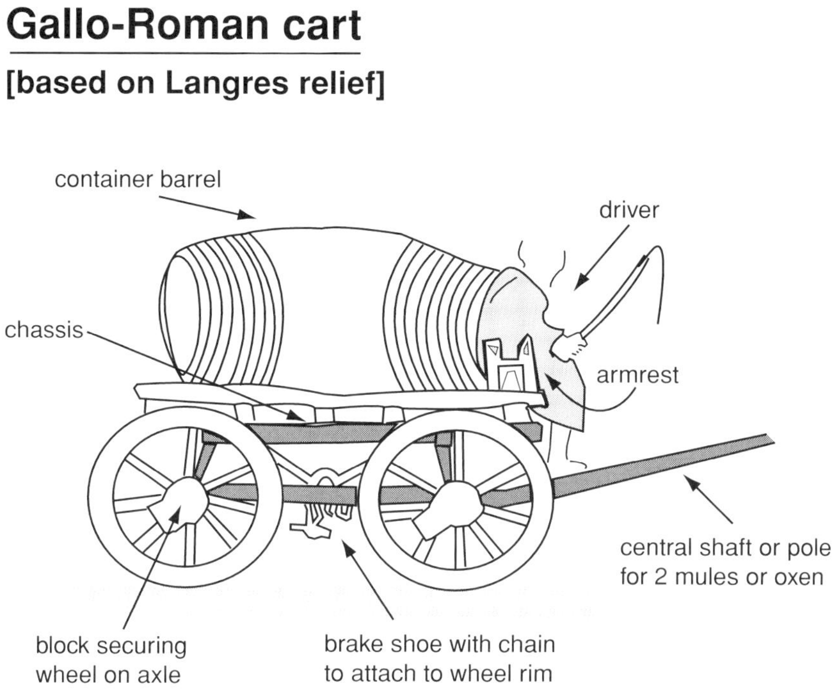

Figure 57 Gallo-Roman cart

wheels may have been enough to get them round right-angle turns in town, yet swivelling axles were known; were they really not used?

Light passenger vehicles could travel considerable distances. Daily journeys of 40–60km were not uncommon. Well-designed vehicles, reliable roads and an infrastructure to support them made it possible. The state gave a lead by converting what was originally just an expression of power – the requirement of locals to provide lodging, food and carriages for those on official business – into a system for state-subsidized travellers (still provisioned of course by locals), consisting of *mansiones*, or overnight stops, and *mutationes*, where they could change their *carrum* (two-wheel) and *raeda* (four-wheel) carriages and their mules or horses (see PETIT ST BERNARD). The system emerged in the first and still existed in the fifth century. Sidonius, in a letter to his friend Heronius (I, 5, 2) explains how he used this *cursus publicus*:

> When I passed the gates of our native Rhodanusia [Lyon] I found the state post at my disposal as one summoned by an imperial letter, and, moreover, the homes of intimate friends and relations lined the route; delays on my journey were due not to scarcity of post-horses but to the multiplicity of friends.

But there were also commercial taverns and many roadside *vici* (see SAVERNE) which would have supplied lodging in addition to lock-up yards, animal feed, grooms, vets, and so on needed by both long-distance and local carriers of people and goods. Itineraries, stylized maps for travellers, existed to specify these different kinds of stopping points over long journeys.

Usage of the transport network would have been most intensive during the years of peace and stability during the second century; the third probably saw some decline without significant revival in the fourth and fifth centuries. Banditry would always have been a risk, but this must have grown as the increased use of the para-military *stationarii* in the countryside suggests. Most cities were experiencing decline by the 230s, demand must have been reduced, and the dislocation caused by inflation would have further undermined business optimism; warfare made it worse. Payment in kind, leading to the large-scale movement of grain to feed armies, may have compensated to some extent, but the trend to self-sufficiency both on villa estates and in frontier areas would surely have minimized its impact. Yet Roman Gaul's excellent complementary transport system continued as the foundation for the 'barbarian' successor states. African ware could still be imported; the Irish Saint Columbanus (see LUXEUIL) could journey across Gaul many times and still sail along the upper Rhine; Sidonius could happily write letters to be delivered not only all over Gaul but also in Italy, and in his 460s letter to Hesparius (II, 10) he encapsulates the continuing vitality of the network near Lyon:

> On the one side is the noisy high road, on the other the echoing Arar [Saône]; on the first the traveller on foot, or on horse and the drivers of creaking carriages turn round; on the other, the company of barge hauliers, their backs bent to their work.

Notes

1 **Ath Museum/L'espace Gallo-Romain**. 2 Rue de Nazareth, 7800 Ath, Belgium. Closed Monday. Tuesday–Friday, 10a.m.–noon; 1–5p.m.; Saturday, Sunday 2–6p.m. Barge, canoe, displays and restoration workshop.

2 **Musée d'Yverdon-les-Bains**. Le Château, Place Pestalozzi, Yverdon, Switzerland. Closed Monday. Tuesday–Sunday; June–September 10a.m.–noon, 2–5p.m.; October–May 2–5p.m. The fourth-century AD boat.

3 **Mainz Museum für Römische Schiffahrt**. Markhalle, Holzhofstrasse, Mainz, Germany. Closed Monday. Tuesday–Sunday 10a.m.–6p.m. Remains and full-scale re-creations of seven varied ships belonging to the Rhine fleet.

3

THE SITES OF CHAMPAGNE, THE ARDENNES, LORRAINE AND ALSACE

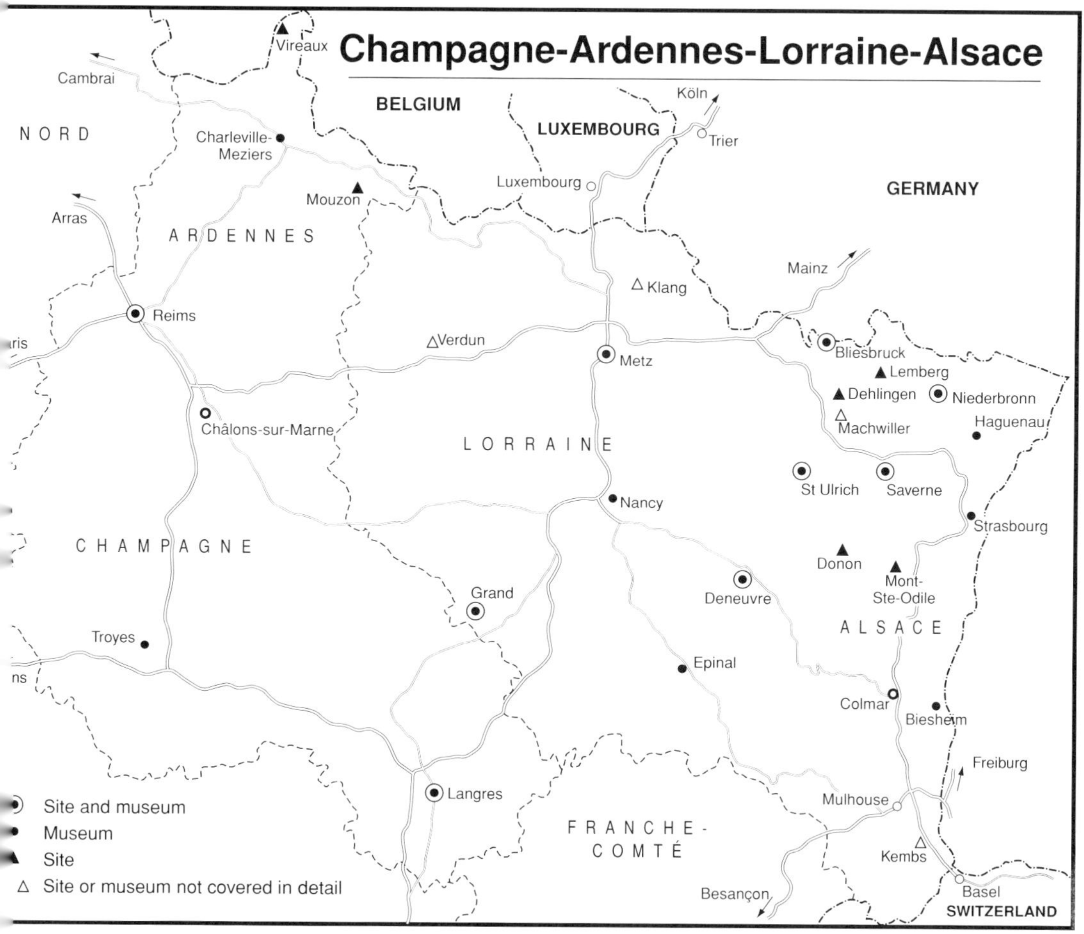

Figure 58 Regional map: Champagne, the Ardennes, Lorraine and Alsace

BIESHEIM, Haut-Rhin

Museum.

3km north of Neuf-Brisach by the D468, 18km east of Colmar.

This is a small place, but it has the best archaeological museum in the region. Here objects are displayed to communicate both what has been learnt and what currently is being learnt. When you have reviewed the archaeological desert that constitutes the south of Alsace – or even STRASBOURG, with its awkward labels and intermittent and generalized panels – then the outstanding nature of Biesheim is clear.

The Roman site was a military base, relay post and *vicus* on the road from Augst to Mainz, paralleling the Rhine waterway. The road itself is followed today (roughly) by the D468. Between the conquest and the 70s, this was the road, providing rapid communications up and down the *limes* or frontier zone, secured by strongpoints like this, largely manned by troops from the fortress at Strasbourg, though occasionally detachments came down from Mainz. Even between the 70s and the 260s, when the Decumates was occupied, it retained a military presence. During the fourth century, when the Rhine again became the heart of western imperial defence, the Prima Martia legion manned a new fort here (see MANDEURE).

Sondages began (1960s) in the fields between Biesheim and Kunheim where the village of Oedenburgheim died in the Thirty Years War (1638). These revealed its Roman origins and led to serious excavations from 1976 onwards. Early results have revealed most about the *vicus*, though knowledge of the Augustan settlement (a few huts?) is still minimal. During the first century *pisé* houses were built along a grid of streets, eventually being replaced with buildings using stone from east of the Rhine; in the second century the streets got drains and porticoes, some of the houses cellars. Aerial photographs suggest an extensive formally laid out town, perhaps covering as much as 60ha. Its size and position on the main road make it more likely that this, rather than Horbourg, is the Argentovaria of the itineraries.

Excavators have found the usual bronze workshop and butchers, but also a *sigillata*-filled cellar, interpreted as the shop of the tableware salesman. Local resources were exploited to vary diet: a pool believed to have functioned as a fishpond for the local fishmonger and a vat found filled with peach and plum stones, pine nuts and grape pips, suggesting both viticulture and sophisticated food preparation. The shocks of the third century were felt, but the site was not abandoned; a large cemetery filled up and a *mithraeum* functioned throughout the fourth century.

Until recently the army has been known primarily through its stamped bricks rather than their forts. At least three forts have now been identified in aerial photographs and geophysical survey work. Since 1996 excavations have tried to clarify what was actually built, when and by whom. The later first-century fort, using a double wall of timber with an earth infill and a double ditch in front, is likely to have been the work of Legio XXI Rapax which has provided most stamped bricks. Prima Martia produced the second largest group and a fourth-century *castellum* has been confirmed. The large number of fourth-century coins and late Roman burials show that Oedenburgheim was considered an essential part of Roman defences until the disastrous incursions at the beginning of the fifth century, when it was abandoned to the Alamanni and Franks.

Musée Gallo-Romain, Le Capitole

Place de la Mairie
68600 Biesheim

Hours:	Wednesday, Friday, Saturday, Sunday	2–6p.m.
	closed Monday, Tuesday	
	Thursday	9–1p.m.

The prize find is a **superbly cut agate** picturing Commodus (180–92) thrusting his lance down at a supplicant woman, symbolizing imperial triumph over a defeated people. It is in a fourth- or fifth-century gold setting and no doubt once decorated the neck of someone rich, but it was an easy thing to lose. On the other hand, soldiers rarely mislay their equipment in camp, therefore most finds are insignificant or rubbish: a few lance and *pilum* heads, a battered *gladius* and broken examples of the stamped bricks. A rarity is the **silver ingot**, used for pay in the fourth century; only fifteen are known, eleven from frontier forts in Britain.

The minutiae of daily life in the *vicus* are vividly recalled by a bone cheese-drainer; the little bronze animals, simple attributes of gods, perhaps decorated household shrines. Changing personal adornment is embodied in two tiny brooches: one a distinctly Gallo-Roman **boat brooch**, its bow shaped as a curving creature's head and carrying three people, the other a fifth-century Germanic **aviform brooch**, its red stone eye picked out in the gilded setting, one of the last things left here.

Last, the museum points to some of the techniques called upon by archaeologists, such as expertise in bone analysis to look at not only diet, but also how bones have been cut, chewed or subsequently used. Panels are being used to explain the current digs, with spaces left for subsequent years. A museum that for once manages to present archaeology as a contemporary and dynamic process.

BLIESBRUCK, Moselle

Sites.

The Parc Archéologique Européen is 75km east of Metz and 15km south-east of Saarbrücken, beside the D82 north to Reinheim.

The EU flag flies over the shining roof protecting the Roman baths. It is a place where symbolism and reality converge. Bliesbruck – in France – and Reinheim – in Germany – are frontier villages 800m apart which have found a Gallo-Roman settlement and villa lying between them. Since 1984 there has been an international multi-disciplinary team – BLESA – to oversee work here and in 1988 the Parc Archéologique Européen was created to reflect the urban and rural exploitation revealed by the archaeology. The practical advantages have been many. Money has been generated for extensive excavations, led locally by J.P. Petit and J. Schaub (French) and A. Miron and W. Reinhard (German), research and experimental archaeology, and eventually a common museum/presentation centre. Yet surprisingly few reflections have emerged on the inter-relationship of villa and settlement, something cross-border co-operation would surely have encouraged?

The Blies flows south to join the Saar, through gentle rolling hills dominated by pasture and trees. Its alluvium is sandy and it was the exploitation of the sand, creating the now water-filled pits by the river, that led to the first major archaeological discovery here in 1954. German quarrying stopped when the diggers cut into a rich burial chamber: it was an exceptional Iron Age tomb, created for a woman of high status around 400 BC, a 'Rhine–Moselle Celtic princess' burial. The finds included a wonderful gold torc, bracelets, fibulae and a bronze flagon 'masterpiece' of Celtic engraving. But little suggests that there was significant Iron Age settlement immediately before the Romans arrived. Traces of a Roman bridge had been found in 1850 – no one now knows where – and haphazard burrowing identified Reinheim villa in the nineteenth century, but the Bliesbruck excavations have left exposed more remains of a Roman small town than almost anywhere else in France and stimulated the full-scale investigation and restoration of the villa.

The Bliesbruck site has no Gallo-Roman name: it is not mentioned on any itinerary and has produced no inscription. In Mediomatrices territory, by a winding minor river, settlement straggled beside a secondary north–south road in a region of mainly east–west arterial roads. The known area of the small town is 15–20ha, but it might have been bigger; possibly more lies under modern Bliesbruck. The earliest levels found date to the 30s or 40s AD. Its peak development is unusually late – yet to be explained – during the first half of the third century; the villa, too, reached its fullest extent in this period. They were hard hit by both fire and destruction in the third quarter, but there was marked revival in the town during the early fourth century, though occupying a more limited zone; the villa experienced

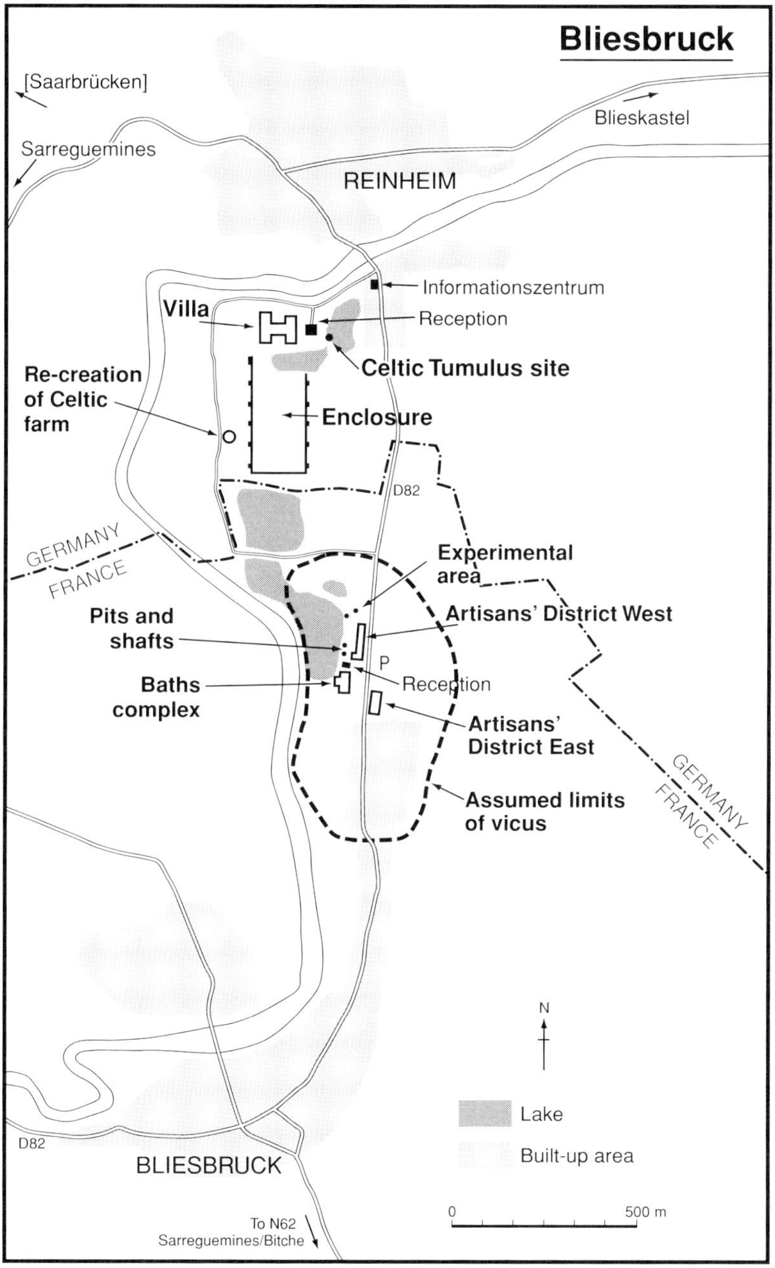

Figure 59 Bliesbruck: local plan

a much more partial recovery. In the fifth century came progressive abandonment, though two Merovingian cemeteries indicate that the area was not deserted; ultimately, two separate medieval communities were to evolve.

The entrance and baths

An elegant modern structure covers the baths and houses the *parc* reception. Stairs and walkways take you through the tastefully, though heavily, restored baths. Excellent panels in English, as well as French and German, explain each section.

The complex is the only public building so far identified in the town, if you discount the open area that formed what might have been the central 'square' separating the baths from the road. Built at the end of the first century, it could have been the first serious use of stone for building here, with a core of three bathing rooms, an outside swimming pool in an exercise area, an entrance hall and a row of porticoed shops on each side. It is a building that suggests a high level of Romanization: a great landowner's donation to the settlement?

Over time it was modified and expanded, plastered and extensively painted in red. The entrance hall was enlarged twice, taking it from a small room beside the *tepidarium*, to a great hall, then adding large heated rooms; the *caldarium* was expanded with a new western apse and relocated stoking chamber,

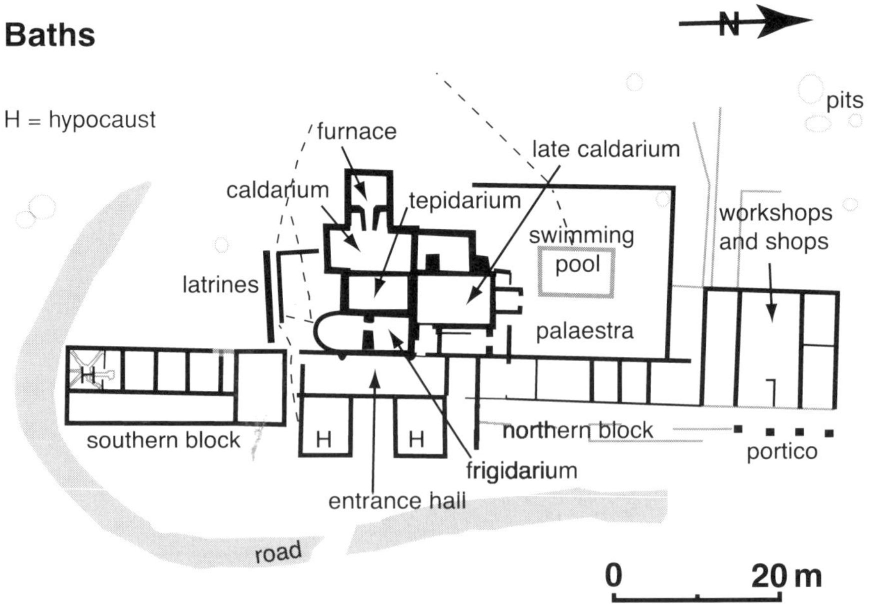

Figure 60 Bliesbruck: baths

which also allowed the addition of an extra *caldarium* and furnace; the swimming pool was converted to a cistern and finally filled in (too cold perhaps). The southern block of shops perhaps became one or more habitations with heated rooms, and a large building to the north which seems to have had more shops and workshops was linked to the baths. While the network of channels to remove water is evident (and the location of the associated latrines), nothing has come to light of the supply: surely it needed an aqueduct?

Experimental area

During the summer months, Bliesbruck conducts a number of Gallo-Roman re-creation activities. There are kilns to make Gallo-Belgic style pots; a treadmill driving a millstone to grind corn for baking in 'Gallo-Roman' ovens; and growing all the year are the traditional crops; Reinheim villa has a small timber 'Gallic' farm and a few goats.

Artisans' district: west

It is easiest to start at the northern end as the buildings are numbered from here: 1–14. They face the **Roman road**, a mix of herringbone foundations covered by sand and gravel; traces are visible by the modern D82. The buildings have narrow frontages and form long, side-by-side strips; all have a large main room and all have living rooms at the rear, but this is their final form, developed over 200+ years. The **north** (1–7) and the **south** (8–14) show different building histories. This reflects contrasting approaches to property development, reflecting different plot owners, but also how the buildings were used.

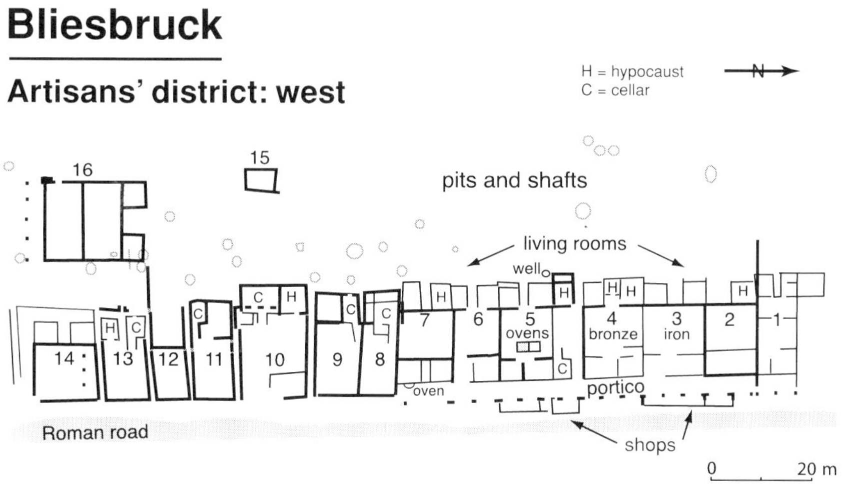

Figure 61 Bliesbruck: artisans' district

The north: a craft sector

This zone was developed AD 30/40 as one block of six buildings, each with a big central room, a shop at the front and a portico by the road; living accommodation was probably on a second floor. Stone was used for the main walls, but others were of perishable materials, including the fronts, probably shop counters. *Second-century* rebuilding began with number 1: it retained the basic structure but was more substantial both in size and materials, using more stone and having a larger portico; it was soon followed by buildings 2–6, again as a block with a common portico (7 was added when building 8 was constructed). The sizes of their frontages varied and were still open, but solid *petit appareil* was used for much of the walling. In the *late second/third century* living rooms were added to the rear: in many cases these have concrete floors and hypocausts with painted plaster walls, two added cellars along the front. They also encroach on the road, adding shop-fronts on the other side of the portico.

Individual buildings. The first three dealt in iron. 3 provided the best evidence with an open hearth, ovens, slag, fragments of iron and tools (hammers and tongs). It is possible that the smith also carried out smelting, though he would have usually obtained blooms – iron with some of the impurities removed by smelters near the iron ore sources. 4 was occupied by a bronze specialist, demonstrated by finding two furnaces, small crucibles, traces of bronze, even rare moulds for casting the metal; he made fibulae and pins, small statuettes and tableware. Two hypocausts suggest that he may have had his hot baths in the back. 5 has a cellar at the front with a lip to help sacks to be poured down: this was a baker's. One of the two ovens in the main room has been restored. A broken millstone was found here along with grain residue. 7 has lots of oven remains, but despite the presence of stone weights it is not clear what product was made – perhaps cooked food?

The south: a commercial sector

The earliest phase only had a scatter of insubstantial building. In the *second century* nearly all construction was of independent buildings, separated by narrow passages, gradually filling the plot. They had no shop fronts, but large main rooms and small rear rooms – storage and offices? A street portico linked them to the north. In the *final phase*, living rooms were added to the rear, like those in the north, but sometimes with cellars.

Individual buildings. There is little to indicate the products handled here. However, 10 had a large cellar in which many amphorae were found – perhaps the owner dealt in Mediterranean wine or oil. 14 still has three stone bases for pillars to hold up the massive roof necessary over the main room.

The pits and shafts zone

The area behind and to the south-west of the western artisans' district is limited by the water of a sandpit, but still scattered here are many of the pits and *shafts* – deeper with neat drystone walling. 100 pits and 50 shafts (there were many more) have been examined; they seem to have been carefully filled in layers and, in the case of the shafts, then plugged; some even contained complete vases. Were they part of a local ritual? Yet other exactly similar shafts elsewhere on the site were used as latrines. Two buildings in the zone, 15 and 16, have no clear function, and may just be detached houses; 16 has precisely proportioned rooms.

Artisans' district: east

Despite modern road construction destroying the fronts of most of these eight buildings, it is clear that they were, during the third century at least, very similar to those in the western artisans' district: constricted fronts, extended backs and a mix of the joined and narrowly separated. The early phases have not been published yet, but even in the third century numbers of rooms were still of beaten earth; half the houses have hypocaust rooms and all seem to have large work rooms, but little evidence has been found of the type of activity undertaken; significantly more have cellars with light shafts and double niches. As elsewhere, fire swept through them in the second half of the third century, and once again there is evidence of reoccupation in the fourth century on a reduced scale.

Individual buildings. 5 is probably the best preserved of the houses. In the fourth century, the cellar and room above were rebuilt. There is a large paved courtyard to the rear and holes seem to have been silos and latrines. Traces of cereal seeds found hint at agricultural associations.

The Reinheim villa complex

Follow the D82 800m across the border into Reinheim and turn left before the bridge for the Europäischer Kultur Park. The reception contains a reproduction of the Celtic princess burial. The information panels here are more limited than in Bliesbruck, but excavation continues.

The **villa** has two residential wings linked by a *central section* of two porticoes with a court or garden in between. The pool that ran beside the northern portico was filled in during the third century. The best-preserved part of *the western wing* is the cellar with the usual light shafts and niches, but with a separate staircase, containing carbonized remains demonstrating the equally usual destruction of the third century. It was filled with rubbish in the fourth century, suggesting that the villa had a shorter life than the *vicus*. The heated rooms in the south-west suggest this may have been the winter quarters

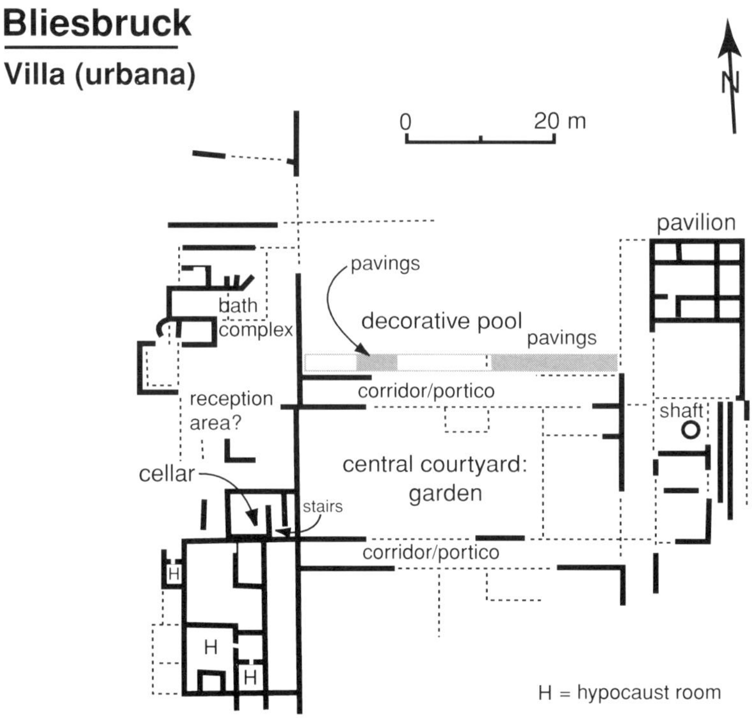

Figure 62 Bliesbruck: villa

of the household. The most interesting features in *the eastern wing* are the drystone shaft and the symmetrical rooms of the 'pavilion' area: the meaning of both is still obscure.

A **'U'-shaped enclosure** stretches out in front of the villa, 300m long, the open end facing the villa. Along each side were six symmetrically placed rectangular structures. The larger north-west building has been exposed and all the smaller structures down the western side, together with a road sweeping round the outside. They seem to be too well planned and too well constructed to house farm workers; perhaps the enclosure was an ornamental display for a great aristocrat separating him/her from the working town? What must have been an imposing gate stood at the centre facing Bliesbruck.

Reinheim Informationszentrum

Finds and reproductions are mixed rather confusingly. Note also that the pre-1980s finds from the villa were dispersed, the largest single collection going to **Speyer** (Historisches Museum der Pfalz) and the originals of the

Celtic burial are in **Saarbrücken** (Museum für Vor- und Frühgeschichte). There is, though, an excellent model of the whole Bliesbruck–Reinheim site and there are good examples of Gallo-Belgic pottery made here; agricultural and other *iron tools*; keys and even a lock mechanism; a crucible, bronze figurines and a phallus amulet; and, most attractive of all, *enamelled fibulae* found in the baths. A proper museum is projected for the park.

DEHLINGEN, Bas-Rhin

IGN 3613 ET
956.4/2453.5

Villa site.

22km south-west of Sarreguemines by the D919 to Oermingen and then the D123 to Dehlingen. From the church it is 1.5km. Through the village to the T-junction and turn right to the pond. Take the left-hand track, *c.*600m to the excavation area.

Gurtelbach villa was first discovered and reported in 1862 by the parish priest – and then forgotten. During ploughing, the villa was rediscovered in 1993 and this time excavated by the local archaeological society. The **foundations**, some 3–4 courses high, reveal a small to medium-sized **courtyard villa** with a gallery in front, looking out over the vale where a number of other buildings have been identified in sondages; they were presumably farm outbuildings. There are the remains of an oven in the middle of the court and a kiln in the rear. Finds suggest that there must have been an Iron Age farm in the vicinity, but the first stone villa was built under the Flavians. After some sections of the villa were pulled down in the 180s, it was rebuilt in an expanded form under Severus. After the familiar destruction of the later third century it was roughly put in order around the courtyard and reoccupied in the fourth until what seems to have been a final destruction at the time of Theodosius (379–95). The **depot** used to store finds is under the fire station opposite the church and is sometimes open to visitors.

DENEUVRE, Meurthe-et-Moselle

Museum and site.

50km south-east of Nancy to Baccarat; Deneuvre is the village/suburb on the southern bank of the Meurthe, overshadowed by its neighbour.

Although there were periodic excavations from 1868 to 1890, it is the work of Gérard Moitrieux in 1967–1987, and the subsequent decision to build a special museum for the finds, that makes Deneuvre worth visiting. Moitrieux

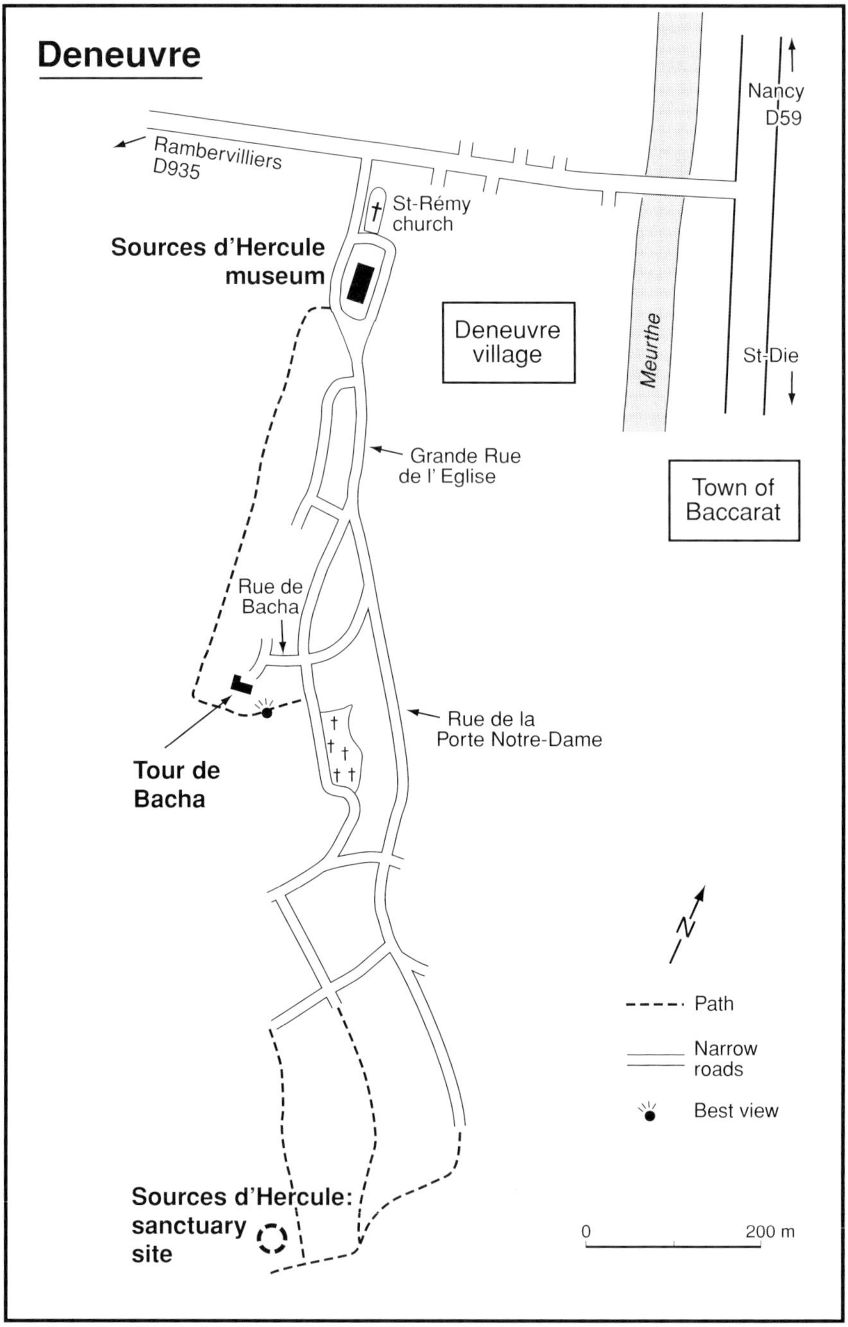

Figure 63 Deneuvre: town plan

Plate 25 Deneuvre. Hercules relief, fourth century. Musée Les Sources d'Hercule. Photograph: D. Joannes.

revealed that this was more than a small river crossing settlement linking Leuci communities across the valley; here was a rare spring sanctuary dedicated to Hercules: indeed, a third (fifty-three) of all the representations of this god found in Gaul have been found here.

Little is known of the settlement. Evidence suggests that it had both potteries and a tilery. Quarrying was probably significant as well as forestry, as implied by a relief of men sawing (see NANCY). Visitors to the springs no doubt brought additional prosperity, particularly in the later second and fourth centuries. The sanctuary was wrecked in the late 360s/early 370s. The burning of the roofs and fallen columns could be the work of barbarians, but the face-down, disfigured reliefs suggest deliberate Christian work. It marked the end of the Gallo-Roman settlement as a whole: no occupation is known from the fifth to the eighth century.

Musée Les Sources d'Hercule

Grande Rue de l'Eglise

Hours:	May–October	10a.m.–noon, 2–6p.m.
	November–April	2–5p.m. Saturday and Sunday only

The museum opened in 1996, designed around the partial re-creation of the sanctuary. Excavations revealed that the springs were channelled using wooden pipes and organized into three pools, originally made of wood and clay but, by 175, replaced with stone basins; two of these were protected with roofs each supported by four columns. Seriously damaged during the third century, the sanctuary was rebuilt, one of the pools getting a new surround; it is this site that is re-created here. A path lined with Hercules reliefs, presumably paid for by hopeful pilgrims seeking his support, approached the pool area. Hercules was the Roman god of victory in battle, but he was also seen as compassionate and good natured, with healing associations, perhaps based on his descent into the underworld, so conquering death, as described in one of his twelve labours. He is known at AIX-LES-BAINS and at Bourbonne-les-Bains, but in both cases linked with the Gallic Borvo/Bormo. Here he is the benevolent intermediary – Hercules Salutis – to the unnamed spring goddess. His portrayals vary considerably from classical to the most provincial Gallic. Among the many altars, five statues have been restored; all would have been painted. One shows Hercules, a serpent clasped to his chest, not only recalling the snake sent by Hera to kill him, which he survived, but also its widespread healing connotations. Finds show that the pilgrims would have washed themselves using pottery bowls and left offerings of food, white clay figurines, money and jewellery.

Fouilles Archéologiques

Rue de la Chantier

About 1.25km from the museum south via the Grande Rue de l'Eglise and the Rue de la Porte Notre-Dame. A gentle grass slope surrounded by woodland is dotted with water marking the spring outlets; one pond still has a few stones from the Gallo-Roman pool surround.

Tour de Bacha

Rue de Bacha

A modern house sits on a rocky outcrop at the top of the village. It partially hides traces of a square double wall, the inner with 12m sides, the outer with 25–30m sides, each some 1–1.8m thick. A tall section of the inner wall rises above the house. The best view can be found by taking the nearby Rue de Cemetière – signposted to the 'Ruines Eglise XIVe' – and the path 30m on the right. From here the lower external walling can be seen. It has been interpreted variously. The stonework is clearly Gallo-Roman. It dominates the region and traditionally has been seen as a late Roman *castellum*. However, there is no record of the site in the *Notitia Dignitatum* and alternatives have been sought such as a secure storage depot for the late Roman army or, as the shape also suggests, it could be a *fanum* temple.

DONON, Bas-Rhin

IGN 3616 OT
956.2/2401.5

Mountain-top temple site.

11km north-west of the N420 Strasbourg–St Die road by the D392, 2km after Grandfontaine. At the Col du Donon take the D993, 1km to parking and track for Donon mountain. The walk to the top is steadily upwards, rather than steep, and takes about three-quarters of an hour. Explanatory panels help the visitor.

Standing on a summit some 1,000m high and looking out over mountains and plain is inevitably awe-inspiring, but here it is enhanced by the awareness of the antiquity of the experience. Adventurous antiquaries noted ruins here from the seventeenth century; sculpture and reliefs were being removed and from at least 1832 onwards various museums acquired their share, particularly Strasbourg and Epinal; this phase came to a climax with the construction in 1862 of the 'Greek temple' on the peak itself. Serious excavation, led by Fanny Lacour, began in the 1930s after First World War

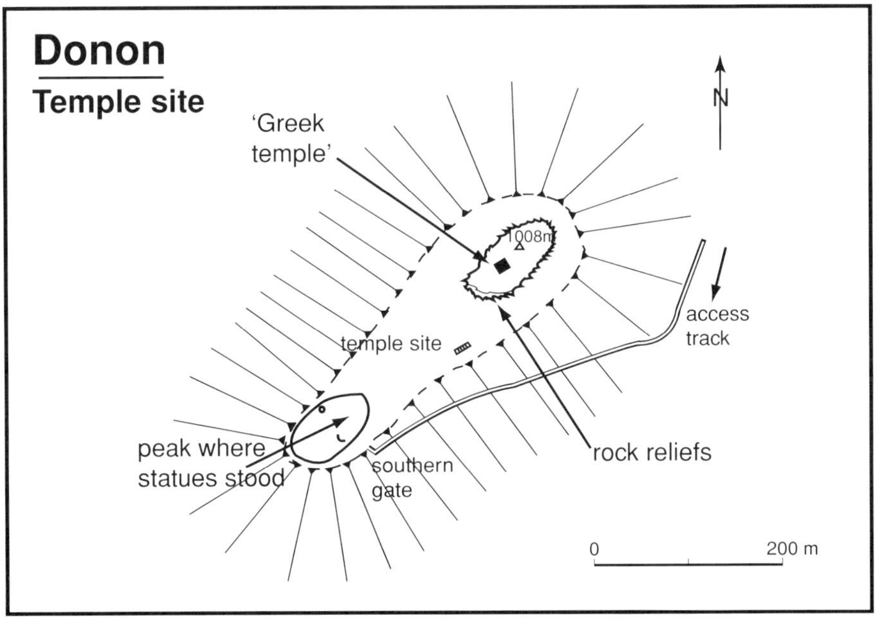

Figure 64 Donon: site plan

trenches had revealed that traces of the ancient sanctuary site still existed. Her work was refined and extended by François Petry in the 1970s.

The Donon lay at a natural meeting place of both north–south and east–west routes and lay on the borders of three tribes, the Mediomatrices, the Triboci and the Leuci: it may have been an especially dramatic confederate sanctuary, already old, as material going back to at least the Bronze Age was found here. Defined by a pre-Roman enclosure wall around the two peaks and the flat ridge between, the sanctuary was at its most developed in the Gallo-Roman era.

Access is through the ancient southern gate by the lower south-east peak; **massive rectangular blocks** may represent the reception point for pilgrims. A spring supplied water nearby. A **large hole**, deliberately cut, could have been a tomb, though a cistern with a cult role seems more likely. Overlooking the flat ridge between the peaks stood a circular wooden building – a *fanum?* Fragments of at least five Jupiter–giants were found on the south-east peak, suggesting that this crest was dedicated to the great sky god, particularly worshipped in the Vosges. Eight reproduction altars here, dedicated to other gods (originals in EPINAL), actually stood round the higher north-west peak.

The flat ridge was no doubt used for religious ceremonies and there is evidence of paved pathways. The north-west peak is surrounded by a rocky outcrop: despite the 'Greek temple', there has never been any evidence for a temple on the peak itself. Excavations exposed remains of a timber building with a stone tiled roof facing the ridge, perhaps used for sacrifices. In **alcoves round the outcrop**, there were altars and reliefs, some cut in the rock itself. A reproduction relief of a lion and wild boar face each other (see EPINAL). An inscription names Bellicus and Surbur: gods or dedicators? The stag god representation stood here (see STRASBOURG). However, most of the material can be related to Mercury (also largely in STRASBOURG). No doubt he offered prosperity and fertility, but these are very non-classical representations and most writers identify this Mercury as a god of the region, Vosegus.

EPINAL, Vosges

Museum.

Musée Départemental d'Art Ancien et Contemporain

1 Place Lagarde
88000 Epinal
Hours: 10a.m.–6p.m. Closed Tuesday

This severe museum was designed as a minimalist art gallery: objects must speak for themselves – labels and information are a rarity. It works best looking at the fine **Jupiter-giant column** (see CUSSY-LA-COLONNE), found in the Moselle near Portieux in 1870, strikingly reconstructed here. The god-emperor/horseman and anguished monster can best be seen from the first floor. Other stonework deserves more help. The Sommercourt pair are dressed in Roman tunics and carved with assurance. A **cross-legged god** with curling hair, a torc round his neck and two snakes with goats' heads hanging from his shoulders is possibly Cernunnos; note two holes on his head, which could have held horns, perhaps removable to allow a seasonal ritual. A **seated headless female** carries a cornucopia and wears a snake belt with a ram's head. The similarity of style suggests they were a divine couple. The **'Medritina' tombstone relief** shows a seated woman surrounded by barrels and tubs, behind her another woman stirring a bowl: since 1841 it has been interpreted as the goddess of pharmacists. Minimalism patently does not work when faced with presenting Gallo-Roman brooches: laid out to form beautiful pointless patterns, they are deprived of context and meaning.

Above all, nothing is done to give context to the material from Grand. **Tiny bronze legs**, presumably brought by the sick appealing to Apollo Grannius for help, are lost on a shelf of bronzes. A very rare ivory **Egyptian zodiac table** (its twin is in St Germain-en-Laye, PARIS) is provided with a

Epinal

Egyptian zodiac table

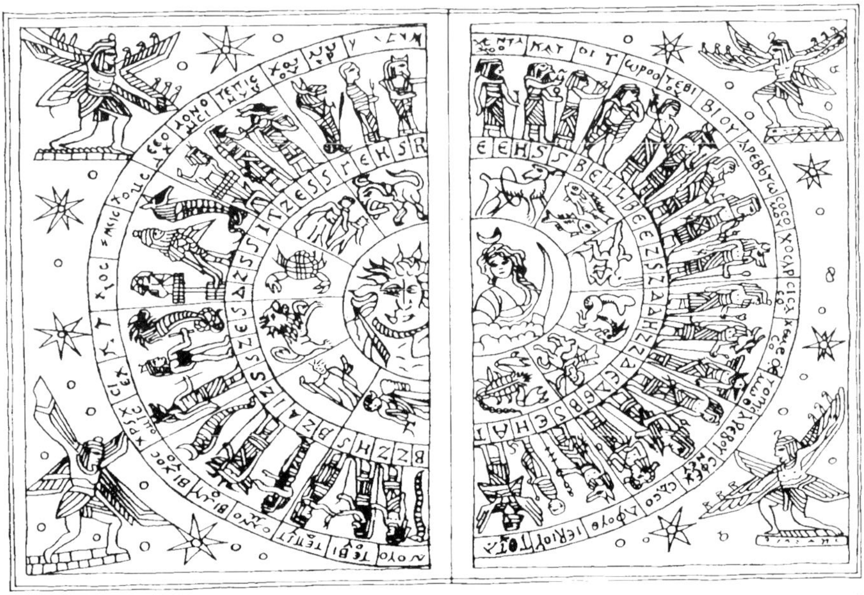

Figure 65 Epinal: zodiac table. Drawn by M. Nicole.

magnifying glass, but why is no attempt made to explain what you can see and provide a historical background? The table takes the form of ovals in the centre of which are the sun god Apollo and the moon goddess Selene; around them are the twelve zodiacal months. Distinctively Egyptian are the 'decans'. These are ten-day segments in which events are governed by a specific Egyptian god, each shown as an upright figure named above in old coptic. It is thought the tables would have been used as part of the consultation for cures at the sanatorium, a normal element in a major healing sanctuary. Astrology had been increasingly accepted in the early empire to function alongside divination, and, in the uncertain world of the late empire, became even stronger until attacked by Christian emperors. These diptychs were discovered smashed in a well, the stratigraphy suggesting a date of *c.* 170; the context for their deliberate destruction is unknown.

GRAND, Vosges

IGN 3217 O/3217 E

Major site.
www.exagonline.com/grand

30km west of Neufchâteau by the N74 to Liffol-le-Grand, then D427 and D71.

Whenever I search for Grand on the map, it seems to be for the first time. When I finally spot it, I cannot understand how it has not been obvious, so many minor roads seem to arrive here and it even has its own *périphérique*: pointers to its past significance. The old name for the encircling road is *la voie close* and, like an English cathedral close, it suggests a religious enclosure. This was once a ditch that became a road; it was the religious boundary, the *pomerium*, of what may have been the most important sanctuary in Roman Gaul.

The Hauts-Pays plateau is *c.*350m high, cold and bleak in winter, stormy in summer. This is a land of karst, a porous limestone, producing an endemic shortage of water: a strange place, apparently, for a water sanctuary. Although the heavy rainfall quickly disappears into the ground, it has created fissures in which undergound streams run, one of which passes directly under Grand. Here the water hit harder stone and, rising to the surface, formed a small 'lake' before rapidly falling into a new fissure and travelled on underground to the Routeuil spring 3km away. Though virtually no Iron Age material has been found, it seems likely that this pool was already a holy place before the Roman period.

Until the modern excavations, Grand was difficult to explain. Here was a massive amphitheatre, first excavated by J.-B. Prosper Jollois in the 1820s; an enormous mosaic in a basilica, revealed by Félix Voulot in 1883; and a rampart, known about since the twelfth century. Scholars could only be puzzled by what seemed to be obvious signs of urbanization. The 1960–88 programme, directed by R. Billoret and then J.-P. Bertaux, revealed decoration, reliefs and statue remnants from what had to be a temple, and, adding a new inscription fragment find to an old one, revealed that Apollo Grannius was worshipped here. The strange shape of the rampart became clearer, new towers and gateways were found, roads identified and a large portico around the lake area recognized. A joint archaeological, speleological, and finally hydrographic survey revealed a vast network of underground aqueducts, estimated to cover at least 15km, bringing together at Grand the water of three separate basins; enough to provide a regular supply of water for the lake, the main baths complex and three other baths in the area.

A much clearer picture has emerged. The underground channels are dated to the Flavian period and in themselves constitute a massive investment;

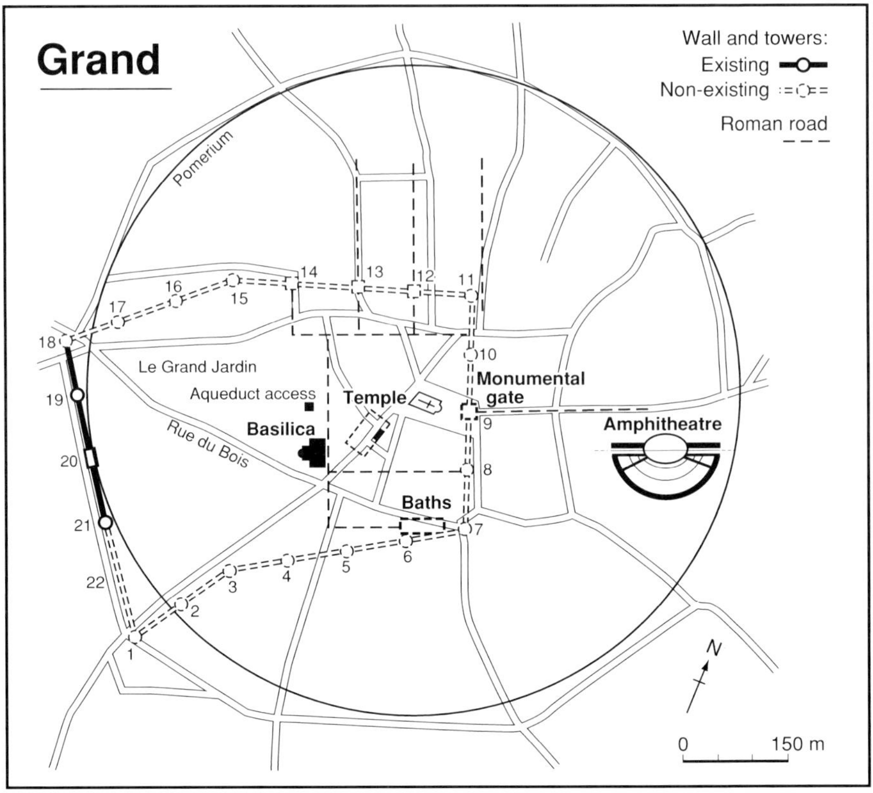

Figure 66 Grand: local plan

most of the other buildings seem to have been Trajanic and completed by the early years of the second century. There are suggestions of late second-century destruction here, as at Liffol (see page 286–7), but the basilica was certainly restored if not built by the Severans and a portico inscription mentions M [A] ANTONINUM – that is, Caracalla (211–17). Dio (*Roman History*, LXXVIII, 15, 5–6) describes the pathological emperor as having sought help for his body and soul from three gods, Asclepius at Pergamon, Serapis at Alexandria and Apollo Grannius in Gaul: surely at Grand. An anonymous panegyric (*PL*, VII, 21, 3–4) to Constantine indicates that he also came: it refers to his visiting 'the most beautiful temple in the whole world' to see his protector Apollo. Here he had a vision of his long future life as emperor. This has led some writers to see Grand as a place where priests combined Mediterranean and Gallic intellectual mysticism (see

LYON) in the worship of Apollo Grannius. This was a sanctuary that practised 'incubation' or healing through dreams, a natural place therefore for someone to experience a vision. Here a priesthood would have been able to interpret, advise on and divine from the sleep experiences of pilgrims in the sanctuary: the discovery of an Egyptian zodiac table (see EPINAL) shows that they were able to draw upon practice far across the empire.

Apollo Grannius was not the only god recognized at Grand. Heads and reliefs have been interpreted as representing Apollo's healing heirs, his son Asclepius, and Hygia, his granddaughter; they also hint at the cult of Dionysus with its imagery of fertility, often a reason for seeking the help of the gods. A raised imperial hand could suggest the imperial cult. Other gods are represented round the site, including Jupiter riding down representatives of the earth force.

The sick, the hypochondriacal, the passionate believers and the curious must have come. They would have cleansed themselves, maybe sought out the altar of a favourite god within the *pomerium*, attended a ceremony in the amphitheatre and then entered within the rampart. One interpretation of its strange shape suggests that it reflects a star pattern, thus linking the astrological interest of the priests and the use of a zodiac table. Within this sanctuary area, the empty western side could have been a sacred wood; if so, a sign that Druidic beliefs were a component at Grand. Perhaps this was a purified form, made less threatening to Roman authority by the stress on Apollo with his long oracular tradition at Delphi; it is even possible that descendants of Druid families came here after Claudius banned Druidism and helped create the sanctuary. Richer pilgrims would have met in the great hall, or basilica, and perhaps slept in a nearby building; all would have walked and talked with the priests in the portico and spelt out their needs. They would have bought gifts at the shops lining the street between the amphitheatre and the monumental gate and left these for Apollo. But where? Hardly any votive offerings or plaques have been found (see EPINAL); is there a major cache waiting for future archaeologists below the church or in the unexcavated areas around the temple – or did early Christians destroy them all?

Grand was not abandoned and medieval tradition, recorded in twelfth-century hagiography, ascribes the martyrdom here of Sainte Libaire to the Emperor Julian (361–3). An interesting feature of the story is that she picked up her severed head and bathed it in the lake before expiring, so Christianizing the holy waters of Apollo Grannius. The writer reports that an earthquake occurred at the same time; there is no evidence for activity of this kind, however, during storms when the water rushes through the fissures and tunnels there is underground rumbling: a nerve-tingling experience for both the pagan sick and the credulous early Christian.

The amphitheatre

Rue de l'Amphithéâtre
D71E, road for Midrevaux
Hours: 1 April–30 September 9a.m.–noon, 2–7p.m. Closed Tuesday
1 October–31 March 10a.m.–noon, 2–5p.m.
Closed 15 December–14 January

During the 1990s millions of francs were spent on wooden seating for 3,000, supported by concrete pillars and a metal frame suspended over the south-west end of the amphitheatre, to present summer 'spectacles' (and so help bring visitors to the Vosges). A serious amount of 'rubble' was removed in the process, though on balance, by inhibiting future degradation and bringing renewed life to the amphitheatre, this has been worth while.

The amphitheatre was built of *petit appareil* stone facings and fill to hold an estimated 17,000 in the early second century. The *grand appareil* in the north-west is believed to be Constantinian repairs, implying continued use in the fourth century. Roger Billoret's excavations from 1963 onwards demonstrated this was really an amphitheatre and not a theatre as well. The confusion had arisen because only one side forms a full half oval; however, the arena is complete and there is no stage building in the other half, which does have some lower seating.

For the ***cavea***, the builders used the shape of the valley, the natural surface being lined with courses of thin, slanting, upright stones to support the seat pavings (continuous removal through the nineteenth century accelerated weathering). Around the upper section at the back, a vaulted gallery provided access through the *vomitoria*; above ran a portico, probably arcaded. The radial walls by **the corridors** into the arena not only contain the changing rooms for performers, but also heavy buttressing to help contain the pressures created by the rubble filling used to support the *cavea* at each end.

The parish church

Place des Halles

The site of the 'lake' is marked by the parish church. Two access covers on the north-west of the portal mark the place where the stream water and channels arrived, now passing under the portal to depart south; all undergound today, but in the eighteenth century there was still a pool exposed on the eastern choir side of the church.

The temple

Rue de la Mosaïque

Nothing survives except a low mound of rubble commemorating the 1960s sondages that identified the 31 × 62m building. It, too, experienced a reconstruction at the end of the second century.

Basilica, mosaic and museum

Rue de la Mosaïque
Hours: as amphitheatre

Outside are traces of consolidated **basilica walls** with buttresses and a **gutter** beyond. Excavation suggested a five-nave structure facing an apsed extension forming a 'tribunal'.

The **mosaic** is 224sq m, one of the largest in the western provinces. Sadly, the central emblema is three-quarters destroyed. In the surviving section, a man covers his face with a mask and holds a crook, probably representing a pilgrim. He is welcomed by another figure: a priest of Apollo? At the corners of the emblema are wild beasts. The surround, creating a carpet look, uses patterns of triangles, dentils and guilloche. The apse has a dog's tooth pattern with an acanthus scroll and more geometric figures. It is a design popular throughout the third century and associated with Trier.

The surrounding wall survives for a few centimetres; it was once covered with sixty different marbles, mostly imported, and stucco, its style suggesting the end of the second century. However, the building's foundations use the same herringbone method found at the amphitheatre; initial construction could then be Trajanic with renovation for or following Caracalla's visit.

Some **excavation finds** in surrounding cases include marble wall facing; stone roof slating; a candle holder; statuettes; evidence of Merovingian occupation; and five manacles (with skeletons) found in a Roman cellar in the early nineteenth century – and immediately christened a prison.

The ramparts

Rue de la Voie Close

Only the western side has visible traces. Take the Rue du Bois (sacred wood?) *c.*500m to the crossroads with the D19 to Trampot; turn left into the encircling road. Fifty metres down on the left find the base of a tower and a stretch of rampart wall. This is **tower '19'**, though only seven towers and four gates of the supposed twenty-two are known definitely. It is a solid round tower sitting astride the wall, built with fine *petit appareil* facing with neat sloping courses marking the junction of the rampart proper and the foundations. It was probably 6m high, but only survives to 1m at best. The style is typical early empire, often built more to impress than for defence. Some 90m further along a clump of trees marks the site where a number of Roman tiles were found set in concrete over a water access point. **Tower 21** is poorly preserved and surrounded by nettles; **tower 22** is even more overgrown.

The underground aqueducts

Hours:	July–August	afternoon guided visits (*c.* 1hr), 2–6p.m. helmet and rubber boots provided

Not for the claustrophobic, lit only by helmet lights, requiring squeezing stooped in a space periodically less than shoulder width, walking in inches of water, but this is the opportunity to enter a Roman environment unchanged in 2,000 years.

The tunnels were all cut in the marl, clay-like material deposited between the more broken surface karst strata and the deeper, firmer karst level, where most of the water was trapped. This means the channels vary from 4m to 9m metres deep and their design alters according to two factors: the surface proximity (they were made by cut and cover methods, or tunnelling) and the pressure created by the two kinds of rock on the walls (a sinuous path was sometimes adopted as well to limit the effects). Along the channel there are crossbar stones to reinforce the walls' resistance to pressure. On the basis of pottery finds in the access holes, these underground aqueducts were the earliest large-scale constructions in Grand, AD 50–70; the last mix of rubble and pottery shows maintenance ended in the mid-fourth century.

Musée de Liffol-le-Grand

3 Route de Joinville
88350 Liffol-le-Grand.
Hours: 10a.m.–noon, 1.30–6p.m.

Liffol-le-Grand is 12km south-east from Grand. It was therefore about a day's journey by cart from the great sanctuary and a little less from the main Lyon–Trier road. Although it may have had a *mansio* – remains of a large building have been observed under the parish church – settlement does not seem to have significantly depended on the great sanctuary. Extended research still needs to be done, but the community seems widely spread, with workshops and farms scattered around this minor crossroads exploiting the natural resources of the Meuse valley and the Hauts-Pays plateau. It may have had its own sanctuary. A large villa utilized La Goulotte spring 1.5km north of the modern village. Workshops have been found for making tiles, cement, pottery, ironmongery and smoking meat. The settlement suffered destruction at the end of the second century; only reduced occupation continued in the third and none in the fourth.

The museum is small and has good touches in its display. The villa was certainly luxurious, but the evidence is thin: plaster fragments, painted with delicate stemmed green and black flowers and tiny pieces of Greek and Italian marble; the main mosaic found here is in Epinal. Most impressive is the rich evidence for craft activity. There is a wide range of woodworking equipment, including a **foot-long ruler**; butchers' cleavers and knives; agricultural tools, including a fruitpicker's tree hook; fishermen's hooks and lead weights; and minute stone and metal **candle holders**: a reminder of workers' dependence on daylight. Large photographs illustrate the tileworks site with a wide range of tiles (see VILLERS-FARLAY). The best display is the **meat smokehouse** found in the mid-third-century villa farmyard, with models to clarify both context and operation. Smoking preserved meat in general and ensured valuable nutrients over the winter months. Note the **branding irons** to record ownership on the meat.

Musée Soulosse-sous-St-Elophe

La Mairie
St Elophe

Hours:	1 April–30 September	9a.m.–noon, 2–7p.m.
	1 October–31 March	2–5p.m.

On the N74, 19km east from Grand, by the D71E to Midrevaux and D3 via Coussey.

The Roman main Lyon–Trier road, like the N74, went through Soulosse to Toul, the *civitas* capital of the Leuci. When the museum is open (it has been known to close for summer holidays), the collection here is more interesting than that in Toul itself.

Soulosse is the site of a straggling Gallo-Roman *vicus*, Solimariaca. As the eighty tombstones of its inhabitants illustrate, it was clearly a small town of artisans, though nineteenth-century sondages mentioned temples and a basilica as well as houses. It seems to have prospered in the second and early third centuries, perhaps due in part to the turning for Grand. Two **milestones** dedicated to Constantine's sons Crispus (died 326) and Constantine II (died 340) measure in leagues from Grand, possibly at that time more important than Toul. These were found, with the tombstones, in a *castrum* rampart, built to protect the Vair crossing in the later fourth century (nothing visible). The local population seem to have withdrawn to the small plateau above, which became St Elophe. According to their hagiographer, this brother of Sainte Libaire was also decapitated by Julian.

The **tombstones** vary from early empire Roman realism (country style) to extremely schematic late Roman works. They depict a range of artisans including a butcher with his cleaver, a travelling merchant with his cart, leather workers and moneychangers. Mercury, particularly valued for his support for trade and travellers, is the most popular god depicted.

HAGUENAU, Bas-Rhin

Museum.

Haguenau is a medieval foundation and a modern industrial and commercial town. The museum has an excellent, small, well-displayed Gallo-Roman collection, largely drawn from along the Rhine, especially Seltz, where there was a *vicus* on the Strasbourg–Mainz military road.

Musée Historique

9 Rue du Maréchal-Foch
675000 Haguenau

Hours:	weekdays	10a.m.–noon, 2–6p.m. Closed Tuesday
	weekends	3–5.30p.m.

The most compelling exhibit is a **late Roman greave**. This is a soldier's bronze shin-guard transformed into a magnificent work of art: its silver and gold gilt is the very essence of glittering imperial splendour. In a famous passage, Ammianus (*History*, XVI, 10, 8) describes Constantius II in 357 on a golden cart, resplendent, iconic, at the centre of a parade through Rome surrounded by gleaming infantry and cavalry, who would have worn greaves such as this; this greave would have exemplified the power of Rome. The decoration also embodies the late Roman revival of pagan myth: Aeneas carries his blind father Anchises away from burning Troy to found the eternal city. The greave, found in a gravel pit near the Rhine, was perhaps once worn in a ceremony to intimidate the Alamanni, though without lasting effect.

Nothing equals the greave, but there is a fine first-century AD **Mannheim Coolus-type helmet** (see CHALON). The basic bronze cone has been improved with an extensive neck-guard and strengthened with a bar across the front. Decoration was added with a knob for the crest and tubes on each side for feathers. On the neck-guard are names of soldiers in Legio IV Macedonica, based in Mainz in 43–69, implying use by a number of men and finally lost by one while on detachment in the Haguenau area. It was probably made by an armourer in Gaul; its origins could have been early in the century. There are also some legionary fibulae for holding their cloaks.

Melting down old material was common among bronze- and ironsmiths. In 1866 the cellars of two Seltz workshops were discovered filled with objects. There was a fine mix of **bronze statues and tableware**. Among the most striking are a Neptune holding a porpoise in one hand, a strange twisted tree and flowers, decorated oval dishes, casseroles and sieves, a wine jug with a beautiful figured handle and a massive cauldron for serving wine at a banquet. Even the pottery finds are presented effectively.

LANGRES, Haute Marne

Museum and sites.

Langres sits on a steep promontory ridge rising more than 100m above the valleys to the east and west. Its Gallo-Roman name, Andemantunnum, and the nature of the site strongly suggest that this was an important *oppidum* of the Lingones. Few Iron Age remains have been turned up and little is known about the tribe. According to Livy, they were among the Celts who migrated to northern Italy and some at least settled there in the fourth century BC. The territory where Caesar found them was on the watershed between north/south draining rivers and the most direct land route from the Saône basin to the Moselle. The Langres plateau holds water badly and lacks good arable soil, probably limiting Iron Age settlement, though its extensive pasture may explain why Caesar asked the the Lingones to provide him with horsemen. They were the most consistent of allies, remaining loyal to the Romans throughout the wars and were rewarded with 'federate' status. They later provided cavalry who served on the imperial frontiers, including Britain, based in forts at High Rochester and Wallsend. The *civitas* was also known for its coarse woollen cloak, the *bardocucullus*, suggesting the pasture supported herds of sheep.

Not much of the Roman city has been revealed. The lack of either visible remains or much knowledge of the Roman town's topography is the product of weak local interest and limited urban development. The one major modern excavation, from the late 1960s to the 1980s in the Place d'Etats-Unis/Place Bel'Air area, suggests the town developed rapidly in the early first century AD with wide roads and imposing stone structures. Sadly, little more is known about Andemantunnum. No forum has been identified, no temple site, no public baths, no amphitheatre or theatre and no full house plan. Fragments of Roman road imply Rue Longeporte/Rue Diderot formed the main *cardo*, and on the town limits at least two triumphal arches are known. A rampart was constructed at the end of the third century on the northern tip of the promontory, enclosing a third of Andemantunnum, largely replaced since by medieval and Renaissance walls.

Despite it being rewarded with the title of *colonia*, modern estimates put Andemantunnum at a maximum extent of only 70ha, a third of the area of Autun. Its administrative evolution also suggests a certain disdain from the imperial authorities: initially placed in Belgica, it was transferred to Upper Germany in the 80s, and in the late Roman period to Lugdunensis Prima. Only two senators from the *civitas* are known, both fifth century. One of them, Gregorious, started the trend for bishops to reside in Dijon, where he had estates, a sign that Langres had become a backwater. It became part of the short-lived Alamanni state in the 450s, but by the 480s was under the rule of Chilperic, king of the Burgundians.

Langres supplies a footnote to the history of the empire. During the civil wars at the death of Nero, the Lingones made the mistake of supporting Vitellius (AD 69) as he was beaten by Vespasian; they were then inspired by a local noble, Julius Sabinus, to join the Civilis revolt in creating an independent Gallic empire. On his own initiative, he began a private war with the Sequani and lost. He then faked a suicide, apparently dying in a burning farmstead, but in reality going into hiding with his wife Epponina, where they had two children. Nine years later, they surrendered. Vespasian was unforgiving and, despite Epponina's passionate pleading, they were executed. Plutarch records it as an example of love, Tacitus and Dio as a political lesson.

La Porte Romaine

Belle Allée

The ornamental arch is 19.95m wide, pierced by two semi-circular arches with Corinthian decoration, and covered with a frieze from which nearly all the original relief work – arms and shields – has disappeared. The only dating evidence, a single coin found between stones in 1775 and lost long ago (even the paper recording this was destroyed in a fire in 1892!), gave an Antonine date; it could be much earlier. This arch became a gate when it was enclosed in a 3.5m-thick rampart built largely of reused stone. In the first years of the fourth century, Constantius Chlorus was campaigning near here against the Alamanni. In a surprise attack, Constantius had to flee for protection in the city, but the gates were shut. Ropes were thrown over the rampart and the Caesar rapidly climbed up. Later, when reinforcements arrived, Constantius swept the Alamanni before him 'killing 60,000' (Eutropius, *Digest*, IX, 23). Despite such losses the Alamanni were to return: in the 350s the rampart did not stop them and bishop Desiderius was killed, to become the Saint Didier of later hagiographers.

Porte Longe-Porte

Rue Longe-Porte

Nothing is visible now, but in the nineteenth century traces of arch and frieze were found, then destroyed by a new gateway covering the foundations. This arch and gate took the Roman traveller out to the precipitous hillside road for Metz and Trier, undoubtedly dangerous and exhausting for people and animals.

Musée de Langres

St-Didier
Place du Centenaire
Hours: 10a.m.–noon; 2–6p.m. Closed Tuesday

Most of the reliefs and sculptures from the rampart are badly battered and only one mosiac, the **polychrome Bacchus**, deserves attention. Half a dozen **tombstones**, found in the same part of the citadel cemetery, depict in flat relief an altar between two pillars and a pediment; they are clearly by the same mason: a rare occurrence. Three seem to be public slaves or freedmen; perhaps they all were and the mason was retained by their burial club. Another tombstone records an unusual profession, a *derisor*: Lollius Geminus Gemellus was a jester. The **cart carrying a large barrel**, the most important relief (see Figure 57), once decorated a mausoleum. This could have carried an estimated 300 litres of wine or beer. Despite the heavy bodies, the ears, faces and necks of the animals strongly suggest two mules, not oxen. Only showing his head, behind them is a third held by loose reins; he must be there to encourage the others on steep climbs; the side relief shows the spare team held by a groom using a chain. Below the cart, note the brake shoe on its chain, used to slow the vehicle on a descent (see METZ). However, there seems to have been little to stop a cart from crashing helplessly if it began to slip backwards on a hill.

Faverolles mausoleum

IGN 3119 O/3119 E
816/2333.2

20km north-west of Langres by the N19, D155 and D256. Well signposted on all approaches to the village, taking you to the Atelier Archéologique. The remains of a large tower mausoleum were found in 1980 overlooking a fine section of the Roman road from Langres to Reims. It is still being excavated.

Atelier Archéologique. The reliefs, pilasters and decorative features are preserved here. A model shows that the mausolem was a tall three-tiered structure, similar to the tomb of the Julii at Glanum/St Rémy-de-Provence. Particularly good is the head of a bearded man, his hair sprinkled with flowers. It is thought to be of a leading Lingones estate owner who died at the time of Tiberius (14–37).

The **site** is in the Blaise valley forest. Follow the Rue des Templiers north 1.5km, passing the church, under the electrical grid, to a very minor cross-roads; take the forest track *c.*500m; a path on the right points to the mausoleum and a picnic site (5 minutes).

The square core of rubble is impressive, 57.3sq m, and *grand appareil* blocks, some with mouldings, stand around the mausoleum; it is protected by a shed roof. Nearby sections of **Roman cobbled road** evoke a vivid picture of the bumpy ride for Gallo-Roman travellers, though the surface would have been in much better condition then. As they passed by what once must have been a striking memorial, they could look forward to the long uphill struggle to Langres and some good refreshment.

LEMBERG, Moselle

IGN 3713 ET

Rock carvings.

Lemberg is 9km south-west of Bitche by the D37. There are three sites within 2km of the village. The pleasure is not the quality of the sculpture – you will see much better in museums. Instead, the tall beech trees, the pale canopy of branches and the open, leaf-covered ground provide a natural context for the reliefs, giving a sense of meeting people in the past.

Source St Hubert (Pompöser Bronn) (968.9/2458.1). From the village centre taking the D37, 1.2km north to the first turning on left for parking place. Follow the track towards the Schlossberg hill and then left on the white cross and red circle path. Joined by the red triangle path near two benches, your path divides, but both lead to the spring *c.*150m further on where there is a panel.

The spring is named after an eighth-century bishop of Liège, the patron saint of huntsmen. The carved rock has lost its upper half, but enough survives

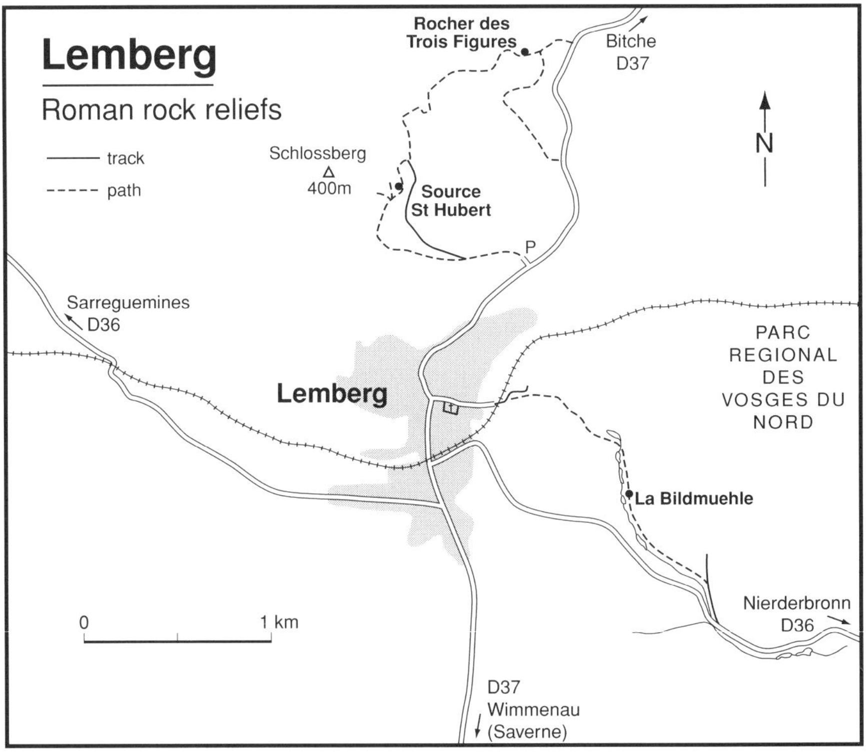

Figure 67 Lemburg: area map

Plate 26 Lemberg. Rock carvings at St Hubert spring. Photograph: James Bromwich.

to explain why it became linked with Saint Hubert. On the right two stags fight; next to them stands the woodland god Silvanus, possibly holding a lance, and beside him the huntress Diana with her bow. At their feet are a wild boar and four dogs. Above seems to be a nymph and a child. In front are traces of canalization at the spring. The Roman writer Arrian (*De venatione*, IV) pointed out that for Celts hunting was not simply for food or a pastime but an exercise in skill and needed divine approval.

Rocher des Trois Figures (Dreibilderthal) (969.7/2459). This can be approached in two ways. Carry on from the Source St Hubert, taking the red triangle path north. This rejoins the track and then bears right when the track turns sharply left; it is a further 1.25km. Carry on the red triangle path to reach the car-park (1.5km). Alternatively, from the source St Hubert walk back to the car-park and drive to the next left turn off the D37 (2km); the walk from here is about 500m.

Some metres above the path on a rocky projection are two figures, *c.* 1.4m high; they are not easy to make out. One is a woman with a diadem, the other a man in a long tunic; they are thought to be a divine couple: a mother-goddess/Diana and a woodland god. A third (very) faint figure may be a nymph.

La Bildmuehle (970.2/2456.2). This rock carving is a twenty-minute walk south-east of Lemberg. From the village centre go east past the cemetery to the bridge under the railway, then by the white circle path along a pool-filled valley (1.5km) to find a tiny relief by a spring, once hidden by a mill.

A veiled goddess sits in a niche (35cm high), carrying a corn of abundance and a patera. For her worshippers, she offered abundance and protected the spring.

METZ, Moselle

Museum and sites.

My image of Metz had always been of a city with the misfortune to be the capital of a much disputed province buffeted between German and French nationalism, a dark and dismal place made worse by the blight of heavy industry to the north. Not true: Metz is an attractive and historic city with one of the finest Gallo-Roman museums in France.

A third-century BC cemetery, traces of huts and a short section of *murus gallicus* rampart point to a late Iron Age *oppidum* at the junction of the Seille and Moselle. The rampart enclosed 35ha, but much of this was marshland, the rest Ste Croix hill. Dendrochronology shows the original timber frame of the rampart was built in 112–14 BC. It was renovated in 55 BC, but the Mediomatrices are hardly mentioned by Caesar: clearly they did not provide serious resistance to the Roman armies. The tribe seems to have been little more than a federation of peoples or *pagi*, then covering the lands

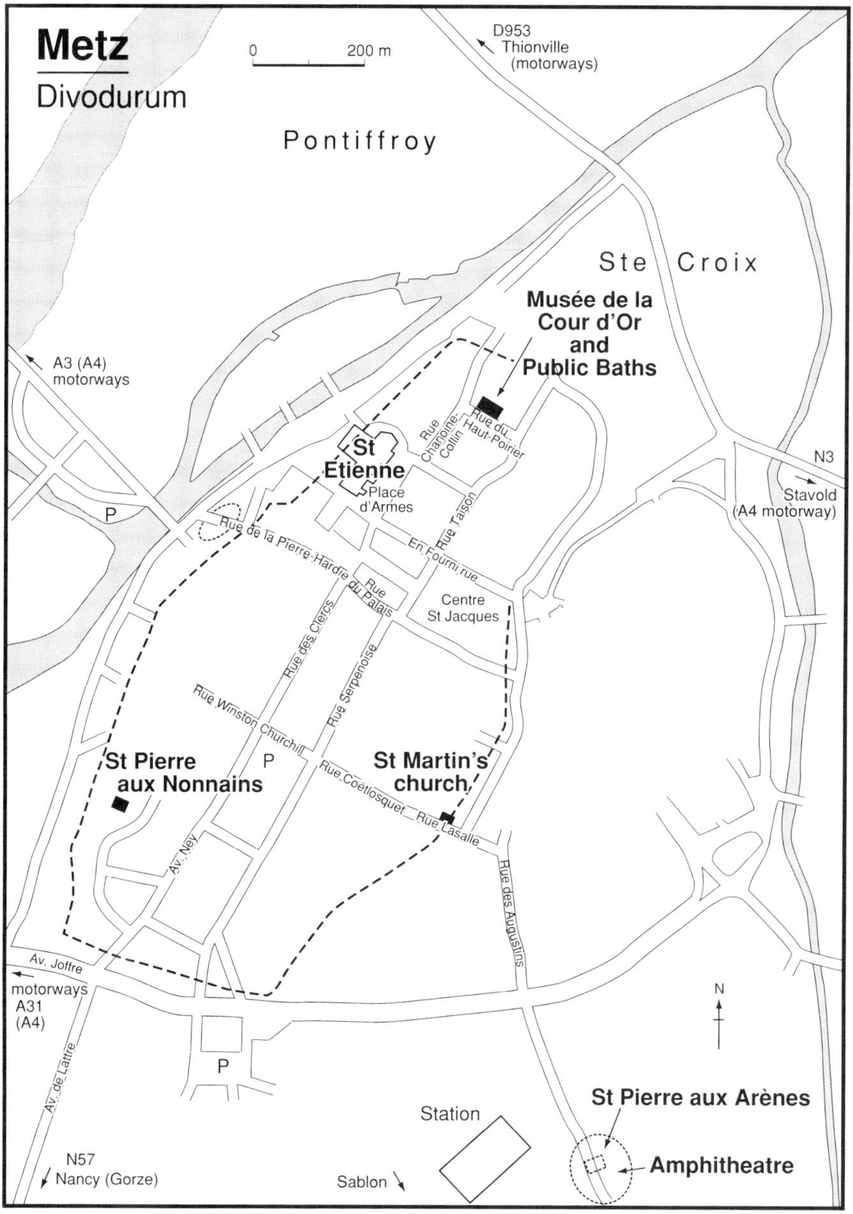

Figure 68 Metz: town plan

between the Meuse and the Rhine, though under Augustus or Tiberius, the Triboci and Nemetes were given the Rhine valley.

The Roman town

Initially a scatter of buildings crept down the gentle southern slopes of Ste Croix. Under Augustus a grid was laid out. It stretched to what became known as the citadel hill, the earliest of three known grids. The first-century AD housing was almost entirely of timber and earth. Fire deposits have been linked to the Florus revolt (AD 21) and the fighting in Gaul after the death of Nero (68–70): if these really represent widespread destruction, they do not seem to have had a long-lasting impact. Divodurum was made the *civitas* capital and may have become a 'colony' with Latin rights, making available a few more positions to local notables, who from the late first and early second centuries began to have more impressive city houses built beside the new stone public buildings. Unfortunately most of the latter were excavated some time ago and dated on thin evidence; virtually none has left visible remains. Close by St Etienne cathedral, the 'Maison Quarrée' was pulled down in the eighteenth century; associated with a portico, it is thought to have been part of the forum, perhaps a temple or maybe a basilica. An amphitheatre, outside the town itself, was finally flattened in the seventeenth century. The foundations were excavated in 1902–3 revealing that it had been very large, supporting two **tiers** with a capacity of up to 40,000 people; the stonework suggested a Trajanic date. A curved structure beside the Moselle, excavated at the same time, was interpreted as 'a small amphitheatre': both building and date remain obscure. At least three public baths are known; only those in the museum are visible. The need for additional water entailed aqueducts: one is known from Gorze, another presumed for the elevated Ste-Croix. The Gorze distribution *castellum* has been associated with two sites, close by St Pierre-aux-Nonnains and in the Sablon suburb, neither conclusively. The first could be a *nymphaeum* and the second an underground water sanctuary dedicated to the goddess Iconellauna.

Despite such frustrating evidence, it is clear Divodurum had become a significant Roman town with a population of 10,000 or more, spread over 100ha with suburbs at both Sablon and Pontiffroy. Though there were regional resources that Divodurum exploited, good land and fishing from the river, iron to the north and salt to the south, clay for potteries both in the town and in the vicinity producing Gallo-Belgic ware and *sigillata*, the fundamental factor in the prosperity of the town must have been trade. Boats carrying goods for the largest city of Belgica, Trier, and the armies on the Rhine frontiers beyond would have rested and resupplied here. It was also a major road junction where the Lyon–Trier highway met the increasingly important road from Strasbourg to Reims. Inscriptions record both *nautae* and *negotiatores*, but most powerful in conveying an image of a prosperous town are the reliefs decorating the tombs of the well-to-do inhabitants. This top 5–10 per cent were local people (foreign names and fully Romanized forms are rare), drawn from trade, farming and the ownership of workshops. Dressed in their thick tunics, they are surrounded by evidence of their business or home life; they exhibit a lifestyle distant from the struggles of the poor who would have surrounded them in the town and countryside – and equally far from the great estate owners of Gaul.

Due to its strategic position, despite losing the Verdun *pagus*, the relative importance of late Roman 'Civitas Mediomatricorum' was enhanced. Unusually, most of Mettis (the increasingly popular abbreviated name) was enclosed by a rampart, embracing *c.*70ha and stretching 3km. This has not been securely dated, though it was certainly after 300. Second city to Trier in Belgica Prima, its supply role continued to be important. In addition to the earlier evidence for production, the *Notitia Dignitatum* mentions a *fabrica* for the woollen industry. The aqueduct was repaired. Even new public building was undertaken with the basilica of St Pierre-aux-Nonnains, certainly in the fourth century, though dating evidence is uncertain. Usage also is uncertain, but it was probably part of a bath complex. Whether the large amphitheatre operated is also debated. Building was undertaken in the arena cellars in the late third century: renewal *or* church building? This was indeed the site of St Pierre-aux-Arènes, associated with Saint Clement, the third-century first bishop of Metz, but the 1890s excavations failed to clarify if the church elements were a precocious third or fifth century. By the 450s there were other churches, particularly associated with the southern cemetery, but their distribution suggests settlement was gradually becoming more suburban anyway.

From the 350s onwards the evidence for occupation within the walls is minimal; the direct and indirect impact of the Alamanni and Frankish wars had dramatically reduced the ability to maintain town life. In 451 Attila's Huns sacked the city. A recent study of Metz argued that this remained in folk memory because so many churches and churchmen suffered: they were outside the walls. St Stephen's oratory 'miraculously' survived because it was inside, a reminder for the locals and their bishop that the cathedral and his residence should be within the rampart. As a town it re-emerged when, in the mid-sixth century, Sigebert recognized that Metz lay at the centre of his Austrasian Merovingian kingdom and made it his chief residence.

Musée de La Cour d'Or/d'Art et d'Histoire

2 Rue du Haut-Poirier
57000 Metz

Hours:	summer	10a.m.–noon, 2–6p.m. Closed Tuesday
	winter	10a.m.–noon, 2–5p.m. Closed Tuesday

This is a great museum, filled with pleasures. Nowhere else in eastern France gives a better picture of Gallo-Roman people and their lives. It is laid out with historical awareness and precision, linking sculpture and smaller finds together, lit to highlight exhibits and providing basic information.

Entry area

The **tombstone relief** of a Gallo-Roman family is the epitome of the prosperous middling sort, only to be found again a thousand years later (for their clothes see DRESS AND APPEARANCE). The ***Nike*** or Victory statue was found near the water sanctuary in Sablon and may have decorated part of the sanctuary. Though technically one of the finest figures in the museum, it is a provincial replica of a Greek original.

Basement

The Roman public baths. These were excavated first in the 1930s and again in the 1960s. It was clear that they were extensive and grand, but not enough survived to reveal how they functioned. The staircase down takes you past one of a series of semi-circular and rectangular apses that decorated a large bathing chamber, probably a *tepidarium*. In the main room, a bathtub filled one apse. Contrasting marble linings must have made a magnificent environment. Beyond this chamber a massive tunnel took waste water into a complex underground drainage system. A further section, with its walkways on each side for maintenance, can be entered from room 6 on the ground floor.

Exhibits. The most important are related to water supply. There are cone clay pipes and rare square-sectioned, mould-made, concrete pipes, possibly to resist high pressure. Most important must be the **pump** found in Sablon in 1910. This is exactly as Vitruvius, the first-century BC architect and engineer, described one. There are sections on navigation, on toiletry (using broken sculpture to illustrate hair-styles) and a good section on medicine with a small relief of a pilgrim, arm in a sling, and memorials to **male and female doctors**.

Ground floor: 'daily life' rooms

Normally it is the small finds which give an insight into the commonplace and these are displayed here, but few other museums have so many fine reliefs that are skilful enough to portray human sensibilities, illustrating people at work and in their homes. Dress and travel are covered too, but exhibits here are referred to in special chapters in this book. For the rest, I provide a selection of those that engaged me: undoubtedly you will find others.

While reliefs such as those of a woman ladling from a barrel and men sawing timber show the reality of work – and some pride in it – the **mealtime** tombstone is one of the most evocative (actually acquired from Arlon, Belgium). The commemorative feast was a feature of Roman funerals, but

Plate 27 Metz. A funeral relief with adults and children enjoying meals.© Metz, Musées de la Cour d'Or. Photograph: Jean Munin, all rights reserved.

the meals being eaten here are not stiff, formal occasions. A group of adults sit on chairs, not couches; on the left, a woman has a cushion on hers. The circular table has a cloth; on top lies a plate with a chicken: they are clearly eating this with their fingers – perhaps it is soaked in a spicy sauce; a shelf behind them carries jars. Below is a group of children. One plays a double pipe, the others are also eating. They sit on the floor around their bowl with a begging dog: one holds him back and another raises a stick to hit him; it is a vivid picture full of the noise and movement of young children. Nearby are actual stone tables, bottles, goblets, spoons and lamps. Other tombstone reliefs show a child playing with a dog and a baby wrapped in swaddling clothes; poignant reminders of the harsh reality of early death for so many.

In the **shop scene relief**, a seated baker holds a rolling pin (?) on his knee; he leans forward as his customer checks a cake. Round loaves are spread on the counter and small cakes are stacked in garlanded boxes. A relief from Soulosse (see GRAND) illustrates what must have been another tradesman: the husband proudly carries a large set of scales while his wife cradles a box. Nearby are scales, weights and a tile marked with cursive Latin, the normal script for daily use.

Another, the **tax-collector**, has a man in his basket chair writing in a large book perched on the counter. In front of him lies a pile of money from which a second man seems to be checking a coin – maybe to see if it had been clipped. On a side relief, a man perhaps holds a corn measure; if so, this would suggest the main scene depicts a treasury official responsible for the *annona* (corn tax). Other conjectures include an estate rent collector or even a banker.

The **ceremonial knife** is a stark reminder of formal temple sacrifices, so much part of Gallo-Roman life, a natural way to thank Mercury for giving prosperity or Epona after a safe return from delivering loaded carts to market.

Corridor room

Various types of tombstones and some fine lead coffins lead to the impressive reassembled remains of a **circular tomb**. This must have once housed an extremely wealthy person – and gives some idea of just how big the recently discovered tomb in Strasbourg must have been: it had a diameter of 60m, this was 8m. Inside are hidden three **Jupiter-giant figures**. The largest, from Merten near the German border, is perched on a capital, column and sculptured base, originally estimated to have stood 12m. The two forces of earth and sky are tied in their eternal struggle, but the impassive imperial god of light triumphs over the agonized monster (see CUSSY-LA-COLONNE). Beyond is an enormous **Mithras panel** from a Mithraeum at Sarrebourg found in 1895. A handcuffed skeleton was found in front and clearly the panel has been smashed: late fourth-century Christians? Barbarians? Looters? Mithras is in his standard pose, red cloak trailing, releasing the blood of life by stabbing the great bull in a cave. Like Jupiter, he too is a god of light. But he is more; he is the life-giver and the salvation of souls. The Graeco-Roman pantheon is embraced, including Jupiter who can be seen in the centre of the lintel above, but their overall insignificance is apparent from their relative size. In the main scene battered faces appear in the corners, the four winds; on the left Cautopates, the daytime torchbearer, is reasonably clear, night-time Cautes is barely visible. Supporting the lintel on each side are scenes portraying the life of Mithras; the clearest shows Sol, the Roman sun god, clasping hands with Mithras. Below the bull is a lion, the name and symbol of the fifth level in the faith, and associated with the planet Jupiter; the lion is aligned with the god on the lintel. The whole reflects the complex 'mystery' of both the story and the cult practices of Mithraism.

Craft rooms

The art of building in antiquity is attractive without being exceptional: there are some **gladiator mosaics**, one of which has survived reasonably. More interesting perhaps is the smiths' and carpenters' room. The **blacksmith's tombstone** shows a collection of tools of his trade in a delicate light relief; there are numerous examples of the real things. Their contributions to other trades are indicated by the collection of farmers' and butchers' equipment. Downstairs are brought together the work of bonecarvers, glassmakers and regional potters. Though the Gallo-Belgic ware is attractive, most interesting is the eastern Gaul *sigillata* from Chamery. Numerous **mould stamps** show how bowls could be decorated with cherubs, animals, hunters and gods.

Popular art and Merovingian art

The catch-all term 'popular' is used to display clumsily executed Gallo-Roman tombstones and altars, often marked by crude, box-like figures, possibly home-made. A passage, used to evoke barbarian invasions, leads to the Merovingian. It is the usual display of cemetery finds: swords, damascened buckles, throwing axes, but a magnifying glass is provided to examine inlaid rings and fibulae and period costumes are re-created. The palaeo-Christian section puts together the primitive inscription evidence and an impressive evocation of **the interior of St Pierre-aux-Nonnains** basilica church, with the eighth-century stone balustrade from the chancel.

St Pierre-aux-Nonnains

Rue de la Citadelle
Hours: these change frequently. Ask in the Arsenal or tourist office. Note that the interior is post-Roman and the Merovingian fittings are in the museum.

The external frame is late Roman and though much restored, *petit appareil* can be seen to a considerable height in some places. Until the 1960s it was difficult to comprehend why this building could have been built; the shape is that of a basilica, but it could hardly be a civic structure so far from the town centre. Excavating around it revealed buildings that could have been a bath complex: this would have been an exercise hall replacing a traditional outside *palaestra* (see PARIS where the Cluny baths had two halls). It was converted to a church in the fifth century, though whether before or after the Huns came is not clear. It became an abbey church in the seventh century.

St Martin's church

Place St Martin/Rue Lasalle

Outside the entrance are the sole visible remains of the late Roman rampart, with a few metres of distinctive small, well-cut, facing stonework. On the left it is only 0.5m wide, but rises *c.*6m. The rampart may have been part of the restructuring of northern defences associated with the defeat of the Alamanni by Julian in the 350s.

The Gorze aqueduct

IGN 3313 E

An aqueduct supplied Divodurum from the beginning of the second century with water from the Boissons springs below Gorze, 22km south of Metz, dropping down first into the Moselle valley, crossing the river, using 110–120 arches to do it (1.125km long), and finally reaching a *castellum* somewhere on the gentle slope of the citadel. An inscription records how six *seviri Augustales*, priests of the imperial cult usually drawn from wealthy freedmen, funded works on a spring and *nymphaeum*; it may mean they paid for the whole aqueduct. In 1769, two Benedictine monks accurately plotted the aqueduct's route.

'Buried' section. D12, 4km from Gorze, signposted with a roadside pull-in. Two short sections of the buried channel are visible where recent road widening cut away a curve. Clearly apparent are the standard arched structure of cut-and-cover building and the waterproof cement lining.

West bank arches and tank. Ars-sur-Moselle. D6, *c.*1km south, roadside parking space by the isolated last aqueduct pier. Built in decreasing tiers to ensure their stability, the arches are wider than usual because they were carrying a double channel. The highest still rises 23.5m, with the channel; the central arches would have stood *c.*30m high. A path leads up past the 1870 war burials, *c.*250m to the arched rectangular settling tank. An overflow channel leads down on the northern side; excess flows after days of rain would put intense pressure on the tank and bridge, something that two channels might also have been designed to reduce as well as easing maintenance.

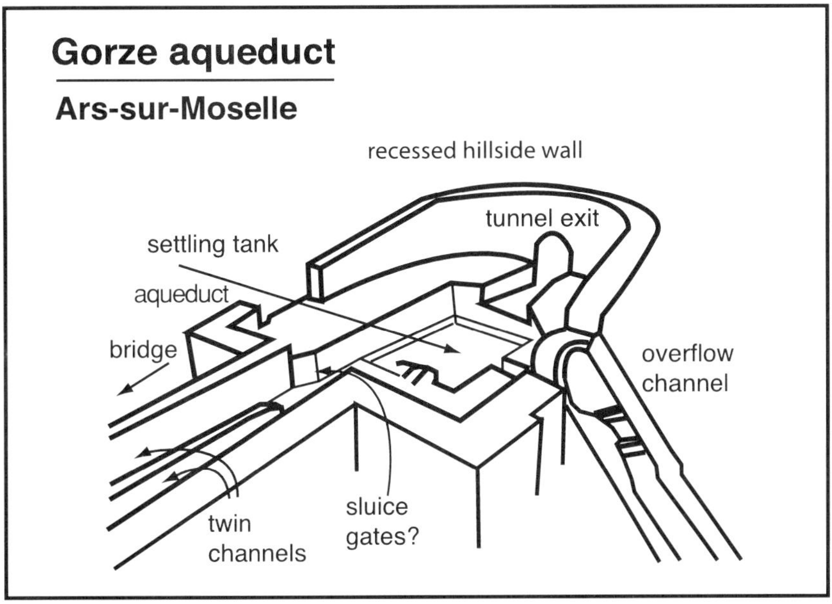

Figure 69 Metz: Gorze aqueduct

East bank arches and tank. Jouy-aux-Arches. The arches here cross the main street, the N57. They are heavily (excessively?) restored and few genuine facing stones survive. The distribution tank is 100m up the hill and sign-posted. It is circular, perhaps as the aqueduct tunnel here takes a right turn northwards.

MONT STE-ODILE, Bas-Rhin

IGN 3716 ET
974.7/2393.7

Rampart.

Mont Ste-Odile is in a cluster of hills and twisting narrow valleys on the eastern edge of the Vosges. Access by car has to be from the west (the old narrow eastern road is now one-way). Parking is available at the point where the road from Klingenthal meets the road up from Barr.

Three high points, Bloss peak (823m), the Hohenbourg or Rocher du Couvent, and the Stollberg ridge, are enclosed by the *mur païen*, a sinuous, intermittent rampart *c.*10km long, enclosing an oblong of some 118ha. There is thick tree cover, dark and damp; below, the bedrock is a 'red' Bunter sand-stone mixed with a conglomerate. Erosion has produced a distinct outcrop

Plate 28 Metz. Seventeen arches of the Gorze–Metz aqueduct at Jouy-aux-Arches. Photograph: James Bromwich.

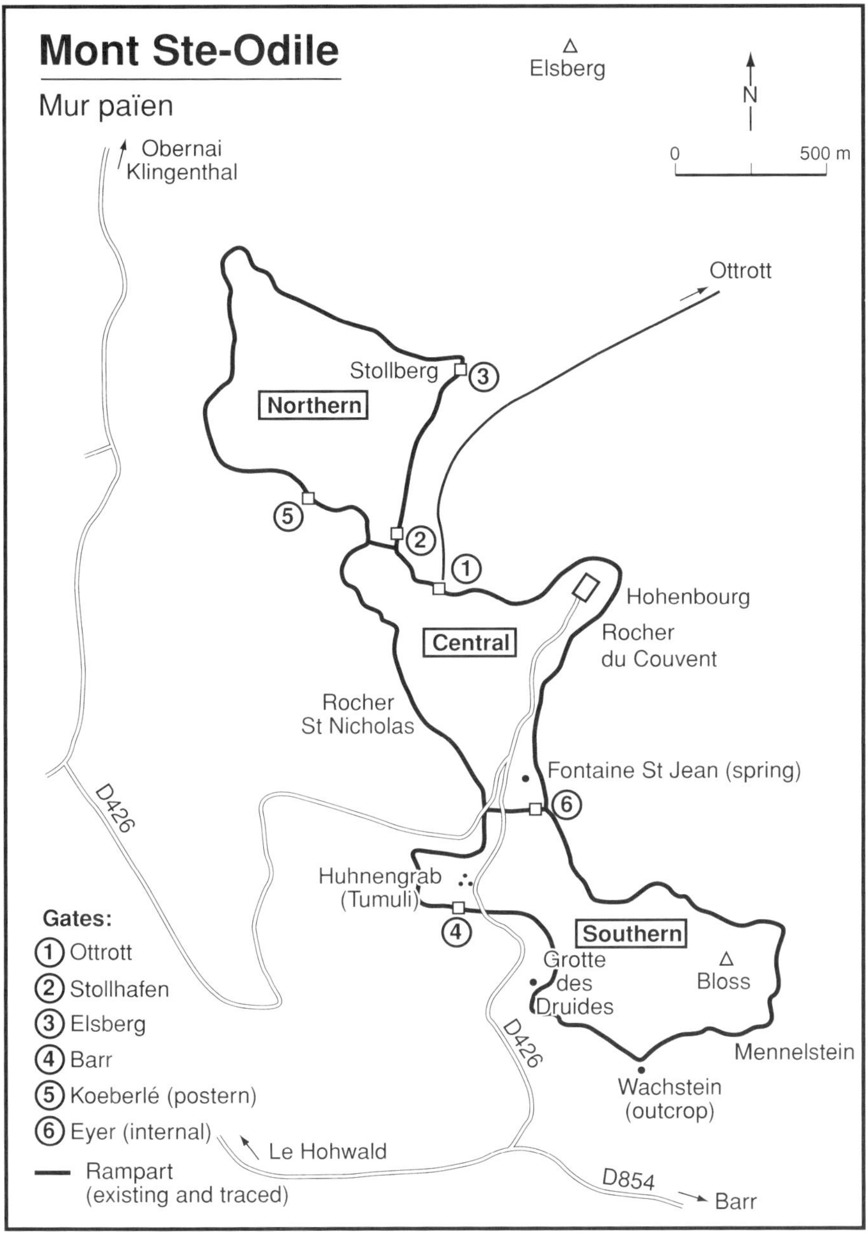

Figure 70 Mont Ste-Odile: site plan

edge that the rampart builders used to give a high firm base for their walling. But much of the erosion has been uneven, leaving flat rocks, tall rocks, leaning rocks and rocks so undercut by weathering they appear to sit on others; the 'Grotte des Druides' is only the best known of these phenomena. The mountains, the gloom, the strange natural shapes, the rampart and the legends surrounding the life of the seventh-century Saint Odile and her convent, all have helped inspire the romantic imagination and myth surrounding the site.

Evidence for occupation has been found for the Neolithic, Bronze Age, Hallstatt, La Tène, Roman and early medieval. Since archaeology began, arguments have been put forward for almost all these inhabitants to have been responsible for building the rampart. They have ranged from the Bronze Age by Mediterranean-inspired builders (1200–1100 BC), to the Merovingians (AD 6–750), not excluding a Nazi-inspired effort in 1943 to see the whole site as a pre-Christian Germanic creation against the Celts. The problem has been the thinness of dated material relating directly to the rampart itself. However, there is a strong case for both a Roman context and a Roman role in construction.

The *mur païen*

Two internal walls divided the enclosed area into three 'camps'. The central camp has a large flat rock outcrop on the east, the Hohenbourg, where the convent was to be built, but which is believed to have previously formed an acropolis.

The external ramparts are 1.6–1.8m thick and survive to a height of 1–1.5m, thought originally to have been 2–4m high, probably with a wooden structure on top; because it was built on the edge of the outcrop it must have seemed much higher. Large rocks were incorporated in the line, which will have functioned as watchtowers. Building blocks vary in size, but for the southern camp they are particularly massive, some in the lower courses being nearly 2m long. For the centre and the north, the average size is smaller. The stonework was secured not by cement or timbers, but by tenons or small pieces of wood, joining oblong holes cut into the blocks above and below.

Occasionally tenons have survived: carbon-14 dating gave a range of 251–425, suggesting 350 as a mean, confirming heavy concentrations of late Roman coins found by the gates. Therefore the main gates were constructed at a time of considerable threat to the local population. But was this renovation? An estimated quarter million blocks were needed for the circuit and at least thirty quarries have been identified, yet the rampart is not even continuous. Clearly stonework has been removed for later building – for example in the surrounding medieval castles – but it is also possible that the rampart was never completed, particularly along the north face of the northern camp. Such a massive enterprise in a traditional dry-stone style is seen as more likely to have been built in the equally dangerous late second or first centuries BC, when so many other large *oppida* were being built (e.g. SAVERNE). Was it conceived by a *pagus* of the Mediomatrices? Or the Leuci? Or the Triboci (and so perhaps 'Germanic')? A fortress to resist the Romans? Modern research may eventually find answers.

Visit

The whole length can be done in five hours, but shorter circuits are signposted, e.g. the southern circuit is 4.5km, designated with yellow cross markers of the Club Vosgien. One section is described below.

The Barr or Zumstein Gate and nearby rampart: the D426 cuts through the rampart about 600m below the Merovingian tumuli burials. 40m west a hole in the rampart marks the medieval road from Barr. Zumstein revealed the late Roman gateway a few metres further west. The lintels and doorjambs of a double gate are visible across the front and the foundations of the two internal walls survive, forming the corridor. The much thicker southern wall probably supported a staircase to the rampart and the roof over the gate. The rampart rises sharply to the south, green moss and lichen covering the widely varying stonework, and double mortise holes can be seen on fallen blocks.

MOUZON, Ardennes

IGN 3110 O

Sanctuary site and museum.

South-east of Sedan by the D964 to Stenay, 4km beyond Mouzon. South of the main road, hidden in Le Fevrier wood, are the remains of a sanctuary site protected from the weather by a steel and glass structure.

Mouzon itself was a small Roman town, or *vicus*, at the Meuse crossing for one of the most important roads in Belgica, the highway linking Reims and Trier. Le Flavier sanctuary lay not far from the road, on a then unforested slope visible from many miles away. It must have attracted both locals and travellers.

The major features of the sanctuary are clear to the visitor. At the centre was a rectangular *fanum*, built in the second century. Excavation revealed it had a solid concrete floor, its walls were plastered and painted and the roof covered with tiles; traces of paving suggest a classic gallery surrounded it. The sanctuary was enclosed by a wall (*peribolus*), of which part must have had a portico with pillars and tile roof. Contemporary with these were other buildings that perhaps stored or supplied offerings and maybe housed a temple guardian.

What has become increasingly apparent is that the site has had a long and complex history, starting from at least the early first century BC and continuing up to the late fourth century. Excavation has taken place here off and on since 1966, but disentangling both the stratigraphy and the evolving shape of the sanctuary has proved difficult. The central *fanum* is only one in a sequence of buildings on this spot. Some post-holes of La Tène period are still visible; this seems to have been the 'temple' used through to the Augustan period. A small square stone building, a replacement or subsidiary temple, was in use during the early and middle years of the first century. It has a strange elliptical pathway on its northern entrance side, conceivably used for processions. If the site's complexities can be disentangled, then it might increase our knowledge of the changes brought by Romanization to Gallic religious practice. Finds displayed in Mouzon itself and in the Musée de l'Ardenne, Charleville-Mézières, already highlight one local adaption.

Musée de la Tour

Porte de Bourgogne
08210 Mouzon

Hours:	mid-May–mid-September	3–6p.m.
	mid-September–mid-May	3–6p.m. Weekends only

The main attractions of the museum are the votive offerings from Le Fevrier. They include pottery, figurines and fibulae, but the most important relate to the early years following the Gallic wars. While the large number of Remi and Treviri coins are not unexpected, the discovery in the 1970s of masses of miniature armaments – more than 600 – was important. The majority are iron swords and shields (such as the Celtic hexagonal design), fewer bigger than 10–12cm. Though a local phenomenon, it shows how the old Gallic warrior culture with its gifts of weapons and, at some sites, slaughtered animals and people, was being forced to adapt to the Roman peace. Even this modified practice had disappeared by the mid-first century AD.

NANCY, Meurthe-et-Moselle

Museum.

Nancy is best known for its splendid eighteenth-century Place Stanislas and its art nouveau. As it is a medieval foundation there are no Roman remains in the city, but it does hold a largely nineteenth-century collection of Roman material from the Lorraine departments.

Musée Lorrain de Nancy

Palais Ducal
64 Grand Rue
54000 Nancy

Hours:	2 May–September	10a.m.–6p.m. Closed Tuesday
	October–April	10a.m.–noon, 2–5p.m.

The archaeological collection looks as if no money has been spent here for many years, being both unimaginative and uninformative: it deserves better. Both the Iron Age and the Merovingian are well represented, but rarely distinguished by helpful labelling.

Better presentation would really help the statues and reliefs of the Gallo-Roman section. There are three **Jupiter–giant statues**. The Dommartin example is badly preserved, but the equally conventional one from Hammert, with the usual serpent-tailed giant being ridden down by an impassive emperor-like Jupiter, is well proportioned in a schematic way. The third is from GRAND and despite heavy restoration – it was found in forty-two pieces – is unique. Although not very well proportioned, this still does not explain the tiny figure of a winged man instead of a suffering giant. It is thought that he could have held Jupiter's thunderbolt with his right hand, so formally stressing that the two figures are part of the same divine force, but why wings if he represents the earth?

Among the other gods portrayed, there are numerous **Mercuries**, recognizable by his attributes; none is remarkable. Nor are the two **Apollo** reliefs, but one is puzzling. He is conventionally identified by his lyre, but here a griffin replaces the usual bird (associated with his prophecy role): an unexplained attribute not associated with the great healing god. There is also the curious almost child-like **Chaligny figure**: is it a spring god or a pilgrim seeking a cure? His cloaked nudity suggests a divinity, yet one hand touches his forehead (headaches?) and the other holds a cask on his stomach, implying a pilgrim.

Even some exhibits portraying daily life are enigmatic. The widely reproduced **sawing scene**, apparently showing two woodcutters at work, has been challenged. The saw has no teeth and the structure they are working on seems very awkward. No alternative interpretation has been offered. Another tombstone relief shows a man holding a hipposandal in one hand: he must have been a groom or vet. The bronze work is varied. An outstanding **statue of Dionysus**; attractive small figures of a child holding a ball and a man in his *cucullus*; a bronze case frame decorated with faces; and some bronze name stamps.

NIEDERBRONN-LES-BAINS, Bas-Rhin

IGN 3714/3814 ET

Museum and surrounding sites.

Niederbronn is a small spa town 38km north-north-west of Strasbourg in the northern Vosges. The exploitation of its two mineral springs, the 'Celtic' and 'Roman', was given new life in the eighteenth and nineteenth centuries by the Dietrich family, a leading dynasty in the Alsatian iron industry. Until recently very little was known about Roman Niederbronn. Isolated finds of walling, hypocaust, tiles and pools confirmed there was a Roman settlement here, but only in the 1990s did M.P. Prévost-Bouré's excavations reveal the existence of a very large bath system on the left bank of the river by the Rue des Romains. The linear design of the bath system is similar to others in the frontier zone, so it was possibly established as a recuperation spa for the troops. Its most vital phase was mid-second century. Though abandoned by the mid-third, it had some kind of re-occupation in the first half of the fourth century. Finds indicate that Niederbronn was also able to depend on passing traffic using the Falkenstein valley route, linking Strasbourg and Trier. The resources of the surrounding area were exploited, though their focus may have been the *vicus* at Reichshoffen. Villa farms suggest market-based agriculture, pottery workshops with a regional distribution and presumably the exploitation of iron ore. Nearby sanctuaries flourished.

Maison de l'Archéologie

44 Avenue Foch
67110 Niederbronn-les-Bains

Hours:	1 March–30 October	2–6p.m. Closed Tuesday
	1 November–28 February	Sunday only 2–5p.m.

The Maison, created in 1989, is a mix of museum and regional research centre. Its integrated nature and open structure allows for more dynamic change than most museums (see also BIESHEIM).

There are two rooms covering the Gallo-Roman period. The first brings together finds from the Frohret forest villa farms and from the Wasenbourg sanctuary. There are pieces of the temple entablature and (battered) Mercury altars; the latter are strongly Gallic, but his attributes, the staff or *caduceus* and purse, confirm his identity. The second contains material from the bath complex, including plans and photographs. There is a clear reconstruction of a villa hypocaust together with clay and lead piping and some small finds. Among the sculpture there are a marble Janus that once decorated the Roman spa, the head of an old man, and reliefs recognizable as Diana and Apollo, Venus and Abundance.

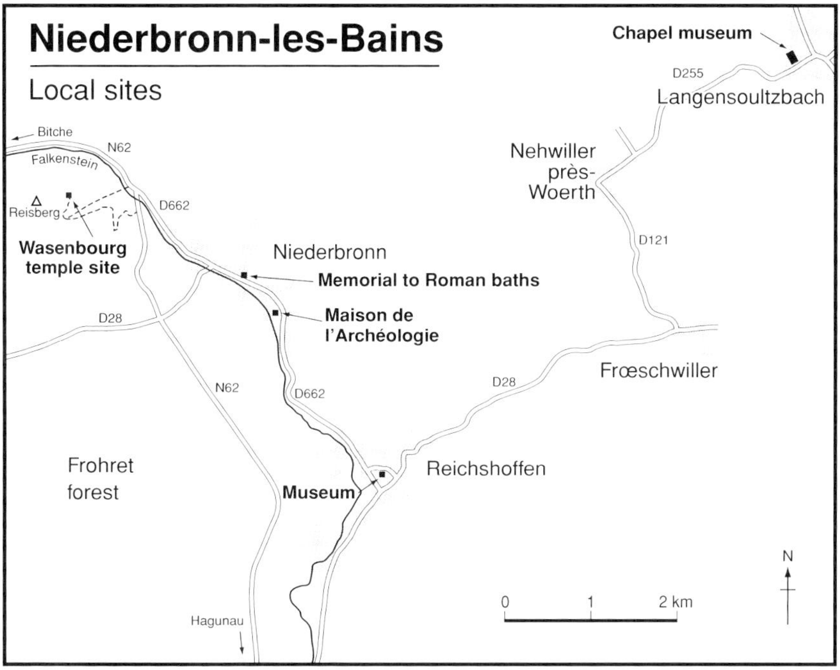

Figure 71 Niederbronn-les-Bains: area map

Wasenbourg

986.4/2454.5

Take the Avenue de la Libération and the Allée des Teuls south of the station west towards the N62. Cross the main road and follow the footpath up to Wasenbourg château ruins (*c.*600m walk). The hill-top sanctuary spread along the ridge, and was partly destroyed by the medieval castle and partly by pillaging; altars have ended up as far away as Mulhouse. A **rock-cut inscription**, noted by Goethe, an early visitor here, records Severinus, son of Caius, making his dedication to Mercury by paying for a temple building. Beside the castle, a 'reconstruction' of the **sanctuary building** is no more than a pile of architectural elements. The view is splendid.

Reichshoffen

IGN 3814 ET

3km south-east via the D662. This small town, overshadowed by the Dietrich ironworks, contains a **museum** in the big presbytery. Inevitably dominated by ironmaking, the basement contains a collection of **pottery** from a workshop specializing in commonware goblets. Other finds suggest the settlement covered *c.*20ha during the Roman period, deriving its modest wealth from the Falkenstein valley road, toolmaking, producing cloth and leather and its proximity to the Niederbronn spa and its visitors.

Langensoutzbach

IGN 3814 ET

14km via Reichshoffen, Frœschwiller and Nehwiller. The chapel at the rear of the village church is used for a modern display illustrating Gallo-Roman cults. Reliefs and statuary include a Jupiter–giant, a Vosegus and Tribans, unknown elsewhere. (Open April–October inclusive, Sundays and holidays.)

REIMS, Marne

City sites and museum.

Perhaps it is appropriate that the symbolic birthplace of the Merovingian state, embodied in the baptism of Clovis by Saint Remigius in 496, should be Reims. It demonstrates how the local people recognized the realities of power in the fifth century AD, just as they had in the first century BC when they chose to support Caesar the moment his forces appeared in the region.

The Remi occupied the plains bordering the hilly forests of the Argonne to the east and the Ardennes to the north. To the west the plateau leading down to the Ile de France was cut by rich river valleys, such as the Aisne, while the heartland of the chalky tufa plains provided excellent north–south routes. Remi is considered to be the Gallic for 'first', but it does not reflect their real status in northern Gaul at the beginning of the first century BC. Caesar mentions (*Gallic Wars*, II, 4) that when he first encountered the Remi, 'in living memory' they had been dependants of the Suessiones, but, probably benefiting from growing trade with Roman merchants from Narbonensis, the area showed signs of new wealth in the first century BC. There were renewed aristocratic chariot burials (reviving this early La Tène practice in the Champagne region) associated with significant imports of Roman amphorae and the sudden emergence of *oppida* at Vieux Laon, Vieux Reims (20km north of Reims at Condé-sur-Suippe) and Durocortorum, Reims itself.

The chronology of these sites is not yet clear enough, and perhaps never will be, to distinguish whether the *oppida* preceded or followed the Remi's alliance with Rome. Caesar noted that the Remi were 'extremely important to us' in his campaigns. They provided a strategic base for his campaigns in Belgica and winter quarters for his troops and remained loyal throughout the wars, even when the Aedui deserted to Vercingetorix. Again in 44–43 BC,

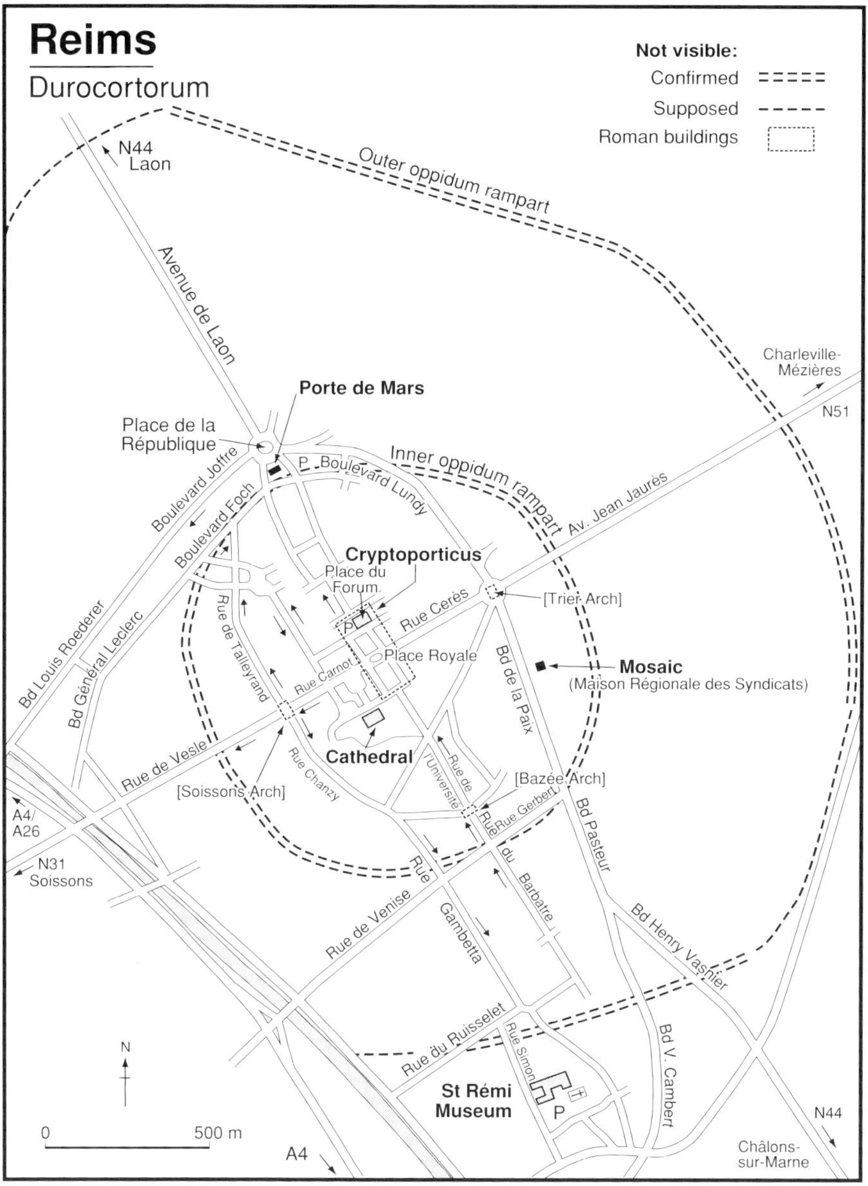

Figure 72 Reims: town plan

Hirtius used the area as a base against rebellious Belgae. Their new status was proclaimed with the most numerous of all tribal bronze coinages: it adopted a Roman type with a spear-bearing warrior in his Gallic torc and a Roman elephant on the reverse. In addition, Durocortorum had two ramparts. The inner, some 3,000m long with a massive embankment of chalk fronted by a wide and deep ditch, enclosed about 90ha, and the outer some 550ha, the largest area anywhere in Gaul: an assertion of their leadership among the Belgae tribes, just as the Romans used city walls in the early empire to proclaim their supremacy.

There is little real sign of Romanization until the first century AD, simply the usual earth and timber houses; yet their loyalty to the new regime was endorsed by the construction of a monument to the 'princes of youth', the adopted sons of Augustus, recorded on an inscription, though sadly no remains of any building have been found (see the Maison Carrée at Nîmes). Their reward was to be made provincial capital, the residence of both the governor and the procurator of Belgica; the latter was particularly important as he was also paymaster for the Rhine army. Two famous men have been connected with the position, Tacitus' father and the great Elder Pliny. Rapid and large-scale growth of Durocortorum followed the decision. Under Tiberius (AD 14–37), well-made streets were constructed using a formal grid covering the area within the inner rampart. By 100 the rampart was being flattened to allow further expansion and ribbon development along the main roads was already extending to the outer rampart, which formed a sort of *pomerium*, or city boundary, beyond which lay the cemeteries.

During the second century much of this outer area filled with suburban housing and the inner city took on a monumental appearance. Many of the streets were furnished with pavements and porticoes. A massive forum was built across the central *decumanus* and *cardo*. Inscriptions record at least one public baths, traces of which have been found in the south of the city. Excavations on the northern side of the cathedral in the 1920s uncovered what was then identified as an early baptistery, but is now thought to be the vestibule of a baths. In the north another inscription was found recording an amphitheatre and there was probably a theatre near the forum. No *praetorium* or governor's residence has been recognized, but rich houses complete with mosaics, marble floors and porticoed courtyards were being built by mid-first century and the number of mosiacs found in the city is second only to that in Trier. A few of the leading citizens became senators but none appears to have been prominent in the administration or politics of the early empire. At the end of the second century, the Porte de Mars and three other massive arches were built, one each on the main roads out of the city, proclaiming the benefits of Roman rule in a typically grandiose Severan way that must have satisfied Remi attitudes as well.

Even though the problems experienced by the empire in the third century certainly hurt Durocortorum, Reims emerged in the late Roman period as capital of Belgica Secunda and with a city wall enclosing 90ha, a far larger area than most. Traces of the wall have been found on a number of sites and show an oval shape linking the monumental arches that now became gateways to the city. The suburbs were largely abandoned and in the south particularly, new cemeteries cover earlier housing. However, inside the walls, unlike other cities, public buildings remained in use. An inscription records Constantine rebuilding the baths, which suggests there must still have been good water supplies and an aqueduct in use. The *Notitia Dignitatum* mentions that Reims had state factories for manufacturing arms and high-quality gold and silver thread for the ceremonial clothes of high officials.

There is also rather more evidence of early Christianity than usual for the north. While the claim for a third-century church is unsubstantiated, a bishop went from Reims to the Gallic church council at Arles in 314 and a fourth-century church has been identified in the southern cemetery. When the public baths fell into disuse in the later fourth century, a part of the old building was converted into a church dedicated to Saint Symphorian, the Autun martyr. Recent excavations in the nave of the cathedral have revealed a church and baptistery dating to the early fifth century with a continuous history from then onwards.

Gallic nobility continued to see Reims as an important centre. Jovinus, *magister equitum*, master of the horse, a leading general in the mobile army during the 360s, chose to retire here. At what point in the fifth century Reims became part of the Frankish kingdom is unclear – perhaps the inhabitants did not even know, as the change from having a Roman governor to ruling in the name of Rome and then just ruling was a subtle one; there were still landowners who considered themselves 'Romans', such as the father of Remigius, who owned four estates in the region in the mid-fifth century. But it was a limited Roman world: by the beginning of the sixth century there were perhaps seven churches in Reims and urban society clustered around these 'public' buildings. Bishop Remigius was typical of the new generation of bishop aristocrats who provided a major element of continuity and made the change from late Roman to early medieval so difficult to distinguish. The events of 496 can be taken as a sign of (almost) seamless change, for the city of Reims at least.

Cryptoporticus

Place du Forum
Hours: 15 June–15 September 2–5p.m. Closed Monday

Forums of a grand type (see BAVAY) were constructed with a partially sunken basement which enabled the architect to create a level platform for the portico of the forum square, where the temple and basilica and any other buildings surrounding the open square itself could stand out on a flat and true surface. Sadly none of the upper structures or even the floor of the forum

Reims

Cryptoporticus

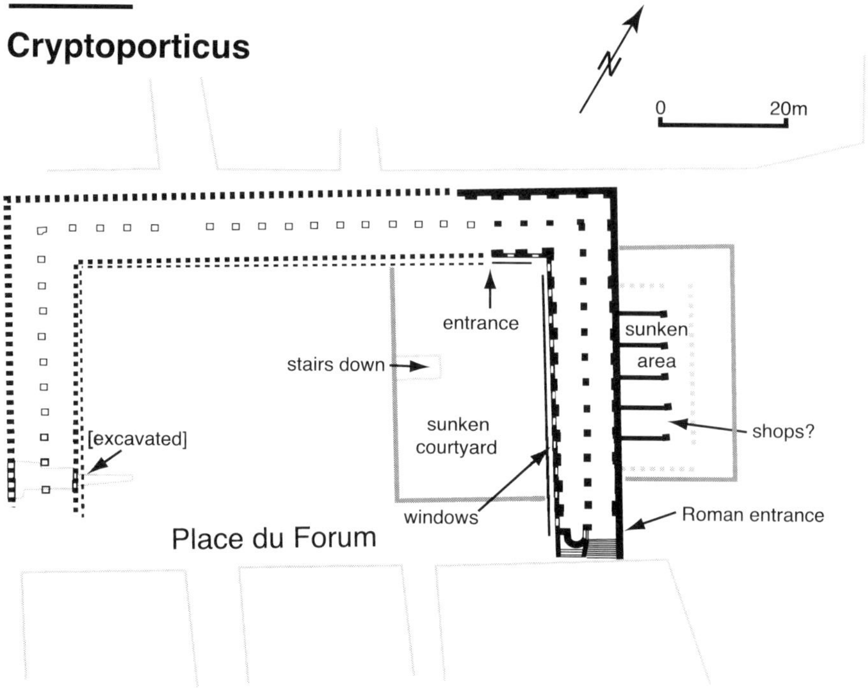

Figure 73 Reims: *cryptoporticus*

square have survived, only this U-shaped 'crypt' that was designed to raise the lower end of the forum.

Discovered originally in 1838 by Brunette, the town's architect, it was partially explored, then left. Revealed again by First World War bombardment, it lay unexamined until the 1930s, when it was excavated inadequately and without proper publication. Limited excavations were again conducted at the end of the 1960s and improved understanding. Only the eastern and a small section of the northern gallery have been fully examined and opened to the visitor.

The galleries were constructed with an interior width of 9.5m, divided down the middle by pillars forming a double nave 5.7m high, with pink cement vaults springing from the pillars and parallel pilasters on the outer walls. The brick courses are the only obvious adornment, set at the point where the vault moulding on the pilasters begins, but the walls were covered with painted plaster; fragments survive at the base of some pilasters and sections of the exterior eastern gallery wall. Outside was a series of rooms, probably shops, facing a road beside the forum. Between each vault on the interior west wall are windows that were set at ground level; the sloping inner frame ensured as much light as possible reached these cellars. The 1967/8 excavations showed that there was an entrance at the southern end of the gallery. On its east side, stairs once rose to a landing and turned back up to reach the portico above. There may have been another more monumental entrance at the centre of the northern side; medieval and modern cellars made it impossible to confirm.

Dating is uncertain, but the not very good stonework and the extensive use of bricks have suggested a Severan date; no stratigraphic evidence has been found. If the eastern entrance is the only one (perhaps replicated for the western gallery, but no one knows), then its simple functional appearance could mean that this *cryptoporticus* was primarily for storage. Pottery finds show it was still used in the fifth century, but that it soon became a rubbish and rubble dump – fortunately helping ensure its partial preservation.

Porte de Mars

Place de la République

This triumphal arch is one of the largest known in the Roman world. The width is impressive (32m), but the height must once have been equally striking with both an attic and a statue group. And there were three other gateway arches like this in Reims. The Porte Bazée still stood in the eighteenth century and its foundations were partially excavated in the 1970s and 1990s: it was on a similar scale. The design with a larger central arch, but all imposts set at the same height, is thought to have been used first in the second century, the style and iconography late second century. Such a grandiose assertion of the benefits of imperial rule is most associated with the early Severans (193–217), who were responsible for the last great phase of public building in the early empire.

Unfortunately, the closer one gets, the more obvious it becomes that the Porte de Mars has suffered over the centuries. Many of the reliefs that decorated the surface have disappeared entirely; the survivors are battered and incomplete or heavily restored. It is an inevitable result of its history. When the late Roman walls were constructed all the arches were converted to gates and were presumably fortified on top. In the twelfth century, earth was heaped over the Porte de Mars to form the base for a castle; the arch itself was only rediscovered in the seventeenth century long after the castle had been burnt and pulled down. Some of the earth and trees were removed in 1812, much more when Brunette made a major effort, but, because of fears about its possible collapse, he only revealed, then restored, the northern side. The south was exposed in the 1860s and the ground was only finally cleared to the Roman surface by a German archaeologist in the Second World War. Further conservation work was carried out in the 1960s.

The north front. The four piers have undecorated plinths surmounted by engaged Corinthian columns, between which are pedimented niches. The

Plate 29 Reims. The Porte de Mars triumphal arch, Place de la République. Photograph: James Bromwich.

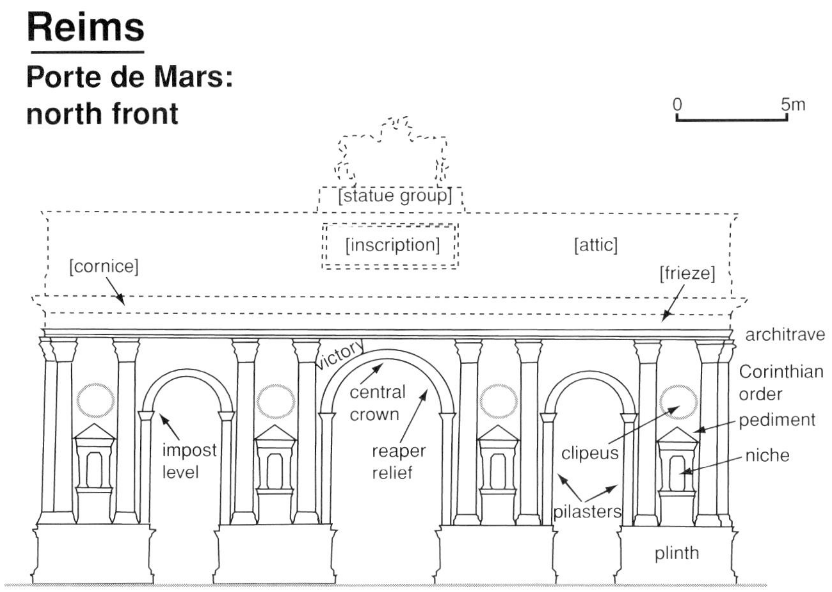

Figure 74 Reims: Porte de Mars arch

reliefs below the niches are impossible to read, and most of the niches are empty. The best preserved is that at the eastern end. Drawings made in the seventeenth or eighteenth century have helped identification, though in some cases there is the fear that imagination filled missing elements. Above the niches are *clipei* – shield-like disks with projecting heads – supported by cupids, symbolizing the triumph of life over death. Above are crossed *caducei*, the herald's staff carried by the god Mercury, and above them are two further cupids drawing back curtains. Nothing survives on top of the architrave. Each arch is defined by floral pilasters. Above the lateral arches and on each side of the central arch are fragmentary winged victories.

The side arcades. No reliefs have been observed below impost level. The vaulting on both follows the same format: a small mythological scene in a central zone at the top, Romulus and Remus suckling at the wolf in the east arcade and Leda and the swan in the west. Immediately surrounding the scenes are octagons and squares filled with roses. Forming wide borders are friezes of arms and shields with winged figures – victories? – in each corner.

The central arch. No side reliefs survive here either. The main focus is the vault and about half the decoration survives: it is of exceptional interest. Not so much the lower figures supporting swags, overflowing fruit bowls or swans above the imposts. Nor the central crown, which is equally conventional; a square filled with a roundel formed from a Greek key design, inside which are acanthus leaf swirls, at the centre a headless Abundance figure with her cornucopia, surrounded by four figures representing the seasons, no doubt echoing the message of the Arch as a whole – the empire as peace and prosperity. The interest lies in the reliefs between, depicting a calendar, unknown on any other arch. January to May have been totally lost, June to December survive in varying states. These reliefs seem to reflect local northern Gallic interests as the rural year depicted differs from conventional calendar mosaics (see PARIS, Louvre). June is represented by horse breeding, the very battered July relief has haymaking using the two-handed scythe, while the slightly better August depicts a **reaper harvesting wheat**. September embodies the sharp social division of the era (and many after it): while the peasant ploughs, the rich man hunts. Almost nothing survives of October, but it is probably grape pressing. November is characterized by pig slaughtering, reflecting the importance of this animal in the region. The shattered remains of December might have shown bulls pulling a cart.

The reaper relief. Carliste, the great nineteenth-century architect who worked on the Orange triumphal arch, visited Reims in the 1840s and, looking at the August relief, suggested that it might depict the Gallic reaper described by both the Elder Pliny and the fifth-century Palladius. His comments were forgotten and it was described as a hoeing scene until the end of the 1950s. Then a relief was found in Belgium at Buzenol near Virton, which showed in much more detail the front of what was quite clearly the machine described by the ancient writers, a *vallus*. It now became obvious

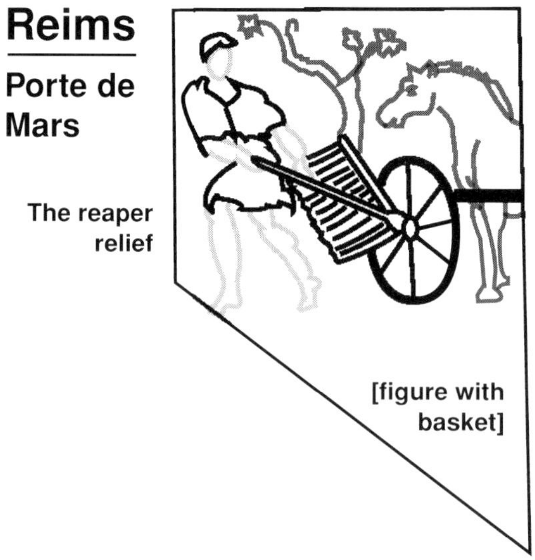

Figure 75 Reims: Porte de Mars reaper relief

that the Reims scene depicted a machine only attempted again in the modern era. Like that developed by nineteenth-century reapers in Scotland and widely used on the North American plains, this was horse-driven, but pushed, not pulled. As an artistic rather than realistic portrayal, only one shaft and one wheel are shown. The long teeth of the reaper form a comb that was thrust through the wheat just below the ears; these ran down between the teeth and were wrenched off to fall into a box attached behind: this is clear from both the written descriptions and the Buzenol relief. Clogging must have been frequent and a man is shown with a rod of some kind – knife-like at the end? – for pushing the ears back and into the box. Not seen is the man holding the shafts behind the horse to steer beast and machine across the field. The stubble left behind would have been a ready food for the pigs.

Because of slavery, the ancient world is often dismissed as uninterested in technology, yet this view needs to be treated with some reserve. Both the Elder Pliny and Palladius stress the reaper's labour-saving advantages. It clearly replaced the large numbers of workers usually needed for harvesting, often paid labour specially hired; equally it could only be easily used on large flat fields and there must have been heavy wastage of ears. All the reliefs showing the reaper have been found in the north-east of Gaul, where the landscape and climate (unreliable August put a premium on speed) suited this machine. The fact that Pliny describes it in the first century AD not only implies that it was a local labour-saving device, like the scythe rather than sickle, and used over a number of centuries, but that its origins might have been Gallic rather than Gallo-Roman. A model scene reproduces the reaper in action in St Rémi museum.

Mosaic

Maison Régionale des Syndicats
Boulevard de la Paix

At the corner of the Rue César-Poulain, when the site was being rebuilt in the 1960s, rescue excavations revealed Gallo-Roman domestic occupation where an elegant *domus* replaced wooden housing. Three rooms with mosaics faced onto a portico looking out into a court with two garden pools. It was decided to preserve the best surviving mosaic. It is based on squares and rosettes, and though largely monochrome, some yellow and red provides a little colour. It is *in situ,* inside the main entrance.

Cathedral

Outside, on the northern side of the nave, a small excavated area is preserved under a canopy. Under the very complex mix of walling could be the entrance to a Gallo-Roman public baths. Inside the cathedral, the Chapelle du Rosaire in the south transept contains a re-laid Roman mosaic.

Musée St Rémi

5 Rue Simon
51100 Reims

Hours:	Monday–Friday	2–6.30p.m.
	weekends	2–7p.m.

The Gallo-Roman collection is displayed in the seventeenth- and eighteenth-century buildings of the Abbaye Royale de St Rémi. On the ground floor, the old refectories and kitchen have been used for exhibiting the larger material, while upstairs rooms 20–24 are used for the smaller pieces covering pre-Roman, 'Gallo-Roman crafts', early Christian and Merovingian phases. Material is well labelled and small models are used revealingly.

Ground floor

A model of Gallo-Roman Reims represents the state of research in the mid-1980s; around this the themes taken up are water supply (note the bronze snake water spout), the city grid and the road system. A poorly cut **mile-stone** found at Château Brumont, 9km north of Reims, is dedicated to the short-lived Gallic ruler Victorinus (269–71), whose main claim to fame is the siege of AUTUN. Interestingly, this expression of Remi loyalty uses the Gallic league rather than the Roman mile (1.5 Roman miles or 2,222m).

The richly coloured **gladiator mosaic** is the finest in the museum. This heavily armed 'Thracian' is from a once magnificent carpet mosaic covered with panels, each filled with a different gladiator or hunter from the arena. It was smashed in the 1917 bombardment of Reims. Two large mosaics are preserved in the main room, one a rather dull series of geometric designs with a central emblem of two idealized combatants. Another more crudely assembled work focuses on the hero Bellerophon.

One of the most striking features is a reconstructed **Jupiter–giant column** (see CUSSY-LA-COLONNE). Another example of Gallo-Roman syncretism is the **Cernunnos relief**. The overall quality of the sculpture, together with the two figures Apollo and Mercury, is strongly classical. But Cernunnos dominates. His name meant 'the horned one' and his antlers, broken off here, the torc round his neck and the cross-legged pose, emphasize his Gallic character. Here is stressed not so much his mysterious animal spirit but his role as bringer of well-being, reinforced by taking over from Mercury the function of distributing prosperity, with coins pouring from his bag to the 'drinking' stag and bull below. The rat in the pediment warns of more sinister forces, perhaps death. A further Gallic twist is provided by the presence of three Gods: the Remi in particular seem to have been keen to enhance the power of their gods by triplism.

A more down-to-earth realism is seen in the **clogmaker's tombstone**, where he sits astride his bench working on a clog, a rack of other carpentry tools to hand on his workshop wall, a basket below for his finished work. The

'Jovinus' sarcophagus is both an embodiment of the opposite end of the social spectrum and the finest piece of Roman art in the museum. Superb marble relief work decorates the front of the stone coffin and is thought to have been made in the third century in Rome, though the heads were probably finished in the fourth. It portrays a mythologized hunting scene. On the left, a man stands in the stiff pose of a Roman general, a child in front of him; a Diana-like figure in her plumed helmet stands by him; servants hold his horse. Below them are the animals of the conventional hunt, dogs and wild boars. On the right an exotic hunt is taking place: a lion leaps, a long-haired companion has fallen beneath it, another companion is poised to strike, but the short-haired general is riding forward thrusting his (broken) lance. The sides of the sarcophagus have light relief featuring the hunters' servants and horses subtly linked to the main scene. Brought from a Reims church where it stood from the early Middle Ages, it has always been ascribed to Jovinus, the commander who had fought for both Julian and Gratian during the 360s, before retiring to Reims, where he was converted late in life.

Upstairs

The Augustan cenotaph dedicated by the Remi to Gaius and Lucius is reconstructed here, yet more impressive is the display of the painstakingly restored **wall painting** of the death of Adonis, recovered from a late second-century mausoleum, even if the effect is that of a fuzzy photograph. The elite families of the Remi are epitomized by the tall **bronze lamp standard** and the **cake mould** recalling their taste for rich food; the agricultural section embodies the underpinning of their wealth: the ownership of vast estates. The early Christian and Merovingian collection in the corridor has models of burials and houses (based on Juvincourt – see SOISSONS), metal decorations from a large purse, some chunky necklaces and a range of glass and weapons.

ST ULRICH/HAUT-CLOCHER, Moselle

IGN 3614 ET

Villa site.

From Sarrebourg take the D27 for Haut-Clocher and after 3km turn right for the convent (1.5 km) for access to the site.

Hours:	July–August only	11a.m.–1p.m., 1.30–6p.m. Closed Tuesday
		Sunday and Monday: afternoons only

St Ulrich villa is one of the largest in France. Not only have 138 rooms been counted in the main complex, but also more than thirty other buildings have been identified on the gentle slopes of the valley to the north-east: this was clearly the heart of a major estate. The presence of Roman material was well known in the nineteenth century, encouraging Karl Wichmann, a Metz history teacher, to carry out extensive and very rapid digs in 1894–7, inevitably focusing on the villa itself. Little attention was paid to stratigraphy and even many dividing walls were missed. New work began in 1963 led by Marcel Lutz. When this ended in 1981 there was still much untouched. Exposed are the central areas of the villa and stone markers have been placed on the outbuildings, many hidden by surrounding woods.

The modern excavations demonstrated that the villa had an unusually early start (beginning of the first century) using a peristyle design: this suggests either an immigrant building on confiscated land or a leading family of the Leuci tribe using an imported architect. The latter seems more likely as it developed in a more typically provincial way. A grandiose U-shaped court replaced the peristyle, then new rooms, courtyards and a large bath complex were added. A heavily buttressed corridor was shown to cover a *cryptoporticus* – interpreted both as an 'Italian' feature and as recalling Iron Age pit storage practice in Gaul! Growth continued in the second century and after some destruction in the 160s–70s the villa was restored in the early third century, though the decor was inferior (for example, mosaics were replaced by pottery-filled cement flooring). Occupation lasted until at least the 360s–70s.

Most interpretations of St Ulrich have seen this as the luxurious great house of a powerful Leuci landowner, probably the home villa of a widely spread estate. A particularly grand bath, a library, columned peristyles with painted wall galleries, exceptionally big reception rooms, one internal court probably functioning as a garden and wings or walls create vistas of control. Beyond lay dependent buildings. One at least was a subsidiary villa, re-excavated by Lutz. This started as a two-room house but in the second century had new rooms and baths added. An estate manager (*vilicus*) or a tenant farmer, expected to live near his lord, just as Louis XIV's nobles lived at Versailles? Of the others, one was a small *fanum*, some were certainly agricultural (livestock, grain, corn drying, sheds, etc.), yet others workshops, and some must have been accommodation for labourers; it is regrettable that they have not been closely examined. Possibly more estate labourers lived at Pons Saravis (Sarrebourg), which must have also served as a market and distribution centre for the villa's produce along the Metz–Strasbourg road. The town may even have been part of the estate's property.

It has been argued by J.T. Smith (*Roman villas*, 1997) that this villa demonstrates shared ownership, a form of Celtic tenure known in early post-Roman Welsh laws. He pointed to a wall apparently dividing the house down the middle and argued that the two main courts represent the homes of two families. There is only one obvious opening and that only gives access to one room. I think that this can only be unproven. There appears to be only one bath complex and the lack of doors is not conclusive: many sites lack lintels.

Perhaps most important, as the excavations by Lutz showed in the sections he re-examined, the design presented by Wichmann is of all the walls he found without recognizing that over nearly 400 years considerable changes were made.

Musée du Pays de Sarrebourg

13 Avenue de France
57400 Sarrebourg

Hours:	June–September	8a.m.–noon, 2–6p.m. Closed Tuesday
	October–May	as above, but closed Tuesday and Sunday

Most of the 1890s St Ulrich villa finds are dispersed and Sarrebourg's major discovery, a Mithraic panel, also found in the 1890s, was removed to METZ. However, the artefacts recently excavated at St Ulrich are exhibited here, together with material from lesser villas in the area, from Vosgian culture villages to the east and from Tarquimpol, a large *vicus* and sanctuary site, *c.*30km to the west among the lakes by the Roman Metz road. Finally, there is pottery from Mittelbronn and bronze from Attilloncourt and a few finds from Sarrebourg itself. The display is by theme rather than by site.

From St Ulrich are the painted plaster fragments with delicate deer and birds on a red background; **hanging oil lamps** and a tiny chandelier; attractive, simple, inlaid brooches, including a **curious sea-horse** (first to third centuries); door fittings, keys, locks, and iron agricultural tools. From Tarquimpol comes a fine bronze cauldron and wine scoop and other metalware ('the peasant hoard'). Among the rest of the collection, note the ceramic **baby feeding jars** and the **inlaid pincers** found in a surgical kit, no doubt for tooth extraction.

SAVERNE, Bas-Rhin

IGN 3715 OT

Vicinity sites and museum.

The easiest way up to the Lorraine plateau from the Rhine plain is through the Saverne gap. The pass is only 410m high and divides the more mountainous southern Vosges from the hills of the north. During the later Iron Age, when the tribes Caesar knew emerged, the north-east Vosges became part of the territory of the Mediomatrices (see METZ). In contrast to other *oppida* in the area, such as Heidenstadt (25ha), the centre of local power clearly lay at this strategic point where an enormous *oppidum* (170ha) was created, straddling the pass itself and known today as the Fossé des Pandeurs, after the name given to the large rampart defending a vulnerable northern stretch. It is likely that in the immediate aftermath of conquest troops were based here; excavations at Ussbann (now covered by a parking area) have shown that by 10 BC houses were built to the north of the Fossé alongside the new Roman road. No *mansio* was identified, but it is likely there was a private enterprise stop, or *taberna*, at this site. Undoubtedly there were others lower down the pass. By the late empire, Saverne was described on the Peutinger table as Tres Tabernae.

The Col de Saverne also became a boundary. First the Mediomatrices lost their part of the Alsace plain to the Triboci tribe and then, with the Flavian restructuring of provinces, it became the Belgica/Germania Superior border. Probably a customs post was established here like that at MANDEURE, but this may have been in the *vicus* below the pass by the river Zorn, which became modern Saverne. Little is known archaeologically about the *vicus* and there are no visible remains. However, the community must have prospered supplying the needs of both military and civilian road users. During the first and second centuries, it would also have been a major regional centre for the exchange of goods between the hill people of the Vosges and the villa farmers and townspeople of the Rhine plain.

The growing insecurity of the third century undermined the local economic structure but stressed the strategic role of Saverne. The medieval walls, traces of which still survive, enclosed an area south of the Zorn (8ha); reused Roman tombstones and altars have been found in the foundation levels and clearly the rampart and towers were constructed on top of the late Roman predecessors. This fortification may date from the late second century but needed strengthening in the third and fourth centuries. According to Ammianus (XVI, 11, 11) Julian, campaigning in 357,

> turned to the task of repairing the fortifications of the strongpoint known as Tres Tabernae which the enemy had recently destroyed by a determined attack. Its rebuilding guaranteed that the Germans could no longer penetrate into the heart of Gaul.

IGN Map 3715 OT is very useful and pamphlets describing walks are available from the Office de Tourisme, 37 Grand'rue, 67700 Saverne.

Jardin Botanique

967.7/2428.5

N4, Col de Saverne

Hours: weekdays 9a.m.–5p.m.
Saturday (July–August only) and Sunday 2–6p.m.

On the left *c.*2.5km up from Saverne, parking on right. There are about 3m of Roman road by the chalet in this beautiful garden.

Saut du Prince Charles

967.7/2428.4

N4, Col de Saverne

Take the first footpath left above the Jardin Botanique, descending *c.*100m. Passing below an outcrop, the battered Roman road is cut into the pink sandstone bedrock. Wheel tracks helped secure the carts on the road. This was only one of the roads known in the pass. A sixteenth-century inscription still reminds people of the local bishop.

Fossé des Pandeurs

967.0/2429.3

N4, Col de Saverne

A marked track parallel with the rampart, *c.*5km on the left up from Saverne. Parking area on the left 100m beyond. Despite the forest cover, the rampart and ditch are clear. Using the *route forestière* and designated paths, it is possible to follow the boundaries of the entire hill-fort; very little of the interior has been excavated and nothing is visible of the Iron Age settlement.

Wasserwald

964.1/2424.4

Forêt Domaniale de Saverne

8km south-east of Saverne, by the D132 to Stambach; turn right at the sign to Château de Ochsenstein. Cross the railway and take the right turn to Hultehouse (*c.*150m). At the fork take the *route forestière* on the left (not Domaine de Stombach). Follow for about 3km to a track on the right. There is a pedestrian signpost to Wasserwald and both here and at the turning right *c.*500m along the track, there are empty yellow circle footpath markers. The path climbs a gentle slope; traces of the settlement begin here in the woodland and the cleared forest that follows.

Wasserwald, excavated in the 1970s, is one of around 100 '**Vosgian culture**' sites in the north-east Vosges. This means little more than that the Gallo-Roman here had a greater Gallic content than elsewhere. The inhabitants occupied the high land with its poor soil by combining a below subsistence agriculture with a forest and pasture economy linked to supplying the plain and plateau dwellers with timber and pink sandstone. Some villages like Wasserwald, and other small hamlets and farmsteads, flowered from the time of Augustus, but collapsed and were abandoned during the third-century crisis. Possibly the timber and stone supply roles were important enough to justify many of the villages being part of an imperial estate forming a buffer between the two provinces of Belgica and Germania. Two public land boundary stones found in the region could support this theory.

The walled **path** itself was a local Gallo-Roman road, this kind of dry-stone walling providing a framework for the settlement. It meets the main east–west 'street' where a footpath crosses (signpost); scraps of walling indicate the walled enclosures of the various holdings within the village. A small square Celtic sanctuary was excavated, but the best preserved site is **farm T**, *c.*50m south-south-east of the crossroads signpost. A rectangular wall forms a courtyard for a linear building with rooms along the eastern side. The method of building derives from the Iron Age. The walls were covered with a gabled roof of timber and thatch; in some cases, flat-topped pyramid stones made bases for beams supporting a large overhang as well. Remains of a Jupiter–giant column were found at farm T; did these indigenous inhabitants identify with Jupiter, or the giant?

Heidenstadt

969.4/2432.3

5km from Saverne by the D115 to St Jean Saverne, taking the turning left out of the village signposted for Chapelle St Michel and Croix de Langenthal. Park at either of these and take the footpath for Heidenstadt *oppidum*. **Roman road**: on the southern flank of the hill-fort there is a well-preserved section called the *Plattenweg*, cut with both narrow- and wide-gauge cart track climbing up the hillside. **Roman land marker**: outside and south of the eastern entrance to the *oppidum* is a stone marked AGER PRIVATUS/AGER PUBLICUS, indicating perhaps where a vast public, that is imperial, estate began.

Musée Archéologique

Château des Rohan
Place du Général de Gaulle
67700 Saverne

Hours:	mid June–mid-September	10–noon, 2–6p.m. Closed Tuesday
	Rest of year	2–5p.m.

The château's basement, traditionally used as a prison, naturally houses the archaeological collection. The stonework is drawn primarily from two sources, the foundations of Saverne's late Roman rampart and from Wasserwald: the main interest lies in the latter. The **house-tombstones** from the necropolis are particularly associated with 'Vosgian culture' and the Mediomatrices. Generally about 60cm high but occasionally much larger, these miniature gabled houses are decorated with circles, rosettes and wheels all thought to suggest a particular affinity with sun worship. The small **Jupiter–giant** from farm T is preserved here.

STRASBOURG, Bas-Rhin

Museum.

Before the Roman armies arrived in the valley of the Rhine there was no more than transient settlement on the Strasbourg site. Indeed, until the nineteenth century, the Rhine constantly changed its course in a flood plain normally 8km wide, making settlement a risky matter. When the Roman armies began their German campaigns in 12 BC, what Drusus and his troops saw here was a tangle of riverbeds meeting in a marsh-ridden alluvium, though by some firmer loess terrace. Drusus chose Mainz for his main base for campaigning in free Germany, but he also decided to establish a fort here. The reason was strategic. Behind lay Saverne, an easy pass through the Vosges, and so a major supply route from the interior of Gaul, while across the Rhine was the Kinzig valley leading into southern Germany and across to the Danube.

The position of the earliest fort is not precisely known, but after the disaster of AD 9 and the end of the dream of German conquest, the Strasbourg site was chosen for a major base, half way between the fortresses of Mogontiacum (Mainz) and Vindonissa (Windisch) with a new military road linking them together. By AD 12 Legio II Augusta had erected a timber-and-earth wall topped with a palisade enclosing an area of 20ha; a civilian community (*canabae*) followed and grew rapidly. The fortress was on land above the flood plain, so avoiding most of the dampness and periodic inundations that plagued the civilian settlement. Though in no sense a hill, it might have led to the choice of the name: Argentorate, an eminence set in silver (the Rhine was known to leave deposits of silver and gold).

In AD 43 Legio II departed for Britain; reduced numbers on the German frontier led to Argentorate being manned by detachments of Legio XXI and Legio IV until the civil wars and Civilis revolt in 69–70: Tacitus' description of the fear, chaos and breakdown is reflected in widespread evidence of burning. The fortress was reoccupied – and no doubt repaired – by a detachment from Mainz (Legio XIV). Meanwhile, the long-term security problem was worked out: this evolved in the 70s into the creation of an advanced military zone covering the triangle of land between the Rhine and Danube, the Agri Decumates, with a new military support road running from Strasbourg to Augsburg through the Black Forest.

As panic over Gallic loyalty subsided, so the fortress at Mirabeau in Burgundy was decommissioned and Argentorate once again became the base for a full legion, Legio VIII. Starting at the end of the 80s, they, rather than Legio XIV, built the first rampart in stone. They used limestone blocks for the 0.9m-thick walls on top of basalt foundations (the latter from across the Rhine). This remained their headquarters till the third century. The *canabae* grew considerably during the long period of peace, Argentorate ultimately stretching over 3.5km from west to east covering some 240ha, significantly more than medieval Strasbourg. There was a heavy concentration of habitation immediately to the west, then a mixture of cemeteries and occupation where the main road – the Route des Romains – ran along the rim of the loess to Koenigshoffen, where there was another large area of settlement. The civilian *canabae* became important enough to gain *vicus* status and therefore have its own magistrates.

The Alamanni incursion of 236, the constant call for troops from warring generals and then the withdrawal from the Agri Decumates (260) hurt Argentorate badly; there is a virtual stratigraphic hiatus for the rest of the century. A milestone dated to 306/7 on the road west to Tres Tabernae (Saverne) suggests that confidence was reviving, but this was now very much a frontier zone with regular warfare taking place. Ammianus (*History*, XVI, 12) reports the loss of cities in 352 and Eutropius (*Digest*, X, 14) describes Julian retaking Argentorate in 357. A massive new rampart was built in front of the old wall, making it 3.5m thick; it is believed to have stood over 9m high; there were new, regularly spaced, semi-circular projecting towers. Perhaps Julian ordered its construction. In the 390s, Stilicho may have been responsible for creating a general (or *comes*, a count) responsible for the Strasbourg region, but he could not stop the Vandals crossing the Rhine in the winter of 406/7 and the numerous fifth-century fire levels show Argentorate suffered heavily in the following years. Occasional bishops are known from 346, but virtually nothing about their achievements and no early churches survive. The struggle between the Alamanni and Franks for control remains historically and archaeologically impossible to pin down. However, it seems unlikely the town was ever abandoned. Patchy fifth- and sixth-century evidence of occupation has been found in both the fortress and the Koenigshoffen areas, burials continue throughout the period and in the sixth century a cathedral and a royal palace were established here. Its new name Strateburgo, 'town of roads', makes the point: it survived as a town but with a new Germanic identity.

Serious research began in the eighteenth century, flourished in the late nineteenth and then languished. Jean-Jacques Hatt revitalized archaeology in Strasbourg after the Second World War, bringing a strict approach to stratigraphy, a precision to epigraphy and a new awareness to the subtleties of Celtic and Roman religious beliefs. From the 1960s, urban renewal put increasing pressures on archaeologists and after Hatt departed as Director of Antiquities (1970), Erwin Kern led numerous rescue digs, but the era of the team was beginning. Current work is characterized by a wide input of expertise, close working with developers and prompt publication, such as the Line B tram research in 1999, published in 2000!

What are the major achievements? The fortress ramparts and main internal roads have been confirmed by excavation: the Rue de Dôme covers the *via principalis* and the Rue des Hallebardes/Rue des Juifs sit on the *via praetoria*. Rich rooms, thought to be officers' quarters, and a bath complex (rare inside a fortress) have been recognized. So far little else is known in the fortress. Outside to the north, fragmentary foundations are thought to be a theatre or amphitheatre; the only temple known is still the Mithraeum in Koenigshoffen; timber and stone remains, considered to be port installations, have been found in both central Strasbourg and in Koenigshoffen. The legionary tileworks has just been firmly identified on the western outskirts of Koenigshoffen. Wells were dug widely and an aqueduct brought water from springs 20km away at Kuttolsheim.

What have been found extensively are burials and ordinary housing. In 1995 an enormous circular mausoleum, 60m in diameter, was discovered. It must have stood some 20m high, and visible from the fortress, 3.5km to the east. A famous legate? An imperial family member? Cemetery enclosures along the Route des Romains are interpreted as group owned, by societies (*collegia*), which could share the costs of decent burial. The nature of houses in the *canabae* is now well known, but excellent examples of early style timber building were found during the 1999 tramline excavations. They were largely wood framed (as houses in Alsace continued to be until the twentieth century) with a fill of rough-cast clay/earth, which was plastered and painted. Floors were of gravel or beaten earth and poorly roofed with thatch. Microscopic investigation revealed that high humidity and foul damp were ever present: people must have suffered. Later houses used stones to support their uprights with carefully insulated gravel and sand foundations below timber flooring; some had timber-lined cellars, a few hypocausts. Broadly this better building evolved from the mid-first century, but the Mésange tram site houses are dated to the 80s: they are seen as the homes of recent arrivals, civilian back-up for a detachment of Legio VIII building the new stone fortress, unable to devote the time and effort needed to combat the insalubrious environment!

Today's Strasbourg is a leading European city, constantly packed with administrators, politicians, business people and tourists. Like many rapidly growing and rich cities, urbanization has been a mixed blessing for archaeologists. Its French and German past has perhaps encouraged a long history of interest in the city's development and today it has one of the best organized and most dynamic urban archaeology services in France, but Roman remains have not been allowed to stand in the way of modern building. Certainly many of the Gallo-Roman structures were not built in stone, making preservation difficult; certainly much of the Roman stonework was robbed and reused; and certainly some sites are covered by major medieval building (e.g. the cathedral), but there are no visible remains at all. The choice has always been that progress rather than preservation should take priority. Argentorate is a place for the imagination. For the physical evidence that gives form to the mind's eye, there is the museum.

Musée Archéologique

Palais Rohan
2 Place du Château
67000 Strasbourg
Hours: 10a.m.–noon; 2–6p.m. Closed Tuesday
Sunday 2–6p.m.

Despite updating in 1992, the museum is still lacking. There remain rooms untouched by a modern curatorial eye. And many panels (with English translations) tackle general themes without reference to specific exhibits, while many of these have only summary labels. However, this is a major collection and the display of new excavations in temporary exhibitions is commendably quick.

Rooms 1–7 cover Prehistoric and Iron Age archaeology. Most striking is the re-creation of the Ohnenheim Hallstatt chariot burial.

Room 8. The theme is the Roman army in Alsace: stamped bricks identify the different legions based here; milestones symbolize the key link between roads and troop movements; metalwork their world of warfare. There is a fine example of a *gladius hispaniensis* or 'Mainz' sword blade, short, slightly waisted (from sharpening?) with a long triangular point, and its fine **bronze openwork scabbard** – good enough for the maker to emboss his name at the top. It is thought that the soldier who somehow mislaid his sword in the Koenigshoffen *vicus* had bought it in the early first century AD from the Q. Nonienus Pudens workshop, probably in Lyon. A bronze socket used to hold the pole and crosspiece from which hung a *vexillum*, or flag of a military detachment, is believed to be later third century and therefore more likely lost in battle. It is exuberantly decorated with Roman gods. In contrast a **bronze cockerel** sounds victory down a circular horn, one of the army's instruments used both in processions and for signalling in battle.

Contrasting **tombstones** depict soldiers who once lived in Argentorate. The memorial to the 37-year-old legionary, **Caius Largennius** of the Legio II Augusta, is confident and extrovert. His hairstyle and double belt show his early first-century date, his pose is relaxed and his 'apron' of leather thongs decorated with round metal studs hangs over his inscription, surely supporting the argument that it was not really to protect the abdomen, but for decorative effect (and maybe the jingle it made on the march). **Lepontius** too is shown full on, but he is fourth century: cruder, far less realistic, remembered with no more than a single name. He too was a legionary, but with new weapons – long sword, massive round shield and lance; his troop insignia, a cockerel, beside him. Another relief shows a legionary driving a cart carrying bales (kit-bags?) urges on his two mules (see TRAVEL AND COMMUNICATIONS).

Rooms 9–10 supposedly reflect Alsace rural settlement and Argentorate. On display is a curious **sundial**: the top has been cut with a half-cone and marked with lines to tell the hours, but so poorly done they would have been ineffective (see AIX-LES-BAINS and LOUVRE for other examples). There are bulbous **face urns** thought to be military; perhaps soldiers felt they gave their ashes a more human identity. Massive clay pipes represent the 8,000+ used to make the aqueduct from Kuttolsheim.

Room 11. Two reconstructed rooms symbolize prosperous Argentorate. The kitchen area on the right gives some impression of the exterior as well, most interesting being the **iron grille** across the window. On the left is a room with **wall paintings**. Unfortunately these are difficult to see; not only are they rather indistinct anyway, but one depicting the 'Judgement of Paris' is also tucked away at the back. The nearest fragment has an ecstatic Bacchus and a follower with corn sprouting from her ears.

Rooms 12 and 13. The tombstone of the charming **peasant couple** in their pleated tunics and coats exemplifies the 'everyday'. Among the pins, fibulae, brooches, metal box fittings, keys and weights displayed, note the less provincial Nubian balsam jar, shaped as a bearded, heavily moustached, African head. Easily missed are the rare bone parts from a **lyre** (see AUTUN). This was a harp-like instrument, developed by the Greeks and associated with Apollo, to accompany song and poetry; the pegs were used to adjust the strings. Unfortunately the pottery and glassware displays retain the nineteenth-century style of over-filled cases with minimal explanation.

Room 14. This is devoted to the site of DONON. There are crude Mercuries and battered Jupiter–giant figures, but easily the most impressive relief work is the **stag god**. A beautiful stag peers from behind the legs of a male figure, reflecting the mystical love of the hunter for the hunted. He wears a wolf skin and carries a bag of pine cones and a curved axe: the very spirit of a forest god.

Rooms 15 and 16 contrast local interpretations of Roman gods with those imported from the eastern borders of the empire. In Celtic myth, Teutates protects the boy Esus; here these gods are interpreted as **Mercury and Bacchus**. The protector/tutor, bringer of prosperity, holds a child Bacchus in his arm, while the boy carries his purse. Mercury is clearly identified with his wand and by the cockerel at his feet. Mercury also appears with his Gallic wife, Rosmerta. Both hold purses, symbols of a prosperous life, while she also has a *mappa* or napkin, a token marking a successful start to life.

Mithraism, like other mystery faiths, attracted those who sought exclusive and highly ritualized groups meeting in secretive conditions, in this case small crypt-like places restricted to men and rarely more than 20–30 of them. They would feast stretched out on benches facing a panel that embodied the central myth of the youthful Iranian god. The few fragments from the panel found at Mackwiller villa Mithraeum have a finely sculpted head of Mithras. Much more survived of the panel found in the **Koenigshoffen Mithraeum** and a full-scale re-creation stands opposite. In a frame topped with a lintel, Mithras is shown killing the bull. There is an excellent figure of Cautopates, one of his twin acolytes, who represent the dawn and sunset of life on each side of the scene. Mithras worship may have been brought by a troop who had been on detachment in the east at the end of the first century, or perhaps by merchants from Rome via the Rhône; the quality of relief work has been taken to indicate Italian sculptors were engaged here.

Rooms 17 and 18 are catch-all rooms for Roman and Gallic gods, mainly bronze. These include an elegant dancing **lar familiaris figure** (see even better in MONTBELIARD); heavy unrealistic thug-like Hercules figures; and a fair side-saddle goddess Epona. Curiously, **Room** 19 is the Merovingian room, a typical but unexceptional cemetery collection, apart from a **silver-inlaid helmet**, while **Room 20** fails to bring any imagination to Strasbourg's extensive Gallo-Roman necropolis research. However, the corridor and stairwell exhibits, **Rooms 21** and **21B**, are more compelling. There is a 'Vosgian culture' (see SAVERNE) double-gabled house tomb from Wasserwald together with site information, and, in the small side room, the **Father Rhine altar**. Found in a well, this is likely to have come from a temple used by sailors of the Rhine fleet and trading ships. It is the earliest known reference to the Rhine as a god, but reflects both Celtic and German religious feelings. The altar is classically presented: libation jug and *patera* on one side, on the other a sacrificial axe and a case of knives. The inscription is simple but the lettering excellent. Ottius Severus came from a wealthy Italian family and as legate commanding Legio VIII in the 130s, represented the emperor and Rome; taste, status and local political and religious needs were being satisfied.

TROYES, Aube

Museum.

The Tricasses emerged from the Gallic wars as a small border *civitas* in the province of Lugdunensis. Their capital, Augustabona, developed on a pre-Roman site, but must have been helped by the major Roman north–south road from Autun to Reims crossing the Seine here. Until two major rescue excavations, very little was known about the early Roman town: fragmentary houses, what could be the public baths discovered near the cathedral, and traces of an aqueduct.

The 1980s Les Halles dig made it clear that there was a proper town grid with a wide (10m) *cardo maximus* and roads equipped with drainage ditches, good chalk foundations and a gravel finish. The extensive La Chaillonet excavations in the early 1990s showed that the city developed rapidly. One house covered more than 4,000sq m. It had a central peristyle with a fountain and, in addition to its sumptuously decorated rooms, a row of shops along a porticoed street: a classic city *domus*, on the Italian model. Mosaics and paintings here have been dated to the first half of the first century AD. There were more typical early imperial timber-and-clay houses as well and, like the *domus*, these lasted a considerable time. Evidence of the commercial exploitation of the Seine was also provided: a meander was cut off by a canal with both a road and a haulage track beside it. During the third century fire swept the area, the canal broke down and flooding followed. The excavators found an enormous hoard of forged coins of the last Gallic emperor, Tetricus (270–73). Was it locally produced money rendered unusable when Aurelian restored central control? The 186,200 coins were still being investigated at the time of writing.

Fortifications were constructed and the reduced city, renamed Tricasini, was increasingly exposed to invaders. Ammianus describes (XVI, 2, 5) the appearance of his hero, the young Caesar Julian, at Troyes in 356: 'his arrival was so unexpected that when he was practically knocking at the gates, the inhabitants, who lived in dread of the host of barbarians spread about the country, opened them only after serious hesitation . . .'. The threat was worse a hundred years later. In 451 Attila and his great army were rolling westwards. Metz and Reims had been sacked already, but Troyes was apparently saved by its bishop.

Lupus is another of the Gallo-Roman aristocrats who saw future leadership in terms of ecclesiastical power. From eastern France, where his family owned estates which he sold when he parted from his wife *c.*426, he left to become a monk in the Lerins Islands monastery off the coast from Cannes. He accompanied Germanus to Britain in 429 (see AUXERRE), corresponded with Sidonius Apollinaris and remained an active bishop until his death in 479. According to the very suspect *Life of Saint Lupus*, he offered himself as hostage to Attila for the people of Troyes, and his sanctity so impressed Attila that instead of sacking the city the great leader asked for prayers to be said for him.

However, Gaul as a whole was saved from Attila's overlordship by his defeat at the **battle of the Catalaunian Fields**. This took place somewhere between Troyes and Chalons. Aëtius, the Danubian Roman general, who had previously co-operated with the Huns, now led a massive coalition against them consisting of his own troops and all the major military groups in Gaul, primarily the Visigoths but also Burgundians, Franks, Alamanni and even Armoricans from Brittany: as Cassiodorus wrote, the Huns were seen as 'the common enemy of all mankind'. Yet Attila's army was also a coalition of Huns and Germanic tribes, including Goths and Franks. The battle was decisive, not perhaps because Attila's losses were dramatic – he retreated in good order and invaded Italy the following year – but because it broke the Huns' aura of invincibility. After Attila's death in 453 (a burst blood vessel on taking another young bride), his empire quickly collapsed. The victorious Aëtius was then murdered by the Emperor Valentinian III. For the inhabitants of Troyes, it meant they were left to be absorbed into the Frankish kingdom of Clovis in the 480s.

Musée des Beaux Arts et d'Archéologie

Abbaye St Loup
1 Rue Chrestien-de-Troyes
10000 Troyes
Hours: 10a.m.–noon, 2–6p.m. Closed Tuesday

The museum's archaeology collection was modernized with little inspiration in the 1970s; perhaps the influx of new finds will stimulate more imagination.

The fifth-century BC Etruscan bronze flagon (*oenochoe*) supports changing connections between Champagne and the Mediterranean world (see HISTORICAL DEVELOPMENT). The metre-high bronze **Vaupoisson Apollo**, found in 1813, looks almost Greek in its well-proportioned and impassive pose, though it must have stood in a Gallo-Roman temple. Other smaller bronzes include another Apollo, with a snake (his healing symbol), though the best is a **bull's head** with extended horns. No one has satisfactorily explained the curious knobs on the end, though admiration for the bull – or ox – as a symbol of strength and fertility goes back for thousands of years before the Romans. Daily life comes most alive with the tiny bronze sandals, probably part of a lamp, while real sandals and clogs were made on the **shoemaker's last**, which would have been pegged in a bench, on which he sat and worked (see REIMS).

The range of Merovingian weapons is good and there is quality in the ornamental buckles and fibulae, but really exceptional is the **Pouan treasure**. In 1842 a day labourer, working in a field outside the village of Pouan, chanced upon a sword and a scramasax, together with the metal elements from their scabbards, all richly decorated with garnets inlaid in gold, as well as inlaid buckles, a massive gold ring inscribed HEVA, gold bracelets and a gold torc. They were immediately seen as the burial goods of a princely warrior, perhaps even the Visigothic king Theodoric, killed in the great battle. Current interpretation based on comparative study suggests that the weapons are typical of styles popular among the elite from the Black Sea to eastern Gaul. The jewellery is more specifically Germanic and most likely Frankish. The dating suggests the 480s rather than the 450s. This, then, might have been one of king Clovis's nobility or even a Gallo-Roman estate owner keen to show how he had adopted modern symbols of power.

VIREUX-MOLHAIN, Ardennes

IGN 3007 O

Late Roman fortress site and museum.

45km north of Charleville-Mézières by the D988/N51 towards Givet and Dinant, following the Meuse.

The Meuse valley was not simply a means of communication among the hills and forests of the Ardennes. Even in the Roman period it was an industrial

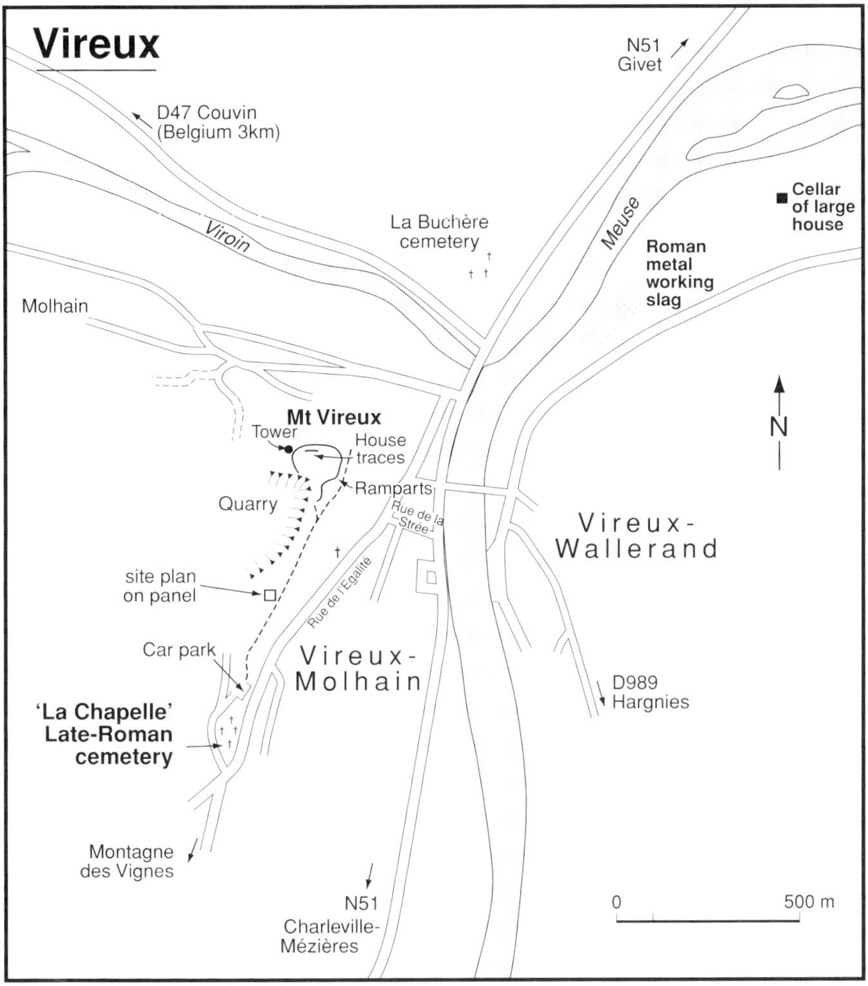

Figure 76 Vireux: local plan

area, though set in a beautiful environment. In **Vireux-Wallerand**, on a terrace by the right bank, stretched a 400m-long slag-heap and the remains of numerous circular iron furnaces, used from the first to the sixth century. Workers were buried in the nearby La Buchère cemetery and in the mid-third century someone hid coins here, perhaps when a large house nearby (the works' manager's?) was destroyed by fire, sealing its well-crafted cellar of stone and brick with a sloping window and vaulted alcoves. The site was re-occupied in the fourth century when a kind of peace returned.

Major excavation has been concentrated on the hill-top behind **Vireux-Molhain**. Some time after the first serious invasions of the 250s, but before AD 300, the summit of Mont Vireux was made into a fortress, to guard the iron and its workers – it may even have been their own private initiative. It was abandoned and then reoccupied in the 330s to 360s. This also culminated with hoards and burning, probably due to Alamanni attacks. Peace was restored in the area, no doubt following Julian and Valentinian's campaigns, but troops were to return in the 380s and lived here for the next 60–70 years. As the nearby cemetery demonstrates, these were clearly Franks and the excavator, J.-P. Lémant, has called this phase 'Proto-Merovingian'. The lifestyle of these soldiers of the Roman empire clearly differed little from their 'barbarian' foes, though there are hints of an army style. They lived in simple huts, set, barrack-like, in a line against the rampart. They buried their dead in a cemetery at La Chapelle/Montagne-des-Vignes and on the Rue de l'Egalité, where a single burial chamber may mark another cemetery. These show they used the same weapons, including the throwing axe, but the existence of an officer class is hinted at by the highly decorated belts typical of the Roman Germanic higher command of this period. They are likely to have been a group of full-time frontier troops or *limitanei*. No doubt the local population formed a part-time force, as even these could have been *laeti* settlers, bound to fight in defence of the empire in return for land; they are known to have been settled in the region.

Mont Vireux fortress site

Coming from Charleville-Mézières along the N51/Avenue Roger Posty, the site is signposted along the Rue de la Strée. After the railway bridge, turn left up Rue de l'Egalité to La Chapelle, where there is a sharp turn right into the Rue des Trieux, continuing up the hill to the car park. Follow the signs along the ridge to Mont Vireux (*c.*500m).

Ramparts. Much of the surviving walling is Carolingian, but it sits on the line of the late Roman foundations. Excavation revealed these used a wood, earth and stone construction method called *murus gallicus* (see BIBRACTE or VERTAULT) suggesting a revival of pre-Roman construction techniques. Panels indicate the traces of the flimsy but comfortable wood-and-daub huts (glass windows) built against the rampart used by the late Roman troops.

North-west tower. This was a circular structure projecting out at the steep, sharp corner looking up the valley. It is now little more than a tumble of roughly cut stone, but the reinforced slope or *glacis* and the steepness of the ramp rising to the gateway by the tower are apparent. The 100m ramparts beyond the tower have more late Roman work than elsewhere. Having been excavated to bedrock, the heavier, offset foundation stonework is more obvious. The modern quarry brutally ends the wall.

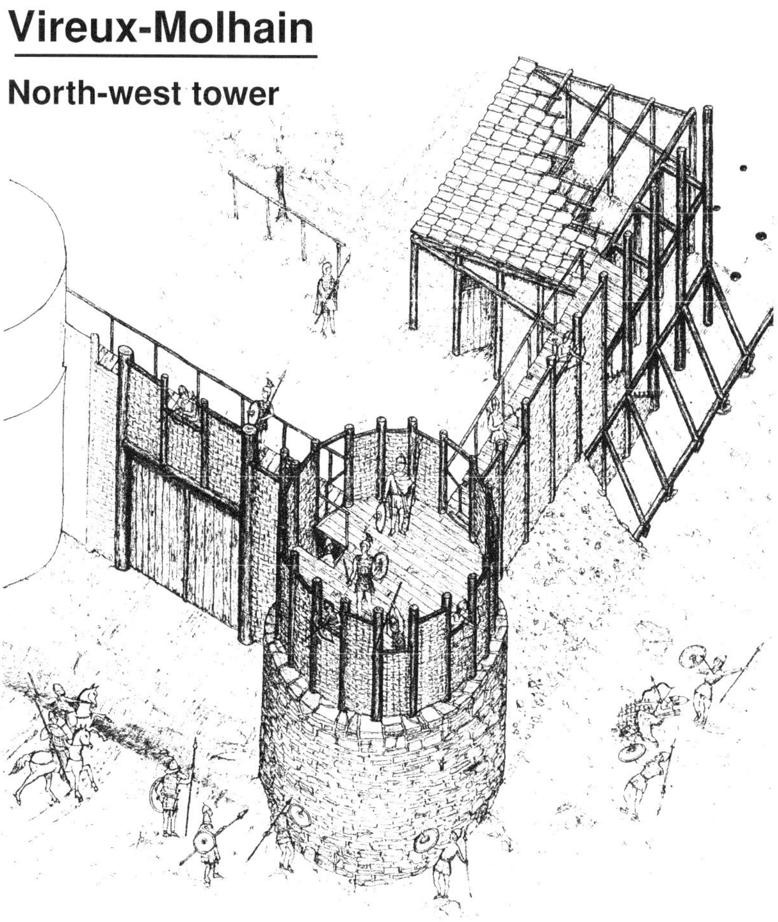

Figure 77 Vireux: north-west tower reconstruction. Note: with permission J.-P. Lémant and B. Squevin.

Musée de l'Ardenne

31 Place Ducale
08000 Charleville-Mézières
Hours: 10a.m.–noon, 2–6p.m. Closed Monday

The museum is installed in a corner of the seventeenth-century Place Ducale. It opened in 1994. Old houses and recent additions have been incorporated in a seamless modern design integrating stone, concrete and wood. The archaeological collection is labelled – but with little attempt to give material any context. In a strange reversion to a nineteenth-century practice, the Gallo-Roman stonework comes first before the Palaeolithic material. There is a battered four-sided upper base and capital from a **Jupiter–giant column**, four heads peering out from the capital's acanthus leaves; this was found in what once must have been a sanctuary area on a hill above Charleville. In the Gallo-Roman section proper, there is material from MOUZON and more miniature offerings from the site of Baâlons-Bouvellemont, showing the localized distribution of this practice in early Romano-Celtic sanctuaries.

The **Vireux sites** are represented by grave goods from the Germanic soldiers' burials at La Chapelle. Sadly there are no maps, pictures, reconstructions or explanations to enliven the display. However, the high status of the men and the two women buried on Mont Vireux at the end of the fourth and in the early fifth centuries is quite clear from their good-quality bronzeware, the Cologne-made 'snake' decoration **glass goblet** and a particularly fine **large jug**.

OTHER SITES

Nothing significant survives of the early Roman town of **Châlons-sur-Marne**, but the museum contains important Iron Age material. The Unterlinden Museum in **Colmar** has an inadequately displayed Gallo-Roman collection, but two interesting tombstone reliefs. The Rhineland *vicus* of **Kembs** (Haut-Rhin) was extensively excavated in the 1980s/90s; the Hôtel-de-Ville displays finds and a model. In **Klang** forest (Moselle) near Kédange-sur-Canner (IGN3411E) there is a rock carved goddess carrying a cornucopia. At **Mackwiller** (Bas-Rhin) are the heavily restored remains of villa baths and a large circular mausoleum. **Verdun** (Meuse) was a late Roman town and, despite the absence of visible remains, has a good new museum.

DRESS AND APPEARANCE IN ROMAN GAUL

The Gauls of the pre-Roman era

Curiously, the one certain eye-witness account, Julius Caesar's *Gallic Wars*, contains remarkably little about the appearance of the people whom he fought. We are driven to turn to the more distant Greek sources. However, there are limitations. Describing unfamiliar cultures it is tempting to notice only the most general and the strange; we operate in stereotypes, often reflecting more on the fears and prejudices of our own society than any real features of those whom we meet. For Greeks and Romans all peoples beyond the Mediterranean basin were automatically barbaric and 'uncivilized'. Diodorus Siculus, a contemporary of Caesar's, summarizes the general image (*History*, V, 28):

> The Gauls are tall of body, with rippling muscles, and white of skin, and their hair is blond, and not only naturally so, but they also make it their practice by artificial means to increase the distinguishing colour which nature has given it. For they are always washing their hair in limewater, and they pull it back from the forehead to the top of the head and back to the nape of the neck, with the result that their appearance is like that of Satyrs and Pans, since the treatment of their hair makes it so heavy and coarse that it differs in no respect from the mane of horses. Some of them shave the beard, but others let it grow a little; and the nobles shave their cheeks, but they let the moustache grow until it covers the mouth.

Though in the first century BC cremation was the norm in Gaul, just as in Rome, and therefore checking Diodorus' assertion about height is difficult, skeletons that have been found as well as earlier Iron Age inhumations suggest that Gauls were not significantly taller than Mediterranean peoples. The 'rippling muscles' hints at a condescending 'brawn but no brains', while the paleness of skin and blond hair are no more than trite comments that they were not Mediterranean-dark. To a Roman or Greek audience, long hair, apparently unkempt, and an unshaven face would seem gross and primitive: Gallia Comata, 'long-haired Gaul', was a scathing epithet for Gaul outside *provincia* before the conquest. Yet pre-Roman reliefs and statuary in the south of France suggest highly decorative hairstyles for men, no more nor less a social and fashion statement than the Roman aristocratic male's 'short back and sides' hair and completely shaven face.

On Celtic women, Greek and Roman writers provide even less genuine insight. The comment that 'the women of the Gauls are not only like men in their great stature but they are a match for them in courage as well' (Diodorus Siculus, 5, 32) may sound approving, but is more likely making a contrast with an ideal of modest, refined Greek and Roman women. The reality is that noble daughters and sisters were used as pawns in the tribal politics of Gaul (see Caesar, *The Gallic War*, I, 3) just as they were in Rome. Strong Celtic women like Boudicca were no more typical than Messalina, the nature of their independent actions being governed by their different political contexts. This is not to suggest that courageous and intelligent women were rare in Gaul – or Rome – simply that the sources do not provide evidence from which we can make genuine cultural distinctions between societies.

Pre-Roman clothes

If general comments on appearance and character have to be treated with reserve, it is possible to be slightly more positive about dress, though little pre-Roman clothing has been found in Gaul. The written sources describe clothes made largely of wool, but also of linen, men in short tunics and breeches (despised in first-century BC Rome), the women wearing a tunic and wrap-around skirt, though more commonly a peplos-type dress – two rectangles of cloth to cover the body, each side secured by fastenings, a brooch pinning each shoulder (permitting easy lowering for breast feeding). For protection in a colder, damper climate, a cloak of coarse wool would often be worn. Though no significant remains of clothes have been found in archaeological contexts in pre-Roman France, Iron Age finds in Danish and British bogs suggest that such dress was common throughout temperate Europe. It also confirms a feature noted by Mediterranean writers: the love of bright colours and chequered patterns or tartans. Variations in these designs, and the shape and use of bronze and gold brooches, pins, torcs, belts, armlets, earrings would have told contemporaries clan and tribal affiliations, probably marital status and certainly class, as well as allowing for changes in fashion. Cosmetics were not unknown either. Propertius (20s BC) makes this clear with his prim comment 'all beauty is best as nature intended it: Belgian rouge is shameful on a Roman face' (*Poems*, II, 18, 26).

The Gallo-Romans of the first three centuries (50 BC–AD 250)

Textiles are among the rarest materials found by archaeologists. It is remarkable that, more than 100 years after its discovery in 1893, only the burial site of Les Martres-de-Veyre, Puy-de-Dôme, has produced a complete set of clothing,[1] though finds of much smaller pieces of cloth, such as the rags used for caulking boats found in the Saône, have helped extend understanding of textile techniques (see CHALON). Our knowledge of what people wore is based on something that had not existed before: the stone memorial. It was only after the conquest that named burials and representations of the dead appear, above all else providing vivid images of how people wished to be seen by others and how they defined themselves.

Large individual mausolea and commemorative structures were built for the wealthiest, though few survive (see AUTUN, LYON, LANGRES, METZ). Here, when portrayed, most men would be shown dressed in the toga, a sign of their true 'Romanitas'. But togas are rare on the reliefs decorating the common upright marker tombstone, found in virtually every Roman collection in France, where both men and women wear clothes that derive from pre-Roman styles.

There are limitations. Not all tombstones had representational reliefs and they are restricted by class and by time. The poorest got no memorial; the poorer perhaps got wooden ones (which have not survived), or their stone

Figure 78 Roman toga

memorials were made by unskilled craftsmen, home-made, crude and uninformative. The earliest tend to be those groups who wished to assert strongly their Roman identity (such as soldiers and freedmen). From the end of the first to the early third century there was a flowering of memorials to those wishing to proclaim that they had led successful lives. We must assume many were landed property owners but there is a surprising number of merchants, craftsmen and shopkeepers.

The north-east (Lorraine and Champagne) and Burgundy have the most remarkable. In the north-east there are more full-scale scenes showing how people have lived happy lives (see METZ for the most vivid), or surrounded by the tools of their business; in Burgundy, there are examples revealing their occupations (see DIJON), but more characteristic are the individuals or couples carrying attributes like goblets, scrolls (proclaiming literacy or for keeping accounts?) or money boxes – symbols of both success and their ability to make offerings for their after-life. The women here carry bottles (for scents?), small sheets, fans and mirrors, all signs of femininity; the children, fruits or toys, the embodiment of their brief lives.

Even without the paint that would have then demonstrated their continued love of both checked materials and bright colours, it is possible to recognize a common Gallo-Roman dress being widely worn. We have an overriding impression of a regional people, confidently at home in the Roman empire.

Gallo-Roman clothes: men

The **toga** was a strip of woven natural wool (with a red or purple stripe for magistrates); being typically 5.75m long and over 2m wide, an assistant was needed to help drape it correctly. It could not be worn by working people and signified Roman citizenship and status; apart from governors and their entourages, it is very unlikely to have been worn outside formal occasions such as the gatherings of the *civitas* priests at the Gallic altar in Lyon.

The **Gallic tunic** or **'coat'**. This was cut from a single length of cloth with projections for the sleeves and a hole for the head. It would be folded in half and sewn at the seams on each side. Normally it fell just below the knee, its loose folds vaguely reminiscent of the toga, but much easier to wear. This was the standard male attire throughout the Gallic provinces and Germania Superior. The fullness of the folds (and so the amount of material used), the quality of wool, the weave and the dyes, the newness, would help distinguish status. Some were decorated with fringes.

The **Gallic *sagum*** and ***cucullus***. The semi-circular *sagum*, a cape joined at the front, and the separate *cucullus*, a hood, provided extra cover when outside in bad weather. The cape is often depicted rolled up over one shoulder to allow easier movement. Sometimes men have a scarf tucked under the cape. A *bardocucullus*, a particularly large hood and cape down to the feet, was associated with the poor – at least in Rome.

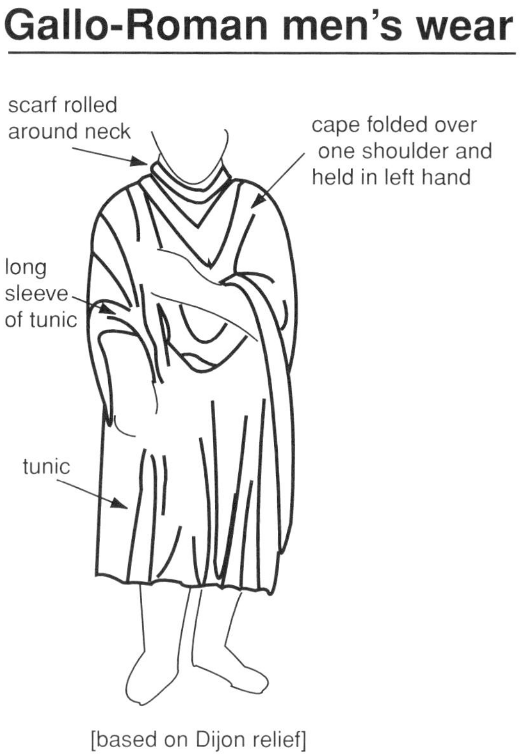

Figure 79 Gallo-Roman men's wear

Underclothing and **leg wear**. A delivery invoice from the Roman fort of Vindolanda in Britain includes a consignment of socks and pants; soldiers along the Rhine frontier are equally likely to have been provided with them. Whether they were common wear for civilians is less certain. Gallic trousers may have disappeared, though the unrecorded poor could well have wisely continued to wear them in northern France.

Gallo-Roman clothes: women

The **Gallic tunic** or **robe**. Similar to the men's coat, but reaching to the ankles, it could be caught at the waist with a belt or girdle. Some women are shown wearing the skirt heavily pleated and sometimes fringe decoration appears around the hem.

The **cloak**. This was rectangular and draped over the shoulders like a stole or used to cover the head like a shawl. In Rome, a similar cloak was called the *paenula*.

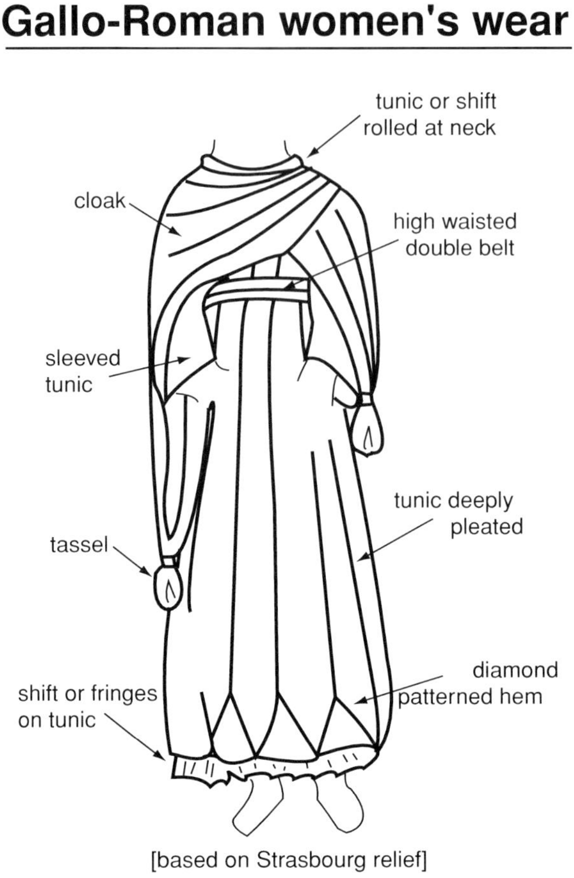

Figure 80 Gallo-Roman women's wear

Underclothing. Some reliefs show women wearing a shift below the tunic, emerging at the ankles and/or at the neck. This would be made of linen or the finest wool. Young women wearing 'bikinis' decorate a mosaic at Piazza Armerina, Sicily, and leather briefs (laced at the side) have been found in London: perhaps such garments were restricted to dancers. Triangles of cloth are thought to have been used during menstruation. Breastbands, long narrow pieces of material, were used either to cover or support the breasts and are known elsewhere in the empire.

Stockings and socks. The length of dress usually restricts visibility on tombstone reliefs. A young woman in Les Martres burial had a pair of thick woollen stockings, held below the knee with cord; fringes hung over the tops. It is likely that socks and stockings were worn at times and could have

Plate 30 Funeral relief of couple and child, Metz. © Metz, Musées de la Cour d'Or. Photograph: Jean Munin, all rights reserved.

been shown with paint on the tombstones. Men and women, particularly in the country, would protect their legs from cold and brambles with lengths of cloth wrapped round the lower leg.

Accessories. Fibulae, rings, necklaces, make-up and hairstyles all changed over time. While some show their reconciliation of Gallic and Roman fashion by wearing torcs, others wore the latest hairstyles, spread by the statues of the imperial family. The emerging Gallo-Roman identity is perhaps best shown by the most commonly found fibulae: safety-pin, animal, circular and cross-bar brooches.

Shoes. Rarely portrayed clearly in reliefs, shoes have survived much better than clothes, making it feasible to outline their evolution. The most ubiquitous was the sandal or *solea*. This had a sole made up from one, two or three strips of leather, attached to the foot with straps, one of which normally went between the big and second toes. In the early empire, nailing was the most common way of securing the soles together. The *caliga* was the army variant: a thick sandal covered in hobnails with a pierced upper.[2] By the early second century, there seems to have been little difference between this and the strong sandals produced for civilians. The *Gallica* is considered to be the basic, widely produced and probably sturdy sandal of Gaul.

Other shoes enclosed the foot (the *calcei*); some shoes had added wedges at the heel; while wooden clogs held by straps, with or without a leather shoe inside, must have been quite widely used. Considerable opportunities were available to the cobbler to vary strapping, to give a fretted top, stamp impressions on leather fronts, or to enclose the ankles with a boot form. Women's and men's fashion diverged in the second century: women's sandals becoming small and pointed, men's gradually widening at the front: at CHALON a third-century sole has such a wide front that it looks unusable. The decisive trend was the switch to sewn rather than nailed shoes. *Carbotina* was the name for a mocassin-type, made from one piece of leather. It became popular in the third century on the Rhine frontier and continued into the late empire, when the technique became widespread. Nailing continued, often with the same style of upper, but ultimately the sewn type became the dominant mode for centuries.

Textiles: a Gallic industry

The evidence of reliefs in the north-east and inscriptions such as those commemorating a *sagarius* (*sagum* dealer) in LYON and *cucullarius* at SENS suggest clothes were not generally made within each household but that there were organized businesses co-ordinating production and distribution. Experiments at Samara suggest that spinning enough yarn for a tunic could take forty-four days. Though it would have undoubtedly been quicker in antiquity, it was still not something a working family could easily undertake. Pliny's measured comments in the 60s AD (*Natural History*, VIII, 192–8) on wool products drawn from all over the empire show that Gaul was known for its *scutula*, or check pattern cloth, its quality dyeing (mainly vegetable), its tough felts and its linen sailcloth. At the end of the century Martial was scorning long Gallic cloaks: 'So a Lingonian bardocucullus put among city tyrianthines contaminates them with its greasy wool' (*Epigrams*, I, 53, 4–5). Juvenal, too, could sneer, 'I sometimes have a greasy cloak given me that will save my toga – a coarse and crudely dyed garment that has been ill-combed by the Gallic weaver' (*Satires*, IX, 30). However, he has let slip what was obviously the key attraction of Gallic cloaks: the thick and hard-wearing material could get soaked but still kept the rain off other clothes.

Many museums have reliefs illustrating clothes; textile manufacturing can be found in METZ, REIMS and SENS while AMIENS (Samara), the ARCHEODROME and BLIESBRUCK do regular re-creations of spinning and weaving techniques; CHALON-SUR-SAONE and Montbéliard (MANDEURE) have particularly good collections of textile industry finds.

The late Roman empire

The third century inevitably saw a dramatic decline in the production of tombstones; the fashion for realistic reliefs depicting individuals and daily life had gone. The elite used sarcophagi where they could, often heavily decorated but with scenes from classical myth and biblical stories, or lines of officials and saints. On the upright tombstones of the less wealthy we see crudely sketched formalized figures, or, in the late fourth and fifth centuries, lightly drawn symbols of the Christian faith such as the dove. Conversely, we have more bodies. Since the late second century, inhumation had increasingly become the norm. The burying of goods with individuals provides dress accessories and shows the position they were worn. Traces of clothes, though, suggest many were specially prepared for the dead, such as the shroud. Nevertheless, the cumulative evidence from burials, tombstones, mosaics and the sporadic comments of contemporaries, indicates a period retaining features of earlier dress while making fundamental changes.

Men

The Gallic tunic and *sagum* undoubtedly continued in use throughout the period and well on into the early Middle Ages. Late Roman tunics normally had sleeves, short and long. The most obvious contrast with the earlier era was that covered legs had become the norm throughout society. As German soldiers wearing tight-fitting trousers became the backbone of the army defending and operating in Gaul, throughout the empire there was a growing popularity for leggings, probably cut from woollen cloth rather than knitted, though this technique was known. Status could be clearly indicated by such accessories as brooches and belts. A large crossbow brooch (long-piece upwards), used to clasp a cloak on the shoulder, was, during the third and fourth centuries, a symbol of officer status, together with a standard wide belt with a buckle, decorated plate and metal fittings along the leather using repeat patterns. By the later fourth century the brooch in particular had become a symbol of adminstrative officers as well. The toga had lost any role except for those who still looked to a career in Rome.

Women

The major development was the fashion for sleeved tunics. The *dalmaticus* was a T-shaped dress with wide sleeves, decorated with stripes and sometimes fringes. The style was loose, without a belt. It may have been particularly associated with Christianity. Longer dresses with wider arms in rich fabrics adopting this style were clearly for the wealthier. In the late fourth century, tying under the breasts came into fashion again, together with a tight-fitting, long-sleeved, under tunic.

Late antiquity and the Germanic impact

> Their eyes are faint and pale, with a glimmer of greyish blue. Their faces are shaven all round, and instead of beards they have thin moustaches which they run through with a comb. Close fitting garments confine the long limbs of the men; they are drawn up so high so as to expose the knees, and a broad belt supports the narrow middle.
>
> (Sidonius on the Franks, *Poems*, V, 237–50)

There is a whiff of the 500-year-earlier Diodorus in Sidonius' comments, while the description of dress hardly differs from that of any late Roman soldier, except for the bare legs: perhaps the leggings were removed for this wedding, perhaps it is a fancy of Sidonius, writing far away from the event. Appearances certainly changed in the 400s and 500s and undoubtedly the German element in society played an important role, but it is extraordinarily difficult to unravel in any precise way. What is now widely agreed is that fashions spread among people who might call themselves Frank, Roman or any other group, but wear very similar dress (not unlike today?).

Men

The central piece of clothing in late antiquity remained the tailored tunic. Those of high status would wear a linen shirt underneath and trousers and perhaps a cloak over it. The belt, too, continued to be an obvious accessory, deriving its prestige from late Roman use. After 500 it began to develop regionally distinct features, though only broadly reflecting the political divisions between the Frankish and Burgundian kingdoms, the Visigothic south-west, and the lands to the east.

Women

During the fifth and sixth centuries the mix of tunics with long inner and short outer sleeves remained characteristic. For German women there was a more fundamental change (and unnoticed by contemporaries) – the final abandonment of garments dependent on pins and brooches to hold them together – they too adopted tunics. Brooches become true ornaments, naturally at first placed in traditional positions, such as on the shoulders, but becoming free to decorate other parts of the figure, such as the breasts.

Early Merovingian decoration in the fifth and sixth centuries

This was a dynamic phase for dress accessories. The bow brooch developed in new ways, using, instead of arms, a semi-circular plate with knobs attached, a flat arch and projecting foot, that during this period, in eastern France, was normally long and straight-sided and is found in both men's and women's burials. After dispensing with the large ugly conical *tutulus* brooch, popular in the late fourth and early fifth centuries, women, too, wore pins, rings and brooches utilizing the same techniques and themes apparent in men's accessories.

Chip-carving. This involved making sharp ridges and hollows in metal deliberately to highlight the ribbon patterns, spirals, keys, interlaced nets, birds and other stylized animals. The bronze and iron belts using this technique would have been available to the less wealthy.

Damascening. A technique of inlaying gold or silver wire in furrows cut in the surface of iron and hammering firmly in place. It was most commonly used on belt fittings, especially the plate behind the buckle, particularly in areas first occupied by the Burgundians, though many were made after the kingdom was conquered by the Franks. Some of the belt buckles and plates were massive: clearly for display.

Cloisonné work. The most striking decoration used this technique. Decorative gold cells (*cloisons*) were either inlaid with cut and polished stones, most frequently garnets, or they were enamelled. They appear first in the second half of the fifth century and were possibly made by old Roman Rhineland workshops freed from traditional constraints. The work is found on sword grips, buckles, brooches and pin heads. When animals are portrayed, they are often dislocated.

> The most interesting sites and museums for looking at the changes taking place in late antiquity are MARLE and CAMBRAI for evidence and displays that focus on ordinary people; NUITS-ST-GEORGE and CHAMPAGNOLE for the Burgundian strand; and PARIS for much of the finest Frankish jewellery. Most museums contain collections of Merovingian accessories.

Notes

1 Those of a young woman (first century AD). See Musée Bargoin, Clermont-Ferrand.

2 The Emperor Gaius (37–41) wore versions as a child when travelling with his father Germanicus, commander of the Rhine army – getting his nickname 'Caligula' or 'small boot' from the soldiers.

Figure 81 Regional map: the Rhône and Savoy

4

THE SITES OF THE RHONE AND SAVOY

AIME, Savoie

Museum and site.

Aime is 89km from Chambéry on the N90 to Aosta (Italy) via the Petit-St-Bernard pass.

Axima was the capital of the Alpes Graiae province. The Isère valley widens here to become the Tarentaise, something of a suntrap, allowing agriculture and even viticulture. To this could be added the normal alpine resources of pasture and forestry and also minerals: silver-bearing lead was soon being exploited in the area, which could also function as a centre for the more distant upland copper-mining in the Beaufortain. However, its key role was in controlling the local alpine population and protecting the vital road artery down from the PETIT-ST-BERNARD pass.

By 2 BC, the Roman town was established on and below St Sigismund hill, a knoll overlooking the valley. It had been occupied since the Neolithic and excavation suggests it may have been a small tribal hillfort for the widely spread Ceutrones. **Axima** became both the official residence of the governor and the capital of the tribe when Claudius made it Forum Claudii Ceutronum with Latin rights. Little of the town is actually known. Although in the nineteenth century a local priest, the Abbé Trémey, claimed there was a large marble paved forum, this was not found until 1992. It is now covered by an old people's home. Evidence of Roman occupation has been located over a square kilometre, though no other clearly recognizable public buildings have been identified. By the fourth century, the forum area was abandoned and other sites below the hill show similar decline: walling on the hillside suggests that Aime had become a *castrum*, protecting the way-stop identified on the Peutinger table, or travellers' map. The fifth-century St Sigismund church perhaps confirms the activities of Saint James of Assyria, supposedly responsible for the conversion of the valley in 427; more definitely it shows the site was never entirely abandoned.

Musée Basilique St Martin

Avenue de Tarentaise
73210 Aime
Hours: 1 July–31 August 9a.m.–noon, 2–6p.m.

This fine Romanesque church was built on the site of a Carolingian chapel. This in turn stood on part of a Gallo-Roman building, which 1980s work has shown was clearly not a temple, though too small an area was excavated to reveal its real identity.

The museum has one of the best-displayed collections of inscriptions anywhere, some 30 of the 50 known for the whole Graiae province. The explanatory panels are excellent: clarity and logic prevail! A number refer to the PROC. AUG., the procurator governor, while others mention the 'Foro Clausienses', or the people of Axima, helping confirm that this was the capital of the province. One of the longest inscriptions honours the procurator **T. Flavius Geminus**, outlining his career or *cursus* (he had been in Thrace and Syria), though it uses the alternative name of 'Atrectiennes' for Graiae province. There are insights, too, into the enclosed and harsh alpine environment. An altar records the procurator Titus Pomponius Victor dedicating a poem to Silvanus, the Roman god of the countryside, slyly demonstrating his longing for his homeland; another acclaims the work of the emperor Verus in restoring the area after floods (see PETIT-ST-BERNARD); on a tombstone, a mother describes how she has brought back across the mountains the remains of her 16-year-old son who died in the course of his studies in Poenina (probably at Martigny), so that they could be buried together. Their crudely worked and damaged busts decorate the memorial.

Musée Pierre Borrione

Chapelle St Sigismond (on the hill).
Hours: 1 July–31 August 10a.m.–noon, 2–6p.m.

The mayor and amateur archaeologist, Pierre Borrione, started modern research at Aime in the 1960s when he explored the crypt of the derelict St Sigismond, discovering the fifth-century remains visible here. The collection of historical material he brought together is dominated by the Gallo-Roman: there is nothing very impressive, but enough to suggest typical provincial Romanization. Note the inscription recording Augustus, used to date the origins of the town, and, upstairs, the lamp found in the La Plagne lead mine.

AIX-LES-BAINS, Savoie

Remains and museum.

The 1930s Thermes Nationaux project a massive, rather dour, gravity over the centre of Aix-les-Bains; the influence of the hot springs was as great in the Roman period, when it was known simply as Aquae. The water issues from two sources, the Alun and the Soutre, as a soda-filled sulphuric mixture at between 41° and 45°C. Springs such as these attracted both Gallic and Roman interest, as a mystical embodiment of godly power at the junction of the known and unknown represented by this unusual water, springing from the earth with curative powers (it is considered to help rheumatism and respiratory problems particularly).

Interest in the Roman role at Aix grew in the eighteenth century when the Princes of Savoy encouraged its development as a spa. As mania about Pompeii grew, so awareness of Aix's own heritage was stimulated. The temple of 'Diana' was recognized as Roman – and misnamed; the arch of Campanus appeared in many engravings, and in the 1780s Roman building was recognized in the houses around the springs. The creation of a modern spa led both to discovery and destruction; little was preserved until the major rebuilding of the Thermes Nationaux in 1931–5, when P. Wuilleumier carried out excavations leading to the preservation of *c.*40 × 25m *in situ*. It is essentially these remains that the visitor sees, though they were re-examined in 1988–9 by Alain Canal, when he carried out a rescue excavation for a car park underneath Place Mollard and the Hôtel de Ville.

Aix sits on an alluvial slope below Mont Revard overlooking the Bourget lake. Given the widespread evidence of Gallic spring sanctuaries elsewhere, it would be extraordinary if this was not one before the arrival of the Romans; the 1989 excavation has confirmed some late La Tène occupation in front of the springs; no doubt there must have been more, perhaps still to be discovered, though more likely destroyed by modern spa constructions.

First-century AD partial remains could be part of a polygonal Romano-Celtic *fanum* contemporary with the construction of the first basins and pools around the springs. Full Romanization came in the second century: a rectangular podium-based temple was built over the earlier structure and the spring site became a classic Roman bathing establishment complete with marble décor and statues. Column finds, the statue of a distinguished Roman lady, and a section of walling interpreted as a *peribolus*, imply the enhancement of a formal zone between the springs/baths and the temple; the arch of Campanus will have formed part of this. A huge storm wrecked the baths in the third century, after which they were rebuilt, but to lower standards. They then fell into gradual decline; there is no evidence of the landslide mentioned by earlier writers. During the early fifth century among the widespread rubbish, common ware was being made in furnaces constructed near the

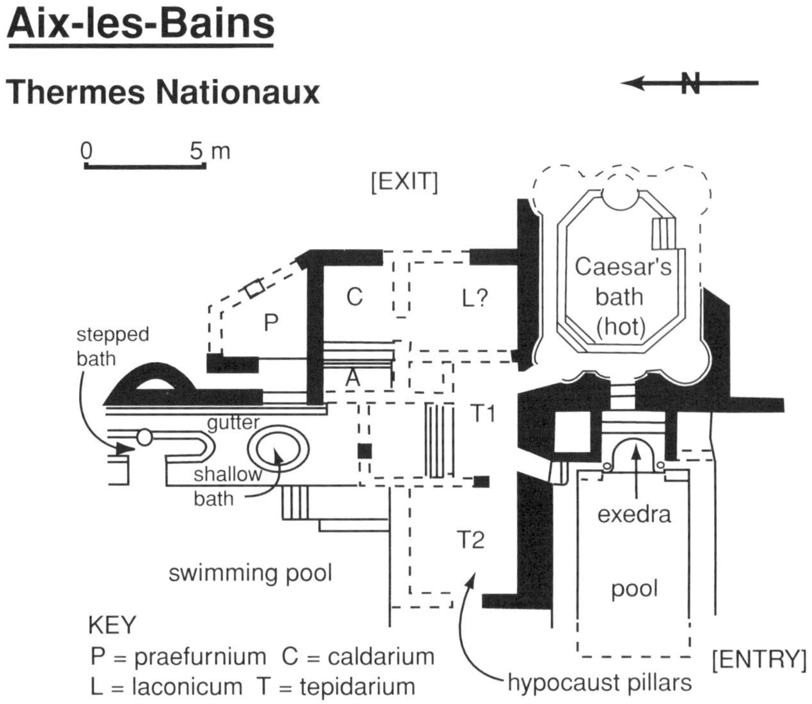

Figure 82 Aix-les-Bains: baths

temple. That the sanctuary simply lost its meaning is supported by the calcareous build-up on spring stonework: signs of abandonment rather than destruction. However, the baths were not forgotten. In the Middle Ages, one pool re-emerged as 'the Royal Bath' to become 'Caesar's Bath' in the later spa.

Thermes Nationaux

Place Maurice Mollard

Access for visitors is only by group tour, which needs to be booked at the Tourist Office, not the Thermes. The tour takes *c.* 1½ hours, the Roman material coming at the end.

The remains constitute at most a quarter of the Roman establishment. Due to the slope, the modern building spreads above and below the Roman, the remains being therefore at first-floor level. It is not easy to see much because lighting is arranged for a 'subterranean' effect, making it difficult to bring sense to the surviving traces of the various rooms, baths and pools.

'Caesar's Bath' and the ***exedra* pool** form a monumental area. The former has a magnificent set of hypocaust pillars, a hundred of which supported the pool itself, and many more supported the surrounding floor once covered with mosaic. The walls were filled with *tubuli*, and the western end of the room had three niches, probably once filled with statues. Maybe the muses kept in the museum came from here. The water flowed down from the bathroom via two flat *tubuli* into pipes that once led to gargoyles decorating the *exedra*. This was a richly decorated *nymphaeum* with two small decorative pools, a dolphin, marble and piers.

Separated from the *exedra* pool by a *tepidarium* (T2), is a large swimming pool thought to have been filled with cold water and open to the sky; only the corner survives. Beside it are a footbath and a stepped bath to lounge around. An open gully and a wall divided the swimming pool from a furnace (P) that carried hot air under and up the walls of the *caldarium* (C) with a hot plunge bath (A), and into the hot dry *laconicum* (L) and the two warm *tepidaria* (T1 and 2). Wuilleumier removed the furnace or *praefurnium* and much of the seriously damaged walls in the 1930s.

The Campanus Arch

Square du Temple de Diane

The archway itself is 6m high by 3.5m wide, and the overall height reaches 9.15m; it is smaller than most public arches and is notably thin, only 0.75m. The main inscription was once clear enough and records that 'Lucius Pompeius Campanus built [this while] living'. The other inscriptions have always been a pleasing challenge to antiquarians, but clearly named his ancestors. This is the proud statement of a leading family, one of the *possessores* of Aquae referred to in inscriptions found here, probably one of the *decemlecti*, who controlled Aquae in the absence of standard *vicus* magistrates.

Arches without specific imperial references are notoriously difficult to date, particularly on stylistic grounds. After his 1989 work here, A. Canal proposed a second-century date; this seems likely given the overall chronological development of the site. It used to be seen simply as a funerary arch, but Canal suggests that it is the donation of a wealthy man putting his family into the privileged portico zone between the life-giving spring and the godly control emanating from the temple.

Temple of 'Diana'

La Mairie
Place M. Mollard

The temple is built into the side of what has now become the Hôtel de Ville; its vestibule is the Office de Tourisme.

The exterior. Its *grand appareil* stone stands out clearly on the exposed northern and western sides. These rise 9.75m and are crowned with a plain architrave; the tympanum of the pediment at the western end is also undecorated. It was a simple but handsome Tuscan style temple, its vestibule formed by extending the lateral walls and placing two columns between. Although smaller than the temples at Nîmes and Vienne, it is still one of the best preserved outside the south of France, especially when it is remembered that it stands on a podium over 3m high, now covered by the modern ground level.

The interior. The rough chisel work of the Gallo-Roman masons would of course have been covered with internal plaster. No evidence has emerged to tie the temple to any specific god. The most likely seems to be the Celtic Bormo/Borvo, to whom a dedication was found in the spring; but there are bronzes of Hercules, the mother-goddesses, and some possibly imperial statuary, hinting at that cult as well.

Musée Lapidaire

Temple de Diane
Office de Tourisme

This is the archaeological collection of Aix-les-Bains and sadly the three cases of small finds are limited indeed. The inscriptions ranged round the walls of the temple are worth looking at to find **Bormo/Borvo** and the ***possessores*** – what a significant name for the elite! – and an inscription recording the donation to Aquae of a sacred wood with its vines. There is a scoop **sundial** (modern pointer), marked with the twelve hours of the day; note a horizontal line marking winter and summer: the hours will have varied in length during the seasons.

Yet it is the marble statuary found in the baths that hints most strongly of all at the importance of Aquae. Most overpowering is the naked **male torso**, perhaps Hercules, perhaps an emperor. The impressive naturalism of its strongly defined musculature is far removed from crude Hercules statues generally found in Gaul (see DENEUVRE). The **head**, set next to it, is striking too, due to its square, staring quality: it is much more like the imperial portrayals developed at the end of the third century; it does not quite fit the dimensions of the torso. The delicately portrayed **headless 'muse'** is identified on the basis of pose and costume. Her tunic hangs in heavy folds tied under her breast, contrasting with a delicate, lightweight cloak. A **female head**, thought to belong to another muse, has a young, beautiful, rather ethereal look. Baths were often seen as inspirational places! Still unlabelled years after its discovery (1989) is the headless **Empress** figure, found in the car-park excavation, her imposing form dressed in a delicately modelled tunic over a heavily pleated under-dress, tied at the waist.

My own favourite is the **Silvanus relief**. His pine-cone crown, his fruit basket and cooking pot, his mix of young stubby athletic body and old face identify the god: perhaps embodying health and safe return (see AIME for another rare reference to Silvanus found in Gaul). This relief was reused: the back has an early Christian inscription to Vahlo, who died in 508: evidence of the collapse of the old beliefs surrounding the springs.

Around Aix-les-Bains

Portout. The site of a late Roman hamlet/villa and workshop manufacturing sub-*sigillata* pottery *c.* AD 375–425 is 18km north of Aix, at the north-west corner of the lake by a delightfully set *auberge*. The re-creation furnaces and demonstration firings are being renewed and a small exhibition room of finds reopened.

Conjux. 2km south beyond Portout. The chapel contails a Cybele altar. This eastern mother-goddess cult is likely to have come to the Aix region via the valley of the Rhône, where evidence of a temple and *taurobolium* (bull sacrifice altar) has been found.

Marigny-St-Marcel. 18km towards Annecy, via Albens. Albinus is the only known *vicus* on the road from Aquae to Condate (Seyssel). Serious research has only just begun at Albinus itself and the three inscriptions on the exterior walls of Marigny church remain the best visible evidence of its existence. Caius Sennius Sabinus records how he has provided Albinus with a baths, an aqueduct, a *palaestra* and a portico (none of which has been identified).

ALBERTVILLE, Savoie

IGN 3432 ET

Museum and sites.

The Lauzière mountains force the Isère northwards until a major tributary, the Arly, joins it and the enlarged river once again turns south into the wide and flat Combe de Savoie. In the pre-Roman and Roman period the Ceutroni (see AIME) occupied the upper Isère, but the Allobroges controlled both the Val d'Arly to Lac Leman and the Combe as far as the Rhône, with their capital at Vienne. This natural junction was to become under the Romans 'Ad Publicanos', a stopping place and tax-collection point on what was a provincial as well as tribal border. Exactly where and quite what sort of settlement there was is only gradually becoming clear.

Henry Barthélémy has argued convincingly that on the basis of current archaeological evidence there were in fact three sites. First, an *oppidum* overlooking the junction itself – subsequently the medieval village Conflans. Second, an as yet undiscovered customs post and *mansio*, below St Sigismond hill, on the north bank of the Arly by the Roman bridge that must have linked it with the PETIT-ST-BERNARD road that ran along the left bank of the Isère. Third, a widely spread *vicus* at Gilly, 4km down the Combe. This was initially suspected from the many chance finds, now mainly lost, then known for its villa site; finally a major survey (1990s) revealed a large porticoed square, a religious centre with at least two *fana*, and perhaps a theatre. It seems very likely, too, that navigation could begin here on the Isère, and this was therefore a major transfer site for the heavier goods carried in the wagons and mule trains down from the Petit-St-Bernard. This would have stimulated the *vicus* as a market centre and explains the large square.

Musée d'Ethnographie et d'Histoire de Conflans

Maison Rouge
Grand Place
73200 Conflans (Albertville)

Hours:	1 June–30 September	10a.m.–noon, 2–7p.m.
	1 April to 31 May, 1 October to 3 November	2–5p.m. Closed Tuesday
	rest of year: school vacations only	2–5p.m.

The outstanding find displayed here is the largest set of **Roman scales** discovered in Europe. It was their discovery in 1975 in an excavation by the local *lycée* that led the professional archaeologists to Gilly. Up to 200kg could be weighed: were they once used by the customs officials, or to resolve disputes in the market square? The other three cases are taken up with old-fashioned displays of material from the Gilly villa excavations.

Figure 83 Albertville: scales

Gilly villa

902.8/2080.3

By the D990 south from Albertville, passing Gilly church for the Grand Verger housing estate.

The villa, a fine peristyle house, was excavated by Barthélémy in the 1980s. The surviving low wall courses, heavily consolidated, were made of river stone roughly squared; gravel outlines the portico. The baths are no longer exposed except for the large pool. The home of a rich landowner, or the official running the tax office? It was largely out of use in the fourth century. (See GRENOBLE model.)

Fréterive

902.8/2072.6

Continue by the D990 *c.*16km towards Chambéry to the 'chef-lieu de Fréterive'. There is an inscription by the mill.

There are three pleasures in coming this way: you are roughly following the Roman road with very little other traffic; there are wonderful views of the mountain scenery; and you will get a sense of an individual Gallo-Roman family on their home soil. By the roadside opposite a fountain, there is an **inscription**, capped with a pine cone, commemorating Marinus, Martius and Marcellinus of the Iulii family. Another two inscriptions of this family are in CHAMBERY museum, also from Fréterive. They were important enough to be *duoviri* in Vienne, but this was their home estate. The baths of what must have been their villa were excavated in Fréterive but are not visible.

ANSE, Rhône

Late Roman ramparts and museum.

Traditionally, Anse has been a travellers' stop between the Lyon basin and the Beaujolais – Napoleon, on his way to Waterloo, supposedly ate an egg here in 1815. Now, as the continuous roar from the A6 and the steady flow of traffic on the N6 show, few stop to explore this attractive, sleepy small town clustered around a late Roman *castellum.*

The Antonine Itinerary mentions an 'Asa Paulini' stop. Albert Grenier suggested that this meant an estate owned by Paulinus, convincing because in 1843 a magnificent villa had been found at La Grange du Bief, 1.5km south of Anse on the western slopes of the Azergues valley. Thirteen plus mosaics were discovered, some in superb condition: virtually all have disappeared, the farmer alone is supposed to have destroyed at least four. In 1845 the Conseiller-Général intervened and managed to save one. Serious

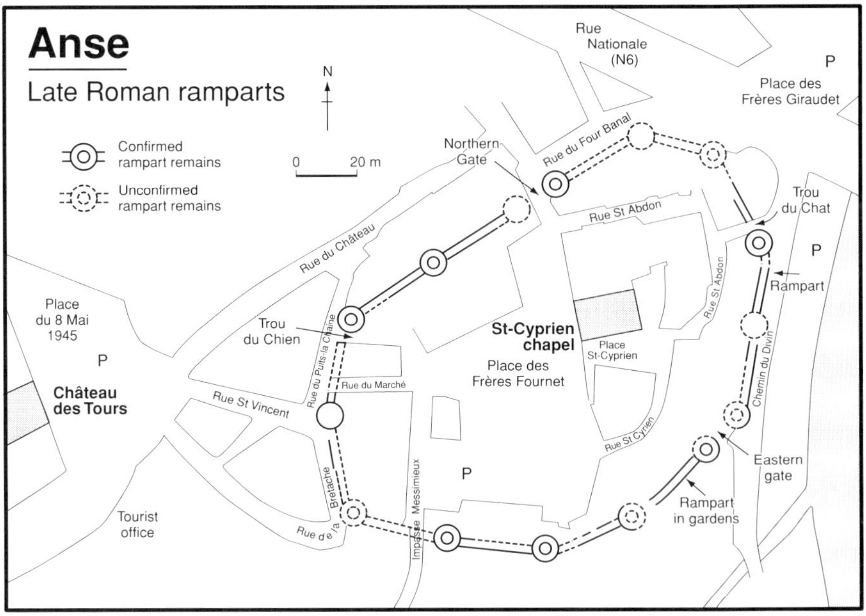

Figure 84 Anse: town plan (ramparts)

excavation resumed in the 1960s, led by Roger Perraud, revealing a bath complex, a gallery more than 170m long and a number of rooms, some with fine wall paintings. Work done in the 1980s, together with aerial photography, has shown this was not simply a large mansion and its working farm, but part of a *vicus* spread over at least 15ha. Finds indicate occupation from the first to fifth centuries. No remains are currently exposed.

However, the bridge carrying the 'Agrippa' road was nearer the junction with the Saône and the *castellum* was needed here. It was only 1.25ha, an oval 170 × 107m, therefore not a fortified town, rather a fortress/warehouse. Road posts like this, guarding the transit of supplies, are known from the time of Aurelian (270–75). Its design is typical of late Roman military construction in Lugdunensis Prima, similar to the known but unpreserved fortifications at Tournus and Mâcon. Here, circular towers, copied from the Augustan examples at Autun, stood astride very thick (3.5m) ramparts.

During the fifth century the *castellum* became the focus for a community that evolved into the medieval village of Anse. Early Christian tombstones have been found and a building considered to be an early sixth-century Burgundian church.

The ramparts

The number of towers has been a matter of some uncertainty, but a recent study argued there must have been fifteen, set 30m apart along the walls. The **Trou du Chien**, in the Rue du Puits la Chaine, was a postern gate, that is, a door (now a street) set beside a single tower. Though the tower has been changed externally, its circular internal shape is quite clear. This plastered tower was once the eastern half of the northern gate. The **'Trou du Chat'** in the east, another postern gate, begins the major section of exposed material. Local tradition explains its name as the result of the discovery of an inscription, of course lost, with the surviving letters 'CATO', from an original 'dedicato'. Only tower core is preserved, further disfigured by its medieval extension joining it to buildings outside the *castellum*. Extending to the south, the Chemin du Divin rampart is exposed rubble core with tile courses. The **eastern gate** has two towers, filled between with later stonework. Some *petit appareil* facing survives here, but the best section of walling is the **rampart on the south side**, rising some 8–9m.

St-Cyprien chapel

Place St-Cyprien

Used as a general shed since the eighteenth century, this rectangular structure is certainly the oldest building within the ramparts. It has obviously been patched many times since the end of the fifth century and the original tiny semi-circular windows have been filled in.

St-Pierre church

Rue Septembre 1944

Inside the entrance set in the right-hand wall are fragments of early tombstones. The longest, most complete and earliest records Proba, a girl of 5 years 8 months who died in 498. Her epitaph is decorated with scrollwork and two doves.

Musée Archéologique

Château des Tours
Place du 8 mai 1945
Hours: July and August guided tours 3.30p.m. Saturday
4.30p.m. Wednesday
for other times consult Office du Tourisme opposite

The castle, built by the Archbishop of Lyon in 1213 to defend his territory against Beaujolais, houses the small collection. The villa **carpet mosaic** once filled a room 16 × 11m (now 9 × 4m). It is made up from simple geometric shapes; the wide border has three sections of which the outer is most interesting, with ships' prows in arcades. Is it simply a decorative motif or was the owner once a shipper? Using white, black and red *tesserae*, it is the product of a Lyon workshop, probably in the Severan period. Even more impressive are the **frescoes**, one a bird perched on a branch, the other a Mediterranean swamp hen, once found in the Camargue. There are also a few finds from the villa, early Christian epitaphs and a fine Merovingian buckle.

AOSTE, Izère

Museum and site.

Unlike the Italian Aosta (Aoste in French, both derived from Augusta), this was not an imperial colony to secure Roman domination over recently conquered people – that was already done by the colonies at Lyon and Vienne – but a *vicus*. An inscription identifying Aoste as a Roman *pagus* centre hinted at earlier Iron Age importance and at last evidence is emerging of an *oppidum* nearby. But its prime importance in the Roman era was as a way station for the two St Bernard routes from Italy, before they crossed the varied lowland of the Bas Dauphiné to Vienne and Lyon. A fourth road went to the bridge at nearby Cordon, so joining the north bank route along the Rhône; it is likely that, close by, there was a landing stage for river traffic as well. Once the long-distance rationale for this site disappeared in late antiquity it allowed other better-placed centres with a regional focus to take over and Aoste never recovered its former position.

Antiquarian interest began in the sixteenth century but only in the last few years has Vicus Augusta become more than a shadow. No *mansio* or public buildings are known, temples are only hinted at, and habitation is defined in terms of a 'zone' rather than houses. Ditches found in 1998 support the view that Gallo-Roman limestone walls are rare because many were later removed to make cement. The *vicus* covered at least 20ha and had two large cemeteries. It is its industrial history that is best known, with evidence for lead and bronze working, glass manufacture and pottery workshops. It was Colette Laroche's work in the 1970s and 1980s on the potteries which led to the creation of an excellent small modern museum (1988); excavations in the 1990s encouraged further updating with a new extension, opened in 2001. It is dynamic and imaginative.

Musée d'Aoste

Rue de Musée (via Rue Champs de Mars)
38490 Aoste
Hours: 10a.m.–noon, 2–6p.m. Closed Tuesday
closed December

Many small towns in Gaul were centres of artisan production for the local market and some like Aoste became larger producers. During the first century AD they manufactured over a hundred designs of fine and common ware, suitable for the table, kitchen and cooking use. Their top fine ware, a virtuoso black jar with décor using twenty-two different mould markers, found a market outside the region, but their key kitchen product, the ***mortaria***, was the major export success, being found as far away as south Wales and Devon. Some *mortaria* are signed, one name being Atisii, an elite Allobrogian family, who no doubt owned workshops here and organized shippers and carriers. *Mortaria* had a sand-grit base which provided a final grating for sauce mixes including numerous herbs and spices, so important for flavouring such dishes as brine-preserved fish.

Displays demonstrate in models and panels how the pottery industry operated. The basalt handmill would have been imported; it could have been used by the potters to grind fire-clay – or for grinding corn. Following the food theme, the museum also has a **re-creation kitchen**. Corked glass bottles shown here could be used to keep milk, oil or vinegar. New finds of glass confirm the curator J.-P. Jospin's conviction that glass was used more widely than traditionally assumed; note the exceptional elegant, first-century **flared jug**.

The **coin collection** is varied, a sign of Aoste's active market role. A **battered altar** is believed to have stood at the town centre, symbolizing Aoste as a crossroads, its four niches once filled with representations of Mercury, the travellers' god and one widely venerated in the region. An empty plinth records the town's patron, **Lucius Julius Fronto**, a magistrate in Vienne and a member of the Julii family who owned estates at Fréterive (see ALBERTVILLE). There is a tombstone to **Claudia Albina**, whose father commanded a ship in the Rhine fleet based at Mainz, now presented in a vivid display on funerary customs.

Gallo-Roman kiln

Signposted 'Le Four Gallo-Romain'. Opposite the Hôtel de Ville, behind the car-park is an old people's home. Beside it, in another parking area is a landscaped concrete bunker with windows protecting the kiln.

The sun-dried brick kiln was constructed at one end of a rectangular pit. Pots were stacked on the perforated floor above the chamber. The kiln was originally covered with a vaulted roof, but this had to be broken after each firing to remove the pots; none has survived anywhere and the actual shape is unknown. To carry out the firing, wood was stacked up outside the chamber, lit, then only gradually pushed in to try to control the heat. Batches that failed fill holes where clay has been cut from the ground. This was one of eight excavated kilns forming a workshop; a further five are known elsewhere in Aoste. There are excellent explanatory panels in French and English.

St-Didier church

3km north of Aoste by the D592.

Grand appareil, brought from a public building in Aoste or from the Roman bridge at Cordon only a couple of hundred metres away, is used to decorate the front, providing a good excuse for visiting this beautiful, simple Romanesque church.

BRIORD, Ain

IGN 3231 OT

Sites and museum.

The Rhône forms the boundary between the bumpy plains stretching west to Lyon, and the Bugey, the first outcrop of the Jura, around which the river takes a big loop. One settlement on this loop, accessible to both river traffic and the Roman road from Lyon to Geneva, was Briorate, named on one of the sixteen Gallo-Roman inscriptions found in the area. Little survives in Briord: perhaps the church was constructed on a temple, and there is fragmentary Gallo-Roman walling and reused stonework around the village; finds indicate a villa in nearby Buison. Nevertheless, there is a local aqueduct, the foundations of an early Christian church, an *in situ* tombstone and a small museum packed with material from a modern necropolis excavation.

The early Christian church and cemetery (843.4/2092.2). 'Les Plantées' site is by the roadside of the D19 indicated by a tourist panel. From the south on the left, 800m north of the D79A turning for Briord. The church is a third- to seventh-century structure; one arm of the Latin cross may have utilized an earlier mausoleum. These foundation walls are mainly river-washed stones. The surrounding area was covered with a large necropolis, hundreds of burials having been identified, covering the period from early empire through to Burgundian and Merovingian. The church is a product of a phase when paganism lived on and Christian worshippers focused their activities in cemetery churches.

The aqueduct tunnel. Take a torch if possible. Opposite 'Les Plantées', across the D19 follow the track leading into the hillside 200m, including a sharp turn to the left after 150m. The 230m tunnel taps the Brivaz on the other side of Bruyarettes hill. Insecurely dated, but a Mercury figurine, now in Grenoble, was found here. There is another local effort like this in Le Bugey at Vieu (not open), and technically, it seems about right: a bend in the middle looks like two teams had problems meeting – a not unknown difficulty. It is roughly finished, but varies between 1.5 and 1.8m high and is over 2.7m wide, making it quite accessible.

Tombstone (843.6/2091.5). On the northern side of the D79A, 50m towards Briord from the junction known as 'sur Plaine'. In what was a

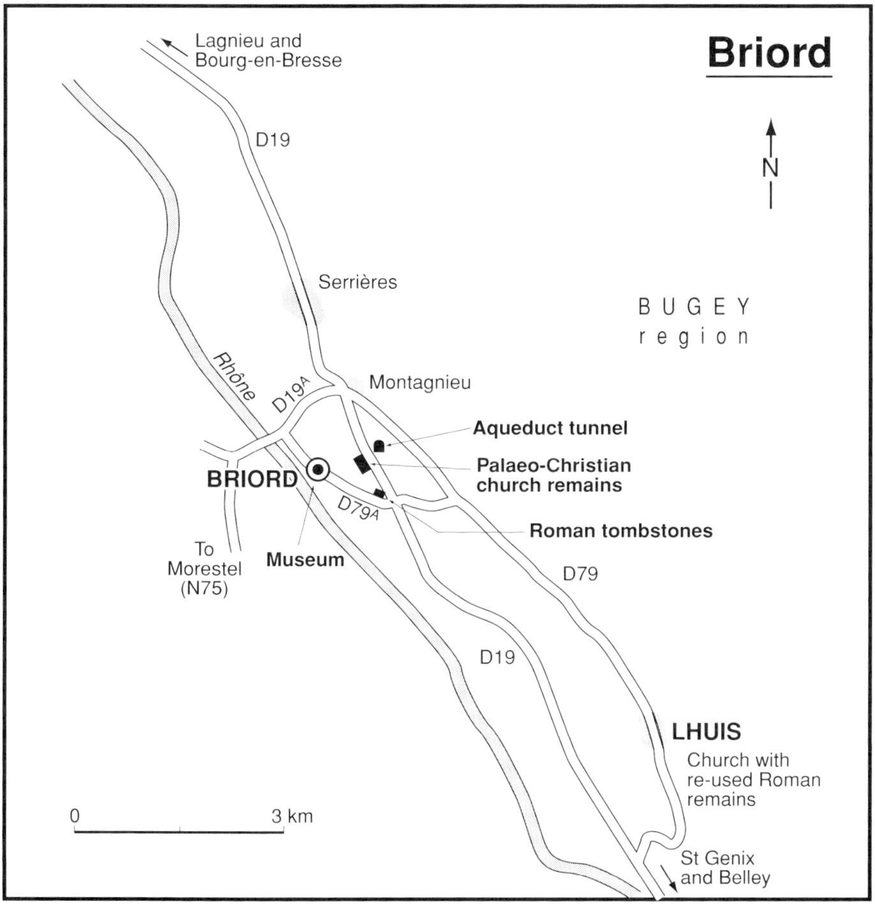

Figure 85 Briord: local map

necropolis created above a support wall that stretched beside the Roman road are preserved a number of tombstones including one dedicated by **Connia Nicen[a]** to her husband Connius Tyticus. The undergrowth has been cleared and once again this third-century memorial can remind us of her feelings.

Musée

Place de la Mairie

Hours:	1 May–30 September	3–6p.m. Sunday, some Saturdays and holidays

Almost the entire collection displayed here is from the necropolis excavations of 1958–81. It is old-fashioned but thoughtfully done with photographs and models and clearly demonstrates the evolution of contemporary funeral practices. Interesting individual burial finds include a small Gallo-Roman braid weaving plate for separating the warp and weft; a second-third-century carved bone pin demonstrating contemporary hairstyling; some attractive pendant jewellery; two fifth-century dog-design fibulae and a classic Merovingian zoomorphic bird. Last, there is a bizarre skull, extended by binding during childhood in a practice derived by the Burgundians from the Huns.

Lhuis. 11km south-east of Briord on the D79 via Montagnieu. The village church has built into the choir an inscription, on which a Catullus makes a dedication, probably to the mother-goddesses, at a *fanum* that may have been under the church. Outside, an altar decorated with a rayed wheel or sun recalls the Gallic Apollo. Another hint of Gallic traditions can be seen in one of the Romanesque capitals, where a man is being devoured by a monster, notably represented by the Noves statue in the Musée Calvet, Avignon.

CHAMBERY, Savoie

Museum.

Chambéry is an important junction town today and the Peutinger table names a 'Lemencum' that should be here. Local place-names like Lemenc hill, a district called 'Mercury', and Gallo-Roman burials hint at a settlement, yet excavations have proved sterile on the hill and little significant has been found elsewhere in Chambéry.

Musée Savoisien

Square Lannoy de Bissey
73000 Chambéry
Hours: 10a.m.–noon, 2–6p.m. Closed Tuesday

The Lac de Bourget settlement finds of the late Bronze Age and early Iron Age are presented imaginatively with modern display panels, something sadly missing with the Gallo-Roman material in badly lit upright glass cases. Presentation gives prominence to neither significant artefacts nor important excavations. No comment is made on the importance of horseshoes in the Alps; fine marble pilaster facings from the Mérende villa at Arbin are not put in the context of the two finest mosaics found in the Savoie hidden in the private Batie château. Even less comprehensible is the case devoted to religion, with no discussion of Châteauneuf, where a large-scale rescue excavation in the early 1980s revealed a major sanctuary *vicus* (subsequently covered by the A43), yet both a Mercury figurine and a votive plaque from the site are displayed.

There are interesting individual exhibits. Mercury was widely worshipped in the region and is best represented here by what must have been a giant statue, judging from the size of the ***caduceus***, or wand, once held in the massive fingers. Note the tiny tortoise, sacred to Mercury. For quality – and here the lighting is most frustrating – see the **two statues of Venus**. One is a 15cm-high bronze of a young, feminine, innocent Venus, perhaps a girl's treasure, as a gold thread (ear?) ring has been attached to her arm. The other is a fine Roman marble copy of Venus at her most enticing, her robe, falling round her thighs, prominently knotted at the front. There is a subtle drunken Hercules (Hercules-Bibax), brought from AIME. There are beautifully carved bone pinheads and good glass goblets. Among the pottery there is a selection

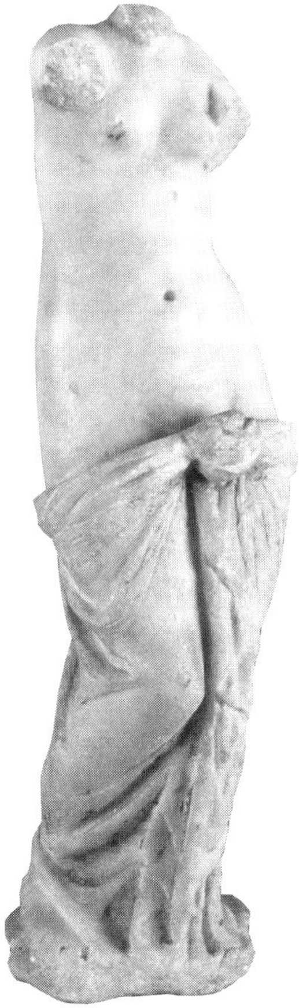

Plate 31 Chambéry. A classic Venus. Collection Musée Savoisien, Chambéry. Service photographique.

of dark Allobrogian ware, often signed by workers, and a separate case for the late Roman Portout ware (see AIX-LES-BAINS), enlivened by the fine leather shoe found here.

DINGY-ST-CLAIR, Haute Savoie

IGN 3431 OT
900.8/2109.0

Roadside inscription.

This inscription is situated some 10km east of Annecy, by the D16. Two kilometres short of Dingy itself, the road crosses the Gier by a narrow bridge over the steep 'Défilé de Dingy'. Turn left for Naves-Parmelan, and you are now on the Roman road. On the right, about 150m up the road, *c.*4m above road level, is an inscription carved in the rock face. The road is narrow but it is possible to park either beyond the inscription or by the bridge.

In a rectangular moulded frame with pointed handles on both sides, is engraved LUCIUS TINCIUS PACULUS/PERVIUM FECIT, the first line clearer than the second. It is generally translated as 'L.T. Paculus made this passage [steep road]' and interpreted as a statement by the local landowner that he has organized the cutting of this road along the side of the gorge to make access to his estates easier. The masons' chisel marks are clear as are the undercutting horizontal lines, parallel to the road, for breaking away the rock. It is an evocative personal statement embedded in the Savoyard countryside.

FAVERGES, Haute Savoie

Site and museum.

19km north-west of Albertville by the N212/N508 and 27km south-east of Annecy.

The valleys of the Arly and Chaise form the basis of one of the main routes from Albertville to Annecy and Geneva, in the north of Allobrogian territory. In the small basin between the Massif des Bauges and the Aravis chain, the Antonine Itinerary mentions Casuaria as a *mansio* stop. It was a local excavation, chancing upon a bronze jar filled with silver coins, which encouraged modern research. An excavation of Viuz church revealed that it stood on a large Gallo-Roman building (perhaps a temple?), and was followed by an early but large Merovingian church *c.*600. At the same time, serious survey work was being carried out in the whole area, and on the other side of Faverges at Le Thovey a bath complex was discovered (1981). The decision to build a by-pass for the N508 led to the major rescue digs of 1988 and the early 1990s. These

Plate 32 Dingy. A plaque celebrates an estate owner's pride in cutting this ravine road. Photograph: James Bromwich.

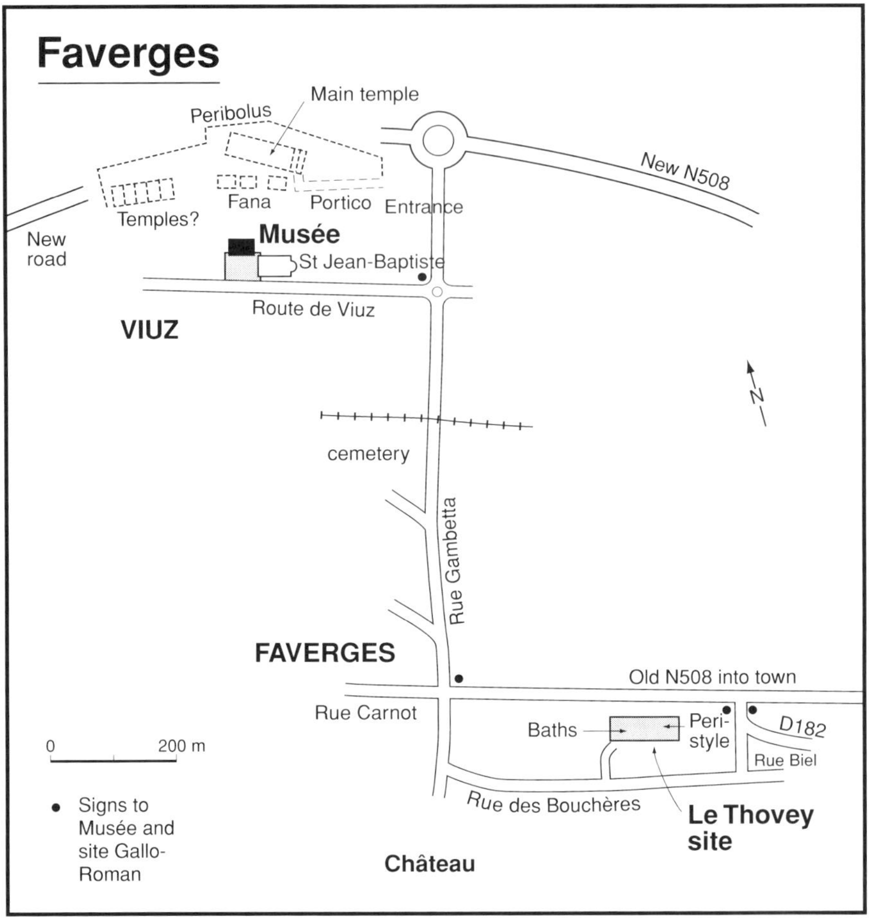

Figure 86 Faverges: local plan

disclosed an astonishing sanctuary filled with temples, before the new road once again hid them from view – their importance at least led to the decision to raise the level of the road and so limit its destructiveness.

A colonnaded ceremonial entrance on the east led to the largest temple, 30m long, with a portico and internal niches, perhaps once filled with statues of gods; a central square wall may have formed another statue base. Nearby is a line of square structures, clearly *fana*, and in the south-west corner, another row of buildings seem best explained as temples with sacrificial furnaces or ovens inside – there are no industrial remains to explain them in any other way. There were votive deposits, a couple of moulded arms, but mainly coins. There was evidence of Augustan building and maybe pre-Roman occupation, which seems very likely. The coins suggest it peaked in the second to fourth centuries. Only lucky future archaeologists of the post-N508 era will reveal more about this major site.

Why was this sanctuary built at Viuz? First, the Col du Marais to the north-east gives a rare view of Mont Blanc: surely this will always have provoked awe. Second, the site lay on the borders between the Allobroges and the Ceutroni: sanctuaries provided a mechanism for the peaceful intermingling of peoples – marriage, the settlement of disputes and the exchange of goods could all be pursued along with worship.

Le Thovey

Signposted on the D182/Rue Biel off the old N508 into Faverges from Albertville. Take the right fork immediately off the D182 and also at T-junction. The site is 200m further on right.

On my visit the site badly needed restoration work, but this is expected to take place with the consolidation of **the baths**. From the vestibule (V), bathers could use the wet-heat *tepidarium* (T) and *caldarium* (C), the cold plunge bath in the *frigidarium* (F) and then use the independently heated massage room. The baths were decorated with marble and painted walls. The complex was in use from the end of the first to the beginning of the third century, when it was seriously damaged by a torrential flood. Attached to the baths was **a portico** with Tuscan pillars; recent excavation to confirm

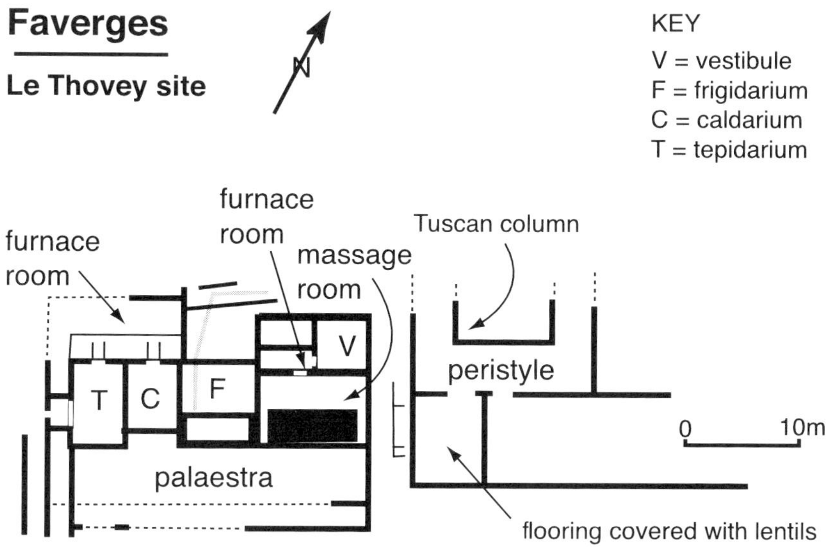

Figure 87 Faverges: Le Thovey

that this was a villa **peristyle** have only shown it was much bigger than expected. The floor of a room beside the portico, perhaps a kitchen, was covered with lentils.

Some way from Viuz, and so part of the road system rather than the sanctuary, the baths would logically be a wing of the *mansio*; equally, they might form part of a grand villa: this is an uncertainty that may be resolved in the near rather than distant future.

Musée Archéologique

Route de Viuz
St Jean-Baptiste church
74210 Faverges

Hours:	summer	2.30–6.30p.m.
	rest of year	4.30–6.30p.m. Monday to Friday

This is a small but interesting collection because, despite limited resources, Les Amis de Viuz-Faverges have set out to communicate and there is a knowledgeable guide. There are imported Iron Age amber necklaces and grave goods from a Merovingian cemetery, but the rest is Gallo-Roman, nearly all from Le Thovey. Naturally used in the construction of the baths were *tubuli* imported from the regional specialist brick and hypocaust supplier, Clarianus; a *tegula* tile has the stud imprint of a Roman worker's shoe. Outstanding is the massive **bronze cauldron**, better than the very similar one found at Gilly (see ALBERTVILLE). Savoie was already famous for cheese; perhaps this was used for an early version of fondue? Note also the large iron saw, a tiny filigree gold brooch, a small stubby-legged bronze dog and the bronze jar with some of the *denarii* and *antoniniani* found in 1971 by the amateurs, one of them Michel Duret, then aged 16, now the proud president of Les Amis.

FEURS, Loire

IGN 2831 E

Museum and site.

Feurs is 70km east of Lyon by the N7/N89. An unremarkable town today, as Forum Segusiavorum it was the *civitas* capital of the Segusiavi tribe. It replaced an Iron Age village, the leading settlement between the two hill-fort *oppida* of Essalois and Crêt-Châtelard since the second century BC. It was built on a right-bank terrace set back from the river Loire at the natural crossing for the Aquitaine road from Lyon to Clermont. Its foundation can be dated to shortly after the construction of the road network.

In 1851 the Abbé Roux published a remarkable book, suggesting that Feurs had Gallic origins, a formal Roman grid and a forum that he outlined pretty accurately. Until the 1970s, others did little to expand on his conclusions, while the town itself managed to demolish most of its surviving remains. The pioneering archaeology of Paul Valette confirmed Roux's deductive work with a series of rescue digs. It is now possible to claim that the forum is one of the best known in France and to provide a broad picture of the Roman town. It grew rapidly in the first and second centuries AD, to decline dramatically at the beginning of the third century, never to recover. It was never very prosperous. The roads were gravel and compacted sand and the porticoed housing was predominantly brick and wattle-and-daub rather than stone, though there were grander houses with mosaics and garden pools. The number of wells suggests these rather than an aqueduct were the main water supply, though there was a bath complex, possibly linked to a sanctuary. It had a theatre, but claims for an amphitheatre seem less likely.

It is clear the town had a regional role and its responsibility for road maintenance is signified by four milestones dedicated to Maximinus (235–8), plus a blank, found together in Feurs, suggesting that a workshop here was preparing new milestones for this section of the Aquitaine road. Less clear is the Roman town's relationship with the river Loire. Though it seems there was no bridge, whether the river was open to traffic here is unresolved. To the north, downstream, lay the Seuil de Neulise, the ridge creating the rapids between the plain of the Forez and that of Roanne, which may or may not have formed a barrier to river traffic. Waterside research may yet expose landings or warehouses and settle whether Feurs was a major transit port for Rhône/Loire traffic.

The forum area

Place de la Boaterie

The only visible remains are the much-reduced buttressed walls of the *curia* that stood at one end of the forum. Regrettably, as photographs show, investigation during 1952–6 was accompanied by considerable demolition. Hidden below ground, and in the cellars surrounding the square, are traces of a *cryptoporticus*, the large central drain and other isolated pieces of paving and walls that permitted the model reconstruction in the museum.

Musée d'Assier

3 Rue Victor-de-Laprade
42110 Feurs
Hours: 2–6p.m. Closed Tuesday

The archaeological collection fills **two rooms** and a 'Roman portico'. The first room contains the second- and first-century BC Iron Age material, mainly pottery from the necropolis; the large forum model dominates the second.

This demonstrates how the forum followed the standard north Italian design adopted by the Augustan/Tiberian builders over the Alps (Augst is often taken as the type site). At the western end is the temple, about the same size as that in Nîmes, surrounded by a portico constructed on top of a *crypto-porticus*. The wall separating the temple area from the central square is now believed to be a mistake. The square would have been filled with a variety of statues; fragments of a Jupiter–giant column found in a well perhaps stood here. The eastern end embodied civil power. A great basilica, identified from the surviving column bases and some walling, was accompanied by two grand staircases on each side of the *curia*. Here leading citizens dispensed justice as *duumviri* (magistrates) or met as *decuriones* (councillors) to settle town affairs.

The **stone weight** of 10 pounds 'P[ondo] X', with its dedication to the communal god Segata, implies it was once used in the forum as a standard weight to settle disputes. The small **bronze inscription** to Sextus Julius Lucanus introduces us to the only known *duumvir* of Feurs. The memorial was put up by his six *apparitores*: freedmen assistants appointed by the council. Among the small finds, those associated with the personal religion of a leading citizen who has fully adopted Roman styles, the sort of objects belonging in a house *lararium*, are the most interesting. One is a copy: the fine classical **seated Mercury** (original in Munich). Another is an **officiating priest** in his toga.

The garden portico. Few **stone inscriptions** have been found in Feurs. The theatre inscription records a dedication to Claudius by a *sacerdos Augusti*, or priest of the imperial cult, called Tiberius Claudius Capito ('big-head'), who funded the new stone theatre. Another is dedicated by the city builders to the *numen Augusti*, the imperial soul that is linked here with the god Silvanus, evidence of the provincial imperial cult. The fine C[aius] Jul[ius] Jull[us] inscription is more unusual, as he is called a *princeps* or prince – perhaps a tribal title. The *nomen gentile* (tribe name) Julius suggests Caesar himself may have rewarded him with citizenship. There is also an **octagonal mosaic** and pictures illustrating the construction of the town.

Salt-en-Donzy. 5km east of Feurs by the D89 and D10. On the front of the old priory house (split by a dangerous crack) are the brick traces of projecting apses that once decorated a monumental wall. A parallel plain wall survives on the eastern side of the rear grass enclosure. These are the visible remains of building(s), which stood on a terrace projecting from the hillside. Roman masonry round a hot spring – 'Gourd Chaud' – provides the rationale for a sanctuary here and the presence of a bath complex, but further remains need to be discovered.

Crêt-Châtelard *oppidum*

940.6/2096.7

15km north of Feurs by the N82 and then D83, signposted to Pinay. 1.5km to the left branch for Le Châtelard. Cross the deep railway cutting. Park at the derelict houses where the narrow rough tarmac becomes track.

The derelict houses are just beyond the artificial mound, or crest, created to protect the *oppidum* on the vulnerable eastern side. In front of the 'crêt' is a wide ditch, with gnarled outcrops where the stone has been cut out. Impenetrable bracken now covers the crest itself. This was a promontory fort with sharp 70m-high slopes overlooking the Loire by the start of the Seuil de Neulise (rapids). A stone-and-earth rampart enclosing the rest of the *oppidum* was built *c.*75 BC and was destroyed or collapsed during the early Augustan period. Dwellings have been recognized but not excavated. However, examination of the many wells shows late Iron Age occupation and a Gallo-Roman village here from the first to third centuries.

GRENOBLE, Isère

Sites and museums.
www.musée-dauphinois.fr

In 43 BC, Plancus, in a letter to his friend Cicero, outlined his journey to Vienne to deal with the revolt that culminated in the foundation of the new colony at Lyon. He mentions *Cularo*, a river crossing where alluvium, built up by both the slower moving Isère coming down from the north and the faster moving Drac, created a site shallow enough for a ford and then a bridge. This became a Roman settlement on the main Mont Genèvre route to Vienne, where a secondary road joined it from the Petit-St-Bernard road. Although some ninety inscriptions suggest its importance – including those concerning a number of Allobrogian magistrates – archaeological knowledge about the settlement is minimal for its early history.

The imperial crisis and restructuring of the late third and fourth centuries transformed its status; it was of course its strategic significance in the defence of two roads from Italy into Gaul that led to this. First, a massive rampart was constructed in the 280s, then Gratian (367–83) made the city a *civitas* capital with a new name: Gratianopolis – from which its modern name is derived. Gratian was a passionate Christian: perhaps the new city name and status was, in part at least, a reward for its early Christian community. It was absorbed by the Burgundians in the later fifth century, followed by the Franks in the sixth century. Though evidence is almost as thin for the late empire, recent excavations have revealed important 'palaeo-Christian' remains from late antiquity.

The ramparts

During 1962 construction of an apartment block and underground car-park in the Rue Lafayette a superb stretch of rampart was discovered – and promptly destroyed, the only record being some photographs: an act of urban renewal at any cost typical of the time. A determination to record accurately the rampart's shape, form and path has been a major feature of recent work. Apart from the remains within the new Musée de l'Ancien Evêché, there is little to see.

Rue Lafayette. At Passage Ste-Claire, a tower bereft of facing stones.

Jardin de l'Hôtel de Ville. A section of walling on the site of 'la treille de Stendhal'.

Notre-Dame area. (1) a short section supports a terrace behind the apse of the cathedral choir; (2) a partial tower, also without facing stones, is visible in the Rue Chinoise.

Musée de l'Ancien Evêché

2 Rue Trés-Clôitres
off Place Notre Dame
38000 Grenoble
Hours: 10a.m.–7p.m. Closed Tuesday

For the visitor this is the most obvious result of recent 'heritage investment', following the decision to drive a new tramway through Place Notre Dame. Its archaeological importance was known: on the edge of the *place* had stood the rampart's 'Porte Viennoise', while the modern cathedral area was thought to cover early church building. The work carried out from 1988 to 1998 brought major discoveries and this expensively fitted new museum.

Crypte archéologique

The excavations revealed a fine section of rampart, confirmed this as the site of the first cathedral, exposed a palaeo-Christian baptistery and revealed other buildings associated with the complex. The crypt is vividly evocative of the past, with excellent models and panels to clarify what was a very complicated excavation.

Rampart section. The excavations particularly demonstrated the care with which the **foundations** were laid. Stakes were rammed in the soil, establishing a preliminary base for the first blocks, then covered by a water-insulating mortar, followed by more blocks (including reused stone from public buildings and cemeteries), culminating in 3–6 courses of smaller limestone blocks forming a horizontal base for the rampart itself. This had the classic rubble mortar core with *petit appareil* facing, some 2.5m wide (the foundations could be double); it stood an estimated 8m high. A ditch 6m wide and 2m deep lay outside. A **postern gate**, giving access to people, not vehicles, is discernible next to a **semi-circular tower**, beyond which lay one of the two main gates, the Porte Viennoise. This stood until demolished in 1804 with an inscription proclaiming Diocletian authorized the rampart's construction.

The baptistery. For Françoise Boucheron, the archaeologist in charge, the real discovery was that, like Lyon and Geneva, Grenoble had once had an imposing fourth-/fifth-century baptistery. Excavation revealed an apsed rectangular area paved with marble and a central octagonal pool; subsequent alterations and repairs included reducing the pool's size and replacing the pavement. Early baptism was undertaken by adults (which accounts for the pool's size) and was the key Christian act in a period when many were still pagans. Only the bishop had the power to baptize and people came to the cathedral to be received into the Church. Before the sixth century the priesthood was limited largely to assistants, living close by; creating a parish system came later with delegated priestly powers to enforce Christianity on the *pagani* – the country people. It was a long process, particularly with fresh barbarian influxes during the fifth, sixth and seventh centuries.

Gallo-Roman museum gallery

Sadly, the design specialists have been allowed too free a hand here. Artefacts are set awkwardly low, writing is small and difficult to read, and the creation of context is minimal: almost a modern Victorian approach. It is not really clear why there are two very good models here: Vienne (an incentive perhaps to visit it?) and **Gilly villa** – but why is this not in Conflans museum, Albertville, where the best of the artefacts are displayed?

However, there are major pieces. There is a Gallic wars legionary helmet, affording much more limited protection than later versions; an attractive unprovenanced bronze Venus in a case devoted to gods; most interesting, a **bronze veterinary tool** for scraping horses' hooves, which happens to be decorated with a Minerva bust, as well as a lion's head and a man leading a horse: a name scratched on the side was perhaps the owner's, Stratilates. There is a delightful and brightly coloured mosaic of two parrots from Vienne and a **marble head**, with grapes hanging from a band round his curly hair (Bacchus?). Finally, in the link room to the medieval, a superb **gilded helmet**, perhaps a prince's, found at Vézeronce, where the Burgundians fought the Franks in 524, shortly before the collapse of their state.

St-Laurent church

Rue St-Laurent
38000 Grenoble
Hours: 10a.m.–noon, 2–6p.m. Closed Tuesday

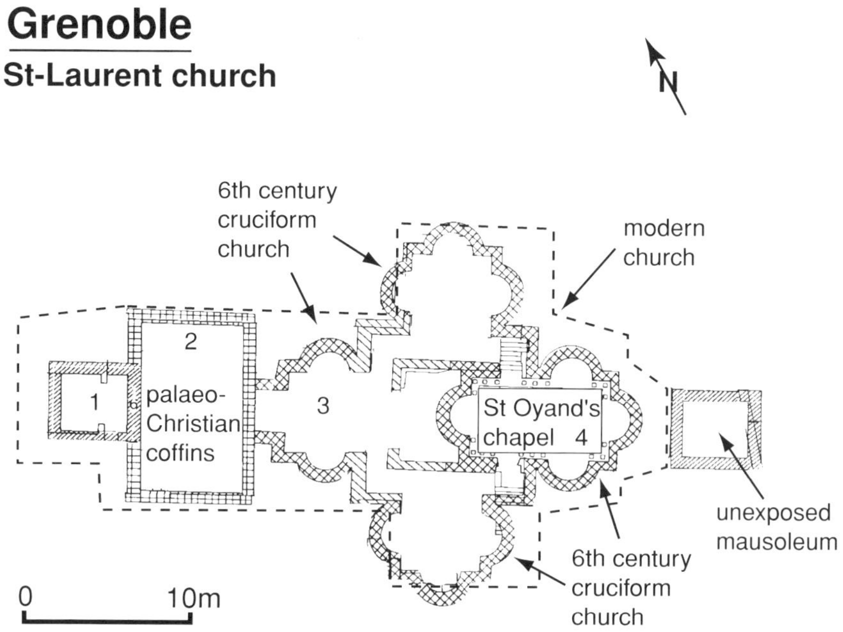

Figure 88 Grenoble: St-Laurent church

Raymond Girard began the modern excavations that culminated with Renée Colardelle's work (1970s–80s), making this one of the most thoroughly studied churches in France. Notwithstanding display panels and specially made see-through walkways, it is not easy for the visitor, though it demonstrates very effectively just how complicated archaeological stratigraphy usually is! St Laurent evolved as a typical cemetery church where Christians could feel close to their early, venerated ancestors. My concern is with the first three phases only, taking us into the seventh/eight centuries.

The earliest structures were Christian mausolea or *memoriae* erected in a late Roman necropolis. One mausoleum (1), built in the late third or fourth century, was included as part of the later church, under the bell-tower. Another (2), built in the early fifth century, contained well-made late Roman coffins, probably of an important local family: perhaps their veneration led to the decision to build the church here in the sixth/seventh century; its rectangular frame and its array of coffins can be picked out below the transparent platform. The western end of the cruciform church (3) joins the rectangle, which then became a vestibule. No other branches of the cruciform are visible, but below the eastern arm was constructed a crypt, St Oyand's (4). Its shape exactly reflects the apsed cruciform arm that once stood above, now hidden by the much later altar area. The crypt is beautiful, though it was the Carolingian colonnade which persuaded Prosper Merimée to press for its preservation (1850–1): it was being used as a wine cellar at the time.

The southern exterior has been more recently explored. Like the church itself, it is filled with fifth- to eighth-century coffins, most of them the typical undecorated trapezoidal design of the period.

HIERES-SUR-AMBY, Isère

IGN 3131 E

Sites and museum.

The Isle Crémieu limestone forms a triangular plateau almost surrounded by rivers. To the north-east and north-west the Rhône, to the south the Bourbre; in addition, much of the land at the foot of the slopes is, or was, fen. The limestone makes for good building stone, though it slices thinly, helping in the development of its use for roofing, producing the distinctive *lauze* tiles

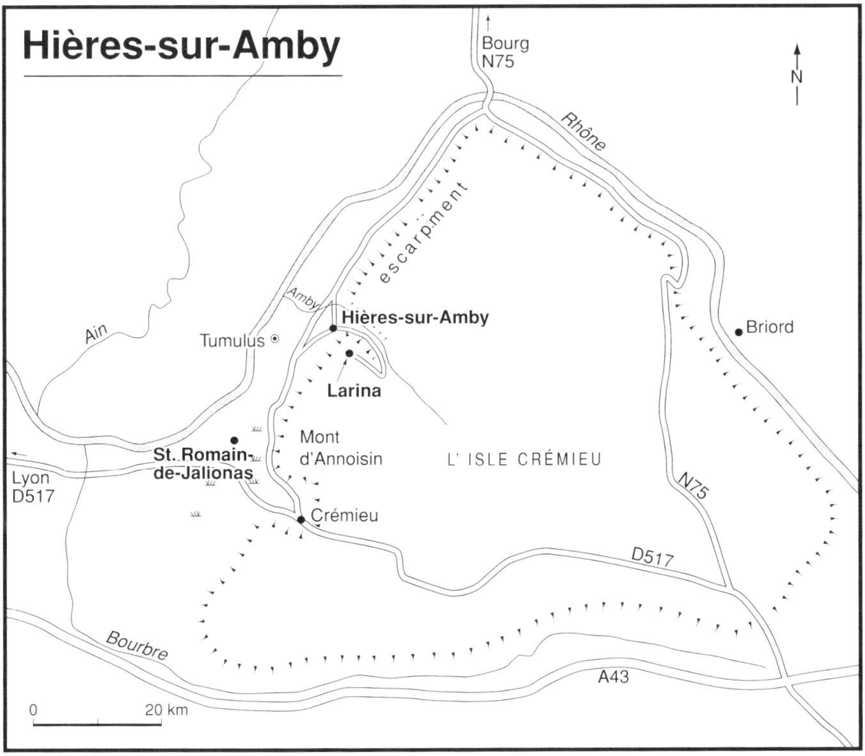

Figure 89 Hières-sur-Amby: area map

of the district. The north-western section of the Isle, with its narrow marsh plain and sharp bluffs, provides a compelling insight into the contribution archaeology can make to understanding political and economic change within a regional environment over a long period, straddling the Gallo-Roman era.

St Romain-de-Jalionas Roman villa

940.6/2096.7

Rue de l'Eglise.

4.5km north-west of Crémieu by the D517, follow the signs in the hamlet for the church or *site archéologique*, *c.*250m.

Though discovered in 1967, major work only commenced here in 1994. It quickly became clear that the villa was extremely large: 1.5ha for the *villa urbana* alone, a further 4.5ha for the *villa rustica*. The house had dozens of rooms; the farm had great barns, cowsheds and workshops, even a mill. It was also a major establishment from its surprisingly early beginning around 40 BC, virtually contemporary with the foundations in Vienne and Lyon, perhaps a rich colonist? Most difficult to understand is the choice of site: many of the rooms needed waterproofing in this damp, fenland environment and there is evidence of the need for extensive canalization on the estate and an aqueduct to bring fresh clean water from the nearest Crémieu hill, Mont d'Annoisin. Presumably the estate included upland pasture and the marshland must have been heavily exploited. Perhaps this enigma will be solved as the excavation progresses. Each year a new part is tackled and earlier work is covered over. When exposed, the baths were shown to be mainly second century, but they were also expanded unusually late in the fourth/fifth centuries. They had the standard hot and cold system, but with added pools and gardens for relaxation.

The church covers the walls of an apsed section of the villa and it is clear that this part was adapted for Christian worship while the villa was still occupied; a coffin was found inside – the first, or the last, Christian Gallo-Roman aristocrat? The villa was abandoned in the sixth century, though the church was replaced, using the earlier structure's walls for foundations: this is the church you see, with later modifications. Clearly the villa and the social structure it represented could survive Burgundian rule but not Frankish. No doubt there were people who lived nearby and worshipped here in the Merovingian period, but only a hut has been found on the site.

Maison de Patrimoine

Place de l'Eglise
318118 Hières-sur-Amby
Hours: 10a.m.–noon, 2–6p.m. (summer 7p.m.)

The 'Heritage House' focuses on changing patterns of resource exploitation, but a big stimulus to the creation of the museum was the discovery in 1987 of a late Bronze Age 'prince's' burial under one of the tumuli near the Rhône in the commune of St Romain-de-Jalionas. The **tomb** is re-created here; in death he shows his finery: a gold pin fixing his cloak, a necklace and pendant, a superb bracelet, beside him his sword and wooden sheath (fragments were found), a decorated plate at his head and, at his feet, remains of beef and a sacrificial knife made of very early iron. The importance of this burial was its implication that in the eighth century BC a 'prince' was able to command a big enough surplus to trade with both southern and central Europe, in a fashion rather like the later Celtic 'princes' of Vix (see CHATILLON). It is likely that his centre of power lay on Larina hill, though further research is needed.

Relatively little is known of early Iron Age material, but from the second and first centuries BC, more finds have been made, traces of a rampart and the 'rubbish dump' at La Chuire. This has a significant amount of metalwork, some deliberately bent. Normally this suggests a ritual context, with largely warrior material, but here we have hooks, sickles and keys. One interpretation is that **Larina** was not a conventional living site or *oppidum*, indeed few Iron Age habitations have been found here, but a site for fairs. With the emergence of the Allobroges tribe and then the Romans in the 120s, this became a frontier zone: Larina was a place for meeting and exchange between Gallia Comata, Alpine peoples and the Mediterranean world. The political scene was once again transformed by Roman conquest. Gallic fairs now gave way to the markets of city, *vicus* and villa. An enigmatic **Roman inscription dedicated to Mercury**, the god of commerce and travel, could mean that a temple replaced the fair in the 40s. This inscription is built into a wall by the church above the Maison (unreadable today). More research is needed, particularly on the role of Larina's rampart; late Roman reuse of earlier material has not made its phases easy to follow.

The museum completes its display with a brief survey of Gallo-Roman occupation in the area and a study of the later evolution of Larina showing the development of the late Roman/Burgundian occupation to the Merovingian.

Parc Archéologique de Larina

830.7/2092.3

Signposted in Hières by footpath (very steep climb) or car (6km).
Hours: open access

The visitor is helped round the site by good guide boards and display panels with reconstruction drawings.

The view westwards from here, especially in the early evening, is breathtaking, if you can somehow exclude the nuclear power station. You can imagine the sense of security the escarpment must have given to those who fled here in the late Roman period. Alternatively they could have been *coloni*, tied labourers, sent here to cut stone for more fortified centres elsewhere; they themselves using only wattle-and-daub on gravel for their simple houses. These huts disappear in the sixth century, reinforcing the picture given at St Romain-de-Jalionas villa that real cultural change came with the Franks, not the Burgundians. The new Merovingian buildings suggest a very different social structure: one massive building was constructed in stone with a *lauze* roof; it measured 38 × 9m, and was divided into various living spaces around the hearth, though inevitably modified over the three centuries it was occupied. Nearby was another large stone structure: a 'barn', not simply for animals but also workshops. This was a semi-self-sufficient community surviving on poor pasture and difficult agriculture. A harsh environment, deserted once again in the Carolingian era (early ninth century), when life became less precarious down below. It is one of the rare Merovingian living sites known.

IZERNORE, Ain

IGN 3228 OT
848.7/2141.0

Site and museum.
5.5km north-west of Nantua, by the D18; 40km due east of Bourg-en-Bresse.

A Roman secondary road through Sequani territory down one of the long north–south valleys in the Jura linked Lons-le-Saunier with the Geneva road to Lyon. On a plateau at the southern end, Izernore was a sizeable settlement with a large temple, extensive bath complex, widely spread housing including a shop and forge, a grid street system and a number of associated villas. In a region without major cities, Izernore must have been a market centre and sanctuary of some significance. What it offers is a picture of exploration without much archaeology, despite the heroic efforts of R. Chevallier in the 1960s and early 1970s.

Temple

Road to Le Voërle, 300m east of the village centre.

The temple at Izernore is a genuine ruin, bruised and battered. In the first excavations in the early eighteenth century about the only positive achievement was to rebuild three of the corner pillars. It was pillaged for the next 150 years; the removal of building stone and the search for inscriptions, coin hoards or bronzes (two ended up in the British Museum) left a confusing wreck that even R. Chevallier had difficulty sorting out, although he was able to show it had at least one rebuilding and probably more. You can tell it was once an impressive sight: 32 × 19m in size, built of massive blocks and decorated with fine marble and limestone facings. It probably had an internal *cella* surrounded by a gallery, consisting of pillars with engaged columns. Lateral walls may have projected to form the sides of a front staircase, but the actual design remains obscure. The site is still covered with a mixture of well-cut and unfinished blocks (once hidden in the structure), mouldings and even an inscription commemorating a vow made by Tutellus to Mercury. The bath complex was 100m to the north, but was dug and re-covered in the nineteenth century.

Musée Gallo-Romain

Mairie
01580 Izernore
Hours: on application to the Mairie, except Tuesday

The geophysical surveys, aerial photography and sondages helped give a grasp of the settlement as a whole over its first- to fifth-century history, but the museum is still one largely of scraps. From the temple are marble and floral painted plaster fragments and a finger from a bronze statue. More interesting are the finds from the nearby **Bussy and Pérignat villas**, both excavated shortly before the First World War. The gallery villa at Bussy produced a sundial, though this does not seem to be displayed. From Pérignat came a considerable amount of metalwork showing the range of rural life: sickles, pruning knives and billhooks, artisans' hammers and gouges, firedogs for the house. Most striking, though, is the large lead basin, decorated with lions chasing gazelles, and part of the water distribution system (for a bath?) with a sprinkler head on the end of a pipe.

LYON, Rhône

Blay-Foldex: Lyon

Sites and museums.
www.marie-lyon.fr

Forget your horror of big-city driving and do not despair at the confusion created by two rivers and their many bridges. To neglect Lyon is to miss one of the truly breathtaking settings for a Roman theatre and one of the great museums.

Lyon offers many more pleasures, though tinged with regret that so much has been lost. Tensions between those insisting on modernization and those wishing to preserve physical evidence of our past are ever-present, but they have been especially characteristic of Lyon's development. It is not surprising

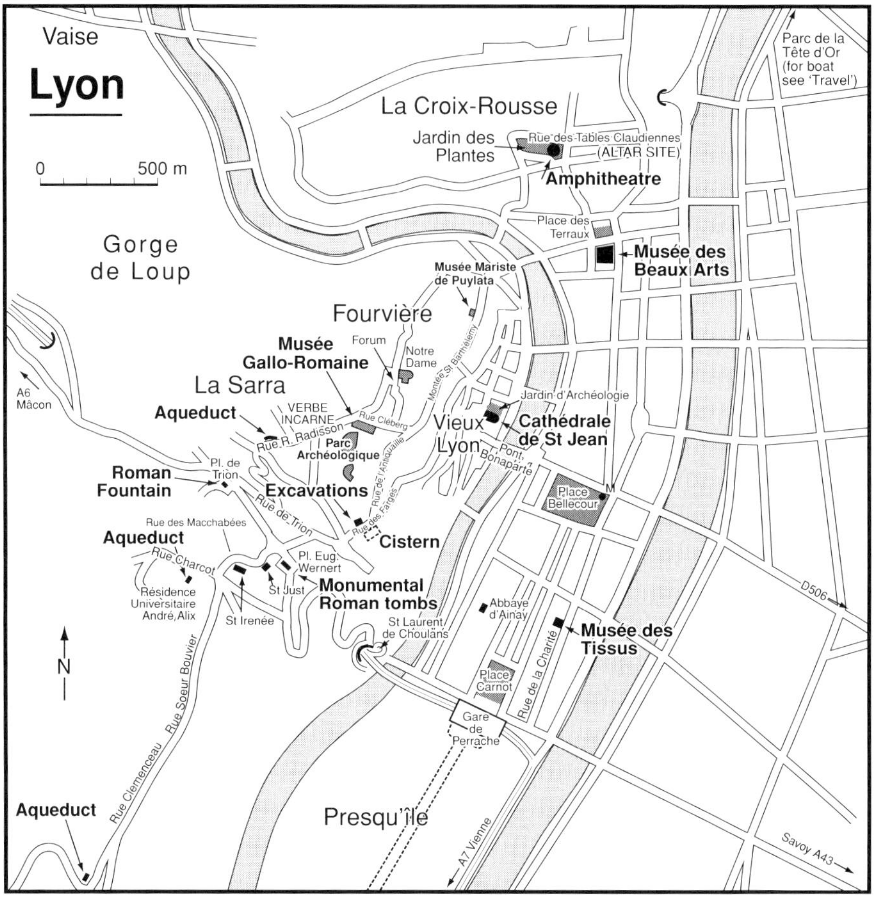

Figure 90 Lyon: town plan

perhaps that the forum site became a quarry when the new medieval Gothic cathedral of St Jean was built, or that the abbey church (St Martin's) of Ainay used Egyptian marbles (cut in half) to line its nave: those are the products of an era when a single-faith society could take brutal and simplistic decisions without reflection. Preservation is still pitifully limited. The largest excavation of the 1980s (Verbe Incarné) resulted in three column drums being used as a nondescript decorative feature at the entrance to new private apartments and the re-erection of a Claudian fountain half a mile away. Yet it is better now than in the 1960s and 1970s: then the new metro lines were driven through with a conscious disdain for Lyon's heritage, 'un véritable désastre', not redeemed by the one mosaic rescued and displayed in Bellecour station.

Nevertheless, both Germain de Montauzon and Amiable Audin have been publicly honoured. Montauzon's magisterial survey of the Lyon aqueducts helped preserve many surviving sections. Audin, who dominated Lyon archaeology from the 1930s to the 1970s, established the Parc Archéologique from his great Fourvière hillside excavations revealing the theatre and odeon, housing, streets, shops and temples. At the same time he organized the exploration and conservation of the surviving half of the amphitheatre. He was rightly rewarded with the curatorship of the new museum in 1975. Audin was possibly the last of the great classical archaeologists whose assumptions have been severely challenged by the generation emerging at the end of the 1970s, who came from the professional and science-based tradition. Leading figures have included Bernard Mandy, who organized the Verbe Incarné excavations, and Armand Desbat, who undertook investigations of Lyon pottery workshops and with a CNRS team carried out new sondages in the Parc Archéologique. Lyon has at least been prepared to fund these rescue digs and their publication, even if relatively little of their work has resulted in new visible evidence.

Since Strabo's day, Lyon has seemed demonstrably the hub of communications between the north and south of Gaul together with reasonable east–west links (see TRAVEL AND COMMUNICATIONS). It had an obvious strongpoint in Fourvière hill; multiple riverside banks with plenty of space for the development of quays, warehouses and housing; and available for exploitation were the river valleys, the Ain plain and the Monts du Lyonnais, a rich variety of land for agriculture and industry. There is no evidence that these merits were obvious to the Gauls: Fourvière was high and had no water; the alluvium below was unstable and liable to flooding. No evidence has been found of Gallic settlement anywhere in the core areas of the Roman city. Transitory and fragmentary Iron Age remains have been found, but in the suburban area of Vaise. Admittedly we have a Gallic name: Lug. If a god, no temple has been found and opinion now favours a word origin describing a hill (*dunum*) of 'luminous light': a perfect name for a hill that looked due east, upon which the sun glows with such a bright intensity.

Pre-Roman political reality also may have helped prevent occupation. It was on the fringe of two tribes whose focus lay elsewhere: the Segusiavi in the Loire and the Allobroges, whose heartland was the Savoy Alps, already had a Rhône capital further south at Vienne. The Rhône–Saône junction was at this time a marker, not a heart.

Did the Romans immediately see the strategic value of the Lyon site? Perhaps. The Roman colony of Lugdunum was founded by Lucius Munatus Plancus, governor of Gallia Comata in 43 BC. He had been a legate with Caesar fifteen years before during the Gallic wars; possibly he was fulfilling a proposal of Caesar's. There may have been a temporary base here during the wars, but current opinion sees chance playing a part. In 44/43 BC the Allobroges drove the Roman colonists from Vienne; they fled to the security offered by Lyon. On their arrival, Plancus and his colleague Lepidus, governor of Transalpine Gaul, faced the sensitive question of restoring order without exacerbating antagonisms. The solution was a compromise: the settlers were not reimposed on the Allobroges and Vienne was permitted to retain its 'Latin' colony status; the settlers were given Lyon and the surrounding territory together with the highest status possible, that of a 'Roman' colony. Perhaps it mollified revenge, but not suspicions.

It was Agrippa in 39 BC who made Lyon the axis of Roman Gaul by creating the major road arteries to complement the rivers. It was Augustus himself who made this an imperial capital, when the three-province structure was established, probably when he came to Gaul in 26 BC. The Gallo-Roman city developed in three main areas. First, on Fourvière hill: this was the colony itself and the centre of imperial administration. Second, on the lower slopes of Croix-Rousse hill, Condate: the meeting place of the Gallic peoples. Third, the settlement on Presqu'île, Canabae: often mistakenly seen as simply a commercial centre. In addition there were the suburbs, close by the riverbanks or mixing with the cemeteries beyond the formal city limits. In the second century, the population may have been anything between 50–100,000.

Modern excavations have clarified just how dramatic growth was in the early years. Traces of ditches on Fourvière were probably those made by the first colonists (though further discoveries might clarify the question of any earlier Roman military occupation). Both Verbe Incarné and Rue des Farges excavations showed houses, workshops and shops being built of earthen bricks, cob and wood between 40 and 20 BC. Formal roads with pavements and porticoes marked a second phase. Main roads were angled to minimize the gradient, but on top *insulae* were being built on a regular grid pattern and terracing with stone supporting walls was taking the town down the hillside. New housing was replacing old, initially still earth and wood, but with painted plaster interiors and constructed around peristyles, typical of southern Roman Gaul. To appreciate such homes, it is essential to go 30km south to Lyon's traditional 'enemy' and see the homes of the rich of Vienne where the foundations of the suburb at St Romain-en-Gal have been superbly excavated, peristyle gardens re-created, and their mosaics and wall paintings preserved in a gleaming 1990s museum. Here you can see how the elite of Lyon must have lived.

Colonia Copia ('prosperous') Felix ('happy') Munatia was built to impress. The Augustan and Tiberian programme of enhancement of the Gallic capital was remarkable. We know a great forum was laid out on the site of the later Nôtre Dame de Fourvière; we can see the scale of the theatre and odeon; the excavations of Verbe Incarné have revealed that an enormous temple, dedicated to the imperial cult, was constructed under Tiberius, and the most costly Lyon public structure of all, the Gier aqueduct, is now considered to be early first century (as well as the much smaller Mont d'Or aqueduct). The Gier must have been finished by the time of Claudius (41–54), as both public baths and fountains were opened on the hill as part of his programme to

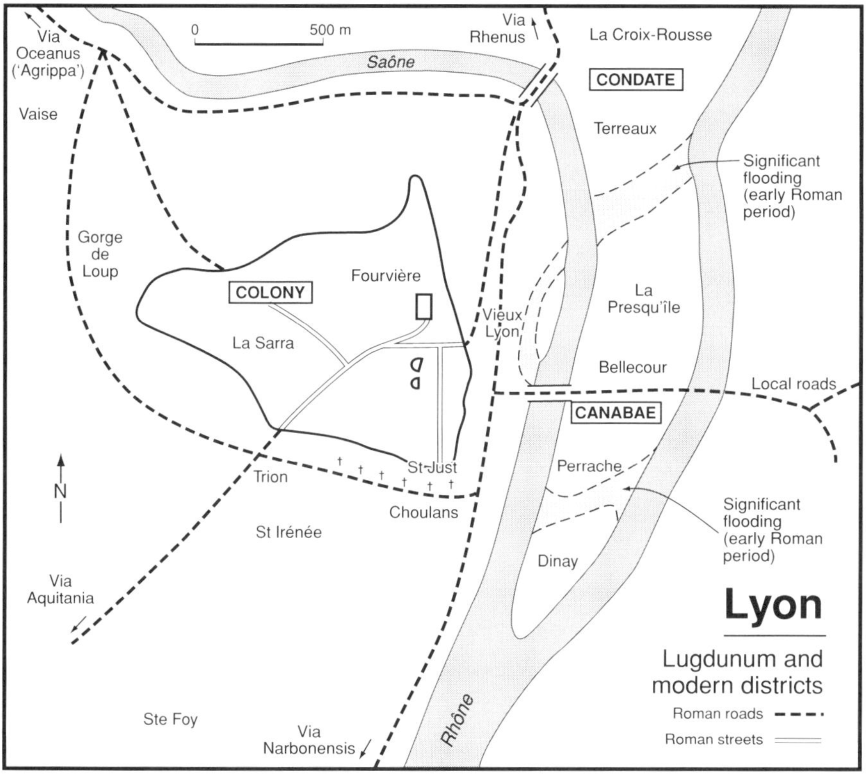

Figure 91 Lyon: Roman town and districts

celebrate the city of his birth, newly named Colonia Copia Claudia Augusta Lugdunum. The high status of the governor here was ensured by the presence of troops, initially drawn from the Rome legions, subsequently replaced in the second century by an urban cohort, an elite force with only one other cohort based outside Rome (in Carthage); these men provided a mix of governor's guard and civil service administrators. Lyon was probably used as the main tax collection centre for the Gallic provinces; certainly a mint was maintained here for many years. At some time and presumably in the Trion area, the only flat site large enough, a circus was built. No rampart has been found and no triumphal arches; it is difficult to believe that the city did not have these as well.

Condate sanctuary was an even more overtly imperial initiative. Augustus came again to Gaul in 16–15 BC to prepare for the German conquest. One of the initiatives he took must have been to order the grandiose altar at which the tribes of Gaul could dedicate themselves to Rome and its emperor. In 12 BC, Drusus, Augustus' stepson, on the brink of leading an army into

Germany came to meet the tribal delegates and lead the proceedings. Short-term, it must have been to strengthen loyalty while the legions campaigned and to win acceptance from those who would raise tribute (taxes) in Gaul; long-term, it would be to convert any surviving traditions of common tribal interests into a harmless demonstration of loyalty and a lesson in Roman rewards by title: being a *sacerdos* (priest) for this altar became a major attribute recorded on your tomb. The amphitheatre built beside the altar served both as a meeting place and for games celebrating the dedications. The arrival in August of the great men and their retinues from the provinces must have provided a sounding board for imperial officials concerning Gallic opinion – and a major source of income for Lyon's business people. Inevitably the slopes of La Croix-Rousse were covered with buildings. It was linked to the colony by a bridge across the Saône.

Presqu'île had never been a stable environment, but from the first century onwards it became less disturbed. This seems to have been partly the result of river dynamics (the turbulent Rhône cutting its own deeper course) and partly the Roman effort to make it habitable. Excavations at four new metro stations in the early 1990s showed that Presqu'île was probably not divided into different islands but had hollows that earlier were subject to flooding, but increasingly secured with embankments and insulating layers of amphorae. Canabae undoubtedly had workshops and warehouses but also rich houses, perhaps the residences of leading merchants. The magnificent circus mosaic (see pages 409–13) comes from a *domus* in Rue Jarente near Bellecour. A bridge crossed the Saône from below Fourvière and then crossed the Rhône to the east. The banks of both rivers must have been lined with quays for the trans-shipment of goods coming up from Arles. Equally Gallic textiles from Belgica and building stone from up the Rhône at Belley would be loading and unloading here.

During the early empire, demand from the frontiers of Germany and Britain must have been especially important in stimulating growth. The need for food and wine, first from Italy and then from Spain, the need for fine pottery and metalware, all stimulated trade and local production. As the inscriptions of Lyon show, it was a cosmopolitan place, a true corridor of commerce. Though the military began to satisfy some of its own needs (eg Köln glass), Lyon had established itself as the cornerstone entrepôt of the Gallic provinces and it is debatable how significant economic difficulties were before the third century. The martyrdoms of 177 might have a social and economic basis; the defeat of Albinus and Lyon's mistake in supporting him against Severus in a battle outside their city in 197 certainly hurt the colony: it did not benefit from the Severan building bonanza of the 200s. A number of the Fourvière sites show that hill-top homes were being steadily abandoned. Equally fewer delegates came to Condate and with growing unwillingness. Conversely, settlement by the rivers continued and even grew. The focus of Lyon became the right bank of the Saône and the south of Presqu'île. Here was the future centre of Lyon.

No coherent picture of late Roman Lyon has yet emerged, but it did not suffer catastrophic decline in the way many towns experienced it further north. Large houses continue to be occupied and the scale of tombs put up in fourth-century cemeteries surely reflects some continued prosperity. Convincing remains of late Roman defences have not been found, but fourth- and fifth-century writers mention ramparts; it has been presumed that these must have been under the later medieval walling, destroyed in the seventeenth century. Yet decline did occur. The impact of the restructuring of the empire carried out by Diocletian (281–304) reduced Lyon's status significantly, and increased that of Vienne. As tax-collecting was replaced by collection in kind, so the massive warehouses of Vienne took over and it became the key imperial city of the Rhône corridor. Lyon was reduced to the status of capital of the small province of Lugdunensis Prima, replaced by Trier for the diocese covering northern Gaul; Vienne was made first city of the new southern diocese.

Some sense of these changes is provided by J.-F. Reynaud's examination of early church building in Lyon. His work has shown that those structures put up in the late fourth and early fifth century during the final years of unstable imperial rule were poorly made, but from the mid-fifth century improvements began which were not hurt by Burgundian rule (469), confirming Sidonius Apollinaris' letters admiring their splendour. The 177 martyrdom confirms there was a bishop in the second century, though the names suggest this was an Eastern/Greek community and therefore likely to have been small; but there is a continuous and accepted bishops' list showing that the community was not destroyed and by the late fourth and fifth century was strong enough to create a major episcopal centre and a number of churches in the new neighbourhoods. Reynaud notes another fall in the quality of church construction in the mid-sixth century; following Frankish conquest in 534, Lyon simply became a town on the southern fringe of the Merovingian world.

THE SITES

Jean Burdy and André Pelletier's excellent *Guide de Lyon Gallo-Romain* (1997) provides a comprehensive description of every scrap of Roman stone exposed in the city. Jean-François Reynaud's *Lyon: aux premier temps chrétiens* (1986) is also still useful.

THE RIGHT BANK OF THE SAONE

Forum

Place de Fourvière

The enormous Augustan Forum Vetus (140 × 75m) was the political and social centre of the colony. It is now covered by the Place. The shining white

Nôtre Dame rises up on the foundations of a temple, whose stones were removed to help build the cathedral complex below in Vieux Lyon. Nothing equals the view from here for making clear the contrasting elements of hills, rivers and plain in the origins and growth of the city.

Sanctuary of the Three Gauls. It is far easier to imagine from here than anywhere else. Strabo describes how 'the temple that was dedicated to Caesar Augustus by all the Gauls in common is situated in front of the city at the junction of the two rivers' (IV, 3, 2). The diorama by the balcony identifies the amphitheatre in the Jardin des Plantes, below and to the right of the Bon Pasteur bell-tower. Massive foundation blocks were found running eastwards from the amphitheatre supporting an esplanade of over 300m in length and at least 70m wide, now covered by the Rue Burdeau and Rue des Tables Claudiennes. It must have been awe-inspiring: a great garlanded altar, sixty statues representing the tribes of Gaul, perhaps a great statue of Augustus, victories and a series of subsidiary alcoves and columns. Surrounding it would have been dedications from the various delegations attending their annual council to celebrate the triumph of Rome. This was an image of imperial power using the hillside of Croix-Rousse to maximize the lustre of bronze, marble and limestone.

Verbe Incarné site

24 Rue Roger Radisson to Rue P.M. Jelicot

This prosperous modern estate covers the most extensive (4ha) excavation carried out in recent years in Lyon. See the pitiful jumble of Gallo-Roman stonework tastefully collected at one of the entrances.

Evidence was found here of occupation from 40 BC onwards. The initial modest wooden houses were soon followed by an Augustan grid of porticoed roads dividing the area into a series of *insulae* on which new housing was built. Under Tiberius a great **imperial cult sanctuary** was constructed at the western end, subsequently linked under Claudius with the forum by a new monumental road. At the same time, the arrival of aqueduct water must have eased living up here. The surrounding *insulae* showed mixed occupation ranging from densely occupied double-storied houses, to a **peristyle *domus***, traces of which were first found in the 1920s when it was considered a possible imperial palace, now maybe a special dining house for the *seviri*, the imperial cult priests. From the early third century the area was being abandoned: part of a general decline or a break in aqueduct supplies? Or was it simply the inconvenience of life here as the town's focus moved down to the riverside?

Parc Archéologique

Rue Cléberg or Rue de l'Antiquaille

Free access.	15 April–16 September	7a.m.–9p.m.
	15 September–14 April	7a.m.–7p.m.

'Temple of Cybele'. The park above the terrace walling is dominated by the foundations of a large precinct (86 × 53m). Around this was a range of buildings, some shops, others finely decorated, as the re-erected column drums suggest. Finding a crowned marble head of a woman, usually associated with Cybele, and nearby a *taurobolium*, the altar recording a bull sacrifice associated with her cult, led Audin to describe this as one of the largest

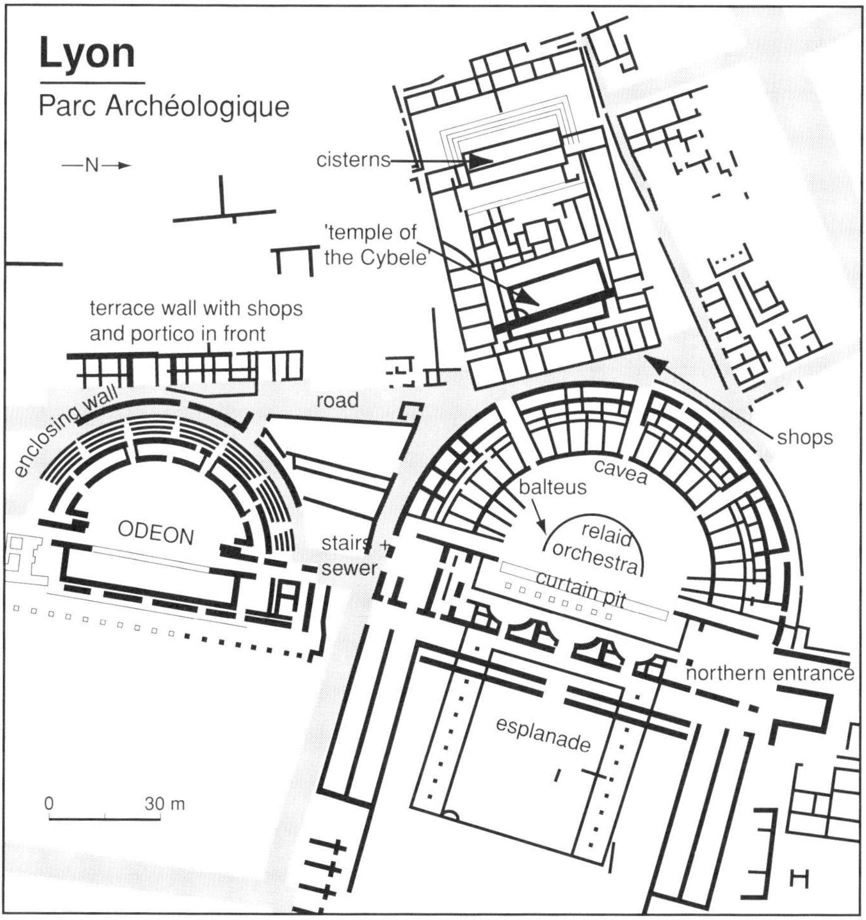

Figure 92 Lyon: Parc Archéologique

Cybele sanctuaries found. He presumed it was dated by the *taurobolium* to AD 160. New sondages made by Desbat suggest the identification of these complex remains is wrong.

First, the shops facing the road at the front belonged to a large building preceding the precinct. This was a sumptuous *domus* built *c.*20 BC, so grand that Desbat was tempted to suggest it could have been a governor's palace or Agrippa's residence. Some of the lower walling belongs to the *domus*. Second, dating evidence suggests the precinct is not AD 160, but AD 10–20. Work continues on identifying it, but it is widely agreed now to be too early for a Cybele temple and the supporting evidence is much too weak.

Reservoir. Much easier to recognize are the two big chambers of a water cistern, constructed late in the first century, which must have been filled by the Gier aqueduct. Note the various supply and drainage tunnels in the area where current work might bring greater understanding of the distribution system from here, both original and modified. The reservoir was barrel vaulted and originally had two compartments above as well (this is why no access point can be seen). The drain in the middle of the concave floor allowed sediment to be cleared; the red cement lining was highly waterproof.

Roads and shops. Between the terrace wall and the road was a line of shops and portico. Successive remodelling and the construction of the odeon changed the road. One shop with a basin might have been a laundry or fuller's.

Plate 33 Lyon. The theatre and odeon dominate the Parc Archéologique. Photograph: François Guy, Agence d'Urbanisme, Lyon.

Theatre. Audin's excavation and restoration of the theatre took place between 1933 and 1943. The **leading citizens' places** are re-laid and so are the marble pavings of the **orchestra floor**; the ***balteus*** (the wall behind the seats of honour) is re-erected. The ***cavea* seats** are all replacements and the blocks with names are copies of those in the museum. The stage machinery pit is covered most of the time with a wooden platform. Of the great *scaena* building that would have backed the stage only a few blocks survive (see Orange for the real thing). The restoration has enabled many to enjoy live entertainment as their Gallo-Roman predecessors did, but inevitably it has been frustrating for archaeologists as new excavation and sondages have been difficult. Even so, modern sondages and careful re-examination of 1930s photographs have not undermined the belief that the original theatre was Augustan. We now know this covered earlier housing and was twice modified later. It always had a diameter of 108.5m, but there was a wooden upper tier carried at first on timber, then on the semi-circular stone vaulted rear corridor. This in turn was replaced by stone seating with **strengthening radiating foundations** cutting up the **corridors**. Best preserved is the large **northern entrance**: traces of marble veneer hint at how the theatre must have sparkled in the sun; 10,500 could enjoy performances here.

Odeon. The odeon is later, probably mid-second century. Holding 3,000, this too was big: Lugdunum must have had a cultured audience indeed if it really was used for lectures, poetry and music. The *cavea*'s sixteen-row **lower tier** has survived, but only the **huge foundations and rear-enclosing wall** of the upper tier remain. The strength of this walling, some of it with apertures, suggests the odeon had rafters to carry roofing. The **five doors** from the back street still have their thresholds. The two lateral doors led to the free top tier; the middle two led down to the closer seats and would have had pay desks. The flooring of the **orchestra** has been re-set with its mix of marbles from Italy, Greece and Egypt. Again, a fragment of the *balteus* has been re-erected to indicate where only the most privileged could sit. A hidden gutter carried rainwater under the building.

Odeon esplanade. Leading down between the theatres were stairs and a sewer to a latrine area. These steps then led on to an esplanade, a suitable monumental frame for the theatres. Crossing this area brings you to the Rue de l'Antiquaille entrance.

Other sites on the right bank

Rue des Farges remains

6–10 Rue des Farges

On the north side of the street below the Lycée Jean Moulin, behind a block of modern housing; access via pedestrian passages to rear of building. Signposted 'Thermes Romains'.

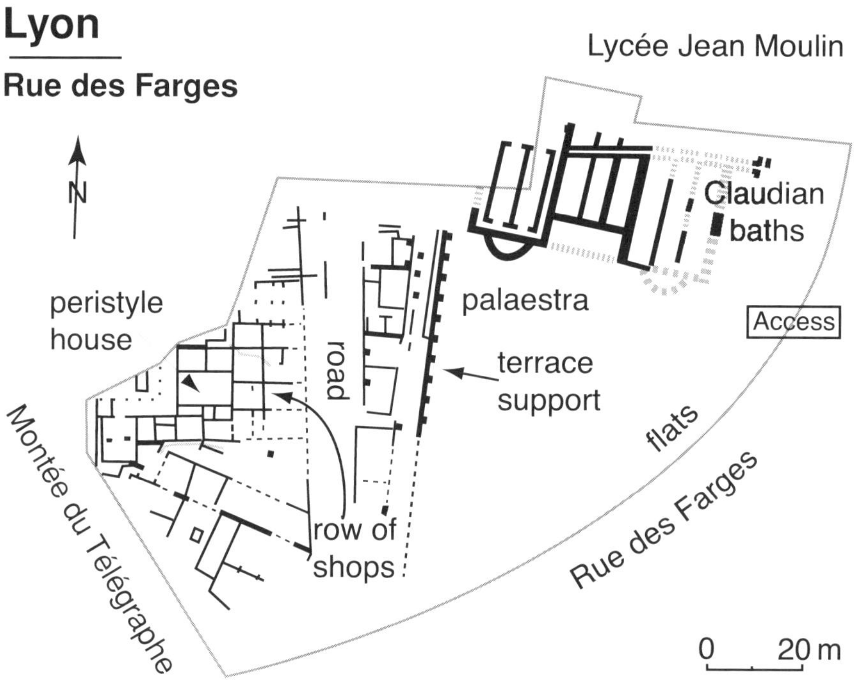

Figure 93 Lyon: Rue des Farges site

This site saw the first extended excavations in Lyon (1974–80) outside the Parc Archéologique, though permission was denied to link the two sites together. When the *lycée* was built, it became clear that large Roman baths existed in the area. The new building scheme next door led to the exposure of the south-west corner of the **Claudian public baths** and further west on the hill-slope, **Roman terracing** which is split by a **road**, running at an angle to ensure a gradual gradient.

The best view is from the top (useful table plan) looking down over three terraces, now covered by grass, but occasionally exposing the stone bulwarks holding the terracing in place. Excavation showed occupation from the early years of Augustus, suggesting the colony had rapidly filled the hilltop itself. The first houses, shops and storage rooms here were wood, earth and plaster, but from the second and third decades of the first century AD stone housing was replacing these. On the top terrace there was even a peristyle house, decorated with theatre masks.

The baths transformed the bottom terrace in the 40s/50s. A new terrace support became the outside wall of the *palaestra*. Drains and culverts indicate the water supply and disposal needs of the baths. On the east side the apsed and vaulted foundations of cellars, probably used for storing fuel, must have been below a hot bath system (*caldarium* and *tepidarium*); the excavators found the collapsed remains of mosaic and marble flooring and fine painted plaster walling. A municipal tile stamp confirmed the baths' public status.

Esplanade of the Lycée de St-Just

Rue des Farges

Beneath the esplanade are the best Gallo-Roman remains of Lyon: the large cistern called La Grotte Berelle. Perhaps one day it may be opened to visitors.

It is possible the garrison barracks stood here and the cistern was theirs, though no single piece of evidence is very convincing. The cistern has been compared with a known military example in Gaul; a mess-room altar was found here; and, in the sixteenth century, a coining blank was found nearby. If this indicates the presence of the mint, then the army must have been close.

Military tombstone

43 Rue des Farges

A few metres down the alley, on the right hand side, is an epitaph to a soldier belonging to Legio XXX. It seems the administrative posting suited him: he died aged 90!

Grandiose tombs

Place Eugène-Wernert

Five of the largest mausolea discovered in an early empire cemetery during railway construction work along the line of the Trion were reconstructed here shortly afterwards. The largest has a frieze of bulls' heads and garlands. The finest commemorates Quintus Calvius Turpio, a *sevir* or priest of the imperial cult. The statue was found near to the mausoleum rather than in the alcove. The other three tombs are smaller; one mentions a Julia.

Early Christian church ('St-Just')

13–15 Rue des Macchabées

An open site by the new residential block of Les Minimes, looking out to the Saône and Rhône rivers. Excavated by Reynaud during the 1970s.

The Trion road marked the limits of the colony proper. In the fourth century this suburb was abandoned for burials. The body of a well-known ascetic, Saint Justus, who had died in the Egyptian desert, was returned to his birthplace for burial. By his tomb, **a late fourth-/early fifth-century**

small apsed church was built. No trace of the mausoleum remains, but the outline of the church is preserved with red metal structures; Sidonius Apollinaris (*Letters*, V, 17), a prominent Lyon aristocrat, bishop and great letter writer, describes a sumptuous commemorative service (469) in an underground gallery on the west of the church. Yellow metal is used to recall the larger **transept-style sixth-century church**. Lined up on the east and south are numbers of simple fourth- and fifth-century **sarcophagi**. Skeletal studies showed that, though a number of people reached their seventies (more men than women), the majority had life expectancies in the twenties. Note the nineteenth-century **fountain with the reused *taurobolium***, a water pipe projecting from the bull's mouth.

St-Irenée church

63 Rue des Macchabées
Crypt open Saturday 3–5p.m. The *curé* may open it at other times.

This nineteenth-century church stands on a crypt once itself a fifth-century church; however, the crypt was heavily restored in 1863. It is a gloomy place.

Audin excavated here, followed by Reynaud in the late 1970s. St-Irenée, like St-Just, developed as a necropolis church. Although Irenaeus was an early fourth-century bishop, he only really became a cult figure in the fifth century (mentioned by Gregory of Tours). The earliest remains found were fifth century, but building went through many subsequent phases.

In the courtyard are reused sarcophagi. One records the 'sanctissimi Ordini' that is the *ordo* or council of decurions, the municipal government of the colony. A dark, narrow, sloping passage leads down to the crypt and is lined with early Christian memorials. Not only is it a less clinical context than the Musée Gallo-Romain, but also there are French translations of the inscriptions, which the museum lacks. Among the oldest are 'Merola Clarissima Femina' (Merola, most distinguished lady) and, 'Procula a terra ad martyres' (Procula, interred beside the martyrs). In the crypt itself, the bishop's tomb stood in an apse, the (restored) polygonal version of which was fashionable in the seventh century.

See LYONNNAIS AQUEDUCTS for the remains in Fort St-Irenée.

Roman fountain

Place de Trion

The Place marks the junction of the Aquitaine, Narbonensis and Ocean roads. In the tiny tree-shaded park stands a large basin bubbling with piped water to form a fountain much as it must have been in the first century AD – but not here. On the pillar behind the fountain, CL AUG can be seen cut into the stone (once filled with bronze letters), recording its erection by Claudius

(44–54) – on the top of La Sarra hill inside the city. It was found when the Verbe Incarné site was excavated and was crucial in demonstrating the Gier aqueduct must have been early first century and not mid-second century. At least here it gives pleasure in a lively environment more like a Roman city street than a modern apartment estate.

St-Laurent-de-Choulans

Quai Fulchiron

Remains preserved at the foot of an office block constructed inside a curve of motorway access road by the Pont Kitchener. Large glass windows surround most of the excavation, but a staircase leads up to a walkway inside the building from which you can look down on to the preserved plan of this early church.

Investigated by Audin, then Reynaud, it is a late sixth-/early seventh-century church with apse, transept, side naves and external porticoes on each side. The most striking feature of the surviving remains is the large number of stone coffins filling the aisles and the portico areas (see also GRENOBLE).

Cathedral of St-Jean and Jardin d'Archéologie

Place St-Jean, Vieux Lyon

The medieval cathedral is attractive in an incoherent way and a careful look along the front suggests the reuse of Roman brick and stone. Bishops are known fairly continuously from the later second century, and Christian Lyon was important enough to hold a number of church councils from 470 onwards. Sidonius describes (*Letters*, II, 2) the cathedral at the time of this first council. It is clear this was not one church but a complex consisting of two main churches, **St-Jean** and **Ste-Croix**, and a baptistery church, **St Etienne**.

Inside St-Jean, 2m under the transept cross, are the remains of the fifth-century apse, the only section of Sidonius' church that is known (nothing is visible and at the time of writing the crypt is dangerous due to asbestos). During the Revolution, both Ste-Croix and St-Etienne were severely damaged. Nothing survives of the early Ste-Croix, though a late Roman heated room was found when clearing the site; it is the medieval Gothic Ste-Croix that is partially restored in the Jardin.

The **fourth-century baptismal font** lay at the heart of St Etienne and was the second built here. It is octagonal and had eight pillars around it. The battered side is original; the other, faced with marble, is modern. The lead pipe, with its typical Roman triangular section, brought the water in and a drain opposite took it out. Large fonts were necessary in the early Christian world: baptism was undertaken relatively late in life as sins committed thereafter were considered to result in eternal damnation.

Riverfront wall (30m). During the early empire, the zone below Fourvière that eventually became Vieux Lyon was only gradually consolidated with fill and embanking. During the second century housing and commercial property filled the area. This wall was first constructed in the late Roman period and served as a quay, church enclosure and rampart. However, it is not quite what it seems. Fear of vandalism led the excavators to remove the massive blocks, brought from the Sanctuary of the Three Gauls, to the safety of the museum and to substitute reproductions.

Canabae

For those involved in commerce the advantages of a location between the rivers were obvious despite the risks of flooding and Canabae was occupied from early on. Traces of quays and warehousing, low-quality accommodation and fine *domus* have been found in many parts of the Presqu'île. Whether the unpredictable Rhône changed course in the late Roman period, or less was being done to secure the land, overall occupation declined, though in the central zone the third century saw intensive use and there were still many people living here in the fifth and sixth centuries. Of the remains, fleetingly revealed, only one has been preserved even near its find spot.

Bellecour metro station mosaic

Entrance in Place Bellecour for Line A to Bonnevay. The mosaic has been set upright in the wall. It comes from what was a luxurious house excavated in Place Ampère. Using black, white and red *tesserae*, designed with a series of geometric patterns around a central area, it takes a carpet-like form. This kind of decoration was used extensively by Rhône valley mosaic workshops in the second century.

CONDATE

Amphitheatre

Jardin des Plantes

Subsidence on the steep slope, the removal of good stonework and later building have led to the disappearance of most Roman building on Croix-Rousse. Audin's 1950s excavation in the old Jardin des Plantes revealed traces of two-thirds of the original elliptical shape. Unfortunately, fencing keeps visitors from entering the dusty red arena and exploring the remains closely.

The amphitheatre of AD 19 was relatively small by later standards, with an arena of 68 × 42m and a single tier of seating around it, though even this involved cutting into the hillside and shoring up the south side. Some thirty years after building, the podium securing the onlookers from the arena was embellished with massive limestone blocks and a parapet, painted red and probably topped with a metal grill. In the 130s, Caius Julius Celsus, Hadrian's procurator, the financial administrator for Lugdunensis, massively modified it. More bedrock had to be cut out and new foundations constructed to the south to support two rows of arcades and an expanded seating area to include another tier and probably an attic above: it could now hold 20,000 people. Its later history is not known.

The amphitheatre was an adjunct of the altar (see Forum), where the delegates could hold meetings and then watch the annual August festival. There is little to show how the amphitheatre was used for the delegates' meetings though loyal speeches must have formed a part. Suetonius (*Lives*, IV, 20) explains that Caligula held oratory contests here – perhaps training for panegyrics – as well as games. Amphitheatres were often used to assert the state's power. Common criminals would be held after trial in the governor's prison, to be brought here and fed to the beasts or killed in other dramatic ways as part of the summer's entertainment. Among the many hundreds who must have died as public warnings was Mariccus, 'a champion of the people' and self- proclaimed god, who led a rising among the Boii in AD 69 and died here on the orders of the Emperor Vitellius. In 177, six Christians were arrested. Eusebius (*c.*260–340) describes how the 90-year-old bishop Pothius died after a beating in his prison and depicts the slaughter of the rest in graphic detail (Ecclesiastical History, V, 1). The post erected in the arena today recalls how one – Blondina – was displayed, then whipped, grilled and finally gored to death by a bull. The body was then exposed for six days, burnt, and the ashes thrown in the Rhône. More prosaically, if Eusebius can be trusted, it shows an organized church in second-century Lyon, even if limited to its Greek community.

Musée de la Civilisation Gallo-Romaine

17 Rue Cléberg
Hours: 10a.m.–6p.m. Closed Monday

For me, this museum is one of the great successes of 1960s design, enhancing as it does a great collection. Built in the then fashionable concrete, it is refined and smooth, the overriding sense of pale grey merging with the gentle, worn, almost ivory-yellow of the Roman stonework, only occasionally broken by other colours. This is not a museum setting out to re-create the life and vitality of the past, but rather the reflective sense of time and continuity. The entry is from above, and the visitor passes down through three floors, broadly following a chronological ramp, but still divided into 'rooms', really open sections separated by low walls and joined by short staircases, each with its own theme.

Rooms I–IV. These rooms deal with Lugdunum's beginnings, its topography and how, through Condate, it embodied Gaul's relationship as a whole with Rome and its emperor. The most important material on Lyon's birth comes from Italy: the imposing aristocratic **statue of Plancus** is a copy and the key **inscription** recalling his foundation of the colony comes from his great circular mausoleum in Gaeta (Latium). Plancus was a survivor, who, as a leading Caesarian senator during the late Republic, following Caesar's assassination wisely took up his governorship of Gallia Comata. Although he supported Antony during the 30s he sensibly kept away from the Senate and avoided the proscriptions that destroyed so many of his class. Seeing defeat was likely at Actium, he joined Octavius and spent his final years enjoying good eating and good poetry.

The large, deliberately stylized model of Lugdunum (1970s) is unsatisfying; it is out of date and lifeless, providing only a generalized vision of the Roman city. More interesting in this section are the **aqueduct photographs**, demonstrating just how dramatic the surviving remains are (see LYONNAIS AQUEDUCTS) and the memorials representing the three main sectors of Lugdunum: the colony, through the epitaph of a young wife who had enjoyed visiting the Apollo baths (*CIL*, XIII, 1983); Canabae, through a patron of the wine merchants (*CIL*, XIII, 1954) – as much part of Lyon life then as now; and an inscription recording the *pagus* of Condate.

Room IV brings together material associated with the **Three Gauls altar** and the **amphitheatre**. We have little difficulty in visualizing an amphitheatre, and the partial survival of the building itself helps; the problem is the altar. The delicately carved **garlanded blocks** suggest its quality and the style is very similar to the Ara Pacis in Rome, constructed by Augustus only a year before; the **bronze victory** dredged from the Saône in 1866 is thought to have come from the altar. Together with the massive terracing foundations, they imply a huge and splendid monument, but the only portrayals that have survived are the inevitably stylized versions on **coins**. These depict a rectangular altar, inscribed 'Rome and Augustus' set between two columns topped with victories. Given the constraints of a coin, the inscription is likely to be only the key words. Equally, the figures along the top of the altar may be representative of the sixty statues symbolizing the submission of the tribes, actually standing there or shown in some kind of perspective, or, of course, this might be decoration and the figures stood below on the esplanade!

The **delegates' inscriptions**, many beautifully executed, that once stood in Condate by the altar, represent the leading men from tribes all over Gaul. They assert their sacred loyalty, they are here as priests of a cult of the person of the emperor and the state of Rome; at the same time they proclaim their personal importance. In the early inscriptions some still look back, linking themselves to the old Gaul as descendants of companions of Vercingetorix. By the second century it is their role as decurions, patrons or imperial functionaries that matters. **Caius Julius Rufus**, one of the early delegates, proclaims his wealth by funding the construction of the amphitheatre, but he also recalls his Gallic noble ancestry. **Caius Julius Celsus**, when he paid for the remodelling of the amphitheatre under Hadrian, simply asserts his purely Roman persona as an imperial procurator.

Delegates had their own **reserved seating**; thirteen are known, for example the TRI or Tricasses, down from Troyes. **Butchers' guild graffiti** demonstrate local claims on seats as well. The widely produced gladiatorial lamps reflect the entertainment role clearly enough. Less common is **the epitaph of Callimorphus**, a gladiator with a typical stage name meaning 'pretty boy' who had received the *rudis* or wooden sword, a sign that he had fought with success and gained his freedom, and, in this case, *secunda rudis* – he must have gone back and won it again. How long he lasted is not apparent.

The most interesting example of the relationship between Gaul's leading citizens and the emperors is the **Claudian Table**. In 1526 Roland Gribaud found two pieces of a broken bronze plaque in his vineyard on the slopes of the Croix-Rousse. Covered in two columns of beautifully cut Latin script, they turned out to be part of a speech to the Senate given by Claudius in AD 48 and actually summarized by the Roman historian Tacitus (*Annals*, XI, 223–25). The emperor is seeking the support of the Senate for the admission of Gaul's leading citizens to their number. Senatorial status in itself would bring prestige to these new men, but it would also enable the ambitious to obtain jobs and titles denied to non-senators. In his speech Claudius stresses his own birth in Lyon, the growing wealth of Gaul and its great men, and how Augustus and Tiberius had already raised individuals to the Senate, and that although Italians would always remain superior, opportunity must be given to all rich and good men.

The 'Table' must have been copied from the papyrus records and proudly decorated a sanctuary wall. The Aeduan delegates had put forward the measure to a council meeting, which had taken it up with Claudius, who, finding increasing difficulty in getting senators to attend and to take on the lesser magistracies (they cost a lot of money), was attracted by the idea. However, the senators, as Tacitus points out, had an instinctive suspicion of Gauls, and, as well over a hundred might qualify, Claudius backed down and limited the privilege to the Aedui. It is therefore suggested the plaque was only displayed after his death when the principle was quietly extended to all the Gallic *civitates*.

Rooms V–VI. These two rooms present material showing other aspects of imperial government. The city administration is represented by various inscriptions recording the lives of the *duoviri* (magistrates) or the *decuriones* (councillors) of the colony. The most striking is that of **Quintus Acceptius Venustus**, a decurion (*CIL*, XIII, 1910). The inscription reveals that he was only 11 years old (officially there was an age limit of 25). His death 'left his parents with endless pain' – a reminder that however frequent child death was in the ancient world, the suffering was still acute, but it also demonstrates what drove the provincial rich during the early empire. His battered, but clearly very grand, sarcophagus echoes the family's wealth and the status and prestige which his membership of the council brought. The many *sevir* inscriptions show how the ambition of freedmen was channelled to the imperial cult and a model recalls the great temple found at the Verbe Incarné site.

The emperor's personal representatives in the province of Lugdunensis were the governor, answerable above all for law and order, and the provincial procurator, responsible for finance. One of them was **Gaius Furius Sabinus Aquila Timositheus**, governor during the later Severan period (220s–30s). Not only was an inscription found here recording his career (*cursus*) to this point, but a fine **bust** which is believed to depict him. The historical sources describe him as cultured and he was certainly well travelled, with dazzling switches from one end of the empire to the other. He must have been ambitious and talented. His career took off when as a centurion he was promoted to an equestrian post as an infantry unit prefect in Spain. He became a procurator in Belgica before transferring to Arabia; he then used his financial skills in Rome as chief of the inheritance tax office, before returning to the East where in Syria and Palestine he collected special imperial taxes. Back to the West again, he was appointed as one of the new equestrian governors in Lower Germany. After a switch to Asia Minor, he arrived in Gaul to look after Aquitania and Lugdunensis. His career climaxed in 241 as praetorian prefect: it meant he had become chief adviser to the 16-year-old emperor, Gordian III, to whom he promptly married his daughter Tranquillina, before going off to the East to lead the imperial armies fighting the Persians. He recovered Syria and conquered Mesopotamia but died in the East, perhaps murdered.

There would have been hundreds of lesser administrators in Lugdunum. Mining was contracted from or administered directly by a special procurator; one imperial freedman accountant in this office commemorates his chief Celsus, another dedicates a memorial to his two daughters. There were also those officials connected with the governors' assizes. An unusual figure recorded on another inscription was the key holder of the prison. Lyon's jail itself is unknown, but is unlikely to have been big: prison was for holding until trial. Punishments were fines and banishment for the 'honest' (meaning wealthy), whipping, condemnation to the games or mines, and summary execution for the rest.

Room VII. Lyon had its own garrison, which, in a cosmopolitan metropolis, must have been an attractive posting; most of the time would have been spent on escort duty or seconded to the governor's administration. Funerary inscriptions commemorate these men, particularly the second-century garrison of the thirteenth urban cohort. Occasionally they were called into action: in the disturbances of 21, the civil war of 69 and that of 197. The last is most vividly brought to life by a **military burial** displayed in a glass case. Here are a soldier's bones, legionary's sword, sword belt and the coins for the ferryman across the Styx. The coins reach 194, and therefore he is likely to have fallen in the 197 battle outside Lyon when Severus triumphed over Albinus, the governor of Britain, his last challenger for the imperial title. His belt buckle inscribed [UT]ERE FELIX is a 'good luck' token typical of the Danubian troops: he must have fought for Severus. The Lyon cohort, which had declared for Albinus, was dissolved and replaced by loyal legionary detachments, particularly from the XXII Primigenia.

One man who perhaps escaped the destruction of the thirteenth urban cohort was the veteran S. Egnatius Paulus, who retired in 192 and whose **diplomata militaria** are preserved here. These are two small bronze plates, held together with wire, which a veteran could carry as proof of his honourable discharge after twenty-five years' service and the privileges attached. It copied the legal text kept in Rome, demonstrating his citizenship with its rights of ownership, special procedures in court and the ability to make a will and so avoid inheritance tax; it also recognized his marriage (and therefore subsequent children's citizenship as well).

Room VIII. There is a good representative collection of the three religious strands in pre-Christian Roman Gaul. The religion and myths of classical Rome are embodied in the almost life-size bronze figure of **Neptune** (no trident) dredged from the Rhône; the very fine bronze statuette of **Fortuna** (lost cornucopia) from AOSTE; the relief of Dionysus/Bacchus, Silenus and an intoxicated maenad with Sol above; and another image of Dionysus provided by the **four seasons' mosaic** seen from here through the well. The Gallic triple mother-goddesses and Mercury altars mix with new religions from the East, such as the Egyptian figurines or the *taurobolium* altar of AD 160, recalling the sacrifice of a bull over the committed believer in a pit below, part of the March festivities of the Cybele cult. A glimpse of the world of luck and spells is perhaps provided by the perplexing twelve-faced (months?) bronze **dodecahedron**, one of ninety-three found mainly in Gaul and Germany.

Most fascinating is the **Coligny calendar**. This was found in a field, shattered, probably once wrapped in a bag and by a broken bronze statue of a male god. They must have been saved/ransacked from a temple, maybe VILLARDS D'HERIA, where pieces of another calendar were found in the lake. Here, 153 pieces of bronze form about two-fifths of the original which would have been displayed inside the temple complex. It shows a *lustrum*, or five-year cycle, of sixty lunar months and two additional intercalary months, inserted to add the extra days needed to overcome the conflict between the cycles of the sun and moon. The months are presented in sixteen columns; the first, of only three months, starts with an unnamed intercalary; the ninth has the other intercalary headed 'CAILLOS'; the remaining columns all have four months. The year began with the month of 'SAMON', generally believed to be the equivalent of November.

Plate 34 Lyon. The Coligny Gallic calendar (detail). Photograph: Ch. Thioc, Musée de la Civilisation Gallo-Romaine, Lyon.

This is the longest Gallic inscription known. At first it seems to embody the survival of the Celtic spirit, yet it also shows how Gallic religion was tamed and adapted to Roman ways. The Druidic tradition was entirely oral; this is written, and it has adopted Roman counting in days, not nights. While the Roman Julian calendar was adopted to make more sense of the year and is clearly solar in inspiration, this attempts to reconcile the lunar and solar cycle in a far less practical way. A recent interpretation sees it as the product of brilliant astronomical minds interested in godly and secular time, the key being the long-term cycle and a predictive power involving covering equinoxes and eclipses. Others have been more sceptical, seeing it as embodying calendar-based divination, an alternative to consulting *haruspices* ('gut-gazers') or oracles. The stress here is on the 'good' and 'bad' days for people: hardly an exceptional activity for priests where astrology was the common currency of the whole ancient world. Masses of people, from emperors down, believed heavenly bodies impacted on human destiny and therefore it was wise to consult experts at interpretation. The fascination of this calendar, then, is the complex application of mathematics to make the days fit the years and the hints through the peg-holes and difficult-to-interpret abbreviations and symbols. Supplicants would have been tremendously impressed by the temple priests' pseudo-scientific calculations to explain the future.

Room IX. Devoted to the theatre and odeon, this is perhaps the least satisfying section in the museum. Two dull models, a large out-of-date plan and a battered statue of Apollo found in the 1950s excavations, inspire few thoughts. Certainly there is a good model (with a handle to work it) of the counterpoise weight system used to raise the *aulaeum* (curtain) from the trench at the front of the stage. However, the room evokes none of the exuberance of performance, nor the rowdy audience participation described by contemporary writers. There is nothing to show how the curtain would hide and then reveal special scenery with collapsing panels; the seething actors, singers and gymnasts marshalled into dramatic poses; or the striking, colourful costumes and dramatic masks combined with the musical effects and the booming voices of the star actors.

Room X. This room contains one of the finest circus mosaics in the Roman world. Over 5m long and 3m wide, it was found on a site south of Bellecour in 1806, somewhat damaged but in few crucial places, allowing virtually complete restoration. It has life, detail and colour – above all it tells the story of chariot racing.

The artist has made some adjustments to fit the circus into a rectangular frame. Both ends of the arena have been modified. On the right, it was always curved, not rectangular. On the left, the starter stalls or ***carceres*** fill the whole space; in reality they would have formed a slight curve facing towards the right-hand track. This was actually wider than the left-hand track because the barrier was set at an angle to allow the chariots to follow equal length lanes to reach the break-line. Instead, the mosaicist is able to depict detail, especially as he has reduced the standard twelve *carceres* to only eight. The *carceres* are clearly wooden, strongly suggesting that he was portraying his local circus: copyists, basing themselves on Rome's Circus Maximus, always show stone.

THE ROMAN CIRCUS AUDIENCE

As in modern mass sports, the circus developed its partisan fans who dressed in the colours and came to chant at the races. It even had its hooligans, though fewer than the notoriously ill-disciplined theatre-goers. Fans ranged from slaves to emperors; those prone to excess elsewhere did not disappoint at the circus. Caracalla (198–215) was so offended in the Circus Maximus by the jeers against his favourite Blue charioteer that he set soldiers to find the offending Green fans; indiscriminate killing followed. Caligula and Nero had been equally passionate – for the Greens – if not quite so violent, and most emperors let it be known which team they favoured. A few found it impossible to show any commitment: Marcus Aurelius (161–80) refused to be involved and Julian (361–3) wrote 'I hate the Games . . .'. Pliny the Younger (*Letters*, IX, 6), writing in the later first century AD, epitomizes the incomprehension of all non-fans down the ages:

> The Races were on, a type of spectacle which has never had the slightest attraction for me. I can find nothing new or different in them: once seen is enough, so it surprises me all the more that so many thousands of adult men should have such a childish passion for watching galloping horses and drivers standing in chariots, over and over again. If they were attracted by the speed of the horses and the drivers' skill one could account for it, but in fact it is the racing colours they really support and care about, and if the colours were to be exchanged in mid-course during a race, they would transfer

By *c.*225 AD, when this was mosaic was probably made, circuses had developed to a standardized design. The track would have been about 400–450m long, surrounded by a podium to secure spectators from out-of-control chariots. No seating is depicted and probably at Lyon this was mainly constructed of wood, except for those entitled to sit at the centre of the stadium whose stone seats could be reserved (see the nearby inscription recording the restoration of some seats by a firemen's guild). The audience brought or hired cushions (*pulvini*). The most privileged had special boxes: the emperor had his *pulvinar*, though it was normally occupied by the governor, while the judges sat opposite in their ***tribunal***.

The mosaicist gives one of the clearest pictures anywhere of the arena itself. It was divided down the middle by a barrier called the ***euripus***, after the large pools of water that filled the two main sections. In Rome, the their favour and enthusiasm and rapidly desert the famous drivers and horses whose names they shout as they recognize them from afar.

Lyon was a provincial capital and had a circus from at least the 120s, but did it have professional teams and fans? It may be that local patrons put on amateur races from their own stables and with their own slave charioteers, but there is some evidence that on major occasions, such as imperial cult festivals, professional teams from Rome may well have come to Lyon. Lamps and appliqué medallions made in the Rhône valley not only had pictorial representations, but also supporters' slogans like 'Prasine Vincas' (Green to win!). From the numbers featuring 'prasina' it appears that here, as in Rome, the Greens were the most popular faction.

Circus racing continued in Gaul for what might seem a surprising length of time. Lyon's circus may well have declined in the fourth century, but only 30km south at Vienne the circus was at its peak, and Sidonius was watching races at Arles in the 460s. According to Gregory of Tours (*History*, V, 17), the Frankish king Chilperic was building circuses at Paris and Soissons in the later sixth century. The explanation can perhaps be found in the subtle change that took place in the relationship between the emperor and the circus during the late empire. Funded and only put on by emperors, it had become an expression of the emperor's power. No longer a method of sharing a sport *with* the people, it was a method of showing oneself *to* the people; the teams had become part of the imperial entourage. Chilperic was simply demonstrating his own 'imperial' style.

surrounding walling, called the ***spina***, was covered with statues and monuments. The Lyon mosaicist has not shown any here, which may mean there were none, or that he wanted to give a clear view of the pool fixtures. In the longer left-hand pool stands an obelisk, probably, like that at Vienne, a copy of the Egyptian original in Rome. In both pools there is standard lap counting equipment: on the left seven **dolphins**, weighed down by water flowing through them, on the right seven **eggs**. Both ends of the barrier were marked by ***metae***, sets of three stone cones capped with spheres. They had cemetery associations and, of course, the corners were the most dangerous points in the arena.

The charioteers entered the circus arena through a passage at the centre of the *carceres* under a balcony box covered by an awning. Three starter judges sit here, the one in the centre drops a white cloth to begin the race. One

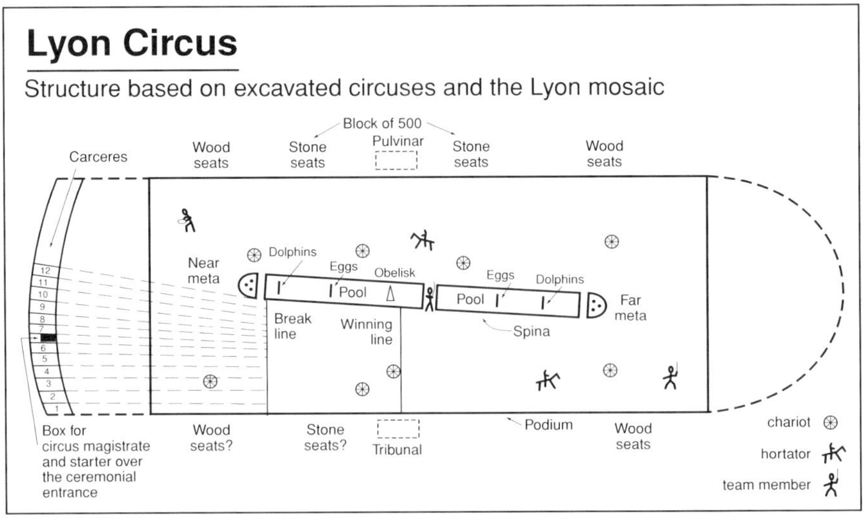

Figure 94 Lyon: circus

Plate 35 Lyon. The circus mosaic (central scene). Photograph: Ch. Thioc, Musée de la Civilisation Gallo-Romaine, Lyon.

man pushes a lever to spring open the *carceres* doors and the chariots tear out, then another quickly moves to shut them. At the **break-line** (*c.*150m), the chariots race for the best line. The artist has omitted the lane markers, no doubt to avoid spoiling the harmony of the design. For seven laps they hugged as near to the *euripus* as they could manage. Flipping the eggs over would add to the tension as increasingly tired, frantic horses swerved, touched and collided with each other or the barrier. Two of the eight chariots have crashed: one is smashed to pieces, while, as his horse trips, another driver flies out of his lightweight lattice-sided chariot. Outriders, ***hortatores***, try to inspire their teams to greater efforts. Other team members rush about on foot throwing water on the horses to cool them. Finally a chariot crosses the **winning-line**. Two figures wait in the corridor between the pools; one carries a palm of victory, the other a crown or trumpet. The charioteer will win the accolade; the *dominus*, or team leader, the prize money.

Circuses were built for professional sport. There were four racing teams (factions), each denoted by a colour: Green, Blue, Red and White. Races normally involved four-horse rigs – *quadrigae* – though some races were run with two-horse *bigae*. Up to three chariots per team could race, though here it had to be two. Damage to the mosaic has made it difficult to distinguish some ribbons, jacket and hat colours that both charioteer and horses wore. The faction supplied the charioteers – usually slaves or freedmen – and their chariots, horses – often from imperial or other stud farms in Spain – and fodder, grooms, vets, doctors, etc. The top charioteers became famous and moved between teams like Grand Prix drivers, no doubt for large fees. There were also the judges, starters, sweepers, etc., all part of the package that the patron paid for: circus spectacles were big business.

Rooms XI–XIII. Artefacts can tell us a great deal about the life of work and, in a conventional way, the cases of pottery indicate the wide range found in Lyon – *sigillata*, red **appliqué medallions**, creamy Alliers ware, lamps, etc., yet they give little idea of Lyon's own role as a production centre. There are the foundations of a furnace found at La Muette, one of a number of workshops along the banks of the Saône, but nothing to give any idea of the scale and significance of the industry. From the earliest years, Lyon attracted craftsmen from Arezzo – perhaps operating in subsidiaries – and soon had its own skilled men, stimulated by the potential of both a metropolis and a major distribution centre. It grew rapidly until the end of the first century AD, when competition from other centres severely reduced the scale of the industry, though local coarse ware production went on into the fourth century.

Other crafts are served much better, if only by providing some sense of the variety demanded by a Roman city. Stepping down into Room XII takes one on to the vast **'swastika' mosaic**, one of eleven found in one Fourvière house. Its chequered pattern of rather colourless and formulaic geometric squares is typical of an early third-century Rhône workshop. The walls display

Plate 36 Lyon. The Vaise treasure. Photograph: Ch. Thioc, Musée de la Civilisation Gallo-Romaine, Lyon.

examples of plaster wall painting and marble décor. The **Vaise treasure** was an unexpected pleasure for archaeologists surveying the Roman suburb in 1992. Found hidden, perhaps by the owner, perhaps by thieves, in two bags in the corner of a room, weights and names scratched on, it is probably linked to the disorders associated with Frankish and Alamanni incursions (260s). The coins, silver plate, cutlery and gold jewellery suggest a wealthy family. The silver statuettes of Fortuna are beautiful; the gold earrings with emeralds, garnets and pearls are exquisite.

The inscriptions kept in this room introduce a range of craftsmen: locksmiths, silver workers, goldsmiths, embroiderers, glassblowers, clothmakers, their corporations and patrons. For me the most engaging is that of **Matila Donata**, one of only four *medicae* known in France; she was clearly highly honoured, as the decurions funded her memorial. It is likely she specialized in gynaecology and obstetrics and, like the more widely known midwives, would have been both literate and have had an extended practical knowledge. Despite the prevalence of disease and early death, the quality of medicine in this field was high and the writings of the great second-century Greek doctor Soranus would have been a standard text for her. This work is filled with much accurate anatomy and consistently sensible advice: 'One should not forbid their use, for even if the amulet has no direct effect, still through hope it will possibly make the patient more cheerful' (quoted in Jackson, *Doctors and Diseases in the Roman Empire*, 1988, page 88). Finally note the **oculist's instrument box**. More widely found in Gaul than elsewhere, this kit, found buried with the oculist, is more complete than many.

In Room XIII crafts merge with trade. Though a set of scales is a reminder of the goods handled by traders, this room is filled with fascinating inscriptions. More than anything else in the museum they epitomize how Lugdunum stood at the centre of a commercial network. Each one records a person and often a guild or corporation, reflecting the variety of Lugdunum's contacts and the many individuals from the rest of Gaul attracted here by its opportunities, ranging from Caius Latinius Reginus, a Remi merchant dealing in sagums (see DRESS AND APPEARANCE) or Marcus Attonius Restitutius (*CIL*, XIII, 2018), who brought salt down from Alsace. (Many more are introduced in TRAVEL AND COMMUNICATIONS.)

Rooms XIV–XV. The international theme continues. Thaemus Julianus and **Julianus Euteknios** were two Greek immigrants from Syria. Among much high-flown third- or fourth-century Greek, the second is complimented on his 'persuasive tongue': clearly a faultless wheeler-dealer. A pity it does not make clear what he traded in, but eastern Mediterranean high-value products ranged from spices to superb textiles. Two soldiers, **Marcus Aurelius Primus** and his fellow legionary from Köln, chose to retire here together. But the focus moves on in a series of inscriptions, for example **Antonius Sacer**, showing how the wealthy Gallo-Roman family was an extended hierarchy. He was a *dominus* for his immediate family, their slaves and freedmen and women – still considered dependent, if only to repay the gift of freedom – and, as patron, he drew together clients who supported him and received his 'protection'.

Domestic life is recalled less coherently by a case of unlabelled bronzes, a fine bronze candelabra, an unlabelled model of the Rue des Farges excavations and an early third-century carpet **mosaic**, enlivened with a watery surround filled with fish and imaginary aquatic creatures. Room XV has more mosaics, the best of which are the **Four seasons with Dionysus mosaic** (late second century), and the **Pan and Cupid mosaic** (early third). The first, found in Fourvière next to the owner's swimming pool, is brightly coloured, especially the green, though the figure work is not especially good. The second has a central panel in which the symbols of fertility (Pan) and love (Eros) face each other like boxers. Silenus is acting as referee and holds the palm of victory. Perhaps the pillar (herm) on the left has a bust of Venus. On this mosaic are placed a brazier and a reconstructed bed; as this has no arm, it may be an extravagant bed for sleeping rather than eating. The **brazier** has been heavily restored, some of the masks and heads are totally nineteenth century; but, clearly of high quality, it must have once heated a wealthy family's home, though it seems unlikely it would have stood on an unprotected mosaic when ashes could damage it so easily.

Last, two different visions of married life, one shocking, the other poignant. *CIL*, XIII, 2182 honours the memory of a woman murdered by her husband after twenty-eight years' marriage. The **relief of Primilla**, *CIL*, XIII, 2242, recalls the life of a beloved daughter, dressed in her earrings and necklace, clasping her jewel box. Placed nearby is a case of jewellery.

Rooms XVI–XVII. The final two rooms are devoted to changes in recording the dead. Yet more inscriptions, but some happier images of love are provided by *CIL*, XIII, 2120, dedicated to 'the sweetest of souls' and *CIL*, XIII, 1897, where Tertius remembers Cirilla, 'my beloved and excellent wife of 18 years and 20 days'. Note the widespread use of the *ascia*, a carpenter's adze, much disputed in meaning, but perhaps a symbol of consecration.

The contrast with the Christian memorials is remarkable: the decline in the art of stone-cutting is obvious – related more to the empire's difficulties than the triumph of Christianity. The cutting is often closer to scratching than engraving, the letters uneven and child-like; even the blocks appear unfinished, but they have charm and joyfulness. The chalice, chi–rho or cross, the symbols of faith, are frequently supported by the True Vine, or the Church's teaching, at which the doves – the faithful – feed. Sometimes peacocks replace doves: their flesh was considered incorruptible. The earliest of the inscriptions, from the fourth century, usually use a simple 'Hic Iacet . . .' (here lies) followed by the name, day and month of death with the year defined by the consulship. This formula is gradually expanded during the fifth century; more details are supplied of the person and a brief expression of sorrow might be included. As the empire became shadowy, year dating got difficult; some inscriptions write of years since the last consul, others drop the practice. As the barbarian kingdoms became the reality, so, in the sixth century, dating by the king's name became the norm. Sadly the display is simply in rows unrelated to the list provided – it is a disappointing conclusion to the main exhibits.

Musée des Beaux Arts

Palais St Pierre
20 Place des Terreaux
Hours: 10a.m.–6p.m. Closed Tuesday
10.30a.m.–6p.m. Thursday

Formed in 1801 from older public collections and Revolutionary confiscations, the holdings were built up during the nineteenth century through donations and acquisitions from art dealers; there is exciting material for the visitor to see.

Le Médaillier/coin collection. One of the finest in France and still presented in classic cabinets. More than 17,000 coins cover the Gallic,

Roman, early Byzantine and Merovingian periods; those on display are some of the finest in France and provide one of the most comprehensive introductions available.

A run of Massilliot coins demonstrates the Greek origins of coinage in Gaul, followed by examples of Philip II of Macedonia staters, the master coin from which the various tribal series derived. Examples from all over Gaul display Celtic dislocation and iconic representations that replaced the chariot on the reverses. They culminate with **Vercingetorix**, his idealized head recalling Alexander, and, on the reverse of the Auvergne coin, an elongated Celtic horse with the last four letters of his name.

The emperors, including many short-lived pretenders, are all here. The **Hadrianic coins** are particularly impressive, not only the superb quality of the portraiture, but also the enormous variety of the reverses: the propaganda machine of the Roman state at work. In cabinets 19 and 20 are products of the Lugdunensis mint; between 15 BC and AD 64 it supplied a significant amount of the bronze currency used in Gaul and it remained an intermittent producer into the fifth century. Undoubtedly the most important coins are those depicting the **Three Gauls altar** – a regular feature in the early years and a crucial element in asserting Roman triumph and Gallic acceptance.

After the disastrous collapse of the debased currency in the third century, a new coinage was created in the late Roman period that continued into the Byzantine era. Note the **gold *solidus*** introduced by Constantine and the appearance of Christian symbols, including the earliest known chi–rho in Gaul (353, Magnentius). In the fifth century the Greek east provided the only serious currency circulating in Gaul: stylized Byzantine emperor heads with reverses of Christian cruciform shapes or symbols. When a new workshop opened in Lyon in the early 500s, the **Burgundian kings** Gondeband, Sigismund and Gondomar simply copied the Byzantine originals. After the Frankish conquest (534) the practice continued, but with a king's monogram added on the reverse. Only at the end of the sixth century did a king's head replace the emperor's: a concrete example of how the social and cultural sense of being Roman did not fit any neat political model of change.

The Ruffieu treasure and Merouville bowl. A treasure trove found in France and acquired by the museum from dealers in the early and mid-nineteenth century. This fine silverware was buried in the 260s/270s. Note the casserole handle decorated with elephants' heads and the gold rings with a squirrel and a kitten cut in the stone.

The Fine Art Gallery. All the material displayed is from Italy or unprovenanced. However, it includes a stunningly beautiful small **marble Venus** torso; a **bronze balsam jar** in the shape of a wrestler's grizzly head and a fine marble **bust of Julia Domna**, the wife of Severus. A strong and influential woman from Syria, she encouraged the last great upsurge in the popularity of eastern religions in the empire during the early third century. She is depicted here as a middle-aged woman.

Musée des Tissus

34 Rue de la Charité
Hours: 10a.m.–5.30 p.m. Closed Monday

Hanging here is a glorious second- or third-century **Roman tapestry** cloth of linen and wool found in Antinous, Egypt, portraying a wide variety of Mediterranean fish swimming in a softly changing green sea. The luminosity and depth of colour, the vitality of its realism, are stunning. When the survival of any Gallo-Roman cloth is so rare, this is a breathtaking reminder of the beauty of the textiles that could be imported from the east of the empire for the very wealthy, perhaps by the Syrian merchants resident in Lyon.

Musée Mariste de Puylata

4 Montée St Barthélemy

Rarely open, this small private museum brings together a collection of small finds made at the foot of Fourvière in Vieux Lyon.

LYONNAIS AQUEDUCTS, Rhône/Loire

IGN 2932 E/3032 O
IGN 2931 E/3031 O
Blay-Foldex: Lyon

Extensive remains of four aqueducts.

These four form the best concentration of aqueduct remains in eastern France. They do not just constitute the greatest mileage of aqueduct building in Gaul as a whole, but also demonstrate a technical competence found in very few other places in the Roman world; such magnificent engineering must be visited.

Lyon was of course a major city in the western empire: it had the status of virtual capital of the Gallic provinces with one of the largest populations. While a small town could satisfy its living needs through wells and cisterns, a city such as Lyon could not. The public baths, the formal fountains, the large private houses (and their gardens), the street-corner fountains, the water to wash out the sewers, demanded external supplies, and building these aqueducts enabled emperors to proclaim the power and wealth of the Roman state. Nothing is known of the costs – but two miles, let alone 150, is known to have bankrupted an eastern city; they must have been financed from the imperial purse.

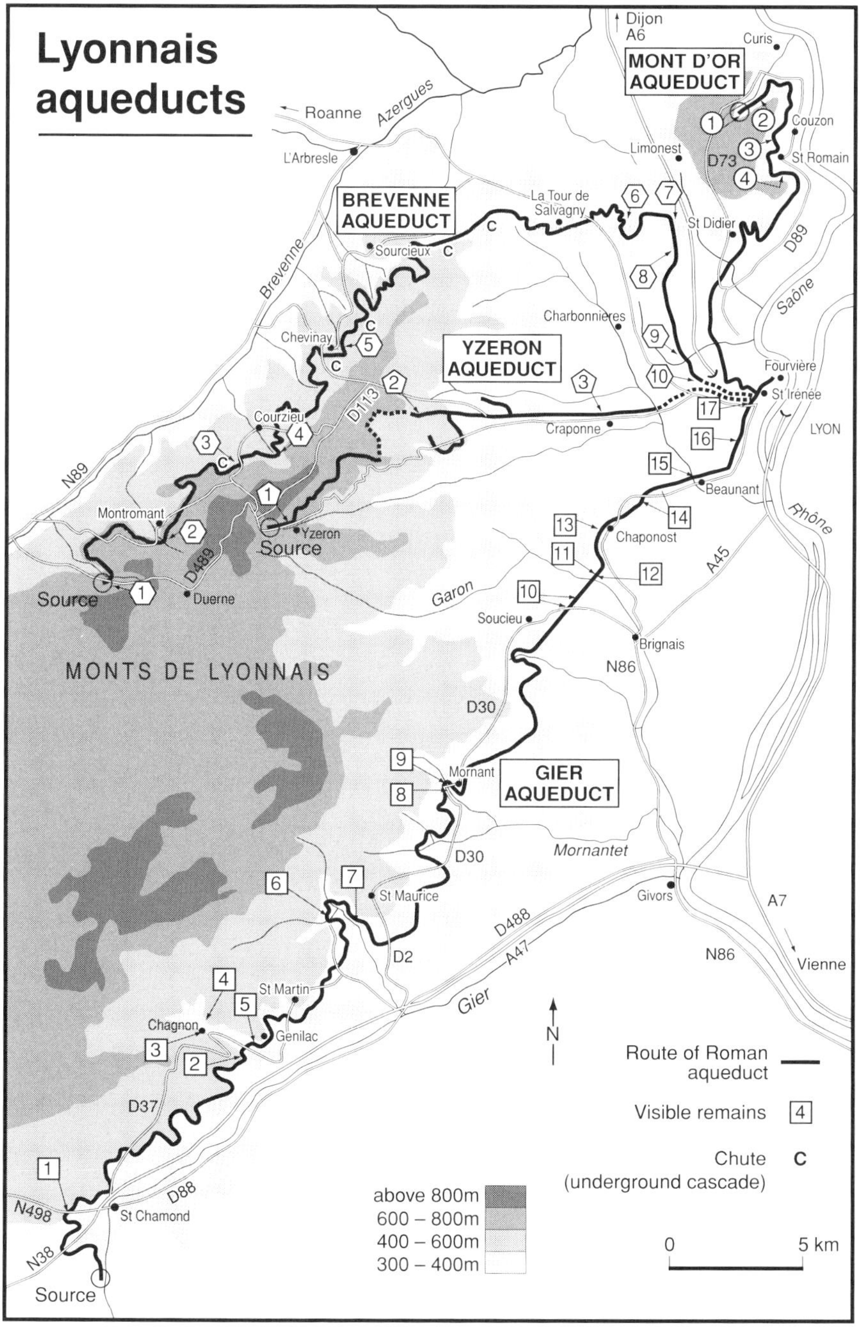

Figure 95 Lyonnais aqueducts: map

The Rhône and Saône could not provide clean water: the sewage from the many settlements upstream made this impossible. To supply the city using gravity as the driving force, the Roman surveyors had to seek pure, constant and voluminous sources in the Mont d'Or, the Monts de Lyonnais and the Mont Pilat massif.

Most aqueducts used contouring, going round valleys rather than across them. This usually involved cutting a ditch, constructing in it a stone channel with concrete and waterproof cement lining (normally vaulted but sometimes roofed with flat pavings), then covering it again with soil: a 'cut and cover' approach minimizing care needs. Sometimes a steep gradient was unavoidable; then a mix of shafts and channels was constructed to create an underground waterfall. Sometimes going round a hill was more costly than going through, so a tunnel was built. In other places, a valley might be too long and it became more economic to construct an arcade linking the two sides. Arcades were frequently necessary for the final stage to reach the chosen high point in the city, the *castellum divisorium*. The Lyonnais aqueducts have something different: they have siphons. In profusion. There are two dozen known in the Roman world, nine of them on the Lyon aqueducts.

To approach Lyon from the north and west entailed crossing deep, wide and unavoidable valleys. Crossed by arcades like the Pont du Gard on the Nîmes aqueduct, the bridges would have been much bigger, the largest ten times its size! A. Trevor Hodge, in his wonderful book on Roman aqueducts (1992), argues that the Romans preferred arcading because it was cheaper as long as the valley was not too deep. However, above a depth of 50m they chose another method: the siphon bridge.

A siphon bridge (formally a U-shaped inverted siphon) uses the principle that water rises to its own level. Pipes could therefore be run down one side of a valley, across the bottom, and up the other side. The aqueduct siphon was not a Roman innovation as it had been used widely in the Hellenistic East and it is perhaps via their second-century BC contacts with Pergamon that the Romans learnt the technique. However, the Romans were able to move far larger quantities of water in their siphons than the Greeks ever achieved. The full flow and pressures created were contained in lead pipes, each 25–30cm wide. On the Gier, where the best siphon towers survive, sets of nine or ten pipes ran together. The bridge at the bottom helped reduce pressure at the corners, where the water hit with the most thrust, though they were probably encased in concrete as well.

Some idea of the scale of this engineering is suggested by the calculation that 2,000 tons of lead were needed for the Beaunant siphon alone, stretching 2.6km across the Yzeron valley, and that thousands of 3m pipes had to be soldered together on site. Sadly the lead has all been removed. The pipes' size and presence have been deduced from the holes left in the header and receiver tanks and the great wide venter bridges that supported them.

Lyonnais Aqueducts

A siphon

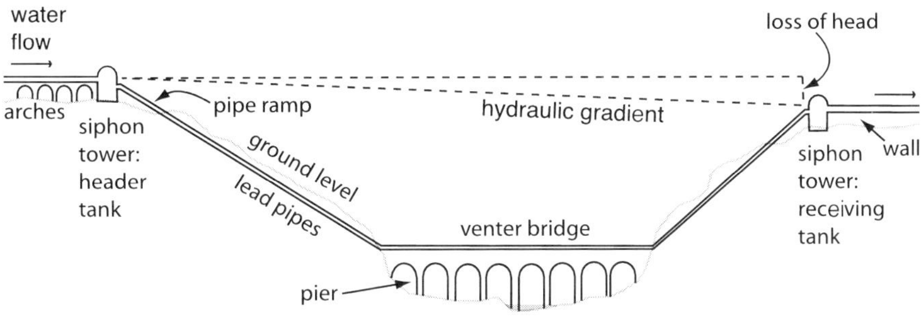

Figure 96 Lyonnais aqueducts: a siphon

Bold numbers in the text refer to Figure 95, but *IGN Série Bleue* maps (1:25,000) and the *Blay-Foldex* Lyon map are essential. Jean Burdy has produced a number of popular as well as academic works to supplement my account below. For tunnel exploration, *torch* and (wellington) *boots* are useful.

Gier aqueduct

This is easily the best preserved of all Lyon's aqueducts and there are a significant number of points where it is possible to examine tunnels, arcading and the dramatic siphon header towers.

De Montauzan in *Les Aqueducs antiques de Lyon* (Paris, 1909) argued, on the basis of an inscription at Chagnon, that the Gier aqueduct was built by Hadrian (118–38) and was therefore the last of the four. Evidence is accumulating that this is wrong. The Gier aqueduct often uses a diamond pattern for its stonework (reticulation), a style fashionable between the later first century BC and first half of the first century AD. Recent excavations in Lyon on the top of Fourvière hill revealed a public fountain of the 50s AD; without an aqueduct it could not have functioned, but none of the other aqueducts could supply this high. Recent sondages of the Cybele reservoir suggest this could be late Augustan. The Gier aqueduct is likely therefore to have been either part of Augustus' determination to make Lyon a great capital city or Claudius' sentiment towards the city of his birth (10BC–AD 50). Certainly it was built in one great effort and must have taken years. Recent study suggests the builders used the 'Roman foot' as their measure, but a longer

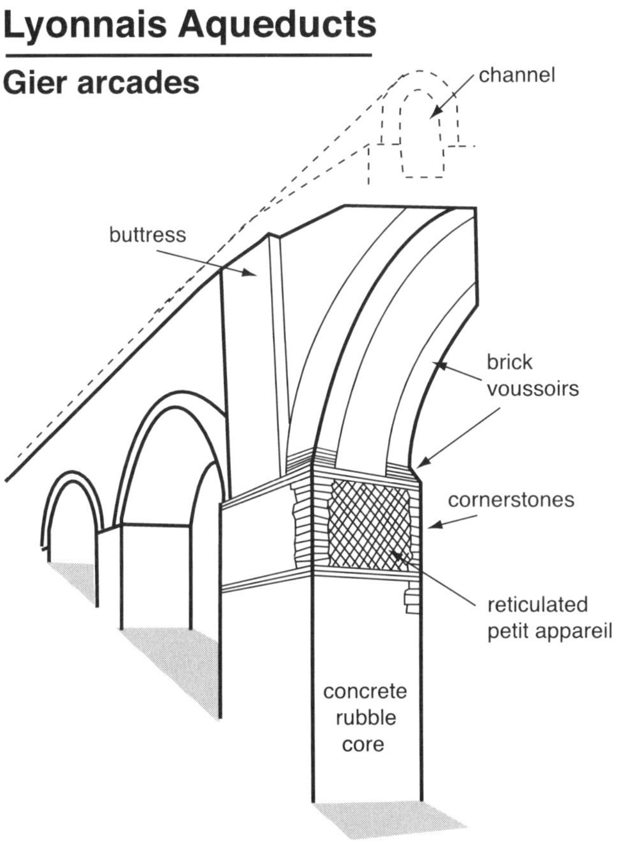

Figure 97 Lyonnais aqueducts: Gier arcades

local version of *c.*32cm (not 29.6cm). Cleaning and repair work was done through manholes at 77m intervals (their double *actus*) – as recommended by Pliny the Elder, regardless of dangerous arcades. All along its length there are distinct decorative elements around the basic concrete rubble core: double or single tile levels and, most obviously, the reticulation.

The aqueduct tapped the sources of the river Gier on Mont Pilat, 42km south-west of Lyon. It crossed the plateau separating the Rhône valley vineyards from the Monts de Lyonnais to the west. Though not really flat, with many hills and gullies for most of its length, it was reasonably easy to maintain a steady slope of 1.47m per km from the 440m spring height to the 260m of the Fourvière hill in Lyon; inevitably it followed a sinuous path over 75km. However, in choosing this route the Roman engineers had to face the problem of four particularly deep and wide valleys; the solution in all cases was the siphon.

St Chamond. South of the N498, 1km west of the town, park in a wide untended roadside area after a renovated restaurant. The remains are of **bridge arcades (1)** that crossed the Langonand valley, about 7km from the many collecting points on the slopes south of Izieux. The surviving section stands to a height of about 10m at a right angle to the road beside, and partly hidden by, the restaurant. On the other side of the road the aqueduct entered a tunnel (not visible).

Chagnon. IGN 2933 E. The aqueduct reaches the Durèze valley at the half dozen houses of 'Les Mûres', south-east of Leymieux, on the D37 towards Rive-de-Gier. The aqueduct split here, one route heading down to a siphon and the 700m pipe bridge, the other taking 10km to follow the valley head round Chagnon to reach the slope below Genilac.

The siphon header tower (2) (774.5/2060.9). This stands on the slope below Les Mûres amid orchards of peach, apple and pears. On top of the pillar, made of a concrete core and reticulated stonework, the aqueduct channel entrance is outlined on the back of the header tank and seven of the ten pipe holes survive on the front. Pink waterproof lining cement covers much of the tank, but lead pipes and vaulted roof have gone.

In the precipitous village of Chagnon (773.2/2061.6), under the school portico, is an **inscription (3)**, 'La Pierre Romaine', recording that, under the authority of the Emperor Hadrian, no one should work, sow or plant the land by the aqueduct (on the Nîmes aqueduct there is extensive evidence of farmers working the land and diverting water). Through the village and over the medieval bridge turn left and by the last house on the right is a sign-posted footpath to 'La Cave du Curé' (773.1/2062.1). This is a **60m tunnel (4)** cut into the rock within which the aqueduct channel was set; pools of water can make it unpleasant. Recent work on the contour route suggests this was built after the siphon, so explaining the Hadrianic inscription, but undermining previously held certainties. Reinterpreted, the siphon was not a logical short cut; rather, it seems, less reliable than originally hoped.

The siphon bridge (5) (774.5/2060.9). Follow the D65 from Chagnon to Rive de Gier. Take the first tarmac turning left, unsignposted but heading towards Genilac. At the bridge (*c.*1km), covered in ivy – though there are plans to remove it – are remains of the supports that held the water pipes. Most of the facing stones have been removed but the alternating single and double tiling layers stabilizing and decorating the core are still clear.

Bozançon valley (IGN 2932 E). After Chagnon, the aqueduct wound its way to rather inaccessible wooded valleys of the Grand and Petit Bozançon (really torrents). Take the D6 from Genilac and D77 to St Martin-la-Plaine, followed by the D37 and D30 to Bissieux, descending to the Grand Bozançon, where, 200m downstream from the bridge, hidden in trees, are a tall **pier and broken arch (6)** (777.0/2066.1) on the north bank of the river. It is then necessary to backtrack, circling round to reach the eastern banks of the Petit Bozançon below **St Maurice-sur-Dargoire**. Here are four different sites **(7)**, well hidden again by trees and poorly signposted down tracks leading off the narrow road from the D2E at Les Granges to La Chandelle, Jurieux and La Billannière farms. (i) **Finely preserved bridge** (778.8/2066.2). Walk from just before La Chandelle farm following the track with traces of blue footpath markings (map 'Ruines d'Aquc'). (ii) **A three-arch bridge** (778.2/2066.6). Third track after La Chandelle, walk down past old quarry (map 'Ruines d'Aquc'). From below La Billannière, a track leads down into the valley where there are two further marked sites (777.5/2067.0). (iii) A **small bridge** and (iv) a **tall pier**, a kilometre beyond up the Petit Bozançon, amid thick undergrowth and trees.

Mornant. IGN 2932 E. The channel crossed two streams and negotiated a low hill on which Mornant is situated through the longest tunnel on the whole aqueduct (825m). From the D34/D30 roundabout, some 600m up the road to La Plaine, are the **bridge ruins (8)** (781.8/2071.0) over the Condamine. Much more splendid is the surviving section crossing the Mornantet at the D34/D63 junction due west of the town. **A 15m-high arch and pier leads to a solid wall (9)** (781.9/2071.7) that carries the channel by a sharp right turn along the hillside and into the tunnel under the town. The setting is idyllic, the aqueduct towering over the stream, a splendid backcloth for an old building and vegetable garden, surrounded by rich green grass and trees. A buried section of channel has been left exposed on the other side of the D34; a railing protects the **rectangular inspection manhole** and its capping stone. One of more than fifty known on the Gier aqueduct, they were used for clearing debris and making repairs. In Mornant, access shafts down into the tunnel have been found in house cellars; during the Second World War these made useful hiding places.

Soucieu-en-Jarrest. IGN 3032 O. East 1.5km by the D25 to Grandchamp. As the slope begins into the Garon valley, the channel was carried on **a large section of both solid walling and a run of arches to the siphon tower (10)** (785.4/2078.1). There are three sections. (i) Where the D25 cuts the aqueduct remains at a right angle, solid wall and low arches. (ii) Taking the track past Grandchamp and by the orchards, arcading gradually rises on this long stretch. (iii) The siphon header tower, 4m high with ten pipe holes, locally called 'la Gerle', is heavily restored with modern brickwork and is slightly smaller than that at Chagnon. The siphon needed to be over a kilometre long to carry the water across the ravine to the receiving tower on the slope below Chaponost. It is not possible to cross by foot.

Brignais. IGN 3032 O/3031 O. Take the Garon road 2km north-north-west out of Brignais. The potholed Chemin de Barret passes through the **arches of the venter bridge (11)** (786.8/2079.5). The water rushed down the pipes in a fall that dropped 93m, over a 200m long bridge carried by twenty-three arches and up a rise of 80m to the receiving tank. The width of the surviving arches and piers is striking; those nearest the slope to Chaponost have blind central arches. From the meadow, you can get a clearer

Plate 37 Arcades on the Gier aqueduct at 'Le Plat de l'Air', Chaponost, Lyonnais. Photograph: James Bromwich.

Plate 38 Aqueduct siphon header tower and pipe ramp, Chaponost, Lyonnais. Photograph: James Bromwich.

view of bridge foundation stones in the river and the arches on the other side. There is a footpath up the very steep slope but driving round to Chaponost is advised.

Chaponost. IGN 3032 O/3031 O. (i) 'La Gagère' **receiving tower (12)** (787.0/2080.0) is marked on the IGN map – though mis-spelt with a 'C' – at the end of the Chemin de la Gagère by the junction with Rue Antoine. It is not very well preserved though the elements of tower, tank and channel exit are clear; 30m to the rear, a section of solid channel support has been used as a retaining wall. Most dramatic is the view over the valley to the clearly visible Soucieu tower. (ii) In La Colombe area due north of La Gagère, a long stretch has been cut by the Chemin du Guichardet, off Rue Louis Martel. From the grass space signposted 'Les Genêts' about 250m of **solid wall and arches (13)** (786.9/2081.5) are preserved. Most of the channel has disappeared.

The 'Plat de l'Air', 550m with **72 arcades and header tower (14)** (788.8/2082.7 and Blay-Foldex Lyon, B-26). This is the longest and finest aqueduct section in the Lyonnais. Passing through Chaponost, along the D50/Rue du Dr Penard towards Lyon, on the right just before the junction with Avenue de Verdun, park in the Rue des Framboisiers. The aqueduct stretches away into the orchards beside the main road before bending to the right to reach the tower marking the start of the siphon carrying the water across the Yzeron valley. I personally prefer the consolidated straight section, with its variety of colours in stone, cement and tiles, and find the restored curve disturbing; though it may give a better vision of what Roman engineers and farmers saw. The tower has a well-preserved arched ramp that supported a concrete casing for the lead pipes; the incline is striking. The vaulted roof of the header tank is partially preserved.

Beaunant. Blay-Foldex Lyon, E-24 (IGN 3031 O: 7904/2083.5). The immense 2.6km long siphon fell 123m and crossed a bridge in the valley floor nearly 270m long supported by **thirty massive venter bridge arches (15)**. Follow the D50 down (Route des Aqueducs, Route de Chaponost) and turn left into the Route de la Libération. The great Roman arches lie straight ahead obviously once supporting a bridge, running beside the Chemin de Verzieux Ducarré. Supports have survived on both the southern and northern sides of the valley. Again the width of the arches is striking; the taller have cross-wise open arcades, those nearest the slope are blind. Note the survival of a very few large projecting blocks which once supported the concrete-encased pipes themselves.

Ste-Foy-lès-Lyon. Blay-Foldex Lyon, I-22/H-23. Climbing up the Ste-Foy hill by the Chemin de Montray turn right down Rue du Nerard and right again down Chemin de Narcel. **Scraps of arcade and pillars (16)** are used here in domestic walling. At the end of Boulevard de Narcel admire the view, and the civil engineering feats of the Romans. Along Rue Deshay, turn right – round the fort – into Rue G. Clemenceau (Blay-Foldex Lyon, I-20). At a block of flats in the Chemin du Fort (no. 63), **two pillars** have been used in the walling.

St Irénée. Blay-Foldex Lyon J-18. Descending the Rue Soeur Bouvier to another old fort, now converted into the André Alix University residence. The **header tower and a ramp arch (17)** of the final siphon are preserved inside the grounds (open access). Another view is possible in Rue Charcot. No remains have survived of the bridge or the receiving tower taking the siphon 600m across the Trion hollow to Fourvière hill.

Fourvière. Blay-Foldex Lyon K-17. Coming up the hill from the Rue de Trion and into the Place Radisson, at the beginning and along Rue R. Radisson remains of **arcading pillars** built into domestic walling, crossing from right to left and then curling round to the right towards the reservoirs on the hill (see LYON: Parc Archéologique).

Yzeron (Craponne) aqueduct

The aqueduct takes its name from the river valley in the Monts de Lyonnais where a line of springs was exploited. However, many others fed into the aqueduct, and it is not yet clear which were the earliest or the most important. It is therefore sometimes known as the Craponne aqueduct, named after the area where important remains have been found. De Montauzan argued this was among the earliest, built at the time of Augustus, but there is no substantial evidence for this and it could be as late as the end of the second century. Its twisting route round the numerous gullies on its steep descent to Lyon, a fall of over 400m in 25km, has made it difficult to identify; undoubtedly there were numbers of underground hydraulic staircases. It is not even known if it was vaulted or simply covered with flat pavings.

The craggy village of **Yzeron (1)** is attractive though busy with visitors at the weekend. Aqueduct **channel** was found here by the D498, but the boules park and tennis courts took priority and nothing visible survives. The line along the road embankment gives a rough idea of the route. About 1km north-north-east of Vaugneray, by the hamlet of **Le Recret (2)**, a team led by Jean Burdy found **two shafts** of an underground waterfall with a drop of 38m, to moderate the speed of the water. They consider there were other shafts in between forming a 'hydraulic staircase' (see also AUTUN aqueducts).

Craponne. IGN 3031 O, 786.7/2086.0. The aqueduct first had to pass over the Tupinier depression, second the valley after Craponne, then on into Lyon. All that survives are **dual siphon towers**, 'Les Tourillons' **(3)**. They once linked receiver and header tanks that stood at the middle of the two siphons. Traces of the ramp downstream have been found, but these visible remains stand 10m and 12m high, heavy with ivy, on very private and well-protected ground. At the traffic lights, turn north from the main road through Craponne (D489) into the Rue des Tourillons. They can be seen from Rue Aqueducs or even better from the Voie Romaine. With this double siphon a distance of around 6km was covered by siphoning: sadly, nothing survives of the pipes, bridges, or other header and receiver towers. After reaching St Irénée, the aqueduct is believed to have crossed to a distribution point on the south-west slope of Fourvière.

The Brévenne aqueduct

Like the Yzeron, the source of this aqueduct lay in the Monts de Lyonnais, but for part of the way it follows the path of the Brévenne river along the western slopes in a wide arc to enter Lyon from the north. Its sinuous route has been traced 66km. Yet the path was steep, a total fall of 350m, and in five places it is believed hydraulic staircases must have been used. Dating evidence is still slight: while de Montauzan considered it to be Claudian, it could be Antonine. Although there are no dramatic sections of remains to see, there are real pleasures to be had in perfect views across the hills scattered with isolated farmsteads and hamlets among woodland, pasture and the yellow of precipitous cornfields. For this reason alone it is worth looking at **Orjolle** hillside, between Ste-Foy-L'Argentière and Duerne (D489) but there is no visible evidence of Roman workings at this **spring site (1)** (IGN 2932 E, 769.0/2078.8). There is also the satisfaction of finding hidden evidence of channels and tunnels deep in such countryside.

Montromant. IGN 2932 E, 770.5/2080.2. On the western side of the village, off the D25, a turning south leads to La Grand Goutte, an old mill.

A footpath signposted for Duerne leads up from the mill across the stream (avoid the track with yellow markers) and, about 100m further on, the aqueduct crossed the road following the gradient round this small valley. In the wood on the left of the footpath a series of holes reveal the **aqueduct channel** below **(2)**; in some cases the displaced top paving stones expose the interior cement and stonework.

Courzieu. IGN 2931 E, 773.9/2084.8. The hamlet of Sortizon is 2km south-south-west of Courzieu, but is best approached by the road down from the D25, reflecting the route taken by the aqueduct from Montromant. Your steep descent is followed by the short climb into Sortizan taking the sharp right turn up to the wooden cross. 10m from the cross is a large stone believed to have formed a **sediment basin (3)**, perhaps related to the hydraulic staircases likely to have been used to deal with the considerable gradient here, a 50–60m drop. From Courzieu itself, 800m along the unsignposted Biternay road via Le Bourbon, on the right hand side, 20m beyond 'Chasse Gard' signs, is an **aqueduct tunnel (4)** (774.4/2084.2) along which it is possible to walk *c.*25m (bring torch).

Chevinay. IGN 2931 E, 776.9/2087.7. The attractive way to approach the village is along the top by the cols and down using the D24 and then onto the D24E. Through Chevinay, passing the cemetery, there is a sharp bend and then a long curve. 70m into the curve, on the left in the undergrowth is a series of holes exposing the **aqueduct channel** below **(5)**. From here the aqueduct route gradually turned eastwards. When the Charponnay power station was built, 150m of arcading foundations were found and soon covered over.

Dardilly. The Roman surveyors took the aqueduct round the hill of what has become the Lyon suburb of Dardilly. There are three places where traces are visible. **(6)** IGN 3031 O, 786.5/2093.7. West of Dardilly by the road linking la Brochetière on the D77 with the estate area of le Clair. 'La Fouillouse' field contains a **large vaulted tunnel**, *c.*25m long, hidden in a bramble bush by an enormous chestnut tree. Only possible to crawl in, it was used as a shelter in 1940. **(7)** Blay-Foldex Lyon, B-3. At the back of the hotel parking area, 11 Chemin Gargantua, a short section of aqueduct **channel** protrudes from the bank. The careful lining of cement inside the stone frame of the channel and its vaulted roof are well restored. **(8)** Blay-Foldex Lyon, C-4. In the courtyard of the Lycée Rabelais, Chemin du Dodin, there is a piece of **short vaulted channel** heavily consolidated.

Ecully. Blay-Foldex Lyon, E-15. A siphon was necessary for the aqueduct to cross Ecully valley. At the bottom of Rue Pierre Dupont, park in the Chemin du Vieux Moulin by the electricity relay station. On private land obscured by tree foliage (access possible across the stream in summer), are the remains of a **header siphon tower (9)**. The larger of the piers supporting the tank and the ramp can just be made out. This siphon alone carried the water 3.5km coping with a drop of nearly 90m.

Lyon. Blay-Foldex Lyon, F–16. A **siphon tower slope**, 6m high **(10)** once took the pipes down from a receiver tank. It was photographed in the 1860s, but then enclosed by a house only re-exposed following 1970s construction work. It stands on the north side of the corner of Rue de Boyer and Rue des Aqueducs. From here, the aqueduct completed another 2km into St Irénée. How it crossed the Trion valley is not known.

Mont d'Or aqueduct

The Mont d'Or hills have been heavily quarried for limestone, which has wiped out major parts of the aqueduct. It is believed to have been 25–28km long and almost entirely buried. The local stone split easily for pavings and this may have led to the decision not to vault but to give the channel a flat roof. This made access manholes unnecessary though it was more vulnerable to collapse. De Montauzan considered this the earliest and the spring's proximity to Lyon (only 10km away) makes construction in the time of Augustus appear likely, possibly even ordered by Agrippa in 19 BC, but there is no firm evidence for this. It is believed siphons were the only way that the last part of the aqueduct could have reached Lyon, first to cross the Rochecardon ravine (420m) and then once again the Ecully valley (3.5km) to reach the Minimes area of Fourvière where there were large public baths. The thrill is the search for evidence rather than the impressiveness of the finds!

Polymieux-au-Mont-d'Or. IGN 3031 O, 791.0/2097.5. Using the D73 up through St Didier will bring you up into the combe or valley top where an ancient spring has been identified in Le Quartier Gambins. A track on the right, opposite the Montée de Chevanées, leads 150m down to a **modern spring collection tank (1)**. When built in 1934, Gallo-Roman workings were found.

Curis-au-Mont-d'Or. IGN 3031 O. Continue down the D73, taking the branch right into Curis and then turn right and right again into the Rue des Combes. Passing the Curis château park, follow the Rue du Bois des Cieux to the small wood on the right, 50m before the sharp turn where there is a house (no. 395) and a walker's signpost. Looking closely at the roadside bank, find semi-buried traces of **aqueduct channel with its top pavings (2)** (792.8/2099.1). It is quickly lost in the wood.

Couzon-au-Mont-d'Or. IGN 3031 O, 792.5/2096.9. The aqueduct, having gone north-east to reach Curis, curved round to the south following the heavily indented hillsides, to reach the deep Vinouve gully east of Couzon. A road, identified as an *impasse*, ends under dangerous-looking electricity pylons and becomes a track (blue footpath 57). The track rises to cut the aqueduct in two, exposing some **100m of channel (3)** on both sides, uncovered on the left, paved on the right and fragments on the track itself.

St Romain-au-Mont-d'Or. IGN 3031 O, 792.7/2095.2. From Couzon, take the road for St Romain and follow the D89 in the direction of Collanges, but turning right up to the cemetery on the northern flank of Mont Cindre. Drive to the top with the cemetery on the right. Park where the road turns right to become a track. About 400m up the track there is a sharp turn left into the wood. From here *c.*150m a mound of stones on the right indicates where the **aqueduct channel** (4) ran. A few metres of uncovered channel can still be recognized.

MONTBRISON (MOINGT), Loire

IGN 2832 O

Sites and museum.

In the seventeenth century, Roman remains were recognized in Moingt, a medieval village below the Monts du Forez, now a suburb of Montbrison. They were excavated by the local archaeologist, Théodore Rochigneux, very quickly in the 1880s, but 1990s work has largely confirmed his discoveries. Aqua Segetae was once an imposing sanctuary, dedicated to Segeta, one of the many Gallic gods about whom virtually nothing is known, though her name occurs on a number of inscriptions in Segusiavi territory (e.g. the weight in FEURS museum). Sadly, there are only hints as to its former magnificence; it clearly had a splendid bath complex. Among other buildings identified here are a theatre and traces of large structures that might have been important residences or pilgrims' hostels. At Chézieux (near St Romain-le-Puy), 3km south, strung out beside the Roman road turning to the sanctuary, was a large settlement without any public buildings; it is interpreted as the 'other half' of the town, where the people lived who worked at and exploited the opportunities offered by a significant spring sanctuary. Pottery dating at both sites suggests the sanctuary was being actively used between the mid-first and the beginning of the third century.

The cult centre and baths

Site Archéologique/Prieuré du Palais et Chapelle Ste-Eugénie
Avenue Thermale
Moingt

Remains of the sanctuary have been examined along the eastern side of the main road from Montbrison. Visible Gallo-Roman remains form part of the delapidated medieval priory. Money for restoration work ran out and the premises are locked up. However, Moingt Boules Club in the Rue Neuve backs on to the area behind the priory. Ask the barman for access.

The priory clearly used the best surviving rooms of the bath complex, as the even courses of medium-sized Roman stonework can be traced *c.*10–12m high on the eastern wall. The baths must have been impressive with evidence

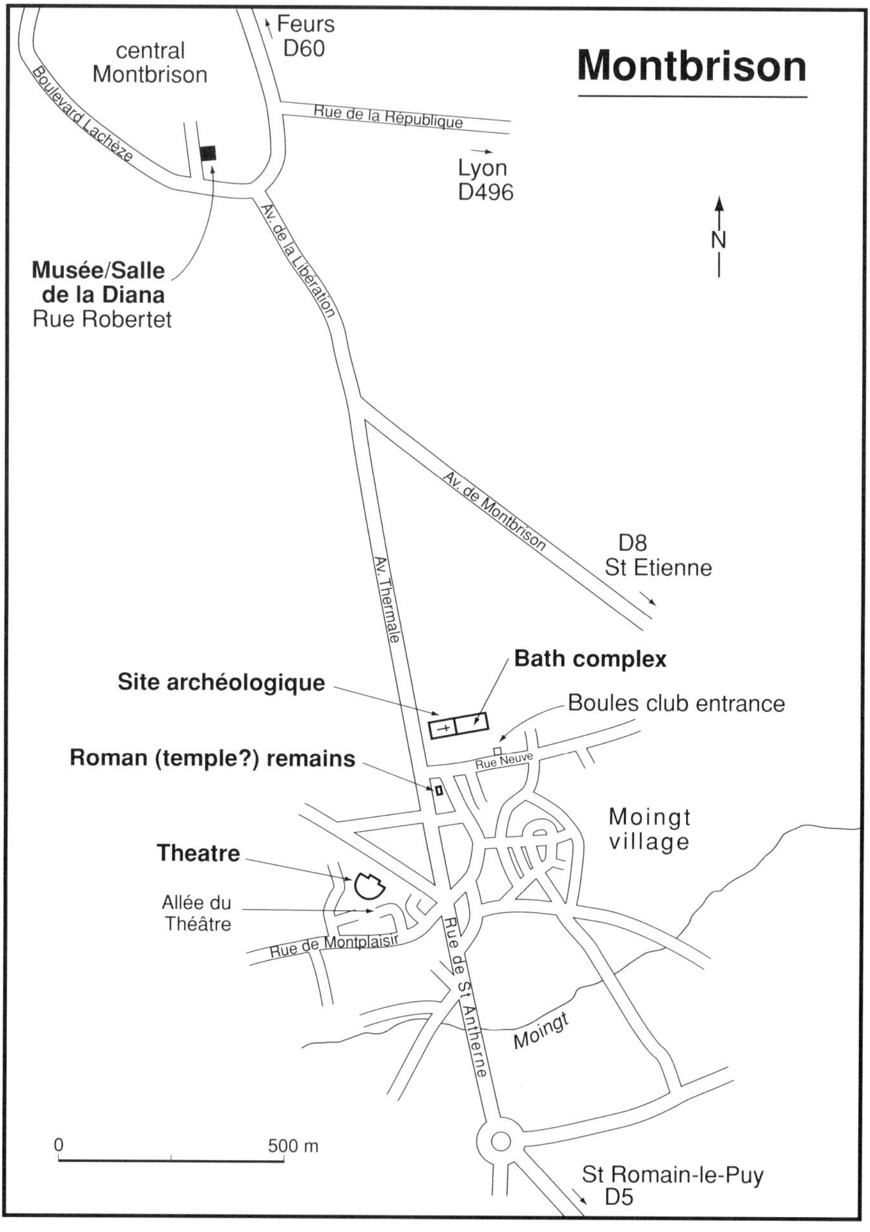

Figure 98 Montbrison: local plan

for marble facing, stucco décor and mosaic flooring. Outside there was a large pool with an *exedra*. Channels were found linking the baths with a local spring. The recent work revealed there was at least one rebuilding and their destruction occurred at the end of the second/start of the third century.

Across the Rue Neuve, in the yard of the clinic at 15 Avenue Thermale, are fragments of *grand appareil* stonework; a wall of *petit appareil* is now hidden. These could be the remnants of temple buildings.

The theatre

Allée du Théâtre,
off Rue de Montplaisir

At the end of the *allée* is a small public garden and beyond, the theatre remains. The north-west exterior buttressed *cavea* wall has the best-preserved masonry, rising some 10m with a *vomitorium* archway and side wing. The radius of 42m implies it might have held as many as 8,000. Now it is filled with no more than a meadow, blooming with dandelions in the spring. The absence of any trace of stone points to timber seating. Fragmentary foundations were interpreted as a large orchestra that could have functioned as an arena as well as fronting a stage. Recent sondages have shown there were many alterations.

St Romain-le-Puy

6km south-east of Moingt, St Romain stands out clearly on the Forez plain: a solitary basalt cone-shaped hill with an early Romanesque priory church perched on top.

J.-F. Reynaud (see LYON) excavated here in the 1980s and discovered a late Roman burial chamber, covered in *tegulae*, and two Merovingian coffins. They were enclosed by a small triple-apsed church (fifth–seventh centuries), over which the later tower was built. Gallo-Roman building stone has been extensively reused, suggesting there were other Late Roman early Christian buildings here, or perhaps fortifications. The church contains a case of minor finds from Chézieux farmstead, the settlement site at the Aqua Segetae turning off the main Feurs/Rodez Roman road.

Musée de La Diana

Rue Florimond-Robertet
42600 Montbrison

Hours:	Guided tours	2–5p.m. Tuesday
		9a.m.–noon, 2–7p.m. Wednesday and Saturday

La Diana, the historical society dedicated to the history of the Forez, is based in the Salle Héraldique, a thirteenth-century building roofed with heraldic devices (heavily restored). The rooms beside the Salle house a small but interesting museum. There are capitals from Moingt and a badly scored Maximinus (235–38) milestone, used to mark the 'L[euga] VIIII' distance from Chézieux to Feurs: Gallic leagues were used alongside miles in the Roman period. There are Iron Age and Gallo-Roman small finds from Essalois, Crêt-Châtelard, Chézieux and other sites in the Forez. The finest material is an excellent **small marble head**, perhaps Galba (AD 68–9), a cruel and short-reigning emperor who fought for the succession after Nero's death, and some attractive metalwork including **delicate silver spoons**, tin plates and bronze sieves, mainly from Chalain d'Uzore.

Essalois *oppidum*

20km south-east from Montbrison by the D8 then the D108 from St Rambert. Turn left at a sign for 'Château d'Essalois' – a sixteenth-century castle used this site as well. A parking area (1.5km) is two further turnings left. It is then a pleasant and easy walk.

The *oppidum* sits on a promontory 600m high and 100m above the left bank of the Loire with magnificent views across the cliffs that surround the twisting river and out over the Forez plain to the north. The **inner rampart** made of irregular dry-stone walling encloses 6.5ha and, despite the gorse and pine trees, is still visible along *c.*500m. Finds indicate occupation in the Final La Tène from the early second century to *c.*25 BC.

PETIT-ST-BERNARD ROMAN ROAD, Savoie

IGN 3531 ET

Sites.

Follow the N90 in France from Albertville to Pont-St-Martin in Italy by the S26.

The conquest of northern Italy (Cisalpine Gaul) brought the Romans into contact with the massive bulk of the Alps and the tough mountain peoples who inhabited its valleys. However, during the third and second centuries BC the focus remained Mediterranean; transalpine Gaul was seen as a coastal periphery to their Spanish conquests and only in the 120s BC did they take long-term control of the Montgenèvre route into what became Narbonensis. Caesar's conquest of the rest of Gaul dramatically changed the situation: secure control of the key passes became essential, and, after the civil wars, Augustus completed the conquest of the entire alpine region. Good roads were part of the process and a result of the new secure conditions. According to Strabo, the Petit-St-Bernard was the major route across the Alps into Gaul

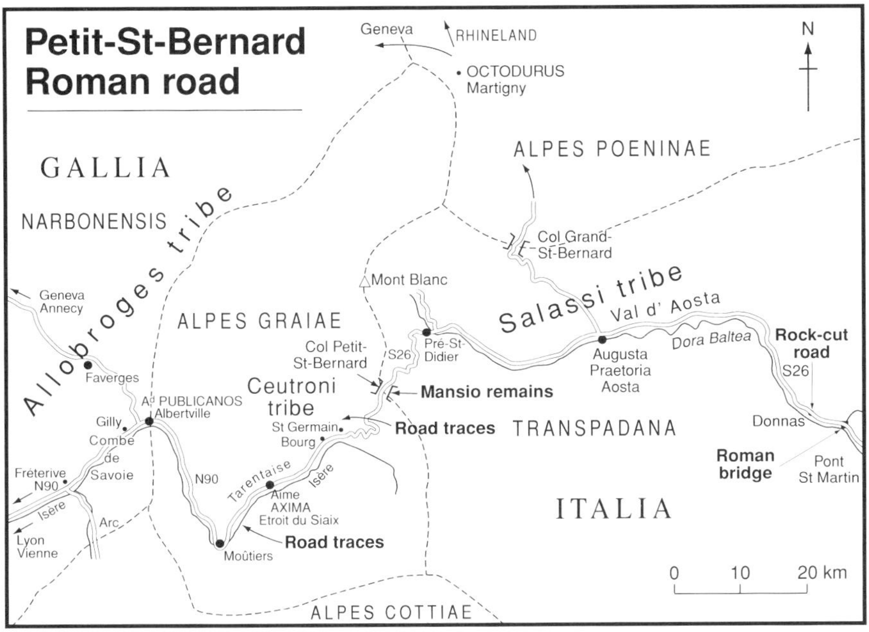

Figure 99 Petit-St-Bernard road: map

that could take wheeled traffic, and therefore one of the most important, linking Vienne and Lyon with Milan and Rome.

On the Italian side, the Dora Baltea cut the deep Val d'Aosta far into the mountains, while on the French side, some 50km to the south, the Isère takes a longer, less direct route through the various massifs of the western Alps on its way to join the Rhône at Vienne. Between the valleys is a line of peaks, the highest of which was the furthest north: Mont Blanc. This could be avoided by going deeper into the Alps through the Grand-St-Bernard pass, and the Romans used this route to reach Lyon via Lake Geneva, though it was primarily used by the military going to the Rhine frontier. Alternatively, as they found in the final years BC, the Petit-St-Bernard pass provided the easiest way – a relative term – into the heart of Gaul.

The Salassi of the Val d'Aosta were crushed in a series of campaigns in 34–25 BC and 25,000 taken as slaves: punishment for revealing Roman vulnerability to Alpine peoples by collecting a toll from Brutus to allow his army through their valley in 43 BC. The Ceutroni of the Tarentaise valley are not mentioned on the Tropaeum Alpium, the great victory monument at La Turbie (near Nice) recording the conquest of the alpine tribes by the armies of Augustus; they had probably made their peace with the Romans when they saw what happened to the Salassi. Augusta Praetoria (Aosta) was founded as a military colony to secure the first stretch of the road. But the upper valleys were treated differently. Small provinces governed by procurators were created with the key function of securing the passes and the roads beyond. The Alpes Poeninae controlled the top of the Grand-St-Bernard (Summo Poenini) and Alpes Graiae guarded the road from the Petit-St-Bernard pass (Alpis Graia). Perhaps Agrippa (died 12 BC), credited with so much of the early Gallic road construction, also began the process of surveying and constructing this great road. Despite the destructive capacity of the alpine environment, traces are still visible.

The French side

The frontier between Gaul and Alpes Graiae was at Ad Publicanos (see ALBERTVILLE), where the road entered the wide valley of the Combe de Savoie. Nothing remains of the actual customs post, but the name shows that this was where the Gallic 'Fortieth' was collected, a duty on goods crossing the external frontiers of the whole of Gaul. The Roman road has been traced in the valley to Moûtiers, but, in the much steeper climb up the Tarentaise, clear evidence of Roman work has been found in the **Etroit du Siaix** and in recent excavations at AIME. Beyond the stop at Bourg-St-Maurice, listed on the Peutinger table (itinerary) as Bergintrum (no visible remains), the road enters the pass. Here its zig-zag climb can be seen from the main road on **the northern slopes beyond St Germain** as a track above the skiing pistes.

Col du Petit-St-Bernard

Mansio site.

The St Bernard monks from the Hospice observed Roman remains around them, but the first professional excavations were carried out by P. Barocelli in the 1920s and 1930s. He exposed the two major sites here, correctly identifying the western *mansio*, but mistook the second for a temple as a hoard of temple treasure was found buried here. Between them, he suggested, further building foundations might represent a Roman military checkpoint of some kind. Since then, the 'temple' has been re-examined (in 1993) and clearly recognized as another *mansio*.

All who arrived here must have been deeply conscious of how fortunate they were and no doubt thanked Graius, the god of the pass, and probably Jupiter, the sky and thunder god. Jupiter features in the hoard and the 'Joux' column, 4.5m high, is a corruption of Jovis (Jupiter). Saint Bernard's statue is a nineteenth-century addition. The structure on the southern side of the eastern *mansio* is half a *fanum* (the rest was destroyed by the modern road) from which the treasure must have been taken. It has been suggested that this was the state *mansio* for officials and imperial post messengers, while the

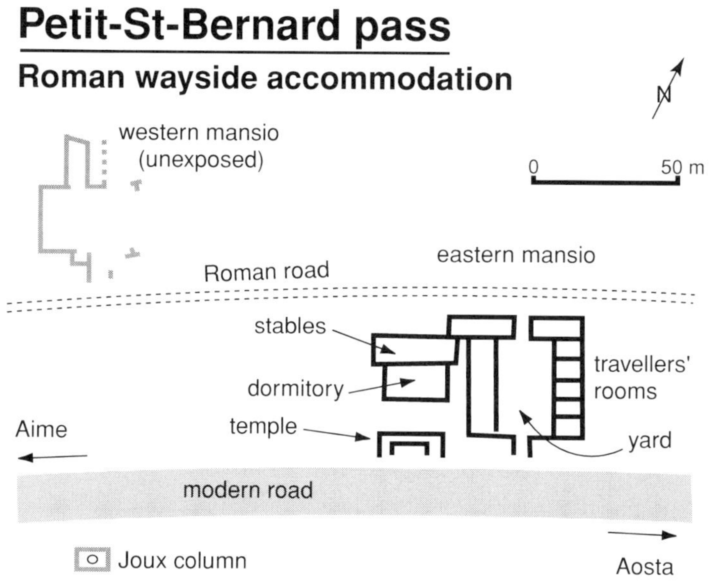

Figure 100 Petit-St-Bernard road: *mansio* sites

less substantial western *mansio* was really more an inn for others. How were all the officers accommodated when Legio XIV crossed here in AD 69 on its way to Britain, or did some have to shiver with the men in their tents?

The pass is snow-covered seven or eight months a year and patches last through the summer; the *lombarde*, a terrible winter wind, can blow up drifts 5–10m deep; the flash floods of the torrents could sweep down and wash away roads, bridges and travellers. Local guides were essential to avoid getting lost and tumbling down nightmare slopes. These *mansiones* with their warmth, food and rest for people and animals – before an equally perilous descent – were a vital part of the road system. Finds suggest that they fell into disrepair in the fourth century. 'Sacrificial fires' found in the western *mansio* were more likely lit by late Roman travellers taking shelter here. The pass was certainly in use during the fifth century as Saint Germain of AUXERRE's remains were brought back to Gaul this way in 448. Although a new rest-place was constructed in the eighth century, it was Saint Bernard's hospice in the eleventh century that finally gave permanence to the *mansio* concept.

The Italian side

The Roman road down to la Chiele is marked on maps as the *mulattiere*, but there is nothing significant in the Val d'Aosta until **Aosta** is reached, where there are imposing remains of the Roman colony. The town layout here has

Plate 39 Petit-St-Bernard pass. The eastern *mansio*. Photograph: James Bromwich.

been seen as a model used by Gallo-Roman town planners. In the context of the road, there is the heavy and **imposing gateway** and the **Museo Archeologico**, where the best material from the Italian Petit-St-Bernard *mansio* excavations is displayed. These include the superb **silver bust of Jupiter** and the votive plaques, found together in the hoard.

Donnas

Impressive Roman road and arch.

45km further down the S26 by the river dam, a parking pull-in is signposted 'Strada Romana'. The Dora Baltea must have been so dangerous that the Roman engineers decided to cut the road from the rock itself above the river – *c.*200m of this road survives. They left a milestone and an unnecessary, but proud, arch, both cut out of the rock. Tracks created to prevent cartwheels from slipping off the smooth rock and into the river have been deepened with use. The later graffiti, including some from the 1470s, is vivid evidence of this long-lasting achievement of Roman civil engineering.

Five kilometres beyond, near the entrance to the Val d'Aosta, a fine single-span bridge crosses the river Lys at **Pont St Martin**. There would have been numerous others over the tributaries and torrents, many would have been wood. They have long since been swept away.

Plate 40 Petit-St-Bernard pass. The rock-cut road in the Dora Baltea valley, Donnas (Italy). Photograph: James Bromwich.

ROANNE, Loire

IGN 2830 O

Museum and site.

In the Roman period the capital of the Loire department was the small town of Rodumna which had a modest prosperity in the first century AD. As at FEURS, there was a Gallic village here from which the Roman settlement expanded due to its position on one of the main roads from Lyon to Autun. However, as a regional market centre, typically represented by its local pottery workshops, the Gallic village appears to have expanded significantly up to the 50s AD, then stagnated until the mid-second century with the suggestion of a late revival until, like Feurs, it collapsed dramatically in the third century. It could have been a transit port for traffic from the Rhône to the Loire, but its restricted growth and the lack of any evidence of wharfs or warehouses seem to be against this. Only one public building is known; identified as a bath complex in the nineteenth century, it was reinterpreted as a possible *fanum* in a rescue dig before the surviving stone walling disappeared under telecom offices.

The home town of one of the great founding fathers of French archaeology, Joseph Déchelette, it now has adventurously renovated galleries for its growing archaeological collection. The creation of a departmental archaeological service stimulated a major leap forward in the 1980s. It focused initially on the Gallic period, particularly well represented in the displays.

Musée Joseph Déchelette

22 Rue Anatole France
42300 Roanne
Hours: 10a.m.–noon, 2–6p.m. Closed Tuesday
10a.m.–6p.m. Thursday
2p.m.–6p.m. Sunday

Joseph Déchelette (1862–1914), whose family made a fortune in textiles, bought this mansion at the end of the 1880s. He worked in the family business. Using his European-wide sales work and skill in modern European languages as well as Latin and Greek, he built up an unrivalled knowledge of both prehistory and the classical world by visiting major archaeological sites and museums. He assembled a reference collection, excavated in Roanne and the Allier, became the museum's curator in 1892, and then took over at MONT BEUVRAY. He finally became a full-time scholar in 1899, rapidly writing the first synthesis of Gallo-Roman pottery, to be followed in 1908–13 by five volumes of the *Manuel d'archéologie préhistorique, Celtique et Gallo-Romaine,* a magisterial study of French archaeology and a key reference work for years. He was a reserve captain, called up and killed within two months of the start of the First World War.

The Iron Age. A tasteful display is graced with very attractive local painted ware and less appealing grey smoked tableware. The zoomorphic baked clay rams' heads and the beautiful tiny **bronze statuettes of a horse and boar** from Joeuvre are reminders of the mystical animalistic Celtic world. That this continued strongly into the Roman period is apparent in an isolated find from St Maurice-lès-Châteauneuf, *c.*30 km north-east of Roanne. A limestone fragment which appears to be a seated man's back is decorated with a ram, boar and eagle perched on a face set in a disc, perhaps also connecting it with the old Gallic severed-head cult.

The Déchelette room. This shows how Déchelette used his collection of Lezoux pottery – put together by the Abbé Constancias in the 1820s-40s and then bought by Déchelette – to demonstrate for the first time the use of moulds in creating the distinctive *sigillata* décor. The material has only been properly catalogued in the 1990s! There are also some of Déchelette's original notebooks.

The Gallo-Roman town. The displays are organized round themes. The first and most important is **the pottery section** divided according to types. The fine wares are mainly from other regions: rich and varied metallic wares; leaded wares from the Allier; and, unsurprisingly, *terra sigillata*, from both Lezoux and La Graufesenque. The local painted and smoked wares continue to be made and surely the former are finer than any of the imports. The common wares are presented in a reconstructed kitchen display.

Upstairs, other themes examined include **glass** with some fine globular funerary finds, then products of the local **bronze and iron workshops**. Elegant face decorated roof **antefixes** hint at the town's houses; aspects of domestic life are featured in **toiletry** and ***fibulae***, while the Allier-produced cream terracotta Venuses and suckling mother goddesses give **religion** an equally homely look. The **writing** display serves to show how in a small town it was rarely a public matter: only two fragmentary inscriptions have turned up, but graffiti suggests that literacy was not confined to the very few.

Fours de Potiers

Rue du Château

Behind the apse of St Etienne church, below ground by a small garden beside the Place de Lattre de Tassigny. Obtain keys from the Joseph Déchelette Museum.

The **four furnaces** were excavated in 1959–65 and represent the only complete workshop found, though nine other furnaces have been identified in Roanne. All four follow a standard pattern: a circular brick chamber, 0.9–1.3m diameter, set in a pit. The floor, which held the ceramics, was supported by pillars and once covered with a dome. In front, a passage led down to a vaulted hearth that fed directly into the chamber. These four were in use for some fifty years in the second century. The products here were common ware: ovoid jars, flagons, cooking pots and so on.

Joeuvre *oppidum*

10km south of Roanne via Le Coteau and Commelle Vernay, using the D43 then D56, to the turning for Chevenet and Joeuvre. The hillfort overlooks the last meander before the Neulise gorges. On the north side of the plateau's steep slopes, the excavators found a ditch and mound, and associated iron nails indicating a *murus gallicus*. As at Chêt-Châtelard (see FEURS), there was a late Iron Age community here; numerous amphorae have been found as well as the fine bronzes in Roanne museum. A small Roman occupation followed, probably a farm, finally destroyed in the sixth century.

OTHER SITES

Annecy (Haute Savoie) museum has been closed for renovation, but there are traces of a Roman bath system. In the Chartreuse, a mountain walk (not for children) leads to the site of **St Bernard du Touvet** (Isère), an inscribed estate marker on the Crête des Lances de Malissard (IGN 3334 OT).

GLOSSARY

actus: A Roman measurement mainly used for an area, but also for distance on aqueducts. 120 Roman feet (*c.*36m).

amphora: A large two-handled storage jar. The wide variations in shape and size were first catalogued and numbered by Dressel.

angon: The Frankish version of the Roman *pilum*.

appareil: (in masonry) *Grand appareil* consists of large rectangular blocks; *petit appareil* refers to small rectangular blockwork, 10–15cm long, often used as a facing for a rubble core.

appliqué: Decorative material made to be added to another.

architectural orders: The four major classical styles: Corinthian, Doric, Ionic and Tuscan.

Arian: A form of Christianity based on the views of Arius of Alexandria asserting the Son must be secondary to the Father. Arianism was a widely held belief in the Church in the fourth century but succumbed to the Catholic Trinity (in the Nicene Creed), but not before the Arians converted many barbarians including the Burgundians and Visigoths, but not the Franks.

Arretine: See *sigillata*.

Bacchus: See *Dionysus*.

Baetica: A rich province in Spain famous for its large-scale olive exports.

balteus: A wall that separated leading citizens from the rest as in the theatre or that isolated the arena from the onlookers in the amphitheatre.

caldarium: The hot, wet-heat, room of a bath system.

Campanian ware: A black gloss pottery from southern and central Italy exported to Gaul in the third to first centuries BC.

canabae: A civilian settlement outside a fortress. The name canabae for the Presqu'île area of Lyon, contrasted its mixed inhabitants with the ex-legionaries and Roman officials in the colony on Fourvière.

***cardo* (*maximus*)**: The main road running north–south in a Roman town.

castrum, castellum: A Roman fort and fortlet; in France they generally refer to late Roman strongpoints or refuges.

cavea: The seating area of a theatre or amphitheatre.

cella: The cult room inside a temple.

Cernunnos: A Gallo-Roman god. 'The horned one' was always shown with antlers, often sitting cross-legged, wearing a torc. Emphasizing his lordship of the forest, he was sometimes portrayed with animals or a ram-horned snake. He offered prosperity, fertility and well-being.

chi–rho: A monogram in Greek of the first two letters of Christ's name.

cinerary urn: A jar holding cremation ashes.

***civitas*:** A community seen ideally by the Romans as a self-governing unit, based on a city with its surrounding, supporting countryside. Gallic tribes were recognized and organized as *civitates*, despite varying traditions and levels of urbanization.

***comes*:** A vague late Roman army title, often a general.

***comitatus*:** The late Roman mobile field army (see *Limitanei*).

common ware and fine ware: Very broad terms distinguishing kitchen from tableware.

Corinthian: The most decorative architectural order with an acanthus-based capital.

corporation or *collegium*: A guild bringing together groups of craft workers, merchants or artists. Corporations also functioned as burial societies and cult associations.

***cryptoporticus*:** A semi-subterranean vaulted corridor, often under a forum.

***curia*:** The place where municipal *decurions* met.

Cybele: An Earth goddess native to Phrygia in modern Turkey. Associated with fertility.

***decumanus* (*maximus*):** The main road running east–west through a town.

***decurio*:** A member of municipal council (for life).

Dionysus: The Greek god of wine and ecstasy. His semi-divine male and female followers were known as Bacchi and Bacchae. See also *Silenus*.

***domus*:** A rich town house with Roman features.

Doric: A classical architectural order with a plain capital and fluted column.

DRAC: Direction Régionale des Affaires Culturelles; the DRAC co-ordinates archaeological work for the Ministry of Culture.

***duovir* or *duumvir*:** A municipal magistrate and chief local administrator.

***dux*:** A late Roman military commander of frontier forces in one or more provinces.

Epona: The Gallo-Roman 'horse goddess' who usually appears mounted side-saddle on a mare. Associated with fertility, healing and looking after the dead. Among the Aedui she was often shown with a foal, stressing the importance of horses in Gallic society. Adopted widely in the Roman world.

***Equites*:** The second rank in Roman society after senator. Based on wealth, it gave many provincials the opportunity to gain status and prestige in their communities or follow a career in the Roman army and administration.

***exedra*:** A semi-circular or rectangular recess in a wall or colonnade.

***fanum*, *fana*:** Romano-Celtic temple(s), typically of square design with a *cella* and surrounding portico.

feoderati: Barbarian groups allied to the Romans. In the late empire they were increasingly allowed to settle within the empire on condition that they defended it, but controlled by and fighting under their own leaders.

foot (Roman): 0.296m or 11.6 inches.

forum: A central open space surrounded by public buildings.

francisca: A short battle-axe often thrown. Made famous by the Franks.

frigidarium: The cold-water room in a bath system.

Hellenistic: Greek, especially of the third and second centuries BC. Associated with 'baroque' artistic style.

herm: A four-cornered pillar surmounted by a head.

hipposandal: A horseshoe tied round the hoof.

Jupiter column: A lone column surmounted by a horseman riding down a monster; its base was decorated with reliefs of gods.

imbrex **(plural** *imbrices***):** A roof tile. See *tegula*.

in situ: Used by archaeologists to describe (a) artefacts found in their place of original use, or (b) artefacts where they were discovered.

insula, insulae: Normally rectangular street block(s).

Ionic: An architectural order using capitals decorated with scrolls or volutes.

itineraries: Diagrammatic maps listing stops (e.g. *mansiones* or way-stations). The Antonine was probably second third/century and the Peutinger Table a third- to fifth-century compilation. The fourth-century Bordeaux was for pilgrimages.

laconicum: A dry hot room in a bath system.

laeti: Barbarians given land on condition that they provided men to fight for the empire. They were supervised and commanded by a Roman prefect.

lares (*familiares*): The household guardian gods or spirits with a shrine in the house. There were also *lares* of crossroads or even cities.

liberti, libertinae: Freedmen or women; ex-slaves often still with close ties to the *dominus* who had freed them.

limitanei: Late Roman frontier troops.

macellum: A covered market for farmers and merchants.

mansio: A post-inn where those carrying imperial letters could stay and change horses.

matrona(e): A mother goddess, often shown in threes, the Celtic reiforcing triplism; associated with fertility, well-being and locality.

Mercury: A god in Gaul depicted with Mercury's Roman attributes including his wand or *caduceus*, his winged hat and a purse, embodying commercial prosperity and success. He often appears with a consort, usually Rosmerta; as a divine couple they provide well-being at home and work.

Merovingian: Family name of Frankish kings from *c.*450 onwards claiming descent from 'Merovech', a probably mythical ancestor. Also used to describe the late fifth- to eighth-century period.

Mithras: A Persian god whose cult spread throughout the Roman empire; associated with secret rites and a complex mythology. Mithraism is called a 'mystery religion'.

mortaria: Mixing bowls used in the kitchen and on the table with a rough surface to help break up cereals.

murus gallicus: A method of constructing ramparts used by Celts, based on a mix of logs, rubble/earth and facing stones. Precise designs varied.

names/*nomina*: *Romans* generally had three or more names: *praenomen*: the forename; *nomen*: the family name; *gens*: the tribal name – omitted by the late second century; *cognomen*: surname – an extra name to help distinguish people. Adoptions and re-marriages led to changing the *cognomen* or adding more names.

Gauls had one name, but when they obtained Roman citizenship they added the names of their patron (often an emperor).

Slaves had one name, plus 'of' their master. Freed slaves (*liberti*) normally took the *praenomen* and *nomen* of their former masters.

Notitia (Dignitatum): A document listing late Roman military commands, thought to reflect the position in the late fourth and early fifth centuries.

nymphaeum: A decorative shrine associated with water nymphs.

oppidum/oppida: A Latin name for a settlement or settlements, used by archaeologists to define large non-Roman settlements with a range of urban features. During the Iron Age many in Gaul were hill-forts.

oscillum: An engraved marble disc used as a decoration.

palaeo-Christian: Used in France to mean early Christian of the fourth to sixth centuries.

palaestra: An exercise courtyard associated with public baths.

pagus: A lesser tribe or clan associated with a defined territory, generally rural. Their people were 'pagani'.

panegyrics: Orations praising emperors or other major figures. Only one collection has survived with twelve panegyrics, probably for those learning rhetoric during the late empire. Roman Gauls were famous for their oratorical skills.

patera: The saucer-shaped bowl used for religious offerings.

peribolus: The enclosing wall of a temple precinct or *temenos*.

peristyle: An internal display garden, often porticoed, around which rooms were laid out.

phalera: A decorative disc used on harness fittings, particularly in the army.

pilum, pila: Roman throwing spear(s).

pisé: Clay or mud laid directly on a wall in house building.

podium: A wall separating an audience from danger or the elite from the rest; a high platform on which a Roman temple was built.

pomerium: A sacred strip of land encircling a town or sanctuary forming a boundary.

postern: A small doorway in a rampart.

prefect/*praefectus*: A title used for imperial officials of widely differing status and powers.

***pulpitum*:** A timber stage for actors.

scaena and ***frons scaenae*:** The stage building and its decorative front.

scramasax: A single-bladed weapon, shorter than a conventional sword, used by Franks.

***sevir*:** A priest of the imperial cult; generally a wealthy freedman.

sherd: A broken fragment of pottery.

(*terra*) *sigillata*: The most widely found fine ware in the empire. A glossy red to pink pottery called Samian in Britain. First made in Italy and called Arretine, then manufactured in Gaul on a large scale, starting in Lyon and La Graufesenque, later Lezoux and then the Rhineland.

Silenus: A demi-god depicted as a wise but drunken old man and often linked with Dionysus.

sondages: Test-holes investigating a restricted area of a site. Usually sampling to establish answers to specific questions.

stela(e): Upright stone block(s), often inscribed and generally tombstone(s).

stratigraphy: Analysing and placing in chronological sequence the levels or deposits found in an archaeological excavation.

strigil: A curved metal tool used in the bath to scrape sweat, dirt and soap off the body.

Sucellus: 'The Good Striker' is a mature god with rich, curling hair and beard, in Gallic tunic and cloak, carrying a mallet or hammer; this perhaps marked the renewal of life and nature. A people's god, he supports the harvest. Sometimes with a consort, Nantosuelta, when they jointly reinforce the gift of plenty.

***tegula*:** A flat roof tile with ridges on two sides. The curved *imbrex* fitted over adjacent ridges.

***tepidarium*:** The warm room in a bath system.

***tesserae*:** The tiny blocks used to make a mosaic.

torc/torque: An open-ended neck-ring, sometimes twisted, made of gold or bronze. Particularly popular in the late Iron Age Celtic world.

Tuscan: A simplified version of the Doric order with an unfluted column and plain entablature.

***vicus*:** The smallest unit of self-government in the Roman provinces, the *vici* were villages and small towns, each with its own magistrates.

villa: A large house or mansion in the country. Sometimes the farming and living areas are distinguished as *rustica* and *urbana*. Occasionally the term is used as an alternative for *domus*.

***vomitorium*:** A tunnel entrance into an (amphi)theatre.

votive: An offering left for god(s).

SELECT BIBLIOGRAPHY

It should be noted that many more texts are available in specialist libraries, especially regional academic journal series. However, I have included references that have summarized important work, particularly from more widely available magazines. Museum guides are largely excluded. The following abbreviations are used:

AECR Association pour l'Etude de la Civilisation Romaine
BAR British Archaeological Reports
CNRS Centre National de la Recherche Scientifique

MAJOR ORIGINAL SOURCES MENTIONED IN THE TEXT

Many are available either as Penguin Classics or in the Loeb Classical Library series.

Ammianus Marcellinus, *History*
Anon, *Lives of the Caesars* (*SHA – Scriptores historiae Augustae*)
Ausonius, *The Moselle*
Caesar, *Gallic Wars* (*De Bello Gallico*)
Corpus Inscriptionum Latinarum (*CIL*) – volume XIII contains most of the inscriptions found in Gaul
Diodorus Siculus, *Library of History*
Eutropius, *Digest*
Gregory of Tours, *History of the Franks*
Juvenal, *The Satires*
Pliny, *Natural History*
Sidonius (Apollinaris), *Poems* and *Letters*
Strabo, *The Geography*
Suetonius, *Lives of the Twelve Caesars*
Tacitus, *Annals, Histories, Agricola, Germania*
Various, *Panegyrici Latini* (*PL*). See Nixon, C.E.V. and Rodgers, B.S. (1994) *In Praise of Later Roman Emperiors: The Panegyrici Latini*, Berkeley: University of California Press.

GALLO-ROMAN STUDIES

Bedon, R., Chevallier, R. and Pinon, P. (1988) *Architecture et urbanisme en Gaule Romaine*, tomes 1 et 2, Paris: Errance.
Bedon, R. *et al.* (1998) 'Les Villes et leurs faubourgs', *Dossiers d'Archéologie*, 237.
Brunaux, J.L. (1988) *The Celtic Gauls: Gods, Rites and Sanctuaries*, London: Seaby.
Carroll, M. (2001) *Romans, Celts, and Germans*, Stroud: Tempus.
Chevallier, R. (1972; 2nd edn 1997) *Les Voies romaines*, Paris: Picard.
Collis, J. (1984) *The European Iron Age*, London: Batsford.
Croom, A.T. (2000) *Roman Clothing and Fashion*, Stroud: Tempus.
Cunliffe, B. (1988) *Greeks, Romans and Barbarians*, London: Batsford.
Drinkwater, J. F. (1983) *Roman Gaul*, London: Croom Helm.
Esperandieu, E. (1907–66) *Recueil général des bas reliefs, statues et bustes de la Gaule romaine*, Paris: Imprimerie Nationale.
Fichtl, S. (2000) *La Ville celtique*, Paris: Errance.
Geary, P.J. (1988) *Before France and Germany*, Oxford: Oxford University Press.
Green, M. (1986) *The Gods of the Ancient Celts*, Gloucester: Alan Sutton.
—— (1989), *Symbol and Image in Celtic Religious Art*, London: Routledge.
—— (ed) (1995), *The Celtic World*, London: Routledge.
Grenier, A. (1931–60) *Manuel d'archéologie gallo-romaine*, vols I–IV, Paris: Picard.
Hatt, J.J. (1989) *Mythes et dieux de la Gaule*, Paris: Picard.
Hodge, A. Trevor (1992) *Roman Aqueducts and Water Supply*, London: Duckworth.
Izarra, F. de (1993) *Hommes et fleuves en Gaule romaine*, Paris: Errance.
James, E. (1988) *The Franks*, Oxford: Oxford University Press.
Johnson, S. (1983) *Late Roman Fortifications*, London: Batsford.
King, A. (1990) *Roman Gaul and Germany*, London: British Museum.
Knight, J.K. (1999) *The End of Antiquity*, Stroud: Tempus.
Mackintosh, M. (1995) 'The divine rider in the art of the western Roman Empire', *BAR International Series* 607, Oxford.
Meijer, F. and vann Niif, O. (eds) (1992) *Trade, Transport and Society in the Ancient World*, London: Routledge.
Nerzic, C. (1989) *La Sculpture en Gaule romaine*, Paris: Errance.
Petit, J.-P. and Mangin, M. with Brunella, P. (1994) *Atlas des agglomérations secondaires de la Gaule Belgique et des Germanies*, Paris: Errance.
Reddé, M. (1996) *L'Armée romaine en Gaule*, Paris: Errance.
Reece, R. (1999) *The Roman Empire: An Archaeology AD 150–600*, Stroud: Tempus.
Roche-Bernard, G. (1993) *Costumes et textiles en Gaule romaine*, Paris: Errance.
Stern, H. *et al.* (1956–94) *Recueil général des mosaïques de la Gaule*, *Gallia* Supplément 10, Paris: CNRS.
Swift, E. (2000), *The End of the Western Empire: An Archaeological Investigation*, Stroud: Tempus.
Wells, P.S. (1999) *The Barbarians Speak*, Princeton: Princeton University Press.
White, K.D. (1984) *Greek and Roman Technology*, Ithaca, N.Y.: Cornell.
Wightman, E.M. (1985) *Gallia Belgica*, London: Batsford.
Wild J.P. (1968) *Clothing in the NW Provinces of the Roman Empire*, Bonn: offprint from *Bonner Jahrbücher*.
Wiseman, A. and Wiseman, P. (1980) *The Battle for Gaul*, London: Chatto and Windus.
Woolf, G. (1998) *Becoming Roman: the Origins of Provincial Civilisation in Gaul*, Cambridge: Cambridge University Press.

Journals. The following have national coverage: *Gallia* (journal); *Gallia Informations* (current reports); *Caesarodunum*; and the more popular *Archéologia, L'Archéologue* and *Les Dossiers d'Archéologie*.

REGIONAL BIBLIOGRAPHIES

Details on sites and museums not specifically mentioned can often be found in the general regional texts. Many museums produce material not included here.

1 THE PARIS REGION AND NORTHERN FRANCE

General:

Agache, R. (1978) *La Somme pré-romaine et romaine*, Amiens: Société des Antiquaires de Picardie.

Cartes Archéologiques de la France: *Nord* 59 (1996); *Oise* 60 (1995); *Pas-de-Calais* 62 (1994); *Paris* 75 (1998).

Exhibition catalogue (1984) *Gallo-Romains en Ile-de-France*, [Sceaux]: Association des Conservateurs des Musées d'Ile-de-France.

Frezouls, E. (1982) *Les Villes antiques de la France I, la Belgique*, Strasbourg: AECR.

Musée des Beaux Arts de Valenciennes (1997) *Trésors archéologiques du nord de la France*, Valenciennes.

Journals: *Revue du Nord (RN) and Revue archéologique de Picardie (RAP)* are particularly useful.

Some sites:

Bayard, D. and Massy, J.-L. (1983) *Amiens romain: Samarobriva Ambianorum*, RAP.

Belot, E. (1994) 'Le Renouveau de l'archéologie Boulonnais', *Archéologia*, 301: 42–51.

Buchez, N. and Gemehl, D. (1997) 'Amiens, découvertes récentes', *Archéologia*, 333: 48–54.

Cholet, L and Delestre, X. (1992) 'Le Sanctuaire gallo-romain de Genainville', *Archéologia*, 278: 54–59.

Durand, M. (1984) 'Etat des recherches archéologiques gallo-romaines dans Senlis', *RAP*, 3–4: 193–203.

Fémolant, M. (1998) 'L'Archéologie à Beauvais', *Archéologia*, 346: 32–41.

Magnan, D. and Marion, S. (1999) 'Le Sanctuaire antique des Meldes', *L'Archéologue*, 42: 38–42.

Nice, A. (1994) 'L'Habitat Mérovingian de Goudelancourt' and 'Archéologie experimentale à Marle (Aisne)', *RAP*, 1–2.

Piton, D. (ed.) (1993) Vendeuil-Caply, *Nord-Ouest Archéologie*, 5.

Thollard, P. (1994) 'Le Développement urbain à Bavay à la lumière des recherches récentes', *RN*, LXXVI, 308: 21–35 and subsequent issues.

Velay, P. (1992) *From Lutetia to Paris*, Paris: CNRS.

Woimant, G.P. (1993) 'Le Sanctuaire antique de Champlieu', *RAP*, 1–2: 63–198.

2 BURGUNDY AND THE FRANCHE COMTE

General:

Anon. (1999) 'La Bourgogne archéologique' *L'Archéologue*, 43, Août–Septembre.

Bénard, J. *et al.* (1994) *Les Agglomérations antiques de Côte d'Or*, Paris: Les Belles Lettres.

Bonnamour, L. (2000) *Archéologie de la Saône*, Paris.

Cartes Archéologiques de la France: *Autun* 71/1 (1993); *Nièvre* 58 (1996); *Saône-et-Loire* 71/4 (1994).

Delor, J.-P. and Rolley, C. (eds) (1990) *L'Yonne et son passé*, Arny-le-Duc: Expo-Archéo 89.

Exhibition catalogue (1992) *Dans le Jura gallo-romain*, Lons-et-Saunier: Cercle Giradot.
Frezouls, E. (1988) *Les Villes antiques de la France II, Germanie Supèrieure 1*, Strasbourg: AECR.
Frezouls, E. (ed.) (1997) *Les Villes Antiques de la France III, Lyonnaise 1*, Paris: De Boccard.

Journals: *Revue d'Archéologie de l'Est et du Centre-Est de la France*; *Archéologia* is produced in Dijon.

Some sites:
Bonnamour, L. (forthcoming) 'Le Port antique de Chalon-sur-Saône', *Caesarodunum*, 33.
Breton, C. (2001) 'Six années de recherche Européene au Mt Beuvray', *Archéologia*, 380: 20–26.
Deyts, S. (1983) *Les Bois sculptés des Sources de la Seine*, *Gallia* Supplément xlii, Paris: CNRS.
Exhibition catalogue (1991) *Luxovium: retour aux sources*, Besançon: Centre Régional de Documentation archéologique.
Goudineau, C. (ed.) (1998) 'L'Année terrible: 52 avant JC', *L'Archéologue*, Hors-Série 1.
Gruel, K. and Vitali, D. (eds) (1998) 'L'Oppidum de Bibracte', *Gallia* 55: 1–140.
Joffroy, R. (1979) *Vix et ses trésors*, Paris: Libraire Jules Talendier.
Laurent, P. (1996) 'Le Site antique d'Escolives-Ste-Camille', *Archéologia*, 329: 54–9.
Le Gall, J. (1985) *Alesia*, Guides Archéologiques 4, Paris: Imprimerie Nationale.
Lerat, L. (1990) *Besançon antique*, Guides Archéologiques 18, Paris: Imprimerie Nationale.
—— (1998) *Les Villards d'Héria, I-II,* Paris: Diffusion les Belles Lettres.
Mangin, M. and Mangin, M.-J. (1995) 'Vertault, un site lingon à redécouvrir', *Archéologia*, 310: 62–6.
Mougin, P. and Mougin, C. (2000) *Le Théâtre antique de Mandeure*, Montbéliard: Editions du Patrimoine.
Pinette, M. and Rebourg, A. (1986) *Autun*, Guides Archéologiques 12, Paris: Imprimerie Nationale.
Planson, E. and Pommeret, C. (1986) *Les Bolards*, Guides Archéologiques 7, Paris: Imprimerie Nationale.
Rebourg, A (1998) 'L'Urbanisme d'Augustodunum', *Gallia*, 55: 141–236.
Roussel, L and Olivier, A. (1988) 'Mâlain', *Archéologia*, 237: 62–81.

3 CHAMPAGNE, THE ARDENNES, LORRAINE AND ALSACE

General:
Berton, R. *et al.* (2001) 'La Moselle archéologique', *L'Archéologue*, 52: 4–31.
Cartes Archéologiques de la France: *Haut-Rhin* 68 (1998).
Frezouls, E. (1982) *Les Villes antiques de la France I, La Belgique*, Strasbourg: AECR.
—— (1988) *Les Villes antiques de la France II, Germanie Supèrieure 1*, Strasbourg: AECR.
Schnitzler, B. (1996) *Cinq siècles de civilisation romaine en Alsace*, Strasbourg: Musées de Strasbourg.

Journals: *Les Cahiers Alsaciens d'Archéologie, d'Art et d'Archéologie*; *L'Archéologie Ardennaise*; *Les Cahiers Lorrains.*

Some sites:
Baudaux, J. *et al.* (2000) *Strasbourg: Fouilles archéologiques de la ligne B du tram* (Fouilles Récentes en Alsace, 5), Strasbourg: Musées de Strasbourg.

Bertaux, J.P. (1994) *La Plaine vosgienne à l'époque gallo-romaine*, Nancy: Editions Serpenoise.
Berthelot, F. and Neiss, R. (1994) 'Reims antique et médiévale', *Archéologia*, 300: 50–57.
Colardelle, M. *et al.* (1991) 'Grand. Prestigieux sanctuaire de la Gaule', *Dossiers d'Archéologie*, 162: 1–83.
Fleury-Alcaraz, K. (1997) 'Aux sources d'Hercule', *Archéologia*, 332: 5–55.
Halsall, G. (1995) *Settlement and Social Organisation: The Merovingian Region of Metz*, Cambridge: Cambridge University Press.
Hatt, J.J. (1993) *Argentorate Strasbourg*, Lyon: Presses Universitaires de Lyon.
Lémant, J.-P. (1993) 'Les Sites de Vireux à l'époque romaine', *L'Archéologie Ardennaise*, 3: 71–6.
Moitrieux, G. (1992) *Hercules Salutaris: Hercule au sanctuaire de Deneuvre*, Nancy: Presses Universitaire de Nancy.
Petit, J.-P. and Schaub, J. (1995) *Bliesbruck Reinheim parc archéologique européen*, Guides Archéologiques 32, Paris: Imprimerie Nationale.
Petry, F. (1988) *Mont-Ste-Odile*, Guides Archéologiques 16, Paris: Imprimerie Nationale.

4 LYON AND SAVOY

General:

Barthélémy, H., Mermet, C. and Rémy, B. (1997) *La Savoie gallo-romaine: histoire et archéologie*, Chambéry: Société Savoisienne.
Cartes Archéologiques de la France: *Ain* 01 (1990); *Isère* 38/1 (1994); *Loire* 42 (1997); *Savoie* 73 (1996).
Davier, D. (1985) *Les Romains en Savoie*, Rennes: Ouest-France.
Grange, P. and Viviant, C. (1996), *Itinéraires gallo-romains en Rhône-Alpes*, Lyon: EMCC.

Journals: *L'Histoire en Savoie*; *Revue Archéologique de Narbonnaise*; *Documents d'Archéologie en Rhône-Alpes* (DARA).

Some sites:

Arland, C. *et al.* (1993) 'Les Fouilles de la Presqu'île à Lyon', *Archéologia*, 294: 58–66.
Audin, A (1965; 2nd edn 1979) *Lyon, miroir de Rome*, Paris: Fayard.
Bedon, R. (ed.) (1997) *Les Aqueducs de la Gaule romaine et des régions voisines*, Caesarodunum 31: Presses Universitaires de Limoges.
Burdy, J. and Pelletier, A. (1997) *Guide du Lyon Gallo-Romain: Français–Anglais*, Lyon: Editions Lyonnaises d'Art et d'Histoire.
Burdy, J. *et al.* (1966; 3rd edn 1992) *Les Aqueducs romains de Lyon*, Messimy en Lyonnais: L'Araire.
Colardelle, R. (1986) *Grenoble aux premiers temps chrétiens*, Guides Archéologiques 9, Paris: Imprimerie Nationale.
Fleury-Alcaraz, K. (1998) 'Grenoble, le musée de l'Ancien Evêché', *Archéologia*, 351: 20–25.
Guichard, V. and Valette, P. (1990) *Feurs antique*, Roanne: Fédération Archéologique de la Loire.
Jospin, J.-P. and Bleu, S. (2001) 'Aoste antique', *Archéologia*, 378: 28–35.
Miquel, A. (1996) 'Du temple de Cybèle au prétoire d'Agrippa', *L'Archéologue*, 25: 44–7.
Prieur, J. (1978) *Aix-les-Bains dans l'antiquité*, Aix-les-Bains: P. Jacques.
Reynaud, J.-F. (1986) *Lyon aux premiers temps chrétiens*, Guides Archéologiques 10, Paris: Imprimerie Nationale.

INDEX

(**Bold** used for listed sites and main entries in text)